FIFTH EDITION

The Norton
Field Guide
to Writing

Richard Bullock

WRIGHT STATE UNIVERSITY

W. W. NORTON & COMPANY

New York • London

W. W. Norton & Company has been independent since its founding in 1923, when William Warder Norton and Mary D. Herter Norton first published lectures delivered at the People's Institute, the adult education division of New York City's Cooper Union. The firm soon expanded its program beyond the Institute, publishing books by celebrated academics from America and abroad. By mid-century, the two major pillars of Norton's publishing program—trade books and college texts—were firmly established. In the 1950s, the Norton family transferred control of the company to its employees, and today—with a staff of four hundred and a comparable number of trade, college, and professional titles published each year—W. W. Norton & Company stands as the largest and oldest publishing house owned wholly by its employees.

Editor: Sarah Touborg
Project Editor: Christine D'Antonio
Associate Editor: Claire Wallace
Assistant Editor: Madeline Rombes
Manuscript Editor: Jude Grant
Managing Editor, College: Marian Johnson
Managing Editor, College Digital Media: Kim Yi
Production Manager: Liz Marotta
Media Editors: Erica Wnek, Samantha Held
Media Project Editor: Cooper Wilhelm
Media Assistant Editor: Ava Bramson

Ebook Production Manager: Danielle Lehman
Marketing Manager, Composition: Lib Triplett
Design Director: Hope Miller Goodell
Book Designer: Anna Palchik
Photo Editor: Catherine Abelman
Photo Research: Dena Digilio Betz
Permissions Manager: Megan Schindel
Permissions Clearing: Bethany Salminen
Composition: Graphic World
Manufacturing: LSC Communications, Crawfordsville

Permission to use copyrighted material is included in the Acknowledgments section of this book, which begins on page A-1.

Library of Congress Cataloging-in-Publication Data
Names: Bullock, Richard H. (Richard Harvey) author.
Title: The Norton field guide to writing / Richard Bullock, Wright State University.
Description: Fifth edition. | New York ; London : W. W. Norton & Company, [2019]
Identifiers: LCCN 2018004993 | **ISBN 9780393655773** (paperback)
Subjects: LCSH: English language—Rhetoric—Handbooks, manuals, etc. | English language—Grammar—Handbooks, manuals, etc. | Report writing—Handbooks, manuals, etc.
Classification: LCC PE1408 .B883824 2019 | DDC 808/.042—dc23 LC record available at https://lccn.loc.gov/2018004993

W. W. Norton & Company, Inc., 500 Fifth Avenue, New York, N.Y. 10110
www.wwnorton.com

W. W. Norton & Company Ltd., 15 Carlisle St., London W1D 3BS

3 4 5 6 7 8 9 0

Preface

The Norton Field Guide to Writing began as an attempt to offer the kind of writing guides found in the best rhetorics in a format as user-friendly as the best handbooks, and on top of that, to be as brief as could be. I wanted to create a handy guide to help college students with all their written work. Just as there are field guides for bird watchers, for gardeners, and for accountants, this would be one for writers. In its first four editions, the book has obviously touched a chord with many writing instructors, and it remains the best-selling college rhetoric—a success that leaves me humbled and grateful. Student success is now on everyone's mind. As a teacher, I want my students to succeed, and first-year writing courses offer one of the best opportunities to help them develop the skills and habits of mind they need to succeed, whatever their goals may be. Success, though, doesn't end with first-year writing; students need to transfer their knowledge and skills to other courses and other writing tasks. To that end, I've added new chapters on reading and writing across fields of study and new guidance on writing literature reviews. I've also added "Taking Stock" questions to each Genre chapter to help students develop their metacognitive abilities by reflecting on their work.

The Norton Field Guide still aims to offer both the guidance new teachers and first-year writers need and the flexibility many experienced teachers want. In my own teaching I've seen how well explicit guides to writing work for students and novice teachers. But too often, writing textbooks provide far more information than students need or instructors can assign and as a result are bigger and more expensive than they should be. So I've tried to provide enough structure without too much detail—to give the information college writers need to know while resisting the temptation to tell them everything there is to know.

Most of all, I've tried to make the book easy to use, with menus, directories, a glossary/index, and color-coded links to help students find what they're looking for. The links are also the key to keeping the book brief: chapters are short, but the links send students to pages elsewhere in the book if they need more detail.

What's in the Book

The Norton Field Guide covers 14 genres often assigned in college. Much of the book is in the form of guidelines, designed to help students consider the choices they have as writers. The book is organized into eight parts:

1. ACADEMIC LITERACIES. Chapters 1–4 focus on writing and reading in academic contexts, summarizing and responding, and developing academic habits of mind.

2. RHETORICAL SITUATIONS. Chapters 5–9 focus on purpose, audience, genre, stance, and media and design. In addition, almost every chapter includes tips to help students focus on their rhetorical situations.

3. GENRES. Chapters 10–23 cover 14 genres, 4 of them—literacy narrative, textual analysis, report, and argument—treated in greater detail.

4. FIELDS. Chapters 24–26 cover the key features of major fields of study and give guidance on reading and writing in each of those fields.

5. PROCESSES. Chapters 27–34 offer advice for generating ideas and text, drafting, revising and rewriting, editing, proofreading, compiling a portfolio, collaborating with others, and writing as inquiry.

6. STRATEGIES. Chapters 35–46 cover ways of developing and organizing text—writing effective beginnings and endings, titles and thesis statements, comparing, describing, taking essay exams, and so on.

7. RESEARCH/DOCUMENTATION. Chapters 47–55 offer advice on how to do academic research; work with sources; quote, paraphrase, and summarize source materials; and document sources using MLA and APA styles. Chapter 54 presents the "official MLA style" introduced in 2016.

8. MEDIA/DESIGN. Chapters 56–60 give guidance on choosing the appropriate print, digital, or spoken medium; designing text; using images and sound; giving spoken presentations; and writing online.

What's Online for Students

Ebooks. All versions of *The Norton Field Guide* are available as ebooks and include all the readings and images found in the print books. Highlighted links are active in the ebook so students can quickly navigate to more detail as needed. The ebook is accessible from any computer, tablet, or mobile device and lets students highlight, annotate, or even listen to the text.

InQuizitive for Writers. With InQuizitive, students learn to edit sentences and practice working with sources to become better writers and researchers. InQuizitive is adaptive: students receive additional practice on the areas where they need more help. Links to *The Little Seagull Handbook* and explanatory feedback give students advice, right when they need it. And it's formative: by wagering points, students think about what they know and don't know. Visit inquizitive.wwnorton.com.

Norton/write. Just a click away with no passcode required, find a library of model student papers; more than 1,000 online exercises and quizzes; research and plagiarism tutorials; documentation guidelines for MLA, APA, *Chicago*, and CSE styles; MLA citation drills—and more. All MLA materials reflect 2016 style. Access the site at wwnorton.com/write.

What's Available for Instructors

A Guide to Teaching with *The Norton Field Guides*. Written by Richard Bullock and several other teachers, this is a comprehensive guide to teaching first-year writing, from developing a syllabus to facilitating group work, teaching multimodal writing to assessing student writing. Free of charge.

Coursepacks are available for free and in a variety of formats, including *Blackboard*, *D2L*, *Moodle*, *Canvas*, and *Angel*—and work within your existing learning management system, so there's no new system to learn, and access is free and easy. The *Field Guide* Coursepack includes model student papers; reading comprehension quizzes; reading strategy exercises; quizzes and exercises on grammar and research; documentation guidelines; and author biographies. Coursepacks are ready to use, right from the start—but are also easy to customize, using the system you already know and understand. Access the Coursepack at wwnorton.com/instructors.

PowerPoints. Ready-made PowerPoints feature genre organization flowcharts and documentation maps from the book to help you show examples during class. Download the PowerPoints at wwnorton.com/instructors.

Worksheets available in Word and PDF can be edited, downloaded, and printed with guidance on editing paragraphs, responding to a draft, and more. Download the worksheets at wwnorton.com/instructors.

Highlights

It's easy to use. Menus, directories, and a glossary/index make it easy for students to find what they're looking for. Color-coded templates and documentation maps even make MLA and APA documentation easy.

It has just enough detail, with short chapters that include color-coded links sending students to more detail if they need more.

It's uniquely flexible for teachers. Short chapters can be assigned in any order—and color-coded links help draw from other chapters as need be.

What's New

A new part on fields of study with 3 new chapters on reading and writing in the disciplines (Part 4):

- A new chapter on the fields of study surveys the distinctions among the major discipline areas and includes an overview of why a general education matters. (Chapter 24)
- A new chapter on reading across fields of study includes short examples drawn from a variety of courses and genres, along with tips, techniques, and key terms specific to each. (Chapter 25)
- A new chapter on writing in academic fields includes summaries of the key features of writing in the major disciplines, along with descriptions and short examples of typical writing assignments in each. (Chapter 26)

New advice on detecting "false news" and unreliable sources, including how to read sources with a critical eye and how to use the elements of a rhetorical situation to determine whether or not a potential source is genuine and reputable. (Chapter 49)

A new section on reviews of scholarly literature with advice on how to develop, organize, and write a literature review. This section also includes an overview of the key features of the genre, as well as a new student example. (Chapter 15)

New "Taking Stock of Your Work" questions: each Genre chapter now ends with a series of questions to help students develop their metacognitive abilities by thinking about their writing processes and products.

New guidelines for peer review with detailed advice on how to read and respond to peers' drafts. (Chapter 32)

Expanded coverage of synthesizing ideas: a new sample essay that shows students how to synthesize multiple sources. (Chapter 50)

New advice on arguing with a hostile audience, including how to use Rogerian argument techniques to engage with audiences who may not share students' perspectives or values. (Chapter 38)

12 new readings: new essays in nearly every genre, including a literacy narrative on working in an auto repair shop, a report on popcorn, a rhetorical analysis of a speech by former president Barack Obama, a profile of the modern-day plastic straw, and many more. In addition, there is a new APA research paper on the benefits of nurseries in women's prisons.

Ways of Teaching with The Norton Field Guide to Writing

The Norton Field Guide is designed to give you both support and flexibility. It has clear assignment sequences if you want them, or you can create your own. If, for example, you assign a position paper, there's a full chapter. If you want students to use sources, add the appropriate research chapters. If you want them to submit a topic proposal, add that chapter.

If you're a new teacher, the Genre chapters offer explicit assignment sequences—and the color-coded links will remind you of detail you may want to bring in. The instructor's manual offers advice on creating a syllabus, responding to writing, and more.

If you focus on genres, there are complete chapters on all the genres college students are often assigned. Color-coded links will help you bring in details about research or other writing strategies as you wish.

If you organize your course thematically, Chapter 29 on generating ideas can help get students thinking about a theme. You can also assign them to do research on the theme, starting with Chapter 48 on finding sources, or perhaps with Chapter 27 on writing as inquiry. If they then write in a particular genre, there will be a chapter to guide them.

If you want students to do research, there are 9 chapters on the research process, including guidelines and sample papers for MLA and APA styles.

If you focus on modes, you'll find chapters on using narration, description, and so on as strategies for many writing purposes, and links that lead students through the process of writing an essay organized around a particular mode.

If you teach a stretch, ALP, IRW, or dual credit course, the academic literacies chapters offer explicit guidelines to help students write and read in academic contexts, summarize and respond to what they read, and develop academic habits of mind that will help them succeed in college.

If you teach online, the book is available as an ebook—and a companion Coursepack includes exercises, quizzes, video tutorials, and more.

Acknowledgments

As I've traveled around the country and met many of the students, teachers, and WPAs who are using *The Norton Field Guide*, I've been gratified to hear that so many find it helpful, to the point that some students tell me that they aren't going to sell it back to the bookstore when the term ends—the highest form of praise. As much as I like the positive response, though, I am especially grateful when I receive suggestions for ways the book might be improved. In this fifth edition, as I did in the fourth edition, I have tried to respond to the many good suggestions I've gotten from students, colleagues, reviewers, and editors. Thank you all, both for your kind words and for your good suggestions.

Some people need to be singled out for thanks, especially Marilyn Moller, the guiding editorial spirit of the *Field Guide* through all five editions. When I presented Marilyn with the idea for this book, she encouraged me and helped me conceptualize it—and then taught me how to write a textbook. The quality of the *Field Guide* is due in large part to her knowledge of the field of composition, her formidable editing and writing skills, her sometimes uncanny ability to see the future of the teaching of writing— and her equally formidable, if not uncanny, stamina.

Editor Sarah Touborg guided me through this new edition with good humor and better advice. Just as developmental editor John Elliott did with the third and fourth editions, Sarah shepherded this fifth edition through revisions and additions with a careful hand and a clear eye for appropriate content and language. Her painstaking editing shows throughout the book, and I'm grateful for her ability to make me appear to be a better writer than I am.

Many others have contributed, too. Thanks to project editor Christine D'Antonio for her energy, patience, and great skill in coordinating the tightly scheduled production process for the book. Claire Wallace brought her astute eye and keen judgment to all of the readings, while Maddy Rombes managed the extensive reviewing process and took great care of the manuscript at every stage. *The Norton Field Guide* is more than just a print book, and I thank Erica Wnek, Samantha Held, Kim Yi, Ava Bramson, and Cooper Wilhelm for creating and producing the superb ebook and instructors' site. Anna Palchik designed the award-winning, user-friendly, and attractive interior, Pete Garceau created the beautiful new cover design, and Debra Morton Hoyt and Tiani Kennedy further enhanced the design and coordinated it all, inside and out. Liz Marotta transformed a scribbled-over manuscript into a finished product with extraordinary speed and precision, while Jude Grant copyedited. Megan Schindel and Bethany Salminen cleared text permissions, coping efficiently with ongoing changes, and Catherine Abelman cleared permission for the images found by Dena Digilio Betz. Steve Dunn, Lib Triplett, Elizabeth Pieslor, and Doug Day helped us all keep our eyes on the market. Thanks to all, and to Roby Harrington, Drake McFeely, and Julia Reidhead for supporting this project in the first place.

I have many, many people at Wright State University to thank for their support and assistance. Jane Blakelock taught me most of what I know about electronic text and writing on and for the web and assembled an impressive list of useful links for the book's website. Adrienne Cassel (now at Sinclair Community College) and Catherine Crowley read and commented on many drafts. Peggy Lindsey (now at Georgia Southern University) shared her students' work and the idea of using charts to show how various genres might be organized. Brady Allen, Debbie Bertsch (now at Columbus State Community College), Vicki Burke, Melissa Carrion, Jimmy Chesire, Carol Cornett, Mary Doyle, Byron Crews, Deborah Crusan, Sally DeThomas, Stephanie Dickey, Scott Geisel, Karen Hayes, Chuck Holmes, Beth Klaisner (now at Colorado State University), Nancy Mack, Marty Maner, Cynthia Marshall, Sarah McGinley, Kristie McKiernan, Michelle Metzner, Kristie Rowe, Bobby Rubin, Cathy Sayer, David Seitz, Caroline Simmons, Tracy Smith, Rick Strader, Mary Van Loveren, and A. J. Williams responded to drafts, submitted good models of student writing, contributed to the instructor's manual, tested the *Field Guide* in their classes, provided support, and shared with me some of their best teaching ideas. Henry Limouze and then Carol Loranger, chairs of the English Department, gave me room to work on this project with patience and good humor. Sandy Trimboli, Becky Traxler, and Lynn Morgan, the secretaries to the writing programs, kept me anchored. And I thank especially the more than 300 graduate teaching assistants and 10,000 first-year students who class-tested various editions of the *Field Guide* and whose experiences helped — and continue to help — to shape it.

Thanks to the teachers across the country who reviewed the fourth edition of the *Field Guide* and helped shape this fifth edition: Elizabeth Acosta, El Paso Community College; Thomas Barber, City College of New York; Keri Behre, Marylhurst University; David Bell, University of North Georgia; Dean Blumberg, Horry–Georgetown Technical College; Abdallah Boumarate, Valencia College; Tabitha Bozeman, Gadsden State Community College; Laurie E. Buchanan, Clark State Community College; Ashley Buzzard, Midlands Technical College; Emma Carlton, University of New Orleans; Danielle Carr, City College of New York; Toni I. Carter, Ivy Tech Community College of Indiana; Carla Chwat, University of North Georgia; Marie Coffey, Northeast Lakeview College; Stephanie Conner, College of Coastal Georgia; Robert Derr, Danville Community College; Cheryl Divine, Columbia College; Amber Duncan, Northwest Vista College; Gloria Estrada, El Paso Community College; Kevin Ferns, Woodland Community College; Dianne Flickinger, Cowley County Community College; Michael Flood,

Horry–Georgetown Technical College; Dan Fuller, Hinds Community College–Utica; Robert Galin, University of New Mexico–Gallup; Jennifer P. Gray, College of Coastal Georgia; Julie Groesch, San Jacinto College; Elizabeth Hair, Trident Technical College; Mark Hankerson, Albany State University; Pamela Hardman, Cuyahoga Community College; Michael Hedges, Horry–Georgetown Technical College; Michael Hill, Henry Ford College; Lorraine M. Howland, New Hampshire Technical Institute, Concord's Community College; Alyssa Johnson, Horry–Georgetown Technical College; Luke Johnson, Mesabi Range College; Elaine M. Jolayemi, Ivy Tech Community College of Indiana; George Kanieski, Cuyahoga Community College; Elizabeth Kuehne, Wayland Baptist University; Matt Laferty, Cuyahoga Community College; Robin Latham, Nash Community College; Adam Lee, Concordia University Irvine; Bronwen Llewellyn, Daytona State College; Chelsea Lonsdale, Henry Ford College; Jeffery D. Mack, Albany State University; Devona Mallory, Albany State University; Katheryn McCoskey, Butler Community College; Jenny McHenry, Tallahassee Community College; James McWard, Johnson County Community College; Eileen E. Medeiros, Johnson & Wales University; Kristina Meehan, Spartanburg Community College; Cathryn Meyer, Tallahassee Community College; Josephine Mills, Arapahoe Community College; James Minor, South Piedmont Community College; Erin O'Keefe, Allen Community College–Burlingame; Jeff Owens, Lassen Community College; Anthony Guy Patricia, Concord University; Brenda Reid, Tallahassee Community College; Emily Riser, Mississippi Delta Community College; Emily Rosenblatt, City College of New York; Kent Ross, Northeastern Junior College; Jessica Schreyer, University of Dubuque; Sunita Sharma, Mississippi Delta Community College; Taten Sheridan, Kodiak College; Ann Spurlock, Mississippi State University; Derrick Stewart, Midlands Technical College; Pamela Stovall, University of New Mexico–Gallup; James D. Suderman, Northwest Florida State College; Harun K. Thomas, Daytona State College; Alison Van Nyhuis, Fayetteville State University; Anna Voisard; City College of New York; Elisabeth von Uhl, City College of New York; Ellen Wayland-Smith, University of Southern California; James Williams, Soka University; Michael Williams, Horry–Georgetown Technical College; Mark W. Wilson, Southwestern Oregon Community College; and Michelle Zollars, Patrick Henry Community College.

Thanks also to those instructors who reviewed the *Field Guide* resources, helping us improve them for the fifth edition: Jessica Adams, Clark State Community College; Megan Anderson, Limestone College; Jamee Atkinson, Texas State Technical College; David Bach, Northwest Vista College; Ryan Baechle, University of Toledo; Aaron Barrell, Everett Community College; Soky Barrenechea, Penn State Abington; Lauren Baugus, Pensacola State College; Kristina Baumli, University of the Arts; Kay Berry, Dixie High School; Marie Bischoff, Sierra Community College; Matt Bloom, Hawkeye Community College; Allison Brady, Toccoa Falls College; Hannah Bingham Brunner, Oklahoma Christian University; Sybil Canon, Northwest MS Community College; Marie Coffey, Northeast Lakeview College; Susan Cowart, Texas State Technical College; Kennette Crockett, Harold Washington College; Anthony D'Ariea, Regis College; Mary Rutledge-Davis, North Lake College; Courtney Doi, Alamance Community College; Zona Douthit, Roger Williams University; Amber Duncan, Northwest Vista College; Michelle Ellwood, Keuka College; Michael Esquivel, Tarrant County College; Julie Felux, Northwest Vista College; Monika Fleming, Edgecombe Community College; Dianne Flickinger, Cowley County Community College; Barbara Z. Flinn, Youngstown State University; P. Foster, Alabama State University; Darius Frasure, Mountain View College; Robert Galin, University of New Mexico; Chanda Gilmore, Immaculata University; William Godbey, Tarrant County College; Deborah Goodwyn, Virginia State University; Ben Graydon, Daytona State College; Lamarr Green, Northwest Vista College; Marie Green, Northern VA Community College; Ricardo Guzman, Northwest Vista College; Lori Hicks, Ivy Tech Community College; Lana Highfill, Ivy Tech Community College; Lorraine M. Howland, NHTI, Concord's Community College; N. Luanne J. Hurst, Pasco Hernando State College; Judith Isakson, Daytona State College; Jeanine Jewell, Southeast Community College; Lori Johnson, Rappahannock Community College; Randy Johnson, Capital Community College; Wesley Johnson, Pasco-Hernando State College; Kelsea Jones, Treasure Valley Community College; Lisa Jones, Pasco-Hernando State College; Erin Kalish, Bridgewater State University; Amber Kovach, Boise State University; Julie Kratt, Cowley College; Robin Latham, Nash Community College; Stephanie Legarreta, El Paso Community College; Amy Ludwig, College of the Canyons; Carol Luvert, Hawkeye Community College; Barbara Lyras, Youngstown State University;

Crystal Manboard, Northwest Vista College; Margaret Marangione, Blue Ridge Community College; Kristen Marangoni, Tulsa Community College; Christina McCleanhan, Maysville Community and Technical College; Sara McDonald, Saint Cloud Technical and Community College and Saint Cloud State University; Kelly McDonough, Clarendon College; Shannon McGregor, Des Moines Area Community College; Lisa McHarry, West Hills College, Coalinga; Craig McLuckie, Okanagan College; James McWard, Johnson County Community College; Eileen Medeiros, Pasco-Hernando State College; Kristy Meehan, Spartanburg Community College; Jason Melton, Sacramento State University; John Miller, Ivy Tech Community College; Erik Moellering, Asheville Buncombe Technical Community College; Michael Murray, Columbus State Community College; Briana Murrell, Fayetteville State University; Anthony Nelson, El Paso Community College; Andrew Nye, Minnesota State University Mankato; Alison Van Nyhuis, Fayetteville State University; Oluwatosin Ogunnika, Virginia State University; Judith Oster, Valley Community College; Deb Paczynski, Central New Mexico Community College; Susan Passmore, Colquitt County High School; Diane Paul, Southeast Community College; Patricia Penn, Cowley College; Mike Peterson, Dixie State University; Larissa L. Pierce, Eastfield College; David Pittard, Fossil Ridge High School; Robert Ramos, City College; Cynthia Fox Richardson, Clark State Community College; Alice Waits-Richardson, Southern State Community College; Maurisa Riley, Tarrant County College NW; Stephanie Roberts, Georgia Military College; Adrian Rosa, Jackson College; Erin Mahoney-Ross, Tarrant County College Northwest Campus; Jennifer Royal, Santa Rosa Junior College; Julia Ruengert, Pensacola State College; Shirley Rutter, Johnson & Wales University; Eli Ryder, Antelope Valley College; Jessica Schreyer, University of Dubuque; Jennifer Scowron, Youngstown State University; Claudia Skutar, University of Cincinnati Blue Ash College; Jennifer Smith, Pepperdine University; Michael Stewart, University of Alabama; Michelle Sufridge, Madison-Plains High School; Harun Karim Thomas, Daytona State College; Zainah Usman, Tarrant County College; Jennifer Vega, El Paso Community College; Ashley Waterman, Community College of Aurora; Ann Henson Webb, Moraine Valley Community College; Maggie M. Werner, Hobart and William Smith College; Kaci L. West, Abraham Baldwin Agricultural College; Cassandra Wettlaufer, Tarrant County College; Holly

White, Cuyahoga County Community College; Casey Wiley, Penn State University; Karen Wilson, Hawkeye Community College; Sabine Winter, Eastfield College; Jonathan Wood, College of Western Idaho; and Marilyn S. Yamin, Pellissippi State Community College.

The Norton Field Guide has also benefited from the good advice and conversations I've had with writing teachers across the country, including (among many others) Maureen Mathison, Susan Miller, Tom Huckin, Gae Lyn Henderson, and Sundy Watanabe at the University of Utah; Christa Albrecht-Crane, Doug Downs, and Brian Whaley at Utah Valley State College; Anne Dvorak and Anya Morrissey at Longview Community University; Jeff Andelora at Mesa Community College; Robin Calitri at Merced College; Lori Gallinger, Rose Hawkins, Jennifer Nelson, Georgia Standish, and John Ziebell at the Community College of Southern Nevada; Stuart Blythe at Indiana University–Purdue University Fort Wayne; Janice Kelly at Arizona State University; Jeanne McDonald at Waubonsee Community College; Web Newbold, Mary Clark-Upchurch, Megan Auffart, Matt Balk, Edward James Chambers, Sarah Chavez, Desiree Dighton, Ashley Ellison, Theresa Evans, Keith Heller, Ellie Isenhart, Angela Jackson-Brown, Naoko Kato, Yuanyuan Liao, Claire Lutkewitte, Yeno Matuki, Casey McArdle, Tibor Munkacsi, Dani Nier-Weber, Karen Neubauer, Craig O'Hara, Martha Payne, Sarah Sandman, and Kellie Weiss at Ball State University; Patrick Tompkins at Tyler Community College; George Kanieski and Pamela Hardman at Cuyahoga Community College; Daniela Regusa, Jeff Partridge, and Lydia Vine at Capital Community College; Elizabeth Woodworth, Auburn University–Montgomery; Stephanie Eason at Enterprise Community College; Kate Geiselman at Sinclair Community College; Ronda Leathers Dively at Southern Illinois University; Debra Knutson at Shawnee State University; Guy Shebat and Amy Flick at Youngstown State University; Martha Tolleson, Toni McMillen, and Patricia Gerecci at Collin College; Sylva Miller at Pikes Peak Community College; Dharma Hernandez at Los Angeles Unified School District; Ann Spurlock at Mississippi State University; Luke Niiler at the University of Alabama; and Jeff Tix at Wharton County Junior College.

I wouldn't have met most of these people without the help of the Norton travelers, the representatives who spend their days visiting faculty, showing and discussing the *Field Guide* and Norton's many other fine textbooks.

Thanks to Kathy Carlsen, Scott Cook, Marilyn Rayner, Peter Wentz, Krista Azer, Sarah Wolf, Mary Helen Willett, Susyn Dietz, and all the other Norton travelers. Thanks also to regional sales managers Paul Ducham, Dennis Fernandes, Deirdre Hall, Dan Horton, Katie Incorvia, Jordan Mendez, Annie Stewart, Amber Watkins, and Natasha Zabohonski. And I'd especially like to thank Mike Wright and Doug Day for promoting this book so enthusiastically and professionally.

Finally, with this fifth edition comes an opportunity to thank Barb, my wife, for her love, support, and patience over the last 40 years. She is my best friend and my best teacher.

How to Use This Book

There's no one way to do anything, and writing is no exception. Some people need to do a lot of planning on paper; others write entire drafts in their heads. Some writers compose quickly and loosely, going back later to revise; others work on one sentence until they're satisfied with it, then move on to the next. And writers' needs vary from task to task, too: sometimes you know what you're going to write about and why, but need to figure out how to do it; other times your first job is to come up with a topic. *The Norton Field Guide* is designed to allow you to chart your own course as a writer, offering guidelines that suit your writing needs. It is organized in eight parts:

1. **ACADEMIC LITERACIES**: The chapters in this part will help you know what's expected in the reading and writing you do for academic purposes, and in summarizing and responding to what you read. One chapter even provides tips for developing habits of mind that will help you succeed in college, whatever your goals.

2. **RHETORICAL SITUATIONS**: No matter what you're writing, it will always have some purpose, audience, genre, stance, and medium and design. This part will help you consider each of these elements, as well as the particular kinds of rhetorical situations created by academic assignments.

3. **GENRES**: Use these chapters for help with specific kinds of writing, from abstracts to lab reports to memoirs and more. You'll find more detailed guidance for four especially common assignments: literacy narratives, textual analyses, reports, and arguments.

4. **FIELDS**: The chapters in this part will help you apply what you're learning in this book to your other general education courses or courses in your major.

5. **PROCESSES**: These chapters offer general advice for all writing situations—from generating ideas and text to drafting, revising and rewriting, compiling a portfolio—and more.

6. **STRATEGIES**: Use the advice in this part to develop and organize your writing—to write effective beginnings and endings, to guide readers through your text, and to use comparison, description, dialogue, and other strategies as appropriate.

7. **RESEARCH / DOCUMENTATION**: Use this section for advice on how to do research, work with sources, and compose and document research-based texts using MLA and APA styles.

8. **MEDIA / DESIGN**: This section offers guidance in designing your work and using visuals and sound, and in deciding whether and how to deliver what you write on paper, on screen, or in person.

Ways into the Book

The Norton Field Guide gives you the writing advice you need, along with the flexibility to write in the way that works best for you. Here are some of the ways you can find what you need in the book.

Brief menus.   Inside the front cover you'll find a list of all the chapters; start here if you are looking for a chapter on a certain kind of writing or a general writing issue. Inside the back cover are directories on MLA and APA styles.

Complete contents.   Pages xix–xxxvii contain a detailed table of contents. Look here if you need to find a reading or a specific section in a chapter.

Guides to writing.   If you know the kind of writing you need to do, you'll find guides to writing 14 common genres in Part 3. These guides are designed to help you through all the decisions you have to make—from coming up with a topic to editing and proofreading your final draft.

Color-coding.   The parts of this book are color-coded for easy reference: light blue for **ACADEMIC LITERACIES**, red for **RHETORICAL SITUATIONS**, green for **GENRES**, pink for **FIELDS**, lavender for **PROCESSES**, orange for **STRATEGIES**, blue for **RESEARCH / DOCUMENTATION**, and gold for **MEDIA / DESIGN**. You'll find a key to the colors on the front cover flap and also at the foot of each left-hand page. When you see a word highlighted in a color, that tells you where you can find additional detail on the topic.

Glossary / index. At the back of the book is a combined glossary and index, where you'll find full definitions of key terms and topics, along with a list of the pages where everything is covered in detail.

Directories to MLA and APA documentation. A brief directory inside the back cover will lead you to guidelines on citing sources and composing a list of references or works cited. The documentation models are color-coded so you can easily see the key details.

Ways of Getting Started

If you know your genre, simply turn to the appropriate genre chapter. There you'll find model readings, a description of the genre's Key Features, and a Guide to Writing that will help you come up with a topic, generate text, organize and write a draft, get response, revise, edit, and proofread. The genre chapters also point out places where you might need to do research, use certain writing strategies, design your text a certain way—and direct you to the exact pages in the book where you can find help doing so.

If you know your topic, you might start with some of the activities in Chapter 29, Generating Ideas and Text. From there, you might turn to Chapter 48, for help Finding Sources on the topic. When it comes time to narrow your topic and come up with a thesis statement, Chapter 36 can help. If you get stuck at any point, you might turn to Chapter 27, Writing as Inquiry; it provides tips that can get you beyond what you already know about your topic. If your assignment or your thesis defines your genre, turn to that chapter; if not, consult Chapter 27 for help determining the appropriate genre, and then turn to that genre chapter.

Contents

Part 1   Academic Literacies   1

1 Writing in Academic Contexts   3

2 Reading in Academic Contexts   10

13   Arguing a Position   157

KEY FEATURES   170

A GUIDE TO WRITING   172

14   Abstracts   185

INFORMATIVE ABSTRACTS   185

PROPOSAL ABSTRACTS   186

Part 4   Fields   289

Part 7   Doing Research   477

Part 8   Media / Design   637

part 1

Academic Literacies

Whenever we enter a new community—start a new job, move to a new town, join a new club—there are certain things we need to learn. The same is true upon entering the academic world. We need to be able to **READ** and **WRITE** in certain ways. We're routinely called on to **SUMMARIZE** something we've heard or read and to **RESPOND** in some way. And to succeed, we need to develop certain **HABITS OF MIND**—everyday things such as asking questions and being persistent. The following chapters provide guidelines to help you develop these fundamental academic literacies—and know what's expected of you in academic communities.

Academic Literacies

Writing in Academic Contexts   **1**

Write an essay arguing whether genes or environment do more to determine people's intelligence. Research and write a report on the environmental effects of electricity-generating windmills. Work with a team to write a proposal and create a multimedia presentation for a sales campaign. Whatever you're studying, you're surely going to be doing a lot of writing, in classes from various disciplines—the above assignments, for example, are from psychology, environmental science, and marketing. Academic writing can serve a number of different purposes—to **ARGUE** for what you think about a topic and why, to **REPORT** on what's known about an issue, to **PROPOSE A SOLUTION** for some problem, and so on. Whatever your topics or purposes, all academic writing follows certain conventions, ones you'll need to master in order to join the conversations going on across campus. This chapter describes what's expected of academic writing—and of academic writers.

157–84
131–56
246–55

What's Expected of Academic Writing

Evidence that you've considered the subject thoughtfully. Whether you're composing a report, an argument, or some other kind of writing, you need to demonstrate that you've thought seriously about the topic and done any necessary research. You can use various ways to show that you've considered the subject carefully, from citing authoritative sources to incorporating information you learned in class to pointing out connections among ideas.

3

academic literacies
rhetorical situations
genres
fields
processes
strategies
research MLA / APA
media / design

An indication of why your topic matters. You need to help your readers understand why your topic is worth exploring and why your writing is worth reading. Even if you are writing in response to an assigned topic, you can better make your point and achieve your purpose by showing your readers why your topic is important and why they should care about it. For example, in the prologue to *Our Declaration*, political philosopher Danielle Allen explains why her topic, the Declaration of Independence, is worth writing about:

> The Declaration of Independence matters because it helps us see that we cannot have freedom *without* equality. It is out of an egalitarian commitment that a people grows—a people that is capable of protecting us all collectively, and each of us individually, from domination. If the Declaration can stake a claim to freedom, it is only because it is so clear-eyed about the fact that the people's strength resides in its equality.
>
> The Declaration also conveys another lesson of paramount importance. It is this: language is one of the most potent resources each of us has for achieving our own political empowerment. The men who wrote the Declaration of Independence grasped the power of words. This reveals itself in the laborious processes by which they brought the Declaration, and their revolution, into being. It shows itself forcefully, of course, in the text's own eloquence.

By explaining that the topic matters because freedom and equality matter—and language gives us the means for empowering ourselves—Allen gives readers reason to read her careful analysis.

A response to what others have said. Whatever your topic, it's unlikely that you'll be the first one to write about it. And if, as this chapter assumes, all academic writing is part of a larger conversation, you are in a way adding your own voice to that conversation. One good way of doing that is to present your ideas as a response to what others have said about your topic—to begin by quoting, paraphrasing, or summarizing what others have said and then to agree, disagree, or both.

For example, in an essay arguing that organ sales will save lives, MIT student Joanna MacKay says, "Some agree with Pope John Paul II that the selling of organs is morally wrong and violates 'the dignity of the human person.'" But she then responds—and disagrees, arguing that "the morals we hold are not absolute truths" and that "peasants of third-world countries" might not agree with the pope.

A clear, appropriately qualified thesis. When you write in an academic context, you're expected to state your main point explicitly, often in a THESIS STATEMENT. Joanna MacKay states her thesis clearly in her essay "Organ Sales Will Save Lives": "Governments should not ban the sale of human organs; they should regulate it." Often you'll need to QUALIFY your thesis statement to acknowledge that the subject is complicated and there may be more than one way of seeing it or exceptions to the generalization you're making about it. Here, for example, is a qualified thesis, from an essay evaluating the movie *Juno* by Ali Heinekamp, a student at Wright State University: "Although the situations *Juno's* characters find themselves in and their dialogue may be criticized as unrealistic, the film, written by Diablo Cody and directed by Jason Reitman, successfully portrays the emotions of a teen being shoved into maturity way too fast." Heinekamp makes a claim that *Juno* achieves its main goal, while acknowledging at the beginning of the sentence that the film may be flawed.

387–89

388–89

Good reasons supported by evidence. You need to provide good reasons for your thesis and evidence to support those reasons. For example, Joanna MacKay offers several reasons why sales of human kidneys should be legalized: there is a surplus of kidneys, the risk to the donor is not great, and legalization would allow the trade in kidneys to be regulated. Evidence to support your reasons sometimes comes from your own experience but more often from published research and scholarship, research you do yourself, or firsthand accounts by others.

Compared with other kinds of writing, academic writing is generally expected to be more objective and less emotional. You may find *Romeo and Juliet* deeply moving or cry when you watch *The Fault in Our Stars*—but when you write about the play or the film for a class, you must do so using evidence from the text to support your thesis. You may find someone's ideas deeply offensive, but you should respond to them with reason rather than with emotional appeals or personal attacks.

Acknowledgment of multiple perspectives. Debates and arguments in popular media are often framed in "pro/con" terms, as if there were only two sides to any given issue. Once you begin seriously studying a topic, though, you're likely to find that there are several sides and that each of them deserves serious consideration. In your academic writing, you need to represent fairly the range of perspectives on your topic—to explore three, four, or more positions on it as you research and write. In her report, "Does Texting Affect Writing?," Marywood University student Michaela Cullington, for example, examines texting from several points of view: teachers' impressions of the influence of texting on student writing, the results of several research studies, and her own survey research.

A confident, authoritative stance. If one goal of academic writing is to contribute to a larger conversation, your tone should convey confidence and establish your authority to write about your subject. Ways to achieve such a tone include using active verbs ("X claims" rather than "it seems"), avoiding such phrases as "in my opinion" and "I think," and writing in a straightforward, direct style. Your writing should send the message that you've done the research, analysis, and thinking and know what you're talking about. For example, here is the final paragraph of Michaela Cullington's essay on texting and writing:

> On the basis of my own research, expert research, and personal observations, I can confidently state that texting is not interfering with students' use of standard written English and has no effect on their writing abilities in general. It is interesting to look at the dynamics of the arguments over these issues. Teachers and parents who claim that they are seeing a decline in the writing abilities of their students and children mainly support the negative-impact argument. Other teachers and researchers suggest that texting provides a way for teens to practice writing in a casual setting and thus helps prepare them to write formally. Experts and students themselves, however, report that they see no effect, positive or negative. Anecdotal experiences should not overshadow the actual evidence.

Cullington's use of simple, declarative sentences ("Other teachers and researchers suggest…"; "Anecdotal experiences should not overshadow…")

and her straightforward summary of the arguments surrounding texting, along with her strong, unequivocal ending ("texting is not interfering with students' use of standard written English"), lend her writing a confident tone. Her stance sends the message that she's done the research and knows what she's talking about.

Carefully documented sources. Clearly acknowledging sources and documenting them carefully and correctly is a basic requirement of academic writing. When you use the words or ideas of others—including visuals, video, or audio—those sources must be documented in the text and in a works-cited or references list at the end. (If you're writing something that will appear online, you may also refer readers to your sources by using hyperlinks in the text; ask your instructor if you need to include a list of references or works cited as well.)

Careful attention to correctness. Whether you're writing something formal or informal, in an essay or an email, you should always write in complete sentences, use appropriate capitalization and punctuation, and check that your spelling is correct. In general, academic writing is no place for colloquial language, slang, or texting abbreviations. If you're quoting someone, you can reproduce that person's writing or speech exactly, but in your own writing you try hard to be correct—and always proofread carefully.

What's Expected of College Writers: The WPA Outcomes

Writing is not a multiple-choice test; it doesn't have right and wrong answers that are easily graded. Instead, your readers, whether they're teachers or anyone else, are likely to read your writing with various questions in mind: does it make sense, does it meet the demands of the assignment, is the grammar correct, to name just a few of the things readers may look for. Different readers may notice different things, so sometimes it may seem to you that their response—and your grade—is unpredictable. It should be good to know, then, that writing teachers across the nation have come to some agreement on certain "outcomes," what college students should know and be able to do by the time they finish a first-year writing course. These outcomes have been defined by the National Council of Writing Program Administrators (WPA). Here's a brief summary of these outcomes and how *The Norton Field Guide* can help you meet them:

Knowledge of Rhetoric

- *Understand the rhetorical situation of texts that you read and write.* See Chapters 5–9 and the many prompts for Considering the Rhetorical Situation throughout the book.
- *Read and write texts in a number of different genres, and understand how your purpose may influence your writing.* See Chapters 10–22 for guidelines on writing in thirteen genres and Chapter 23 on mixing genres.
- *Adjust your voice, tone, level of formality, design, and medium as is necessary and appropriate.* See Chapter 8 on stance and tone and Chapter 9 for help thinking about medium and design.
- *Choose the media that will best suit your audience, purpose, and the rest of your rhetorical situation.* See Chapters 9 and 56.

Critical Thinking, Reading, and Composing

- *Read and write to inquire, learn, think critically, and communicate.* See Chapters 1 and 2 on academic writing and reading, and Chapter 27 on writing as inquiry. Chapters 10–23 provide genre-specific prompts to help you think critically about a draft.
- *Read for content, argumentative strategies, and rhetorical effectiveness.* Chapter 7 provides guidance on reading texts with a critical eye, Chapter 11 teaches how to analyze a text, and Chapter 49 shows how to evaluate sources.
- *Find and evaluate popular and scholarly sources.* Chapter 48 teaches how to use databases and other methods to find sources, and Chapter 49 shows how to evaluate the sources you find.

- *Use sources in various ways to support your ideas.* Chapter 38 suggests strategies for supporting your ideas, and Chapter 51 shows how to incorporate ideas from sources into your writing to support your ideas.

Processes

- *Use writing processes to compose texts and explore ideas in various media.* Part 5 covers all stages of the processes writers use, from generating ideas and text to drafting, getting response and revising, and editing and proofreading. Each of the thirteen genre chapters (10–22) includes a guide that leads you through the process of writing in that genre.
- *Collaborate with others on your own writing and on group tasks.* Chapter 28 offers guidelines for working with others, Chapter 32 provides general prompts for getting and giving response, and Chapters 10–23 provide genre-specific prompts for reading a draft with a critical eye.
- *Reflect on your own writing processes.* Chapters 10–23 provide genre-specific questions to help you take stock of your work, and Chapter 31 offers guidance in thinking about your own writing process. Chapter 34 provides prompts to help you reflect on a writing portfolio.

Knowledge of Conventions

- *Use correct grammar, punctuation, and spelling.* Chapter 33 provides tips to help you edit and proofread for your writing. Chapters 10–23 offer genre-specific advice for editing and proofreading.
- *Understand and use genre conventions and formats in your writing.* Chapter 7 provides an overview of genres and how to think about them. Part 3 covers thirteen genres, describing the key features and conventions of each one.
- *Understand intellectual property and document sources appropriately.* Chapter 52 offers guidance on the ethical use of sources, Chapter 53 provides an overview of documentation styles, and Chapters 54 and 55 provide templates for documenting in MLA and APA styles.

2 Reading in Academic Contexts

We read newspapers to know about the events of the day. We read text-books to learn about history, chemistry, and other academic topics—and other academic sources to do research and develop arguments. We read tweets and blogs to follow (and participate in) conversations about issues that interest us. And as writers, we read our own writing to make sure it says what we mean it to say and proofread our final drafts to make sure they say it correctly. In other words, we read many kinds of texts for many different purposes. This chapter offers a number of strategies for various kinds of reading you do in academic contexts.

TAKING STOCK OF YOUR READING

One way to become a better reader is to understand your reading process; if you know what you do when you read, you're in a position to decide what you need to change or improve. Consider the answers to the following questions:

- What do you read for pleasure? for work? for school? Consider all the sorts of reading you do: books, magazines, and newspapers, websites, *Facebook*, texts, blogs, product instructions.

- When you're facing a reading assignment, what do you do? Do you do certain things to get comfortable? Do you play music or seek quiet? Do you plan your reading time or set reading goals for yourself? Do you flip through or skim the text before settling down to read it, or do you start at the beginning and work through it?

- When you begin to read something for an assignment, do you make sure you understand the purpose of the assignment—why you must

academic
literacies

rhetorical
situations

genres

fields

processes

strategies

research
MLA / APA

media /
design

read this text? Do you ever ask your instructor (or whoever else assigned the reading) what its purpose is?

- How do you motivate yourself to read material you don't have any interest in? How do you deal with boredom while reading?

- Does your mind wander? If you realize that you haven't been paying attention and don't know what you just read, what do you do?

- Do you ever highlight, underline, or annotate text as you read? Do you take notes? If so, what do you mark or write down? Why?

- When you read text you don't understand, what do you do?

- As you anticipate and read an assigned text, what attitudes or feelings do you typically have? If they differ from reading to reading, why do they?

- What do you do when you've finished reading an assigned text? Write out notes? Think about what you've just read? Move on to the next task? Something else?

- How well do your reading processes work for you, both in school and otherwise? What would you like to change? What can you do to change?

The rest of this chapter offers advice and strategies that you may find helpful as you work to improve your reading skills.

READING STRATEGICALLY

Academic reading is challenging because it makes several demands on you at once. Textbooks present new vocabulary and new concepts, and picking out the main ideas can be difficult. Scholarly articles present content and arguments you need to understand, but they often assume that readers already know key concepts and vocabulary and so don't generally provide background information. As you read more texts in an academic field and begin to participate in its conversations, the reading will become easier, but in the meantime you can develop strategies that will help you read effectively.

Thinking about What You Want to Learn

To learn anything, we need to place new information into the context of what we already know. For example, to understand photosynthesis, we need to already know something about plants, energy, and oxygen, among other things. To learn a new language, we draw on similarities and differences between it and any other languages we know. A method of bringing to conscious attention our current knowledge on a topic and of helping us articulate our purposes for reading is a list-making process called KWL+. To use it, create a table with three columns:

K: What I _Know_	W: What I _Want_ to Know	L: What I _Learned_

Before you begin reading a text, list in the "K" column what you already know about the topic. Brainstorm ideas, and list terms or phrases that come to mind. Then group them into categories. Also before reading, or after reading the first few paragraphs, list in the "W" column questions you have that you expect, want, or hope to be answered as you read. Number or reorder the questions by their importance to you.

Then, as you read the text or afterward, list in the "L" column what you learned from the text. Compare your "L" list with your "W" list to see what you still want or need to know (the "+")—and what you learned that you didn't expect.

Previewing the Text

It's usually a good idea to start by skimming a text—read the title and subtitle, any headings, the first and last paragraphs, the first sentences of all the other paragraphs. Study any illustrations and other visuals. Your goal is to get a sense of where the text is heading. At this point, don't stop to look up unfamiliar words; just mark them in some way to look up later.

Adjusting Your Reading Speed to Different Texts

Different texts require different kinds of effort. Some that are simple and straightforward can be skimmed fairly quickly. With academic texts, though, you usually need to read more slowly and carefully, matching the pace of your reading to the difficulty of the text. You'll likely need to skim the text for an overview of the basic ideas and then go back to read it closely. And then you may need to read it yet again. (But do try always to read quickly enough to focus on the meanings of sentences and paragraphs, not just individual words.) With visual texts, too, you'll often need to look at them several times, moving from gaining an overall impression to closely examining the structure, layout, and other visual features—and exploring how those features relate to any accompanying verbal text.

Looking for Organizational Cues

As you read, look for cues that signal the way the text's ideas are organized and how each part relates to the ones around it.

The introductory paragraph and thesis often offer a preview of the topics to be discussed and the order in which they will be addressed. Here, for example, is a typical thesis statement for a report: *Types of prisons in the United States include minimum and medium security, close security, maximum security, and supermax.* The report that follows should explain each type of prison in the order stated in the thesis.

391 ◆

Transitions help GUIDE READERS in following the direction of the writer's thinking from idea to idea. For example, "however" indicates an idea that contradicts or limits what has just been said, while "furthermore" indicates one that adds to or supports it.

Headings identify a text's major and minor sections, by means of both the headings' content and their design.

Thinking about Your Initial Response

Some readers find it helps to make brief notes about their first response to a text, noting their reaction and thinking a little about why they reacted as they did.

What are your initial reactions?   Describe both your intellectual reaction and any emotional reaction, and identify places in the text that caused you to react as you did. An intellectual reaction might consist of an evaluation ("I disagree with this position because . . ."), a connection ("This idea reminds me of . . ."), or an elaboration ("Another example of this point is . . ."). An emotional reaction could include approval or disapproval ("YES! This is exactly right!" "NO! This is so wrong!"), an expression of feeling ("This passage makes me so sad"), or one of appreciation ("This is said so beautifully"). If you had no particular reaction, note that, too.

What accounts for your reactions?   Are they rooted in personal experiences? aspects of your personality? positions you hold on an issue? As much as possible, you want to keep your opinions from interfering with your understanding of what you're reading, so it's important to try to identify those opinions up front.

Dealing with Difficult Texts

Let's face it: some texts are difficult. You may have no interest in the subject matter, or lack background knowledge or vocabulary necessary for understanding the text, or simply not have a clear sense of why you have to read the text at all. Whatever the reason, reading such texts can be a challenge. Here are some tips for dealing with them:

Look for something familiar.   Texts often seem difficult or boring because we don't know enough about the topic or about the larger conversation surrounding it to read them effectively. By skimming the headings, the abstract or introduction, and the conclusion, you may find something that relates to something you already know or are at least interested in—and being aware of that prior knowledge can help you see how this new material relates to it.

Look for "landmarks."   Reading a challenging academic text the first time through can be like driving to an unfamiliar destination on roads you've never traveled: you don't know where you're headed, you don't recognize anything along the way, and you're not sure how long getting there will take. As you drive the route again, though, you see landmarks along the way that help you know where you're going. The same goes for reading a difficult text: sometimes you need to get through it once just to get some idea of what it's about. On the second reading, now that you have "driven the route," look for the ways that the parts of the text relate to one another, to other texts or course information, or to other knowledge you have.

Monitor your understanding.   You may have had the experience of reading a text and suddenly realizing that you have no idea what you just read. Being able to monitor your reading—to sense when you aren't understanding the text and need to reread, focus your attention, look up unfamiliar terms, take some notes, or take a break—can make you a more efficient and better reader. Keep these questions in mind as you read: What is my purpose for reading this text? Am I understanding it? Does it make sense? Should I slow down, reread, annotate? skim ahead and then come back? pause to reflect?

Be persistent.   Research shows that many students respond to difficult texts by assuming they're "too dumb to get it"—and quit reading. Successful students, on the other hand, report that if they keep at a text, they will come to understand it. Some of them even see difficult texts as challenges: "I'm going to keep working on this until I make sense of it." Remember that reading is an active process, and the more you work at it the more successful you will be.

Annotating

Many readers find it helps to annotate as they read: highlighting keywords, phrases, sentences; connecting ideas with lines or symbols; writing comments or questions in the margin or on sticky notes; circling new words so you can look up the definitions later; noting anything that seems noteworthy or questionable. Annotating forces you to read for more than just the surface meaning. Especially when you are going to be writing about or responding to a text, annotating creates a record of things you may want to refer to.

Annotate as if you're having a conversation with the author, someone you take seriously but whose words you do not accept without question. Put your part of the conversation in the margin, asking questions, talking back: "What's this mean?" "So what?" "Says who?" "Where's evidence?" "Yes!" "Whoa!" or even ☺ or ☹ or texting shorthand like LOL or INTRSTN. If you're reading a text online, you may be able to copy it and annotate it electronically. If so, make your annotations a different color from the text itself.

academic literacies

rhetorical situations

genres

fields

processes

strategies

research MLA / APA

media / design

What you annotate depends on your **PURPOSE**, or what you're most interested in. If you're analyzing a text that makes an explicit argument, you would probably underline the **THESIS STATEMENT** and then the **REASONS** and **EVIDENCE** that support that statement. It might help to restate those ideas in your own words in the margins—in order to understand them, you need to put them in your own words! If you are trying to **IDENTIFY PATTERNS**, you might highlight each pattern in a different color or mark it with a sticky note and write any questions or notes about it in that color. You might annotate a visual text by circling and identifying important parts of the image.

55–56

387–89
400–401
401–8

23–25

There are some texts that you cannot annotate, of course—library books, some materials you read on the web, and so on. Then you will need to use sticky notes or make notes elsewhere, and you might find it useful to keep a reading log for this purpose.

Coding

You may also find it useful to record your thoughts as you read by using a coding system—for example, using "X" to indicate passages that contradict your assumptions, or "?" for ones that puzzle you. You can make up your own coding system, of course, but you could start with this one*:

✔ Confirms what you thought

X Contradicts what you thought

? Puzzles you

?? Confuses you

! Surprises you

☆ Strikes you as important

➔ Is new or interesting to you

You might also circle new words that you'll want to look up later and highlight or underline key phrases.

---

*Adapted from Harvey Daniels and Steven Zemelman, *Subjects Matter: Every Teacher's Guide to Content-Area Reading*.

A Sample Annotated Text

Here is an excerpt from Justice: What's the Right Thing to Do?, *a book by Harvard professor Michael J. Sandel, annotated by a writer who was doing research for a report on the awarding of military medals:*

What Wounds Deserve the Purple Heart?

✔

On some issues, questions of virtue and honor are too obvious to deny. Consider the recent debate over who should qualify for the Purple Heart. Since 1932, the U.S. military has awarded the medal to soldiers wounded or killed in battle by enemy action. In addition to the honor, the medal entitles recipients to special privileges in veterans' hospitals.

PTSD increasingly common among veterans.

Since the beginning of the current wars in Iraq and Afghanistan, growing numbers of veterans have been diagnosed with post-traumatic stress disorder and treated for the condition. Symptoms include recurring nightmares, severe depression, and suicide. At least three hundred thousand veterans reportedly suffer from traumatic stress or major depression. Advocates for these veterans have proposed that they, too, should qualify for the Purple Heart. Since psychological injuries can be at least as debilitating as physical ones, they argue, soldiers who suffer these wounds should receive the medal.

Argument: Vets with PTSD should be eligible for PH because psych. injuries are as serious as physical.

No PH for PTSD vets? Seems unfair!

After a Pentagon advisory group studied the question, the Pentagon announced, in 2009, that the Purple Heart would be reserved for soldiers with physical injuries. Veterans suffering from mental disorders and psychological trauma would not be eligible, even though they qualify for government-supported medical treatment and disability payments. The Pentagon offered two reasons for its decision: traumatic stress disorders are not intentionally caused by enemy action, and they are difficult to diagnose objectively.

Argument: PTSD is like punctured eardrums, which do get the PH.

Did the Pentagon make the right decision? Taken by themselves, its reasons are unconvincing. In the Iraq War, one of the most common injuries recognized with the Purple Heart has been a punctured eardrum, caused by explosions at close range. But unlike bullets and bombs, such explosions are not a deliberate enemy tactic intended to injure or kill; they are (like traumatic stress) a damaging side effect of battlefield action. And while traumatic disorders may be more difficult

academic literacies rhetorical situations genres fields processes strategies research MLA / APA media / design

to diagnose than a broken limb, the injury they inflict can be more severe and long-lasting.

As the wider debate about the Purple Heart revealed, the real issue is about the meaning of the medal and the virtues it honors. What, then, are the relevant virtues? Unlike other military medals, <u>the Purple Heart honors sacrifice, not bravery</u>. It requires no heroic act, only an injury inflicted by the enemy. The question is what kind of injury should count.

PH "honors sacrifice, not bravery." Injury enough. So what kind of injury?

A veteran's group called the Military Order of the Purple Heart opposed awarding the medal for psychological injuries, claiming that doing so would "debase" the honor. A spokesman for the group stated that "shedding blood" should be an essential qualification. He didn't explain why bloodless injuries shouldn't count. But Tyler E. Boudreau, a former Marine captain who favors including psychological injuries, offers a compelling analysis of the dispute. He attributes the opposition to a deep-seated attitude in the military that views post-traumatic stress as a kind of weakness. "The same culture that demands tough-mindedness also encourages skepticism toward the suggestion that the violence of war can hurt the healthiest of minds . . . Sadly, <u>as long as our military culture bears at least a quiet contempt for the psychological wounds of war, it is unlikely those veterans will ever see a Purple Heart</u>."

Wow: one vet's group insists that for PH, soldier must <u>bleed</u>!

☆

So the debate over the Purple Heart is more than a medical or clinical dispute about how to determine the veracity of injury. At the heart of the disagreement are rival conceptions of <u>moral character and military valor</u>. Those who insist that only bleeding wounds should count believe that post-traumatic stress reflects a weakness of character unworthy of honor. Those who believe that psychological wounds should qualify argue that veterans suffering long-term trauma and severe depression have sacrificed for their country as surely, and as honorably, as those who've lost a limb. The dispute over the Purple Heart illustrates the moral logic of Aristotle's theory of justice. We can't determine who deserves a military medal without asking what virtues the medal properly honors. And to answer that question, we have to assess competing conceptions of character and sacrifice.

Argument based on different ideas about what counts as a military virtue.

— Michael J. Sandel, *Justice: What's the Right Thing to Do?*

Summarizing

Writing a summary, boiling down a text to its main ideas, can help you understand it. To do so, you need to identify which ideas in the text are crucial to its meaning. Then you put those crucial ideas into your own words, creating a brief version that accurately sums up the text. Here, for example, is a summary of Sandel's analysis of the Purple Heart debate:

> In "What Wounds Deserve the Purple Heart?," Harvard professor Michael J. Sandel explores the debate over eligibility for the Purple Heart, the medal given to soldiers who die or are wounded in battle. Some argue that soldiers suffering from post-traumatic stress disorder should qualify for the medal because psychological injuries are as serious as physical ones. However, the military disagrees, since PTSD injuries are not "intentionally caused by enemy action" and are hard to diagnose. Sandel observes that the dispute centers on how "character" and "sacrifice" are defined. Those who insist that soldiers must have had physical wounds to be eligible for the Purple Heart see psychological wounds as reflecting "weakness of character," while others argue that veterans with PTSD and other psychological traumas have sacrificed honorably for their country.

READING CRITICALLY

When we read critically, we apply our analytical skills in order to engage with a text to determine not only what a text says but also what it means and how it works. The following strategies can help you read texts critically.

Believing and Doubting

One way to develop a response to a text is to play the believing and doubting game, sometimes called reading with and against the grain. Your goal is to LIST or FREEWRITE notes as you read, writing out as many

332–33
331–32

reasons as you can think of for believing what the writer says (reading with the grain) and then as many as you can for doubting it (reading against the grain).

First, try to look at the world through the writer's perspective. Try to understand their reasons for arguing as they do, even if you strongly disagree. Then reread the text, trying to doubt everything in it: try to find every flaw in the argument, every possible way it can be refuted—even if you totally agree with it. Developed by writing theorist Peter Elbow, the believing and doubting game helps you consider new ideas and question ideas you already have—and at the same time see where you stand in relation to the ideas in the text you're reading.

Thinking about How the Text Works: What It Says, What It Does

Sometimes you'll need to think about how a text works, how its parts fit together. You may be assigned to analyze a text, or you may just need to make sense of a difficult text, to think about how the ideas all relate to one another. Whatever your purpose, a good way to think about a text structure is by **OUTLINING** it, paragraph by paragraph. If you're interested in analyzing its ideas, look at what each paragraph *says*; if, on the other hand, you're concerned with how the ideas are presented, pay attention to what each paragraph *does*.

335–37

What it says.   Write a sentence that identifies what each paragraph says. Once you've done that for the whole text, look for patterns in the topics the writer addresses. Pay attention to the order in which the topics are presented. Also look for gaps, ideas the writer has left unsaid. Such paragraph-by-paragraph outlining of the content can help you see how the writer has arranged ideas and how that arrangement builds an argument or develops a topic. Here, for example, is an outline of Michael Granof's proposal,

"Course Requirement: Extortion"; the essay may be found on pages 246–49. The numbers in the left column refer to the essay's paragraphs.

1	College textbooks cost several times more than other books.
2	However, a proposed solution to the cost problem would only make things worse.
3	This proposal, to promote sales of used textbooks, would actually cause textbook costs to rise, because the sale of used books is a main reason new texts cost so much.
4	There is another way to lower costs.
5	Used textbooks are already being marketed and sold very efficiently.
6	Because of this, most new textbook sales take place in the first semester after they're published, forcing publishers to raise prices before used books take over the market.
7	In response, textbooks are revised every few years, whether or not the content is outdated, and the texts are "bundled" with other materials that can't be used again.
8–9	A better solution would be to consider textbooks to be like computer software and issue "site licenses" to universities. Once instructors choose textbooks, the university would pay publishers fees per student for their use.
10	Publishers would earn money for the use of the textbooks, and students' costs would be much lower.
11	Students could use an electronic text or buy a print copy for additional money. The print copies would cost less because the publisher would make most of its profits on the site license fees.
12	This arrangement would have no impact on teaching, unlike other proposals that focus on using electronic materials or using "no frills" textbooks and that might negatively affect students' learning.
13	This proposal would reduce the cost of attending college and help students and their families.

What it does. Identify the function of each paragraph. Starting with the first paragraph, ask, What does this paragraph do? Does it introduce a topic? provide background for a topic to come? describe something? define something? entice me to read further? something else? What does the second paragraph do? the third? As you go through the text, you may identify groups of paragraphs that have a single purpose. Here is a functional outline of Granof's essay (again, the numbers on the left refer to the paragraphs):

1	Introduces the topic by defining a problem
2	Introduces a flawed solution
3	Explains the flawed solution and the problem with it
4	Introduces a better solution
5–7	Describes the current situation and the dynamics of the problem
8	Outlines the author's proposed solution
9–10	Explains the proposed solution
11–12	Describes the benefits and effects of the proposed solution
13	Concludes

Identifying Patterns

Look for notable patterns in the text—recurring words and their synonyms, as well as repeated phrases, metaphors and other images, and types of sentences. Some readers find it helps to highlight patterns in various colors. Does the author repeatedly rely on any particular writing strategies: **NARRATION**? **COMPARISON**? Something else?

462–70
424–31

Another kind of pattern that might be important to consider is the kind of evidence the text provides. Is it more opinion than facts? nothing but statistics? If many sources are cited, is the information presented in any patterns—as **QUOTATIONS**? **PARAPHRASES**? **SUMMARIES**? Are there repeated references to certain experts or sources?

526–38

In visual texts, look for patterns of color, shape, and line. What's in the foreground, and what's in the background? What's completely visible, partly visible, or hidden? In both verbal and visual texts, look for omissions and anomalies: What isn't there that you would expect to find? Is there anything that doesn't really fit in?

If you discover patterns, then you need to consider what, if anything, they mean in terms of what the writer is saying. What do they reveal about the writer's underlying premises and beliefs? What do they tell you about the writer's strategies for persuading readers to accept the truth of what they are saying?

See how color-coding an essay by *New York Times* columnist William Safire on the meaning of the Gettysburg Address reveals several patterns in the language Safire uses. In this excerpt from the essay, which was published just before the first anniversary of the September 11, 2001, terrorist attacks, Safire develops his analysis through several patterns. Religious references are colored yellow; references to a "national spirit," green; references to life, death, and rebirth, blue; and places where Safire directly addresses the reader, gray.

> But the selection of this poetic political sermon as the oratorical centerpiece of our observance need not be only an exercise. . . . Now, as then, a national spirit rose from the ashes of destruction.
>
> Here is how to listen to Lincoln's all-too-familiar speech with new ears.
>
> In those 266 words, you will hear the word *dedicate* five times. . . .
>
> Those five pillars of dedication rested on a fundament of religious metaphor. From a president not known for his piety—indeed, often criticized for his supposed lack of faith—came a speech rooted in the theme of national resurrection. The speech is grounded in conception, birth, death, and rebirth.
>
> Consider the barrage of images of birth in the opening sentence. . . .
>
> Finally, the nation's spirit rises from this scene of death: "that this nation, under God, shall have a new birth of freedom." Conception, birth, death, rebirth. The nation, purified in this fiery trial of war, is resurrected. Through the sacrifice of its sons, the sundered nation would be reborn as one. . . .
>
> Do not listen on Sept. 11 only to Lincoln's famous words and comforting cadences. Think about how Lincoln's message encompasses but goes beyond paying "fitting and proper" respect to the dead and the bereaved. His sermon at Gettysburg reminds "us the living" of our "unfinished work" and "the great task remaining before us"—to resolve that this generation's response to the deaths of thousands of our people leads to "a new birth of freedom."

The color coding helps us to see patterns in Safire's language, just as Safire reveals patterns in Lincoln's words. He offers an interpretation of

Lincoln's address as a "poetic political sermon," and the words he uses throughout support that interpretation. At the end, he repeats the assertion that Lincoln's address is a sermon, inviting us to consider it differently. Safire's repeated commands ("Consider," "Do not listen," "Think about") offer additional insight into how he wishes to position himself in relation to his readers.

READING RHETORICALLY

To read academic texts effectively, you need to look beyond the words on the page or screen to the **RHETORICAL CONTEXT** of the text and the argument it makes. Academic texts—both the ones you read and the ones you write—are parts of ongoing scholarly conversations, in which writers respond to the ideas and assertions of others in order to advance knowledge. To enter those conversations, you must first read carefully and critically to understand the rhetorical situation, the larger context within which a writer wrote, and the argument the text makes.

▲ 116–17

Considering the Rhetorical Situation

As a reader, you need to think about the message that the writer wants to articulate, including the intended audience and the writer's attitude toward that audience and the topic, as well as about the genre, medium, and design of the text.

PURPOSE   What is the writer's purpose? To entertain? inform? persuade readers to think something or take some action? What is *your* purpose for reading this text?

■ 55–56

AUDIENCE   Who is the intended audience? Are you a member of that group? If not, should you expect that you'll need to look up unfamiliar terms or concepts or that you'll run into assumptions you don't necessarily share? How is the writer addressing the audience—as an expert addressing those less knowledgeable? an outsider addressing insiders?

■ 57–60

61–65 **GENRE** What is the genre? Is it a report? an argument? an analysis? something else? Knowing the genre can help you to anticipate certain key features.

66–68 **STANCE** Who is the writer, and what is their stance? Critical? Curious? Opinionated? Objective? Passionate? Indifferent? Something else? Knowing the stance affects the way you understand a text, whether you're inclined to agree or disagree with it, to take it seriously, and so on.

69–71 **MEDIA / DESIGN** What is the medium, and how does it affect the way you read? If it's a print text, what do you know about the publisher? If it's on the web, who sponsors the site, and when was it last updated? Are there any headings, summaries, or other elements that highlight key parts of the text?

Analyzing the Argument

All texts make some kind of argument, claiming something and then offering reasons and evidence as support for any claim. As a critical reader, you need to look closely at the argument a text makes—to recognize all the claims it makes, consider the support it offers for those claims, and decide how you want to respond. What do you think, and why? Here are some questions to consider when analyzing an argument:

387–89
5
400–401
401–8

- *What claim is the text making?* What is the writer's main point? Is it stated as a **THESIS** or only implied? Is it limited or **QUALIFIED** somehow? If not, should it have been?
- *How is the claim supported?* What **REASONS** does the writer provide for the claim, and what **EVIDENCE** is given for the reasons? What kind of evidence is it? Facts? Statistics? Examples? Expert opinions? Images? How convincing do you find the reasons and evidence? Is there enough evidence?

413
410–11

- *What appeals besides logical ones are used?* Does the writer appeal to readers' **EMOTIONS**? try to establish **COMMON GROUND**? demonstrate their **CREDIBILITY** as trustworthy and knowledgeable? How successful are these appeals?

◆ 401–13

- *Are any* **COUNTERARGUMENTS** *acknowledged?* If so, are they presented accurately and respectfully? Does the writer concede any value to them or try to refute them? How successfully does the writer deal with them?

◆ 411–12

- *What outside sources of information does the writer cite?* What kinds of sources are they, and how credible do they seem? Are they current and authoritative? How well do they support the argument?

- *Do you detect any* **FALLACIES**? Fallacies are arguments that involve faulty reasoning. Because they often seem plausible, they can be persuasive. It is important, therefore, that you question the legitimacy of such reasoning when you run across it.

◆ 414–16

Considering the Larger Context

All texts are part of ongoing conversations with other texts that have dealt with the topic of the text. An essay arguing for an assault-weapons ban is part of an ongoing conversation on gun legislation, which is itself part of a conversation on individual rights and responsibilities. Academic texts document their sources in part to show their relationship to the ongoing scholarly conversation on a particular topic. In fact, any time you're reading to learn, you're probably reading for some larger context. Whatever your reading goals, being aware of that larger context can help you better understand what you're reading. Here are some specific aspects of the text to pay attention to:

Who else cares about this topic?   Especially when you're reading in order to learn about a topic, the texts you read will often reveal which people or groups are part of the conversation—and might be sources of further reading. For example, an essay describing the formation of Mammoth Cave in Kentucky could be of interest to geologists, cave explorers, travel writers, or tourists. If you're reading such an essay while doing research on the cave, you should consider how the audience to whom the writer is writing determines the nature of the information provided—and its suitability as a source for your research.

What conversations is this text part of? Does the text refer to any concepts or ideas that give you some sense that it's part of a larger conversation? An argument on airport security measures, for example, is part of larger conversations about government response to terrorism, the limits of freedom in a democracy, and the possibilities of using technology to detect weapons and explosives, among others.

What terms does the writer use? Do any terms or specialized language reflect the writer's allegiance to a particular group or academic discipline? If you run across words like *false consciousness*, *ideology*, and *hegemony*, for example, you might guess that the text was written by a Marxist scholar.

What other writers or sources does the writer cite? Do the other writers have a particular academic specialty, belong to an identifiable intellectual school, share similar political leanings? If an article on politics cites Paul Krugman and Gail Collins in support of its argument, you might assume that the writer holds liberal opinions; if it cites Ross Douthat and Jennifer Rubin, the writer is likely a conservative.

READING VISUAL TEXTS

Photos, drawings, graphs, diagrams, and charts are frequently used to help convey important information and often make powerful arguments themselves. So learning to read and interpret visual texts is just as necessary as it is for written texts.

Taking visuals seriously. Remember that visuals are texts themselves, not just decoration. When they appear as part of a written text, they may introduce information not discussed elsewhere in the text. Or they might illustrate concepts hard to grasp from words alone. In either case, it's important to pay close attention to any visuals in a written text.

Looking at any title, caption, or other written text that's part of a visual will help you understand its main idea. It might also help to think about its purpose: Why did the writer include it? What information does it add or emphasize? What argument is it making? See, for example, how a psychology textbook uses visuals to help explain two ways that information can be represented:

Analogical and Symbolic Representations

When we think about information, we use two basic types of internal representations: analogical and symbolic.

Analogical representations usually correspond to images. They have some characteristics of actual objects. Therefore, they are analogous to actual objects. For example, maps correspond to geographical layouts. Family trees depict branching relationships between relatives. A clock corresponds directly to the passage of time. **Figure 2.1a** is a drawing of a violin from a particular perspective. This drawing is an analogical representation.

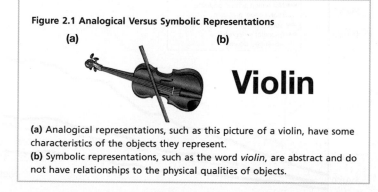

Figure 2.1 Analogical Versus Symbolic Representations

(a)   **(b)**

Violin

(a) Analogical representations, such as this picture of a violin, have some characteristics of the objects they represent.
(b) Symbolic representations, such as the word *violin*, are abstract and do not have relationships to the physical qualities of objects.

By contrast, **symbolic representations** are abstract. These representations usually consist of words or ideas. They do not have relationships to physical qualities of objects in the world. The word *hamburger* is a symbolic representation that usually represents a cooked patty of beef served on a bun. The word *violin* stands for a musical instrument **(Figure 2.1b)**.   — Sarah Grison, Todd Heatherton, and Michael Gazzaniga, *Psychology in Your Life*

The headings tell you the topic: analogical and symbolic representations. The paragraphs define the two types of representation, and the illustrations present a visual example of each type. The visuals make the information in the written text easier to understand by illustrating the differences between the two.

Reading charts and graphs. To read the information in charts and graphs, you need to look for different things depending on what type of chart or graph you're considering. A line graph, for example, usually contains certain elements: title, legend, x axis, y axis, and source information. Figure 2.2 shows one such graph taken from a sociology textbook.

Other types of charts and graphs include some of these same elements. But the specific elements vary according to the different kinds of

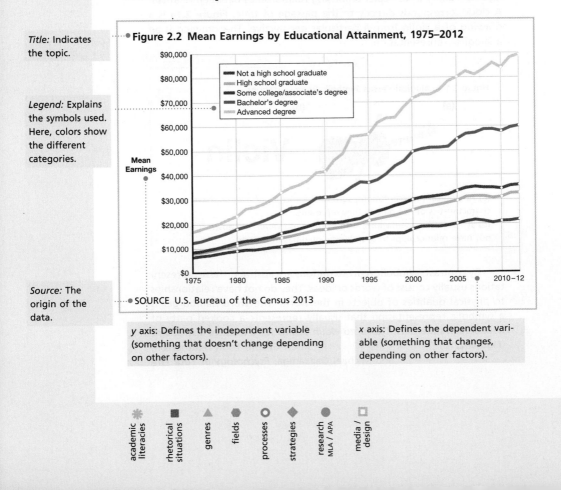

Title: Indicates the topic.

Legend: Explains the symbols used. Here, colors show the different categories.

Figure 2.2 Mean Earnings by Educational Attainment, 1975–2012

Legend:
- Not a high school graduate
- High school graduate
- Some college/associate's degree
- Bachelor's degree
- Advanced degree

Source: The origin of the data.

SOURCE U.S. Bureau of the Census 2013

y axis: Defines the independent variable (something that doesn't change depending on other factors).

x axis: Defines the dependent variable (something that changes, depending on other factors).

academic literacies · rhetorical situations · genres · fields · processes · strategies · research MLA / APA · media / design

Figure 2.3 Women's Participation in the Labor Force in the United States, 1948–2012

*Women in the labor force as a percent of all civilian women age sixteen and over.
†Women in the labor force as a percent of the total labor force (both men and women) age sixteen and over.

SOURCE U.S. Bureau of Labor Statistics 2014

information being presented, and some charts and graphs can be challenging to read. For example, the chart in Figure 2.3, from the same textbook, includes elements of both bar and line graphs to depict two trends at once: the red line shows the percentage of women in the United States who were in the labor force over a sixty-five-year period, and the blue bars show the percentage of U.S. workers who were women during that same period. Both trends are shown in two-year increments. To make sense of this chart, you need to read the title, the y-axis labels, and the labels and their definitions carefully.

Reading Onscreen

Research shows that we tend to read differently onscreen than we do when we read print texts: we skim and sample, often reading a sentence or two and then jumping to another site, another text. If we need to scroll the page to continue, we often don't bother. In general, we don't read as carefully as we do when reading print texts, and we're less likely to reread or take other steps if we find that we don't understand something. Following are some strategies that might help you read effectively onscreen.

Adjust your reading speed and effort to your purpose.   Many students use the web to get an overview of a topic and find potential sources. In that case, skimming and browsing are sensible and appropriate tactics. If you're reading to evaluate a source or find specific information on a topic, though, you probably need to read more slowly and carefully.

Keep your purpose in mind as you read.   Clicking on hyperlinks and jumping from site to site can be tempting. Resist the temptation! Making a list of specific questions you're seeking to answer can help you stay focused and on task.

Print out longer texts.   Some people find reading online to be harder on their eyes than reading pages of print, and many find that they comprehend and remember information in longer texts better if they read them in print. Reading a long text is similar to walking through an unfamiliar neighborhood: we form a mental map of the text as we read and then associate the information with its location in the text, making remembering easier. Since forming such a map is more difficult when reading an electronic text, printing out texts you need to read carefully may be a good strategy.

IF YOU NEED MORE HELP

511–18 ●
331–39 ○
343–47
348–55
356–60

See Chapter 49, **EVALUATING SOURCES** , for questions to help you analyze a text's rhetorical situation. See also Chapter 29 on **GENERATING IDEAS AND TEXT**; you can adapt those methods as ways of looking at texts, especially clustering and cubing. And see also Chapter 31 on **ASSESSING YOUR OWN WRITING**, Chapter 32 on **GETTING RESPONSE AND REVISING** , and Chapter 33 on **EDITING AND PROOF-READING** if you need advice for reading your own writing.

Summarizing and Responding:
Where Reading Meets Writing

3

Summarizing a text helps us to see and understand its main points and to think about what it says. Responding to that text then prompts us to think about—*and say*—what we think. Together, summarizing and responding to texts is one way that we engage with the ideas of others. In a history course, you might summarize and respond to an essay arguing that Civil War photographers did not accurately capture the realities of the battlefield. In a philosophy course, you might summarize Plato's "Allegory of the Cave" and respond to its portrayal of knowledge as shadows on a wall.

And in much of the writing that you do, you'll need to cite the ideas of others, both as context for your own thinking and as evidence to support your arguments. In fact, unless you're Adam, there's probably no topic you'll write about that someone else hasn't already written about—and one way of introducing what you have to say is as a response to something others have said about your topic. A good way of doing that is by summarizing what they've said, using the summary as a launching pad for what you say. This chapter offers advice for summarizing and responding, writing tasks you'll have occasion to do in many of your college classes—and provides a short guide to writing a summary/response essay, a common assignment in composition classes.

SUMMARIZING

In many of your college courses, you'll likely be asked to summarize what someone else has said. Boiling down a text to its basic ideas helps you focus on the text, figure out what the writer has said, and understand (and remember) what you're reading. In fact, summarizing is an essential academic skill, a way to incorporate the ideas of others into your own writing. Following are some guidelines for summarizing effectively:

Read the text carefully.   To write a good summary, you need to read the original text carefully to capture the writer's intended meaning as clearly and evenhandedly as you can. Start by **SKIMMING** the text to get a general sense of what it's saying. If some parts don't make sense, don't worry; at this point, you're reading just to get the gist. Then reread the text more slowly, **ANNOTATING** it paragraph by paragraph. If there's an explicit **THESIS** stating the main point, highlight it in some way. Then try to capture the main idea of each paragraph in a single sentence.

12–13 ❋

16–17 ❋
387–89 ◆

State the main points concisely and accurately.   Summaries of a complete text are generally between 100 and 250 words in length, so you need to choose your words carefully and to focus only on the text's main ideas. Leave out supporting evidence, anecdotes, and counterarguments unless they're crucial to understanding the text. For instance, in summarizing "A Brief History of the Modern-Day Straw, the World's Most Wasteful Commodity" (see p. 233), Ernie Smith's essay explaining why drinking straws are wasteful, you would omit its description of the invention of the rye straw in the nineteenth century.

Describe the text accurately and fairly—and using neutral language.   Present the author's ideas evenhandedly and fairly; a summary isn't the place to share your opinion of what the text says. Use neutral verbs such as *states*, *asserts*, or *concludes*, not verbs that imply praise or criticism like *proves* or *complains*.

535–38 ●

Use SIGNAL PHRASES to distinguish what the author says from what you say.   Introducing a statement with phrases such as "he says" or "the essay concludes" indicates explicitly that you're summarizing what the author said. When first introducing an author, you may need to say something about their credentials. For example:

> In "Our Declaration," political philosopher Danielle Allen analyzes the language of the Declaration of Independence.

> Daniel Felsenfeld, a music composer who also writes about music, describes how he developed a passion for twentieth-century classical music in "Rebel Music."

Later in the text, you may need to refer to the author again as you summarize specific parts of the text. These signal phrases are typically briefer: *In Felsenfeld's view . . . , Allen then argues . . .*

Use quotations sparingly, if at all. You may need to **QUOTE** keywords or memorable phrases, but most or all of a summary should be written in your own words, using your own sentence structures.

    DOCUMENT any text you summarize in a works-cited or references list. A summary of a lengthy work should include **IN-TEXT DOCUMENTATION** noting the pages summarized; they aren't needed with a brief text like the one summarized below (see p. 143).

● 528–31

● 544–47

MLA 551–57

APA 600–604

An Example Summary

> In "The Reason College Costs More than You Think," Jon Marcus, a higher-education editor at the *Hechinger Report*, reports that a major reason why college educations are so expensive is the amount of time students stay in college. Although almost all first-year students and their families assume that earning a bachelor's degree will take four years, the reality is that more than half of all students take longer, with many taking six years or more. This delay happens for many reasons, including students changing majors, having to take developmental courses, taking fewer courses per term than they could have, and being unable to register for required courses. As a result, their expenses are much greater—financial aid seldom covers a fifth or sixth year, so students must borrow money to finish—and the additional time they spend in college is time they aren't working, leading to significant losses in wages.

This summary begins with a signal phrase stating the author's name and credentials and the title of the text being summarized. The summary includes only the main ideas, in the summary writer's own words.

RESPONDING

When you summarize a text, you show that you understand its main ideas; responding to a text pushes you to engage with those ideas—and gives you the opportunity to contribute your ideas to a larger conversation. You can respond in various ways, for instance, by taking a **POSITION** on the text's argument, by **ANALYZING THE TEXT** in some way, or by **REFLECTING** on what it says.

157–84
98–130
256–63

Deciding How to Respond

You may be assigned to write a specific kind of response—an argument or analysis, for instance—but more often than not, the nature of your response is left largely up to you. If so, you'll need to read closely and critically to understand what the text says, to get a sense of how—and how well—it does so, and to think about your own reaction to it. Only then can you decide how to respond. You can respond to what the text says (its ideas), to how it says it (the way it's written), or to where it leads your own thinking (your own personal reaction). Or you might write a response that mixes those ways of responding. You might, for example, combine a personal reaction with an examination of how the writing caused that reaction.

If you're responding to what a text says, you might agree or disagree with the author's argument, supporting your position with good reasons and evidence for your response. You might agree with parts of the argument and disagree with others. You might find that the author has ignored or downplayed some important aspect of the topic that needs to be discussed or at least acknowledged. Here are some questions to consider that can help you think about what a text says:

- What does the writer claim?

400–401
401–8

- What **REASONS** and **EVIDENCE** does the writer provide to support that claim?

✳ academic literacies
■ rhetorical situations
▲ genres
✸ fields
○ processes
◆ strategies
● research MLA / APA
▢ media / design

- What parts of the text do you agree with? Is there anything you dis-agree with—and if so, why?
- Does the writer represent any views other than their own? If not, what other perspectives should be considered?
- Are there any aspects of the topic that the writer overlooks or ignores?
- If you're responding to a visual text, how do the design and any images contribute to your understanding of what the text "says"?

Here is a brief response to Jon Marcus's "The Reason College Costs More than You Think," one that responds to his argument:

> It's true that one reason college costs so much more is that students take longer than four years to finish their degrees, but Jon Marcus's argument in "The Reason College Costs More than You Think" is flawed in several ways. He ignores the fact that over the past years state governments have reduced their subsidies to state-supported colleges and universities, forcing higher tuition, and that federal scholarship aid has declined as well, forcing students to pay a greater share of the costs. He doesn't mention the increased number of administrators or the costs of fancy athletic facilities and dormitories. Ultimately, his argument places most of the blame for higher college costs on students, who, he asserts, make poor choices by changing majors and "taking fewer courses per term than they could." College is supposed to present opportunities to explore many possible career paths, so changing majors should be considered a form of growth and education. Furthermore, many of us are working full-time to pay the high costs of college, leaving us with little extra time to study for four or five courses at once and sometimes forcing us to take fewer classes per term because that's all we can afford. Marcus is partly right—but he gets much of the problem wrong.

If you're focusing on the way a text is written, you'll consider what elements the writer uses to convey their message—facts, stories, images, and so on. You'll likely pay attention to the writer's word choices and look for any patterns that lead you to understand the text in a particular way. To think about the way a text is written, you might find some of these questions helpful:

- What is the writer's message? Is there an explicit statement of that message?

- How well has the writer communicated the message?

- How does the writer support what they say: by citing facts or statistics? by quoting experts? by noting personal experiences? Are you persuaded?

- Are there any words, phrases, or sentences that you find notable and that contribute to the text's overall effect?

119–25 ▲

- How does the text's design affect your response to it? If it's a **VISUAL TEXT**—a photo or ad, for example—how do the various parts of the text contribute to its message?

Here is a brief response to Marcus's essay that analyzes the various ways it makes its argument:

> In "The Reason College Costs More than You Think," *Time* magazine writer Jon Marcus argues that although several factors contribute to high college costs, the main one is how long it takes students to graduate. Marcus introduces this topic by briefly profiling a student who is in his fifth year of school and has run out of financial aid because he "changed majors and took courses he ended up not needing." This profile gives a human face to the topic, which Marcus then develops with statistics about college costs and the numbers of students who take more than four years to finish. Marcus's purpose is twofold: to inform readers that the assumption that most students finish college in four years is wrong and to persuade them that poor choices like those this student made are the primary reason college takes so long and costs so much. He acknowledges that the extra costs are "hidden" and "not entirely the student's fault" and suggests that poor high school preparation and unavailable required courses play a role, as do limits on financial aid. However, his final paragraph quotes the student as saying of the extra years, "That's time you're wasting that you could be out making money." As the essay's final statement, this assertion that spending more time in school is time wasted and that the implicit goal of college is career preparation reinforces Marcus's argument that college *should* take only four years and that students who take longer are financially irresponsible.

If you're reflecting on your own reaction to a text, you might focus on how your personal experiences or beliefs influenced the way you understood the text or on how it reinforced or prompted you to reassess some of those beliefs. You could also focus on how it led you to see the topic in new ways—or note questions that it's led you to wonder about. Some questions that may help you reflect on your own reaction to a text include:

- How did the text affect you personally?
- Is there anything in the text that really got your attention? If so, what?
- Do any parts of the text provoke an emotional reaction—make you laugh or cry, make you uneasy? What prompted that response?
- Does the text bring to mind any memories or past experiences? Can you see anything related to you and your life in the text?
- Does the text remind you of any other texts?
- Does the text support (or challenge) any of your beliefs? How?
- Has reading this text given you any new ideas or insight?

Here is a brief response to Jon Marcus's essay that reflects on an important personal issue:

> Jon Marcus's "Why College Costs More than You Think" made me think hard about my own educational plans. Because I'm working to pay for as much of my education as I can, I'm taking a full load of courses so I can graduate in four years, but truth be told I'm starting to question the major I've chosen. That's one aspect of going to college that Marcus fails to discuss: how your major affects your future career choices and earnings—and whether or not some majors that don't lead immediately to a career are another way of "wasting" your time. After taking several courses in English and philosophy, I find myself fascinated by the study of literature and ideas. If I decide to major in one or both of those subjects, am I being impractical? Or am I "following my heart," as Steve Jobs said in his Stanford commencement speech? Jobs did as he told those graduates to do, and it worked out well for him, so maybe majoring in something "practical" is less practical than it seems. If I graduate in four years and am "out making money" but doing something I don't enjoy, I might be worse off than if I take longer in college but find a path that is satisfying and enriching.

WRITING A SUMMARY / RESPONSE ESSAY

You may be assigned to write a full essay that summarizes and responds to something you've read. Following is one such essay. It was written by Jacob MacLeod, a student at Wright State University, and responds to a *New York Times* column by Nicholas Kristof, "Our Blind Spot about Guns" (see p. 162).

JACOB MacLEOD

Guns and Cars Are Different

In "Our Blind Spot about Guns," *The New York Times* columnist Nicholas Kristof compares guns to cars in order to argue for sensible gun regulation. Kristof suggests that gun regulations would dramatically decrease the number of deaths caused by gun use. To demonstrate this point, he shows that the regulations governments have instituted for cars have greatly decreased the number of deaths per million miles driven. Kristof then argues that guns should be regulated in the same way that cars are, that car regulation provides a model for gun regulation. I agree with Kristof that there should be more sensible gun regulation, but I have difficulty accepting that all of the regulations imposed on cars have made them safer, and I also believe that not all of the safety regulations he proposes for guns would necessarily have positive effects.

Kristof is right that background checks for those who want to buy guns should be expanded. According to Daniel Webster, director of the Johns Hopkins Center for Gun Policy and Research, state laws prohibiting firearm ownership by members of high-risk groups, such as perpetrators of domestic violence and the mentally ill, have been shown to reduce violence. Therefore, Webster argues, universal background checks would significantly reduce the availability of guns to high-risk groups, as well as reducing the number of guns diverted to the illegal market by making it easier to prosecute gun traffickers.

Kristof also argues that lowering the speed limit made cars safer. However, in 1987, forty states raised their top speed limit from 55 to 65 miles per hour. An analysis of this change by the University of California Transportation Center shows that after the increase, traffic fatality rates on interstate highways in those forty states decreased between 3.4 percent and 5.1 percent. After the higher limits went into effect, the study suggested, some drivers may have switched to safer interstates from other, more dangerous roads, and highway patrols may have focused less on enforcing interstate speed limits and more on activities yielding greater benefits in terms of safety (Lave and Elias 58–61). Although common sense might suggest that lowered speed limits would mean safer driving, research showed otherwise, and the same may be true for gun regulation.

Gun control advocates argue that more guns mean more deaths. However, an article by gun rights advocates Don B. Kates and Gary Mauser argues that murder rates in many developed nations have bear no relation to the rate of gun ownership (652). The authors cite data on firearms ownership in the United States and England that suggest that crime rates are lowest where the density of gun ownership is highest and highest where gun density is lowest (653) and that increased gun ownership has often coincided with significant reductions in violence. For example, in the United States in the 1990s, criminal violence decreased, even though gun ownership increased (656). However, the authors acknowledge that "the notion that more guns reduce crime is highly controversial" (659).

All in all, then, Kristof is correct to suggest that sensible gun regulation is a good idea in general, but the available data suggest that some of the particular measures he proposes should not be instituted. I agree that expanding background checks would be a good way to regulate guns and that failure to require them would lead to more guns in the hands of criminals. While background checks are a good form of regulation, however, lower speed limits and trigger locks are not. The problem with this solution is that although it is based on commonsense thinking, the empirical data show that it may not work.

Works Cited

Kates, Don B., and Gary Mauser. "Would Banning Firearms Reduce Murder and Suicide? A Review of International and Some Domestic Evidence." *Harvard Journal of Law and Public Policy*, vol. 30, no. 2, Jan. 2007, pp. 649–94, www.law.harvard.edu/students/orgs/ jlpp/ Vol30_No2_KatesMauseronline.pdf. Accessed 4 Oct. 2017.

Kristof, Nicholas. "Our Blind Spot about Guns." *The New York Times,* 31 July 2014, www.nytimes.com/2014/07/31/opinion/nicholas -kristof-our-blind-spot-about-guns.html. Accessed 4 Oct. 2017.

Lave, Charles, and Patrick Elias. "Did the 65 mph Speed Limit Save Lives?" *Accident Analysis & Prevention*, vol. 26, no. 1, Feb. 1994, pp. 49–62, www.sciencedirect.com/science/article/ pii/000145759490068X. Accessed 4 Oct. 2017.

Webster, Daniel. "Why Expanding Background Checks Would, in Fact, Reduce Gun Crime." Interview by Greg Sargent. *The Washington Post,* 3 Apr. 2013, www.washingtonpost.com/blogs/plum-line/wp/2013/04/03/why-expanding-background-checks-would-in-fact-reduce-gun-crime/. Accessed 5 Oct. 2017.

In his response, MacLeod both agrees and disagrees with Kristof's argument, using several sources to support his argument that some of Kristof's proposals may not work. MacLeod states his thesis at the end of the first paragraph, after his summary, and ends with a balanced assessment of Kristof's proposals. He cites several sources, both in the text with signal phrases and in-text documentation and at the end in a works-cited section.

Key Features of Summary / Response Essays

A clearly identified author and title.   Usually the author and title of the text being summarized are identified in a signal phrase in the first sentence. The author (or sometimes the title) may then be referred to in an abbreviated form if necessary in the rest of the essay: for example, "Kristof argues . . ." or "according to 'Our Blind Spot about Guns' . . ."

A concise summary of the text.   The summary presents the main and supporting ideas in the text, usually in the order in which they appear. MacLeod, for example, reduces Kristof's argument to four sentences that capture Kristof's main points while leaving out his many examples.

An explicit response.   Your essay should usually provide a concise statement (one sentence if possible) of your overall response to the text.

- *If you're responding to the argument,* you'll likely agree or disagree (or both), and so your response itself will constitute an argument, with an explicit thesis statement. For example, MacLeod first agrees with Kristof that "there should be more sensible gun regulation," but then introduces a two-part thesis: that not all automobile regulations have made cars safer and that not all gun regulations would make guns safer.

- *If you're analyzing the text,* you'll likely need to explain what you think the author is saying and how the text goes about conveying that message. An analysis of Kristof's text, for example, might focus on his comparison of automobile regulations with gun regulations.

- *If you're responding with a reflection,* you might explore the ideas, emotions, or memories that the text evokes, the effects of its ideas on your own beliefs, or how your own personal experiences support or contradict the author's position. One response to Kristof's essay might begin by expressing surprise at the comparison of guns to cars and then explore the reasons you find that comparison surprising, leading to a new understanding of the ways regulations can work to save lives.

Support for your response. Whatever your response, you need to offer reasons and evidence to support what you say.

- *If you're responding to what the text says,* you may offer facts, statistics, anecdotal evidence, and textual evidence, as MacLeod does. You'll also need to consider—and acknowledge—any possible counterarguments, positions other than yours.

- *If you're responding to the way the text is written,* you may identify certain patterns in the text that you think mean something, and you'll need to cite evidence from the text itself. For example, Kristof twice invokes a popular slogan among gun rights advocates, "Guns don't kill people. People kill people," changing "guns" to "cars" to advance his argument that regulating guns may make them safer, just as has happened with cars.

- *If you're reflecting on your own reaction to the text,* you may connect its ideas with your own experiences or beliefs or explore how the text reinforced, challenged, or altered your beliefs. A staunch gun-rights advocate, for example, might find in Kristof's essay a reasonable middle ground too often lacking in polarized debates like the one on gun control.

Ways of Organizing a Summary and Response Essay

You can organize a summary and response essay in various ways. You may want to use a simple, straightforward structure that starts out by

387–89 ◆

summarizing the text and then gives the **THESIS** of your response followed by details that develop the thesis.

[Summary, followed by response]

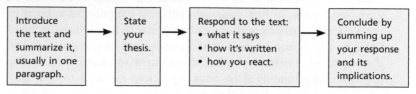

| Introduce the text and summarize it, usually in one paragraph. | → | State your thesis. | → | Respond to the text:
• what it says
• how it's written
• how you react. | → | Conclude by summing up your response and its implications. |

Or you may want to start out with the thesis and then, depending on whether your response focuses on the text's argument or its rhetorical choices, provide a paired summary of each main point or each aspect of the writing and a response to it.

[Introduction and thesis, followed by point-by-point summary and response]

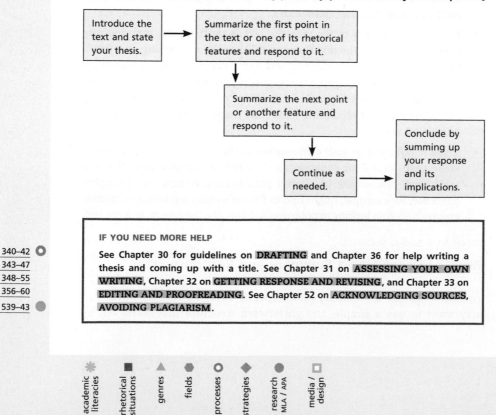

| Introduce the text and state your thesis. | → | Summarize the first point in the text or one of its rhetorical features and respond to it. |

Summarize the next point or another feature and respond to it.

Continue as needed. → Conclude by summing up your response and its implications.

IF YOU NEED MORE HELP

340–42 ○
343–47
348–55
356–60
539–43 ●

See Chapter 30 for guidelines on **DRAFTING** and Chapter 36 for help writing a thesis and coming up with a title. See Chapter 31 on **ASSESSING YOUR OWN WRITING**, Chapter 32 on **GETTING RESPONSE AND REVISING**, and Chapter 33 on **EDITING AND PROOFREADING**. See Chapter 52 on **ACKNOWLEDGING SOURCES, AVOIDING PLAGIARISM**.

Developing Academic Habits of Mind **4**

A little advice from Serena Williams: "Stick to it and work hard." She wasn't just talking about tennis, and her words resonate for all of us, for everything we set out to do. And here's Michael Jordan, who tells us "Never quit!" and then goes on to issue a warning: "If you quit once, it becomes a habit." Serena Williams and Michael Jordan may be two of the greatest athletes ever, but neither of them was born a champion. They became great by working hard, hanging in there, never giving up.

They succeeded, in other words, by developing certain habits of mind that can serve us all well—and that are especially valuable when it comes to succeeding in school. This chapter is about developing *academic habits of mind*. Just as Serena Williams wasn't born with her powerful serve, none of us was born knowing how to write academic papers or ace exams. But we too can learn and can develop the habits we need to succeed. This chapter offers advice for developing habits of mind that writing teachers nationwide have identified as essential for college success.

Engage

We all know people who see school as a series of hoops to jump through, who seem uninvolved—and even bored. We also know people who are passionate about something—a video game, a hobby, a profession—and who invest themselves, their time, and their emotions wholeheartedly in those activities. Successful students make that investment in school.

In other words, they engage with what they're studying, what they're doing, and what they're learning.

Think about your purpose for being in college. What are your goals? To get a degree? To qualify for a particular job or profession? To find intellectual stimulation? To explore life? Try to define why you are in school, both in larger terms ("to get a degree in accounting") and in terms of the specific courses you are taking ("Learning to write better will help me be a better student in general and communicate effectively at work").

Fight off boredom. Every job, including the job of being a student, involves some tasks that are dull but need to be done. When you encounter such a task, ask yourself how it helps you reach a larger goal. Shooting a hundred free throws for practice may not seem interesting, but it can help you win games. When you're listening to a lecture or reading a textbook, take notes, highlight, and annotate; doing that forces you to pay attention and increases what you remember and learn. Trying to identify the main ideas as you listen to a lecture will help you stay focused. When you're studying, try alternating between different tasks: reading, writing, doing problem sets, drawing, and so on.

If you get distracted, figure out ways to deal with it. It's hard to engage with what you're reading or studying when you're thinking about something else—paying a tuition bill, the last episode of *The Walking Dead*, whatever. Try taking a few moments to write out what's on your mind, in a journal or somewhere else. Sometimes that simple act frees your mind to think about your work, even if it doesn't solve anything.

Raise your hand. When you think you know the answer to a teacher's question (or when you yourself have a question), raise your hand. Most teachers appreciate students who take chances and who participate in class. At the same time, be polite: don't monopolize discussion or interrupt others when they're speaking.

Get involved. Get to know other students; study with them; join a campus organization. People who see themselves as part of something larger, even just a study group with three or four others, engage more in what they're doing than those who try to go it alone.

Be Curious

When we're young, we're curious about everything, and we learn by asking questions (why? why *not?*) and by exploring our surroundings (digging holes, cutting up magazines, investigating attics and basements). As we get older, though, we focus on things that interest us—and may as a result start to ignore other things or even to forget how to explore. In college, you'll be asked to research, study, and write about many topics you know nothing about. Seize the opportunity. Be curious! And take a tip from Dr. Seuss: "The more that you read, the more things you will know. / The more that you learn, the more places you'll go."

Ask questions. It's tempting to stay within our comfort zones, thinking about things we know and like, listening to those whose views we tend to agree with—to say what we already believe rather than to stop and think. Resist that temptation! Take every opportunity to ask questions, to learn more about things you're already interested in, and especially to learn about things you don't (yet) know anything about. As marine biologist Sylvia Earle says, "The best scientists and explorers have the attributes of kids! They ask questions and have a sense of wonder. They have curiosity. Who, what, where, why, when, and how! They never stop asking questions, and I never stop asking questions, just like a five year old."

Listen! Pay attention to what others say, including those who you don't necessarily agree with. The words and ideas of others can challenge the way we think, prompt us to rethink what we think—and spark our curiosity: Why does X think that? What do I think—*and why?* Why do my neighbors oppose the Common Core? What do educators think about it? Paying attention to all sides of an argument, doing research to find out what others have said about a topic, or searching social media to see the latest postings on a trending topic are all ways you can listen in on (and engage in) conversations on important issues of all kinds.

Be Open to New Ideas

No matter where you're in school, you're going to encounter ideas and concepts and even facts that challenge your own beliefs; you're also likely to meet people whose backgrounds and ways of looking at life are very different from your own. Be open-minded, open to new ideas and to what others think and say. Consider the perspectives and arguments of others. Learning involves accepting new ideas, acknowledging the value of different perspectives, and coming to understand our own beliefs in new ways. Listen to what others say, and think before you respond.

- *Treat the ideas of others with respect,* whether you agree with them or not, and encourage others to do the same. We don't open up if we don't feel safe.

- *Try to withhold judgment.* Be willing to listen to the thoughts of others and to consider ideas that may at first seem alien or weird (or wrong). Remember that your weird is likely someone else's normal—and the reverse.

- *Look for common ground between your perspectives and those of others—* places where you can agree, even in the midst of serious disagreement.

Be Flexible

Being flexible means being adaptable. In college, you'll likely face novel situations and need to find new ways to address problems, such as juggling school, work, and family; adjusting to roommates and making new friends; and figuring out how to do unfamiliar new assignments and how to take tests. You'll even have to do new kinds of writing: lab reports, reflections, literacy narratives, and many, many more; if your school writing up until this point has usually (or always) called for a five-paragraph theme, that's not going to be the case anymore.

Look for new ways to do things. As the saying goes, "If all you have is a hammer, everything looks like a nail." Look for other tools to add to your toolbox: try solving math problems with words or by drawing, or starting a writing project by sketching out the parts.

Try not to see things as right or wrong, good or bad. Be willing to consider alternative points of view and to withhold judgment. Often ideas or actions can only be judged in context; they may be true in some cases or in part, and you often need to understand the larger situation or take into account various perspectives. For example, you may believe that lying is wrong, but is it excusable if telling the truth will cause someone pain? You find a required reading assignment boring and useless, but why, then, did your instructor assign it?

Approach academic assignments rhetorically. Analyze each assignment's purpose, intended audience, and the rest of its RHETORICAL SITUATION. Think about what's required in terms of content and format—and also about what's appropriate in terms of language and style. And what's expected in the discipline: informal language, sentence fragments, and photographs without captions might be appropriate for a sociology blog, for example, whereas a research project for a history course might have different requirements for how it's organized, formatted, and documented.

■ 53

Be Creative

If you think that creativity is something artists have (and are born with), think again. From the young man selling homemade granola at a local farm market to the woman who puts together an eye-catching outfit from thrift-store bins, many of us are at work expressing ourselves in distinctive ways. Psychologists tell us that acting creatively opens us up to becoming more creative—and it is safe to say that doing so will make your work more productive and very likely more fun.

- *Play with ideas.* Freewrite. Make lists. Try looping, clustering, and the other ways of **GENERATING IDEAS** covered in this book. Take some time to think about the ideas you come up with.

331–39 ◐

- *Don't wait until the last minute.* Some students say they do better under the pressure of a deadline. Don't believe it! It's *always* better to give yourself time to think, to explore ideas, to "sleep on" assignments that first stump you.

- *Take risks!* Explore questions and topics that you haven't thought about before. Try out methods you haven't used previously. Challenge yourself to come up with ten ideas. Or twenty.

- *Ask questions.* And remember that there's no such thing as a dumb question.

Persist

Sometimes the key to success is simply sticking to the task at hand: ignoring distractions, hanging in there, forgetting frustration, getting the work done even in the face of setbacks and failures. Here's some advice from actress and singer Julie Andrews: "Perseverance is failing 19 times and succeeding the 20th."

- *Don't quit.* Assume that you can complete the task, and make up your mind to do it. If you're reading a book that seems hopelessly confusing or over your head, for example, keep at it until it starts to make sense. Reread, **OUTLINE CHAPTERS**, **SUMMARIZE**, **ANNOTATE**, and do whatever else you need to do to understand it.

335–37 ◐
20 ❋
16–17

- *Remember that sometimes you'll encounter setbacks*—and that the goal (a passing grade, a degree, a job) is still reachable if you keep trying. Those who play video games know that failing is an inherent part of playing them; the same is true of many other things as well.

- *Make a plan and establish a schedule,* and stick to them.
- *Break large projects into smaller goals.* Especially with assignments that call for a huge amount of work, approach it in stages: focus on getting through the next chapter, the next draft, the next whatever. It may be good to "keep your eyes on the prize," but it's usually best to take it one step at a time.
- *When you're working on several assignments, tackle the hardest ones first.* Work on them when you're fresh and your mind is clear.
- *If you don't understand something, ask for clarification.* Better to admit to confusion than to act as if you know something when you don't.
- *Ask for help when you need it.* Teachers are usually happy to help students during office hours or by appointment, before or after class, or over email. Get to know your teachers: they're there to help you.
- *Take advantage of whatever help is available* at your school's writing center or learning center and in class. An important part of being persistent is getting help when you need it.

Reflect

Pay attention to the ways you work and make decisions. Reflect on the ways you think and on how you think about the world. This kind of "meta-cognitive" thinking is one of the most important habits of mind, and it's one that will continue to serve you well throughout your life.

- *Figure out when you are most efficient* and do your best work—and try to schedule your work accordingly.
- *Pay attention to what you're reading and how you're doing it.* Think about why you're reading x, and use **READING STRATEGIES** appropriate to your purpose. If you lose the thread of an explanation or argument, figure out where you got lost and why. ✳ 10–32
- *After completing an assignment, reflect in writing* on what you did well, what problems you had, and how you solved them (or not). What would you do differently next time—or if you had more time? You'll

find prompts for "Taking Stock of Your Work" at the end of Chapters 10–23 that can help.

- *Troubleshoot.* Pay attention to bumps in the road as you encounter them. Try to understand what caused the problem, what you did to solve it, how successful you were and why.

- *Try to focus on your achievements, what you can do,* rather than on what you may not be able to do or to do as well as you'd like.

Take Responsibility

In one way or another, all the habits of mind discussed above involve taking responsibility for your own actions. It may be tempting to blame others or society or bad luck for problems in your academic life, but the more you take ownership of your own learning, the more control you have over the results. Some ways you can enhance your sense of responsibility and demonstrate it include these:

- *Acknowledge that how much you learn and what grades you get depend mostly on you.* Teachers often say that they don't *give* grades, students *earn* grades—an important difference.

- *Treat school as you do a job,* one for which you must show up on time, perform tasks at a certain level of competence, and meet deadlines. In college, where your time is mostly unstructured, you have to become your own boss. So attend class regularly, follow instructions, and turn in assignments on time.

- *Get organized.* Maintain a calendar so you know what's due when. Create a schedule for your day that includes time for class, studying, working, and personal activities. Develop a system for organizing your written work and notes for each course you're taking. Learn where to find the materials you need to do your classwork.

526–38
544–47
- *Use research sources responsibly.* QUOTE, PARAPHRASE, and SUMMARIZE the work of others accurately, and DOCUMENT it correctly. Give appropriate credit to those whose ideas and words you are using.

✳ academic literacies ■ rhetorical situations ▲ genres ⬢ fields ○ processes ◆ strategies ● research MLA / APA ▢ media / design

part 2

Rhetorical Situations

Whenever we write, whether it's a text to a friend or a toast for a wedding, an English essay or a résumé, we face some kind of rhetorical situation. We have a PURPOSE, a certain AUDIENCE, a particular STANCE, a GENRE, and a MEDIUM to consider—and, as often as not, a DESIGN. All are important elements that we need to think about carefully. The following chapters offer brief discussions of those elements of the rhetorical situation, along with questions that can help you make the choices you need to as you write. See also the GENRE chapters for guidelines for considering your rhetorical situation in each of these specific kinds of writing.

Rhetorical Situations

Purpose 5

All writing has a purpose. We write to explore our thoughts and emotions, to express ourselves, to entertain; we write to record words and events, to communicate with others, to try to persuade others to believe as we do or to behave in certain ways. In fact, we often have several purposes at the same time. We may write an essay in which we try to explain something to an audience, but at the same time we may be trying to persuade that audience of something. Look, for example, at this passage from a 2012 *New York Times* op-ed essay by economist and editorial columnist Paul Krugman about social and economic trends among "the traditional working-class family"—declining rates of marriage and of male participation in the labor force and increasing numbers of out-of-wedlock births. Krugman asserts that the primary reason for those statistics is a "drastic reduction in the work opportunities available to less-educated men":

> Most of the numbers you see about income trends in America focus on households rather than individuals, which makes sense for some purposes. But when you see a modest rise in incomes for the lower tiers of the income distribution, you have to realize that all—yes, all—of this rise comes from the women, both because more women are in the paid labor force and because women's wages aren't as much below male wages as they used to be.
>
> For lower-education working men, however, it has been all negative. Adjusted for inflation, entry-level wages of male high school graduates have fallen 23 percent since 1973. Meanwhile, employment benefits have collapsed. In 1980, 65 percent of recent high-school graduates working in the private sector had health benefits, but, by 2009, that was down to 29 percent.
>
> So we have become a society in which less-educated men have great difficulty finding jobs with decent wages and good benefits.
>
> —Paul Krugman, "Money and Morals"

Krugman is reporting information here, outlining how the earnings and benefits of less-educated men have dropped over the last forty years. He is also making an argument, that these economic setbacks are a cause of the social ills among working-class Americans and not, as some would have it, the result of them. (Krugman, writing for a newspaper, is also using a style—including dashes, contractions, and other informal elements—that strives to be engaging while it informs and argues.)

Even though our purposes may be many, knowing our primary reason for writing can help us shape that writing and understand how to proceed with it. Our purpose can determine the genre we choose, our audience, even the way we design what we write.

Identify your purpose.　While a piece of writing often has many purposes, a writer usually focuses on one. When you get an assignment or see a need to write, ask yourself what the primary purpose of the writing task is: to entertain? to inform? to persuade? to demonstrate your knowledge or your writing ability? What are your own goals? What are your audience's expectations, and do they affect the way you define your purpose?

Thinking about Purpose

371

73

66–68

637

- *What do you want your audience to do, think, or feel?* How will your readers use what you tell them?
- *What does this writing task call on you to do?* Do you need to show that you have mastered certain content or skills? Do you have an assignment that specifies a particular **STRATEGY** or **GENRE**—to compare two things, perhaps, or to argue a position?
- *What are the best ways to achieve your purpose?* What **STANCE** should you take? Should you write in a particular genre? Do you have a choice of **MEDIUM**, and does your text require any special format or **DESIGN** elements?

academic literacies | rhetorical situations | genres | fields | processes | strategies | research MLA / APA | media / design

Audience 6

Who will read (or hear) what you are writing? A seemingly obvious but crucially important question. Your audience affects your writing in various ways. Consider a piece of writing as simple as a text from a mother to her son:

Pls. take chicken out to thaw and feed Annye. Remember Dr. Wong at 4.

On the surface, this brief note is a straightforward reminder to do three things. But in fact it is a complex message filled with compressed information for a specific audience. The writer (the mother) counts on the reader (her son) to know a lot that can be left unsaid. She expects that he knows that the chicken is in the freezer and needs to thaw in time to be cooked for dinner; she knows that he knows who Annye is (a pet?), what they are fed, and how much; she assumes that he knows who (and where) Dr. Wong is. She doesn't need to spell out any of that because she knows what her son knows and what he needs to know—and in her text she can be brief. She understands her audience. Think how different such a reminder would be were it written to another audience—a babysitter, perhaps, or a friend helping out while Mom is out of town.

What you write, how much you write, how you phrase it, even your choice of **GENRE** (memo, essay, email, text, speech)—all are influenced by the audience you envision. And your audience will interpret your writing according to their own expectations and experiences, not yours.

61–65

When you are a student, your audience is most often your teachers, so you need to be aware of their expectations and know the conventions (rules, often unstated) for writing in specific academic fields. You may make statements that seem obvious to you, not realizing that your instructors may consider them assertions that must be proved with evidence of one sort or another. Or you may write more or less formally than teachers expect. Understanding your audience's expectations—by asking outright, by reading materials in your field of study, by trial and error—is important to your success as a college writer.

This point is worth dwelling on. You are probably reading this textbook for a writing course. As a student, you will be expected to produce essays with few or no errors. If you correspond with family, friends, or coworkers using email and texts, you may question such standards; after all, many of the messages you get in these contexts are not grammatically perfect. But in a writing class, the instructor needs to see your best work. Whatever the rhetorical situation, your writing must meet the expectations of your audience.

Identify your audience.   Audiences may be defined as *known, multiple,* or *unknown. Known audiences* can include people with whom you're familiar as well as people you don't know personally but whose needs and expectations you do know. You yourself are a known, familiar audience, and you write to and for yourself often. Class notes, to-do lists, reminders, and journals are all written primarily for an audience of one: you. For that reason, they are often in shorthand, full of references and code that you alone understand.

Other known, familiar audiences include anyone you actually know—friends, relatives, teachers, classmates—and whose needs and expectations you understand. You can also know what certain readers want and need, even if you've never met them personally, if you write for them within a specific shared context. Such a known audience might include PC gamers who read cheat codes that you have posted on the internet for beating a game; you don't know those people, but you know roughly what they know about the game and what they need to know, and you know how to write about it in ways they will understand.

You often have to write for *multiple audiences.* Business memos or reports may be written initially for a supervisor, who may pass them along to others. Grant proposals may be reviewed by four to six levels of readers—each, of course, with its own expectations and perspectives.

Even writing for a class might involve multiple audiences: your instructor and your classmates.

Unknown audiences can be the most difficult to address since you can't be sure what they know, what they need to know, how they'll react. Such an audience could be your downstairs neighbor, with whom you've chatted occasionally in the laundry room. How will she respond to your letter asking her to sponsor you in an upcoming charity walk? Another unknown audience—perhaps surprisingly—might be many of your instructors, who want—and expect!—you to write in ways that are new to you. While you can benefit from analyzing any audience, you need to think most carefully about those you don't know.

Thinking about Audience

- *Whom do you want to reach?* To whom are you writing (or speaking)?

- *What is your audience's background—their education and life experiences?* It may be important for you to know, for example, whether your readers attended college, fought in a war, or have young children.

- *What are their interests?* What do they like? What motivates them? What do they care about?

- *Is there any demographic information that you should keep in mind?* Consider whether race, gender, sexual orientation, disabilities, occupation, religious beliefs, economic status, and so on should affect what or how you write. For example, writers for *Men's Health*, *InStyle*, and *Out* must consider the particular interests of each magazine's readers.

- *What political circumstances may affect their reading?* What attitudes—opinions, special interests, biases—may affect the way your audience reads your piece? Are your readers conservative, liberal, or middle of the road? Politics may take many other forms as well—retirees on a fixed income may object to increased school taxes, so a letter arguing for such an increase would need to appeal to them differently than would a similar letter sent to parents of young children.

- *What does your audience already know—or believe—about your topic? What do you need to tell them? What is the best way to do so?* Those retirees who oppose school taxes already know that taxes are a burden for them; they may need to know why schools are justified in asking for more money every few years. A good way to explain this may be with a bar graph showing how property values benefit from good schools with adequate funding. Consider which **STRATEGIES** will be effective—narrative, comparison, something else?

371 ◆

- *What's your relationship with your audience, and how should it affect your language and tone?* Do you know them, or not? Are they friends? colleagues? mentors? adversaries? strangers? Will they likely share your **STANCE**? In general, you need to write more formally when you're addressing readers you don't know, and you may address friends and colleagues more informally than you would a boss.

66–68

- *What does your audience need and expect from you?* Your history professor, for example, may need to know how well you can discuss the economy of the late Middle Ages in order to assess your learning; he may expect you to write a carefully reasoned argument, drawing conclusions from various sources, with a readily identifiable thesis in the first paragraph. Your boss, on the other hand, may need an informal email that briefly lists your sales contacts for the day; she may expect that you list the contacts in the order in which you saw them, that you clearly identify each one, and that you briefly say how well each contact went. What **GENRE** is most appropriate?

73 ▲

- *What kind of response do you want?* Do you want readers to believe or do something? to accept as valid your information on a topic? to understand why an experience you once had matters to you?

637 ☐

- *How can you best appeal to your audience?* Is there a particular **MEDIUM** that will best reach them? Are there any **DESIGN** requirements? (Elderly readers may need larger type, for instance.)

academic literacies   rhetorical situations   genres   fields   processes   strategies   research MLA / APA   media / design

Genres are kinds of writing. Letters, profiles, reports, position papers, poems, blog posts, instructions, parodies—even jokes—are genres. For example, here is the beginning of a **PROFILE** of a mechanic who repairs a specific kind of automobile:

▲ 233–45

> Her business card reads Shirley Barnes, M.D., and she's a doctor, all right—a Metropolitan Doctor. Her passion is the Nash Metropolitan, the little car produced by Austin of England for American Motors between 1954 and 1962. Barnes is a legend among southern California Met lovers—an icon, a beacon, and a font of useful knowledge and freely offered opinions.

A profile offers a written portrait of someone or something that informs and sometimes entertains, often examining its subject from a particular angle—in this case, as a female mechanic who fixes Nash Metropolitans. While the language in this example is informal and lively ("she's a doctor, all right"), the focus is on the subject, Shirley Barnes, "M.D." If this same excerpt were presented as a poem, however, the new genre would change our reading:

> Her business card reads
> Shirley Barnes, M.D.,
> and she's a doctor, all right
> —a Metropolitan Doctor.
> Her passion is the Nash Metropolitan,
> the little car produced by Austin of England
> for American Motors between 1954 and 1962.
> Barnes is a legend
> among southern California Met lovers
> —an icon,

a beacon,
and a font of useful knowledge and
freely offered opinions.

The content hasn't changed, but the different presentation invites us to read not only to learn about Shirley Barnes but also to explore the significance of the words and phrases on each line, to read for deeper meaning and greater appreciation of language. The genre thus determines how we read and how we interpret what we read.

Genres help us write by establishing features for conveying certain kinds of content. They give readers clues about what sort of information they're likely to find and so help them figure out how to read ("This article begins with an abstract, so it's probably a scholarly source" or "Thank goodness! I found the instructions for editing videos on my phone"). At the same time, genres are flexible; writers often tweak the features or combine elements of different genres to achieve a particular purpose or connect with an audience in a particular way. Genres also change as writers' needs and available technologies change. For example, computers have enabled us to add audio and video content to texts that once could appear only on paper.

Choosing the Appropriate Genre

How do you know which genre you should choose? Often the words and phrases used in writing assignments can give you clues to the best choice. Here are typical terms used in assignments and the genres they usually call for.

75–97 ▲   **LITERACY NARRATIVE** If you're assigned to explore your development as a writer or reader or to describe how you came to be interested in a particular subject or career, you'll likely need to write a literacy narrative or a variation on one. Some terms that might signal a literacy narrative: *describe a learning experience, tell how you learned, trace your development, write a story.*

98–130 ▲
211–23   **TEXTUAL ANALYSIS** or **LITERARY ANALYSIS** If your assignment calls on you to look at a nonfiction text to see not only what it says but how it works,

you likely need to write a textual analysis. If the text is a short story, novel, poem, or play, you probably need to write a literary analysis. If you are analyzing a text or texts in multiple media, you might choose either genre or mix the two. Some terms that might signal that a textual or literary analysis is being asked for: *analyze, examine, explicate, read closely, interpret.*

REPORT If your task is to research a topic and then tell your audience in a balanced, neutral way what you know about it, your goal is probably to write a report. Some terms that might signal that a report is being asked for: *define, describe, explain, inform, observe, record, report, show.*

131–56

POSITION PAPER or **ARGUMENT** Some terms that might signal that your instructor wants you to take a position or argue for or against something: *agree or disagree, argue, claim, criticize, defend, justify, position paper, prove.*

157–84

SUMMARY If your assignment is to reduce a text into a single paragraph or so, is called for. Some terms that might signal that a summary is expected: *abridge, boil down, compress, condense, recap, summarize.*

EVALUATION If your instructor asks you to say whether or not you like something or whether it's a good or bad example of a category or better or worse than something else, an evaluation is likely being called for. Some terms that might signal that an evaluation is expected: *assess, critique, evaluate, judge, recommend, review.*

202–10

MEMOIR If you're asked to explore an important moment or event in your life, you're probably being asked to write a memoir. Some terms that likely signal that a memoir is desired: *autobiography, chronicle, narrate, a significant personal memory, a story drawn from your experience.*

224–32

PROFILE If your instructor assigns you the task of portraying a subject in a way that is both informative and entertaining, you're likely being asked to write a profile. Some terms that might indicate that a profile is being asked for: *angle, describe, dominant impression, interview, observe, report on.*

233–45

PROPOSAL If you're asked to offer a solution to a problem, to suggest some action—or to make a case for pursuing a certain project, a proposal

246–55

is probably in order. Some terms that might indicate a proposal: *argue for [a solution or action], propose, put forward, recommend.*

256–63 ▲

REFLECTION If your assignment calls on you to think in writing about something or to play with ideas, you are likely being asked to write a reflection. Some terms that may mean that a reflection is called for: *consider, explore, ponder, probe, reflect, speculate.*

Dealing with Ambiguous Assignments

Sometimes even the key term in an assignment doesn't indicate clearly which genre is wanted, so you need to read such an assignment especially carefully. A first step might be to consider whether it's asking for a report or an argument. For example, here are two sample assignments:

> Discuss ways in which the invention of gas and incandescent lighting significantly changed people's daily lives in the nineteenth century.

> Discuss why Willy Loman in Death of a Salesman is, or is not, a tragic hero.

Both assignments use the word *discuss,* but in very different ways. The first may be simply be requesting an informative, researched report: the thesis—new forms of lighting significantly changed people's daily lives in various ways—is already given, and you may be simply expected to research and explain what some of these changes were. It's also possible, though, that this assignment is asking you to make an argument about which of these changes were the most significant ones.

In contrast, *discuss* in the second assignment is much more open-ended. It does not lead to a particular thesis but is more clearly asking you to present an argument: to choose a position (Willy Loman *is* a tragic hero; Willy Loman is *not* a tragic hero; even, possibly, Willy Loman both *is and is not* a tragic hero) and to marshal reasons and evidence from the play to support your position. A clue that an argument is being asked for lies in the way the assignment offers a choice of paths.

Other potentially ambiguous words in assignments are *show* and *explore,* both of which could lead in many directions. If after a careful

✳ academic literacies
■ rhetorical situations
▲ genres
● fields
○ processes
◆ strategies
● research MLA / APA
☐ media / design

reading of the entire assignment you still aren't sure what it's asking for, ask your instructor to clarify the appropriate genre or genres.

Thinking about Genre

- *How does your genre affect what content you can or should include?* Objective information? Researched source material? Your own opinions? Personal experience? A mix?

- *Does your genre call for any specific* **STRATEGIES**? Profiles, for example, usually include some narration; lab reports often explain a process.

◆ 371

- *Does your genre require a certain organization?* **PROPOSALS**, for instance, usually need to show a problem exists before offering a solution. Some genres leave room for choice. Business letters delivering good news might be organized differently than those making sales pitches.

▲ 246–55

- *Does your genre affect your tone?* An abstract of a scholarly paper calls for a different **TONE** than a memoir. Should your words sound serious and scholarly? brisk and to the point? objective? opinionated? Sometimes your genre affects the way you communicate your **STANCE**.

■ 67–68

■ 66–68

- *Does the genre require formal (or informal) language?* A letter to the mother of a friend asking for a summer job in her bookstore calls for more formal language than does an email to the friend thanking him for the lead.

- *Do you have a choice of medium?* Some genres call for print; others for an electronic medium. Sometimes you have a choice: a résumé, for instance, can be printed to bring to an interview, or it may be downloaded or emailed. Some teachers want reports turned in on paper; others prefer that they be emailed or posted in the class course management system. If you're not sure what **MEDIUM** you can use, ask.

□ 637

- *Does your genre have any design requirements?* Some genres call for paragraphs; others require lists. Some require certain kinds of fonts—you wouldn't use **impact** for a personal narrative, nor would you likely use chiller for an invitation to Grandma's sixty-fifth birthday party. Different genres call for different **DESIGN** elements.

□ 637

8 Stance

Whenever you write, you have a certain stance, an attitude toward your topic. The way you express that stance affects the way you come across to your audience as a writer and a person. This email from a college student to his father, for example, shows a thoughtful, reasonable stance for a carefully researched argument:

> Hi Dad,
> I'll get right to the point: I'd like to buy a car. I saved over $4,500 from working this summer, and I've found three different cars that I can get for under $3,000. That'll leave me $1,400 to cover the insurance. I can park in Lot J, over behind Monte Hall, for $75 for both semesters. And I can earn gas and repair money by upping my hours at the cafeteria. It won't cost you any more, and if I have a car, you won't have to come and pick me up when I want to come home. May I buy it?
> Love,
> Michael

While such a stance can't guarantee that Dad will give permission, it's more likely to produce results than this version:

> Hi Dad,
> I'm buying a car. A guy in my Western Civ course has a cool Nissan he wants to get rid of. I've got $4,500 saved from working this summer, it's mine, and I'm going to use it to get some wheels. Mom said you'd freak if I did, but I want this car. OK?
> Michael

The writer of the first email respects his reader and offers reasoned arguments and evidence of research to convince him that buying a car is an action that will benefit them both. The writer of the second, by contrast, seems impulsive, ready to buy the first car that comes along, and defiant—

he's picking a fight. Each email reflects a certain stance that shows the writer as a certain kind of person dealing with a topic in a certain way and establishing a certain relationship with his audience.

Identify your stance.   What is your attitude toward your topic? Objective? Critical? Curious? Opinionated? Passionate? Indifferent? Your stance may be affected by your relationship to your **AUDIENCE**. How do you want them to see you? As a colleague sharing information? a good student showing what you can do? an advocate for a position? Often your stance is affected by your **GENRE**: for example, lab reports require an objective, unemotional stance that emphasizes the content and minimizes the writer's own attitudes. Memoir, by comparison, allows you to reveal your feelings about your topic. Your stance is also affected by your **PURPOSE**, as the two emails about cars show. Your stance in a piece written to entertain will likely differ from the stance you'd adopt to persuade.

■ 57–60

▲ 73

■ 55–56

You communicate (or downplay) your stance through your tone — through the words you use and other ways your text expresses an attitude toward your subject and audience. For example, in an academic essay you would state your position directly — "*The Bachelor* reflects the values of American society today" — using a confident, authoritative tone. In contrast, using qualifiers like "might" or "I think" can give your writing a wishy-washy, uncertain tone: "I think *The Bachelor* might reflect some of America's values." A sarcastic tone might be appropriate for a comment on a blog post but isn't right for an academic essay: "*The Bachelor*'s star has all the personality of a bowling ball."

Like every other element of writing, your tone must be appropriate for your rhetorical situation.

Just as you likely alter what you say depending on whether you're speaking to a boss, an instructor, a parent, or a good friend, so you need to make similar adjustments as a writer. It's a question of appropriateness: we behave in certain ways in various social situations, and writing is a social situation. You might sign an email to a friend with an XO, but in an email to your supervisor you'll likely sign off with a "Many thanks" or "Sincerely." To write well, you need to write with integrity, to say as much as possible what you wish to say; yet you also must understand that in writing, as in speaking, your stance and tone need to suit your purpose, your relationship to your audience, the way in which you wish your audience to perceive you, and your medium.

In writing as in other aspects of life, the Golden Rule applies: "Do unto audiences as you would have them do unto you." Address readers respectfully if you want them to respond to your words with respect.

Thinking about Stance

- *What is your stance, and how does it relate to your purpose for writing?* If you feel strongly about your topic and are writing an argument that tries to persuade your audience to feel the same way, your stance and your **PURPOSE** fit naturally together. But suppose you are writing about the same topic with a different purpose—to demonstrate the depth of your knowledge about the topic, for example, or your ability to consider it in a detached, objective way. You will need to adjust your stance to meet the demands of this different purpose.

  55–56

- *How should your stance be reflected in your tone?* Can your tone grow directly out of your stance, or do you need to "tone down" your attitude toward the topic or take a different tone altogether? Do you want to be seen as reasonable? angry? thoughtful? gentle? funny? ironic? If you're writing about something you want to be seen as taking very seriously, be sure that your language and even your font reflect that seriousness. Check your writing for words that reflect the tone you want to convey—and for ones that do not (and revise as necessary).

- *How is your stance likely to be received by your audience?* Your tone and especially the attitude it projects toward your **AUDIENCE** will affect how they react to the content of what you say.

  57–60

- *Should you openly discuss your stance?* Do you want or need to announce your own perspective on your topic? Will doing so help you reach your audience, or would it be better not to say directly where you're coming from?

Media/Design 9

In its broadest sense, a medium is a go-between: a way for information to be conveyed from one person to another. We communicate through many media, verbal and nonverbal: our bodies (we catch someone's eye, wave, nod); our voices (we whisper, talk, shout, groan); and various technologies, including handwriting, print, telephone, radio, video, and computer.

Each medium has unique characteristics that influence both what and how we communicate. As an example, consider this message: "I haven't told you this before, but I love you." Most of the time, we communicate such a message in person, using the medium of voice (with, presumably, help from eye contact and touch). A phone call will do, though most of us would think it a poor second choice, and a handwritten letter or note would be acceptable, if necessary. Few of us would break such news on a website, with a tweet, or during a radio call-in program.

By contrast, imagine whispering the following sentence in a darkened room: "By the last decades of the nineteenth century, the territorial expansion of the United States had left almost all Indians confined to reservations." That sentence starts a chapter in a history textbook, and it would be strange indeed to whisper it into someone's ear. It is appropriate, however, in the textbook, in print or in an e-book, or as a quotation in an oral presentation.

As you can see, we can often choose among various media depending on our purpose and audience. In addition, we can often combine media to create **MULTIMEDIA** texts. And different media allow us to use different ways or modes of expressing meaning, from words to images to sound to hyperlinks, that can be combined into **MULTIMODAL** formats.

641–42

No matter the medium or media, a text's design affects the way it is received and understood. A typed letter on official letterhead sends a different message than the same words handwritten on pastel stationery. Classic type

654–60 □
sends a different message than *flowery italics*. Some genres and media (and audiences) demand **PHOTOS**, **DIAGRAMS**, or color. Some information is easier to explain—and read—in the form of a **PIE CHART** or a **BAR GRAPH** than in the form of a paragraph. Some reports and documents are so long and complex that they need to be divided into sections, which are then best
650–52 □
labeled with **HEADINGS**. These are some of the elements to consider when you are thinking about how to design what you write.

Identify your media and design needs.   Does your writing situation call for a certain medium and design? A printed essay? An oral report with visual aids? A blog? A podcast? Academic assignments often assume a particular medium and design, but if you're unsure about your options or the degree of flexibility you have, check with your instructor.

Thinking about Media

- *What medium are you using*—print? spoken? electronic? a combination?—and how does it affect the way you will create your text? A printed résumé is usually no more than one page long; an electronic résumé posted on an employer's website has no length limits. An oral presentation should contain detailed information; accompanying slides should provide only an outline.

371 ◆
- *How does your medium affect your organization and* **STRATEGIES**? Long paragraphs are fine on paper but don't work well on the web. On presentation slides, phrases or keywords work better than sentences. In print, you need to define unfamiliar terms; on the web, you can sometimes just add a link to a definition found elsewhere.

- *How does your medium affect your language?* Some print documents require a more formal voice than spoken media; email and texting often invite greater informality.

- *How does your medium affect what modes of expression you use?* Should your text include photos, graphics, audio or video files, or links? Do you need slides, handouts, or other visuals to accompany an oral presentation?

Thinking about Design

- *What's the appropriate look for your* RHETORICAL SITUATION*?* Should your text look serious? whimsical? personal? something else? What design elements will suit your audience, purpose, stance, genre, and medium?

53

- *What elements need to be designed?* Is there any information you would like to highlight by putting it in a box? Are there any key terms that should be boldfaced? Do you need navigation buttons? How should you indicate links?

- *What font(s) are appropriate* to your audience, purpose, stance, genre, and medium?

- *Are you including any* VISUALS? Should you? Will your AUDIENCE expect or need any? Is there any information in your text that would be easier to understand as a chart or graph? If you need to include video or audio clips, how should the links be presented?

653–63
57–60

- *Should you include headings?* Would they help you organize your materials and help readers follow the text? Does your GENRE or MEDIUM require them?

61–65
69–71

- *Should you use a specific format?* MLA? APA?

MLA 548–96
APA 597–636

part 3

Genres

When we make a shopping list, we automatically write each item we need in a single column. When we email a friend, we begin with a salutation: "Hi, Jordan." Whether we are writing a letter, a résumé, or a proposal, we know generally what it should contain and what it should look like because we are familiar with each of those genres. Genres are kinds of writing, and texts in any given genre share goals and features—a proposal, for instance, generally starts out by identifying a problem and then suggests a certain solution. The chapters in this part provide guidelines for writing in thirteen common academic genres. First come detailed chapters on four genres often assigned in writing classes—LITERACY NARRATIVES, TEXTUAL ANALYSES, REPORTS, and ARGUMENTS— followed by brief chapters on NINE OTHER GENRES and one on MIXING GENRES.

Genres

Writing a Literacy Narrative 10

Narratives are stories, and we read and tell them for many different purposes. Parents read their children bedtime stories as an evening ritual. College applicants write about significant moments in their lives. In *psychology* courses, you may write a personal narrative to illustrate how individuals' stories inform the study of behavior. In *education* courses, you may share stories of your teaching experiences. And in *computer science* courses, you may write programming narratives to develop programming skills.

This chapter provides detailed guidelines for writing a specific kind of narrative: a literacy narrative. Writers of literacy narratives traditionally explore their experiences with reading or writing, but we'll broaden the definition to include experiences with various literacies, which might include learning an academic skill, a sport, an artistic technique, or something else. For example, the third narrative in this chapter explores one writer's realization that she needs "automotive literacy" to work in her parents' car repair shop. Along with this essay, this chapter includes two additional good examples, the first annotated to point out the key features found in most literacy narratives.

EMILY VALLOWE

Write or Wrong Identity

Emily Vallowe wrote this literacy narrative for a writing class at the University of Mary Washington in Virginia. In it, she explores her lifelong identity as a writer—and her doubts about that identity.

I'm sitting in the woods with a bunch of Catholic people I just met yesterday. Suddenly, they ask me to name one of the talents God has given me. I panic for a split second and then breathe an internal sigh of relief. I tell them I'm a writer. As the group leaders move on to ques-

Attention-getting opening.

tion someone else, I sit trying to mentally catch my breath. It will take a moment before the terror leaves my forearms, chest, and stomach, but I tell myself that I have nothing to fear. I am a writer. Yes, I most definitely am a writer. *Now breathe,* I tell myself . . . *and suppress that horrifying suspicion that you are actually not a writer at all.*

The retreat that prepared me for my eighth-grade confirmation was not the first time I found myself pulling out the old "I'm a writer" card and wondering whether I was worthy enough to carry this sacred card in the wallet of my identity. Such things happen to people with identity crises.

Clearly described details.

In kindergarten I wrote about thirty books. They were each about five pages long, with one sentence and a picture on each page. They were held together with three staples on the left side or top and had construction paper covers with the book's title and the phrase "by Emily Vallowe" written out in neat kindergarten-teacher handwriting. My mom still has all of these books in a box at the bottom of her closet.

One day at the very end of the school year, my kindergarten teacher took me to meet my future first-grade teacher, Mrs. Meadows. I got to make a special trip to meet her because I had been absent on the day the rest of the kindergarteners had gone to meet their future teachers. Mrs. Meadows's classroom was big and blue and different from the kindergarten class, complete with bigger, different kids (I think Mrs. Meadows had been teaching third or fourth graders that year, so her students were much older than I was). During this visit, Mrs. Meadows showed me a special writing desk, complete with a small, old-fashioned desk lamp (with a lamp shade and everything). I'm not sure if I understood why she was showing me this writing area. She may have said that she'd heard good things about me.

Vallowe traces her identity as a writer through her life.

This handful of images is all I can remember about the most 5 significant event in my writing life. I'm not sure why I connect the memory of my kindergarten books with the image of me sitting in Mrs. Meadows's old classroom (for by the time I had her she was in a room on the opposite side of the school). I guess I don't even know exactly when this major event happened. Was it kindergarten? First grade? Somewhere in between? All I know is that some event occurred in early elementary school that made me want to be a writer. I don't even clearly remember what this event was, but it is something that has actively affected me for the fourteen years since then.

I have wanted to be a writer my entire life—or at least that's what I tell people. Looking back, I don't know if I ever *wanted* to be a writer. The idea might never have even occurred to me. Yet somehow I was marked as a writer. My teachers must have seen something in my writing that impressed them and clued me in on it. Teachers like to recognize kids for their strengths, and at the age of five, I probably started to notice that different kids were good at different things: Bobby was good at t-ball; Sally was good at drawing; Jenny could run really fast. I was probably starting to panic at the thought that I might not be good at anything—and then a teacher came along and told me I was good at writing. Someone gave me a compliment, and I ran with it. I declared myself to be a writer and have clung to this writer identity ever since.

There are certain drawbacks to clinging to one unchanging identity since the age of five. Constant panic is one of these drawbacks. It is a strange feeling to grow up defining yourself as something when you don't know if that something is actually true. By the time I got to middle school, I could no longer remember having become a writer; I had just always been one—and had been one without any proof that I deserved to be called one. By the age of ten, I was facing a seasoned writer's terror of "am I any good?!" and this terror has followed me throughout my entire life since then. Every writing assignment I ever had was a test—a test to see if I was a real writer, to prove myself to teachers, to classmates, to myself. I approached every writing assignment thinking, "I am supposed to be good at this," not "I am going to try to make this good," and such an attitude is not a healthy way to approach anything.

It doesn't help that if I am a writer, I am a very slow one. I can't sit down and instantly write something beautiful like some people I know can. I have been fortunate to go to school with some very smart classmates, some of whom can whip out a great piece of writing in minutes. I still find these people threatening. If they are faster than I am, does that make them better writers than I am? *I thought I was supposed to be "the writer"!*

My obsession with being "the" writer stems from my understanding of what it means to be "the" anything. My childhood was

Ongoing discussion of the central issue: is she a writer or not?

marked by a belief in many abstract absolutes that I am only now allowing to crumble. I was born in Chicago (and was thus the fourth generation of my family to live there), but I grew up in northern Virginia. I came to look down on my Virginia surroundings because I had been taught to view Chicago as this great Mecca—the world's most amazing city to which I must someday return, and to which all other places on earth pale in comparison. Throughout my childhood, I gathered that Chicago is a real city in which average people live and which has an economy historically based in shipping and manufacturing; Washington, D.C., on the other hand, where my dad works, has a population that includes a bizarre mix of impoverished people and the most influential leaders and diplomats in the world—and so manufactures nothing but political power. People in Chicago know how to deal with snow; Virginians panic at the *possibility* of snow. Chicago rests on soil that is so fertile it's *black*; Virginia does not even have soil—it has reddish clay suitable for growing nothing except tobacco. Even Chicago's tap water tastes amazing; D.C.'s tap water is poisoned with lead. I grew up thinking that every aspect of Chicago was perfect—so perfect that Chicago became glorious to the point of abstraction. No other city could compare, and after a while I forgot *why* no other city could compare. I just knew that Chicago was "the" city . . . and that if "the" city exists, there must also be an abstract "the" everything.

I grew up with this and many other abstract ideals that I would 10 defend against my friends' attacks . . . until I learned that they were just abstractions—and so was I. My writing identity was just another ideal, an absolute that I clung to without any basis in fact. I used to use writing as an easy way to define myself on those over-simplistic surveys teachers always asked us to fill out in elementary and middle school—the surveys that assumed that someone could know all about me simply by finding out my favorite color, my favorite TV show, or my hobbies. I used to casually throw out the "I'm a writer" card just to get these silly surveys over with. "I'm a writer" was just an easy answer to the complicated question, "Who are you?" I always thought the surveys avoided asking this question, but maybe I was the one avoiding it. For years, I had been defining myself as "the writer" without really pondering what this writer identity meant. Is a writer simply someone who writes all the time? Well, I often went through long stretches in which I did not write anything, so this definition did not seem to suit me. Is a writer someone who is good at writing? Well, I've

Vallowe examines the roots of her identity as a writer—and why she questions that identity.

already mentioned that I've been having "am I any good?!" thoughts since elementary school, so this definition didn't seem to fit me, either. I was identifying myself as "the writer" as an abstraction, without any just cause to do so.

The funny thing is that I recognized my writing identity as an abstract ideal before I recognized any of the other ideals I was clinging to, but that didn't make the situation any better. It is one thing to learn that dead people have been voting in Chicago elections for decades, and so perhaps Chicago isn't the perfect city, but what happens when the absolute ideal is you? More important, what would happen if *this* absolute were to crumble? It was terrifying to think that I might discover that I was not a writer because to not be a writer was to suddenly be nothing. If a writer was the only thing that I had ever been, what would happen if writing was a lie? I would vanish. Looking back, the logical part of my brain tells me that, if I am not a writer, I am still plenty of other things: I am a Catholic; I am a Vallowe; people tell me that I have other good qualities. But when facing these horrifying spells of writer's doubt, my brain doesn't see these other things. I am driven only by the fear of nothingness and the thought that I have to be a writer because I'm not good at anything else.

Am I really not good at anything else? I used to blame this entire writer's complex on whoever it was that told me I was a writer. If that person hadn't channeled this burdensome identity into me, I might never have expected great literary things from myself, and life would have been easier. I had these thoughts until one day in high school I mentioned something to my mom about the fact that I'd been writing since I was five years old. My mom corrected me by saying that I'd been writing since I was three years old. At the age of three I couldn't even physically form letters, but apparently I would dictate stories to my mom on a regular basis. My mom explained to me how I would run to her and say, "Mommy, Mommy, write my story for me!"

She continues to explore her identity as a writer.

This new information was both comforting and unsettling. On one hand, it was a great relief to know that I had been a writer all along—that I would have been a writer even if no one had told me that I was one. On the other hand, the knowledge that I had been a writer all along drove me into an entirely new realm of panic.

I've been a writer my entire life?

WHAT?!

15

I've been a writer since I was three? Three? *Three* years old: How is that even possible? I didn't know it was possible to be anything at age three, let alone the thing that might define me for my entire life.

I have been taught that each person has a vocation—a calling that he or she must use to spread God's love to others. Yet I've also assumed that one must go on some sort of journey to figure out what this vocation is. If I found my vocation at the age of three, have I skipped this journey? And if I've skipped the journey, does that mean that the vocation isn't real? Or am I just really lucky for having found my vocation so early? Was I really born a writer? Was I born to do one thing and will I do that one thing for my entire life? Can anything be that consistent? That simple? And if I am living out some divine vocation, is that any comfort at all? If I am channeling some divine being in my writing, and everything I write comes from some outside source, where does that leave me? Am I nothing even if I am a writer?

This questioning has not led me to any comforting conclusions. I still wonder if my writer identity has been thrust upon me, and what it means to have someone else determine who I am. If I am a writer, then I am someone who passionately seeks originality—someone who gets pleasure from inventing entire fictional worlds. Yet if someone—either a teacher or a divine being—is channeling an identity into me, then I am no more original than the characters that I create in my fiction. If my identity is not original, then this identity is not real, and if I am not real . . . I can't even finish this sentence.

Ending refers back to the opening anecdote.

I don't know if I really wrote thirty books in kindergarten. It might have been twenty—or fifteen—or ten—or five. I might have made up that part about the special writing desk in Mrs. Meadows's old classroom. I don't know if God predestined me to write masterpieces or if a teacher just casually mentioned that I wrote well and I completely overreacted to the compliment. Questioning my identity as "the writer" has led me to new levels of fear and uncertainty, but this questioning is not going to stop. Even if I one day sit, withered and gray, with a Nobel Prize for Literature proudly displayed on my desk as I try to crank out one last novel at the age of ninety-two, my thoughts will probably drift back to Mrs. Meadows and those books I wrote in kindergarten. In my old age, I still might not understand my writer identity,

Conclusion is tentative (since the end of the story is decades in the future).

academic literacies · rhetorical situations · genres · fields · processes · strategies · research MLA / APA · media / design

but maybe by that point, I will have written a novel about a character with an identity crisis—and maybe the character will have come through all right.

In this literacy narrative, Vallowe reflects on the origins of her identity as a writer: her early teachers, her parents, God, herself. The significance of her story lies in her inability to settle on any one of these possibilities.

DANIEL FELSENFELD

Rebel Music

Daniel Felsenfeld is a composer of classical music, a writer of several books on music, and a contributor to NewMusicBox, a multimedia publication whose mission "is to support and promote new music created in the United States." In this essay, which originally appeared in 2010 in Opinionator, *a commentary blog of the* New York Times, *he explores his journey of becoming literate in classical music.*

Music may be the universal language, but those of us who spend our lives with it are expected to know it in depth, from early on. Many composers, whether traditional or experimental, have been steeped in Western classical music from the cradle. That was not the case with me.

My primal time was the middle of the '80's in Orange County, Calif. I was 17 years old. The O.C. was billed as the ideal suburban community, but when you are raised in a palm-tree lined Shangri-La as I was, it is hard to grasp what's missing without that crucial glimpse beyond. Now I realize: even though we had enough water to keep the manicured lawns just so, I was experiencing a personal drought, an arid lack of culture of all kinds, especially music.

I was by no means unmusical, though any talent I have remains a mystery, coming as I do from perhaps the least musical of families (who would be the first to admit this). To her credit, my mother signed me up for the de rigueur piano lessons. Each week I dazzled poor Ms. Shimizu with either an astonishing performance of a Mozart sonata or a heretofore unseen level of ill-preparedness. I slogged my way through

Chopin Preludes, culminating my high school piano study with a mid-dling performance of Beethoven's "Pathétique" sonata. Probably not unlike most kids' first encounter with formal music study: uninspiring.

Eventually I quit lessons, but had developed chops enough to work in both piano bars (an underage piano man, traveling with my own snifter) and community theater orchestra pits. The music was dull, or at least had a dulling effect on me—it didn't sparkle, or ask questions. I took a lot of gigs, but at 17 I was already pretty detached. I was attracted to music for some reason I lacked vocabulary to explain, and neither *Oklahoma!* nor *Annie* offered answers.

That might have been it—working my way through junior college 5
playing in pits or at Nordstrom's, settling into some career or other—a piano studio, weddings, writing songs for mild amusement. Thankfully, it was not.

Some afternoons I would go to my friend Mike's house at the end of my cul-de-sac to listen to tapes of bands a lot of my friends were listening to: General Public, Howard Jones, the Thompson Twins (or David Bowie, Bauhaus and The Clash in our edgier moments). One day, bored with the music, Mike flipped his double-decked cassette case over to reveal rows of hidden tapes in a concealed compartment.

"Want to hear something really wild?" he said.

"But of course."

At 17, rebellion was of course a staple in my life. The smartest kids I knew took the route of dolling themselves up in anti-establishment finery—goth, punk, straight edge—forming bands, going to clubs in Los Angeles, spouting manifestos. I had auditioned this mode, joining a band (whose name escapes me) and, in one of my great (mercifully unphotographed) late high school moments, taking a long, throbbing solo at a school assembly on one of those bygone over-the-shoulder keyboards.

It seems implausible now, but the "something really wild" Mike 10
held was not goth, metal, or punk. It was a neatly hand-labeled tape of Beethoven's Ninth Symphony. He put it on, and I listened. I think it was then I actually heard music for the first time.

Was this the same Beethoven to whose sonata I had done such violence? It unrolled from the small speakers, this big, gorgeous, unruly beast of a thing, contemporary, horrifying, a juggernaut that moved from the dark to unbearable brightness, soaring and spitting, malin-gering and dancing wildly, the Most Beautiful Thing I Ever Heard. This "symphony" by this Beethoven had a drug-like effect on me. At my insistence we listened again. And again. I wished it would just keep going.

Mike, who was just a kid in the neighborhood with odd—evolved? sophisticated?—taste, had dozens more tapes: Brahms, Mozart, Bach, Prokofiev, Tchaikovsky, Sibelius, Rachmaninoff, Strauss. I may have known that this kind of music was called classical, but I certainly did not understand that it was considered "great" or that it was revered as the foundation of musical culture in the West. I just loved it more than anything I'd heard before, and I must have sensed it was also miles away from Orange County, exactly as far as my adolescent self longed to be. I dubbed Mike's tapes, and listened to them in secret. Driving to school with Beethoven blaring, I'd switch to KROQ as I entered the parking lot, swerving into my spot believing I'd put one over on people again.

My passion for this "other" kind of music felt like the height of rebellion: I was the lone Bolshevik in my army. I loved this new (to me) music, but loved my abstract role in it even more. Rebels sought to break the mold, to do something that was exclusively "theirs," to be weird by way of self-expression. And since I was the only one I knew listening to symphonies and concerti, operas and string quartets, I felt I was the weirdest of them all; it served my adolescent need to be misunderstood. And so I decided, with little prior experience or interest, to become a composer.

Little did I know, right?

All too soon, I came to understand what hard work this was. 15 I studied scores, read biographies, got a serious piano teacher and logged hours a day practicing, traded up Mike's cassettes for the then-novel compact discs, and boarded the spaceship bound for planet New York once or twice (always returning, at least then, to warmer climes). After signing up for theory classes at Fullerton Junior College, I met my first living composers: Brent Pierce taught me counterpoint and harmony (one summer I wrote a daily fugue), and Lloyd Rodgers was my private teacher (who encouraged me to copy out the entire "Well Tempered Clavier" by hand). In the meantime, I heard my first examples of what is called "New Music," that is, classical music written more recently than the 19th century.

Of course, some of my illusions vanished as soon as I realized there were composers I could actually meet. I was no longer a rebellion of one, but this halcyon innocence was traded for the ability to interact with artists who were always taking on the obscene challenge of creating music that was totally new, completely theirs.

Now I live far from the O.C., in New York, having long ago colonized this distant planet and gone native, an active member of a community I once admired from what seemed an impossible distance. And while there are moments I lament not having been raised in a musical family, or my late and clumsy start, I also strive to make my less-than-ideal origins an asset. I've learned I do my best work when I remove myself and try to return to that Age of Wonder when I first heard the gorgeous dissonances of pieces like Samuel Barber's *Hermit Songs* or *Prayers of Kierkegaard*, Elliott Carter's Second String Quartet, Michael Nyman's The Kiss, George Crumb's *Black Angels*, Arnold Schoenberg's *Pierrot Lunaire*, Benjamin Britten's *Turn of the Screw*, John Corigliano's First Symphony, and Stephen Sondheim's *Sweeney Todd*, and took them to be the *same* dissonances, not contrasting sides of a sometimes-contentious or politicized art world. When I am composing, I try to return to that time and place of inexperience when I was knocked sideways by dangerous sounds. Why else write? Why else listen?

Felsenfeld portrays the significance of his narrative as a specific moment: when he first heard Beethoven's Ninth Symphony, which marked a turning point in his life. To capture the evolution of his musical tastes and talent, he provides detailed lists of the musicians and musical pieces that influenced him as a composer and music lover.

ANA-JAMILEH KASSFY

Automotive Literacy

In the following literacy narrative, Ana-Jamileh Kassfy describes an experience that taught her that literacy takes many forms, as well as the importance of knowing what goes on in the family business, auto repair. She wrote this essay in a college writing class at the University of Texas at El Paso and posted it on her class blog.

My father runs a well-known family-owned auto shop here in El Paso, Texas. I come from a family of five, which consists of me, two older brothers, and my parents. My father manages the place, while one of my brothers works as a mechanic in charge of most of the heavy labor and the other spends all day standing by a state inspection machine making sure the cars can run safely on the streets of El Paso. My mother works as the shop's secretary, answering the phone and handling all paperwork. I, on the other hand, was not given the option of being a part of the family business; my job is to graduate from college. And I'll gladly accept going to school and learning in place of spending my days working on cars, even though I spent a lot of time at the shop throughout my childhood.

Since I come from a family whose life revolves around cars, and since I practically lived at the auto shop until I was able to drive, you'd think that I'd understand most of the jargon a mechanic would use, right? Wrong. During my first sixteen years of life, I did manage to learn the difference between a flathead and a Torx screwdriver. I also learned what brake pads do and that a car uses many different colorful fuses. However, rather than paying attention to what was happening and what was being said around me, most of the time I chose to focus on the social aspect of the business. While everyone was running around ordering different pads, filters, and starters or explaining in precise detail why a customer needed a new engine, I preferred to sit and speak with customers and learn their life stories. Being social worked for me—until it didn't.

One day my mother couldn't come to work and decided to have me fill in for her. That was fine with me. I thought to myself, "How hard could it be to answer a phone and say, 'Good afternoon, M & J Service, how may I help you?' or to greet customers and then turn them over to my dad?"

My morning went by pretty smoothly. I thought I had my duties down to a science. I figured aside from the permanent ringing in my ear from the annoyingly loud air compressors, a few minor paper cuts, and the almost perpetual stench of gasoline and burnt oil, my day was going to fly by.

Then, around lunchtime, my dad left to pick up a part at a car ⁵ dealership and my brothers went out for lunch. A woman pulled up in a '01 Hyundai Elantra that was desperately in need of a new paint job and walked into the shop. The woman seemed to be in her late forties and was wearing professional clothing with green eye shadow and bright orange lipstick. Her copper-brown hair was feathered out and she wore extremely large gold earrings. And she was angry. She demanded I tell her why she was having a difficult time starting her car. As I began to dust off the file stored in my memory as "Automotive Terms I Will Never Use," I attempted to calm her down, and then I made the mistake of asking her what the problem was.

She said in a harsh tone, "My car doesn't start, your dad just replaced the spark plugs and the motor head, and now my 'blah blah blah' is making noise! I took it to my friend who's a mechanic and he told me your dad fixed the wrong part."

I took a few seconds and just stood there looking at her, trying to add up what I had learned in my life as a "mechanic" and recall what spark plugs were. But it was useless. After a few moments, I gave up. I told her that I couldn't help her, but that she was more than welcome to wait for a mechanic to return.

After giving me an unpleasant look, she proceeded to say, while waving her hands in front of me, "I want my money back! Here is my receipt. I'm taking my car elsewhere. Your dad screwed me over. I told him it was the 'blah blah blah.' Why did he take out the 'blah blah blah'? WHY CAN'T YOU HELP ME? WHY ARE YOU HERE? BLAH BLAH BLAH!"

I stood there, overwhelmed. I began to fidget and push my hair back nervously as I wished some knowledge would kick in. It seemed unbelievable, but despite growing up in a family that lived and breathed automobiles, there was nothing I could do to help her. And my sixteen years of socializing with customers hadn't even paid off because I couldn't calm her down. When I saw my dad walk in, I sighed with relief, explained the problem to him, and it was resolved. But standing in front of that woman like a deer caught in headlights was so embarrassing. Having somebody shout, "Why can't you help me?" and "Why are you here?" made me feel so ignorant.

Unfortunately, that was only the first of many occasions when people have automatically expected that I know how to take apart and rebuild an engine, or perform some other auto-related task. In reality, I know as much about cars as the next person. After that incident, it became clear to me that I could be literate on very different levels. I'm an expert at running social networks like my *Twitter* feed, and I can zip through and analyze an entire novel written in Spanish, but in other subjects, like automobiles, I am completely illiterate. And when I'm expected to know them, I feel anything but competent.

10

A confrontation with an irate costumer forces Kassfy to realize that she could be very literate in some situations but almost illiterate in others, and that her lack of knowledge in a workplace context put her at a real disadvantage.

Key Features / Literacy Narratives

A well-told story.   As with most narratives, those about literacy often set up some sort of situation that needs to be resolved. That need for resolution makes readers want to keep on reading. We want to know how Kassfy will deal with an irate customer. Some literacy narratives simply explore the role that developing literacy of some kind played at some time in someone's life, as when Felsenfeld "was knocked sideways" by classical music. And some, like Vallowe's, speculate on the origins of the writer's literacy.

Vivid detail.   Details can bring a narrative to life for readers by giving them vivid mental sensations of the sights, sounds, smells, tastes, and textures of the world in which your story takes place. The details you use when describing something can help readers picture places, people, and events; dialogue can help them hear what is being said. We grasp the depth of Felsenfeld's reaction to hearing Beethoven's Ninth Symphony from his description of it: "big, gorgeous, unruly beast of a thing, contemporary, horrifying, a juggernaut." Similarly, we can picture and hear Vallowe as a little girl running to her mother and saying, "Mommy, Mommy, write my story for me!"

Some indication of the narrative's significance.   By definition, a literacy narrative tells something the writer remembers about learning to read, write, or gain competence in a specific area. In addition, the writer needs to make clear why the incident matters to them. You may reveal its significance in various ways. Now a composer, Felsenfeld tries to "return to that Age of Wonder when [he] first heard" what he calls "dangerous sounds." Kassfy comes to understand that to work in an auto repair shop, she needs to understand automotive repair terms. Vallowe's narrative would be less effective if, instead of questioning her identity as a writer from several perspectives, she had simply said, "I became a writer at the age of three."

A GUIDE TO WRITING LITERACY NARRATIVES

Choosing a Topic

In general, it's a good idea to focus on a single event that took place during a relatively brief period of time—though sometimes learning to do or understand something may take place over an extended period. In that case, several snapshots or important moments may be needed. Here are some suggestions for topics:

- any early memory about writing, reading, speaking, or another form of literacy that you recall vividly
- someone who taught you to read or write
- someone who helped you understand how to do something
- a book, video game, recording, or other text that has been significant for you in some way
- an event at school that was related to your literacy and that you found interesting, humorous, or embarrassing
- a literacy task that you found (or still find) especially difficult or challenging
- a memento that represents an important moment in your literacy development (perhaps the start of a **LITERACY PORTFOLIO**)
- the origins of your current attitudes about writing, reading, speaking, or doing something
- learning to text, learning to write email appropriately, creating and maintaining a *Facebook* page or blog

361–70

Make a list of possible topics, and then choose one that you think will be interesting to you and to others—and that you're willing to share with others. If several seem promising, try them out on a friend or classmate.

Or just choose one and see where it leads; you can switch to another if need be. If you have trouble coming up with a topic, try **FREEWRITING**, **LISTING**, **CLUSTERING**, or **LOOPING**.

331–34

Considering the Rhetorical Situation

PURPOSE   Why do you want to tell this story? To share a memory with others? To fulfill an assignment? To teach a lesson? To explore your past learning? Think about the reasons for your choice and how they will shape what you write.

55–56

AUDIENCE   Are your readers likely to have had similar experiences? Would they tell similar stories? How much explaining will you have to do to help them understand your narrative? Can you assume that they will share your attitudes toward your story, or will you have to work at making them see your perspective? How much about your life are you willing to share with this audience?

57–60

STANCE   What attitude do you want to project? Affectionate? Neutral? Critical? Do you wish to be sincere? serious? humorously detached? self-critical? self-effacing? something else? How do you want your readers to see you?

66–68

MEDIA / DESIGN   Will your narrative be in print? presented orally? online? Should you use photos, tables, graphs, or video or audio clips? Is there a font that conveys the right tone? Do you need headings?

69–71

Generating Ideas and Text

Good literacy narratives share certain elements that make them interesting and compelling for readers. Remember that your goals are to tell the story as clearly and vividly as you can and to convey the meaning the incident has for you today. Start by thinking about what you already know about writing a literacy narrative. Then write out what you remember about the

331–39
506–7

setting of your narrative and those involved, perhaps trying out some of the methods in the chapter on **GENERATING IDEAS AND TEXT**. You may also want to **INTERVIEW** a teacher or parent or other person who figures in your narrative.

Explore what you already know about writing a literacy narrative. Think about recent occasions when you've had to narrate a story, either orally or in writing, in school or out. Take a few moments to think about a couple of those occasions, especially ones involving your reading, writing, speaking, or learning to do something. Why and to whom were you telling these stories? How successful do you think your narratives were? What aspects of telling the story did you feel most confident about or do especially well? What could you have done better? What do you still need to learn about writing a literacy narrative?

Describe the setting.   Where does your narrative take place? List the places where your story unfolds. For each place, write informally for a few

443–51

minutes, **DESCRIBING** what you remember:

- *What do you see?* If you're inside, what color are the walls? What's hanging on them? What can you see out any windows? What else do you see? Books? Lined paper? Red ink? Are there people? places to sit? a desk or a table?

- *What do you hear?* A radiator hissing? Leaves rustling? The wind howling? Rain? Someone reading aloud? Shouts? Cheers? Children playing? Music? The chime of a text arriving on your phone?

- *What do you smell?* Sweat? Perfume? Incense? Food cooking?

- *How and what do you feel?* Nervous? Happy? Cold? Hot? A scratchy wool sweater? Tight shoes? Rough wood on a bench?

- *What do you taste?* Gum? Mints? Graham crackers? Juice? Coffee?

Think about the key people.   Narratives include people whose actions play an important role in the story. In your literacy narrative, you are probably one of those people. A good way to develop your understanding of the people in your narrative is to write about them:

- *Describe each person in a paragraph or so.* What do the people look like? How do they dress? How do they speak? Quickly? Slowly? With an accent? Do they speak clearly, or do they mumble? Do they use any distinctive words or phrases? You might begin by describing their movements, their posture, their bearing, their facial expressions. Do they have a distinctive scent?

- *Recall (or imagine) some characteristic dialogue.* A good way to bring people to life and move a story along is with **DIALOGUE**, to let readers hear them rather than just hearing about them. Try writing six to ten lines of dialogue between two people in your narrative. If you can't remember an actual conversation, make up one that could have happened. (After all, you are telling the story, and you get to decide how it is to be told.) Try to remember (and write down) some of the characteristic words or phrases that the people in your narrative used.

◆ 452–56

Write about "what happened." At the heart of every good **NARRATIVE** is the answer to the question "What happened?" The action in a literacy narrative may be as dramatic as winning a spelling bee or as subtle as a conversation between two friends; both contain action, movement, or change that the narrative tries to capture for readers. A good story dramatizes the action. Try **SUMMARIZING** the action in your narrative in a paragraph—try to capture what happened. Use active and specific verbs (*pondered, shouted, laughed*) to describe the action as vividly as possible.

◆ 462–70

● 526–38

Consider the significance of the narrative. You need to make clear the ways in which any event you are writing about is significant for you now. Write a page or so about the meaning it has for you. How did it change or otherwise affect you? What aspects of your life now can you trace to that event? How might your life have been different if this event had not happened or had turned out differently? Why does this story matter to you?

Ways of Organizing a Literacy Narrative

335–37 ○

Start by **OUTLINING** the main events in your narrative. Then think about how you want to tell the story. Don't assume that the only way to tell your story is just as it happened. That's one way—starting at the beginning of the action and continuing to the end. But you could also start in the middle—or even at the end. Daniel Felsenfeld, for example, could have begun his narrative by discussing his influences as a composer and then gone back to the origins of his interest in music at seventeen. Several ways of organizing a narrative follow.

[Chronologically, from beginning to end]

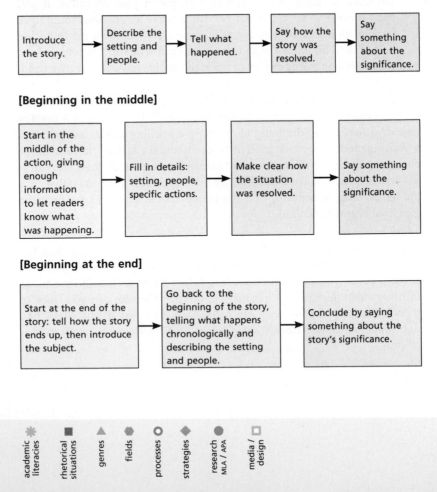

Introduce the story. → Describe the setting and people. → Tell what happened. → Say how the story was resolved. → Say something about the significance.

[Beginning in the middle]

Start in the middle of the action, giving enough information to let readers know what was happening. → Fill in details: setting, people, specific actions. → Make clear how the situation was resolved. → Say something about the significance.

[Beginning at the end]

Start at the end of the story: tell how the story ends up, then introduce the subject. → Go back to the beginning of the story, telling what happens chronologically and describing the setting and people. → Conclude by saying something about the story's significance.

Writing Out a Draft

Once you have generated ideas and thought about how you want to organize your narrative, it's time to begin **DRAFTING**. Do this quickly—try to write a complete draft in one sitting, concentrating on getting the story on paper or screen and on putting in as much detail as you can. Some writers find it helpful to work on the beginning or ending first. Others write out the main event first and then draft the beginning and ending.

◯ 340–42

Draft a BEGINNING.   A good narrative grabs readers' attention right from the start. Here are some ways of beginning:

◆ 373–80

- *Create a question to be answered.* Felsenfeld describes the typical composer's upbringing, but then states that his was not typical—so his narrative should describe his unique introduction to classical music.

- *Describe the context.* You may want to provide background information at the start of your narrative, as Vallowe does with an anecdote exposing her fears that she may not be who she thinks she is.

- *Describe the setting, especially if it's important to the narrative.* Kassfy begins by describing her family's roles working in her father's auto shop.

Draft an ENDING.   Think about what you want readers to read last. An effective ending helps them understand the meaning of your narrative. Here are some possibilities:

◆ 380–85

- *End where your story ends.* It's up to you to decide where a narrative ends. Vallowe ends far in the future, in her imagined old age.

- *Say something about the significance of your narrative.* Vallowe explores the meaning of her experience over several paragraphs, and Kassfy discusses her ignorance and resulting embarrassment. The trick is to touch on the narrative's significance without stating it too directly.

- *Refer back to the beginning.* Vallowe refers back to her kindergarten writing, and Felsenfeld to his first encounter with classical music.

353–55 ○
Consider REWRITING. If you have time and want to explore alternatives, you might try rewriting your draft to see if a different plan or approach might work better.

386–87 ◆
Come up with a title. A good **TITLE** indicates something about the subject of your narrative—and makes readers want to take a look. Kassfy's title joins two terms—"automotive" and "literacy"—that aren't usually seen together. Vallowe uses word play—"Write or Wrong Identity", to question whether she is actually a writer. Felsenfeld captures the irony in calling his secret love of classical music an act of rebellion with his title "Rebel Music."

Considering Matters of Design

You'll probably write your narrative in paragraph form, but think about the information you're presenting and how you can design it to enhance your story and appeal to your audience.

648–49 ▢
- What would be an appropriate **FONT**? Something serious, like Times Roman? Something whimsical, like *Comic Sans*? Something else?

650–52 ▢
- Would it help your readers if you added **HEADINGS** in order to divide your narrative into shorter sections?

653–63 ▢
- Would photographs or other **VISUALS** show details better than you can describe them with words alone? If you're writing about learning to read, for example, you might scan in an image of one of the first books you read. Or if your topic is learning to write, you could include something you wrote. You could even include a video or audio recording. Would your narrative best be conveyed as a multimodal composition that combines written text, images, and video or audio?

❋ academic literacies
■ rhetorical situations
▲ genres
◆ fields
○ processes
◆ strategies
● research MLA / APA
▢ media / design

Getting Response and Revising

The following questions can help you study your draft with a critical eye. **GETTING RESPONSE** from others is always good, and these questions can guide their reading, too. Make sure they know your purpose and audience.

348–50

- Do the title and first few sentences make readers want to read on? If not, how else might you begin?
- Is the sequence of events in the narrative clear? Does it flow, and are there effective transitions? Does the narrative get sidetracked at any point?
- Is anything confusing?
- Is there enough detail, and is it interesting? Will readers be able to imagine the setting? Can they picture the characters and sense what they're like? Would it help to add some dialogue so that readers can "hear" them?
- Are visuals used effectively and integrated smoothly with the written text? If there are no visuals, would using some strengthen the narrative?
- Have you made the narrative meaningful enough for readers so that they wonder and care about what will happen?
- Do you narrate any actions clearly? vividly? Does the action keep readers engaged?
- Is the significance of the narrative clear?
- Is the ending satisfying? What are readers left thinking?

The preceding questions should identify aspects of your narrative you need to work on. When it's time to **REVISE**, make sure your text appeals to your audience and achieves your purpose as successfully as possible.

350–53

Editing and Proofreading

Readers equate correctness with competence. Once you've revised your draft, follow these guidelines for **EDITING** a narrative:

356–59

462–70 ◆

391

- Make sure events are **NARRATED** in a clear order and include appropriate time markers, **TRANSITIONS**, and summary phrases to link the parts and show the passing of time.

- Be careful that verb tenses are consistent throughout. If you start your narrative in the past tense ("he *taught* me how to use a computer"), be careful not to switch to the present ("So I *look* at him and *say* . . . ") along the way.

- Check to see that verb tenses correctly indicate when an action took place. If one action took place before another action in the past, for example, you should use the past perfect tense: "I forgot to dot my i's, a mistake I *had made* many times before."

452–56 ◆

- Punctuate **DIALOGUE** correctly. Whenever someone speaks, surround the speech with quotation marks ("No way," I said). Periods and commas go inside quotation marks; exclamation points and question marks go inside if they're part of the quotation, outside if they're part of the whole sentence:

  INSIDE   Opening the door, Ms. Cordell announced, "Pop quiz!"
  OUTSIDE   It wasn't my intention to announce "I hate to read"!

359–60

- **PROOFREAD** your finished narrative carefully before turning it in.

Taking Stock of Your Work

- How well do you think you told the story?
- What did you do especially well?
- What could still be improved?
- How did you go about coming up with ideas and generating text?
- How did you go about drafting your narrative?

- Did you use photographs or any other visual or audio elements? What did they add? Can you think of such elements you might have used?
- How did others' responses influence your writing?
- What would you do differently next time?

IF YOU NEED MORE HELP

See also **MEMOIRS** (Chapter 18), a kind of narrative that focuses more generally on a significant event from your past, and **REFLECTIONS** (Chapter 21), a kind of essay for thinking about a topic in writing. See Chapter 34 if you are required to submit your literacy narrative as part of a writing **PORTFOLIO**.

▲ 224–32
256–63

● 361–70

11 Analyzing Texts

Both the *Huffington Post* and *National Review* cover the same events, but each one interprets them differently. All toothpaste ads claim to make teeth "the whitest." The Environmental Protection Agency is a guardian of America's air, water, and soil—or an unconstitutional impediment to economic growth, depending on which politician is speaking. Those are but three examples that demonstrate why we need to be careful, analytical readers of magazines, newspapers, blogs, websites, ads, political documents, even textbooks.

Text is commonly thought of as words, as a piece of writing. In the academic world, however, text can include not only writing but images—photographs, illustrations, videos, films—and even sculptures, buildings, and music and other sounds. And many texts combine words, images, and sounds. We are constantly bombarded with texts: on the web, in print, on signs and billboards, even on our clothing. Not only does text convey information, but it also influences how and what we think. We need to read, then, to understand not only what texts say but also how they say it and how they try to persuade or influence what we think.

Because understanding how texts say what they say and achieve their effects is so crucial, assignments in many disciplines ask you to analyze texts. You may be asked to analyze candidates' speeches in a *political science* course or to analyze the imagery in a poem for a *literature* class. In a *statistics* course, you might analyze a set of data—a numerical text—to find the standard deviation from the mean.

This chapter offers detailed guidelines for writing an essay that closely examines a text both for what it says and for how it does so, with the goal of demonstrating for readers how—and how well—the text achieves its effects. We'll begin with three good examples, the first annotated to point out the key features found in most textual analyses.

HANNAH BERRY

The Fashion Industry: Free to Be an Individual

Hannah Berry wrote this analysis of two visual texts, shoe ads, for a first-year writing course at Wright State University.

As young women, we have always been told through the medium of advertisement that we must use certain products to make ourselves beautiful. For decades, ads for things like soap, makeup, and mouthwash have established a sort of misplaced control over our lives, telling us what will make us attractive and what will not. Recently, however, a new generation of advertisement has emerged in the fashion industry, one that cleverly equates the products shown in the ads with the quest for confident individuality. Ads such as the two for Clarks and Sorel discussed below encourage us to break free from the standard beauty mold and be ourselves; using mostly imagery, they remind us that being unique is the true origin of beauty.

The first ad promotes Clarks fashion as band geek chic, quite literally raising a unique personality onto a pedestal, with the subject poised on a decorative stone platform as shown in fig. 1. Photographed in standing profile, this quirky-looking young woman is doing what she loves—playing some kind of trumpet—and looks great doing it. She is wearing her hair in a French twist with a strand tucked behind her ear, as if she recently moved it out of her face to play the music she loves without distraction. The downturn of her nose points to the short gray-black dress that stops several inches above her knees but covers her chest and shoulders modestly, with a collar situated at the base of her neck and sleeves that reach for her elbows. The dress is plain,

Fig. 1. Clarks ad shows a band geek doing what she loves (*Clarks*).

Attention to the context of the ads Berry will analyze.

Clear thesis.

Detailed description of the first text.

Illustrations are labeled in MLA format.

but it is a perfect fit for the personality implied in the photo. Set against the background of a light-tan wall, the model leans back slightly as if supporting the weight of her instrument. Her right knee is bent while her left knee remains straight. The positioning of her legs not only accentuates her unbalanced posture but also points out the pair of simple brown pumps that complete the look. She wears the shoes with a pair of socks in a much darker shade of brown pulled up around her shins. Around her ankles are sandy-colored rings of shaggy fabric that are most likely attached to the socks, giving the whole outfit a sense of nerdy flair. Her expression is a simple mix of calm and concentration. It's as if the photographer happened to take the picture while she was practicing for a school recital.

Analysis of the first text.

Clarks has taken what looks like your average high school student and dressed her in an outfit that speaks to her own distinctive character and talents. The image sparks the idea that her beauty comes from an internal base of secure self-confidence and moves outward to infuse her physical appearance and sense of style. This ad urges us to celebrate individuality with the right look. Using an image alone, Clarks advertises its products with the simple promise that they will support you in doing what you love and keep you original.

Description of the second text.

Taking a narrower perspective on originality, the ad for Sorel boots shown in fig. 2 dramatizes the idea that spontaneity is key to a distinctive personal identity. This abstract idea is depicted in a vividly concrete way, using the featured fur-topped boots as a base for encouraging a bold sense of self. The ad dares us to break free from the mold of society and do something "fearless" (Sorel). It shows us a dark-haired, red-lipped woman sitting in a formal French upholstered chair in a

Fig. 2. Sorel ad flaunts devil-red boots worn by a fearless woman with a shotgun (Sorel).

dark-blue, elaborately paneled parlor. An expression of triumph and mischief adorns her sultry visage. She's wearing a revealing short white dress that overlaps slightly around her chest and falls strategically over her hips so that large portions of her upper thighs are visible. Feathers in autumn colors cover her shoulders, and a gold belt accentuates her waist. Next to her is a polished wood table supporting a lighted candle, a small glass vase of pink and white flowers, and a black-and-white-patterned orb. There is a dormant, ornate fireplace to her left. But what makes this scene extraordinary is what seems to have taken place moments before the picture was taken. One of the young woman's feet, clad in the devil-red black-laced boots being advertised, rests defiantly on top of the shattered remains of a crystal chandelier. In her right hand, the woman holds an old-looking shotgun with her forefinger still resting on the trigger.

Speculation about the story behind the image.

In Sorel's explosive ad, it is apparent that the woman not only shot 5 down the ceiling fixture but also has no regrets about doing so. Her white dress represents a sort of purity and innocence that is completely contradicted by the way she wears it—and by the boots. They gave her the power to shoot down the chandelier, the push she needed to give in to a long-held desire that perhaps she couldn't have indulged in without the extra help. They symbolize her liberty to decide to be herself and do what she wants. Along with the white dress, the formal decor represents the bounds that society tells her she must fit into—but that she decides to take a potshot at instead. Focusing on the beauty of inner power, not just the power of outer beauty, this Sorel ad punctuates its bold visual statement with a single verbal phrase: "Après anything" (Sorel). In the French language, the word *après* means "after." So, the ad suggests, no matter what outrageous or outlandish deed you do, the Sorel boots will be there for you, suitable for slipping into afterward like a negligee.

Analysis of the second text.

With these pioneering fashion ads that celebrate blowing your own horn or shooting up fancy French lighting fixtures for fun, young women are told to accessorize their inner beauty with articles of clothing geared toward their distinctive individual desires. "You don't have to just try to be beautiful in the ways other women do," they say; "you can strike out on your own, and our products will help you do it." The extent to which women will respond to these messages remains to be seen, but certainly the ads themselves achieve a strikingly different look. Whether celebrating individual talents or random acts of defiance in our everyday lives, they dare us to accessorize our personalities.

Conclusion ties together the strands of the analysis.

Works Cited

Clarks. Advertisement. *Lucky*, Sept. 2011, p. 55.

Sorel. Advertisement. *Lucky*, Sept. 2011, p. 65.

Berry summarizes each ad clearly and focuses her analysis on a theme running through both ads: that clothing is an expression of one's individuality. She describes patterns of images in both ads as evidence.

DANIELLE ALLEN

Our Declaration

Danielle Allen is a political theorist, teaches at Harvard University, and directs Harvard's Edmond J. Safra Center for Ethics. This analysis is a chapter from her book Our Declaration: A Reading of the Declaration of Independence in Defense of Equality.

There's something quite startling about the phrase "We hold these truths to be self-evident." Perhaps it can be made visible most easily with a comparison.

The Catholic Church, too, is committed to a set of truths. At every mass priest and parishioners together recite a list of their beliefs called the *Credo*. One version, called the Apostles' Creed, starts like this: "I believe in God, the Father almighty, creator of heaven and earth. I believe in Jesus Christ, his only son and Lord." Each section begins with the words "I believe," and that's why this recitation is called the *Credo*. Latin, "credo" simply means "I believe."

The Declaration launches its list of truths altogether differently. Jefferson and his colleagues do not say, "I believe," or even "we believe," that all men are created equal. Instead, they say, "We hold these truths to be self-evident," and then they give us a set of either three or five truths, depending on how you count.

What's the difference between "We believe" and "We hold these truths to be self-evident"? In the Catholic *Credo*, when one says, "I believe," the basis for that belief is God's revealed word. In contrast, when Jefferson and his colleagues say, "We hold these truths to be self-evident," they are claiming to know the truths thanks to their own powers of perception and reasoning. These truths are self-evident, and so humans can grasp and hold them without any external or divine assistance.

In order to understand what "We hold these truths to be self-evident" really means, then, it is important to know what "self-evident" means. 5

Sometimes people take it to mean that we can instantly understand an idea, but that's not really right. It's true that sometimes the idea of self-evidence is used for things that we simply perceive. For instance, when I look out my window I immediately perceive that the world includes things like trees and flowers. If outside my window there are many different kinds of tree — hickory and maple and oak, for instance — when I look at them, I nonetheless rapidly perceive that they are all the same kind of thing. That many different kinds of a particular sort of growing thing are all trees is self-evident. We can call this self-evidence from sense perception.

The immediacy of perception, though, is not the same as instantly understanding an idea. And, in fact, to call a proposition self-evident is not at all to say that you will instantly get it. It means instead that if you look into the proposition, if you entertain it, if you reflect upon it, you will inevitably come to affirm it. All the evidence that you need in order to believe the proposition exists within the proposition itself.

This second kind of self-evidence comes not from perception but from logic and how language works.

For instance, we define a chair as an object with a seat and some structure of legs to hold that seat up; and the artifact serves the purpose of having someone sit on it. Then, if I say that a chair is for sitting on, I am expressing a self-evident truth based only on the definition of a chair. Of course a chair is for sitting on! That is how I've defined the word, after all. That's a pretty trivial example of self-evidence. If that were all there were to the idea of self-evidence, it wouldn't be very interesting.

So here is where matters get more interesting: one can string together more than one kind of self-evident proposition — let's call them "premises" — in order to lead to a new piece of knowledge, a conclusion, which will also count as self-evident, since it has been deduced from a few basic self-evident premises. 10

Aristotle called this method of stringing together valid premises to yield a self-evident conclusion, a syllogism. Above, I said that "syllogism" is a technical word. Here is a basic example:

FIRST PREMISE: *Bill Gates is a human being.*
SECOND PREMISE: *All human beings are mortal.*
CONCLUSION: *Bill Gates is mortal.*

This is a bit like math. We can use a Venn diagram to show how the syllogism works. Venn diagrams represent sets of things and how they overlap, and the argument of a syllogism can be thought of as expressing facts about sets and their members. Bill Gates is in the set of human beings. And the set of human beings is entirely contained within the set of mortals. It follows that Bill Gates is in the set of mortals. The validity of this syllogism becomes self-evident when those facts are represented as in this Venn diagram:

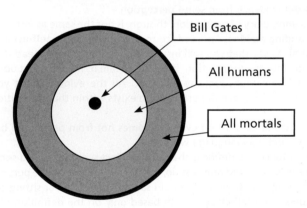

Bill Gates

All humans

All mortals

Now, in this syllogism, our two premises are both self-evident truths based on sense perception. We know Bill Gates is a human being by looking at and listening to him. As to the idea that human beings are mortal, we know that human beings die by seeing it happen all around us and never seeing a counterexample. Then we take these two premises, each self-evident through sense perception, and generate a third self-evident proposition, in this case a conclusion, through deduction. From the two premises, we can deduce the certain conclusion that Bill Gates will die.

The Declaration introduces a similar kind of argument when it says, "We hold these truths to be self-evident." At first glance, it looks as if we just have three separate self-evident truths. But if we look closer, we notice that our truths also represent an argument with two premises, which are true from sense perception, and a conclusion that is deduced from them.

Here's how it works.

After the Declaration says, "We hold these truths to be self-evident," the text proceeds to identify three truths: one about human beings, one about government, and one about revolution. The truth about human beings, though, is a three-part truth.

It is self-evidently true:

> that all men are created equal, that they are endowed by their Creator with certain unalienable Rights, that among these are Life, Liberty and the pursuit of Happiness.

How do these three claims make a single truth? Human beings are equal in all acquiring the same rights at the moment of their creation. From the moment of their emergence as living beings, human beings seek to survive, to be free from domination, and to be happy. This is something we simply observe about human beings. For that matter, we observe it about other animals, too. For instance, I've never seen a cat that didn't want to survive, to be free, and to be happy.

Then, with the next truth, we come to the difference between human beings and animals. The Declaration says, it is self-evidently true

> —That to secure these rights, Governments are instituted among Men, deriving their just powers from the consent of the governed.

This is a truly salient point. The signers are saying that, in contrast to the animal kingdom, the world of human beings is indeed full of kingdoms and other kinds of governments. The so-called animal kingdom is a kingdom only metaphorically. There are no governments among animals. Animals have social hierarchies, and they have their own methods for seeking their survival, freedom, and happiness, but human beings use politics. Human beings display self-conscious thought about social organization, and politics is the activity that flows from

15

that self-consciousness about power. Again, this is simply a matter of observation. From the beginning of time to the present day, human beings have formed governments. Human beings have done this just as regularly as birds build nests.

Then the Declaration puts these first two truths together. Since human beings seek their own survival, freedom, and happiness, and since they have a special tool for doing so—namely, the ability to form governments—it makes sense for them to stick with any particular version of that tool, any particular government, only if it's doing the work it's been built to do. 20

Compare it to a bird with a nest. What's the point of a bird's staying in a nest if it turns out that the nest has been built out of material inimical or poisonous to the bird? What's the use, in other words, of having a government, if it doesn't serve the purposes of protecting life, liberty, and the pursuit of happiness for which governments are set up in the first place?

The Declaration puts it this way: It is self-evidently true

— *That whenever any Form of Government becomes destructive of these ends, it is the Right of the People to alter or to abolish it, and to institute new Government, laying its foundation on such principles and organizing its powers in such form, as to them shall seem most likely to effect their Safety and Happiness.*

From the facts, first, that people are simply wired, as are all animals, to seek their survival, freedom, and happiness, and, second, that human beings use governments as their central instrument for protecting their life, liberty, and pursuit of happiness, we can deduce that people have a right to change governments that aren't working for them.

This makes an argument that goes like this:

PREMISE 1: All people have rights to life, liberty, and the pursuit of happiness.
PREMISE 2: Properly constituted government is necessary to their securing their rights
CONCLUSION: All people have a right to a properly constituted government.

In fact, a philosopher would say that a premise is missing from that ²⁵ argument and that the full formally valid syllogism would look like this:

PREMISE 1: All people have rights to life, liberty, and the pursuit of happiness.

PREMISE 2: Properly constituted government is necessary to their securing these rights.

PREMISE 3: [All people have a right to whatever is necessary to secure what they have a right to].

CONCLUSION: All people have a right to a properly constituted government.

Politicians often craft maxims simply by dropping out pieces of their argument. With the missing premise inserted, the Declaration's truths fit together almost like the pieces of a mathematical equation; we intuitively feel the puzzle pieces snap together. That is how self-evidence should feel.

Allen's analysis focuses on the Declaration's second sentence, unpacking its logic through a careful examination of its key term, "self-evident," and explaining how the rest of the sentence forms a syllogism that "snaps together." She looks carefully at every word, restricting her analysis here to a very brief part of the text—but provides insights that illuminate the whole document.

ROY PETER CLARK

Why It Worked: A Rhetorical Analysis of Obama's Speech on Race

Roy Peter Clark teaches writing at the Poynter Institute. This essay, which Clark describes as "an X-ray reading of the text," appeared online on the Poynter Institute's website, first in 2008 and again in 2017, with a new introduction.

The National Conference of Teachers of English (NCTE) has declared today [October 20, 2017] a National Day on Writing. I celebrate such a day. The introduction of my book *Writing Tools* imagines what America might look like and sound like if we declared ourselves a "nation of writers." After all, what good is freedom of expression if we lack the means to express ourselves?

To mark this day—and to honor language arts teachers everywhere—Poynter is republishing an essay I wrote almost a decade ago. Remember? It was the spring of 2008 and Barack Obama was running for president. Many of us wondered if America was ready to elect an African-American president (a man with the middle name Hussein).

To dispel the fears of some white Americans and to advance his chances for election, Obama delivered a major address on race in America, a speech that was praised even by some of his adversaries. Obama had / has a gift for language. He is a skilled orator. To neutralize that advantage, his opponents—including Hillary Clinton at one point—would characterize Obama's words as empty "rhetoric"—an elaborate trick of language.

The spring of 2008 seems like such a long time ago. A time just before the Great Recession [that affected the U.S. from 2008 to 2009]. A time just before the ascendancy of social networks and the trolls who try to poison them. A time before black lives were said to matter in a more assertive way. A time before fake news was anything more dangerous than a piece of satire in the *Onion*. A time before Colin Kaepernick took a knee—except when he was tired. A time before torch-bearing white supremacists marched through the night in Charlottesville, Virginia.

It feels like the perfect time for a restart on a conversation about   5
race. To prepare us, let's take another look at the words of Barack Obama before he was president. Let's review what he said, and, more important, how and why he said it. My X-ray analysis of that speech is meant not as a final word on that historical moment, but as an invitation, a doorway to a room where we can all reflect on American history and the American language.

Have a great National Day on Writing.

More than a century ago, scholar and journalist W. E. B. Du Bois wrote a single paragraph about how race is experienced in America. I have learned more from those 112 words than from most book-length studies of the subject:

After the Egyptian and Indian, the Greek and Roman, the Teuton and Mongolian, the Negro is a sort of seventh son, born with a veil, and gifted with second-sight in this American world, a world which yields him no true self-consciousness, but only lets him see himself through the revelation of the other world. It is a peculiar sensation, this double-consciousness, this sense of always looking at one's self through the eyes of others, of measuring one's soul by the tape of a world that looks on in amused contempt and pity. One ever feels his two-ness,—an American, a Negro; two souls, two thoughts, two unreconciled strivings; two warring ideals in one dark body, whose dogged strength alone keeps it from being torn asunder.

Much has been said about the power and brilliance of Barack Obama's March 18, 2008, speech on race, even by some of his detractors. The focus has been on the orator's willingness to say things in public about race that are rarely spoken at all, even in private, and his expressed desire to move the country to a new and better place. There has also been attention to the immediate purpose of the speech, which was to reassure white voters that they had nothing to fear from the congregant of a fiery African-American pastor, the Rev. Jeremiah Wright.

Amid all the commentary, I have yet to see an X-ray reading of the text that would make visible the rhetorical strategies that the orator and authors used so effectively. When received in the ear, these effects breeze through us like a harmonious song. When inspected with the eye, these moves become more apparent, like reading a piece of sheet music for a difficult song and finally recognizing the chord changes.

Such analysis, while interesting in itself, might be little more than a scholarly curiosity if we were not so concerned with the language issues of political discourse. The popular opinion is that our current president [George W. Bush], though plain spoken, is clumsy with language. Fair or not, this perception has produced a hope that our next president will be a more powerful communicator, a Kennedy or Reagan, perhaps, who can use language less as a way to signal ideology and more as a means to bring the disparate parts of the nation together. Journalists need to pay closer attention to political language than ever before.

Like most memorable pieces of oratory, Obama's speech sounds better than it reads. We have no way of knowing if that was true of Lincoln's Gettysburg Address, but it is certainly true of Dr. King's "I Have a Dream" speech. If you doubt this assertion, test it out. Read the speech[1] and then experience it in its original setting[2] recited by his soulful voice.

The effectiveness of Obama's speech rests upon four related rhetorical strategies:

1. The power of allusion and its patriotic associations.
2. The oratorical resonance of parallel constructions.
3. The "two-ness" of the texture, to use Du Bois's useful term.
4. His ability to include himself as a character in a narrative about race.

Allusion

Part of what made Dr. King's speech resonate, not just for black people, but for some whites, was its framing of racial equality in familiar patriotic terms: "This will be the day when all of God's children will be able to sing with new meaning, 'My country 'tis of thee, sweet land of liberty, of thee I sing. Land where my fathers died, land of the pilgrim's pride, from every mountainside, let freedom ring.'" What follows, of course, is King's great litany of iconic topography that carries listeners across the American landscape: "Let freedom ring from the snowcapped Rockies of Colorado! . . ."

In this tradition, Obama begins with "We the people, in order to form a more perfect union," a quote from the Constitution that becomes a recurring refrain linking the parts of the speech. What comes next is "Two hundred and twenty one years ago," an opening that places him in the tradition of Lincoln at Gettysburg and Dr. King at the Lincoln Memorial: "Five score years ago."

On the first page, Obama mentions the words democracy, Declaration of Independence, Philadelphia convention, 1787, the colonies, the founders, the Constitution, liberty, justice, citizenship under the law, parchment, equal, free, prosperous, and the presidency. It is not as well known as it should be that many black leaders, including Dr. King, use two different modes of discourse when addressing white vs. black audiences, an ignorance that has led to some of the hysteria over some of Rev. Wright's comments.

Obama's patriotic lexicon is meant to comfort white ears and soothe white fears. What keeps the speech from falling into a pan-

15

1. http://www.americanrhetoric.com/speeches/mlkihaveadream.htm
2. https://archive.org/details/MLKDream

dering sea of slogans is language that reveals, not the ideals, but the failures of the American experiment: "It was stained by this nation's original sin of slavery, a question that divided the colonies and brought the convention to a stalemate until the founders chose to allow the slave trade to continue for at least twenty more years, and to leave any final resolution to future generations." And "what would be needed were Americans in successive generations who were willing to do their part . . . to narrow that gap between the promise of our ideals and the reality of their time."

Lest a dark vision of America disillusion potential voters, Obama returns to familiar evocations of national history, ideals, and language:

— "Out of many, we are truly one."
— "survived a Depression."
— "a man who served his country"
— "on a path of a more perfect union"
— "a full measure of justice"
— "the immigrant trying to feed his family"
— "where our union grows stronger"
— "a band of patriots signed that document."

Parallelism

At the risk of calling to mind the worst memories of grammar class, I invoke the wisdom that parallel constructions help authors and orators make meaning memorable. To remember how parallelism works, think of equal terms to express equal ideas. So Dr. King dreamed that one day his four children "will not be judged by the color of their skin but by the content of their character." (*By the content of their character* is parallel to *by the color of their skin*.)

Back to Obama: "This was one of the tasks we set forth at the beginning of this campaign—to continue the long march of those who came before us, a march for a more just, more equal, more free, more caring and more prosperous America." If you are counting, that's five parallel phrases among 43 words.

And there are many more:

20

". . . we may not have come from the same place, but we all want to move in the same direction."

"So when they are told to bus their children to a school across town; when they hear that an African American is getting an advantage in landing a good job or a spot in a good college because of an injustice that they themselves never committed; when they're told that their fears about crime in urban neighborhoods are somehow prejudiced, resentment builds over time."

". . . embracing the burdens of our past without becoming victims of our past."

Two-ness

I could argue that Obama's speech is a meditation upon Du Bois's theory of a dual experience of race in America. There is no mention of Du Bois or two-ness, but it is all there in the texture. In fact, once you begin the search, it is remarkable how many examples of two-ness shine through:

- "through protests and struggles"
- "on the streets and in the courts"
- "through civil war and civil disobedience"
- "I am the son of a black man from Kenya and a white woman from Kansas."
- "white and black"
- "black and brown"
- "best schools . . . poorest nations"
- "too black or not black enough"
- "the doctor and the welfare mom"
- "the model student and the former gang-banger"
- "raucous laughter and sometimes bawdy humor"
- "political correctness or reverse racism"
- "your dreams do not have to come at the expense of my dreams"

Such language manages to create both tension and balance and, without being excessively messianic, permits Obama to present himself as the bridge builder, the reconciler of America's racial divide.

Autobiography

There is an obnoxious tendency among political candidates to frame their life story as a struggle against poverty or hard circumstances. As satirist Stephen Colbert once noted of presidential candidates, it is not enough to be an average millionaire. To appeal to populist instincts it becomes de rigueur to be descended from "goat turd farmers" in France.

Without dwelling on it, Obama reminds us that his father was black and his mother white, that he came from Kenya, but she came from Kansas: "I am married to a black American who carries within her the blood of slaves and slave owners—an inheritance we pass on to our two precious daughters. I have brothers, sisters, nieces, nephews, uncles, and cousins, of every race and every hue, scattered across three continents, and for as long as I live, I will never forget that in no other country on Earth is my story even possible."

The word "story" is a revealing one, for it is always the candidate's job (as both responsibility and ploy) to describe himself or herself as a character in a story of his or her own making. In speeches, as in homilies, stories almost always carry the weight of parable, with moral lessons to be drawn.

Most memorable, of course, is the story at the end of the speech— 25 which is why it appears at the end. It is the story of Ashley Baia, a young, white Obama volunteer from South Carolina, whose family was so poor she convinced her mother that her favorite meal was a mustard and relish sandwich.

"Anyway, Ashley finishes her story and then goes around the room and asks everyone else why they're supporting the campaign. They all have different stories and reasons. Many bring up a specific issue. And finally they come to this elderly black man who's been sitting there quietly the entire time. . . . He simply says to everyone in the room, 'I am here because of Ashley.'"

During most of the 20th century, demagogues, especially in the South, gained political traction by pitting working class whites and blacks against each other. How fitting, then, that Obama's story points in the opposite direction through an old black man who feels a young white woman's pain.

Clark traces four patterns of rhetorical strategies used by President Obama in his speech: allusion, parallelism, W. E. B. Du Bois's "two-ness," and autobiography. His analysis shows how these strategies combine to provide Obama with the opportunity to address and bring together a broad audience through memorable prose.

Key Features / Textual Analysis

A summary or description of the text. Your readers may not know the text you are analyzing, so you need to include it or tell them about it before you analyze it. Allen's text, the Declaration of Independence, is well known, so she assumes that her readers already know its first sentences. Texts that are not so well known require a more detailed summary or description. For example, Berry includes the ads she analyzes and also describes them in detail.

Attention to the context. Texts don't exist in isolation: they are influenced by and contribute to ongoing conversations, controversies, debates, and cultural trends. To fully engage a particular text, you need to understand its larger context. Clark begins by quoting a 1903 book on race in America, and Berry places shoe ads into the context of fashion advertising.

A clear interpretation or judgment. Your goal in analyzing a text is to lead readers through careful examination of the text to some kind of interpretation or reasoned judgment, sometimes announced clearly in a thesis statement. When you interpret something, you explain what you think it means, as Berry does when she argues that the two ads suggest that our clothing choices enhance our individuality. She might instead have chosen to judge the effectiveness of the ads, perhaps noting that they promise the impossible: uniqueness through mass-produced clothing. Clark argues that through Obama's use of four rhetorical strategies, he "present[s] himself as the bridge builder, the reconciler of America's racial divide."

Reasonable support for your conclusions. Written analysis of a text is generally supported by evidence from the text itself and sometimes from other sources as well. The writer might support their interpretation by quoting words or passages from a verbal text or referring to images in a visual text. Allen, for example, interprets the term "self-evident" by referring to formal logic, Venn diagrams, and the Catholic Credo. Berry examines patterns of both language and images in her analysis of two ads. Clark provides lists of phrases from Obama's speech to support his thesis. Note that the support you offer for your interpretation need only be "reasonable"—there is never only one way to interpret something.

A GUIDE TO WRITING TEXTUAL ANALYSES

Choosing a Text to Analyze

Most of the time, you will be assigned a text or a type of text to analyze: a poem in a literature class, the work of a political philosopher in a political science class, a speech in a history or communications course, a painting or sculpture in an art class, a piece of music in a music theory course. If you must choose a text to analyze, look for one that suits the demands of the assignment—one that is neither too large or complex to analyze thoroughly (a Dickens novel or a Beethoven symphony is probably too big) nor too brief or limited to generate sufficient material (a ten-second TV news brief or a paragraph from *Hillbilly Elegy* would probably be too small). You might also choose to analyze three or four texts by examining elements common to all. Be sure you understand what the assignment asks you to do, and ask your instructor for clarification if you're not sure.

Considering the Rhetorical Situation

PURPOSE	Why are you analyzing this text? To demonstrate that you understand it? To show how its argument works—or doesn't? Or are you using the text as a way to make some other point?	▪ 55–56
AUDIENCE	Are your readers likely to know your text? How much detail will you need to supply?	▪ 57–60
STANCE	What interests you (or not) about your text? Why? What do you know or believe about it, and how will your own beliefs affect your analysis?	▪ 66–68
MEDIA / DESIGN	Will your analysis appear in print? on the web? How will your medium affect your analysis? If you are analyzing a visual text, you will probably need to include an image of it.	▪ 69–71

Generating Ideas and Text

In analyzing a written text, your goal is to understand what it says, how it works, and what it means. To do so, you may find it helpful to follow a certain sequence: read, respond, summarize, analyze, and draw conclusions from your analysis.

Read to see what the text says.   Start by reading carefully, to get a sense of what it says. This means first skimming to **PREVIEW THE TEXT**, rereading for the main ideas, then questioning and **ANNOTATING**.

12–13
16–17
14

Consider your **INITIAL RESPONSE**. Once you have a sense of what the text says, what do you think? What's your reaction to the argument, the tone, the language, the images? Do you find the text difficult? puzzling? Do you agree with what the writer says? disagree? agree *and* disagree? Your reaction to a text can color your analysis, so start by thinking about how you react—and why. Consider both your intellectual and any emotional reactions. Identify places in the text that trigger or account for those reactions. If you think that you have no particular reaction or response, try to articulate why. Whatever your response, think about what accounts for it.

534–35
335–37

Next, consolidate your understanding of the text by **SUMMARIZING** what it says in your own words. You may find it helpful to **OUTLINE** its main ideas. For instance, Allen carefully maps out the parts of the syllogism at the heart of her analysis.

Decide what you want to analyze.   Having read the text carefully, think about what you find most interesting or intriguing and why. Does the argument interest you? its logic? its attempt to create an emotional response? its reliance on the writer's credibility or reputation? its use of design to achieve its aims? its context? Does the text's language, imagery, or structure intrigue you? something else? You might begin your analysis by exploring what attracted your notice.

Think about the larger context.   All texts are part of larger conversations with other texts that have dealt with the same topic. An essay arguing for handgun trigger locks is part of an ongoing conversation about gun regulation, which is itself part of a conversation on individual rights and responsibilities. Academic texts include documentation in part to weave in voices from the conversation. And, in fact, anytime you're reading to learn, you're probably reading for some larger context. Whatever your reading goals, being aware of that larger context can help you better understand what you're reading. Here are some specific aspects of the text to pay attention to:

- *Who else cares about this topic?* Especially when you're reading in order to learn about a topic, the texts you read will often reveal which people or groups are part of the conversation—and might be sources of further reading. For example, an essay describing the formation of the Grand Canyon could be of interest to geologists, environmentalists, Native Americans, travel writers, or tourists. If you're reading such an essay while doing research on the canyon, you should consider how the audience addressed determines the nature of the information provided—and its suitability as a source for your research.

- *Ideas.* Does the text refer to any concepts or ideas that give you some sense that it's part of a larger conversation? An argument on airport security measures, for example, is part of larger conversations about government response to terrorism, the limits of freedom in a democracy, and the possibilities of using technology to detect weapons and explosives, among others.

- *Terms.* Is there any terminology or specialized language that reflects the writer's allegiance to a particular group or academic discipline? If you run across words like *false consciousness*, *ideology*, and *hegemony*, for example, you might guess the text was written by a Marxist scholar.

- *Citations.* Whom does the writer cite? Do the other writers have a particular academic specialty, belong to an identifiable intellectual school, share similar political leanings? If an article on politics cites Michael Moore and Maureen Dowd in support of its argument, you might assume the writer holds liberal opinions; if it cites Rush Limbaugh and Sean Hannity, the writer is likely a conservative.

Write a brief paragraph describing the larger context surrounding the text and how that context affects your understanding of the text.

Consider what you know about the writer. What you know about the person who created a text can influence your understanding of it. Their **CREDENTIALS**, other work, reputation, stance, and beliefs are all useful windows into understanding a text. You may need to conduct an online search to find information on the writer. Then write a sentence or two summarizing what you know about the writer and how that information affects your understanding of the text.

512 ●

Study how the text works. Written texts are made up of various components, including words, sentences, paragraphs, headings, lists, punctuation—and sometimes images as well. Look for patterns in the way these components are used and try to decide what those patterns reveal about the text. How do they affect its message? See the sections on **THINKING ABOUT HOW THE TEXT WORKS** and **IDENTIFYING PATTERNS** for specific guidelines on examining patterns this way. Then write a sentence or two describing the patterns you've discovered and how they contribute to what the text says.

21–23 ✳
23–25

Analyze the argument. Every text makes an argument and provides some kind of support for it. An important part of understanding any text is to recognize its argument—what the writer wants the audience to believe, feel, or do. Here are some questions you'll want to consider when you analyze an argument:

- *What is the claim?* What is the main point the writer is trying to make? Is there a clearly stated **THESIS**, or is the thesis merely implied? Is it appropriately qualified?

387–89 ◆

- *What support does the writer offer for the claim?* What **REASONS** are given to support the claim? What **EVIDENCE** backs up those reasons? Facts? Statistics? Examples? Testimonials by authorities? Anecdotes or stories? Are the reasons and evidence appropriate, plausible, and sufficient? Are you convinced by them? If not, why not?

400–401 ◆
401–8

- *How does the writer appeal to readers?* Do they appeal to your **EMOTIONS**? rely on **LOGIC**? try to establish **COMMON GROUND**? demonstrate **CREDIBILITY**?

413 ◆
398–408
410–11
410–13

- *How evenhandedly does the writer present the argument?* Is there any mention of **COUNTERARGUMENTS**? If so, how does the writer deal with them? By refuting them? By acknowledging them and responding to them reasonably? Does the writer treat other arguments respectfully? dismissively?

  411–12

- *Does the writer use any logical* **FALLACIES**? Are the arguments or beliefs of others distorted or exaggerated? Is the logic faulty?

  414–16

- *What authorities or other sources of outside information does the writer use?* How are they used? How credible are they? Are they in any way biased or otherwise unreliable? Are they current?

- *How does the writer address you as the reader?* Does the writer assume that readers know something about what is being discussed? Does their language include you or exclude you? (Hint: If you see the word *we*, do you feel included?) Do you sense that you and the writer share any beliefs or attitudes? If the writer is not writing to you, what audience is the target? How do you know?

Then write a brief paragraph summarizing the argument the text makes and the main way the writer argues it, along with your reactions to or questions about that argument.

In analyzing a visual text, your goal is to understand its intended effect on viewers as well as its actual effect, the ways it creates that effect, and its relationship to other texts. If the visual text accompanies a written one, you need to understand how the texts work together to convey a message or make an argument.

Describe the text. Your first job is to examine the image carefully. Focus on specific details; given the increasing use of *Photoshop* and other digital image manipulation tools, you can usually assume that every detail in the image is intentional. Ask yourself these questions:

- What kind of image is it? Does it stand alone, or is it part of a group? Are there typical features of this kind of image that it includes—or lacks?

- What does the image show? What stands out? What is in the background? Are some parts of the image grouped together or connected? Are any set apart from one another?

- As you look at the image, does the content seem far away, close up, or in between? Are you level with it, looking down from above, or looking up from below? What is the effect of your viewing position?

- Does the image tell or suggest a story about what has happened (as in Berry's ad for Sorel shoes) or is about to happen?

- Does the image allude to or refer to anything else? For example, the Starbucks logo features the image of a Siren, a mythical being who lured sailors to their doom.

Explore your response.   Images, particularly those in advertisements, are often trying to persuade us to buy something or to feel, think, or behave a certain way. News photographs and online videos also try to evoke

413 ◆ EMOTIONAL responses, from horror over murdered innocents to amusement at cute kittens. Think about your response:

- How does the image make you feel? What emotional response, if any, does the image make you feel? Sympathy? Concern? Anger? Happiness? Contentment? Something else?

- What does the image lead you to think about? What connections does it have to things in your life, in the news, in your knowledge of the world?

- Do the image and any words accompanying seem to be trying to persuade you to think or do something? Do they do so directly, such as by pointing out the virtues of a product (Buick Encore: "Sized to Fit Your Life")? Or indirectly, by setting a tone or establishing a mood (the Clarks shoe ad that Berry analyzes)?

73 ▲ - Does the GENRE affect your response? For example, do you expect to laugh at a comic? feel empathy with victims of a tragedy in a photo accompanying a news story? find a satirical editorial cartoon offensive?

Consider the context. Like written texts, visual texts are part of larger conversations with other texts that have dealt with the same topic or used similar imagery. This editorial cartoon on global warming, for example, is part of an ongoing conversation about climate change and the role our lifestyles play in it:

Consider what you know about the artist or sponsor. Editorial cartoons, like the one above, are usually signed, and information about the artist and their other work is usually readily available on the web. Many commercials and advertisements, however, are created by ad agencies, so the organization or company that sponsored or posted the image should be identified and researched. How does that information affect your understanding of the text?

Decide on a focus for your analysis. What do you find most interesting about the text, and why? Its details and the way they work together (or not)? The argument it makes? The way it uses images to appeal to its audience? The emotional response it evokes? The way any words and images work together to deliver a message? These are just some ways of thinking about a visual text, ones that can help you find a focus.

However you choose to focus your analysis, it should be limited in scope so that you can zero in on the details of the visual you're analyzing. Here, for example, is an excerpt from an essay from 2014 by an art historian responding to a statement made by former president Barack Obama that manufacturing skills may be worth more than a degree in art history:

"I promise you, folks can make a lot more potentially with skilled manufacturing or the trades than they might with an art history degree." President Barack Obama

Charged with interrogating this quote from the president, I Google "Obama art history." I click on the first result, a video from CNN, in which the quote is introduced by a gray-haired man in a dark and serious suit, standing in front of a bank of monitors in a digitally created nonspace. The camera cuts from this man to President Obama, who stands in shirtsleeves, his tie slightly loosened. His undershirt is visible through his buttondown under the intense light from what I assume is the work-day sun.

Behind him is a crowd of men and women in more casual clothing, some wearing sweatshirts that have the name of a union printed across them. Their presence creates a spectrum of skin tones. Each person was clearly vetted for visual effect, as were the president's and the newscaster's costumes, the size of their flag lapel pins, the shape of the microphones they speak into, and the angle of the light on their faces. The president makes the comment in question, immediately declares his love for art history, and says that he doesn't want to get a bunch of angry emails from art historians. The crowd behind him laughs and the clip cuts off abruptly.

A click away, I find a digitized copy of a handwritten note from President Obama, apologizing to an angry art history professor who emailed him to complain about his comments. The card on which the note is written is plain, undecorated save for two lines of text printed in a conservative, serif font in a shade of blue that is just on the vibrant side of navy—THE WHITE HOUSE—and under it in smaller letters, WASHINGTON. Its tasteful, minimal aesthetic pulls double duty, meant to convey both populist efficiency (note the absence of gold gilding) and stern superiority (you know where Washington is, right?). It sets up a productive contrast with the friendliness of the president's own handwriting, particularly his looping signature, soft on the outside with a strong slash through the middle.

Like the video of the president's speech, it is a screen-scale tour de force of political imagecraft, certainly produced with the full knowledge that it would be digitized and go viral, at least among a particular demographic.

—Joel Parsons, "Richness in the Eye of the Beholder"

Parsons begins by describing the images—Obama's clothing, the people standing behind him, the letterhead on his note card, his "looping

Barack Obama speaking at a General Electric plant in Waukesha, Wisconsin, 2014.

THE WHITE HOUSE

WASHINGTON

Ann —

Let me apologize for my off-the-cuff remarks. I was making a point about the jobs market, not the value of art history. As it so happens, art history was one of my favorite subjects in high school, and it has helped me take in a great deal of joy in my life that

I might otherwise have missed.

So please pass on my apology for the glib remark to the entire department, and understand that I was trying to encourage young people who may not be predisposed to a four year college experience to be open to technical training that can lead them to an honorable career.

Sincerely,

Obama's apology note to Ann Johns, art history professor at the University of Texas at Austin.

signature"—followed by an analysis of how every aspect of the video and the note card was "certainly produced with the full knowledge that it would be digitized and go viral." Notice as well that Parsons's analysis focuses more on the visual aspects of the video and note card than on what was said or written. And in a part of his essay not shown here, he notes that his analysis is grounded in "tools . . . he learned in a first-year art history course"—a not-so-subtle response to what President Obama said.

Coming Up with a Thesis

When you analyze a text, you are basically **ARGUING** that the text should be read or seen in a certain way. Once you've studied the text thoroughly, you need to identify your analytical goal: do you want to show that the text has a certain meaning? uses certain techniques to achieve its purposes? tries to influence its audience in particular ways? relates to some larger context in some significant manner? should be taken seriously—or not? something else? Come up with a tentative **THESIS** to guide your thinking and analyzing—but be aware that your thesis may change as you continue to work.

397–417

387–89

Ways of Organizing a Textual Analysis

Examine the information you have to see how it supports or complicates your thesis. Look for clusters of related information that you can use to structure an **OUTLINE**. Your analysis might be structured in at least two ways. You might, as Clark does, discuss patterns, elements, or themes that run through the text. Alternatively, you might analyze each text or section of text separately, as Berry does. Following are graphic representations of some ways of organizing a textual analysis:

335–37

[Thematically]

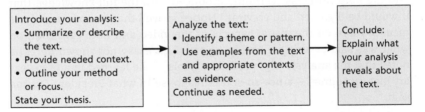

[Part by part, or text by text]

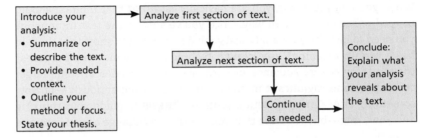

[Spatially, as the text is likely to be experienced by viewers]

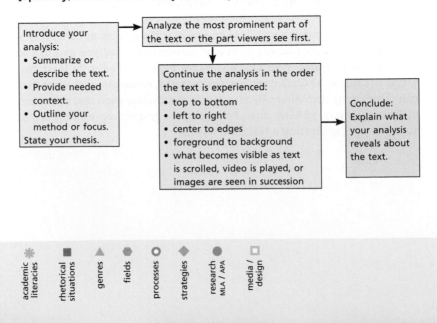

Writing Out a Draft

In drafting your analysis, your goal should be to integrate the various parts into a smoothly flowing, logically organized essay. However, it's easy to get bogged down in the details. Consider writing one section of the analysis first, then another and another, until you've drafted the entire middle; then draft your beginning and ending. Alternatively, start by summarizing the text and moving from there to your analysis and then to your ending. However you do it, you need to support your analysis with evidence: from the text itself (as Berry's analysis of advertisements does), or from **RESEARCH** on the larger context of the text (as Allen does), or by comparing the text you are analyzing to another text (as Clark does).

● 477

Draft a BEGINNING. The beginning of an essay that analyzes a text generally has several tasks: to introduce or summarize the text for your readers, to offer any necessary information on the larger context, and to present your thesis.

◆ 373–80

- *Summarize or describe the text.* If the text is one your readers don't know, you need to **SUMMARIZE** or **DESCRIBE** it early on to show that you understand it fully. For example, Berry begins each analysis of a shoe advertisement with a description of its content.

◆ 534–35

- *Show the text.* If you're analyzing a visual text online, consider starting off with an image, a video, or a link to it or something similar, as Berry does by embedding the ads she analyzes in her text.

- *Provide a context for your analysis.* If there is a larger context that is significant for your analysis, you might mention it in your introduction. Allen does this by comparing the Declaration's statement about self-evident truths to the statements of belief in the Apostles' Creed of the Catholic Church.

- *State your THESIS.* Berry ends her first paragraph by stating her thesis explicitly: These ads "for Clarks and Sorel. . . encourage us to break free from the standard beauty mold and be ourselves; using mostly imagery, they remind us that being unique is the true origin of beauty." Clark promises to analyze "the rhetorical strategies that the orator and authors used so effectively."

◆ 387–89

380–85   **Draft an ENDING.**   Think about what you want your readers to take away from your analysis, and end by getting them to focus on those thoughts.

- *Restate your thesis—and say why it matters.* Berry, for example, ends by asserting that the ads she examines invite women to "be ourselves" by "accessoriz[ing] our personalities."

- *Explain what your analysis reveals.* Your analysis should tell your readers something about the way the text works or about what it means or says. Allen, for example, concludes by noting that "the Declaration's truths fit together almost like the pieces of a mathematical equation; we intuitively feel the puzzle pieces snap together. That is how self-evidence should feel."

386–87   **Come up with a TITLE.**   A good title indicates something about the subject of your analysis—and makes readers want to see what you have to say about it. Berry's title provides a preview of her thesis that the ads she is analyzing are selling a vision of clothing as a vehicle for being unique, while Clark's title straightforwardly announces his topic.

353–55   **Consider REWRITING.**   If you have time and want to explore alternatives, you might try rewriting your draft to see if a different plan or approach might work better.

Considering Matters of Design

544–47

650–52

- If you cite written text as evidence, be sure to set long quotations and **DOCUMENTATION** according to the style you're using.

- If your essay is lengthy, consider whether **HEADINGS** would make your analysis easier for readers to follow.

- If you're analyzing a visual text, include a copy of the image and a caption identifying it.

- If you're submitting your essay electronically, provide links to whatever text you are analyzing.

- If you're analyzing an image or a screen shot, consider annotating elements of it right on the image.

Getting Response and Revising

The following questions can help you and others study your draft with a critical eye. Make sure that anyone you ask to read and **RESPOND** to your text knows your purpose and audience.

348–50

- Is the beginning effective? Does it make a reader want to continue?
- Does the introduction provide an overview of your analysis? Is your thesis clear?
- Is the text described or summarized clearly and sufficiently?
- Is the analysis well organized and easy to follow? Do the parts fit together coherently? Does it read like an essay rather than a collection of separate bits of analysis?
- Does each part of the analysis relate to and support the thesis?
- Is anything confusing or in need of more explanation?
- Are all quotations accurate and correctly documented?
- Is it clear how the analysis leads to the interpretation? Is there adequate evidence to support the interpretation?
- Does the ending make clear what your analysis shows?

Then it's time to **REVISE**. Make sure your text appeals to your audience and think hard about whether it will achieve your purpose.

350–53

Editing and Proofreading

Readers equate correctness with competence. Once you've revised your draft, edit carefully:

- Is your **THESIS** clearly stated?
- Check all **QUOTATIONS**, **PARAPHRASES**, and **SUMMARIES** for accuracy and form. Be sure that each has the required **DOCUMENTATION**.
- Make sure that your analysis flows clearly from one point to the next and that you use **TRANSITIONS** to help readers move through your text.
- **PROOFREAD** your finished analysis carefully before turning it in.

387–89
526–38
544–47
391
359–60

Taking Stock of Your Work

Take stock of what you've written and learned by writing out answers to these questions:

- How did you go about analyzing the text? What methods did you use—and which ones were most helpful?
- How did you go about drafting your essay?
- How well did you organize your written analysis? What, if anything, could you do to make it easier to read?
- Did you provide sufficient evidence to support your analysis?
- What did you do especially well?
- What could still be improved?
- Did you include any visuals, and if so, what did they add? Could you have shown the same thing with words?
- How did other readers' responses influence your writing?
- What would you do differently next time?
- Are you pleased with your analysis? What did it teach you about the text you analyzed? Did it make you want to study more works by the same writer or artist?

IF YOU NEED MORE HELP

340–42 ○
343–47
348–55
356–60
361–70
653–63 ▢

See Chapter 30 for guidelines on **DRAFTING**, Chapter 31 on **ASSESSING YOUR OWN WRITING**, Chapter 32 on **GETTING RESPONSE AND REVISING**, and Chapter 33 on **EDITING AND PROOFREADING**. See Chapter 34 if you are required to submit your analysis in a writing **PORTFOLIO**. See Chapter 58 for help **USING VISUALS**.

✳ academic literacies
■ rhetorical situations
▲ genres
● fields
○ processes
◆ strategies
● research MLA / APA
▢ media / design

Reporting Information 12

Many kinds of writing report information. Newspapers report on local and world events; textbooks give information about biology, history, writing; websites provide information about products (*jcrew.com*), people (*pharrellwilliams.com*), institutions (*smithsonian.org*). We write out a lot of information ourselves, from a note we post on our door saying we've gone to choir practice to a text we send to tell a friend where to meet us for dinner and how to get there.

College assignments often call for reporting information as well. In a *history* class, you may be assigned to report what you've learned about the state of U.S. relations with Japan just before the bombing of Pearl Harbor. A *biology* course may require you to report the effects of an experiment in which plants are deprived of sunlight for different periods of time. In a *nursing* class, you may have to report the changes in a patient's symptoms after the administration of a particular drug.

This chapter focuses on reports that are written to inform readers about a particular topic. Very often this kind of writing calls for some kind of research: you need to know your subject in order to report on it! When you write to report information, you are the expert. We'll begin with three good examples, the first annotated to show the key features found in most reports.

MICHAELA CULLINGTON

Does Texting Affect Writing?

This essay by a student at Marywood University was published in Young Scholars in Writing, *a journal of undergraduate writing published by the University of Missouri–Kansas City.*

It's taking over our lives. We can do it almost anywhere—walking to class, waiting in line at the grocery store, or hanging out at home. It's quick, easy, and convenient. It has become a concern of doctors, parents, and teachers alike. What is it? It's texting!

Text messaging—or texting, as it's more commonly called—is the process of sending and receiving typed messages via a cellular phone. It is a common means of communication among teenagers and is even becoming popular in the business world because it allows quick messages to be sent without people having to commit to a telephone conversation. A person is able to say what is needed, and the other person will receive the information and respond when it's convenient to do so.

Definitions of key terms.

In order to more quickly type what they are trying to say, many people use abbreviations instead of words. The language created by these abbreviations is called textspeak. Some people believe that using these abbreviations is hindering the writing abilities of students, and others argue that texting is actually having a positive effect on writing. In fact, it seems likely that texting has no significant effect on student writing.

Here's the thesis.

Concerns about Textspeak

A September 2008 article in *USA Today* entitled "Texting, Testing Destroys Kids' Writing Style" summarizes many of the most common complaints about the effect of texting. It states that according to the National Center for Education Statistics, only 25% of high school seniors are "proficient" writers. The article quotes Jacquie Ream, a former teacher and author of *K.I.S.S.—Keep It Short and Simple*, a guide for writing more effectively. Ream states, "[W]e have a whole generation being raised without communication skills." She blames the use of acronyms and shorthand in text messages for students' inability to spell and ultimately to write well. Ream also points out that students struggle to convey emotion in their writing because, as she states, in text messages "emotions are always sideways smiley faces."

Analysis of causes and effects.

This debate became prominent after some teachers began to believe they were seeing a decline in the writing abilities of their students. Many attributed this perceived decline to the increasing popularity of text messaging and its use of abbreviations. Naomi Baron, a linguistics professor at American University, blames texting for what she sees as the fact that "so much of American society has become sloppy and laissez faire about

5

the mechanics of writing" ("Should"). Teachers report finding "2" for "to," "gr8" for "great," "dat" for "that," and "wut" for "what," among other examples of textspeak, in their students' writing. A Minnesota teacher of the seventh and ninth grades says that she has to spend extra time in class editing papers and must "explicitly" remind her students that it is not acceptable to use text slang and abbreviations in writing (Walsh). Another English teacher believes that text language has become "second nature" to her students (Carey); they are so used to it that they do not even catch themselves doing it.

Many also complain that because texting does not stress the importance of punctuation, students are neglecting it in their formal writing. Teachers say that their students are forgetting commas, apostrophes, and even capital letters to begin sentences. Another complaint is that text messages lack emotion. Many argue that texts lack feeling because of their tendency to be short, brief, and to the point. Because students are not able to communicate emotion effectively through texts, some teachers worry, they may lose the ability to do so in writing.

To get a more personal perspective on the question of how teachers perceive texting to be influencing student writing, I interviewed two of my former high school teachers—my junior-year English teacher and my senior-year theology teacher. Both teachers stress the importance of writing in their courses. They maintain that they notice text abbreviations in their students' writing often. To correct this problem, they point it out when it occurs and take points off for its use. They also remind their students to use proper sentence structure and complete sentences. The English teacher says that she believes texting inhibits good writing—it reinforces simplistic writing that may be acceptable for conversation but is "not so good for critical thinking or analysis." She suggests that texting tends to generate topic sentences without emphasizing the following explanation. According to these teachers, then, texting is inhibiting good writing. However, their evidence is limited, based on just a few personal experiences rather than on a significant amount of research.

Responses to Concerns about Textspeak

In response to these complaints that texting is having a negative impact on student writing, others insist that texting should be viewed as beneficial because it provides students with motivation to write, practice in specific writing skills, and an opportunity to gain confidence in their writing. For example, Betty Sternberg and her coauthors argue that texting is a good way to motivate students: teens enjoy texting, and if they frequently write through texts, they will be more motivated to write formally. Texting also helps to spark students' creativity, these authors argue, because they are always coming up with new ways to express their ideas (417).

In addition, because they are engaging in written communication rather than oral speech, texting teens learn how to convey their message to a reader in as few words as possible. In his book *Txtng: The Gr8 Db8*, David Crystal discusses a study that concludes that texting actually helps foster "the ability to summarize and express oneself concisely" in writing (168). Furthermore, Crystal explains that texting actually helps people to "sharpen their diplomatic skills . . . [because] it allows more time to formulate their thoughts and express them carefully" (168). One language arts teacher from Minnesota believes that texting helps students develop their own "individual voice" (qtd. in Walsh). Perfecting such a voice allows the writer to offer personal insights and express feelings that will interest and engage readers.

Supporters of texting also argue that it not only teaches elements of writing but provides extra practice to those who struggle with the conventions of writing. As Crystal points out, children who struggle with literacy will not choose to use a technology that requires them to do something that is difficult for them. However, if they do choose to text, the experience will help them "overcome their awkwardness and develop their social and communication skills" (*Txtng* 171). Shirley Holm, a junior high school teacher, describes texting as a "comfortable form of communication" (qtd. in Walsh). Teenagers are used to texting, enjoy doing so, and as a result are always writing. Through this experience of writing in ways they enjoy, they can learn to take pleasure in writing formally. If students are continually writing in some form, they will eventually develop better skills.

Furthermore, those who favor texting explain that with practice comes the confidence and courage to try new things, which some observers believe they are seeing happen with writing as a result of texting. Teenagers have, for example, created an entirely new language—one that uses abbreviations and symbols instead of words, does not require punctuation, and uses short, incomplete phrases throughout the entire

10

Synthesis of various sources of information. Quotations are introduced with signal phrases.

academic literacies
rhetorical situations
genres
fields
processes
strategies
research MLA / APA
media / design

conversation. It's a way of speaking that is a language in and of itself. Crystal, among others, sees this "language evolution" as a positive effect of texting; he seems, in fact, fascinated that teenagers are capable of creating such a phenomenon, which he describes as the "latest manifestation of the human ability" (*Txtng* 175). David Warlick, a teacher and author of books about technology in the classroom, would agree with Crystal. He believes students should be given credit for "inventing a new language ideal for communicating in a high-tech world" (qtd. in Carey).

Methods

I decided to conduct my own research into this controversy. I wanted to get different, more personal, perspectives on the issue. First, I surveyed seven students on their opinions about the impact of texting on writing. Second, I questioned two high school teachers, as noted above. Finally, in an effort to compare what students are actually doing to people's perceptions of what they are doing, I analyzed student writing samples for instances of textspeak.[1]

To let students speak for themselves, I created a list of questions for seven high school and college students, some of my closest and most reliable friends. Although the number of respondents was small, I could trust my knowledge of them to help me interpret their responses. In addition, these students are very different from one another, and I believed their differences would allow for a wide array of thoughts and opinions on the issue. I was thus confident in the reliability and diversity of their answers but was cautious not to make too many assumptions because of the small sample size.

Firsthand research: interviews and survey.

I asked the students how long they had been texting; how often they texted; what types of abbreviations they used most and how often they used them; and whether they noticed themselves using any type of textspeak in their formal writing. In analyzing their responses, I looked for commonalities to help me draw conclusions about the students' texting habits and if/how they believed their writing was affected.

I created a list of questions for teachers similar to the one for the students and asked two of my high school teachers to provide their input. I asked if they had noticed their students using textspeak in their writing assignments and, if so, how they dealt with it. I also asked if they believed texting had a positive or negative effect on writing. Next, I asked if they were texters themselves. And, finally, I solicited their

15

opinions on what they believed should be done to prevent teens from using text abbreviations and other textspeak in their writing.

I was surprised at how different the students' replies and opinions were from the teachers'. I decided to find out for myself whose impressions were more accurate by comparing some students' actual writing with students' and teachers' perceptions of that writing. To do this I looked at twenty samples of student writing—end-of-semester research arguments written in two first-year college writing courses with different instructors. The topics varied from increased airport security after September 11 to the weapons of the Vietnam War to autism, and lengths ranged from eight to ten pages. To analyze the papers for the presence of textspeak, I looked closely for use of abbreviations and other common slang terms, especially those usages which the students had stated in their surveys were most common. These included "hbu" ("How about you?"); "gtg" ("Got to go"); and "cuz" ("because"). I also looked for the numbers 2 and 4 used instead of the words "to" and "for."

Comparison and contrast.

Discussion of Findings

My research suggests that texting actually has a minimal effect on student writing. It showed that students do not believe textspeak is appropriate in formal writing assignments. They recognize the difference between texting friends and writing formally and know what is appropriate in each situation. This was proven true in the student samples, in which no examples of textspeak were used. Many experts would agree that there is no harm in textspeak, as long as students continue to be taught and reminded that occasions where formal language is expected are not the place for it. As Crystal explains, the purpose of the abbreviations used in text messages is not to replace language but rather to make quick communications shorter and easier, since in a standard text message, the texter is allowed only 160 characters for a communication ("Texting" 81).

Summary and quotations of sources.

Dennis Baron, an English and linguistics professor at the University of Illinois, has done much research on the effect of technology on writing, and his findings are aligned with those of my own study. In his book *A Better Pencil: Readers, Writers, and the Digital Revolution,* he concludes that students do not use textspeak in their writing. In fact, he suggests students do not even use abbreviations in their text messages very often. Baron says that college students have "put away such

academic literacies   rhetorical situations   genres   fields   processes   strategies   research MLA / APA   media / design

childish things, and many of them had already abandoned such signs of middle-school immaturity in high school" (qtd. in Golden).

In surveying the high school and college students, I found that most have been texting for a few years, usually starting around ninth grade. The students said they generally text between thirty and a hundred messages every day but use abbreviations only occasionally, with the most common being "lol" ("Laugh out loud"), "gtg" ("Got to go"), "hbu" ("How about you?"), "cuz" ("because"), and "jk" ("Just kidding"). None of them believed texting abbreviations were acceptable in formal writing. In fact, research has found that most students report that they do not use textspeak in formal writing. As one Minnesota high school student says, "[T]here is a time and a place for everything," and formal writing is not the place for communicating the way she would if she were texting her friends (qtd. in Walsh). Another student admits that in writing for school she sometimes finds herself using these abbreviations. However, she notices and corrects them before handing in her final paper (Carey). One teacher reports that, despite texting, her students' "formal writing remains solid." She occasionally sees an abbreviation; however, it is in informal, "warm-up" writing. She believes that what students do in everyday writing is up to them as long as they use standard English in formal writing (qtd. in Walsh).

Summary of survey results with quotations.

Also supporting my own research findings are those from a study which took place at a midwestern research university. This study involved eighty-six students who were taking an Introduction to Education course at the university. The participants were asked to complete a questionnaire that included questions about their texting habits, the spelling instruction they had received, and their proficiency at spelling. They also took a standardized spelling test. Before starting the study, the researchers had hypothesized that texting and the use of abbreviations would have a negative impact on the spelling abilities of the students. However, they found that the results did not support their hypothesis. The researchers did note that text messaging is continuing to increase in popularity; therefore, this issue should continue to be examined (Shaw et al.).

20

Summary of research that supports her own.

I myself am a frequent texter. I chat with my friends from home every day through texting. I also use texting to communicate with my school friends, perhaps to discuss what time we are going to meet for dinner or to ask quick questions about homework. According to my cell phone bill, I send and receive around 6,400 texts a month. In the messages I send, I

Pertinent personal experience.

rarely notice myself using abbreviations. The only time I use them is if I do not have time to write out the complete phrase. However, sometimes I find it more time-consuming to try to figure out how to abbreviate something so that my message will still be comprehensible.

Since I rarely use abbreviations in my texting, I never use them in my formal writing. I know that they are unacceptable and that it would make me look unintelligent if I included acronyms and symbols instead of proper and formal language. I also have not noticed an effect on my spelling as a result of texting. I am confident in my spelling abilities, and even when I use an abbreviation, I know how to spell the word(s) it stands for.

Conclusion: summary of research and restatement of claim.

On the basis of my own research, expert research, and personal observations, I can confidently state that texting is not interfering with students' use of standard written English and has no effect on their writing abilities in general. It is interesting to look at the dynamics of the arguments over these issues. Teachers and parents who claim that they are seeing a decline in the writing abilities of their students and children mainly support the negative-impact argument. Other teachers and researchers suggest that texting provides a way for teens to practice writing in a casual setting and thus helps prepare them to write formally. Experts and students themselves, however, report that they see no effect, positive or negative. Anecdotal experiences should not overshadow the actual evidence.

Note

1. All participants in the study have given permission for their responses to be published.

Works Cited

Baron, Dennis. *A Better Pencil: Readers, Writers, and the Digital Revolution.* Oxford UP, 2009.

Carey, Bridget. "The Rise of Text, Instant Messaging Vernacular Slips into Schoolwork." *The Miami Herald,* 6 Mar. 2007, *Academic OneFile,* search.ebscohost.com/login.aspx?.direct=true&db=edsgao&AN=edsgcl.160190230&site=eds-live. Accessed 27 Oct. 2009.

Crystal, David. "Texting." *ELT Journal,* vol. 62, no. 1, Jan. 2008, pp. 77–83. *Academic OneFile,* search.ebscohost.com/login.aspx?direct=true&db=edsgao&AN=edsgcl.177163353&site=eds-live. Accessed 8 Nov. 2009.

———. *Txtng: The Gr8 Db8.* Oxford UP, 2008.

academic literacies

rhetorical situations

genres

fields

processes

strategies

research MLA / APA

media / design

Golden, Serena. Rev. of *A Better Pencil*. *Inside Higher Ed*, 18 Sept. 2009, insidehighered.com/news/2009/09/18/barron. Accessed 9 Nov. 2009.

Shaw, Donita M., et al. "An Exploratory Investigation into the Relationship between Text Messaging and Spelling." *New England Reading Association Journal*, vol. 43, no. 1, pp. 57–62. *EBSCO Discovery Service for Marywood University*, search.ebscohost.com/login.aspx?direct=true&db=edb&AN=25648081&site=eds-live. Accessed 8 Nov. 2009.

"Should We Worry or LOL?" *NEA Today*, Mar. 2004, p. 12. *ProQuest*, search.proquest.com/docview/198894194?accountid=42654. Accessed 27 Oct. 2009.

Sternberg, Betty, et al. "Enhancing Adolescent Literacy Achievement through Integration of Technology in the Classroom." *Reading Research Quarterly*, vol. 42, no. 3, July–Sept. 2007, pp. 416–20. *ProQuest*, search.proquest.com/docview/212128056?accountid=42654. Accessed 8 Nov. 2009.

"Texting, Testing Destroys Kids' Writing Style." *USA Today Magazine*, vol. 137, no. 2760, Sept. 2008, p. 8. *ProQuest*, search.proquest.com/docview/214595644?accountid=42654. Accessed 9 Nov. 2009.

Walsh, James. "Txt Msgs Creep in2 class; Some Say That's gr8." *McClatchy-Tribune News Service*, 23 Oct. 2007. *ProQuest*, search.proquest.com/docview/456879133?accountid=42654. Accessed 27 Oct. 2009.

Cullington's essay examines whether or not texting affects students' writing. Her information is based on both published scholarship and a small survey of students and teachers.

FRANKIE SCHEMBRI

Edible Magic

In the following report, Massachusetts Institute of Technology student Frankie Schembri explains the science behind how popcorn pops. Her essay was originally published in Angles 2016: Selected Essays from Introductory Writing Subjects at MIT.

Life is studded with little pockets of magic. These are the moments with mysterious emergent qualities, when the whole is greater than the sum of the parts, when one plus one somehow equals three. Such magic is even better when it comes in edible form.

When an unassuming little kernel of corn meets hot oil, it is transformed. It is elevated with an unmistakable "pop!" into a fluffy cloud of goodness ready to be dressed with butter, caramel, or whatever your heart desires.

This magic is called popcorn.

Popcorn exploded in popularity in the early 20th century but surprisingly only made it into movie theaters with the advent of sound films, or "talkies," in 1927. Silent films catered to a smaller, more exclusive clientele and owners worried that the sound of the snack being munched would detract from the experience (Geiling, 2013).

By the 1940s, popcorn had become an inextricable part of going   5
to the movies, and from then on, over half of the popcorn consumed yearly in America was eaten at movie theaters (Geiling, 2013). Fast-forward some 70 years and the relationship remains unbreakable.

Step into any movie theater lobby across America and your senses are bombarded with the unmistakable scent of salt and butter.

Popcorn snuck into the American household in the 1960s with Jiffy Pop, a self-contained stovetop popper including kernels, oil, and even the pan, and it flourished with the popularity of microwave ovens in the 1970s (Smith, 1999, p. 124). Popcorn cultivated an important relationship with microwaves in the latter half of the 20th century, important enough that popcorn was eventually given the rare honor of its own designated microwave button (Smith, 1999, p. 127).

"But how?" you might ask. How do these ordinary kernels magically spring to life with a little heat and oil, enchanting kids and grown-ups alike?

Like most acts of magic, popcorn's "pop" can be understood with a little science.

Botanically speaking, popcorn is a type of maize, the only domesticated subgroup in the genus *Zea*, a group of plants in the grass family. The different types of maize are classified based on their kernel's size, shape, and composition (Smith, 1999, p. 6).

Corn kernels have three main structural components. First, there 10
is the germ (from the Latin *germen*, meaning seed or sprout), a small pocket of genetic material that is essentially a baby corn plant waiting to grow. The germ is surrounded by the endosperm (the Greek *endon*, within, and *sperma,* seed), a larger parcel of water mixed with soft and hard starch granules that make up most of the kernel's weight and would provide food for the corn plant if it were to sprout. Finally, the germ-endosperm complex is surrounded by the pericarp (from the Greek *peri,* around, and *karpos*, fruit), the hard shell that winds up stuck between your molars after you enjoy a bag of popcorn (Ghose, 2015).

Popcorn kernels are unique in that they are relatively small, they have endosperms containing a larger number of hard starch granules, and their pericarps are hard and impermeable, essentially sealing off the contents of the kernel from the outside environment. These characteristics have endowed popcorn kernels with the ability to pop (Ghose, 2015).

In an attempt to better understand the physics of popcorn, aeronautical engineer Emmanuel Virot and physicist Alexandre Ponomarenko, who seem to have also fallen under popcorn's spell (judging by the language of their published report), experimented with the temperature at which a kernel pops. As Virot and Ponomarenko (2015) explain, when heat is applied to the kernels via hot oil on a stovetop or in a microwave, the temperature of the kernels begins to rise accordingly. Most affected by this increase in heat is the water stored between the starch granules in the endosperm. Much like a bubbling pot of water brought to a boil, the water in the kernel begins to change from liquid into gas.

While liquid water is content to stay put, gaseous water in the form of steam craves space to move, but the hard shell of the pericarp effectively keeps the water trapped inside the kernel. As a result, the kernel acts like a tiny steamer and the starch granules inside are cooked into a gooey mass. As the mass gets hotter and hotter, the steam presses harder and harder on the inside surface of the kernel's shell like the hands of a million tiny creatures trapped inside a bubble (Virot & Ponomarenko, 2015).

The tension is palpable. The kernel begins to shake with anticipation. It rocks back and forth, back and forth, faster and faster, and faster still. Then finally . . . pop! The bubble bursts, the lid flies off the pot, and fireworks explode as the hard shell of the pericarp cracks and the steam breaks free from its kernel prison. The starchy goop also bubbles out into the world, where it meets cold, fresh air and rapidly hardens into spongy cloudlike shapes. Just like that, in just one-fifteenth of a second, a new piece of popcorn is born (Virot & Ponomarenko, 2015).

Virot and Ponomarenko (2015) determined that the temperature at which kernels typically pop is 180 degrees Celsius. The pair also determined that the resulting popped kernel can be up to 40 times its unpopped volume, although usually the kernel's radius merely doubles.

But what propels the kernel, with what Virot and Ponomarenko (2015) call "all the grace of a seasoned gymnast," into the air as it pops? When the pericarp fractures, it does so in only one place first, giving some of the steam and starchy goop a head start on escaping. The starch released first extends to create a leg of sorts, off of which the rest of the kernel springboards, launching it somersaulting into the air like an Olympic gymnast. Popcorn jumps typically only reach a height of a few centimeters, but still manage to create endless entertainment for the hungry viewer.

Where does the "pop" sound come from? Arguably the most important part of the whole experience, popcorn's characteristic noise is not, contrary to popular belief, the sound of the kernel's shell breaking open. The popping sound is created by the release of trapped water vapor resonating in the kernel, similar to how, when removed, a champagne cork makes a popping sound that resonates in the glass bottle (Virot & Ponomarenko, 2015).

Making popcorn hardly seems like an opportunity to learn about physics, but the kernels' unique transformation illustrates some principles of thermodynamics, biomechanics, and acoustics, as the properties of different materials dictate how they respond to pressure and heat.

Life is studded with little pockets of magic. From the enticing smell during a night at the movies to the rising staccato sound of a bag coming to life in your microwave, popcorn is magic-meets-science in its most delicious form. And it always leaves you hungry for more.

15

References

Geiling, N. (2013, October 3). Why do we eat popcorn at the movies? *Smithsonian.com*. Retrieved from https://www.smithsonianmag .com/arts-culture/why-do-we-eat-popcorn-at-the-movies-475063/

Ghose, T. (2015, February 10). The secret acrobatics of popcorn revealed. *Live Science*. Retrieved from https://www.livescience.com/49768 -mechanics-of-popcorn.html

Smith, A. (1999). *Popped culture: A social history of popcorn in America*. Columbia, SC: University of South Carolina Press.

Virot, E., & Ponomarenko, A. (2015). Popcorn: Critical temperature, jump and sound. *Journal of the Royal Society Interface, 12*(104). doi:10.1098/rsif.2014.1247

Schembri introduces her subject by placing it in a cultural context of the movies, Jiffy Pop, and microwave popcorn. She then distinguishes popcorn from other varieties of corn or maize and goes on to describe what happens when popcorn kernels are heated, pop, and fly into the air. To explore her subject from these various perspectives, she draws on scientific, historical, and popular sources.

JON MARCUS

The Reason College Costs More than You Think

Writing online for Time *in 2014, Hechinger Report editor Jon Marcus examines the length of time students take to graduate and how that affects the cost of getting a degree.*

When Alex Nichols started as a freshman at the University of Mississippi, he felt sure he'd earn his bachelor's degree in four years. Five years later, and Nichols is back on the Oxford, Mississippi, campus for what he hopes is truly his final semester.

"There are a lot more students staying another semester or another year than I thought there would be when I got here," Nichols says. "I meet people once a week who say, 'Yes, I'm a second-year senior,' or, 'I've been here for five years.'"

The Lyceum, the oldest building at the University of Mississippi.

They're likely as surprised as Nichols still to be toiling away in school.

Nearly nine out of 10 freshmen think they'll earn their bachelor's degrees within the traditional four years, according to a nationwide survey conducted by the Higher Education Research Institute at UCLA. But the U.S. Department of Education reports that fewer than half that many actually will. And about 45 percent won't have finished even after six years.

That means the annual cost of college, a source of so much anxiety   5 for families and students, often overlooks the enormous additional expense of the extra time it will actually take to graduate.

"It's a huge inconvenience," says Nichols, whose college career has been prolonged for the common reason that he changed majors and took courses he ended up not needing. His athletic scholarship—Nichols was a middle-distance runner on the cross-country team—ran out after four years. "I had to get some financial help from my parents."

The average added cost of just one extra year at a four-year public university is $63,718 in tuition, fees, books, and living expenses, plus lost wages each of those many students could have been earning had they finished on time, according to the advocacy group Complete College America.

A separate report by the Los Angeles–based Campaign for College Opportunity finds that the average student at a California State University campus who takes six years instead of four to earn a bachelor's degree will spend an additional $58,000 and earn $52,900 less over their lifetimes than a student who graduates on time, for a total loss of $110,900.

"The cost of college isn't just what students and their families pay in tuition or fees," says Michele Siqueiros, the organization's executive director. "It's also about time. That's the hidden cost of a college education."

So hidden that most families still unknowingly plan on four years 10 for a bachelor's degree, says Sylvia Hurtado, director of the Higher Education Research Institute at UCLA.

Although the institute does not poll parents in its annual survey, "that high percentage of freshmen [who are confident they'll finish in four years] is probably reflecting their parents' expectation—'This is costing me a lot, so you're going to be out in four years.' So the students think, 'Sure, why not?' I don't think the parents even initially entertain or plan for six years or some possible outcome like that."

Yet many students almost immediately doom themselves to taking longer, since they register for fewer courses than they need to stay on track. Surveys of incoming freshmen in California and Indiana who said they expected to graduate in four years found that half signed up for fewer courses than they'd needed to meet that goal, according to a new report by the higher-education consulting firm HCM Strategists.

It's not entirely the students' fault.

More than half of community-college students are slowed down by having to retake subjects such as math and reading that they should have learned in high school, says Complete College America. And at some schools, budget cuts have made it difficult to register for the courses students do need to take. Two-thirds of students at one California State University campus weren't able to get into their required courses, according to a 2010 study by the University of California's Civil Rights Project.

Most state financial-aid programs, meanwhile, cover only four years. 15 "They do not fund a fifth or sixth year," says Stan Jones, president of

Complete College America and a former Indiana commissioner of higher education. "And by that time the parents' resources and the students' resources have run out. So that fifth year is where you borrow."

Students at the most elite colleges and universities tend not to have this problem, which means that schools with some of the highest annual tuition can turn out to be relative bargains. These schools "would have a revolt if their students had to go a fifth year," Jones says. "But that recognition has really not hit the public sector yet, about the hidden cost of that extra year."

Policymakers urge speeding students through remedial classes more quickly, adding more sections of required courses so students can get in when they need them, and encouraging students to take 15 credits per semester instead of the typical 12.

Change won't come soon enough for Nichols, who is determined that it won't take more than one extra semester to finish his degree in integrated marketing communications.

"That's time you're wasting," he says, "that you could be out making money."

Marcus combines information from various research institutes, advocacy groups, surveys, and academic sources to support his argument. His statistics are given a human face by quotations from a student who is taking longer to graduate than he expected.

Key Features / Reports

A tightly focused topic. The goal of this kind of writing is to inform readers about something without digressing—and without, in general, bringing in the writer's own opinions. All three examples focus on a particular topic—texting, popping popcorn, and the cost of college—and present information about the topics evenhandedly.

Accurate, well-researched information. Reports usually require research. The kind of research depends on the topic. Sometimes internet research will suffice, though reports done for college courses may require library research to locate scholarly sources—Cullington, for example, uses various sources available through her university library's databases. Other topics may require or benefit from field research—interviews, observations, surveys, and so on. In addition to doing library and online research, for example, Marcus interviewed a student, and Cullington conducted a survey of students and analyzed twenty samples of student writing.

A synthesis of ideas.   Reports seldom rely on a single source of information. Rather, they draw on several sources, making connections among the facts and ideas found in them. For example, Schembri combines information from a magazine article and a book to provide a brief history of the growth of popcorn's popularity in the United States. Marcus compares undergraduate students' expectations of finishing college in four years with statistics showing that more than half will take longer, using information from a university study and a government report as well as an interview with a student.

Various writing strategies.   Presenting information usually requires various organizing patterns—defining, comparing, classifying, explaining processes, analyzing causes and effects, and so on. Schembri explains the process governing popcorn popping and classifies different kinds of maize. Marcus analyzes the financial effects of delaying graduation, and Cullington analyzes the effects (or lack of effects) of texting on students' writing ability.

Clear definitions.   Reports need to provide clear definitions of any key terms that their audience may not know. Cullington defines both *texting* and *textspeak*. Schembri defines several components of corn kernels, including the germ, endosperm, and pericarp.

Appropriate design.   Reports often combine paragraphs with information presented in lists, tables, diagrams, and other illustrations. When you're presenting information, you need to think carefully about how to design it —numerical data, for instance, can be easier to understand and remember in a table than in a paragraph. Often a photograph can bring a subject to life, as does the photo on page 140, which accompanies "Edible Magic." Online reports offer the possibility of video and audio clips as well as links to source materials and more detailed information.

A GUIDE TO WRITING REPORTS

Choosing a Topic

Whether you get to choose your topic or are working with an assigned one, see if you can approach the topic from an angle that interests you.

If you get to choose. What interests you? What do you wish you knew more about? The possible topics for informational reports are limitless, but the topics that you're most likely to write well on are those that engage you. They may be academic in nature or reflect your personal interests or both. If you're not sure where to begin, here are some places to start:

- an intriguing technology: driverless cars, touchscreens, tooth whiteners
- sports: soccer, snowboarding, ultimate Frisbee, basketball
- an important world event: the Arab Spring, the fall of Rome, the Black Death
- a historical period: the African diaspora, the Middle Ages, the Ming dynasty, the Great Depression
- a common object: hoodies, gel pens, mascara, Post-it notes
- a significant environmental issue: melting Arctic ice, deer overpopulation, mercury and the fish supply
- the arts: rap, outsider art, the Crystal Bridges Museum of American Art, Savion Glover, Mary Cassatt

332–33 ○

LIST a few possibilities, and then choose one that you'd like to know more about—and that your audience might find interesting, too. You might start out by phrasing your topic as a question that your research will attempt to answer. For example:

How is *Google* different from *Yahoo!*?

How was the Great Pyramid constructed?

What kind of training do football referees receive?

academic literacies ✳ rhetorical situations ■ genres ▲ fields ● processes ○ strategies ◆ research MLA / APA ● media / design ▢

If your topic is assigned. If your assignment is broad—"Explain some aspect of the U.S. government"—try focusing on a more limited topic within the larger topic: federalism, majority rule, political parties, states' rights. Even if an assignment seems to offer little flexibility—"Explain the physics of roller coasters"—your task is to decide how to research the topic, and sometimes even narrow topics can be shaped to fit your own interests and those of your audience.

Considering the Rhetorical Situation

PURPOSE	Why are you presenting this information? To teach readers about the subject? To demonstrate your research and writing skills? For some other reason?	■ 55–56
AUDIENCE	Who will read this report? What do they already know about the topic? What background information do they need in order to understand it? Will you need to define any terms? What do they want or need to know about the topic? Why should they care about it? How can you attract their interest?	■ 57–60
STANCE	What is your own attitude toward your subject? What interests you most about it? What about it seems important?	■ 66–68
MEDIA/DESIGN	What medium are you using? What is the best way to present the information? Will it all be in paragraph form, or is there information that is best presented as a chart, table, or infographic? Do you need headings? Would diagrams, photographs, or other illustrations help you explain the information?	■ 69–71

Generating Ideas and Text

Good reports share certain features that make them useful and interesting to readers. Remember that your goal is to present information clearly and accurately. Start by exploring your topic.

Explore what you already know about your topic. Write out what-ever you know or want to know about your topic, perhaps by **FREEWRITING**, **LISTING**, or **CLUSTERING**. Why are you interested in this topic? What questions do you have about it? Such questions can help you decide what you'd like to focus on and how you need to direct your research efforts.

331–34

Narrow your topic. To write a good report, you need to narrow your focus—and to narrow your focus, you need to know a fair amount about your subject. If you are assigned to write on a subject like biodiversity, for example, you need to know what it is, what the key issues are, and so on. If you do, you can simply list or brainstorm possibilities, choose one, and start your research. If you don't know much about the subject, though, you need to do some research to discover focused, workable topics. This research may shape your thinking and change your focus. Start with **SOURCES** that can give you a general sense of the subject, such as a *Wikipedia* entry, a magazine article, a website, perhaps an interview with an expert. Your goal at this point is simply to find out what issues your topic might include and then to focus your efforts on an aspect of the topic you will be able to cover.

489–510

Come up with a tentative thesis. Once you narrow your topic, write out a statement that explains what you plan to report or explain. A good **THESIS** is potentially interesting (to you and your readers) and limits your topic enough to make it manageable. Schembri phrases her thesis as a question: "How do these ordinary kernels magically spring to life with a little heat and oil?" Cullington frames her thesis in relation to the context surrounding her topic: "Some people believe that using these abbreviations is hindering the writing abilities of students, and others argue that texting is actually having a positive effect on writing. In fact, it seems likely that texting has no significant effect on student writing." At this point, however, you need only a tentative thesis that will help focus any research you do.

387–89

Do any necessary research, and revise your thesis. To focus your research efforts, **OUTLINE** the aspects of your topic that you expect to discuss. Identify any aspects that require additional research and develop a research plan.

335–37

Expect to revise your outline as you do your research, since more information will be available for some aspects of your topic than others, some may
prove irrelevant to your topic, and some may turn out to be more than you
need. You'll need to revisit your tentative thesis once you've done any
research, to finalize your statement.

Ways of Organizing a Report

Reports can be organized in various ways. Here are three common organizational structures:

[Reports on topics that are unfamiliar to readers]

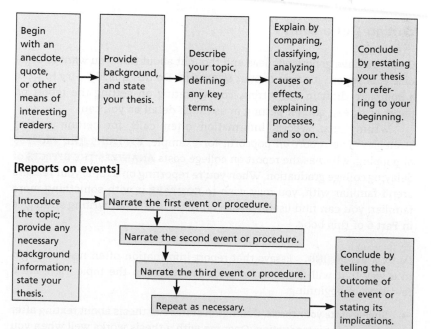

[Reports on events]

[Reports that compare and contrast]

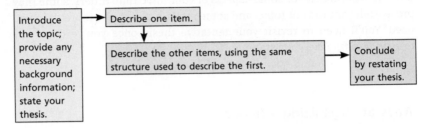

Many reports use a combination of organizational structures; don't be afraid to use whatever method of organization best suits your material and your purpose.

Writing Out a Draft

340–42 ⊙

Once you have generated ideas and thought about how you want to organize your report, it's time to start **DRAFTING**. Do this quickly—try to write a complete draft in one sitting, concentrating on getting the report on paper or screen and on putting in as much detail as you can.

457–61 ◆
392–96

Writing that reports information often calls for certain writing strategies. The report on popcorn, for example, **EXPLAINS THE PROCESS** of popping, whereas the report on college costs **ANALYZES THE EFFECTS** of delaying college graduation. When you're reporting on a topic your readers

424–31 ◆

aren't familiar with, you may wish to **COMPARE** it with something more familiar; you can find useful advice on these and other writing strategies in Part 6 of this book.

373–80 ◆

Draft a **BEGINNING**.   Essays that report information often need to begin in a way that will get your audience interested in the topic. Here are a few ways of beginning:

- *Simply state your thesis.* Cullington states her thesis about texting after only a brief introduction. Opening with a thesis works well when you

academic literacies · rhetorical situations · genres · fields · processes · strategies · research MLA / APA · media / design

can assume your readers have enough familiarity with your topic that you don't need to give much detailed background information.

- *Start with something that will provoke readers' interest.* Marcus's report begins with an anecdote about a college student.

- *Begin with an illustrative example.* Schembri evokes the childhood wonder of popping corn before exploring its history and physics.

Draft an **ENDING**.   Think about what you want your readers to read last. An effective ending leaves them thinking about your topic.

380–85

- *Summarize your main points.* This is a good way to end when you've presented several key points you want readers to remember. Cullington ends this way, summarizing the debate about texting's effects and the results of her research.

- *Point out the implications of your report.* Cullington ends by affirming the importance of researched evidence when drawing conclusions not only about texting but in general.

- *Frame your report by referring to its introduction.* Marcus begins and ends his report by quoting the same student, and Schembri returns to her introductory evocation of popcorn as "little pockets of magic."

- *Tell what happened.* If you are reporting on an event, you could conclude by telling how it turns out.

Come up with a title.   You'll want a title that tells readers something about your subject—and makes them want to know more. Cullington's title, "Does Texting Affect Writing?," is a straightforward description of what's to come. Marcus suggests that his essay will disclose the reason college costs more than you think—but doesn't tell us in the title. See the chapter on **GUIDING YOUR READER** for tips on coming up with titles that are informative and enticing enough to make readers wish to read on.

386–91

Considering Matters of Design

You'll probably write the main text of your report in paragraph form, but think about what kind of information you're presenting and how you can design and format it to make it as easy as possible for your readers to understand. You might ask yourself these questions:

648–49
- What is an appropriate **FONT**? A font like Times New Roman that is easy to read in print? A font like Ariel or Verdana that looks good onscreen? Something else?

650–52
- Would it help your readers if you divided your report into shorter sections and added **HEADINGS**?

649–50
- Is there any information that would be easier to follow in a **LIST**?

656
- Could any of your information be summarized in a **TABLE** or **FIGURE**?

656
- Do you have any data that readers would more easily understand in the form of a bar **GRAPH**, line graph, or pie chart?

653–63
- Would **ILLUSTRATIONS** (diagrams, photos, drawings, and so on), video or audio clips, or links help you explain anything in your report?

Getting Response and Revising

The following questions can help you study your draft with a critical eye. **GETTING RESPONSE** from others is always good, and these questions can guide their reading, too. Make sure they know your purpose and audience.

348–50

- Do the title and opening sentences get readers' interest? If not, how might they do so?
- What information does this text provide, and for what purpose?
- Does the introduction explain why this information is being presented? Does it place the topic in a larger context?
- Are all key terms defined that need to be?
- Do you have any questions? Where might more explanation or an example help you understand something better?

academic literacies | rhetorical situations | genres | fields | processes | strategies | research MLA / APA | media / design

- Is any information presented visually, with a chart, graph, table, drawing, or photograph? If so, is it clear how the illustration relates to the written text? Is there any text that would be more easily understood if it were presented visually?

- Is any information presented through digital media, such as hyperlinks, video clips, or audio files? If so, is the relation of these elements to the written text made clear? Would any aspect of the report be clearer if presented using such elements?

- Does the organization help make sense of the information? Does the text include description, comparison, or any other writing strategies? Does the topic or rhetorical situation call for any particular strategies that should be added?

- If the report cites any sources, are they quoted, paraphrased, or summarized effectively (and with appropriate documentation)? Is information from sources introduced with **SIGNAL PHRASES**? 535–38

- Does the report end in a satisfying way? What are readers left thinking?

These questions should identify aspects of your report you need to work on. When it's time to **REVISE**, make sure your report appeals to your audience and achieves your purpose as successfully as possible. If you have time and want to explore alternatives, you might try **REWRITING** your draft to see if a different plan or approach might work better. 350–53 353–55

Editing and Proofreading

Readers equate correctness with the writer's competence. Once you've revised your draft, follow these guidelines for **EDITING** a report: 356–59

- Check your use of key terms. Repeating key words is acceptable in reports; using synonyms for unfamiliar words may confuse readers, while the repetition of key words or the use of clearly identified pronouns for them can be genuinely helpful.

- Check to be sure you have **TRANSITIONS** where you need them. 391

650–52 ▫
- If you have included **HEADINGS**, make sure they're parallel in structure and consistent in design.

653–63 ▫
- Make sure that any photos or other **ILLUSTRATIONS** have captions, that charts and graphs have headings—and that all are referred to in the main text. Use white space as necessary to separate sections of your report and to highlight graphic elements.

544–47 ●
- Check any **DOCUMENTATION** to see that it follows the appropriate style.

359–60 ○
- **PROOFREAD** and spell-check your report carefully.

Taking Stock of Your Work

- How well did you convey the information? Is it complete enough for your audience's needs?
- What strategies did you rely on, and how did they help you achieve your purpose?
- How well did you organize the report?
- How did you go about researching the information for this piece?
- How did you go about drafting this piece?
- Did you use any tables, graphs, diagrams, photographs, illustrations, or other graphics effectively?
- How did others' responses influence your writing?
- What did you do especially well?
- What could still be improved?
- What would you do differently next time?

IF YOU NEED MORE HELP

361–70 ○
185–89 ▲
233–45

See Chapter 34 if you are required to submit your report in a writing **PORTFOLIO**. See also Chapter 14 on **ABSTRACTS** if your report requires one; and Chapter 19 on **PROFILES**, a report based on firsthand research.

✳ academic literacies
■ rhetorical situations
▲ genres
⬡ fields
○ processes
◆ strategies
● research MLA / APA
▫ media / design

Arguing a Position **13**

Everything we say or do presents some kind of argument, takes some kind of position. Often we take overt positions: "Everyone in the United States is entitled to affordable health care." "The university needs to offer more language courses." "Photoshopped images should carry disclosure notices." But arguments can be less direct and specific as well, from yellow ribbons that honor U.S. troops to a yellow smiley face, which might be said to argue for a good day.

In college course work, you are constantly called on to argue positions: in an *English* class, you may argue for a certain interpretation of a poem; in a *business* course, you may argue for the merits of a flat tax; in a *linguistics* class, you may argue that English is now a global language. All of those positions are arguable—people of goodwill can agree or disagree with them and present reasons and evidence to support their positions.

This chapter provides guidelines for writing an essay that argues a position. We'll begin with three good examples, the first one annotated to point out key features of this kind of writing.

JOANNA MACKAY

Organ Sales Will Save Lives

In this essay, written for a class on ethics and politics in science, MIT student Joanna MacKay argues that the sale of human organs should be legal.

There are thousands of people dying to buy a kidney and thousands of people dying to sell a kidney. It seems a match made in heaven. So why are we standing in the way? Governments should not ban the sale of human organs; they should regulate it. Lives should not be wasted; they should be saved.

Clear and arguable position.

About 350,000 Americans suffer from end-stage renal disease, a state of kidney disorder so advanced that the organ stops functioning altogether. There are no miracle drugs that can revive a failed kidney, leaving dialysis and kidney transplantation as the only possible treatments (McDonnell and Mallon, pars. 2 and 3).

Dialysis is harsh, expensive, and, worst of all, only temporary. Acting as an artificial kidney, dialysis mechanically filters the blood of a patient. It works, but not well. With treatment sessions lasting three hours, several times a week, those dependent on dialysis are, in a sense, shackled to a machine for the rest of their lives. Adding excessive stress to the body, dialysis causes patients to feel increasingly faint and tired, usually keeping them from work and other normal activities.

Kidney transplantation, on the other hand, is the closest thing to a cure that anyone could hope for. Today the procedure is both safe and reliable, causing few complications. With better technology for confirming tissue matches and new anti-rejection drugs, the surgery is relatively simple.

Necessary background information.

But those hoping for a new kidney have high hopes indeed. In the year 2000 alone, 2,583 Americans died while waiting for a kidney transplant; worldwide the number of deaths is around 50,000 (Finkel 27). With the sale of organs outlawed in almost every country, the number of living donors willing to part with a kidney for free is small. When no family member is a suitable candidate for donation, the patient is placed on a deceased donors list, relying on the organs from people dying of old age or accidents. The list is long. With over 60,000 people in line in the United States alone, the average wait for a cadaverous kidney is ten long years.

Daunted by the low odds, some have turned to an alternative solution: purchasing kidneys on the black market. For about $150,000, they can buy a fresh kidney from a healthy, living donor. There are no lines, no waits. Arranged through a broker, the entire procedure is carefully planned out. The buyer, seller, surgeons, and nurses are flown to a predetermined hospital in a foreign country. The operations are performed, and then all are flown back to their respective homes. There is no follow-up, no paperwork to sign (Finkel 27).

The illegal kidney trade is attractive not only because of the promptness but also because of the chance at a living donor. An organ from a cadaver will most likely be old or damaged, estimated

5

academic literacies   rhetorical situations   genres   fields   processes   strategies   research MLA / APA   media / design

to function for about ten years at most. A kidney from a living donor can last over twice as long. Once a person's transplanted cadaverous kidney stops functioning, he or she must get back on the donor list, this time probably at the end of the line. A transplanted living kidney, however, could last a person a lifetime.

While there may seem to be a shortage of kidneys, in reality there is a surplus. In third-world countries, there are people willing to do anything for money. In such extreme poverty these people barely have enough to eat, living in shacks and sleeping on dirt floors. Eager to pay off debts, they line up at hospitals, willing to sell a kidney for about $1,000. The money will go toward food and clothing, or perhaps to pay for a family member's medical operation (Goyal et al. 1590–91). Whatever the case, these people need the money.

Reason (donors need the money) supported by evidence.

There is certainly a risk in donating a kidney, but this risk is not great enough to be outlawed. Millions of people take risks to their health every day for money, or simply for enjoyment. As explained in *The Lancet*, "If the rich are free to engage in dangerous sports for pleasure, or dangerous jobs for high pay, it is difficult to see why the poor who take the lesser risk of kidney selling for greater rewards . . . should be thought so misguided as to need saving from themselves" (Radcliffe-Richards et al. 1951). Studies have shown that a person can live a healthy life with only one kidney. While these studies might not apply to the poor living under strenuous conditions in unsanitary environments, the risk is still theirs to take. These people have decided that their best hope for money is to sell a kidney. How can we deny them the best opportunity they have?

Counterargument (donating a kidney is risky) acknowledged.

Some agree with Pope John Paul II that the selling of organs is 10 morally wrong and violates "the dignity of the human person" (qtd. in Finkel 26), but this is a belief professed by healthy and affluent individuals. Are we sure that the peasants of third-world countries agree? The morals we hold are not absolute truths. We have the responsibility to protect and help those less fortunate, but we cannot let our own ideals cloud the issues at hand.

Counterargument (selling organs is wrong) acknowledged.

In a legal kidney transplant, everybody gains except the donor. The doctors and nurses are paid for the operation, the patient receives a new kidney, but the donor receives nothing. Sure, the donor will have the warm, uplifting feeling associated with helping a fellow human being, but this is not enough reward for most people to part with a

Reason (altruism is not enough) supported by evidence.

piece of themselves. In an ideal world, the average person would be altruistic enough to donate a kidney with nothing expected in return. The real world, however, is run by money. We pay men for donating sperm, and we pay women for donating ova, yet we expect others to give away an entire organ for no compensation. If the sale of organs were allowed, people would have a greater incentive to help save the life of a stranger.

While many argue that legalizing the sale of organs will exploit the poorer people of third-world countries, the truth of the matter is that this is already the case. Even with the threat of a $50,000 fine and five years in prison (Finkel 26), the current ban has not been successful in preventing illegal kidney transplants. The kidneys of the poor are still benefiting only the rich. While the sellers do receive most of the money promised, the sum is too small to have any real impact on their financial situation. A study in India discovered that in the long run, organ sellers suffer. In the illegal kidney trade, nobody has the interests of the seller at heart. After selling a kidney, their state of living actually worsens. While the $1,000 pays off one debt, it is not enough to relieve the donor of the extreme poverty that placed him in debt in the first place (Goyal et al. 1591).

These impoverished people do not need stricter and harsher penalties against organ selling to protect them, but quite the opposite. If the sale of organs were made legal, it could be regulated and closely monitored by the government and other responsible organizations. Under a regulated system, education would be incorporated into the application process. Before deciding to donate a kidney, the seller should know the details of the operation and any hazards involved. Only with an understanding of the long-term physical health risks can a person make an informed decision (Radcliffe-Richards et al. 1951).

Regulation would ensure that the seller is fairly compensated. In the illegal kidney trade, surgeons collect most of the buyer's money in return for putting their careers on the line. The brokers arranging the procedure also receive a modest cut, typically around ten percent. If the entire practice were legalized, more of the money could be directed toward the person who needs it most, the seller. By eliminating the middleman and allowing the doctors to settle for lower prices, a regulated system would benefit all those in need of a kidney, both rich

Counterargument (poor people are exploited) acknowledged.

Reason (regulating organ sales would lead to better decisions).

Reason (fairness to sellers) followed by evidence.

and poor. According to Finkel, the money that would otherwise be spent on dialysis treatment could not only cover the charge of a kidney transplant at no cost to the recipient, but also reward the donor with as much as $25,000 (32). This money could go a long way for people living in the poverty of third-world countries.

Critics fear that controlling the lawful sale of organs would be too 15 difficult, but could it be any more difficult than controlling the unlawful sale of organs? Governments have tried to eradicate the kidney market for decades to no avail. Maybe it is time to try something else. When "desperately wanted goods" are made illegal, history has shown that there is more opportunity for corruption and exploitation than if those goods were allowed (Radcliffe-Richards et al. 1951). (Just look at the effects of the prohibition of alcohol, for example.) Legalization of organ sales would give governments the authority and the opportunity to closely monitor these live kidney operations.

Counterargument (controlling organ sales would be difficult) acknowledged.

Regulation would also protect the buyers. Because of the need for secrecy, the current illegal method of obtaining a kidney has no contracts and, therefore, no guarantees. Since what they are doing is illegal, the buyers have nobody to turn to if something goes wrong. There is nobody to point the finger at, nobody to sue. While those participating in the kidney market are breaking the law, they have no other choice. Without a new kidney, end-stage renal disease will soon kill them. Desperate to survive, they are forced to take the only offer available. It seems immoral to first deny them the opportunity of a new kidney and then to leave them stranded at the mercy of the black market. Without laws regulating live kidney transplants, these people are subject to possibly hazardous procedures. Instead of turning our backs, we have the power to ensure that these operations are done safely and efficiently for both the recipient and the donor.

Reason (fairness to buyers) supported by examples.

Those suffering from end-stage renal disease would do anything for the chance at a new kidney, take any risk or pay any price. There are other people so poor that the sale of a kidney is worth the profit. Try to tell someone that he has to die from kidney failure because selling a kidney is morally wrong. Then turn around and try to tell another person that he has to remain in poverty for that same reason. In matters of life and death, our stances on moral issues must be reevaluated. If legalized and regulated, the sale of human organs would save lives. Is it moral to sentence thousands to unnecessary deaths?

Concludes by asking a question for readers to consider.

Works Cited

Finkel, Michael. "This Little Kidney Went to Market." *The New York Times Magazine,* 27 May 2001, pp. 26+.

Goyal, Madhav, et al. "Economic and Health Consequences of Selling a Kidney in India." *Journal of the American Medical Association,* vol. 288, 2002, pp. 1589–92.

McDonnell, Michael B., and William K. Mallon. "Kidney Transplant." *eMedicine Health,* 18 Aug. 2008, www.emedicinehealth.com/articles/24500-1.asp. Accessed 30 Nov. 2008.

Radcliffe-Richards, J., et al. "The Case for Allowing Kidney Sales." *The Lancet,* vol. 351, no. 9120, 27 June 1998, pp. 1950–52.

MacKay clearly states her position at the beginning of her text: "Governments should not ban the sale of human organs; they should regulate it." Her argument appeals to her readers' sense of fairness; when kidney sales are legalized and regulated, both sellers and buyers will benefit from the transaction. She uses MLA style to document her sources.

NICHOLAS KRISTOF

Our Blind Spot about Guns

In this essay, which first appeared in the New York Times in 2014, columnist Nicholas Kristof argues that if guns and their owners were regulated in the same way that cars and their drivers are, thousands of lives could be saved each year.

If we had the same auto fatality rate today that we had in 1921, by my calculations we would have 715,000 Americans dying annually in vehicle accidents.

Instead, we've reduced the fatality rate by more than 95 percent—not by confiscating cars, but by regulating them and their drivers sensibly.

We could have said, "Cars don't kill people. People kill people," and there would have been an element of truth to that. Many accidents are a result of alcohol consumption, speeding, road rage or driver distraction. Or we could have said, "It's pointless because even if you regulate cars, then people will just run each other down with bicycles," and that, too, would have been partly true.

Yet, instead, we built a system that protects us from ourselves. This saves hundreds of thousands of lives a year and is a model of what we should do with guns in America.

Whenever I write about the need for sensible regulation of guns, 5 some readers jeer: *Cars kill people, too, so why not ban cars? Why are you so hypocritical as to try to take away guns from law-abiding people when you don't seize cars?*

That question is a reflection of our national blind spot about guns. The truth is that we regulate cars quite intelligently, instituting evidence-based measures to reduce fatalities. Yet the gun lobby is too strong, or our politicians too craven, to do the same for guns. So guns and cars now each kill more than 30,000 in America every year.

One constraint, the argument goes, is the Second Amendment. Yet the paradox is that a bit more than a century ago, there was no universally recognized individual right to bear arms in the United States, but there was widely believed to be a "right to travel" that allowed people to drive cars without regulation.

A court struck down an early attempt to require driver's licenses, and initial attempts to set speed limits or register vehicles were met with resistance and ridicule. When authorities in New York City sought in 1899 to ban horseless carriages in the parks, the idea was lambasted in the *New York Times* as "devoid of merit" and "impossible to maintain."

Yet, over time, it became increasingly obvious that cars were killing and maiming people, as well as scaring horses and causing accidents. As a distinguished former congressman, Robert Cousins, put it in 1910: "Pedestrians are menaced every minute of the days and nights by a wanton recklessness of speed, crippling and killing people at a rate that is appalling."

Courts and editorial writers alike saw the carnage and agreed 10 that something must be done. By the 1920s, courts routinely accepted driver's license requirements, car registration and other safety measures.

That continued in recent decades with requirements of seatbelts and air bags, padded dashboards and better bumpers. We cracked down on drunken drivers and instituted graduated licensing for young people, while also improving road engineering to reduce accidents. The upshot is that there is now just over 1 car fatality per 100 million miles driven.

Yet as we've learned to treat cars intelligently, we've gone in the opposite direction with guns. In his terrific new book, *The Second Amendment: A Biography,* Michael Waldman, the president of the Brennan Center for Justice at the New York University School of Law, notes that "gun control laws were ubiquitous" in the nineteenth century. Visitors to Wichita, Kansas, for example, were required to check their revolvers at police headquarters.

And Dodge City, symbol of the Wild West? A photo shows a sign on the main street in 1879 warning: "The Carrying of Fire Arms Strictly Prohibited."

Dodge City, Kansas, 1878. The sign reads, "The Carrying of Fire Arms strictly prohibited."

academic literacies   rhetorical situations   genres   fields   processes   strategies   research MLA / APA   media / design

The National Rifle Association supported reasonable gun control for most of its history and didn't even oppose the landmark Gun Control Act of 1968. But, since then, most attempts at safety regulation have stalled or gone backward, and that makes the example of cars instructive.

"We didn't ban cars, or send black helicopters to confiscate them," 15 notes Waldman. "We made cars safer: air bags, seatbelts, increasing the drinking age, lowering the speed limit. There are similar techno-logical and behavioral fixes that can ease the toll of gun violence, from expanded background checks to trigger locks to smart guns that recognize a thumbprint, just like my iPhone does."

Some of these should be doable. A Quinnipiac poll this month found 92 percent support for background checks for all gun buyers.

These steps won't eliminate gun deaths any more than seatbelts eliminate auto deaths. But if a combination of measures could reduce the toll by one-third, that would be 10,000 lives saved every year.

A century ago, we reacted to deaths and injuries from unregulated vehicles by imposing sensible safety measures that have saved hundreds of thousands of lives a year. Why can't we ask politicians to be just as rational about guns?

Kristof argues that because regulating cars has made them much safer, guns should be regulated similarly. He supports his argument with data on fatality rates and the history of automobile and gun regulation in the United States.

MOLLY WORTHEN

U Can't Talk to Ur Professor Like This

Molly Worthen is an assistant professor of history at the University of North Carolina–Chapel Hill and a frequent contributor to the New York Times, *where this essay arguing that manners and etiquette matter in the college classroom originally appeared.*

At the start of my teaching career, when I was fresh out of graduate school, I briefly considered trying to pass myself off as a cool professor. Luckily, I soon came to my senses and embraced my true identity as a young fogey. After one too many students called me by my first name and sent me email that resembled a drunken late-night *Facebook* post, I took a very fogeyish step. I began attaching a page on etiquette to every syllabus: basic rules for how to address teachers and write polite, grammatically correct emails.

Over the past decade or two, college students have become far more casual in their interactions with faculty members. My colleagues around the country grumble about students' sloppy emails and blithe informality.

Mark Tomforde, a math professor at the University of Houston who has been teaching for almost two decades, added etiquette guidelines to his website. "When students started calling me by my first name, I felt that was too far, and I've got to say something," he told me. "There were also the emails written like text messages. Worse than the text abbreviations was the level of informality, with no address or signoff."

His webpage covers matters ranging from appropriate email addresses (if you're still using "cutie_pie_98@hotmail.com," then "it's time to retire that address") to how to be gracious when making a request ("do not make demands").

Sociologists who surveyed undergraduate syllabuses from 2004 and 2010 found that in 2004, 14 percent addressed issues related to classroom etiquette; six years later, that number had more than doubled, to 33 percent. This phenomenon crosses socio-economic lines. My colleagues at Stanford gripe as much as the ones who teach at state schools, and students from more privileged backgrounds are often the worst offenders.

Why are so many teachers bent out of shape because a student fails to call them "Professor" or neglects to proofread an email? Are academics really that insecure? Is this just another case of scapegoating millennials for changes in the broader culture?

Don't dismiss these calls for old-fashioned courtesy as a case of fragile ivory tower egos or misplaced nostalgia. There is a strong liberal case for using formal manners and titles to ensure respect for all university professionals, regardless of age, race or gender. More important, doing so helps defend the university's dearest values at a time when they are under continual assault.

It's true that the conventions that have, until recently, ruled higher education did not rule from time immemorial. Two centuries ago, students often rejected expectations of deference. In 1834, Harvard students rebelled when some of their classmates were punished for refusing to memorize their Latin textbook. They broke the windows of a teacher's apartment and destroyed his furniture. When the president of the college cracked down and suspended the entire sophomore class, the juniors retaliated by hanging and burning him in effigy and setting off a rudimentary explosive in the campus chapel.

Later in the 19th century, etiquette manuals proliferated in bookstores, and Americans began to emphasize elaborate social protocols. As colleges expanded and academic disciplines professionalized, they mimicked the hierarchical cultures of the German research universities, where students cowered before "Herr Professor Doktor."

The historian John Kasson has noted that back then, formal etiquette was not aimed at ensuring respect for all. It was, in part, a system to enforce boundaries of race, class and gender at a time when the growth of cities and mass transit forced Americans into close quarters with strangers. Codes of behavior served "as checks against a fully democratic order and in support of special interests, institutions of privilege and structures of domination," he writes in his book *Rudeness and Civility*. 10

But today, on the other side of the civil rights revolution, formal titles and etiquette can be tools to protect disempowered minorities and ensure that the modern university belongs to all of us. Students seem more inclined to use casual forms of address with professors who are young, nonwhite and female—some of whom have responded by becoming vocal defenders of old-fashioned propriety.

Angela Jackson-Brown, a professor of English at Ball State University in Muncie, Ind., told me that "most of my students will acknowledge that I'm the first and only black teacher they've ever had." Insisting on her formal title is important, she said: "I feel the extra burden of having to go in from Day 1 and establish that I belong here."

When Professor Jackson-Brown began teaching in the 1990s, most students respected her authority. But in recent years, that deference has waned (she blames the informality of social media). "I go out of my way now to not give them access to my first name," she said. "On every syllabus, it states clearly: 'Please address me as Professor Jackson-Brown.'"

She linked this policy to the atmosphere of mutual respect that she cultivates in her classes. These days, simply being considerate can feel like a political act. "After this recent election, I've had several female students come to me and say, 'I'm noticing differences in how men are treating me.' It's heartbreaking," she said. "We're trying to set standards for them that they may not see outside the classroom, places where you'd think there would be decorum."

This logic resonates with some students. "Having these titles forces everyone to give that respect," Lyndah Lovell, a graduating senior at the College of William & Mary in Williamsburg, Va., said. "They know they have to use these manners with everyone. Even if the underlying thoughts of prejudice will still be there to some extent, you give these thoughts less power." 15

Insisting on traditional etiquette is also simply good pedagogy. It's a teacher's job to correct sloppy prose, whether in an essay or an email. And I suspect that most of the time, students who call faculty members by their first names and send slangy messages are not seeking a more casual rapport. They just don't know they should do otherwise—no one has bothered to explain it to them. Explaining the rules of professional interaction is not an act of condescension; it's the first step in treating students like adults.

That said, the teacher-student relationship depends on a special kind of inequality. "Once I refer to them as I would my best friend, I eliminate that boundary of clarity," Ms. Lovell told me. She recalled how awkward she felt when the head of the research lab where she worked asked undergraduates to call him Willy. "All my friends were saying: 'Oh, man, do we do this? He has a Ph.D. He's a professor. Is it O.K. to do this?' Sometimes I do, but he's a great mentor, and it's confusing. A lot of us like to preserve that distance."

Alexis Delgado, a sophomore at the University of Rochester, is skeptical of professors who make a point of insisting on their title. "I always think it's a power move," she told me. "Just because someone gave you a piece of paper that says you're smart doesn't mean you can communicate those ideas to me. I reserve the right to judge if you're a good professor."

But she ruefully recalled one young professor who made the mistake of telling the class that he didn't care if they used his first name. "He didn't realize how far it would go, and we all thought, this is awkward," she said. "I had no desire to be friends. I only wanted to ask questions."

During office hours, we have frank conversations about career choices, mental health crises and family tribulations. But the last thing most students want from a mentor is the pretense of chumminess. 20

Ms. Lovell said the very act of communicating more formally helps her get some distance on a personal problem. "When I explain my difficulties and struggles, I try to explain in a mature way," she said. "I want to know: How would someone older than me think through this?"

The facile egalitarianism of the first-name basis can impede good teaching and mentoring, but it also presents a more insidious threat. It undermines the message that academic titles are meant to convey: esteem for learning. The central endeavor of higher education is not the pursuit of money or fame but knowledge. "There needs to be some understanding that degrees mean something," Professor Jackson-Brown said. "Otherwise, why are we encouraging them to get an education?"

The values of higher education are not the values of the commercial, capitalist paradigm. At a time when corporate executives populate university boards and politicians demand proof of a diploma's immediate cash value, this distinction needs vigilant defense.

The erosion of etiquette encourages students to view faculty members as a bunch of overeducated customer service agents. "More and more, students view the process of going to college as a business transaction," Dr. Tomforde, the math professor, told me. "They see themselves as a customer, and they view knowledge as a physical thing where they pay money and I hand them the knowledge—so if they don't do well on a test, they think I haven't kept up my side of the business agreement." He added, "They view professors in a way similar to the person behind the counter getting their coffee."

But if American culture in general—including many work- 25 places—has become less formal, are professors doing students a disservice by insisting on old-fashioned manners?

When Anna Lewis left a Ph.D. program in English to work at a technology firm, she had to learn to operate in a different culture. Yet she has noticed that the informality of the tech industry can mislead new millennial employees.

"They see they can call everyone from the C.E.O. down by their first name, and that can be confusing—because what they often don't realize is that there's still a high standard of professionalism," she told me. "At the intern level, these things are basic, but they require reminders: show up to meetings on time; be aware that you, yourself, are fully responsible for your work schedule. No one is going to tell you to attend a meeting." In other words, young graduates mistake informality for license to act unprofessionally.

"There is some value in being schooled in more formal etiquette, developing personal and professional accountability, a work ethic and a level of empathy, which is very much valued in the tech industry," Ms. Lewis said.

Here's an analogy: We should teach students traditional etiquette for the same reason most great abstract painters first mastered figurative painting. In order to abandon or riff on a form, you have to get the hang of its underlying principles.

That means that professors should take the time to explain these principles, making it clear that learning how to write a professional email and relate to authority figures is not just preparation for a job after graduation. The real point is to stand up for the values that have made our universities the guardians of civilization.   30

And if you're going to write an angry email telling me how wrong I am, I beg you: Please proofread it before you hit "send."

Worthen argues that using "formal manners and titles" shows respect for both academic professionals and the ideals for which they stand, protects minorities and women, and is part of a complete education. Much of the support for her position is in the form of testimony from college teachers and students.

Key Features / Arguments

A clear and arguable position. At the heart of every argument is a claim with which people may reasonably disagree. Some claims are not arguable because they're completely subjective, matters of taste or opinion ("I hate sauerkraut"), because they are a matter of fact ("The first *Star Wars* movie came out in 1977"), or because they are based on belief or faith ("There is life after death"). To be arguable, a position must reflect one of at least two points of view, making reasoned argument necessary: Guns should (or should not) be regulated; selling human organs should be legal (or illegal). In college writing, you will often argue not that a position is correct but that it is plausible—that it is reasonable, supportable, and worthy of being taken seriously.

Necessary background information. Sometimes we need to provide some background on a topic we are arguing so that readers can understand what is being argued. MacKay establishes the need for kidney donors before launching her argument for legalizing the selling of organs; Kristof describes the history of automobile regulation.

Good reasons. By itself, a position does not make an argument; the argument comes when a writer offers reasons to back up the position. There are many kinds of good reasons. Kristof makes his argument by comparing cars to guns. MacKay bases her argument in favor of legalizing the sale of human organs on the grounds that doing so would save more lives, that impoverished people should be able to make risky choices, and that regulation would protect such people who currently sell their organs on the black market as well as desperate buyers.

Convincing evidence. Once you've given reasons for your position, you then need to offer evidence for your reasons: facts, statistics, expert testimony, anecdotal evidence, case studies, textual evidence. All three arguments use a mix of these types of evidence. MacKay cites statistics about Americans who die from renal failure to support her argument for legalizing organ sales. Kristof shows how regulating cars led to dramatic decreases in driving deaths and injuries. Worthen offers testimony from several college faculty and students who assert the value of etiquette and manners in the classroom.

Appeals to readers' values. Effective arguers try to appeal to readers' values and emotions. MacKay appeals to basic values of compassion and fairness. These are deeply held values that we may not think about very much and as a result may see as common ground we share with the writers. And some of MacKay's evidence appeals to emotion—her descriptions of people dying from kidney disease and of poor people selling their organs are likely to evoke an emotional response in many readers.

A trustworthy tone. Arguments can stand or fall on the way readers perceive the writer. Very simply, readers need to trust the person who's making the argument. One way of winning this trust is by demonstrating that you know what you're talking about. Kristof offers plenty of facts to show his knowledge of the history of automotive regulation—and he does so in a self-assured tone. There are many other ways of establishing yourself (and your argument) as trustworthy—by showing that you have some experience with your subject, that you're fair, and of course that you're honest.

Careful consideration of other positions. No matter how reasonable and careful we are in arguing our positions, others may disagree or offer counterarguments. We need to consider those other views and to acknowledge and, if possible, refute them in our written arguments. MacKay, for example, acknowledges that some believe that selling organs is unethical, but she counters that it's usually healthy, affluent people who say this—not people who need either an organ or the money they could get by selling one.

A GUIDE TO WRITING ARGUMENTS

Choosing a Topic

A fully developed argument requires significant work and time, so choosing a topic in which you're interested is very important. Students often find that widely debated topics such as "animal rights" or "abortion" can be difficult to write on because they don't feel any personal connection to them. Better topics include those that

- interest you right now
- are focused but not too narrowly
- have some personal connection to your life

331–39 ○

One good way to **GENERATE IDEAS** for a topic that meets those three criteria is to explore your own roles in life.

Start with your roles in life. Make four columns with the headings "Personal," "Family," "Public," and "School." Then **LIST** the roles you play that relate to it. Here is a list one student wrote:

332–33

Personal	Family	Public	School
gamer	son	voter	college student
dog owner	younger	homeless-shelter volunteer	work-study employee
old-car owner	brother	American	dorm resident
male	grandson	resident of Texas	primary-education major
white			
middle class			

Identify issues that interest you. Think, then, about issues or controversies that may concern you as a member of one or more of those groups. For instance, as a primary-education major, this student cares about the controversy over whether teachers' jobs should be focused on preparing kids for high-stakes standardized tests. As a college student, he cares about the costs of a college education. Issues that stem from these subjects could include the following: Should student progress be measured by standardized tests? Should college cost less than it does?

Pick four or five of the roles you list. In 5 or 10 minutes, identify issues that concern or affect you as a member of each of those roles. It might help to word each issue as a question starting with *Should*.

Frame your topic as a problem. Most position papers address issues that are subjects of ongoing debate—their solutions aren't easy, and people disagree on which ones are best. Posing your topic as a problem can help you think about the topic, find an issue that's suitable to write about, and find a clear focus for your essay.

For example, if you wanted to write an argument on the lack of student parking at your school, you could frame your topic as one of several problems: What causes the parking shortage? Why are the university's parking garages and lots limited in their capacity? What might alleviate the shortage?

Choose one issue to write about. Remember that the issue should be interesting to you and have some connection to your life. It is a tentative choice; if you find later that you have trouble writing about it, simply go back to your list of roles or issues and choose another.

Considering the Rhetorical Situation

55–56 **PURPOSE**   Do you want to persuade your audience to do something? Change their minds? Consider alternative views? Accept your position as plausible—see that you have thought carefully about an issue and researched it appropriately?

57–60 **AUDIENCE**   Who is your intended audience? What do they likely know and believe about this issue? How personal is it for them? To what extent are they likely to agree or disagree with you—and with one another? Why? What common ground can you find with them?

66–68 **STANCE**   What's your attitude toward your topic, and why? How do you want your audience to perceive your attitude? How do you want your audience to perceive you? As an authority on your topic? As someone much like them? As calm? reasonable? impassioned or angry? something else?

69–71 **MEDIA/DESIGN**   What media will you use, and how do your media affect your argument? Does your print or online argument call for photos or charts? If you're giving an oral presentation, should you put your reasons and support on slides? If you're writing electronically, should you include audio or video evidence or links to counterarguments or your sources?

Generating Ideas and Text

Most essays that successfully argue a position share certain features that make them interesting and persuasive. Remember that your goal is to stake out a position and convince your readers that it is plausible.

academic literacies   rhetorical situations   genres   fields   processes   strategies   research MLA / APA   media / design

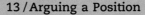

Explore what you already know about the issue. Write out whatever you know about the issue by **FREEWRITING** or as a **LIST** or **OUTLINE**. Why are you interested in this topic? What is your position on it at this point, and why? What aspect do you think you'd like to focus on? Where do you need to focus your research efforts? This activity can help you discover what more you need to learn. Chances are you'll need to learn a lot more about the issue before you even decide what position to take.

331–32
335–37

Do some research. At this point, try to get an overview. Start with one **GENERAL SOURCE** of information that will give you a sense of the ins and outs of your issue, one that isn't overtly biased. *The Atlantic, Time, Slate*, and other online newspapers and magazines can be good starting points on current issues. For some issues, you may need to **INTERVIEW** an expert. For example, one student who wanted to write about chemical abuse of animals at 4-H competitions interviewed an experienced show competitor. Use your overview source to find out the main questions raised about your issue and to get some idea about the various ways in which you might argue it.

498–99

506–7

Explore the issue strategically. Most issues may be argued from many different perspectives. You'll probably have some sense of the different views that exist on your issue, but you should explore multiple perspectives before deciding on your position. The following methods are good ways of exploring issues:

- As a matter of **DEFINITION**. What is it? How should it be defined? How can *organic* or *genetically modified food* be defined? How do proponents of *organic food* define it—and how do they define *genetically modified food*? How do advocates of *genetically modified food* define it—and how do they define *organic food*? Considering such definitions is one way to identify different perspectives on the topic.

432–42

- As a matter of **CLASSIFICATION**. Can the issue be divided into categories? Are there different kinds of, or different ways of, producing organic foods and genetically modified foods? Do different categories suggest particular positions or perhaps a way of supporting a certain position? Are there other ways of categorizing foods?

418–23

424–31 ◆
- As a matter of **COMPARISON**. Is one subject being considered better than another? Is organic food healthier or safer than genetically modified food? Is genetically modified food healthier or safer than organic? Is the answer somewhere in the middle?

457–61 ◆
- As a matter of **PROCESS**. Should somebody do something? What? Should people buy and eat more organic food? More genetically modified food? Should they buy and eat some of each?

Reconsider whether the issue can be argued. Is this issue worth discussing? Why is it important to you and to others? What difference will it make if one position or another prevails? Is **ARGUABLE**? At this point, you want to be sure that your topic is worth arguing about.

397–417 ◆

Draft a thesis. Having explored the possibilities, decide your position, and write it out as a complete sentence. For example:

> Parents should be required to have their children vaccinated.
>
> Pod-based coffeemakers should be banned.
>
> Genetically modified foods should not be permitted in the United States.

Qualify your thesis. Rather than taking a strict pro or con position, in most cases you'll want to **QUALIFY YOUR POSITION**—in certain circumstances, with certain conditions, with these limitations, and so on. This is not to say that we should settle, give in, sell out; rather, it is to say that our position may not be the only "correct" one and that other positions may be valid as well. **QUALIFYING YOUR THESIS** also makes your topic manageable by limiting it. For example:

399 ◆

388–89 ◆

> Parents should be required to have their children vaccinated, with only medical exemptions allowed.
>
> Pod-based coffeemakers should be banned unless the pods are recyclable.
>
> Genetically modified foods should not be permitted in the United States if a link between GMOs and resistance to antibiotics is proven.

Come up with good reasons. Once you have a thesis, you need to come up with good **REASONS** to convince your readers that it's plausible. Write out your position, and then list several reasons. For instance, if your thesis is that pod-based coffeemakers should be banned, two of your reasons might be:

400–401

> The pods cannot be recycled.
>
> Other methods of making coffee are more environmentally sound.

Think about which reasons are best for your purposes. Which seem the most persuasive? Which are most likely to be accepted by your audience? Which seem to matter the most now? If your list of reasons is short or you think you'll have trouble developing them enough to write an appropriate essay, this is a good time to rethink your topic—before you've invested too much time in it.

Develop support for your reasons. Next you have to come up with **EVIDENCE** to support your reasons: facts, statistics, examples, testimony by authorities and experts, anecdotal evidence, scenarios, case studies and observation, and textual evidence. For some topics, you may want or need to use evidence in visual form like photos, graphs, and charts; online, you could also use video or audio evidence and links to evidence in other websites.

401–8

What counts as evidence varies across audiences. Statistical evidence may be required in certain disciplines but not in others; anecdotes may be accepted as evidence in some courses but not in engineering. Some audiences will be persuaded by emotional appeals while others will not. For example, if you argue that foods produced from genetically modified organisms (GMOs) should be allowed to be sold because they're safe, you could support that reason with *facts*: GMOs are tested thoroughly by three separate U.S. government agencies. Or you could support it with *statistics*: A study of 29 years of data on livestock fed GMO feed found that GMO-fed cattle had no adverse health effects on people who ate them. *Expert testimony* might include R. E. Goodman of the Department of Food Science and Technology at the University of Nebraska–Lincoln, who writes that "there is an absence of proof of harm to consumers from commercially available GMOs."

Identify other positions. Now think about positions other than yours and the reasons people are likely to give for those positions. Be careful to represent their points of view as accurately and fairly as you can. Then decide whether you need to acknowledge or to refute each position.

Acknowledging other positions. Some positions can't be refuted but are too important to ignore, so you need to **ACKNOWLEDGE** concerns and objections they raise to show that you've considered other perspectives. For example, in an essay arguing that vacations are necessary to maintain good health, medical writer Alina Tugend acknowledges that "in some cases, these trips—particularly with entire families in tow—can be stressful in their own way. The joys of a holiday can also include lugging around a ridiculous amount of paraphernalia, jet-lagged children sobbing on airplanes, hotels that looked wonderful on the Web but are in reality next to a construction site." Tugend's acknowledgment moderates her position and makes her argument appear more reasonable.

411

Refuting other positions. State the position as clearly and as fairly as you can, and then **REFUTE** it by showing why you believe it is wrong. Perhaps the reasoning is faulty or the supporting evidence inadequate. Acknowledge the merits of the position, if any, but emphasize its shortcomings. Avoid the **FALLACY** of attacking the person holding the position or bringing up a competing position that no one seriously entertains.

413–14

414–16

Ways of Organizing an Argument

Readers need to be able to follow the reasoning of your argument from beginning to end; your task is to lead them from point to point as you build your case. Sometimes you'll want to give all the reasons for your argument first, followed by discussion of any other positions. Alternatively, you might discuss each reason and any opposing arguments together.

[Reasons to support your argument, followed by opposing arguments]

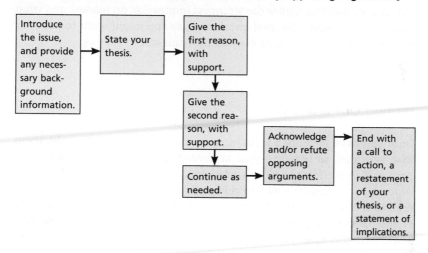

[Reason/opposing argument, reason/opposing argument]

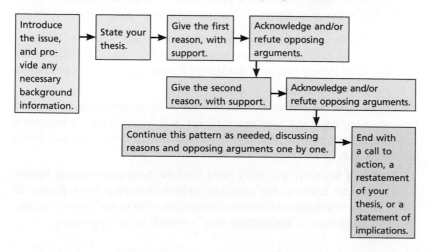

Consider carefully the order in which you discuss your reasons. Usually what comes last makes the strongest impression on readers and what comes in the middle the least impression, so you might want to put your most important or strongest reasons first and last.

Writing Out a Draft

340–42

Once you have generated ideas, done some research, and thought about how you want to organize your argument, it's time to start **DRAFTING**. Your goal in the initial draft is to develop your argument—you can fill in support and transitions as you revise. You may want to write your first draft in one sitting, so that you can develop your reasoning from beginning to end. Or you may write the main argument first and the introduction and conclusion after you've drafted the body of the essay; many writers find that beginning and ending an essay are the hardest tasks they face.

373–85

Here is some advice on how you might **BEGIN AND END** your argument:

Draft a beginning. There are various ways to begin an argument essay, depending on your audience and purpose. Here are a few suggestions:

- *Offer background information.* You may need to give your readers information to help them understand your position. MacKay outlines the extent of kidney failure in the United States and the limits of dialysis as treatment.

- *Begin with an anecdote.* Worthen starts by summarizing her early teaching days and how her students' behavior led her to become a "young fogey" who instructed her students on classroom and email etiquette.

- *Define a key term.* You may need to show how you're using certain keywords. MacKay, for example, defines *end-stage renal disease* as "a state of kidney disorder so advanced that the organ stops functioning altogether," a **DEFINITION** that is central to her argument.

432–42

academic literacies · rhetorical situations · genres · fields · processes · strategies · research MLA / APA · media / design

- *Begin with something that will get readers' attention.* MacKay begins emphatically: "There are thousands of people dying to buy a kidney and thousands of people dying to sell a kidney . . . So why are we standing in the way?"

- *Explain the context for your position.* All arguments are part of a larger, ongoing conversation, so you might begin by showing how your position fits into the arguments others have made. Kristof places his argument about guns in the **CONTEXT** of government regulation of other dangerous technologies.

▲ 114

Draft an ending. Your conclusion is the chance to wrap up your argument in such a way that readers will remember what you've said. Here are a few ways of concluding an argument essay:

- *Summarize your main points.* Especially when you've presented a complex argument, it can help readers to **SUMMARIZE** your main point. MacKay sums up her argument with the sentence "If legalized and regulated, the sale of human organs would save lives."

● 534–35

- *Call for action.* Kristof does this by asking politicians to consider "sensible safety measures." Worthen asks professors to teach the principles underlying etiquette.

- *Frame your argument by referring to the introduction.* MacKay does this when she ends by reiterating that selling organs benefits both seller and buyer. Worthen mentions the need for correct emails in both her first and last few paragraphs.

Come up with a title. Most often you'll want your title to tell readers something about your topic—and to make them want to read on. MacKay's "Organ Sales Will Save Lives" tells us both her topic and position. Kristof's title, "Our Blind Spot about Guns," entices us to find out what that blind spot is. Worthen's "U Can't Talk to Ur Professor Like This" leads us to ask, "Like what?" See the chapter on **GUIDING YOUR READER** for more advice on composing a good title.

◆ 386–87

Considering Matters of Design

You'll probably write the main text of your argument in paragraph form, but think about what kind of information you're presenting and how you can design it to make your argument as easy as possible for your readers to understand. Think also about whether any visual or audio elements would be more persuasive than written words.

648–49 ☐
• What would be an appropriate **FONT**? Something serious like Times Roman? Something traditional like Courier? Something else?

650–52 ☐
• Would it help your readers if you divided your argument into shorter sections and added **HEADINGS**?

649–50 ☐
• If you're making several points, would they be easier to follow if you set them off in a **LIST**?

656 ☐
• Do you have any supporting evidence that would be easier to understand in the form of a bar **GRAPH**, line graph, or pie chart?

653–63 ☐
• Would **ILLUSTRATIONS**—photos, diagrams, or drawings—add support for your argument? Online, would video, audio, or links help?

Getting Response and Revising

At this point you need to look at your draft closely, and if possible **GET RESPONSE** from others as well. Following are some questions for looking at an argument with a critical eye.

348–50 ○

• Is there sufficient background or context?

• Have you defined terms to avoid misunderstandings?

• Is the thesis clear and appropriately qualified?

• Are the reasons plausible?

• Is there enough evidence to support these reasons? Will readers accept the evidence as valid and sufficient?

• Can readers follow the steps in your reasoning?

- Have you considered potential objections or other positions? Are there any others that should be addressed?

- Have you cited enough sources, and are these sources credible?

- Are source materials documented carefully and completely, with in-text citations and a works-cited or references section?

- Are any visuals or links that are included used effectively and integrated smoothly with the rest of the text? If there are no visuals or links, would using some strengthen the argument?

Next it's time to **REVISE**, to make sure your argument offers convincing evidence, appeals to readers' values, and achieves your purpose. If you have time and want to explore alternatives, you might try **REWRITING** your draft to see if a different plan or approach might work better.

○ 348–50

○ 353–55

Editing and Proofreading

Readers equate correctness with competence. Once you've revised your draft, follow these guidelines for **EDITING** an argument:

◎ 356–59

- Check to see that your tone is appropriate and consistent throughout, reflects your **STANCE** accurately, and enhances the argument you're making.

■ 66–68

- Be sure readers will be able to follow the argument; check to see you've provided **TRANSITIONS** and summary statements where necessary.

◆ 391

- Make sure you've smoothly integrated **QUOTATIONS**, **PARAPHRASES**, and **SUMMARIES** from source material into your writing and **DOCUMENTED** them accurately.

● 526–38
544–47

- Look for phrases such as "I think" or "I feel" and delete them; your essay itself expresses your opinion.

- Make sure that **ILLUSTRATIONS** have captions and that charts and graphs have headings—and that all are referred to in the main text.

□ 653–63

- If you're writing online, make sure all your links work.

- **PROOFREAD** and spell-check your essay carefully.

○ 359–60

Taking Stock of Your Work

Take stock of what you've written by writing out answers to these questions:

- What did you do well in this piece?
- What could still be improved?
- How did you go about researching your topic?
- How did others' responses influence your writing?
- How did you go about drafting this piece?
- Did you use visual elements (tables, graphs, diagrams, photographs), audio elements, or links effectively? If not, would they have helped?
- What would you do differently next time?
- What have you learned about your writing ability from writing this piece? What do you need to work on in the future?

361–70 ○
98–130 △
202–10
246–55

IF YOU NEED MORE HELP

See Chapter 34 if you are required to submit your argument as part of a writing **PORTFOLIO**. See also Chapter 11 on **ANALYZING A TEXT**, Chapter 16 on **EVALUATIONS**, and Chapter 20 on **PROPOSALS** for advice on writing those specific types of arguments.

Abstracts **14**

Abstracts are summaries written to give readers the gist of a **REPORT** or presentation. Sometimes they are published in conference proceedings or databases. In courses in the *sciences, social sciences,* and *engineering,* you may be asked to create abstracts of your proposed projects and completed reports and essays. Abstracts are brief, typically 100–200 words, sometimes even shorter. Two common kinds are *informative abstracts* and *proposal abstracts.*

▲ 131–56

INFORMATIVE ABSTRACTS

Informative abstracts state in one paragraph the essence of a whole paper about a study or a research project. That one paragraph must mention all the main points or parts of the paper: a description of the study or project, its methods, the results, and the conclusions. Here is an example of the abstract accompanying a seven-page article that appeared in the *Journal of Clinical Psychology:*

> The relationship between boredom proneness and health-symptom reporting was examined. Undergraduate students ($N = 200$) completed the Boredom Proneness Scale and the Hopkins Symptom Checklist. A multiple analysis of covariance indicated that individuals with high boredom-proneness total scores reported significantly higher ratings on all five subscales of the Hopkins Symptom Checklist (Obsessive–Compulsive, Somatization, Anxiety, Interpersonal Sensitivity, and Depression). The results suggest that boredom proneness may be an

important element to consider when assessing symptom reporting. Implications for determining the effects of boredom proneness on psychological- and physical-health symptoms, as well as the application in clinical settings, are discussed.

—Jennifer Sommers and Stephen J. Vodanovich,
"Boredom Proneness"

The first sentence states the nature of the study being reported. The next summarizes the method used to investigate the problem, and the following one gives the results: students who, according to specific tests, are more likely to be bored are also more likely to have certain medical or psychological symptoms. The last two sentences indicate that the paper discusses those results and examines the conclusion and its implications.

PROPOSAL ABSTRACTS

Proposal abstracts contain the same basic information as informative abstracts, but their purpose is very different. You prepare proposal abstracts to persuade someone to let you write on a topic, pursue a project, conduct an experiment, or present a paper at a scholarly conference. This kind of abstract is not written to introduce a longer piece but rather to stand alone, and often the abstract is written before the paper itself. Titles and other aspects of the proposal deliberately reflect the theme of the proposed work, and you may use the future tense, rather than the past, to describe work not yet completed. Here is a possible proposal for doing research on boredom:

> Undergraduate students will complete the Boredom Proneness Scale and the Hopkins Symptom Checklist. A multiple analysis of covariance will be performed to determine the relationship between boredom-proneness total scores and ratings on the five subscales of the Hopkins Symptom Checklist (Obsessive–Compulsive, Somatization, Anxiety, Interpersonal Sensitivity, and Depression).

Key Features / Abstracts

A summary of basic information. An informative abstract includes enough information to substitute for the report itself, and a proposal abstract gives an overview of the planned work.

Objective description. Abstracts present information on the contents of a report or a proposed study; they do not present arguments about or personal perspectives on those contents. The informative abstract on boredom proneness, for example, offers only a tentative conclusion: "The results *suggest* that boredom proneness *may* be an important element to consider."

Brevity. Although the length of abstracts may vary, journals and organizations often restrict them to 120–200 words—meaning you must carefully select and edit your words.

A BRIEF GUIDE TO WRITING ABSTRACTS

Considering the Rhetorical Situation

PURPOSE	Are you giving a brief but thorough overview of a completed study? only enough information to create interest? a proposal for a planned study or presentation?	55–56
AUDIENCE	For whom are you writing this abstract? What information about your project will your readers need?	55–56
STANCE	Whatever your stance in the longer work, your abstract must be objective.	66–68
MEDIA / DESIGN	How will you set off your abstract from the rest of the text? If you are publishing it online, should it be on a separate page? What format do your readers expect?	69–71

Generating Ideas and Text

Write the paper first, the abstract last. You can then use the finished work as the guide for the abstract, which should follow the same basic structure. *Exception:* You may need to write a proposal abstract months before the work it describes will be complete.

Copy and paste key statements. If you've already written the work, highlight your **THESIS**, objective, or purpose; basic information on your methods; your results; and your conclusion. Copy and paste those sentences into a new document to create a rough version of your abstract.

387–89 ◆

534–35 ●

Pare down the rough abstract. **SUMMARIZE** the key ideas in the document, editing out any nonessential words and details. In your first sentence, introduce the overall scope of your study. Also include any other information that seems crucial to understanding your paper. Avoid phrases that add unnecessary words, such as "It is concluded that." In general, you probably won't want to use "I"; an abstract should cover ideas, not say what you think or will do.

Conform to any requirements. In general, an informative abstract should be at most 10 percent of the length of the entire work and no longer than the maximum length allowed. Proposal abstracts should conform to the requirements of the organization calling for the proposal.

Ways of Organizing an Abstract

Organizing abstracts is straightforward: in a single paragraph, briefly state the nature of the report or presentation, followed by an overview of the paper or the proposal.

academic literacies

rhetorical situations

genres

fields

processes

strategies

research MLA / APA

media / design

[An informative abstract]

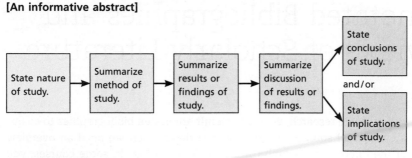

[A proposal abstract]

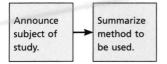

Taking Stock of Your Work

Take stock of what you've written by writing out answers to these questions:

- How did you decide on the type of abstract—informative or proposal—to write?

- How did you identify key statements in your finished work?

- What did you do well in this piece? What could still be improved? What would you do differently next time?

IF YOU NEED MORE HELP

See Chapter 30 for guidelines on **DRAFTING**, Chapter 31 on **ASSESSING YOUR OWN WRITING**, Chapter 32 on **GETTING RESPONSE AND REVISING**, and Chapter 33 on **EDITING AND PROOFREADING**.

340–42
343–47
348–55
356–60

15 Annotated Bibliographies and Reviews of Scholarly Literature

When we do research, we may consult annotated bibliographies to evaluate potential sources and literature reviews when we need an overview of the important research ("literature") on a topic. In some courses, you may be asked to create annotated bibliographies or literature reviews to demonstrate that you have researched your topic thoroughly. This chapter offers advice on writing both.

ANNOTATED BIBLIOGRAPHIES

Annotated bibliographies describe, give publication information for, and sometimes evaluate each work on a list of sources. There are two kinds of annotations, *descriptive* and *evaluative*; both may be brief, consisting only of phrases, or more formal, consisting of sentences and paragraphs. Sometimes an annotated bibliography is introduced by a short statement explaining its scope.

Descriptive annotations simply summarize the contents of each work, without comment or evaluation. They may be very short, just long enough to capture the flavor of the work, like the examples in the following excerpt from a bibliography of books and articles on teen films, published in the *Journal of Popular Film and Television*.

MICHAEL BENTON, MARK DOLAN, AND REBECCA ZISCH

Teen Film$

In the introduction to his book *The Road to Romance and Ruin*, Jon Lewis points out that over half of the world's population is currently under the age of twenty. This rather startling fact should be enough to make most Hollywood producers drool when they think of the potential profits from a target movie audience. Attracting the largest demographic group is, after all, the quickest way to box-office success. In fact, almost from its beginning, the film industry has recognized the importance of the teenaged audience, with characters such as Andy Hardy and locales such as Ridgemont High and the 'hood.

Beyond the assumption that teen films are geared exclusively toward teenagers, however, film researchers should keep in mind that people of all ages have attended and still attend teen films. Popular films about adolescents are also expressions of larger cultural currents. Studying the films is important for understanding an era's common beliefs about its teenaged population within a broader pattern of general cultural preoccupations.

This selected bibliography is intended both to serve and to stimulate interest in the teen film genre. It provides a research tool for those who are studying teen films and their cultural implications. Unfortunately, however, in the process of compiling this list we quickly realized that it was impossible to be genuinely comprehensive or to satisfy every interest.

Doherty, Thomas. *Teenagers and Teenpics: The Juvenilization of American Movies in the 1950s*. Unwin Hyman, 1988. Historical discussion of the identification of teenagers as a targeted film market.

Foster, Harold M. "Film in the Classroom: Coping with 'Teenpics.'" *English Journal*, vol. 76, no. 3, Mar. 1987, pp. 86–88. Evaluation of the potential of using teen films such as *Sixteen Candles*, *The Karate Kid*, *Risky Business*, *The Flamingo Kid*, and *The Breakfast Club* to instruct adolescents on the difference between film as communication and film as exploitation.

Washington, Michael, and Marvin J. Berlowitz. "Blaxploitation Films and High School Youth: Swat Superfly." *Jump Cut*, vol. 9, Oct.–Dec. 1975, pp. 23–24. Marxist reaction to the trend of youth-oriented black action films. Article seeks to illuminate the negative influences the films have on high school students by pointing out the false ideas about education, morality, and the black family espoused by the heroes in the films.

These annotations are purely descriptive; the authors express none of their own opinions. They describe works as "historical" or "Marxist" but do not indicate whether they're "good." The bibliography entries are documented in MLA style.

Evaluative annotations offer opinions on a source as well as describe it. They are often helpful in assessing how useful a source will be for your own writing. The following evaluative annotations are from a bibliography by Kelly Green, a student at Arizona State University. Following her instructor's directions, she labeled each required part of her annotation— summary, degree of advocacy, credibility, and reliability.

KELLY GREEN

Researching Hunger and Poverty

Abramsky, Sasha. "The Other America, 2012: Confronting the Poverty Epidemic." *The Nation,* vol. 294, no. 20, 25 Apr. 2012, https://www.thenation .com/article/other-america-2012-confronting-poverty-epidemic/. Accessed 10 Oct. 2017.

    The author presents the image of American poverty in 2012 with examples from various families living in poverty. The author explores the conditions that make up the new recession and suggests that people in America notice the scale of the issue and take action to solve it [Summary]. The author advocates poverty reform and shows bias toward the interests of low-income families. He acknowledges other perspectives on the issue respectfully [Degree of Advocacy]. Abramsky is a freelance journalist with experience in several magazines and newspapers. He has written several books on the topic of poverty [Credibility]. *The Nation* is one of the oldest-running magazines in the United States and contains opinions on politics and culture [Reliability].

Ambler, Marjane. "Sustaining Our Home, Determining Our Destiny." *Tribal College Journal,* vol. 13, no. 3, Spring 2002, http://www .tribalcollegejournal.org/sustaining-home-determining-destiny/. Accessed 14 Oct. 2017.

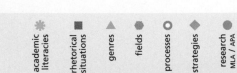

academic literacies   rhetorical situations   genres   fields   processes   strategies   research MLA / APA   media / design

The author examines the causes of poverty on Native American reservations, the factors that lead to solutions to Native American poverty, and the ways in which tribal colleges have helped improve life on reservations [Summary]. The author is strongly biased toward Native American interests and advocates that effective solutions to poverty originate within the reservations, especially in tribal colleges and universities [Degree of Advocacy]. Marjane Ambler was an editor for the *Tribal College Journal* for 9 years and worked in national park service for nearly a decade [Credibility]. This article was published in 2002 in the *Tribal College Journal*, a national magazine published by the American Indian Higher Education Consortium [Reliability].

These annotations not only summarize the sources in detail but also evaluate their bias, or "degree of advocacy"; credibility; and reliability.

Key Features / Annotated Bibliographies

A statement of scope. Sometimes you need or are asked to provide a brief introductory statement to explain what you're covering. The authors of the bibliography on teen films introduce their bibliography with three paragraphs establishing a context for the bibliography and announcing their purpose for compiling it.

Complete bibliographic information. Provide all the information about each source using one documentation system (MLA, APA, or another one) so that you, your readers, or other researchers will be able to find the source easily. It's a good idea to include sources' URLs or **PERMALINKS** to make accessing online sources easier.

● 487
_____

A concise description of the work. A good annotation describes each item as carefully and objectively as possible, giving accurate information and showing that you understand the source. These qualities will help to build authority—for you as a writer and for your annotations.

Relevant commentary. If you write an evaluative bibliography, your comments should be relevant to your purpose and audience. The best way to achieve relevance is to consider what questions a potential reader might have about each source: What are the main points of the source? What is its argument? How even-handed or biased is it? How current and reliable is it? Will the source be helpful for your project?

Consistent presentation. All annotations should follow a consistent pattern: if one is written in complete sentences, they should all be. Each annotation in the teen films bibliography, for example, begins with a phrase (not a complete sentence) characterizing the work.

A BRIEF GUIDE TO WRITING ANNOTATED BIBLIOGRAPHIES

Considering the Rhetorical Situation

55–56 ■	**PURPOSE**	Will your bibliography need to demonstrate the depth or breadth of your research? Will your readers actually track down and use your sources? Do you need or want to convince readers that your sources are good?
57–60 ■	**AUDIENCE**	For whom are you compiling this bibliography? What does your audience need to know about each source?
66–68 ■	**STANCE**	Are you presenting yourself as an objective describer or evaluator? Or are you expressing a particular point of view toward the sources you evaluate?
69–71 ■	**MEDIA / DESIGN**	If you are publishing the bibliography electronically, will you provide links from each annotation to the source itself? Online or offline, should you distinguish the bibliographic information from the annotation by using a different font?

Generating Ideas and Text

Decide what sources to include. You may be tempted to include in a bibliography every source you find or look at. A better strategy is to include only those sources that you or your readers may find potentially useful in researching your topic. For an academic bibliography, you need to consider the qualities in the list below. Some of these qualities should not rule a source in or out; they simply raise issues you need to think about.

- *Appropriateness.* Is this source relevant to your topic? Is it a primary source or a secondary source? Is it aimed at an appropriate audience? General or specialized? Elementary, advanced, or somewhere in between?

- *Credibility.* Is the author reputable? Is the publication, publishing company, or sponsor of the site reputable? Do the ideas more or less agree with those in other sources you've read?

- *Balance.* Does the source present enough evidence for its assertions? Does it show any particular bias? Does it present countering arguments fairly?

- *Timeliness.* Is the source recent enough? Does it reflect current thinking or research about the subject?

If you need help **FINDING SOURCES**, see Chapter 48.

489–510

Compile a list of works to annotate. Give the sources themselves in whatever documentation style is required; see the guidelines for **MLA** and **APA** styles in Chapters 54 and 55.

MLA 548–96
APA 597–636

Determine what kind of bibliography you need to write. Will your bibliography be descriptive or evaluative? Will your annotations be in the form of phrases? complete sentences? paragraphs? The form will shape your reading and note taking. If you're writing a descriptive bibliography, your reading goal will be just to understand and capture the writer's message as clearly as possible. If you're writing an evaluative bibliography, you will also need to assess the source as you read in order to include your own opinions of it.

Read carefully.   To write an annotation, you must understand the source's argument, but when you are writing an annotated bibliography as part of a **PROPOSAL**, you may have neither the time nor the need to read the whole text. Here's a way of quickly determining whether a source is likely to serve your needs:

246–55 △

- Check the publisher or sponsor (university press? scholarly journal? popular magazine? website sponsored by a reputable organization?).
- Read the preface (of a book), abstract (of a scholarly article), introduction (of an article in a nonscholarly magazine or a website).
- Skim the table of contents or the headings.
- Read the parts that relate specifically to your topic.

Research the writer, if necessary.   If you are required to indicate the writer's credentials, you may need to do additional research. You may find information by typing the writer's name into a search engine or looking up the writer in *Contemporary Authors*. In any case, information about the writer should take up no more than one sentence in your annotation.

443–51 ◆

Summarize the work in a sentence or two.   **DESCRIBE** it as objectively as possible: even if you are writing an evaluative annotation, you can evaluate the central point of a work better by stating it clearly first. *If you're writing a descriptive annotation, you're done.*

511–18 ●

Establish criteria for evaluating sources.   If you're **EVALUATING** sources for a project, you'll need to evaluate them in terms of their usefulness for your project, their **STANCE**, and their overall credibility.

66–68 ■

Write a brief evaluation of the source.   If you can generalize about the worth of the entire work, fine. You may find, however, that some parts are useful while others are not, and what you write should reflect that mix.

Be consistent—in content, sentence structure, and format.

- *Content.* Try to provide about the same amount of information for each entry. If you're evaluating, don't evaluate some sources and just describe others.

- *Sentence structure.* Use the same style throughout—complete sentences, brief phrases, or a mix.

- *Format.* Use one documentation style throughout; use a consistent **FONT** for each element in each entry—for example, italicize or underline all book titles.

648–49

Ways of Organizing an Annotated Bibliography

Depending on their purpose, annotated bibliographies may or may not include an introduction. Most annotated bibliographies cover a single topic and so are organized alphabetically by author's or editor's last name. When a work lacks a named author, alphabetize it by the first important word in its title. Consult the documentation system you're using for additional details about alphabetizing works appropriately.

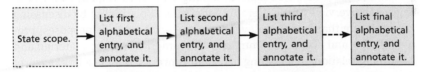

Sometimes an annotated bibliography needs to be organized into several subject areas (or genres, periods, or some other category); if so, the entries are listed alphabetically within each category. For example, a bibliography about terrorism breaks down into subjects such as "Global Terrorism" and "Weapons of Mass Destruction."

[Multicategory bibliography]

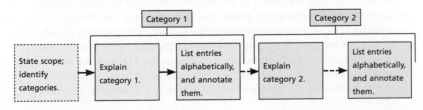

Taking Stock of Your Work

Take stock of what you've written by writing out answers to these questions:

- How did you go about researching the entries in this bibliography?
- How did you decide which sources to include and which to leave out?
- How did you go about drafting your bibliography?
- Did you cite your sources accurately?
- What did you do well? What could still be improved? What would you do differently next time?

REVIEWS OF SCHOLARLY LITERATURE

Reviews of scholarly literature describe and evaluate important research ("literature") available on a topic. In writing a literature review, your goal is to give an overview of the literature on a topic. You do that by discussing the literature that is most relevant to your topic and your purposes, providing clear and accurate summaries of appropriate source material, and describing relationships among facts and concepts. Here is a brief excerpt from a literature review that describes scholarship in zombie movies by a student at the University of Mary Washington.

CAMERON CARROLL

Zombie Film Scholarship: A Review of the Literature

Zombies are the shambling undead creatures that attack in hordes and strike terror into the hearts of moviegoers with their mindless aggression. Monsters on the big screen fascinate American audiences and scholars alike as representations of cultural fears and reflections of public perceptions, and they have done so since they first shuffled into theaters. The walking dead first haunted cinemas in 1932 with the release of *White Zombie* and have gone through cycles of popularity both at the box office and in scholarly debate. Without a doubt, the height of zombie scholarship began in the mid-2000s with only shallow mentions made in horror analyses before then. Only the English discipline gave the zombie credit as a subject worthy of study. As author and English professor Kyle Bishop wrote in 2010, "The zombie phenomenon has yet to be plumbed to its depths by the academic and literary markets."[1] Although significant zombie research has only surfaced in the 2000s, a valiant effort is currently being made to explore zombie symbolism and its historical and cultural context across non-traditional scholarly fields, such as anthropology, psychology, sociology, and philosophy.

. . .

Zombies, as creatures that waver between living and dead, necessarily bring forth questions on the nature of being and thus also fall into the realm of philosophy as seen in *Zombies, Vampires, and Philosophy: New Life for the Undead* published in 2010 and edited by Richard Greene and K. Silem Mohammed, professors of philosophy and English, respectively. Philosophers in the study of zombies seek to answer such questions as, is it better to be undead or dead? Richard Greene argues that since death is a state of non-existence and Undeath is at least a primal existence, the question comes down to the classic "to be, or not to be?" For him, Undeath is the only option for a state of being, since death is non-existence. Existence in any form is inherently better than utterly ceasing to be.[16] Greene's philosophy colleague, William Larkin, counters that zombies are driven to actions seen as evil and mindless, both states that humans do not usually choose. He cites how zombie films repeatedly depict survivors who ask their friends and family to kill them should it appear that they will turn into zombies, so desperate are they to avoid Undeath.[17] Simon Clark, a writer with a master's degree in Fine Arts, discusses morality in relation to zombies: if zombies are non-moral and whether or not they are the freest creatures because of their lack of morality. Clark writes that they become ultimately free in their modern incarnations from turn of the millennium cinema.[18] Zombies break through barriers that survivors put up to keep them confined and are so primal that they cannot be held accountable for their actions, making them truly liberated. A fictional creature encourages real discussions in philosophical debate, demonstrating yet another area that inspires scholars to reexamine their own field because of zombies.

. . .

The message to take away from zombie scholarship is that what it represents is evolutionary and infinitely debatable, but the victory for zombie studies is that zombies are being studied at all. After decades of being underrepresented in horror scholarship, zombies are finally getting their due as a cultural icon, complete with varying opinions and interpretations. Scholarly debate proves that the zombie is a valid resource for understanding American culture and worthy of the enthusiastic pursuit of interdepartmental scholarship. As shown within the scholarly works above, the debate over the meaning of the living dead is quite lively, indeed.

Notes

1. Kyle William Bishop, *American Zombie Gothic: The Rise and Fall (and Rise) of the Walking Dead in Popular Culture* (Jefferson, NC: McFarland, 2010), 7.

. . .

16. Richard Greene and K. Silem Mohammed, eds., *Zombies, Vampires, and Philosophy: New Life for the Undead* (Chicago: Open Court, 2010), 13.
17. Greene and Mohammed, *Zombies, Vampires, and Philosophy*, 20.
18. Greene and Mohammed, *Zombies, Vampires, and Philosophy*, 208.

Carroll begins by establishing a context for her discussion and then focuses on her topic, the scholarship of zombies in film. In her review, she discusses the history of zombie scholarship in general and then in psychology, social trends, fiction, and, in this excerpt, philosophy. A history major, she follows Chicago style; in addition to the notes, she included a bibliography listing all her sources, including the two noted here.

Key Features / Reviews of Scholarly Literature

Careful, thorough research.   A review of scholarly literature demands that you research all the major literature on the topic—or at least the major literature available to you, given the time you have.

Accurate, objective summaries of the relevant literature.   Readers expect a literature review to objectively summarize the main ideas or conclusions of the texts reviewed.

Critical evaluation for the literature. A literature review offers considered selection of the most important, relevant, and useful sources of information on its topic, so you must evaluate each source to decide whether it should be included and then to determine how it advances understanding of the topic.

SYNTHESIS of the scholarship. A literature review differs from an annotated bibliography in that the review identifies key concepts, similarities, and differences within the body of literature, showing how the sources relate to one another by method, study findings, themes, main ideas, or something else.

519–25

A clear focus. Because a literature review provides an overview of your topic's main issues and explains the main concepts underlying your research, it must be carefully organized and clearly focused on your specific topic.

Taking Stock of Your Work

Take stock of what you've written by writing out answers to these questions:

- How did you go about researching the sources you used?
- How did you decide which sources to include and which to leave out?
- What led you to group related sources together as you did?
- How did you go about synthesizing similar sources?
- What did you do well? What could still be improved? What would you do differently next time?

IF YOU NEED MORE HELP

See Chapter 30 for guidelines on **DRAFTING**, Chapter 31 on **ASSESSING YOUR OWN WRITING**, Chapter 32 on **GETTING RESPONSE AND REVISING**, and Chapter 33 on **EDITING AND PROOFREADING**. See Chapter 34 if you are required to submit your bibliography in a writing **PORTFOLIO**.

340–42
343–47
348–55
356–60
361–70

16 Evaluations

TestFreaks evaluates audio equipment and appliances. The *Princeton Review* and *U.S. News & World Report* evaluate colleges and universities. You probably consult such sources to make decisions, and you probably evaluate things all the time—when you recommend a film (or not) or a teacher (ditto). An evaluation is at bottom a judgment; you judge something according to certain criteria, supporting your judgment with reasons and evidence. You need to give your reasons for evaluating it as you do because often your evaluation will affect your audience's actions: they must see this movie, needn't bother with this book, should be sure to have the Caesar salad at this restaurant, and so on.

In college courses, students in *literature, film, drama,* and *art* classes may be assigned to evaluate poems, fiction, movies, plays, and artwork,

TestFreaks *crawls the web for expert reviews and user opinions.*

and those in *business* and *political science* classes may be asked to evaluate advertising or political campaigns or plans for business or public-policy initiatives. In a review that follows, written for *The Daily Bruin*, UCLA's student newspaper, William Thorne offers his evaluation of the film *The Circle*.

WILLIAM THORNE

Movie Review: The Circle

The Circle imagines a world in which internet stardom is just a daily vlog away, and giant tech companies battle governments over privacy issues. Sound familiar?

The latest offering from up-and-coming indie director James Ponsoldt aims to be both a reflection on documenting one's life online and a warning against millennials' unchecked faith in tech giants. But the film falls short of being a well-rounded piece.

If anyone can get millennials to put down their iPhones and listen, it's the film's main star, Emma Watson. Fresh off her all-singing all-dancing performance in the Disney behemoth *Beauty and the Beast*, Watson plays Mae Holland, a frustrated young woman trapped in a dull office job in the modern-day Bay Area. Mae's problems stretch beyond her career concerns, though, as her father, played by the late, great Bill Paxton in his final film role, has multiple sclerosis. And Mae's relationship with her ex-boyfriend Mercer (Ellar Coltrane), a local lad who makes antler chandeliers, doesn't seem to be going anywhere.

The solution to all of Mae's problems? Joining The Circle, a powerful internet company co-founded by Eamon Bailey (Tom Hanks), a bearded, ambitious genius who is a turtleneck and a pair of glasses away from Steve Jobs. Bailey's motto is "Knowing is good. Knowing everything is better," yet somehow hardly anyone at the company can see the creepy, maniacal implications of these two sentences, and so Bailey and his co-founder Tom Stenton (Patton Oswalt) act on their crazy ideas unchallenged.

The Circle starts out as a promising and intriguing sci-fi thriller, 5 exploring the pros and cons of having minute, camouflaged cameras on every street corner. Hanks does a Jobsian job of selling Big Brother surveillance to the audience, channeling a mixture of his trademark

American Dream optimism and "Go get 'em, Woody" attitude. But, as with most Hanks performances, there's more to the character than meets the eye, and Bailey's enthusiasm masks his stalkerish desire to see what everyone is doing.

Some of the best moments in the movie occur when Mae volunteers to wear a tiny camera on her chest and document her every move for the world to see as part of The Circle's latest venture. Although Mae is reluctant at first to expose her life to the online world, she soon becomes addicted to the millions of faceless followers and begins to sacrifice real relationships with her family and friends for superficial interactions with often offensive users. The character adopts a fake smile and exudes nauseating enthusiasm, echoing many of today's *YouTube* vloggers and providing a clever commentary on how online fame can come with a price.

Tonally, however, the film can't quite decide what it wants to be. At one point, Ty Lafitte (John Boyega), who seems to be the only person even slightly worried by The Circle's practices, leads Mae into the sewers underneath The Circle's colossal offices, referred to as "the campus," to warn her about the dangers of the company's omniscience. The

scene suggests that the two will team up to take down the company and escape together in a heart-racing thriller. Yet Ty is subsequently sidelined, and the uneasy sexual tension between him and Mae is left unresolved.

The film's tonal issues begin even earlier, during a scene that critiques millennials' obsession with social media and their trademark fear of missing out on socializing. Two "Circlers," acting under the pretense of getting her settled in at the company, approach Mae and inform her that The Circle's company barbecues and impromptu Beck concerts are not mandatory, but that if she doesn't show up, she'll drop in the company participation rankings. The moment is laugh-out-loud funny, but it makes the seriousness of subsequent scenes dealing with Mae's father's disease and Mercer's detachment feel empty and tasteless.

The Circle lurches from tense thriller to weepy family drama to savvy, knowing comedy from scene to scene, leaving the audience wondering why it couldn't just settle for one of the above. The film only avoids rotten-apple status because of the elements of clever commentary on modern-day surveillance and the power of information in the hands of tech companies, and because of the solid acting. Watson and Hanks both shine, and it's definitely worth getting off *Instagram* for a few hours to see the final film performance from the legendary Paxton.

Thorne quickly summarizes The Circle's *plot and then evaluates the film using clear criteria: the performances of Tom Hanks and Emma Watson, the complexity of their characters, the film's coherence, and its message.*

Key Features / Evaluations

A concise description of the subject.　You should include just enough information to let readers who may not be familiar with your subject understand what it is; the goal is to evaluate, not summarize. Depending on your topic and medium, some of this information may be in visual or audio form. Thorne briefly describes *The Circle*'s main plot points, only providing what readers need to understand the context of his evaluation.

Clearly defined criteria. You need to determine clear criteria as the basis for your judgment. In reviews or other evaluations written for a broad audience, you can integrate the criteria into the discussion as reasons for your assessment, as Thorne does in his evaluation of *The Circle*. In more formal evaluations, you may need to announce your criteria explicitly. Thorne evaluates the film based on the stars' performances, the complexity of their characters, and the film's coherence.

A knowledgeable discussion of the subject. To evaluate something credibly, you need to show that you know it yourself and that you understand its context. Thorne cites many examples from *The Circle*, showing his knowledge of the film, and he draws parallels to other topics, such as Steve Jobs's iconic look, Tom Hanks's tendency to play complicated characters, and modern society's obsession with social media. Some evaluations require that you research what other authoritative sources have said about your subject. Thorne might have referred to other reviews of the film to show that he'd researched others' views.

A balanced and fair assessment. An evaluation is centered on a judgment. Thorne concedes that *The Circle* doesn't quite know what kind of movie it is, so it "lurches from tense thriller to weepy family drama to savvy, knowing comedy." Nevertheless, he thinks the film is worth seeing due to its "clever commentary on modern-day surveillance" and some of the actors' performances. It is important that any judgment be balanced and fair. Seldom is something all good or all bad. A fair evaluation need not be all positive or all negative; it may acknowledge both strengths and weaknesses. For example, a movie's soundtrack may be wonderful while the plot is not.

Well-supported reasons. You need to argue for your judgment, providing reasons and evidence that might include visual and audio as well as verbal material. Thorne gives several reasons for his assessment of *The Circle*—the strong performances by Hanks and Watson, the ways in which "the film can't quite decide what it wants to be"—and he supports these reasons with several examples from the film.

A BRIEF GUIDE TO WRITING EVALUATIONS

Choosing Something to Evaluate

You can more effectively evaluate a limited subject than a broad one: review certain dishes at a local restaurant rather than the entire menu; review one film or episode rather than all the films by Alfred Hitchcock or all seventy-three *Game of Thrones* episodes. The more specific and focused your subject, the better you can write about it.

Considering the Rhetorical Situation

PURPOSE
Are you writing to affect your audience's opinion of a subject? to help others decide what to see, do, or buy? to demonstrate your expertise in a field?
55–56

AUDIENCE
To whom are you writing? What will your audience already know about the subject? What will they expect to learn from your evaluation of it? Are they likely to agree with you or not?
57–60

STANCE
What is your attitude toward the subject, and how will you show that you have evaluated it fairly and appropriately? Think about the tone you want to use: should it be reasonable? passionate? critical?
66–68

MEDIA / DESIGN
How will you deliver your evaluation? In print? Electronically? As a speech? Can you show images or audio or video clips? If you're submitting your text for publication, are there any format requirements?
69–71

Generating Ideas and Text

Explore what you already know. **FREEWRITE** to answer the following questions: What do you know about this subject or subjects like it? What are your initial or gut feelings, and why do you feel as you do? How does
331–32

this subject reflect or affect your basic values or beliefs? How have others evaluated subjects like this?

Identify criteria. Make a list of criteria you think should be used to evaluate your subject. Think about which criteria will likely be important to

57–60
334–35

your **AUDIENCE**. You might find **CUBING** and **QUESTIONING** to be useful processes for thinking about your criteria.

Evaluate your subject. Study your subject closely to determine to what extent it meets each of your criteria. You may want to list your criteria and take notes related to each one, or you may develop a rating scale for each criterion to help stay focused on it. Come up with a tentative judgment.

Compare your subject with others. Often, evaluating something

424–31

involves **COMPARING AND CONTRASTING** it with similar things. We judge movies in comparison with the other movies we've seen and french fries with the other fries we've tasted. Sometimes those comparisons can be made informally. For other evaluations, you may have to do research—to try on several pairs of jeans before buying any, for example—to see how your subject compares.

State your judgment as a tentative thesis statement. Your **THESIS**

387–89

STATEMENT should be one that addresses both pros and cons. "*Hawaii Five-O* is fun to watch despite its stilted dialogue." "Of the five sport-utility vehicles tested, the Toyota 4Runner emerged as the best in comfort, power, and durability, though not in styling or cargo capacity." Both of these examples offer a judgment but qualify it according to the writer's criteria.

Anticipate other opinions. I think Will Ferrell is a comic genius whose movies are first-rate. You think Will Ferrell is a terrible actor who makes awful movies. How can I write a review of his latest film that you will

411
412–13

at least consider? One way is by **ACKNOWLEDGING** other opinions—and **REFUTING** those opinions as best I can. I may not persuade you to see Ferrell's next film, but I can at least demonstrate that by certain criteria

477

he should be appreciated. You may need to **RESEARCH** how others have evaluated your subject.

✳ academic literacies
■ rhetorical situations
▲ genres
◆ fields
○ processes
◆ strategies
● research MLA / APA
□ media / design

Identify and support your reasons. Write out all the **REASONS** you can think of that will convince your audience to accept your judgment. Review your list to identify the most convincing or important reasons. Then review how well your subject meets your criteria and decide how best to **SUPPORT** your reasons: through examples, authoritative opinions, statistics, visual or audio evidence, or something else.

◆ 400–401

◆ 401–8

Ways of Organizing an Evaluation

Evaluations are usually organized in one of two ways. One way is to introduce what's being evaluated, followed by your judgment, discussing your criteria along the way. This is a useful strategy if your audience may not be familiar with your subject.

[Start with your subject]

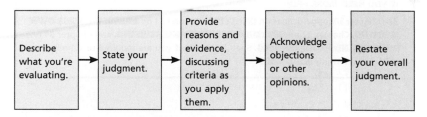

Describe what you're evaluating. → State your judgment. → Provide reasons and evidence, discussing criteria as you apply them. → Acknowledge objections or other opinions. → Restate your overall judgment.

You might also start by identifying your criteria and then follow with a discussion of how well your subject meets those criteria. This strategy foregrounds the process by which you reached your conclusions.

[Start with your criteria]

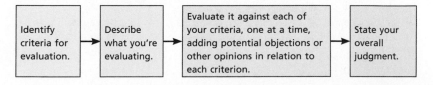

Identify criteria for evaluation. → Describe what you're evaluating. → Evaluate it against each of your criteria, one at a time, adding potential objections or other opinions in relation to each criterion. → State your overall judgment.

Taking Stock of Your Work

Take stock of what you've written by writing out answers to these questions:

- What did you do well in this piece?

- What could still be improved?

- How did you develop criteria for your evaluation?

- How did others' responses influence your writing?

- What would you do differently next time?

- What have you learned about your writing ability or writing processes from writing this piece? What do you need to work on in the future?

340–42
343–47
348–55
356–60
361–70

> **IF YOU NEED MORE HELP**
>
> See Chapter 30 for guidelines on **DRAFTING**, Chapter 31 on **ASSESSING YOUR OWN WRITING**, Chapter 32 on **GETTING RESPONSE AND REVISING**, and Chapter 33 on **EDITING AND PROOFREADING**. See Chapter 34 if you are required to submit your report in a writing **PORTFOLIO**.

academic literacies
rhetorical situations
genres
fields
processes
strategies
research MLA / APA
media / design

Literary analyses are essays that examine literary texts closely to understand their messages, interpret their meanings, appreciate their techniques, or understand their historical or social contexts. Such texts traditionally include novels, short stories, poems, and plays but may also include films, TV shows, videogames, music, and comics. You might read *Macbeth* and notice that Shakespeare's play contains a pattern of images of blood. You could explore the distinctive point of view in Ambrose Bierce's story "An Occurrence at Owl Creek Bridge." Or you could point out the differences between Stephen King's *The Shining* and Stanley Kubrick's screenplay based on that novel. In all these cases, you use specific analytical techniques to go below the surface of the work to deepen your understanding of how it works and what it means.

You may be assigned to analyze works of literature in courses in *English, film, drama,* and many other subjects. Here is a poem by the twentieth-century American poet Robert Frost, followed by a student's analysis of it written for a literature course at the University of South Dakota and chosen as a winner of the 2017 Norton Writer's Prize.

ROBERT FROST

The Road Not Taken

Two roads diverged in a yellow wood,
And sorry I could not travel both
And be one traveler, long I stood
And looked down one as far as I could
To where it bent in the undergrowth;   5

Then took the other, as just as fair,
And having perhaps the better claim,
Because it was grassy and wanted wear;
Though as for that the passing there
Had worn them really about the same,   10

And both that morning equally lay
In leaves no step had trodden black.
Oh, I kept the first for another day!
Yet knowing how way leads on to way,
I doubted if I should ever come back.   15

I shall be telling this with a sigh
Somewhere ages and ages hence:
Two roads diverged in a wood, and I—
I took the one less traveled by,
And that has made all the difference.   20

MATTHEW MILLER

Frost's Broken Roads

"The Road Not Taken" by Robert Frost is arguably one of the most popular poems ever written. Read at graduations, eulogies, even in movies and car commercials, it is often interpreted as an ode to individualism. Frost's image of the road "less traveled" has become synonymous with daring life choices that make "all the difference" in living a fulfilling life (lines 19–20). Some may latch on to this as the poem's deeper meaning. However, this convenient conclusion ignores several conflicting, yet beautiful, details that lead the poem down a path of broken metaphor and temporal inconsistency. To truly recognize what Frost is building in this poem, a few nagging inconsistencies must be considered.

In the first line of the poem, the traveler is depicted hiking in a "yellow wood" wherein he finds a fork in his path (1). This setting is the foundation of a common metaphor, but transposing familiar notions of a figurative fork in the road onto Frost's poem requires acceptance of the traveler's metaphoric natural world and its "temporal scheme," or some form of unified movement through time, as the critic Cleanth Brooks describes it in his classic book on poetic structure, *The Well Wrought Urn* (203). If the path that is covered "[i]n leaves no step had trodden black" (12) makes "all the difference" (20) in a life, common sense indicates the decision to choose that path has to occur early enough during a lifetime to properly affect its outcome. The speaker/traveler affirms this, telling the reader that he "shall be telling" them the story of his decision "with a sigh / Somewhere ages and ages hence" (16–17). In other words, the traveler must be fairly young, otherwise he wouldn't have "ages and ages" (17) left to tell his story. It may not be apparent at a surface level, but this complicates our understanding of the poem's implicit story.

It is common knowledge that morning, the beginning of the day, is often paralleled figuratively with the beginning of other things (e.g. "the dawn of civilization"). In this sense, the setting helps to solidify the poem's established temporal sense; the earliness of the day—"morning" (16)—parallels the early point in life when the traveler makes his life-altering decision. However, the description of the scene, the "yellow wood" (1) where the ground "lay / In leaves" (11–12), indicates that late autumn has set in around the forest. Parallels between seasonal progression and the human life cycle saturate literature and art with such metaphors as the "springtime of youth" and the "hoary winter of old age" (Kammen 23). With that in mind, the end of autumn represents the bitter end of productive years and the first step into the cold and death of winter. So, embedded in the poem is a temporal inconsistency; the traveler is young, with "ages and ages" (17) yet to live, but the autumn setting implies his world is quickly coming to an end.

Another question that complicates a traditional understanding of the poem is that of identity. The narrator claims he is "sorry" he "could not travel both" paths "and be one traveler" (2–3). For him to stray off his path would equal becoming a different person; he "could not travel both / And be one traveler" (2–3, emphasis added). However, one person can easily be two different travelers in a lifetime (i.e. one person can take both a cruise vacation and a backpacking trip: two very different traveling styles). The traveler/speaker even admits this is possible by saying he *could* keep "the first for another day" (13). His excuse for not traveling both paths was not that it was impossible but rather that "knowing how way leads on to way, / I doubted if I should ever come back" (14–15). Although he believes one of the paths has "the better claim, / Because it was grassy and wanted wear" (7–8), in practically the same breath he casts doubt on the claim that it is "less traveled" (19), admitting other travelers have worn down the two trails "really about the same" (10). The speaker in this poem is not Emerson's self-reliant transcendentalist, who can "speak what [he] think[s] to-day in words as hard as cannon balls, and to-morrow speak what to-morrow thinks in hard words again, though it contradict every thing [he] said to-day" (214).

Frost's syntax and punctuation add even more nuance. The poem 5 consists of one sentence that takes up the first two stanzas and part of the third, in which our traveler deliberates and, eventually, makes his decision; and the three sentences of the third and fourth stanzas, in which our traveler lives with his choice. As the poem progresses to the point where our traveler makes his decision, we see punctuation that is irregular when compared with the rest of the poem: an exclamation point when the traveler finally makes a decision (possibly showing excess emotion); an em dash (—) followed by a repeated word when re-telling his story that functions almost like a stutter, possibly showing regret/lack of confidence in his choice. With this in mind, it seems as though our traveler had a tough time making his decision, and afterward, there is no obvious approval or happiness with it, only that it "made all the difference" (20), which could be positive or negative.

Placing the poem in its historical context further complicates these questions. According to an article written for the Poetry Foundation by the poet Katherine Robinson, "The Road Not Taken" was actually written "as a joke for a friend, the poet Edward Thomas."

Indeed, when Frost and Thomas went walking together, Thomas would often choose one fork in the road because he was convinced it would lead them to something, perhaps a patch of rare wild flowers or a particular bird's nest. . . . In a letter, Frost goaded Thomas, saying, "No matter which road you take, *you'll always sigh*, and wish you'd taken another" (Robinson, emphasis added).

Introducing the poet's biography might be considered by many a sin against the work, especially for those espousing Cleanth Brooks' celebration of poetic unity and universal meaning. However, knowing this information fills in several gaps about the poem; instead of confusing inconsistencies and paradoxical meanings, the poem can now be viewed—at least partly—as teasing from a friend. It is easy to imagine an indecisive Thomas, standing and staring down the fork in the path, afraid of what he'll miss if he picks the wrong trail, and then on the way home "telling" Frost, "with a sigh" (16), about all he swore he missed on *the road he didn't take* (16). This being said, Frost published this work knowing full well of its depth and epistemological possibilities, saying in a letter, "My poems . . . are all set to trip the reader head foremost into the boundless" (qtd. in Robinson).

Frost's timeless poem is an elegant narrative, filled with serene imagery and laced with layers of mystery. Readers of this canonical work can easily find themselves slipping into the easy, traditional reading of an ode to individualism. Upon closer inspection, there is only one thing clear about "The Road Not Taken," which is said best in words Frost loved to tell his readers regarding his classic poem: "[Y]ou have to be careful of that one; it's a tricky poem—very tricky" (qtd. in Robinson).

Works Cited

Brooks, Cleanth. *The Well Wrought Urn: Studies in the Structure of Poetry*. Harcourt, 1975.

Emerson, Ralph Waldo. "Self-Reliance." *The Norton Anthology of American Literature*, edited by Robert S. Levine et al., 9th ed., vol. B, W. W. Norton, 2017, pp. 236–53.

Frost, Robert. "The Road Not Taken." *Poetry Foundation,* https://www.poetryfoundation.org/poems/44272/the-road-not-taken. Accessed 8 Nov. 2016.

Kammen, Michael G. *A Time to Every Purpose: The Four Seasons in American Culture*. U of North Carolina P, 2004.

Robinson, Katherine. "Robert Frost: 'The Road Not Taken.'" *Poetry Foundation, 27 May 2016,* https://www.poetryfoundation.org/articles/89511/robert-frost-the-road-not-taken. Accessed 8 Nov. 2016.

Miller focuses his analysis on "tricky" aspects of Frost's poem. In addition, he uses aspects of Frost's biography and letters to resolve some of the seeming contradictions and tensions in the poem.

Key Features / Literary Analyses

An arguable thesis. A literary analysis is a form of argument; you are arguing that your analysis of a literary work is valid. Your thesis, then, should be arguable, as Miller's is: "To truly recognize what Frost is building in this poem, a few nagging inconsistencies must be considered." A mere summary— "Frost writes about someone trying to decide which road to take"—would not be arguable and therefore is not a good thesis.

Careful attention to the language of the text. The key to analyzing a text is looking carefully at the language, which is the foundation of its meaning. Specific words, images, metaphors—these are where analysis begins. You may also bring in contextual information, such as cultural, historical, or biographical facts, or you may refer to similar texts. But the words, phrases, and sentences that make up the text you are analyzing are your primary source when dealing with texts. That's what literature teachers mean by "close reading": reading with the assumption that every word of a text is meaningful.

Attention to patterns or themes. Literary analyses are usually built on evidence of meaningful patterns or themes within a text or among several texts. These patterns and themes reveal meaning. In Frost's poem, images of diverging roads and yellow leaves create patterns of meaning, while the regular rhyme scheme (*wood/stood/could, both/undergrowth*) creates patterns of sound and structure that may contribute to the overall meaning.

A clear interpretation. A literary analysis demonstrates the plausibility of its thesis by using evidence from the text and, sometimes, relevant

academic literacies
rhetorical situations
genres
fields
processes
strategies
research MLA / APA
media / design

contextual evidence to explain how the language and patterns found there support a particular interpretation. When you write a literary analysis, you show readers one way the text may be read and understood; that is your interpretation.

MLA style. Literary analyses usually follow MLA style. Miller's essay includes a works-cited list and refers to line numbers using MLA style.

A BRIEF GUIDE TO WRITING LITERARY ANALYSES

Considering the Rhetorical Situation

PURPOSE	What do you need to do? Show that you have examined the text carefully? Offer your own interpretation? Demonstrate a particular analytical technique? Or some combination? If you're responding to an assignment, does it specify what you need to do?	55–56
AUDIENCE	What do you need to do to convince your readers that your interpretation is plausible and based on sound analysis? Can you assume that readers are already familiar with the text you are analyzing, or do you need to tell them about it?	57–60
STANCE	How can you see your subject through interested, curious eyes—and then step back in order to see what your observations might *mean*?	66–68
MEDIA/DESIGN	Will your analysis focus on an essentially verbal text or one that has significant visual content, such as a graphic novel? Will you need to show visual elements in your analysis? Will it be delivered in a print, spoken, or electronic medium? Are you required to follow MLA or some other style?	69–71

Generating Ideas and Text

Look at your assignment. Does it specify a particular kind of analysis? Does it ask you to consider a particular theme? To use any specific critical approaches? Look for any terms that tell you what to do, words like *analyze*, *compare*, *interpret*, and so on.

Study the text with a critical eye. When we read a literary work, we often come away with a reaction to it: we like it, we hate it, it made us cry or laugh, it perplexed us. That may be a good starting point for a literary analysis, but to write about literature you need to go beyond initial reactions, to think about **HOW THE TEXT WORKS**: What does it *say*, and what does it *do*? What elements make up this text? How do those elements work together or fail to work together? Does this text lead you to think or feel a certain way? How does it fit into a particular context (of history, culture, technology, genre, and so on)?

21–23 ✳

Choose a method for analyzing the text. There are various ways to analyze your subject. Three common focuses are on the text itself, on your own experience reading it, and on other cultural, historical, or literary contexts.

432–42 ◆
443–51 ◆
462–70

- *The text itself.* Trace the development and expression of themes, characters, and language through the work. How do they help to create the overall meaning, tone, or effect for which you're arguing? To do this, you might look at the text as a whole, something you can understand from all angles at once. You could also pick out parts from the beginning, middle, and end as needed to make your case, **DEFINING** key terms, **DESCRIBING** characters and settings, and **NARRATING** key scenes. Miller's essay about "The Road Not Taken" offers a text-based analysis that looks at Frost's treatment of time in the poem. You might also examine the same theme in several different works.

- *Your own response as a reader.* Explore the way the text affects you or develops meanings as you read through it from beginning to end. By doing such a close reading, you're slowing down the process to notice how one element of the text leads you to expect something, confirming earlier suspicions or surprises. You build your analysis on your experience of reading the text—as if you were pretending to drive somewhere for the first time, though in reality you know the way intimately. By closely examining the language of the text as you experience it, you explore how it leads you to a set of responses, both intellectual and emotional. If you were responding in this way to the Frost poem, you might discuss how the narrator keeps trying to assert that one road is preferable to another but admits that both are the same, so that his willful assertion that one is "less traveled by" and that his choice "made all the difference" is no difference at all.

- *Context*. Analyze the text as part of some **LARGER CONTEXT**—as part ◆ 427
of a certain time or place in history or as an expression of a certain culture (how does this text relate to the time and place of its creation?), as one of many other texts like it, a representative of a genre (how is this text like or unlike others of its kind? how does it use, play with, or flout the conventions of the genre?). A context-based approach to the Frost poem might look at Frost's friendship with another poet, Edward Thomas, for whom Frost wrote the poem, and its influence on Thomas's decision to enlist in the army at the start of World War I.

Read the work more than once. Reading literature, watching films, or listening to speeches is like driving to a new destination: the first time you go, you need to concentrate on getting there; on subsequent trips, you can see other aspects—the scenery, the curve of the road, other possible routes—that you couldn't pay attention to earlier. When you experience a piece of literature for the first time, you usually focus on the story, the plot, the overall meaning. By experiencing it repeatedly, you can see how its effects are achieved, what the pieces are and how they fit together, where different patterns emerge, how the author crafted the work.

To analyze a literary work, then, plan to read it more than once, with the assumption that every part of the text is there for a reason. Focus on details, even on a single detail that shows up more than once: Why is it there? What can it mean? How does it affect our experience of reading or studying the text? Also, look for anomalies, details that *don't* fit the patterns: Why are they part of the text? What can they mean? How do they affect the experience of the text? See the **READING IN ACADEMIC CONTEXTS** chapter for several different methods for reading a text.

10–32 ✳

387–89 ◆

Compose a strong thesis. The **THESIS** of a literary analysis should be specific, limited, and open to potential disagreement. In addition, it should be analytical, not evaluative: avoid thesis statements that make overall judgments, such as a reviewer might do: "Virginia Woolf's *The Waves* is a failed experiment in narrative" or "No one has equaled the achievement of *The Lego Movie*." Rather, offer a way of seeing the text: "The choice presented in Robert Frost's 'The Road Not Taken' ultimately makes no difference"; "The plot of *The Lego Movie* reflects contemporary American media culture."

Read the text carefully. When you analyze a text, you need to find specific, brief passages that support your interpretation. Then you should interpret those passages in terms of their language, their context, or your reaction to them as a reader. To find such passages, you must read the text closely, questioning it as you go, asking, for example:

- What language provides evidence to support your thesis?
- What does each word (phrase, passage) mean exactly?
- Why does the writer choose *this* language, *these* words? What are the implications or connotations of the language? If the language is dense or difficult, why might the writer have written it that way?
- What images or metaphors are used? What is their effect on the meaning?
- What patterns of language, imagery, or plot do you see? If something is repeated, what significance does the repetition have?
- How does each word, phrase, or passage relate to what precedes and follows it?
- How does the experience of reading the text affect its meaning?

academic literacies | rhetorical situations | genres | fields | processes | strategies | research MLA / APA | media / design

- What words, phrases, or passages connect to a larger **CONTEXT**? What language demonstrates that this work reflects or is affected by that context?

  ✳ 10–32

- How do these various elements of language, image, and pattern support your interpretation?

Your analysis should focus on analyzing and interpreting your subject, not simply summarizing or paraphrasing it. Many literary analyses also use the strategy of **COMPARING** two or more works.

◆ 424–31

Find evidence to support your interpretation. The parts of the text you examine in your close reading become the evidence you use to support your interpretation. Some think that we're all entitled to our own opinions about literature. And indeed we are. But when writing a literary analysis, we're entitled only to our own *well-supported* and *well-argued* opinions. When you analyze a text, you must treat it like any other **ARGUMENT**: you need to discuss how the text creates an effect or expresses a theme, and then you have to show **EVIDENCE** from the text—significant plot or structural elements; important characters; patterns of language, imagery, or action—to back up your argument.

◆ 397–417

◆ 401–8

Pay attention to matters of style. Literary analyses have certain conventions for using pronouns and verbs.

- In informal papers, it's okay to use the first person: "I believe Frost's narrator has little basis for claiming that one road is 'less traveled.'" In more formal essays, make assertions directly; claim authority to make statements about the text: "Frost's narrator has no basis for claiming that one road is 'less traveled.'"

- Discuss textual features in the present tense even if quotations from the text are in another tense: "When Nick finds Gatsby's body floating in the pool, he says very little about it: 'the laden mattress moved irregularly down the pool.'" Describe the historical context of the setting in the past tense: "In the 1920s, such estates as Gatsby's were rare."

MLA 548–96 ●
528–31
535–38

Cite and document sources appropriately. Use **MLA** citation and documentation style unless told otherwise. Format **QUOTATIONS** properly, and use **SIGNAL PHRASES** to introduce quoted material.

650–52 ☐
391 ◆

Think about format and design. Brief essays do not require **HEADINGS**; text divisions are usually marked by **TRANSITIONS** between paragraphs. In longer papers, though, headings can be helpful.

Organizing a Literary Analysis

[Of a single text]

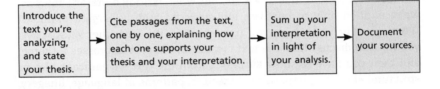

Introduce the text you're analyzing, and state your thesis. → Cite passages from the text, one by one, explaining how each one supports your thesis and your interpretation. → Sum up your interpretation in light of your analysis. → Document your sources.

[Comparing two texts]

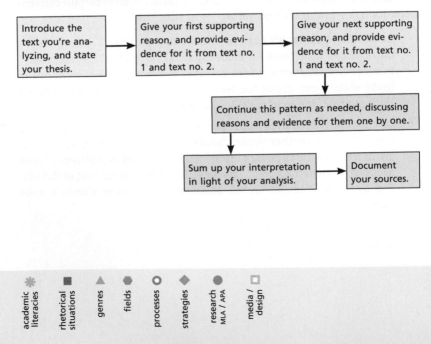

Introduce the text you're analyzing, and state your thesis. → Give your first supporting reason, and provide evidence for it from text no. 1 and text no. 2. → Give your next supporting reason, and provide evidence for it from text no. 1 and text no. 2.

↓

Continue this pattern as needed, discussing reasons and evidence for them one by one.

↓

Sum up your interpretation in light of your analysis. → Document your sources.

※ academic literacies
■ rhetorical situations
▲ genres
● fields
○ processes
◆ strategies
● research MLA / APA
☐ media / design

Taking Stock of Your Work

Take stock of what you've written by writing out answers to these questions:

- How did you go about analyzing the text? Which method did you use? Why?

- Was your thesis specific and limited? Did it offer a way to see the text?

- Did you provide sufficient evidence from the text or its context to support your analysis?

- What did you do especially well? What could still be improved?

- How did other readers' responses influence your writing?

- What would you do differently next time?

- Are you pleased with your analysis? What did it teach you about the text you analyzed? Did it make you want to study more works by the same author?

IF YOU NEED MORE HELP

See Chapter 30 for guidelines on **DRAFTING**, Chapter 31 on **ASSESSING YOUR OWN WRITING**, Chapter 32 on **GETTING RESPONSE AND REVISING**, and Chapter 33 on **EDITING AND PROOFREADING**. See Chapter 34 if you are required to submit your analysis in a writing **PORTFOLIO**.

340–42
343–47
348–55
356–60
361–70

18 Memoirs

We write memoirs to explore our past—about shopping for a party dress with Grandma, or driving a car for the first time, or breaking up with our first love. Memoirs focus on events and people and places that are important to us. We usually have two goals when we write a memoir: to capture an important moment and to convey something about its significance for us. You may be asked to write memoirs or personal reflections that include memoirs in *psychology*, *education*, and *English* courses. The following example is from Pulitzer Prize–winning journalist Rick Bragg's autobiography, *All Over but the Shoutin'*. Bragg grew up in Alabama, and in this memoir he recalls when, as a teenager, he paid a final visit to his dying father.

RICK BRAGG

All Over but the Shoutin'

He was living in a little house in Jacksonville, Alabama, a college and mill town that was the closest urban center—with its stoplights and a high school and two supermarkets—to the country roads we roamed in our raggedy cars. He lived in the mill village, in one of those houses the mills subsidized for their workers, back when companies still did things like that. It was not much of a place, but better than anything we had ever lived in as a family. I knocked and a voice like an old woman's, punctuated with a cough that sounded like it came from deep in the guts, told me to come on in, it ain't locked.

It was dark inside, but light enough to see what looked like a bundle of quilts on the corner of a sofa. Deep inside them was a ghost of a man, his hair and beard long and going dirty gray, his face pale and cut with deep grooves. I knew I was in the right house because my daddy's only

academic literacies
rhetorical situations
genres
fields
processes
strategies
research MLA / APA
media / design

real possessions, a velvet-covered board pinned with medals, sat inside a glass cabinet on a table. But this couldn't be him.

He coughed again, spit into a can and struggled to his feet, but stopped somewhere short of standing straight up, as if a stoop was all he could manage. "Hey, Cotton Top," he said, and then I knew. My daddy, who was supposed to be a still-young man, looked like the walking dead, not just old but damaged, poisoned, used up, crumpled up and thrown in a corner to die. I thought that the man I would see would be the trim, swaggering, high-toned little rooster of a man who stared back at me from the pages of my mother's photo album, the young soldier clowning around in Korea, the arrow-straight, good-looking boy who posed beside my mother back before the fields and mop handle and the rest of it took her looks. The man I remembered had always dressed nice even when there was no cornmeal left, whose black hair always shone with oil, whose chin, even when it wobbled from the beer, was always angled up, high.

I thought he would greet me with that strong voice that sounded so fine when he laughed and so evil when, slurred by a quart of corn likker, he whirled through the house and cried and shrieked, tormented by things we could not see or even imagine. I thought he would be the man and monster of my childhood. But that man was as dead as a man could be, and this was what remained, like when a snake sheds its skin and leaves a dry and brittle husk of itself hanging in the Johnson grass.

"It's all over but the shoutin' now, ain't it, boy," he said, and when 5 he let the quilt slide from his shoulders I saw how he had wasted away, how the bones seemed to poke out of his clothes, and I could see how it killed his pride to look this way, unclean, and he looked away from me for a moment, ashamed.

He made a halfhearted try to shake my hand but had a coughing fit again that lasted a minute, coughing up his life, his lungs, and after that I did not want to touch him. I stared at the tops of my sneakers, ashamed to look at his face. He had a dark streak in his beard below his lip, and I wondered why, because he had never liked snuff. Now I know it was blood.

I remember much of what he had to say that day. When you don't see someone for eight, nine years, when you see that person's life red on their lips and know that you will never see them beyond this day, you listen close, even if what you want most of all is to run away.

"Your momma, she alright?" he said.

I said I reckon so.

"The other boys? They alright?"

I said I reckon so.

10

Then he was quiet for a minute, as if trying to find the words to a question to which he did not really want an answer.

"They ain't never come to see me. How come?"

I remember thinking, fool, why do you think? But I just choked down my words, and in doing so I gave up the only real chance I would ever have to accuse him, to attack him with the facts of his own sorry nature and the price it had cost us all. The opportunity hung perfectly still in the air in front of my face and fists, and I held my temper and let it float on by. I could have no more challenged him, berated him, hurt him, than I could have kicked some three-legged dog. Life had kicked his ass pretty good.

"How come?"

15

I just shrugged.

For the next few hours—unless I was mistaken, having never had one before—he tried to be my father. Between coughing and long pauses when he fought for air to generate his words, he asked me if I liked school, if I had ever gotten any better at math, the one thing that just flat evaded me. He asked me if I ever got even with the boy who blacked my eye ten years ago, and nodded his head, approvingly, as I described how I followed him into the boys' bathroom and knocked his dick string up to his watch pocket, and would have dunked his head in the urinal if the aging principal, Mr. Hand, had not had to pee and caught me dragging him across the concrete floor.

He asked me about basketball and baseball, said he had heard I had a good game against Cedar Springs, and I said pretty good, but it was two years ago, anyway. He asked if I had a girlfriend and I said, "One," and he said, "Just one?" For the slimmest of seconds he almost grinned and the young, swaggering man peeked through, but disappeared again in the disease that cloaked him. He talked and talked and never said a word, at least not the words I wanted.

He never said he was sorry.

He never said he wished things had turned out different.

20

He never acted like he did anything wrong.

Part of it, I know, was culture. Men did not talk about their

academic literacies

rhetorical situations

genres

fields

processes

strategies

research MLA / APA

media / design

feelings in his hard world. I did not expect, even for a second, that he would bare his soul. All I wanted was a simple acknowledgment that he was wrong, or at least too drunk to notice that he left his pretty wife and sons alone again and again, with no food, no money, no way to get any, short of begging, because when she tried to find work he yelled, screamed, refused. No, I didn't expect much.

After a while he motioned for me to follow him into a back room where he had my present, and I planned to take it and run. He handed me a long, thin box, and inside was a brand-new, well-oiled Remington .22 rifle. He said he had bought it some time back, just kept forgetting to give it to me. It was a fine gun, and for a moment we were just like anybody else in the culture of that place, where a father's gift of a gun to his son is a rite. He said, with absolute seriousness, not to shoot my brothers.

I thanked him and made to leave, but he stopped me with a hand on my arm and said wait, that ain't all, that he had some other things for me. He motioned to three big cardboard egg cartons stacked against one wall.

Inside was the only treasure I truly have ever known.   25

I had grown up in a house in which there were only two books, the King James Bible and the spring seed catalog. But here, in these boxes, were dozens of hardback copies of everything from Mark Twain to Sir Arthur Conan Doyle. There was a water-damaged Faulkner, and the nearly complete set of Edgar Rice Burroughs's *Tarzan*. There was poetry and trash, Zane Grey's *Riders of the Purple Sage,* and a paperback with two naked women on the cover. There was a tiny, old copy of *Arabian Nights,* threadbare Hardy Boys, and one Hemingway. He had bought most of them at a yard sale, by the box or pound, and some at a flea market. He did not even know what he was giving me, did not recognize most of the writers. "Your momma said you still liked to read," he said.

There was Shakespeare. My father did not know who he was, exactly, but he had heard the name. He wanted them because they were pretty, because they were wrapped in fake leather, because they looked like rich folks' books. I do not love Shakespeare, but I still have those books. I would not trade them for a gold monkey.

"They's maybe some dirty books in there, by mistake, but I know you ain't interested in them, so just throw 'em away," he said. "Or at

least, throw 'em away before your momma sees 'em." And then I swear
to God he winked.

I guess my heart should have broken then, and maybe it did, a
little. I guess I should have done something, anything, besides mumble "Thank you, Daddy." I guess that would have been fine, would
not have betrayed in some way my mother, my brothers, myself. But
I just stood there, trapped somewhere between my long-standing,
comfortable hatred, and what might have been forgiveness. I am
trapped there still.

*Bragg's memoir illustrates all the features that make a memoir good: how the
son and father react to each other creates the kind of suspense that keeps us
reading; vivid details and rich dialogue bring the scene to life. His later reflections make the significance of that final meeting very clear.*

Key Features / Memoirs

A good story. Your memoir should be interesting, to yourself and others.
It need not be about a world-shaking event, but your topic—and how you
write about it—should interest your readers. At the center of most good
stories stands a conflict or question to be resolved. The most compelling
memoirs feature some sort of situation or problem that needs resolution.
That need for resolution is another name for suspense. It's what makes
us want to keep reading.

Vivid details. Details bring a memoir to life by giving readers mental
images of the sights, sounds, smells, tastes, and textures of the world in
which your story takes place. The goal is to show as well as tell, to take
readers there. When Bragg describes a "voice like an old woman's, punctuated with a cough that sounded like it came from deep in the guts," we can
hear his dying father ourselves. A memoir is more than simply a report of
what happened; it uses vivid details and dialogue to bring the events of
the past to life, much as good fiction brings to life events that the writer
makes up or embellishes. Depending on your topic and medium, you may
want to provide some of the details in audio or visual form.

Clear significance. Memories of the past are filtered through our view from the present: we pick out some moments in our lives as significant, some as more important or vivid than others. Over time, our interpretations change, and our memories themselves change.

A good memoir conveys something about the significance of its subject. As a writer, you need to reveal something about what the incident means to you. You don't, however, want to simply announce the significance as if you're tacking on the moral of the story. Bragg tells us that he's "trapped between [his] long-standing, comfortable hatred, and what might have been forgiveness," but he doesn't come right out and say that's why the incident is so important to him.

A BRIEF GUIDE TO WRITING MEMOIRS

Choosing an Event to Write About

LIST several events or incidents from your past that you consider significant in some way. They do not have to be earthshaking; indeed, they may involve a quiet moment that only you see as important—a brief encounter with a remarkable person, a visit to a special place, a memorable achievement (or failure), something that makes you laugh whenever you think about it. Writing about events that happened at least a few years ago is often easier than writing about recent events because you can more easily step back and see those events with a clear perspective. To choose the event that you will write about, consider how well you can recall what happened, how interesting it will be to readers, and whether you want to share it with an audience.

332–33

Considering the Rhetorical Situation

PURPOSE   What is the importance of the memory you are trying to convey? How will this story help you understand yourself and your readers understand you, as you were then and as you are now?

55–56

57–60 ■ **AUDIENCE**   Who are your readers? Why will they care about your memoir? What do you want them to think of you after reading it? How can you help them understand your experience?

66–68 ■ **STANCE**   What impression do you want to give, and how can your words contribute to that impression? What tone do you want to project? Sincere? Serious? Humorous? Detached? Self-critical?

69–71 ■ **MEDIA / DESIGN**   Will your memoir be a print document? A speech? Will it be posted on a website? Can you include photographs, audio or video clips, or other visual texts?

Generating Ideas and Text

Think about what happened.   Take a few minutes to write out an account of the incident: **WHAT** happened, **WHERE** it took place, **WHO** else was 334–35 ○ involved, what was said, how you feel about it, and so on. Can you identify any tension or conflict that will make for a compelling story? If not, you might want to rethink your topic.

Consider its significance.   Why do you still remember this event? What effect has it had on your life? What makes you want to tell someone else about it? Does it say anything about you? What about it might interest someone else? If you have trouble answering these questions, you should probably find another topic. But in general, once you have defined the significance of the incident, you can be sure you have a story to tell—and a reason for telling it.

Think about the details.   The best memoirs connect with readers by giving them a sense of what it was like to be there, leading them to experience in words and images what the writer experienced in life. Spend some time 443–51 ◆ **DESCRIBING** the incident, writing what you see, hear, smell, touch, and taste when you envision it. Do you have any photos or memorabilia or other **VISUAL** materials you might include in your memoir? Try writing out **DIALOGUE**, things that were said (or, if you can't recall exactly, things that might have been said). Look at what you come up with—is there detail enough to bring the scene to life? Anything that might be called vivid? If you don't have enough detail, you might reconsider whether you recall enough about the incident to write about it. If you have trouble coming up with plenty of detail, try **FREEWRITING**, **LISTING**, or **LOOPING**.

☐ 653–63

◆ 452–56

◯ 331–33

Ways of Organizing Memoirs

[Tell about the event from beginning to end]

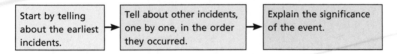

Start by telling about the earliest incidents. → Tell about other incidents, one by one, in the order they occurred. → Explain the significance of the event.

[Start at the end and tell how the event came about]

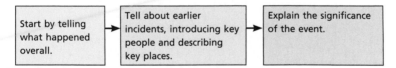

Start by telling what happened overall. → Tell about earlier incidents, introducing key people and describing key places. → Explain the significance of the event.

Taking Stock of Your Work

Take stock of what you've written by writing out answers to these questions:

- How well do you think you told the story?

- How did you go about coming up with ideas and generating text?

- How did you go about drafting your narrative?

- Did you use photographs or any other visual or audio elements? What did they add? Can you think of such elements you might have used?

- How did others' responses influence your writing?

- What did you do especially well? What could be improved? What would you do differently next time?

340–42
343–47
348–55
356–60
361–70

IF YOU NEED MORE HELP

See Chapter 30 for guidelines on **DRAFTING**, Chapter 31 on **ASSESSING YOUR OWN WRITING**, Chapter 32 on **GETTING RESPONSE AND REVISING**, and Chapter 33 on **EDITING AND PROOFREADING**. See Chapter 34 if you are required to submit your memoir in a writing **PORTFOLIO**.

academic literacies · rhetorical situations · genres · fields · processes · strategies · research MLA / APA · media / design

Profiles

Profiles are written portraits—of people, places, events, or other things. We find profiles of celebrities, travel destinations, and offbeat festivals in magazines and newspapers, on radio and TV. A profile presents a subject in an entertaining way that conveys its significance, showing us something or someone that we may not have known existed or that we see every day but don't know much about. In college *journalism* classes, students learn to create profiles using words and, in many cases, photos and video as well. Here is a profile of a common, everyday object: the drinking straw. The writer, Ernie Smith, is a social media journalist, blogger, and founder of the *Tedium* newsletter, where a version of this essay originally appeared. It was revised and reposted on *Atlas Obscura*, an online news site.

ERNIE SMITH

A Brief History of the Modern-Day Straw, the World's Most Wasteful Commodity

The plastic straw is a simple invention with relatively modest value: For a few moments, the device helps make beverages easier to drink. And then, due to reasons of sanitation and ease of use, the straws are thrown away, never to be seen again.

Except, of course, the straw you use in your iced coffee doesn't biodegrade, and stays around basically forever, often as ocean junk. That, understandably, is leading to chatter around banning plastic straws—notably in Berkeley, California, often the first place to ban anything potentially damaging to the environment.

And while the rest of the world won't be banning straws anytime soon, maybe they should start thinking about it, because the problem

with straws is one of scale. According to *National Geographic*, Americans use *500 million* straws every single day—more than one per person daily.

The resulting waste is difficult to recycle and often shows up in landfills, at sea, and on the beach; the plastic is particularly dangerous for marine wildlife.

But it wasn't always this way. The modern day-straw was an 5 attempt to solve the failings of a device that was very much biodegradable. And that replacement was itself biodegradable. The problem, really, is what came after.

Marvin Stone, perhaps more than any other person, deserves credit for making artificial straws useful and popular. But he doesn't deserve the blame for what straws have become.

Stone was a serial inventor who was known for manufacturing a variety of products with a cylinder shape, such as cigarette holders. Born in Ohio in 1842, but based in Washington, D.C., for much of his life, he launched his career as a journalist, but eventually followed his father's inventive spirit into the realm of manufacturing. Being a D.C. resident, he was a big fan of mint juleps, a drink popularized in the city during the 19th century by famed Kentucky Senator Henry Clay. Stone would order the drinks at Aman's, a well-known restaurant in D.C. during the era—though he was disappointed by the rye straws, which had a negative effect on his drink.

Yes, that's right, before plastic straws, we used straws made of rye grass—produced naturally, from the ground. The manufacturing process, according to a *The Small Grains*, a book by Mark Alfred Carleton, was closer to wheat than plastic.

"After bleaching, the straws are assorted by hand, each individual stalk being examined, and the imperfect ones removed," Carleton explained. "They are then cut, the five lower joints only being utilized for drinking purposes. The sheaths are then removed, and the straw washed and bound into bundles ready for the market."

The rye straw, while the first widely used variety of drinking straw, had some significant problems—including that the straws affected the taste of the drink and that they had a tendency to disintegrate into the beverage, leaving sediment at the bottom of the drink.

Stone was just the guy to fix the problem. He was already making cigarette holders at his nearby factory, and had recently patented a fountain pen holder, so he knew a thing or two about building cylinder-shaped objects. So he wrapped a sheet of paper around a pencil, added some glue, and suddenly he had invented the paper straw. He gave his initial supply to Aman's for his own personal use, but found

that people he ran into at the bar were impressed enough with his invention that they wanted their own. That led Stone to patent the device, and within a few years, he had cornered the market on paper straws, which became popular with the rise of soda fountains at pharmacies.

According to a 1889 article from *The Lafayette Advertiser*, Stone's factory was producing 2 million straws per day not long after he filed for that patent. And when he died in 1899, Stone was well-regarded in obituaries.

"Although few pharmacists have had the pleasure of personally meeting Mr. Stone, his name is, nevertheless, known wherever there is a soda fountain," the pharmacy trade publication *The Spatula* wrote at the time.

But the straws had a problem—simply, they weren't as durable as plastic, and while they didn't negatively affect the taste of the soda like rye straws did, they did eventually disintegrate in the beverages. By the 1960s, plastic straws, which initially carried a sense of novelty for the public because they could be made clear, had usurped the paper version entirely.

Good for plastic. Bad for the environment.   15

In 2017, we're perhaps more aware than ever of the weaknesses of the plastic straw, bendable or not. And more than one entrepreneur has tried to create new alternatives that solve the problems of both paper and plastic.

Many of these straw varieties rely on permanence over disposability and biodegradability, which means you'll be carrying a straw around with you—no matter how weird that seems.

Perhaps the most intriguing natural option for straw drinking is the bamboo straw. The company Brush With Bamboo, which makes a bamboo-based toothbrush (and sports support from Ed Begley Jr. on its website), also sells a set of bamboo drinking straws, which are handmade in India and designed to be reused for many years. As a result, the company sells a 12-pack of bamboo straws for $20—or more than a dollar a straw.

Other materials, like metal, have also become common straw vectors. And more than one small-scale manufacturer, like the Michigan company Strawesome, has tried selling straws made from glass. (That said, neither of these straws sound good for your teeth.)

On the disposable front, the primary alternative that's revealed 20 itself is corn, which has perhaps gotten the closest in terms of disposability and flexibility. Eco-Products, a Certified B Corporation, sells plastic materials to stores and other retailers made from Ingeo, a biopolymer often produced from corn that's compostable and renewable.

While not horribly cheap compared to standard plastic straws—they sell for about a quarter a pop in small quantities—Eco-Products' compostable straws are a lot better for the environment.

And hey, if you can't beat 'em, eat 'em—the straws that is. Starbucks earned a whole lot of buzz a couple years ago after it started selling cookie straws to go with its Frappuccinos, and it's not a phenomenon that's completely unheard of—candy straws and beef straws are things that exist. But perhaps the most natural approach to edible straw-making might be ice straws. Just make sure you don't want a refill.

All these alternative materials are great—but the concerns about plastic have brought long-dormant paper straws back from the brink.

And you can thank an eccentric billionaire for that.

A couple years ago, I called Ted Turner "the Steve Jobs of television," as well as a "genius," and emphasized I was not being hyperbolic by making this claim—because what he did for television in the '70s was genuinely groundbreaking. 25

Now, while Turner no longer has the level of influence and power he once did—he no longer owns Turner Broadcasting (which he regrets), and he literally gave a billion dollars to the United Nations in 1997, which probably did a number on his checkbook—he does own a lot of land, and that land contains a lot of bison. And that means that he's well suited for being a restaurant entrepreneur.

Ted's Montana Grill, a chain he started in 2002, is quietly an environmental maverick—the entire chain was built around the idea of ensuring the bison would stick around for generations to come by building business value around the animal. Despite the fact you're eating bison, it's actually hugely beneficial for the species' long-term survival because there's a business case for investing in ranching bison. But beyond that, Turner and his business partner George McKerrow Jr. saw an opportunity to build an eco-friendly legacy even greater than that of *Captain Planet*.

And the straw is kind of the key element of the whole thing. In a 2011 interview with the podcast and news site *Southeast Green*, McKerrow (who is also known for starting the LongHorn Steakhouse and Capital Grille chains) explained how he helped bring the paper straw back to life as a tool of environmentalism—and how it was one of the biggest challenges he faced in his efforts to minimize the amount of plastic used by the chain.

"I remember growing up with a paper straw," McKerrow explained in an interview with the podcast's Beth Bond. "It collapsed a lot, but heck, it was better for the environment than a plastic straw, which might be in a landfill for a hundred-plus years, or for eternity."

McKerrow looked online for info and soon found himself on   30
the phone with the owner of Precision Products Group—the parent
company of Paramount Tube, the direct descendant of Stone's manufacturing company. McKerrow noted that paper straws hadn't been
manufactured anywhere since 1970, but that the firm was willing to pay
top-dollar to get those straws. Precision had the equipment around, but
it had fallen into disuse. But inspired by the phone call, the company
pledged to check to see what was possible.

"About two weeks later, he got back to me, and he said, 'We
found that machine,' and I could hear it in his voice that he was really
excited," McKerrow continued. "He said, 'The engineers think that they
can make it work.' "

And they did. Ted's Montana Grill became the first company to
use paper straws in more than 30 years, but the quality issues with the
straws—made from paper and coated in beeswax—were still apparent, leading to customer complaints. Initially, McKerrow relented for a
time, letting plastic into the cups at the restaurant, but eventually, he
got a hold of Precision again, only to find that the phone call a couple
years prior had led the firm to shift its entire corporate direction.

Precision, seeing a market need for eco-friendly straws, launched
a brand-new subsidiary, Aardvark, to bring their paper straws back to
the market.

"The story goes, we recreated a whole industry, something that
was old became new again, something that was better for the environment by at least 50 percent," McKerrow added.

They aren't cheap—at 1.5 cents each, the cost is far above the   35
commodity price of standard plastic straws. But in some ways, the extra
cost on the front end means it's a whole lot cheaper for the environment.

Like most people, I drink a lot of beverages on an average day,
often out of cups, sometimes with straws. There's something strangely
appealing about the basic disposability of cups that you don't have
to carry around everywhere. We live in a disposable culture and we
probably throw away more disposable cups than anything else.

But there are consequences to that disposability. In 2015, a sea
turtle became the face of a budding anti-straw movement after a gruesome video of that turtle getting a straw removed from its nose drew
millions of views online. (Aardvark launched a new bendy straw, with
sea turtle art, directly inspired by the story.)

That video is one of a few reasons why we're starting to see campaigns to cut back on straw usage pick up in a big way. It's easy fodder for corporate responsibility campaigns—Bacardi, a company that has probably benefited more than most from the existence of straws, started one last year—and multiple nonprofit campaigns have coalesced around the issue, including The Last Plastic Straw and One Less Straw.

Which doesn't mean we have to ban straws to stop them from polluting the environment, but there is a reason to discuss changing habits. How much harder is it to drink your coffee out of a cup that you bring with you? If you end up using a straw, is there a way to get just a little bit more mileage out of that piece of plastic? And if the issue matters to you, does that affect the places you go to buy things? (And no, this isn't a commercial for Ted Turner's restaurant chain.)

The problem with straws are that they're so insignificant that we take them for granted. Perhaps we shouldn't. 40

Smith's profile examines the environmental impacts of a common household and restaurant object, the plastic drinking straw. The writer engages our interest first with the title, which claims that straws, seemingly inconsequential, are "the world's most wasteful commodity." He then provides a history of the drinking straw, alternatives to plastic straws, and a tale of the reemergence of the paper straw.

Key Features / Profiles

An interesting subject.   The subject may be something unusual, or it may be something ordinary shown in an intriguing way. You might profile an interesting person (like billionaire Ted Turner), a place (like the company that makes paper straws), an event (like the rescue of the sea turtle), or an object (like the drinking straw).

Any necessary background.   A profile usually includes just enough information to let readers know something about the subject's larger context. Smith quickly explains the problems with plastic straws: there are billions of them, they don't degrade, and they're hard to recycle, making them dangerous to wildlife, but leaves out other details about straws that don't matter for this profile.

An interesting angle. A good profile captures its subject from a particular angle. Sometimes finding an angle will be fairly easy because your topic—like the history of the drinking straw—is offbeat enough to be interesting in and of itself. Other topics, though, may require you to find a particular aspect that you can focus on. For example, a profile of a person might focus on the important work the person does or a challenging hobby they pursue; it would likely ignore aspects of the person's life that don't relate to that angle.

A firsthand account. Whether you are writing about a person, place, object, or event, you need to spend time observing and interacting with your subject. With a person, interacting means watching and conversing. Journalists tell us that "following the guy around," getting your subject to do something and talk about it at the same time, yields excellent material for a profile. When one writer met Theodor Geisel (Dr. Seuss) before profiling him, she asked him not only to talk about his characters but also to draw one—resulting in an illustration for her profile. With a place, object, or event, interacting may mean visiting and participating, although sometimes you may gather even more information by playing the role of the silent observer.

Engaging details. You need to include details that bring your subject to life. These may include *specific information* ("Americans use 500 million straws every single day—more than one per person daily"); *sensory images* ("[Rye] straws affected the taste of the drink and . . . had a tendency to disintegrate into the beverage, leaving sediment at the bottom of the drink"); *figurative language* (Giving a billion dollars to the UN "did a number on [Ted Turner's] checkbook"); *dialogue* ("He said, 'The engineers think that they can make it work'"); and *anecdotes* ("He wrapped a sheet of paper around a pencil, added some glue, and suddenly he had invented the paper straw"). Choose details that show rather than tell—that let your audience see and hear your subject rather than merely read an abstract description of it. Sometimes you may let them see and hear it literally, by including *photographs* or *video and audio clips*. And be sure all the details create some *dominant impression* of your subject: the impression that we get out of this profile, for example, is of a simple device that is more complicated and destructive than it seems.

A BRIEF GUIDE TO WRITING PROFILES

Choosing a Suitable Subject

A person, a place, an object, an event—whatever you choose, make sure it's something that arouses your curiosity and that you're not too familiar with. Knowing your subject too well can blind you to interesting details. **LIST** five to ten interesting subjects that you can experience firsthand. Obviously, you can't profile a person who won't be interviewed or a place or activity that can't be observed. So before you commit to a topic, make sure you'll be able to carry out firsthand research.

331–32

Considering the Rhetorical Situation

PURPOSE	Why are you writing the profile? What angle will best achieve your purpose? How can you inform *and engage* your audience?
AUDIENCE	Who is your audience? How familiar are they with your subject? What expectations of your profile might they have? What background information or definitions do you need to provide? How interested will they be—and how can you get their interest?

55–56

57–60

66–68 ■ **STANCE**   What view of your subject do you expect to present? Sympathetic? Critical? Sarcastic? Will you strive for a carefully balanced perspective?

69–71 ■ **MEDIA/DESIGN**   Will your profile be a print document? electronic? an oral presentation? Can (and should) you include images or any other visuals? Will it be recorded as an audio file or multimodal text?

Generating Ideas and Text

Explore what you already know about your subject.   Why do you find this subject interesting? What do you know about it now? What do you expect to find out about it from your research? What preconceived ideas about or emotional reactions to this subject do you have? Why do you have them? It may be helpful to try some of the activities in the chapter on 331–39 ○ **GENERATING IDEAS AND TEXT**.

Visit your subject.   If you're writing about an amusement park, go there; if you're profiling the man who runs the carousel, make an appointment to meet and interview him. Get to know your subject—if you profile Ben and Jerry, sample the ice cream! Take photos or videos if there's anything you might want to show visually in your profile. Find helpful hints for 506–8 ● **OBSERVING** and **INTERVIEWING** in the chapter on finding sources.

If you're planning to interview someone, prepare questions.   If Smith had interviewed manufacturers of alternatives to plastic straws, he might have asked questions like "How do you manufacture them?" and "If we're supposed to use them over and over again, how can we clean them?"

Do additional research.   You may be able to write a profile based entirely on your field research. You may, though, need to do some library or web 477 ● **RESEARCH** as well, to deepen your understanding, get a different perspective, or fill in gaps. Often the people you interview can help you find sources of additional information; so can the sponsors of events and those in charge of places. To learn more about a city park, for instance, contact the government office that maintains it. Download any good photos of your subject that you find online (such as the photos of straws and the soda fountain), both to refer to as you write and to illustrate your profile.

Analyze your findings. Look for patterns, images, recurring ideas or phrases, and engaging details. Look for contrasts or discrepancies: between a subject's words and actions, between the appearance of a place and what goes on there, between your expectations and your research findings. Smith probably expected plastic straws to be an environmental problem, but he may not have expected that problem to be as big as it is. You may find the advice in the **READING IN ACADEMIC CONTEXTS** chapter helpful here.

✳ 10–32

Come up with an angle. What's most memorable about your subject? What most interests you? What will interest your audience? Smith focuses on the environmental impact and usability of straws and alternatives to plastic straws. Sometimes you'll know your angle from the start; other times you'll need to look further into your topic. You might try **CLUSTERING**, **CUBING**, **FREEWRITING**, and **LOOPING**, to help you look at your topic from many different angles.

◯ 331–34

Note details that support your angle. Use your angle to focus your research and generate text. Try **DESCRIBING** your subject as clearly as you can, **COMPARING** your subject with other subjects of its sort, writing **DIALOGUE** that captures your subject. Smith, for instance, tells us how rye straws were manufactured and provides an intriguing look at how Ted Turner's desire for an eco-friendly restaurant chain led to the resurgence of the paper straw. Engaging details will bring your subject to life for your audience. Together, these details should create a dominant impression of your subject.

◆ 443–51
424–31
452–56

Ways of Organizing a Profile

462–70 One common way to organize a profile is by **NARRATING**. For example, if you are profiling a chess championship, you may write about it chronologically, creating suspense as you move from start to finish.

[As a narrative]

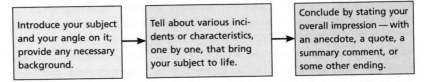

| Introduce your subject and your angle on it; provide any necessary background. | → | Tell about various incidents or characteristics, one by one, that bring your subject to life. | → | Conclude by stating your overall impression — with an anecdote, a quote, a summary comment, or some other ending. |

443–51 Sometimes you may organize a profile by **DESCRIBING** — a person or a place, for instance.

[As a description]

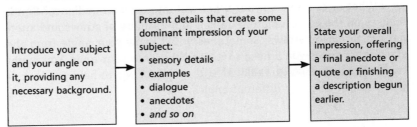

| Introduce your subject and your angle on it, providing any necessary background. | → | Present details that create some dominant impression of your subject: • sensory details • examples • dialogue • anecdotes • and so on | → | State your overall impression, offering a final anecdote or quote or finishing a description begun earlier. |

Taking Stock of Your Work

Take stock of what you've written by writing out answers to these questions:

- How did you go about choosing a subject—and an angle on that subject?
- How did you go about doing the necessary research? Did you encounter any difficulties?

academic literacies | rhetorical situations | genres | fields | processes | strategies | research MLA / APA | media / design

- How did you go about drafting your profile?
- Did you use photographs or any other visual or audio elements? What did they add? Can you think of such elements you might have used?
- How did others' responses influence your writing?
- What did you do especially well? What could still be improved? What would you do differently next time?

IF YOU NEED MORE HELP

See Chapter 30 for guidelines on **DRAFTING**, Chapter 31 on **ASSESSING YOUR OWN WRITING**, Chapter 32 on **GETTING RESPONSE AND REVISING**, and Chapter 33 on **EDITING AND PROOFREADING**. See Chapter 34 if you are required to submit your analysis in a writing **PORTFOLIO**.

340–42
343–47
348–55
356–60
361–70

20 Proposals

Proposals are part of our personal lives: lovers propose marriage, friends propose sharing dinner and a movie, you offer to pay half the cost of a car and insurance if your parents will pay the other half. They are also part of our academic and professional lives: student leaders lobby for lights on bike paths. Musicians, artists, writers, and educators apply for grants. Researchers in all fields of the humanities, social sciences, sciences, and technology seek funding for their projects. In business, contractors bid on building projects, and companies and freelancers solicit work from potential clients. These are all examples of proposals, ideas put forward for consideration that say, "Here is a solution to a problem" or "This is what ought to be done." For example, here is a proposal for reducing the costs of college textbooks, written by an accounting professor at the University of Texas who is chairman of the university's Co-op Bookstore and himself a textbook author.

MICHAEL GRANOF

Course Requirement: Extortion

By now, entering college students and their parents have been warned: textbooks are outrageously expensive. Few textbooks for semester-long courses retail for less than $120, and those for science and math courses typically approach $180. Contrast this with the $20 to $30 cost of most hardcover best sellers and other trade books.

Perhaps these students and their parents can take comfort in knowing that the federal government empathizes with them, and in an attempt to ease their pain Congress asked its Advisory Committee on Student Financial Assistance to suggest a cure for the problem.

246

academic literacies · rhetorical situations · genres · fields · processes · strategies · research MLA / APA · media / design

Unfortunately, though, the committee has proposed a remedy that would only worsen the problem.

The committee's report, released in May, mainly proposes strengthening the market for used textbooks—by encouraging college bookstores to guarantee that they will buy back textbooks, establishing online book swaps among students, and urging faculty to avoid switching textbooks from one semester to the next. The fatal flaw in that proposal (and similar ones made by many state legislatures) is that used books are the cause of, not the cure for, high textbook prices.

Yet there is a way to lighten the load for students in their budgets, if not their backpacks. With small modifications to the institutional arrangements between universities, publishers, and students, textbook costs could be reduced—and these changes could be made without government intervention.

Today the used-book market is exceedingly well organized and efficient. Campus bookstores buy back not only the books that will be used at their university the next semester but also those that will not. Those that are no longer on their lists of required books they resell to national wholesalers, which in turn sell them to college bookstores on campuses where they will be required. This means that even if a text is being adopted for the first time at a particular college, there is almost certain to be an ample supply of used copies.

As a result, publishers have the chance to sell a book to only one of the multiple students who eventually use it. Hence, publishers must cover their costs and make their profit in the first semester their books are sold—before used copies swamp the market. That's why the prices are so high.

As might be expected, publishers do what they can to undermine the used-book market, principally by coming out with new editions every three or four years. To be sure, in rapidly changing fields like biology and physics, the new editions may be academically defensible. But in areas like algebra and calculus, they are nothing more than a transparent attempt to ensure premature textbook obsolescence. Publishers also try to discourage students from buying used books by bundling the text with extra materials like workbooks and CDs that are not reusable and therefore cannot be passed from one student to another.

The system could be much improved if, first of all, colleges and publishers would acknowledge that textbooks are more akin to computer software than to trade books. A textbook's value, like that of a software program, is not in its physical form, but rather in its intellectual content. Therefore, just as software companies typically "site license" to colleges, so should textbook publishers.

Here's how it would work: A teacher would pick a textbook, and the college would pay a negotiated fee to the publisher based on the number of students enrolled in the class. If there were 50 students in the class, for example, the fee might be $15 per student, or $750 for the semester. If the text were used for ten semesters, the publisher would ultimately receive a total of $150 ($15 × 10) for each student enrolled in the course, or as much as $7,500.

In other words, the publisher would have a stream of revenue for as long as the text was in use. Presumably, the university would pass on this fee to the students, just as it does the cost of laboratory supplies and computer software. But the students would pay much less than the $900 a semester they now typically pay for textbooks.   10

Once the university had paid the license fee, each student would have the option of using the text in electronic format or paying more to purchase a hard copy through the usual channels. The publisher could set the price of hard copies low enough to cover only its production and distribution costs plus a small profit, because it would be covering most of its costs and making most of its profit by way of the license fees. The hard copies could then be resold to other students or back to the bookstore, but that would be of little concern to the publisher.

A further benefit of this approach is that it would not affect the way courses are taught. The same cannot be said for other recommendations from the Congressional committee and from state legislatures, like placing teaching materials on electronic reserve, urging faculty to adopt cheaper "no frills" textbooks, and assigning mainly electronic textbooks. While each of these suggestions may have merit, they force faculty to weigh students' academic interests against their fiscal concerns and encourage them to rely less on new textbooks.

Neither colleges nor publishers are known for their cutting-edge innovations. But if they could slightly change the way they do business, they would make a substantial dent in the cost of higher education and provide a real benefit to students and their parents.

This proposal clearly defines the problem—some textbooks cost a lot—and explains why. It proposes a solution to the problem of high textbook prices and offers reasons why this solution will work better than others. Its tone is reasonable and measured, yet decisive.

Key Features / Proposals

A well-defined problem.   Some problems are self-evident and relatively simple, and you would not need much persuasive power to make people act—as with the problem "This university discards too much paper." While some people might see nothing wrong with throwing paper away, most are likely to agree that recycling is a good thing. Other issues are controversial: some people see them as problems while others do not, such as this one: "Motorcycle riders who do not wear helmets risk serious injury and raise health-care costs for everyone." Some motorcyclists believe that wearing or not wearing a helmet should be a personal choice; you would have to present arguments to convince your readers that not wearing a helmet is indeed a problem needing a solution. Any written proposal must establish at the outset that there is a problem—and that it's serious enough to require a solution. For some topics, visual or audio evidence of the problem may be helpful.

A recommended solution.   Once you have defined the problem, you need to describe the solution you are suggesting and to explain it in enough detail for readers to understand what you are proposing. Again, photographs, diagrams, or other visuals may help. Sometimes you might suggest several solutions, weigh their merits, and choose the best one.

A convincing argument for your proposed solution.   You need to convince readers that your solution is feasible—and that it is the best way to solve the problem. Sometimes you'll want to explain in detail how your proposed solution would work. See, for example, how the textbook proposal details the way a licensing system would operate. Visuals may strengthen this part of your argument as well.

Granof's proposal for reducing textbook prices via licensing fees might benefit from a photograph like this one, which provides a comparison of other approaches to the problem, such as buying used books or renting them.

A response to anticipated questions. You may need to consider any questions readers may have about your proposal—and to show how its advantages outweigh any disadvantages. Had the textbook proposal been written for college budget officers, it would have needed to anticipate and answer questions about the costs of implementing the proposed solution.

A call to action. The goal of a proposal is to persuade readers to accept your proposed solution. This solution may include asking readers to take action.

An appropriate tone. Since you're trying to persuade readers to act, your tone is important—readers will always react better to a reasonable, respectful presentation than to anger or self-righteousness.

A BRIEF GUIDE TO WRITING PROPOSALS

Deciding on a Topic

Choose a problem that can be solved. Complex, large problems, such as poverty, hunger, or terrorism, usually require complex, large solutions. Most of the time, focusing on a smaller problem or a limited aspect of a large problem will yield a more manageable proposal. Rather than tackling the problem of world poverty, for example, think about the problem faced by people in your community who have lost jobs and need help until they find employment.

Considering the Rhetorical Situation

PURPOSE	Do you have a stake in a particular solution, or do you simply want to eliminate the problem by whatever solution might be adopted?	◀ 55–56
AUDIENCE	Do your readers share your view of the problem as a serious one needing a solution? Are they likely to be open to possible solutions or resistant? Do they have the authority to carry out a proposed solution?	◀ 57–60
STANCE	How can you show your audience that your proposal is reasonable and should be taken seriously? How can you demonstrate your own authority and credibility?	◀ 66–68
MEDIA / DESIGN	How will you deliver your proposal? In print? Electronically? As a speech? Would visuals, or video or audio clips help support your proposal?	◀ 69–71

Generating Ideas and Text

Explore potential solutions to the problem. Many problems can be solved in more than one way, and you need to show your readers that you've examined several potential solutions. You may develop solutions

477

424–31

on your own; more often, though, you'll need to do **RESEARCH** to see how others have solved—or tried to solve—similar problems. Don't settle on a single solution too quickly—you'll need to **COMPARE** the advantages and disadvantages of several solutions in order to argue convincingly for one.

Decide on the most desirable solution(s).　One solution may be head and shoulders above others—but be open to rejecting all the possible solutions on your list and starting over if you need to, or to combining two or more potential solutions in order to come up with an acceptable fix.

Think about why your solution is the best one.　Why did you choose your solution? Why will it work better than others? What has to be done to enact it? What will it cost? What makes you think it can be done? Writing out answers to these questions will help you argue for your solution: to show that you have carefully and objectively outlined a problem, analyzed the potential solutions, weighed their merits, and determined the reasons the solution you propose is the best.

Ways of Organizing a Proposal

You can organize a proposal in various ways, but always you will begin by establishing that there is a problem. You may then identify several possible solutions before recommending one of them or a combination of several. Sometimes, however, you might discuss only a single solution.

[Several possible solutions]

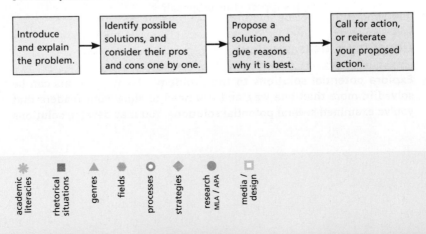

| Introduce and explain the problem. | → | Identify possible solutions, and consider their pros and cons one by one. | → | Propose a solution, and give reasons why it is best. | → | Call for action, or reiterate your proposed action. |

[A single solution]

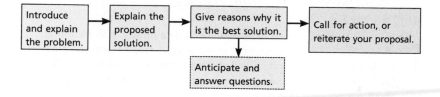

Taking Stock of Your Work

Take stock of what you've written by writing out answers to these questions:

- How did you decide on and limit your topic?
- How did you go about researching your topic?
- How did you determine the best solution to the problem you defined?
- Did you use visual elements (tables, graphs, diagrams, photographs), audio elements, or links effectively? If not, would they have helped?
- What did you do well in this piece? What could still be improved? What would you do differently next time?
- What have you learned about the processes of writing from writing this piece? What do you need to work on in the future?

TOPIC PROPOSALS

Instructors often ask students to write topic proposals to ensure that their topics are appropriate or manageable. Some instructors may also ask for an **ANNOTATED BIBLIOGRAPHY** showing that appropriate sources of information are available—more evidence that the project can be carried out. Here a student proposes a topic for an assignment in a writing course in which she has been asked to take a position on a global issue.

△ 190–98

CATHERINE THOMS

Social Media and Data Privacy

The relationship between social media and data privacy is an issue that has recently risen to the forefront of many social media users' concerns. While we have been posting and sharing online, major companies like Facebook, Twitter, and Google have been silently collecting information about our personal lives and leaving that data vulnerable to potentially harmful exposure. As someone who has had their private information compromised multiple times by large-scale data breaches, I feel compelled to share my research on the dangers of such security breaches and how they can happen.

In this paper, I will argue that it is crucial for consumers to be aware of the ways in which social media platforms can gain access to consumers' private data and what those platforms can do with that data. In March 2018, it was revealed that 87 million Facebook profiles were exposed to manipulation by the political consulting firm Cambridge Analytica during the 2016 presidential election. I will use this scandal as an example of how the unlawful exposure of personal data can have far-reaching effects on external world events, and I plan to analyze how this scandal has functioned as a global catalyst for further scrutiny into the privacy mechanisms of social media.

I will concentrate on the specific ways personal data may be misused. Although sharing thoughts and pictures on social media may not seem like anything to think twice about, many people don't realize just how much is at stake should enough of that personal data fall into the wrong hands. Much of my research will be done on specific social media applications such as Facebook and Google Analytics, as that is where the heart of the issue resides and where consumers can learn the most about their personal data exposure and protection.

Thoms defines and narrows her topic (from data breaches to the specific ways consumers' data may be misused), discusses her interest, outlines her argument, and discusses her research strategy. Her goal is to convince her instructor that she has a realistic writing project and a clear plan.

※ academic literacies ■ rhetorical situations ▲ genres ⬢ fields ○ processes ◆ strategies ● research MLA / APA ▢ media / design

Key Features / Topic Proposals

You'll need to explain what you want to write about, why you want to explore it, and what you'll do with your topic. Unless your instructor has additional requirements, here are the features to include:

A concise discussion of the subject. Topic proposals generally open with a brief discussion of the subject, outlining any important areas of controversy or debate associated with it and clarifying the extent of the writer's current knowledge of it. In its first two paragraphs, Thoms's proposal includes a concise statement of the topic she wishes to address.

A clear statement of your intended focus. State what aspect of the topic you intend to write on as clearly as you can, narrowing your focus appropriately. Thoms does so by stating her intended topic—data breaches—and then showing how she will focus on the specific ways consumers' data may be misused.

A rationale for choosing the topic. Tell your instructor why this topic interests you and why you want to write about it. Thoms both states what made her interested in her topic and hints at a practical reason for choosing it: plenty of information is available.

Mention of resources. To show your instructor that you can achieve your goal, you need to identify the available research materials.

IF YOU NEED MORE HELP

See Chapter 30 for guidelines on **DRAFTING**, Chapter 31 on **ASSESSING YOUR OWN WRITING**, Chapter 32 on **GETTING RESPONSE AND REVISING**, and Chapter 33 on **EDITING AND PROOFREADING**. See Chapter 34 if you are required to submit your proposal in a writing **PORTFOLIO**.

340–42
343–47
348–55
356–60
361–70

21 Reflections

Sometimes we write essays just to think about something—to speculate, ponder, probe; to play with an idea, develop a thought; or simply to share something. Reflective essays are our attempt to think something through by writing about it and to share our thinking with others. If such essays make an argument, it is about things we care or think about more than about what we believe to be "true." In college, you might be asked in courses across the curriculum to write formal or informal reflections in the form of essays, journals, design reports, or learning logs. Have a look at one example of a reflection by Edan Lepucki, a novelist and non-fiction writer. This essay originally appeared on the Op-Ed page of the *New York Times*.

EDAN LEPUCKI

Our Mothers as We Never Saw Them

In one of my favorite photographs of my mother, she's about 18 and very tan, with long, blond hair. It's the 1970s and she's wearing a white midriff and cutoffs. My dad is there, too, hugging her from behind, and from the looks of it, they're somewhere rural—maybe some pastoral patch of small-town New Jersey where they met.

I haven't seen this photo for years, I have no idea where it is now, but I still think of it—and, specifically, my mom in it. She looks really sexy; wars have been waged over less impressive waist-to-hip ratios. And she is so young and innocent. She hasn't yet dropped out of college, or gotten married. The young woman in this photo has no idea that life will bring her five children and five grandchildren, a conversion to Judaism, one divorce, two marriages, a move across the country.

For me, as for many daughters, the time before my mother became a mother is a string of stories, told and retold: the time she got hit by

a car and had amnesia; the time she sold her childhood Barbie to buy a ticket to Woodstock; the time she worked as a waitress at Howard Johnson's, struggling to pay her way through her first year at Rutgers. The old photos of her are even more compelling than the stories because they're a historical record, carrying the weight of fact, even if the truth there is slippery: the trick of an image, and so much left outside the frame. These photos serve as a visual accompaniment to the myths. Because any story about your mother is part myth, isn't it?

After finishing my most recent novel, in part about mother-daughter relationships, I put out a call on social media for photos from women of their mothers before they were mothers. A character in the book, a young artist, does something similar, so I'd thought a lot about what the process might be like. I wasn't prepared, however, for how powerful the images I received would be.

The young women in these pictures are beautiful, fierce, sassy, 5 goofy, cool, sweet—sometimes all at once. I asked contributors to tell me about their moms or the photo submitted, and they often wrote that something specific and special about their present-day mother—her smile, say, or her posture—was present in this earlier version.

Adalena can see her own expression in this image of her mother, Hua Sou, which she contributed to the author's project.

What solace to know that time, aging and motherhood cannot take away a woman's essential identity. For daughters who closely resemble their moms, it must be an even bigger comfort; these mothers and daughters are twins, separated by a generation, and an old photo serves as a kind of mirror: How do I look? Even if there isn't a resemblance, we can't help but compare ourselves to our young mothers before they were mothers.

"I locate something of myself in the slope of her shoulders," said one contributor, Molly. "This makes me feel adjacent to her coolness."

Sometimes, too, a photo deepens the mystery of a mother. Emma, whose mom died when she was 8, says that she "cobbles together" an image of her mother from other people's memories. "Those points only give an outline," she writes, "let alone a shadow or full likeness of a person." She's heard plenty of stories about her mother's childhood, and about her early years as a mother, but very little about the years after her mother graduated college and before she got married. Emma calls this period her mother's "lost years." She notes that she, at age 29, is in that same phase of life now.

Many of us find a breezy toughness in the bygone versions of our mothers, and we envy it. Before a kid or two tied her down, Mom was hitchhiking, or she was playing softball with guys, or like Julia's mom, she was "transcribing tapes from her time as a war reporter like it's the most casual thing in the world." Paria, whose mother fled Iran during the Revolution, notes her mother's resilience; then, as now, her mom maintains a "joie de vivre."

Julia's mother, Anne, during her time as a war reporter.

The photos women sent me offer a key to how we, as daughters, want to perceive young womanhood. Pluck, sex appeal, power, kindness, persistence: We admire and celebrate these characteristics, and we long for the past versions of our moms to embody them. But if these characteristics are a prerequisite for a properly executed womanhood, does becoming a mother divest a woman of such qualities? In studying these photos, and each daughter's interpretation of them, I've come to wonder what traits we allow our mothers to have, and which ones we view as temporary, expiring with age and the beginning of motherhood. Can a woman be both sexual and maternal, daring and responsible, innocent and wise? Mothers are either held up as paragons of selflessness, or they're discounted and parodied. We often don't see them in all their complexity.

For daughters, these old photos of our mothers feel like both a 10 chasm and a bridge. The woman in the picture is someone other than the woman we know. She is also exactly the person in the photo—still, right now. Finally, we see that the woman we've come

Zan submitted this photo of her mother, Darcy, to the project.

to think of as Mom—whether she's nurturing, or disapproving, or thoughtful, or delusional, or pestering, or supportive, or sentimental—is also a mysterious, fun, brave babe.

She's been here all this time.

Photographs of people's mothers when they were young sparks Lepucki's reflection on the lenses through which we see our mothers. She considers the stories our mothers tell and the way photos complement the stories, then examines several photos contributed by others, noting how we compare ourselves to our parents. Finally, her reflections lead her to explore how "we, as daughters, want to perceive young womanhood"—and how the women in the photos combine distance, familiarity, and youthful allure.

Key Features / Reflections

A topic that intrigues you. A reflective essay has a dual purpose: to ponder something you find interesting or puzzling and to share your thoughts with an audience. Your topic may be anything that interests you. You might write about someone you have never met and are curious about, an object or occurrence that makes you think, a place where you feel comfortable or safe. Your goal is to explore the meaning that the person, object, event, or place has for you in a way that will interest others. One way to do that is by making connections between your personal experience and more general ones that readers may share. Lepucki writes about her own and other women's photos of their mothers, and in doing so she raises questions and offers insights about the way people relate to their mothers.

Some kind of structure. A reflective essay can be structured in many ways, but it needs to *be* structured. It may seem to wander, but all its paths and ideas should relate, one way or another. The challenge is to keep your readers' interest as you explore your topic and to leave readers satisfied that the journey was pleasurable, interesting, and profitable. Lepucki begins by describing a remembered photo of her mother and relating it to her mother's stories. She then explores the significance of several photos of other women's mothers and examines the ways daughters interpret photos of their mothers as young women—and how those interpretations may change when those young women become mothers.

Specific details.   You'll need to provide specific details to help readers understand and connect with your subject, especially if it's an abstract or unfamiliar one. Lepucki offers a wealth of details about a favorite photo: "She's about 18 and very tan, with long, blond hair. It's the 1970s and she's wearing a white midriff and cutoffs. My dad is there, too, hugging her from behind." Anecdotes can bring your subject to life. Writing of that photo, Lepucki continues: "And she is so young and innocent. She hasn't yet dropped out of college, or gotten married. The young woman in this photo has no idea that life will bring her five children and five grandchildren, a conversion to Judaism, one divorce, two marriages, a move across the country." Reflections may be about causes, such as how our parents affect our self-images; comparisons, such as when Lepucki compares the photos sent to her; and examples, as the photos included in Lepucki's essay exemplify the "beautiful, fierce, sassy, goofy, cool, sweet" young women she sees in all the photos sent to her.

A questioning, speculative tone.   In a reflective essay, you are working toward answers, not providing them neatly organized and ready for consumption. So your tone is usually tentative and open, demonstrating a willingness to entertain, accept, and reject various ideas as your essay progresses from beginning to end. Lepucki achieves this tone by questioning her own insights: "Any story about your mother is part myth, isn't it?"; and by admitting that she doesn't have all the answers: "In studying these photos, and each daughter's interpretation of them,

I've come to wonder what traits we allow our mothers to have, and which ones we view as temporary, expiring with age and the beginning of motherhood."

A BRIEF GUIDE TO WRITING REFLECTIONS

Deciding on a Topic

Choose a subject you want to explore. Write a list of things that you think about, wonder about, find puzzling or annoying. They may be big things—life, relationships—or little things—quirks of certain people's behavior, curious objects, everyday events. Try **CLUSTERING** one or more of those things, or begin by **FREEWRITING** to see what comes to mind as you write.

333–34
331–32

Considering the Rhetorical Situation

PURPOSE	What's your goal in writing this essay? To introduce a topic that interests you? Entertain? Provoke readers to think about something? What aspects of your subject do you want to ponder and reflect on?
AUDIENCE	Who is the audience? How familiar are they with your subject? How will you introduce it in a way that will interest them?
STANCE	What is your attitude toward the topic you plan to explore? Questioning? Playful? Critical? Curious? Something else?
MEDIA / DESIGN	Will your essay be a print document? an oral presentation? Will it be posted on a website or blog? Would it help to include any visuals or video or audio files?

55–56
57–60
66–68
69–71

Generating Ideas and Text

Explore your subject in detail. Reflections often include descriptive details. Lepucki, for example, describes the aspects of the women in the photos that help her see how daughters want to see young women: as having "pluck, sex appeal, power, kindness, persistence." She also provides details in the form of several photographs. You may also make your point by **DEFINING**, **COMPARING**, even **CLASSIFYING**. Virtually any organizing pattern will help you explore your subject.

432–42
424–31
418–23

Back away. Ask yourself why your subject matters: why is it important or intriguing or significant? You may try **LISTING** or **OUTLINING** possibilities, or you may want to start **DRAFTING** to see where the writing takes your thinking. Your goal is to think on screen (or paper) about your subject, to play with its possibilities.

332–33
335–37
340–42

Think about how to keep readers with you. Reflections may seem loose or unstructured, but they must be carefully crafted so that readers can follow your train of thought. It's a good idea to sketch out a rough **THESIS** to help focus your thoughts. You may not include the thesis in the essay itself, but every part of the essay should in some way relate to it.

387–89

Ways of Organizing a Reflective Essay

Reflective essays may be organized in many ways because they mimic the way we think, associating one idea with another in ways that make sense but do not necessarily form a "logical" progression. In general, you might consider organizing a reflection using this overall strategy:

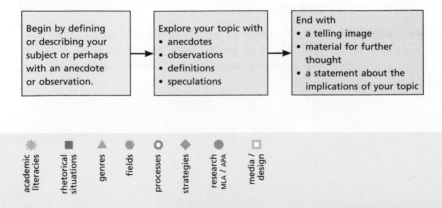

Begin by defining or describing your subject or perhaps with an anecdote or observation. → Explore your topic with
- anecdotes
- observations
- definitions
- speculations

→ End with
- a telling image
- material for further thought
- a statement about the implications of your topic

academic literacies　rhetorical situations　genres　fields　processes　strategies　research MLA / APA　media / design

Another way to organize this type of essay is as a series of brief reflections that together create an overall impression:

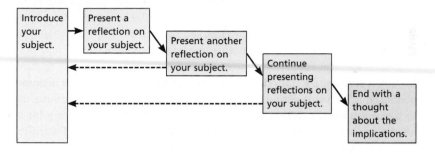

Taking Stock of Your Work

Take stock of what you've written by writing out answers to these questions:

- How did you decide on your topic?
- Why did you organize it as you did?
- Did you use visual elements (photographs, diagrams, drawings), audio elements, or links? If so, what did they add? If not, what might you have used?
- What did you do well in this piece? What could still be improved? What would you do differently next time?
- What have you learned about your writing ability from writing this piece? What do you need to work on in the future?

IF YOU NEED MORE HELP

See Chapter 30 for guidelines on **DRAFTING**, Chapter 31 on **ASSESSING YOUR OWN WRITING**, Chapter 32 on **GETTING RESPONSE AND REVISING**, and Chapter 33 on **EDITING AND PROOFREADING**. See Chapter 34 if you are required to submit your reflection in a writing **PORTFOLIO**.

340–42
343–47
348–55
356–60
361–70

22 Résumés and Job Letters

Résumés summarize our education, work experience, and other accomplishments for prospective employers. Application letters introduce us to those employers. When you send a letter and résumé applying for a job, you are making an argument for why that employer should want to meet you and perhaps hire you. In a way, the two texts together serve as an advertisement selling your talents and abilities to someone who likely has to sift through many applications to decide whom to invite for an interview. That's why résumés and application letters require a level of care that few other documents do. In the same way, sending a thank-you letter following an interview completes your presentation of yourself to potential employers. Résumés, application letters, and thank-you letters are obviously very different genres—yet they share one common purpose: to help you find a job. Thus, they are presented together in this chapter.

Understanding Your Audiences

When you apply for a job, you will likely post your application materials online. They may then be read by a recruiter or a hiring manager. Before that happens, though, your résumé may be searched by an ATS, or applicant tracking system. These systems are designed to ease recruiters' and managers' workloads by ranking applicants, usually on the basis of keywords that appear in their résumés. These keywords usually match the words used in the job posting, so to increase your chances of success, you should describe your skills and experience using the same keywords. One way to do this is to paste the job posting into an online word cloud generator, such as *Wordle, WordItOut,* or *Jobscan.* For example, here is a posting for an internship and a word cloud; the larger the word, the more often it is used in the posting:

academic
literacies

rhetorical
situations

genres

fields

processes

strategies

research
MLA / APA

media /
design

Interns will receive full-on training in their respective departments and be responsible for generating sales, conducting presentations, scheduling promotions, and working within our team.

You will assist Account Executives in their events or retail demonstration and sales and marketing campaigns.

Our company generates over $1 million in revenue through direct marketing campaigns. Interns must be prepared to interact with clients and customers and deliver sales presentations.

This is a hands-on opportunity and interns will gain experience and skills in promotional sales, direct marketing, and working in a team atmosphere and with clients.

Requirements: student mentality; goal-oriented; confidence; self-motivation; punctuality; reliability; strong work ethic; desire to make a difference; passionate about helping people

The word cloud suggests that these words should appear in an applicant's résumé: Sales, *marketing*, *clients*, *business*, *interns*, *team*, and *customers*. (While it's tempting to use "soft skill" terms as listed under the requirements, you're better off describing actions that demonstrate those skills.

For example, "self-motivation" and "passionate about helping people" might be shown by volunteer work at a homeless shelter.)

Social Media and Job Hunting

Social media have become important aspects of finding a job, for both good and ill. In fact, over half of all employers always search for job applicants' online profiles—and in many cases, those profiles reduce the applicants' chances of being hired. So it's important to create or revise your profiles on *Facebook*, *LinkedIn*, and *Twitter*, the three most-searched social media sites, as well as other sites. Emphasize any volunteer or charity work you do, and highlight potential qualifications for and interest in the kind of work you want. Make sure your profiles contain no profanity or references to your sexual activity, or use of alcohol, guns, or illegal drugs—and proofread your posts for grammar and spelling. Your photos of yourself should project a professional image, too. Also, Google yourself to see what a search reveals about you.

You can also use social media to improve your job search. Read the descriptions of positions you would like to have, looking for keywords that describe what employers want in such employees; then use those keywords in your profiles. Also, join *LinkedIn* groups related to your desired job or industry to stay current with the conversations in those fields; then follow the companies where you'd like to work, as new job opportunities are sometimes posted there before they appear in other places.

RÉSUMÉS

A résumé is one of a job seeker's most important tools. If done well, a résumé not only tells potential employers about your education and work history, it says a lot about your attention to detail, writing skills, and professionalism. Taking the time to craft an excellent résumé, then, is time well spent. Here's an example, a résumé written by a college student applying for an internship before her senior year.

academic literacies　rhetorical situations　genres　fields　processes　strategies　research MLA / APA　media / design

Emily W. Williams
Name in boldface.

28 Murphy Lane
Springfield, Ohio 45399
Phone: 937-555-2640
Email: ewilliams22@gmail.com
LinkedIn: www.linkedin.com/EmilyWWilliams

SKILLS

- Communicating in writing and verbally, face-to-face and in various media
- Organizing and analyzing data
- Collaborating with other people on a team to achieve goals within deadlines
- Fluent in French
- Software: Microsoft Word, Microsoft Excel, SPSS, ATLAS.ti, Avid Pro Tools

EDUCATION

Wittenberg University, Springfield, Ohio
- BA in Marketing expected in May 2020
- Minor in Psychology
- Current GPA: 3.67
- Recipient, Community Service Scholarship

Clark State Community College, Springfield, Ohio
- AA in Business Administration, 2018
- GPA: 3.88
- Honors: Alpha Lambda Delta National Honor Society

EXPERIENCE

Aug. 2018–Present: Department of Psychology, Wittenberg University, Springfield, Ohio
Research Assistant
- Collect and analyze data
- Interview research study participants

Work experience in reverse chronological order.

Summer 2018: Landis and Landis Public Relations, Springfield, OH
Events Coordinator
- Organized local charity campaigns
- Coordinated database of potential donors
- Produced two radio spots for event promotion

Summers 2016–17: Springfield Aquatic Club, Springfield, OH
Assistant Swim Coach
- Instructed children ages 5–18 in competitive swimming

Format to fill entire page.

Emily Williams's résumé is arranged to highlight her social media presence and skills; her education and experience are arranged chronologically. Because she is in college, readers can assume that she graduated from high school, so that information isn't needed here. She describes her skills and work responsibilities using action verbs to highlight what she actually did—"communicating," "collaborating," "produced," "instructed"—and so on.

Key Features / Résumés

A structure that suits your goals and experience. There are conventional ways of organizing a résumé but no one right way. You can organize a résumé chronologically or functionally, and it can be targeted (customized for a particular job application) or not. A *chronological résumé* is the most general, listing pretty much all your academic and work experience from the most recent to the earliest. A *targeted résumé* will generally announce the specific goal up top, just beneath your name, and will offer information selectively, showing only the experience and skills relevant to your goal. A *functional résumé* is organized around various kinds of experience and is not chronological. You might write a functional résumé if you wish to demonstrate a lot of experience in more than one area and perhaps if you wish to downplay dates. *Combination résumés*, like Emily Williams's, allow you to combine features from various types of résumés to present yourself in the best light; Emily's initial emphasis on skills is functional, while her education and experience are listed chronologically.

Succinct. A résumé should almost always be short—one page if at all possible. Entries should be parallel but do not need to be written in complete sentences—"Produced two radio spots," for instance, rather than "I produced two radio spots." Use action verbs ("instructed," "produced") to emphasize what you accomplished.

A design that highlights key information. It's important for a résumé to look good and to be easy to skim; typography, white space, and alignment matter. Your name should be bold at the top, and the information you want your readers to see first should be near the top of the page. Major sections should be labeled with headings, all of which should be in one slightly larger or bolder font. And you need to surround each section and the text as a whole with adequate white space to make the parts easy to read—and to make the entire document look professional.

A BRIEF GUIDE TO WRITING RÉSUMÉS

Considering the Rhetorical Situation

PURPOSE   Are you seeking a job? an internship? some other position? How will the position for which you're applying affect what you include on your résumé? — 55–56

AUDIENCE   What sort of employee is the company or organization seeking? What experience and qualities will the person doing the hiring be looking for? — 57–60

STANCE   What personal and professional qualities do you want to convey? Think about how you want to come across— as eager? polite? serious? ambitious?—and choose your words accordingly. — 66–68

MEDIA / DESIGN   Are you planning to send your résumé and letter as PDFs? on paper? as an email attachment? Whatever your medium, be sure both documents are formatted appropriately and proofread carefully. — 69–71

Generating Ideas and Text for a Résumé

Define your objective.   Are you looking for a particular job for which you should create a targeted résumé? Are you preparing a generic chronological résumé to use in a search for work of any kind? Defining your objective as specifically as possible helps you decide on the form the résumé will take and the information it will include.

Consider how you want to present yourself. Begin by gathering the information you will need to include. As you work through the steps of putting your résumé together, think about the method of organization that works best for your purpose—chronological, targeted, functional, or combination.

- *Contact information.* At the top of your résumé, list your full name, a permanent address (rather than your school address), and a permanent telephone number with area code.

- *Your email address.* Your email address should sound professional; addresses like hotbabe334@gmail.com do not make a good first impression on potential employers. If possible, get an address that uses your name and a common provider, such as Gmail, iCloud mail, or Outlook.

- *Your social media presence.* Many employers routinely check applicants' social media presence to evaluate their personality and character, so yours should reflect your professional self and highlight your skills. Anything from an inappropriate photo or reference to drinking to poor writing can hurt your chances, while evidence of communication skills and a professional image can help them, so you should shape your social media presence to highlight or demonstrate your qualifications and skills. Don't scrub your sites and post nothing, though—use your online presence to enhance your employability. That includes checking for jobs on company *Facebook* pages and *Twitter* feeds and in *LinkedIn* groups.

- *Your skills.* What have you learned to do, both in school and in jobs or volunteer work that you've done? Make a list, and phrase each one in terms of what you can *do*, as Williams does. Avoid such phrases as "hard worker," "detail-oriented," and "self-starter." As you revise your résumé to fit different job postings, choose skills from your list that match the job's requirements. As you list your education, experience, and other activities, think in terms of the skills you acquired and add them to your list.

- *Your education.* Start with the most recent: degree, major, college attended, and minor (if any). You may want to list your GPA (if it's over 3.0) and any academic honors you've received. If you don't have much work experience, list education first.

- *Your work experience.* As with education, list your most recent job first and work backward. Include job title, organization name, city and state, start and end dates, and responsibilities. Describe them in terms of your duties and accomplishments. If you have extensive work experience in the area in which you're applying, list that first.

- *Community service, volunteer, and charitable activities.* Many high school students are required to perform community service, and many students participate in various volunteer activities that benefit others. List the skills and aptitudes that participation helped you develop or demonstrate.

- *Other activities, interests, and abilities.* What do you do for fun? What skills do your leisure activities require? (For example, if you play a sport, you probably have a good grasp of the value of teamwork and the drive to practice something until you've mastered it. You should describe your skills in a way that an employer might find attractive.)

Choose references. It's assumed that if you get to the interview stage, employers will ask you to provide references, so you don't need to list them on your résumé or say "References on request." Before you start applying for jobs, ask people to serve as references, so they will be ready. It's a good idea to provide each reference with a one-page summary of relevant information about you (for example, give professors a list of courses you took with them, including the grades you earned and the titles of papers you wrote).

Choose your words carefully. Remember, your résumé is a sales document—you're trying to present yourself as someone worth a second look. Focus on your achievements, using action verbs that say what you've done. Be honest—employers expect truthfulness, and embellishing the truth can cause you to lose a job later.

Consider key design elements.   Make sure your résumé is centered on the page and that it looks clean and clear. It's usually best to use a single, simple **FONT** (Times New Roman, Calibri, Arial, and Cambria are good ones) throughout and to print on white paper. Use bold type and bullets to make the résumé easy to read, and limit it to no more—and no less—than one full page.

648–49

Edit and proofread carefully.   Your résumé must be perfect. Show it to others, and proofread again. You don't want even one typo or other error.

Send the résumé as a PDF.   PDFs look the same on all devices, whereas *Word* or other formats may not. Make sure potential employers see your résumé as you intended.

Ways of Organizing a Résumé

If you don't have much work experience or if you've just gone back to school to train for a new career, put education before work experience; if you have extensive work experience in the area in which you're applying, list work before education.

[Chronological]

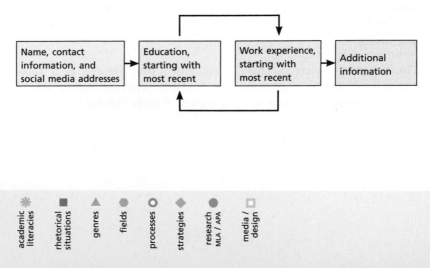

If you have limited work experience, gaps in your employment or education, or wish to focus on your skills, rather than your work history, use a functional résumé.

[Functional]

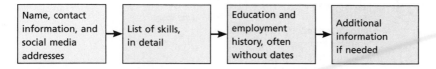

| Name, contact information, and social media addresses | → | List of skills, in detail | → | Education and employment history, often without dates | → | Additional information if needed |

A combination résumé is flexible: it lets you focus on both your skills and your experience by listing skills and also your education and employment history, and it can be tailored to specific job prospects.

[Combination]

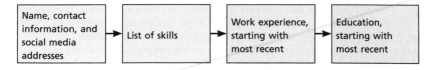

| Name, contact information, and social media addresses | → | List of skills | → | Work experience, starting with most recent | → | Education, starting with most recent |

APPLICATION AND THANK-YOU LETTERS

The application letter argues that the writer should be taken seriously as a candidate for a job or some other opportunity. Generally, it is sent together with a résumé, so it doesn't need to give that much information. It does, however, have to make a favorable impression: the way it's written and presented can get you in for an interview—or not. On the following page is an application letter that Emily Williams wrote seeking a position at the end of her junior year. Williams tailored her letter to one specific reader at a specific organization. The letter cites details, showing that it is not a generic application letter being sent to many possible employers. Rather, it identifies a particular position—the public relations internship—and

Application Letter

Equal space at top and bottom of page, all text aligning at left margin.

Street address, city, state, ZIP, date.

28 Murphy Lane
Springfield, OH 45399
May 19, 2019

Line space.

Recipient's name and title, organization, address.

Barbara Jeremiah, President
Jeremiah Enterprises
44322 Commerce Way
Worthington, OH 45322

Line space.

Re: Public Relations Internship Opening (Ref. ID: 27C)

Subject line with position information.

Salutation, with a colon.

Dear Ms. Jeremiah:

Line space.

Position identified.

I am writing to apply for the public relations internship advertised in the Sunday, May 15, *Columbus Dispatch*. The success of your company makes me eager to work with you and learn from you.

Line space between paragraphs.

Match between experience and job description.

My grasp of public relations goes beyond the theories I have learned in the classroom. I applied those theories last summer at Landis and Landis, the Springfield public relations firm, where I was responsible for organizing two charity events that drew over two hundred potential donors each. I also learned to use sound productions software to produce promotional radio spots. Since

Show knowledge of company.

Jeremiah Enterprises focuses on nonprofit public relations, my experience, training, and initiative will allow me to contribute to your company's public relations team..

Availability.

I will be available to begin any time after May 23, when the spring term at Wittenberg ends. I have attached my résumé, which provides detailed information about my background. I will phone this week to see if I might arrange an interview.

Line space.

Sincerely,

Closing.

Emily W. Williams

4 lines space for signature if mailed. Electronic letters need only typed name.

Emily W. Williams

Sender's name, typed.

stresses the fit between Williams's credentials and the position. Williams also states her availability. Send a thank-you email to each person who interviewed you within twenty-four hours of the interview; follow up by mailing a printed note that follows the same format as the application letter. Doing so is a way of showing appreciation for the interview and restating your interest in the position. It also shows that you have good manners and understand proper business etiquette. Below is an email that Emily Williams sent to the person who interviewed her. Williams thanks the interviewer for her time and the opportunity to meet, and she reiterates her interest in the position and her qualifications for it.

Thank-You Email

Line space.

Dear Ms. Jeremiah: .... *Salutation, with a colon.*

Thank you for the opportunity to meet with you yesterday. I enjoyed talking with you and meeting the people who work with you, and I continue to be very interested in becoming an intern with Jeremiah Enterprises.

Thanks and confirmation of interest.

Line space between paragraphs.

As we discussed, I worked with a public relations firm last summer, and since then I have completed three courses in marketing and public relations that relate directly to the work I would be doing as an intern.

Brief review of qualifications.

Invitation for further contact.

I have attached a list of references, as you requested. If you need any more information, please do not hesitate to contact me by email at ewilliams22@gmail.com or by phone at 937-555-2640. Thanks again; I hope to hear from you soon.

Attachments.

Repeat thanks.

Line space.

Sincerely, ... *Closing.*
Emily W. Williams

Key Features / Application and Thank-You Letters

A succinct indication of your qualifications. In an application letter, you need to make clear why you're interested in the position or the organization—and at the same time give some sense of why the person you're writing to should at least want to meet you. In a thank-you letter, you should remind the interviewer of your qualifications.

A reasonable and pleasing tone. When writing application and thank-you letters, you need to go beyond simply stating your accomplishments or saying thank you. Through your words, you need to demonstrate that you will be the kind of employee the organization wants. Presentation is also important—your letter should be neat and error-free.

A conventional, businesslike format. Application and thank-you letters typically follow a prescribed format. The most common is the block format shown in the examples. It includes the writer's address, the date, the recipient's name and address, a salutation, the message, a closing, and a signature.

A BRIEF GUIDE TO WRITING JOB LETTERS

Generating Ideas and Text for Application and Thank-You Letters

Focus. Application and thank-you letters are not personal and should not be chatty. Keep them focused: when you're applying for a position, include only information relevant to the position. Don't make your audience wade through irrelevant side issues. Stay on topic.

State the reason for the letter. Unlike essays, which develop a thesis over several paragraphs, or emails, which announce their topic in a subject line, letters need to explicitly introduce their reason for being written, usually in the first paragraph. When you're applying for something or thanking someone, say so in the first sentence: "I am writing to apply for the Margaret Branscomb Peabody Scholarship for students majoring in veterinary science." "Thank you for meeting with me."

Think of your letter as an argument. When you're asking for a job, you're making an **ARGUMENT**. You're making a claim—that you're qualified for a certain position—and you need to support your claim with reasons and evidence. Therefore, it's important to read the position's requirements carefully and tailor the letter to show that you meet them. In her letter, for example, Williams shows how her combined education and work experience make her successful in her summer job, and she connects that experience to the specific internship she's applying for.

397–417

Choose an appropriate salutation. If you know the person's name and title, use it: "Dear Professor Turnigan." If you don't know the person's title, one good solution is to address them by first and last name: "Dear Julia Turnigan." If, as sometimes happens, you must write to an unknown reader, your options include "To Whom It May Concern" and the more old-fashioned "Dear Sir or Madam." Another option in such situations might be to omit the salutation completely and instead use a subject line, for example: "Subject: Public Relations Internship Application." Whenever possible, though, write to a specific person; research or contact the organization and find out whom to write to. Once you've had an interview, write to your interviewer.

Consider the medium. If you're applying for a job with a printed letter and résumé, follow standard business-letter format, as Williams does. If you're applying via email, paste your entire letter into the body of the email, but move your contact information below your signature. Also, list the job for which you are applying in your subject line—and if the employer asks for specific information in the subject line, be sure to include it exactly.

Proofread. Few writing situations demand greater perfection than professional letters—especially job letters. Employers receive dozens, sometimes hundreds, of applications, and often can't look at them all. Typos, grammar errors, and other forms of sloppiness prejudice readers against applicants: an employer is likely to think that if this applicant can't take the time and care to **PROOFREAD**, how badly do they want this position? To compete, strive for perfection.

359–60 ○

Ways of Organizing an Application or Thank-You Letter

Application and thank-you letters should both follow a conventional organization, though you might vary the details somewhat. Here are two standard organizations:

[Application letter]

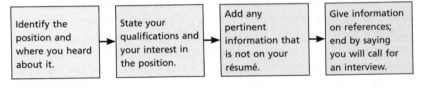

[Thank-you letter]

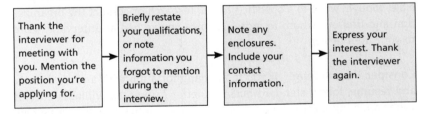

Taking Stock of Your Work

Take stock of what you've written by writing out answers to these questions:

- How did you go about identifying your strengths and qualifications?
- Why did you choose the résumé structure you did?

- Did you maintain an appropriate tone throughout your job letters?
- What did you do well in your résumé and letters? What could still be improved?
- What have you learned about your writing ability and your job qualifications from writing these pieces? What do you need to work on in the future?

IF YOU NEED MORE HELP

See Chapter 30 for guidelines on **DRAFTING**, Chapter 31 on **ASSESSING YOUR OWN WRITING**, Chapter 32 on **GETTING RESPONSE AND REVISING**, and Chapter 33 on **EDITING AND PROOFREADING**.

340–42
343–47
348–55
356–60

23 Mixing Genres

202–10 ▲
233–45
246–55
131–56

Musicians regularly mix genres, blending, for instance, reggae, hip-hop, and jazz to create a unique sound. Like musicians, writers often combine different genres in a single text. An **EVALUATION** of mining practices might include a **PROFILE** of a coal company CEO. A **PROPOSAL** to start a neighborhood watch might begin with a **REPORT** on crime in the area. Here's a column that mixes genres, written by Anna Quindlen for *Newsweek* magazine in 2007.

ANNA QUINDLEN

Write for Your Life

● The new movie *Freedom Writers* isn't entirely about the themes the trailers suggest. It isn't only about gang warfare and racial tensions and tolerance. It isn't only about the difference one good teacher can make in the life of one messed-up kid. *Freedom Writers* is about the power of writing in the lives of ordinary people. That's a lesson everyone needs. The movie, and the book from which it was taken, track the education of a young teacher named Erin Gruwell, who shows up shiny-new to face a class of what are called, in pedagogical jargon, "at risk" students. It's a mixed bag of Latino, Asian, and black teenagers with one feckless white kid thrown in. They ignore, belittle, and dismiss her as she proffers lesson plans and reading materials seriously out of step with the homelessness, drug use, and violence that are the stuff of their precarious existences.

And then one day, she gives them all marbled composition books and the assignment to write their lives, ungraded, unjudged, and the world breaks open.

Textual analysis.

※ academic literacies　■ rhetorical situations　▲ genres　● fields　○ processes　◆ strategies　● research MLA / APA　□ media / design

"My probation officer thinks he's slick; he swears he's an expert on gangs."

"Sorry, diary, I was going to try not to do it tonight, but the little baggy of white powder is calling my name."

"If you pull up my shirtsleeves and look at my arms, you will see 5 black and blue marks."

"The words 'Eviction Notice' stopped me dead in my tracks."

"When I was younger, they would lock me up in the closet because they wanted to get high and beat up on each other."

Ms. G, as the kids called her, embraced a concept that has been lost in modern life: writing can make pain tolerable, confusion clearer and the self stronger.

How is it, at a time when clarity and strength go begging, that we have moved so far from everyday prose? Social critics might trace this back to the demise of letter writing. The details of housekeeping and child rearing, the rigors of war and work, advice to friends and family: none was slated for publication. They were communications that gave shape to life by describing it for others.

But as the letter fell out of favor and education became pro- 10 fessionalized, with its goal less the expansion of the mind than the acquisition of a job, writing began to be seen largely as the purview of writers. Writing at work also became so stylistically removed from the story of our lives that the two seemed to have nothing in common. Corporate prose conformed to an equation: information × polysyllabic words + tortured syntax = aren't you impressed?

Report.

And in the age of the telephone most communication became evanescent, gone into thin air no matter how important or heartfelt. Think of all those people inside the World Trade Center saying goodbye by phone. If only, in the blizzard of paper that followed the collapse of the buildings, a letter had fallen from the sky for every family member and friend, something to hold on to, something to read and reread. Something real. Words on paper confer a kind of immortality. Wouldn't all of us love to have a journal, a memoir, a letter, from those we have loved and lost? Shouldn't all of us leave a bit of that behind?

Reflection.

The age of technology has both revived the use of writing and pro- vided ever more reasons for its spiritual solace. Emails are letters, after all, more lasting than phone calls, even if many of them r 2 cursory 4 u.

And the physical isolation they and other arms-length cyber-advances create makes talking to yourself more important than ever. That's also what writing is: not just a legacy, but therapy. As the novelist Don DeLillo once said, "Writing is a form of personal freedom. It frees us from the mass identity we see in the making all around us. In the end, writers will write not to be outlaw heroes of some underculture but mainly to save themselves, to survive as individuals."

Argument.

That's exactly what Gruwell was after when she got the kids in her class writing, in a program that's since been duplicated at other schools. Salvation and survival for teenagers whose chances of either seemed negligible. "Growing up, I always assumed I would either drop out of school or get pregnant," one student wrote. "So when Ms. G started talking about college, it was like a foreign language to me." Maybe that's the moment when that Latina girl began to speak that foreign language, when she wrote those words down. Today she has a college degree.

One of the texts Erin Gruwell assigned was *The Diary of a Young Girl* by Anne Frank. A student who balked at reading a book about someone so different, so remote, went on to write: "At the end of the book, I was so mad that Anne died, because as she was dying, a part of me was dying with her." Of course Anne never dreamed her diary would be published, much less read by millions of people after her death at the hands of the Nazis. She wrote it for the same reason the kids who called themselves Freedom Writers wrote in those composition books: to make sense of themselves. That's not just for writers. That's for people.

Quindlen argues that writing helps us understand ourselves and our world. She uses several genres to help advance her argument—textual analysis of the film Freedom Writers, *a brief report on the decline of letter writing, and a reflection on the technologies we use to write. Together, these genres help her develop her argument that writing helps us "make sense of [our]selves."*

Key Features / Texts That Mix Genres

One primary genre.   Your writing situation will often call for a certain genre that is appropriate for your purpose—an argument, a proposal, a report, a textual analysis, and so forth. Additional genres then play supporting roles. Quindlen's essay, for example, primarily argues a position and mixes in other genres, including report and reflection, to elaborate her argument and bring it to life.

A clear focus. A text that mixes genres approaches the topic several different ways, but each genre must contribute to your main point. One genre may serve as the introduction, and others may be woven throughout the text in other ways, but all must address some aspect of the topic and support the central claim. Quindlen's analysis of the film *Freedom Writers*, for example, supports her claim that writing is one way we learn about ourselves.

Careful organization. A text that combines several genres requires careful organization—the various genres must fit together neatly and clearly. Quindlen opens by analyzing the theme of *Freedom Writers*, noting that it's about "the power of writing in the lives of ordinary people." She then switches genres, reporting on how "we have moved so far from everyday prose" and then reflecting on the consequences of that move.

Clear transitions. When a text includes several genres, those genres need to be connected in some way. Transitions do that, and in so doing, they help readers make their way through the text. Transitions may include words such as *in addition* and *however*, and they may also consist of phrases that sum up an idea and move it forward. See, for example, how Quindlen ends one paragraph by quoting Don DeLillo as saying that writers write "to save themselves, to survive as individuals" and then begins the next paragraph by referring to DeLillo's words, saying "That's exactly what Gruwell was after."

Some Typical Ways of Mixing Genres

It's possible to mix almost any genres together. Following are some of the most commonly mixed genres and how they combine with other genres.

157–84 ▲
131–56

Memoirs. Sometimes a personal anecdote can help support an **ARGUMENT** or enhance a **REPORT**. Stories from your personal experience can help readers understand your motivations for arguing a certain position and can enhance your credibility as a writer.

131–56 ▲

Profiles. One way to bring a **REPORT** on an abstract topic to life is to include a profile of a person, place, or event. For example, if you were writing a report for your boss on the need to hire more sales representatives, including a profile of one salesperson's typical day might drive home the point that your sales force is stretched too thin.

157–84 ▲

Textual analyses. You might need to analyze a speech or other document as part of an **ARGUMENT**, especially on a historical or political topic. For instance, you might analyze speeches by Abraham Lincoln and Jefferson Davis if you're writing about the causes of the Civil War, or an advertisement for e-cigarettes if you're making an argument about teen smoking.

246–55 ▲

Evaluations. You might include an evaluation of something when you write a **PROPOSAL** about it. For example, if you were writing a proposal for additional student parking on your campus, you would need to evaluate the current parking facilities to discuss their inadequacy.

A BRIEF GUIDE TO WRITING TEXTS THAT MIX GENRES

Considering the Rhetorical Situation

55–56 ■

PURPOSE

Why are you writing this text? To inform? persuade? entertain? explore an idea? something else? What genres will help you achieve your purpose?

57–60 ■

AUDIENCE

Who are your readers? Which genres will help these readers understand your point? Will starting with a memoir or profile draw them in? Will some analysis help them

※ academic literacies ■ rhetorical situations ▲ genres ⬡ fields ○ processes ◆ strategies ● research MLA / APA □ media / design

understand the topic? Will a profile make the topic less abstract or make them more sympathetic to your claim?

GENRE What is your primary genre? What other genres might support that primary genre?

61–65

STANCE What is your stance on your topic—objective? opinion-ated? something else? Will including a textual analysis or report help you establish an objective or analytical tone? Will some reflection or a brief memoir show your personal connection to your topic?

66–68

MEDIA / DESIGN Will your text be an electronic or a print document? an oral presentation? Will it be published on a blog or other website? Should you include illustrations? audio or video clips? Do you need to present any information that would be best shown in a chart or graph?

69–71

Generating Ideas and Text

Identify your primary genre. If you're writing in response to an assignment, does it specify a particular genre? Look for key verbs that name specific genres—for example, *analyze*, *argue*, *evaluate*, and so on. Be aware that other verbs imply certain genres: *explain*, *summarize*, *review*, and *describe* ask for a report; *argue*, *prove*, and *justify* signal that you need to argue a position; and *evaluate* and *propose* specify evaluations and proposals.

If the choice of genre is up to you, consider your **PURPOSE** and **AUDIENCE** carefully to determine what genre is most appropriate. Consult the appropriate genre chapter to identify the key features of your primary genre and to generate ideas and text.

55–56

57–60

Determine if other genres would be helpful. As you write a draft, you may identify a need—for a beginning that grabs readers' attention, for a satisfying ending, for ways to make an abstract concept more concrete or to help in analyzing something. At this point, you may want to try mixing one or more genres within your draft. Determine what genre will help you achieve your purpose and consult the appropriate genre chapter for advice on writing in that genre. Remember, however, that you're mixing genres into your draft to support and enhance it—so your supporting genres may not be as developed as complete texts in that genre would be and may not include all the key features. For example, if you include a brief memoir as part of an argument, it should include a good story and vivid details—but its significance may well be stated as part of the argument rather than revealed through the storytelling itself.

Integrate the genres.   Your goal is to create a focused, unified, coherent text. So you need to make sure that your genres work together to achieve that goal. Make sure that each genre fulfills a purpose within the text. For example, writing that **TAKES A POSITION** rarely jumps into the argument immediately. Instead, it may include several paragraphs in which the context for the disputed position is explained or information crucial to the audience's understanding is reported. Sometimes that **REPORT** will be introduced by a brief **MEMOIR** that makes the topic personal to the writer and so less abstract. And the argument itself may well do much more than simply take a position—it may **EVALUATE** alternatives and end with a **PROPOSAL**, and even include genres in other media, such as a video clip **PROFILING** the subject of the argument. Also, use **TRANSITIONS** to help readers move from section to section in your text.

157–84 ▲

131–56 ▲
224–32
202–10
246–55
233–55
391 ◆

Multigenre Projects

Sometimes a collection of texts can together represent an experience or advance an argument. For example, you might document a trip to the Grand Canyon in an album that contains journal entries written during the trip, photographs, a map of northern Arizona showing the canyon, postcards, an essay on the geology of the canyon, and a souvenir coin stamped with an image of the canyon. Each represents a different way of experiencing the Grand Canyon, and together they offer a multifaceted way to understand your trip.

✳ academic literacies   ◼ rhetorical situations   ▲ genres   ● fields   ○ processes   ◆ strategies   ● research MLA / APA   ▢ media / design

You might also write in several different genres on the same topic. If you begin by **ARGUING** that the government should provide universal health care, for example, writing a **MEMOIR** about a time you were ill could help you explore a personal connection to the topic. Composing a **PROFILE** of a doctor might give you new insights into the issue, and writing a **PROPOSAL** for how universal health care could work might direct you to potential solutions. You could assemble all these texts in a folder, with a title page and table of contents so that readers can see how it all fits together—or you could create an online multimodal text, combining text, images, video, sound, and links to other sites.

397–417
224–32
233–45
246–55

Taking Stock of Your Work

Take stock of what you've written by writing out answers to these questions:

- What led you to choose a mix of genres? How did your mix meet your purpose and your audience's needs?
- How well did you organize your piece?
- What strategies helped you achieve your purpose?
- Did you use visual elements (tables, graphs, diagrams, photographs), audio elements, or links effectively? If not, would they have helped?
- What did you do well in this piece? What could still be improved? What would you do differently next time?
- What have you learned about the processes of writing from writing this piece? What do you need to work on in the future?

IF YOU NEED MORE HELP

See Chapter 31 for guidelines on **DRAFTING**, Chapter 32 on **ASSESSING YOUR OWN WRITING**, Chapter 35 on **BEGINNING AND ENDING**, and Chapter 36 on **GUIDING YOUR READER**.

340–42
343–47
373–85
389–91

part 4

Fields

When we study at a college or university, we take courses in many academic fields of study, or disciplines, in the humanities, social sciences, the sciences, and various career-oriented fields. Each field of study has its own methods of doing research and communicating, requiring us to learn how to **READ** and **WRITE** in the ways appropriate to that field. The chapters that follow offer advice on how to adapt your reading and writing to the demands of various fields of study.

Fields

Fields of Study 24

Most colleges and universities are organized around fields of study, often referred to as *disciplines*, that share ways of seeing the universe, doing research, and presenting information—each through a different lens. Historians examine the way people behave differently than do economists; biologists look for different aspects of the natural world than do physicists. The various majors that colleges and universities offer invite you to learn to see the world in their distinctive ways and join professions that use distinctive skills. Marketing majors, for example, learn ways of influencing human behavior, while education majors learn ways of teaching students and music majors learn the intricacies of playing an instrument or singing. As you immerse yourself in a major, you come to see the world with a particular perspective.

Academic Fields and General Education

Your general education courses have a different goal: to prepare you for the demands of living in a complex and changing world—a world in which you'll need to use your ability to understand a wide range of facts, theories, and concepts to interact with a wide variety of people, work in various jobs, and make important decisions. In other words, these courses are designed to teach you how to learn and think. They are also helpful if you're not sure what you'd like to major in, because you can sample courses in various disciplines to help you decide. In your first couple of years, you will likely take general education courses in the following subject areas:

- the humanities, which include the arts, communications, history, literature, music, philosophy, and religion

academic literacies | rhetorical situations | genres | fields | processes | strategies | research MLA / APA | media / design

- the social sciences, which may include anthropology, economics, political science, geography, psychology, and sociology
- the sciences, which usually include such disciplines as astronomy, biology, chemistry, geology, mathematics, and physics

It's important to note that these lists are far from comprehensive; schools differ in the courses and majors they offer, so some schools may offer courses in fields that are not on any of these lists—and some of these courses won't be available at your school. You may also take courses in career-oriented fields such as education, business, engineering, and nursing.

Studying, Reading, and Writing in Academic Fields

Each field focuses on the study of particular subjects and issues. In *psychology*, you study the human mind—what it is and why we behave as we do. In *sociology*, you study the way society shapes our actions. In *biology*, you study life itself, from bacteria and fungi to organisms interacting with their environment. In *history*, you study the past to understand the present. In *nursing*, you study best ways of providing patient care within the health-care system. In *engineering*, you learn how to solve technical problems and design engineering systems.

Each field also examines the world through a distinctive lens, using its own methods to study and analyze those subjects. For example, scientists test hypotheses with experiments designed to prove or disprove their accuracy; sociologists study groups by using statistical evidence; and historians examine diaries, speeches, or photographs from the past. In addition, disciplines develop technical terms and ways of using language that allow scholars to understand one another—but that can be hard to understand. For example, consider the word *significant*. When people say that something is *significant* in day-to-day conversation, they usually mean that it's important, a big deal; in statistics, though, a *significant* result is one that is probably true—but it may or may not be important.

Disciplines also present information using methods standard in that discipline. In *business* courses, you're likely to read case studies of specific companies and write business cases and other communications. In *education* courses, you'll read and write lesson plans; in *science* courses, you'll read and write laboratory reports; in *English* courses, you'll read fiction, poetry, and plays and write literary analyses. In each, you'll present information in ways used in conversations among scholars in the discipline. And that means that you may need to adapt your reading and writing to the genres, concepts, and methods of the various academic fields you encounter.

THINKING ABOUT READING AND WRITING IN THE FIELDS

- What reading assignments do you have in your other courses?

- What makes them easy or hard to read? What helps you read them?

- Do you enjoy reading some genres or subjects more than others? Why?

- What writing assignments do you have in your other courses?

- Do you alter or adjust your writing processes in different courses? Why or why not?

- What makes writing in some courses hard or easy?

- Do you enjoy writing in certain genres or on certain topics? Why?

25 Reading across Fields of Study

We read shopping lists differently from graphic novels and operating instructions differently from poems. For that matter, we read novels and poems differently—and go about reading textbooks differently still. Just as we write using various processes—generating ideas and text, drafting, getting responses and revising, editing, and proofreading—we vary our reading processes from task to task. We will likely read a mathematics textbook differently from a case study in nursing, and read a speech by Abraham Lincoln in a history course differently from the way we'd read it in a rhetoric course. This chapter offers advice on how to engage with texts in a variety of fields.

Considering the Rhetorical Situation

A good way to approach reading in academic fields is to treat reading as a process that you adapt to the demands of each new situation. Instead of diving in and focusing your reading on the details of the content, it's often useful to take some time to consider the text's purpose, your purpose, the audience, the author, the author's stance, the genre, and the medium. This information can help you decide how to get the most out of the text.

55–56 ■

- *The text's* **PURPOSE**. When was the text written, and why? Is it a textbook? a classic work that lays out concepts that have become fundamental to the field? a work proposing a new way of looking at an issue?

- *Your purpose as a reader*. Why are you reading this text? To study for a test? To find sources for a research project? To learn about something on your own?

academic literacies | rhetorical situations | genres | fields | processes | strategies | research MLA / APA | media / design

- *The* **AUDIENCE**. For whom was the text written? Students like you? Scholars in the field? Interested nonspecialists? Readers who lived at some point in the past or in a particular location? What facts and concepts does the text assume its readers already know and understand?

57–60

- *The author.* Who wrote what you are reading? Does knowing the author's identity matter? Is the author reliable and credible? For example, is the author a respected scholar? Is the author known for a particular point of view?

- *The author's* **STANCE**. What is the author's stance toward the subject? toward the reader? Approving? Hostile? Critical? Passionate? What elements of the text reveal the author's stance?

66–68

- *The* **GENRE**. What is the text's genre? How was it meant to be read? Is that how you're reading it? What are the genre's key features? Knowing the key features of the genre can help you understand the text's content as you read and predict the text's organization.

61–65

- *The* **MEDIUM** *and* **DESIGN**. The medium and design of a text affect how you must read it. You may need to read a textbook differently from an article found on the internet, for example. An online textbook may require different commenting and note-taking strategies from a print text. Understanding the limitations and the advantages of a particular genre, medium, and design will help you get the most out of your reading.

69–71

Advice for Reading across Fields of Study

Becoming knowledgeable in a field of study requires learning its specialized ways of thinking, writing, and reading, including the terminology specific to the field and the kinds of texts the field is likely to produce and study. However, there is some general advice that can help you as you begin to read the kinds of texts you are likely to encounter in college.

Pay attention to vocabulary. All disciplines require that you learn their vocabulary, which includes not only concepts and facts but also the names of important figures in the field and what they represent. Scholars typically write for other scholars in the same field, so they may assume that readers understand these terms and references and refer to them without explanation—and even "popular" writing often makes the same assumption. You'll find that much of the work in all your courses consists of learning terms and concepts. So it's important to take good notes in lectures, writing down terms your instructor emphasizes as they are defined, or, if they aren't, writing them down to look up later. Your textbooks introduce and define key terms and often include a glossary in the back that provides definitions.

In addition, be aware that disciplinary vocabularies use different kinds of words. In the sciences, the language is likely very technical, with many terms based on Greek and Latin roots (for example, the Greek prefix *gastr-* forms *gastropod* [snail], *gastric* [stomach], and *gastroscopy* [examination of the abdomen and stomach]). In the humanities, the vocabulary often alludes to complex concepts. Consider, for example, these sentences from *The Swerve*, a book by literary historian Stephen Greenblatt:

> The household, the kinship network, the guild, the corporation—these were the building blocks of personhood. Independence and self-reliance had no cultural purchase.

Almost every term, from "household" to "guild" to "personhood" to "cultural purchase," carries a wealth of information that must be understood. While understanding the scientific terms requires a good dictionary, these particular terms require an encyclopedia—or the knowledge gained by much reading.

Consider the author—or not. In some disciplines, it's important to know who wrote a text, while in others the identity or **STANCE** of the author is seen as irrelevant. Historians, for example, need to know who the author of a text is, and the perspective that author brings to the text is central to reading history. Literary scholars may try not to consider the author at all, focusing solely on a close reading of the text itself. Scientists may consider the author's identity or the school or lab where the author works

66–68

to decide whether or not to read a text. Mathematicians resolutely ignore the author, focusing solely on the information in the text itself. So to make sense of a text in a discipline, you need to find out how that discipline sees the role of the author.

Identify key ideas and make comparisons.   Whatever the discipline, look for the main ideas its texts present. Rather than highlight or underline them, write out the key ideas in your own words. As you read texts on the same subject, you may want to develop a matrix to help you COMPARE AND CONTRAST as well as SYNTHESIZE the main ideas. The following chart, adapted from one developed by two librarians, presents the main ideas in two sources, and then synthesizes the two versions. This example synthesizes a key idea found in two articles on how social media affects political participation among youths:

424–31
519–25

Source #1: Skorik, M. M. "Youth Engagement in Singapore"	Source #2: Ahmad, K. "Social Media and Youth Participatory Politics"	Synthesis: Main Ideas
Singapore's government has consistently applied controls on traditional media outlets but has left social media outlets untouched and unregulated.	Online participation in political campaigns and issues was almost five times greater than traditional participation. Researches concluded that this "could provide the participant with anonymity, in turn less vulnerability to political vengeance."	Main idea #1: Government control and censorship of mainstream media has caused protesters to look for alternative communication tools.
Key idea in source #1	Key idea in source #2	Synthesis of ideas
Key idea in source #1	Key idea in source #2	Synthesis of ideas

Michelle Chiles and Emily Brown, "Literature Review." Bristol Community College, Fall River, MA, 2015. Unpublished *PowerPoint*.

You might also get into the habit of skimming the works-cited or references list at the end of articles and books. As you do so, you'll begin to see who the most important people are in the discipline and what counts as evidence.

Build a map of the discipline. To make sense of a new idea, we need to have some way of fitting it into what we already know. Reading in an unfamiliar discipline can be hard because we don't have a sense of where the information in the text fits into the conversations of the discipline, its history, or our own goals—what we'd like to know or do in this field. It's useful to visualize the discipline so that we can place readings into the appropriate context. Possible ways of organizing a discipline follow.

Draw a word map. Using your textbook and perhaps some online sources as guides, draw an overview of the field. Here's one for psychology:

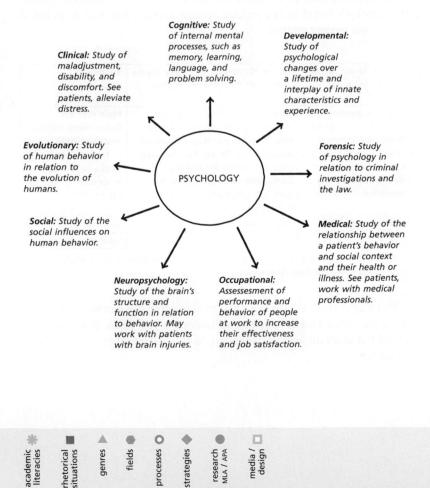

Cognitive: Study of internal mental processes, such as memory, learning, language, and problem solving.

Clinical: Study of maladjustment, disability, and discomfort. See patients, alleviate distress.

Developmental: Study of psychological changes over a lifetime and interplay of innate characteristics and experience.

Evolutionary: Study of human behavior in relation to the evolution of humans.

Forensic: Study of psychology in relation to criminal investigations and the law.

PSYCHOLOGY

Social: Study of the social influences on human behavior.

Medical: Study of the relationship between a patient's behavior and social context and their health or illness. See patients, work with medical professionals.

Neuropsychology: Study of the brain's structure and function in relation to behavior. May work with patients with brain injuries.

Occupational: Assessesment of performance and behavior of people at work to increase their effectiveness and job satisfaction.

Create a timeline.   Sometimes it's helpful to understand how a discipline developed over time, how its research methods or emphases came to be, so you can place its texts and key developments within that history. Here, for example, is a timeline of the behaviorist approach in psychology:

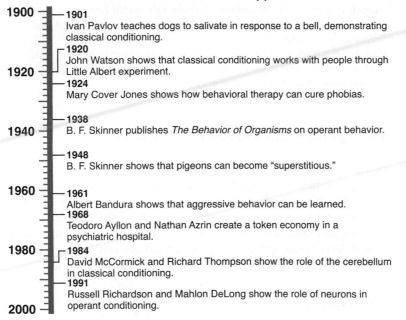

Timeline of the behaviorist approach

1900
— 1901
Ivan Pavlov teaches dogs to salivate in response to a bell, demonstrating classical conditioning.
— 1920
John Watson shows that classical conditioning works with people through
1920
Little Albert experiment.
— 1924
Mary Cover Jones shows how behavioral therapy can cure phobias.

— 1938
1940
B. F. Skinner publishes *The Behavior of Organisms* on operant behavior.

— 1948
B. F. Skinner shows that pigeons can become "superstitious."

1960
— 1961
Albert Bandura shows that aggressive behavior can be learned.
— 1968
Teodoro Ayllon and Nathan Azrin create a token economy in a psychiatric hospital.
1980
— 1984
David McCormick and Richard Thompson show the role of the cerebellum in classical conditioning.
— 1991
Russell Richardson and Mahlon DeLong show the role of neurons in
2000
operant conditioning.

Write a conversation among researchers.   To better understand the similarities and differences among various schools of thought within a discipline, choose some of the most prominent proponents of each school and write a fictional conversation among them, outlining where they agree and disagree and where they published or disseminated their theories and findings. Here, for instance, is a snippet of a dialogue that might have taken place between developmental psychologist Jean Piaget and behavioral psychologist B. F. Skinner:

> **Piaget:** *Children learn by adapting to conflicts between what they already know and challenges to that knowledge.*
>
> **Skinner:** *Bosh! We can't know what's in someone's mind; we have to focus on their behavior.*
>
> **Piaget:** *If a child sees something that doesn't match her preconceptions, she learns from it and through her behavior assimilates the new information into her thinking.*
>
> **Skinner:** *But if we reinforce a certain behavior by rewarding it, the child will do it more, and if we ignore it, the behavior will stop. It doesn't matter what, if anything, the child is thinking.*

TIPS FOR READING IN VARIOUS FIELDS OF STUDY

Though groups of disciplines (the sciences, the arts and humanities, and so on) within each field share many similarities, each discipline has features unique to it. While you should expect to read difficult texts in any field several times, taking notes in your own words, rather than highlighting or underlining, you need to be aware that reading, say, a biology text likely requires different reading techniques than a history text would. Here are some tips that can help you read effectively in various disciplines.

The Humanities

489–90

- Much of the scholarship in the humanities is based on texts of one sort or another—the Constitution, the Bible, Toni Morrison's novels, Mozart's piano concertos, Georgia O'Keeffe's paintings. When reading in the humanities, then, be aware of the differences between reading **PRIMARY SOURCES** like those and **SECONDARY SOURCES** (commentaries; analyses; evaluations; and interpretations of primary).

- When reading a primary source, you may need to ask questions like these: What kind of document is this? Who created it? When and where was the source produced? Who was it intended for? What is

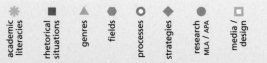
academic literacies — rhetorical situations — genres — fields — processes — strategies — research MLA / APA — media / design

its historical context? Why did the creator of the source create it? How was it received at the time of its creation? Has that reception changed?

- Read primary sources carefully and expect to reread them, perhaps several times. The way a text is organized, its sentence structure, its wording, and its imagery can all contribute to its overall message, and that's true of documents like the Declaration of Independence, the Torah, and Descartes's *Principles of Philosophy*.

- Reading secondary sources requires that you examine them with a critical eye. The questions on pages 513–14 can help you understand the source and evaluate its accuracy, perspective or angle, and usefulness for your own work.

- Similarly, plan to reread secondary sources. The argument of interpretations, analyses, or critical works requires close attention to their logic and use of evidence.

- Remember that in the humanities, "criticism" doesn't necessarily mean looking for flaws and errors. Rather, it's another term for analyzing or evaluating.

- Some key terms you need to know in order to read texts in the humanities include: *analogy, allusion, argument, deductive reasoning, inductive reasoning, irony, metaphor, natural law, natural rights, political rights, premise*. If you don't understand the meaning of any of these terms, be sure to look up their definitions.

The Social Sciences

- As you read writing in the social sciences, you need to pay attention to the hypotheses, claims, reasons, and evidence presented in the texts. Are they persuasive? How do they compare or contrast with other arguments?

- Be sure you understand what a theory in the social sciences is: a way of organizing information to help enhance our understanding of behavior, events, phenomena, or issues. For example, in sociology, social exchange theory assumes that we behave according to our sense of whether we'll be rewarded or punished by those with whom we interact. Remember that a theory is not an unsupported opinion but rather a coherent, logical frame for understanding and describing.

198–201

- Many articles include a **LITERATURE REVIEW** that summarizes and critiques previous work on the topic. Since scholarly work always grows out of the work of others, authors need to connect their work to articles and books previously published on the topic. Many literature reviews discuss imitations and problems in previous studies, ultimately identifying missing elements or gaps in them (often identified with words like *but*, *however*, and *although*), leading to a rationale for why this new work is needed.

- The "Discussion" and "Conclusion" sections (which are sometimes combined into a single section) explain and interpret the results of a study in the context of the previous literature, note any limitations in the current study, and recommend future research to address those limitations. In other words, these sections discuss what the author thinks the study means. As you read, consider possible flaws or omissions in the author's thinking as well as in the research design; for example, the study is too broad, the research question is poorly defined, or the study doesn't address its significance—the "so what?" question. Your insights could lead you to a better understanding of the topic—or to a research project of your own.

- Some key terms you need to know in order to read texts in the social sciences include *adaptation*, *aggregate*, *alienation*, *capital*, *class system*, *deviance*, *interest*, *markets*, *motivation*, *norm*, *power*, *schema*, *supply and demand*, and *value*. If you don't understand the meaning of any of these terms, be sure to look up their definitions.

The Sciences

- Remember that scientific texts are not collections of settled facts. They make claims and argue for them, using reasons and evidence to support those arguments. Scientific texts report the results of studies and experiments and are written by scientists for an audience of other scientists in the same field. These texts are different from science writing, which is often a form of nonfiction sometimes written by scientists, journalists, or other writers and aimed at general audiences to inform about scientific topics.

- If you're examining potential sources for a research project, read selectively: use articles' **ABSTRACTS** to decide whether an article is likely to be useful for your project, and skim the text to find the information relating to your needs. Many scientific articles follow a structure nicknamed IMRaD (Introduction, Methods, Results, and Discussion), so you may need to read only the sections of the article that discuss what you're looking for.

▲ 185–89

- Pay attention to the sample size—the number of units of whatever is being studied that are included in the study (a larger sample size is generally better than a smaller one)—and error bars in graphs, which show the uncertainty in the findings of the study being described.

- Scientists often make their arguments through visuals as much as words, so read images, graphs, and charts as carefully as you would the words in the text.

- For math problems or exercises, read the entire problem. Draw a picture or diagram to help you visualize the problem. Read it again, identifying the most important information; be sure you understand what the problem is asking for. Then decide on a method for solving it and come up with an answer. If you get stuck, think about how you'd deal with this information if it weren't a math problem. How would you go about solving it? Finally, reread the problem and ask yourself if you've answered the question that was asked.

- Some key terms you need to know in order to read texts in the sciences include *skepticism, data, evidence/observation, hypothesis, variables, biodiversity, falsifiability, theory, evolution, experimentation, population, qualitative, quantitative, repeatability, empirical, paradigm, rational/agnostic, cosmos.* If you don't understand the meaning of any of these terms, be sure to look up their definitions.

A Note on Career-Focused Fields

In general, the advice here for reading texts in general-education courses holds for reading in every major, including career-oriented disciplines, such as business administration, nursing, teaching, and education. At the same time, it's worth paying attention to the ways of thinking and the priorities of every field as you read in them. Here are a few examples:

Both business administration and education focus on processes. In business, much reading discusses how businesspeople do things, manage workers, set up systems, follow best accounting practices, and the like; in education, your reading will likely focus on how to write lesson plans, how to present information appropriately, and so on. Drawing flowcharts and diagrams of processes can help you understand the steps involved and help you remember them.

Engineers solve problems. So when reading engineering texts, look for relationships among concepts and ideas, and think about ways those concepts can be used to solve complex problems. Pay close attention to charts, graphs, diagrams, and visuals, as they often pack considerable information into a single image. When reading a graph, for example, consider not only the data as presented but also relationships in the data, and look for inferences and predictions you can make from the data presented.

Engineering and nursing texts contain a lot of information, much of which you won't need right away, so don't try to master every fact or procedure. Instead, read the chapter introductions, summaries, and questions, and skim, looking for the answers to the questions. You might also review a study guide for the NCLEX nursing licensing exam or the NCEES PE exam in engineering and focus your reading on the subject areas the exam focuses on. In general, work to understand the concepts you need rather than trying to memorize an avalanche of information; look for patterns in the information and how concepts are interrelated.

Writing in Academic **26**
Fields of Study

In a *literature* course, you're asked to write an analysis of a short story. In a *biology* course, you must complete several lab reports. In a *management* course, you may create a detailed business plan. In fact, just about every course you take in college will require writing, so to write successfully, you must understand the rhetorical situation of your writing in every course and discipline—to write as if you're an insider, a member of the discipline, even if you're just learning the ropes. This chapter offers help in determining the general expectations of writing done in various academic fields of study.

Considering the Rhetorical Situation

To write in academic fields, you need to use the same processes and strategies you're asked to use in your writing classes, including analyzing the **RHETORICAL SITUATION** in which you're writing. These questions can help:

53

55–56

PURPOSE   Why do people in this discipline write? To share scholarship and research findings? persuade? teach or provide guidance? show learning or mastery? track progress? propose solutions or plans of action? explore ideas or the self? earn grants or other rewards? something else?

57–60 ■

AUDIENCE

To whom do people in this discipline write? To colleagues and other scholars? students? managers? employees? customers? clients? granting agencies? the public? others? What do they already know about the discipline and the topic? What specialized terms or concepts do they understand, and which need to be defined or explained? How much evidence or support is required, and what kinds (empirical data, research findings, logical analysis, personal testimony, something else) will they accept?

61–65 ■

GENRE

What genres—reports, analyses, arguments, instructions, case studies, résumés, to name only a few—are typically used in this discipline? Are they organized in a certain way, and do they contain specific kinds of information? How much flexibility or room for innovation and creativity is allowed? What counts as evidence or support for assertions, and how is it cited (in citations in the text, in footnotes, in a works-cited page, informally in the text, or in some other way)?

66–68 ■

STANCE

What attitude is considered appropriate in this discipline? Objective? Unemotional? Critical? Passionate? Should you write as a good student showing what you can do? an instructor of others? an advocate for a position? someone exploring an idea? something else? Does the discipline require a certain tone? formal or informal language? Can you include your personal perspective and write using "I"? Should you write only in the third person and use passive voice?

69–71 ■

MEDIA/DESIGN

What media are typically used in this discipline? Print? Spoken? Electronic? A combination? Are certain design elements expected? to be avoided? Are visuals commonly used? What kinds—charts, graphs, photos, drawings, video or audio clips, or something else? In which genres? How much design freedom do you have?

✳ academic literacies   ■ rhetorical situations   ▲ genres   ● fields   ○ processes   ◆ strategies   ● research MLA / APA   ▢ media / design

WRITING IN ACADEMIC FIELDS OF STUDY

Generalizing about the requirements of writing in academic disciplines is tricky; what constitutes a discipline is sometimes unclear, and universities group academic fields together in various ways. For example, in some universities psychology is considered a science, while in others it's a social science. Economics is sometimes part of a college of business administration, sometimes in a college of arts and sciences. In addition, the writing required in, say, history, differs from that required in English literature, though both are considered parts of the humanities.

Furthermore, certain genres of writing, like *case studies* and *research reports*, can share the same name but have very different organizational structures and content, depending on the discipline in which they are used. For example, research reports in psychology and the natural sciences include a review of relevant scholarly literature in the introduction; in reports in sociology and other social sciences, the literature review is a separate section. A case study in business identifies a problem or issue in an organization; provides background information; includes a section, "Alternatives," that discusses possible solutions to the problem and why they were rejected; outlines and argues for a proposed solution; and proposes specific strategies for achieving the proposed solution. A case study in nursing, on the other hand, includes three sections: patient status, an overview of the patient's condition and treatment; the nurse's assessment of the patient's symptoms and their possible causes; and a plan for helping the patient improve. The guide below offers general advice on how to write in broad academic disciplines, but as the differences between two disciplines' expectations for case studies show, it's always a good idea to ask each of your professors for guidance on writing for their particular fields.

WRITING IN THE ARTS AND HUMANITIES

The arts and humanities focus on human culture and the expressions of the human mind, and the purpose of writing in these fields is to explore and analyze aspects of the human experience across time and sometimes to create original works of literature, music, and art. The methods used in these disciplines include careful reading, critical analysis, historical research, interpretation, questioning, synthesis, and imitation. Courses in the arts and humanities typically include fine arts, architecture, music, dance, theater, film, photography, literature, history, classical and modern languages, linguistics, and philosophy.

Writing in the arts and humanities is generally done for a broad audience that includes professors and scholars, other students, the general public, and oneself. Genres may include ANNOTATED BIBLIOGRAPHIES, ANALYSES, ARGUMENTS, essays, EVALUATIONS, JOURNALS, personal narratives, REPORTS, PRESENTATIONS, PROPOSALS, REFLECTIONS, and LITERATURE REVIEWS, as well as fiction and poetry. Support is often based on textual and observational evidence and personal insight, though in some fields empirical evidence and data are also valued. Writers in the arts and humanities tend to use modifiers to acknowledge that their insights and conclusions are interpretive, not definitive. Documentation is usually done in MLA or *Chicago* style. Elements of style favored in writing in the arts and humanities may include the use of "I"; the active voice; an informal vocabulary, if appropriate; and vivid language.

190–201 ▲
98–130
157–84
202–10
337–38 ○
131–56 ▲
673–84 □
246–55 ▲
256–63
198–201

MLA 548–96 ●

A Sample of Writing in History: A Researched Essay

Identifies a problem in current understanding of a historical event.

Offers a narrative of a past event.

Demonstrates familiarity with relevant sources.

The Pueblo Revolt of 1680 was one of the most significant yet misrepresented events in the history of American Indians. After three generations of being oppressed by Spanish rule, the Pueblo Indians throughout the southwest region of North America banded together, organizing a widespread rebellion in the blistering summer heat of 1680 and successfully liberating themselves from their oppressors by springtime. When examining the causes of the revolt, the lack of authentic Pueblo voices within the written records challenges the validity of the available sources and makes one wonder if we will ever know what went on through the eyes of the Pueblo. Although in the traditional narrative, the Spaniards are regarded as missionaries sent by God to "save" the "barbaric" Pueblos, the event, if seen from the Pueblo perspective, can be understood as a violent retaliation by the Pueblo against the Spanish oppression. The Pueblo uprisings, from burning down churches to the violent deaths of Catholic friars, reveal spiritual abuse as the major cause of the revolt. Moreover, without texts written by the Pueblo, their architecture and spatial organization provide valuable insight into the causes of the revolt era and help to overcome the veneer of Spanish colonialism.

Offers a strong thesis.

Clear, engaging writing style.

Adapted from "Letting the Unspoken Speak: A Reexamination of the Pueblo Revolt of 1680," by E. McHugh, April 2015, Armstrong Undergraduate Journal of History 5, no. 1, https://www.armstrong.edu/history-journal/history-journal-letting-the-unspoken-speak-a-reexamination-of-the-pueblo-re.

Sources in essay cited in Chicago format.

Typical Organization of Arts and Humanities Essays

Typical essays in the arts and humanities include these elements:

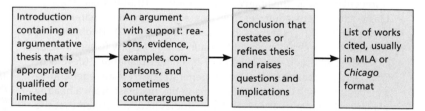

| Introduction containing an argumentative thesis that is appropriately qualified or limited | → | An argument with support: reasons, evidence, examples, comparisons, and sometimes counterarguments | → | Conclusion that restates or refines thesis and raises questions and implications | → | List of works cited, usually in MLA or *Chicago* format |

WRITING IN SCIENCE AND MATHEMATICS

The sciences include biology, chemistry, geology, earth sciences, and physics. Mathematics may include statistics and logic as well. All these fields aim to increase our knowledge of the physical and natural world and its phenomena through observation, experiment, logic, and computation.

185–89
198–201
131–56
157–84
246–55

APA 597–636

Scientists and mathematicians typically write **ABSTRACTS**, **LITERATURE REVIEWS**, **REPORTS**, **ARGUMENTS**, poster presentations, **PROPOSALS**, and lab reports for audiences that may include other researchers, granting agencies, teachers, students, and the general public. Support in the sciences most often consists of repeatable empirical evidence; in mathematics, careful reasoning and the posing and solving of problems; in both, careful attention to the work of previous researchers. The writing in these fields focuses on the subject of the study, not the researcher, so most often the passive voice is used. Source material is paraphrased and summarized and cited in CSE or **APA** style.

A Sample of Scientific Writing: A Scientific Proposal in Biology

Planarians, flatworms widely known for their incredible regenerative capabilities, are able to restore an entire organism from even a small fragment of tissue. This ability to regenerate is attributed solely to neoblasts, pluripotent adult stem cells located throughout the parenchyma of the animal (Newmark & Sanchez Alvarado, 2002). Neoblasts are stimulated to migrate and proliferate in times of injury (Guedelhoefer & Sanchez Alvarado, 2012). Lethally irradiated planarians (devoid of stem cells and therefore unable to regenerate) can restore regenerative capability through transplantation of a single neoblast from a healthy planarian (Wagner et al., 2011). Many studies have concluded that the population of neoblasts is not homogenous (Scimone et al., 2014), and there are different responses to different injury types. Wenemoser and Reddien (2012) observed a body-wide increase in mitotic activity, such as cell division and migration, with any injury.

Careful reference to previous sentence.

Specialized disciplinary vocabulary.

Sources paraphrased and summarized.

Third person, passive voice.

Adapted from "Identifying Genes Involved in Suppression of Tumor Formation in the Planarian Schmidtea mediterranea," by E. Dorsten, 2015, Best Integrated Writing, 2, https://corescholar.libraries.wright.edu/biw/vol2/iss1/6/

Typical Organization of Research Reports in the Sciences

Typical reports in the sciences include elements that follow the IMRaD structure: Introduction, Methods, Results, and Discussion. They also include an abstract and list of references.

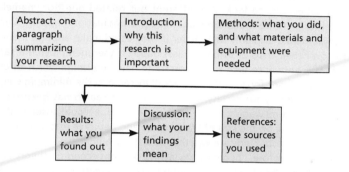

WRITING IN THE SOCIAL SCIENCES

Anthropology, archaeology, criminal justice, cultural studies, gender studies, geography, psychology, political science, and sociology are considered social sciences because they all explore human behavior and society using observation, experimentation, questionnaires, and interviews.

    Social scientists typically write for fellow scholars, teachers, students, and the general public. They may write in several genres: **ABSTRACTS**, **ANNOTATED BIBLIOGRAPHIES**, **ANALYSES**, **ARGUMENTS**, case studies, ethnographies, **LITERATURE OR RESEARCH REVIEWS**, **REPORTS**, **SUMMARIES**, and **PRESENTATIONS**. Claims are typically supported by empirical evidence, fieldwork done in natural settings, observation, and interviews. Writers in these fields strive for an objective tone, often using the passive voice. Sources may be cited in **APA** or *Chicago* style.

▲ 185–89

190–98

98–130

157–84

198–201

131–56

✳ 33–34

▢ 673–84

● APA 597–636

A Sample of Writing in the Social Sciences: A Research Report

Objective tone. ....•

Traditional economic theory states that a minimum wage above the marginal product of labor will lead to increased unemployment. . . . This paper aims to look at a different but related question, namely, whether or not a minimum wage makes a population happier. Since people would arguably be happier if they could make enough money to cover their costs of living and less happy if the unemployment rate rose, the answer to such a question could help determine which effect

Research question. ....•

is the dominant force and if an overall increase in the minimum wage is a good policy for society. Although scant research has been done

Specialized language. ....•

on a minimum wage's effect on happiness, one could assume that research done on the size of the positive and negative effects of minimum wages could indicate whether or not it would leave a population

Literature review. ....•

happier. Therefore, I begin by reviewing relevant economic theory and research on the effects of a minimum wage increase to provide background information and describe what related questions have been

Empirical method. ....•

approached and answered. I then describe the data and method used to answer this question, followed by the interpretation of such results

Analysis and evaluation of results. ....•

as well as the implications.

Adapted from "The Effect of Minimum Wages on Happiness," by J. Nizamoff, Beyond Politics 2014, pp. 85–94, https://beyondpolitics.nd.edu/wp-content/uploads/2015/03/2013-14-Full-Journal.pdf

Typical Organization of a Research Report in the Social Sciences

Typical research reports in social science courses might include the following elements, though the order and names of the elements may differ from discipline to discipline. For example, in psychology, the literature review is part of the introduction, not a separate section as shown here.

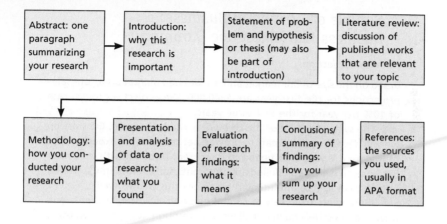

WRITING IN BUSINESS

The focus of the academic discipline of business is business-management principles and their application, and the purpose of writing in business is often to cause readers to make a decision and then act on it. The primary methods used include problem solving, planning, and experiential learning, or learning by doing. Courses typically taught include finance, economics, human resources, marketing, operations management, and accounting.

The audiences for writing in business typically include colleagues, employees in other departments, supervisors, managers, clients, customers, and other stakeholders—often several at the same time as a text moves through an organization. Genres may include memos, emails, letters, case studies, executive summaries, **RÉSUMÉS**, business plans, **REPORTS**, and **ANALYSES**. Support usually takes the form of facts and figures, examples, narratives, and expert testimony, and documentation is usually done in **APA** or *Chicago* style. Elements of style favored in business writing include these features: the main point is presented early; the language used is simple, direct, and positive; and the active voice is used in most cases.

▲ 264–79

131–56

98–130

● APA 597–636

A Sample of Writing in Business: A Business Plan Executive Summary:

Financial Projections

Precise numbers, confidently stated.

Based on the size of our market and our defined market area, our sales projections for the first year are $340,000. We project a growth rate of 10% per year for the first three years.

Clear, direct writing, free of jargon and hedging.

The salary for each of the co-owners will be $40,000. On start up we will have six trained staff to provide pet services and expect to hire four more this year once financing is secured. To begin with, co-owner Pat Simpson will be scheduling appointments and coordinating services, but we plan to hire a full-time receptionist this year as well.

Positive tone.

Already we have service commitments from over 40 clients and plan to aggressively build our client base through newspaper, website, social media, and direct mail advertising. The loving on-site professional care that Pet Grandma will provide is sure to appeal to cat and dog owners throughout the West Vancouver area.

Adapted from "Business Plan Executive Summary Sample," by S. Ward, March 29, 2017, The Balance, https://thebalance.com/business-plan-executive-summary-example-2948007

Typical Organization of Business Plans

A common assignment in business courses is a business plan. Business plans typically include these sections:

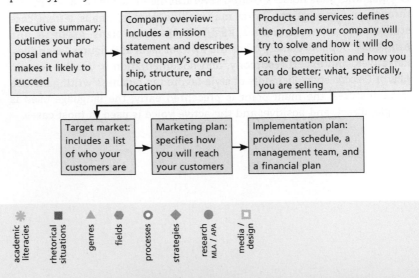

Executive summary: outlines your proposal and what makes it likely to succeed

Company overview: includes a mission statement and describes the company's ownership, structure, and location

Products and services: defines the problem your company will try to solve and how it will do so; the competition and how you can do better; what, specifically, you are selling

Target market: includes a list of who your customers are

Marketing plan: specifies how you will reach your customers

Implementation plan: provides a schedule, a management team, and a financial plan

WRITING IN EDUCATION

The focus of study in education is how people learn and how to teach effectively. Its primary methods include observation, problem solving, and practice teaching. Courses typically center on teaching methods, the philosophy of education, educational measurement and assessment, educational psychology, and instructional technology, among others.

Educators typically write for audiences that include their students, parents, other teachers, administrators, and the public. Genres may include lesson plans, **SUMMARIES**, **REPORTS**, **ANNOTATED BIBLIOGRAPHIES**, **PORTFOLIOS**, and **REFLECTIONS**. Support for claims may include facts, statistics, test scores, personal narratives, observations, and case studies. Sources are documented in **APA** style. Clarity and correctness are important in writing in education; "I" may be used in reflective writing and informal communication, while in formal writing the third person is preferred.

33–34

131–56

190–98

361–70

256–63

APA 600–604

A Sample of Writing in Education: A Teaching Philosophy Statement

My Image of the Child: •···

Sections labeled with headings.

I believe that the student should be at the center of the instructional •·········· process. I have an image of children as strong and capable beings. The classroom is a place where the teacher serves as a facilitator and guide as the students construct their own understanding of the world around them. Although it is the teacher's role to plan lessons and evaluate students' progress, it is of the utmost importance to always take the children and their own unique needs into consideration. For my second field experience, I was placed at Margaret Manson Elementary. Their school motto is that "the children come first." When children are the priority in teaching, an amazing amount of learning can take place. I believe in creating opportunities for students to develop to their fullest potential while developing and expanding their horizons and world-views. In order to accomplish this, there must be a welcoming, positive environment that is open and honest. When students feel comfortable

Argument is constructed to show teaching priorities.

Writing carefully crafted and proofread.

As a reflective piece, "I" is appropriate.

at school they will surely be more engaged and responsive to class activities. I also consider it essential to be passionate and enthusiastic about learning so that the students can have a most relevant and meaningful experience.

Adapted from "Statement of Teaching Philosophy," by K. Tams (n.d.), Kelly Tams' Teaching Portfolio, http://tams.yolasite.com/my-philosophy-of-education.php

Typical Organization of Lesson Plans in Education

Frequent assignments in education courses are lesson plans, which typically include these elements:

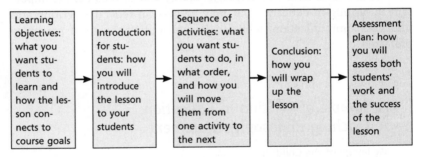

Learning objectives: what you want students to learn and how the lesson connects to course goals → Introduction for students: how you will introduce the lesson to your students → Sequence of activities: what you want students to do, in what order, and how you will move them from one activity to the next → Conclusion: how you will wrap up the lesson → Assessment plan: how you will assess both students' work and the success of the lesson

WRITING IN ENGINEERING AND TECHNOLOGY

In the fields of engineering and technology, the focus is how to create and maintain useful structures, systems, processes, and machines. Engineers and technicians define problems as well as solve them, weigh various alternatives, and test possible solutions before presenting them to clients. This is a broad set of disciplines that may include civil, computer, electrical, mechanical, and structural engineering; computer science; and various technology specialties such as HVAC and automotive technology.

academic literacies · rhetorical situations · genres · fields · processes · strategies · research MLA / APA · media / design

Engineers and technicians typically write for their peers and team members, their clients, and the public. Writing tasks may include **ABSTRACTS**, **EVALUATIONS**, instructions, **LITERATURE REVIEWS**, memos, **PROPOSALS**, **REPORTS**, and **SUMMARIES**. Support usually includes data, examples, mathematical and logical reasoning, and experimental results, and sources are usually cited in **APA** format. Engineers and technicians value writing that includes logical ordering of ideas and precise language. Tables, charts, figures, illustrations, and headings and subheadings within the writing—all ways of quickly and efficiently getting information—are also valued.

▲ 185–89
202–10
198–201
246–55
131–56
✳ 33–34
● APA 597–636

A Sample of Writing in Engineering: A Research Report

2. MATERIALS AND METHODS

Headings used.

To begin testing, an ATV test bed was designed (fig. 1). To secure the machine, a loose rope was attached to the front of the machine and then to the testing platform. An additional rope was then attached at a 90° angle to the front of the machine to act as the lifting force. The test bed platform could be raised to a maximum of 60°, which simulated hills or steep terrain. Each test was started at 0° and then increased by increments of 10 (angles were determined by a digital level attached to platform). Once the machine was at the appropriate angle, a lift force was applied to observe turnover weight. Once the machine's tires lifted off of the platform, the scale was read to determine the amount of weight. Each machine was tested from to rear and side to side.

Charts, graphs, and photos included.

Precise description of procedure.

Technical language used for precision.

Adapted from "Analysis of All Terrain Vehicle Crash Mechanisms," by S. Tanner, M. Aitken, and J. N. Warnock, 2008–10, Journal of Undergraduate Research in Bioengineering, https://www.uweb.engr.washington.edu/education/pdf/tanner.pdf

Typical Organization of Lab Reports in Engineering

Lab reports, a typical assignment in engineering classes, usually include the IMRaD elements, along with an abstract and a list of references. This format may vary depending on the engineering field and the requirements of the experiment or task.

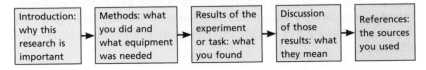

| Introduction: why this research is important | → | Methods: what you did and what equipment was needed | → | Results of the experiment or task: what you found | → | Discussion of those results: what they mean | → | References: the sources you used |

WRITING IN HEALTH SCIENCES AND NURSING

Health sciences and nursing is a broad set of fields that may include nursing, anatomy, physiology, nutrition, and pharmacology as well as athletic training, exercise science, physical or occupational therapy, and speech pathology. Consequently, the methods used are also broad and varied, and they may include study of theories and techniques, observation, roleplaying, and experiential learning.

Writing in these fields may include **ABSTRACTS**, **ANNOTATED BIBLIOGRAPHIES**, **ARGUMENTS**, case studies, instructions, personal narratives, **REPORTS**, **REFLECTIONS**, **REVIEWS**, **SUMMARIES**, and charts **DESCRIBING** patients' conditions and care. The audiences for this writing may include other patient care providers, clinic and hospital administrators and staff, insurance companies, and patients or clients. Support for assertions typically includes scholarly research, observation, and description, and high value is placed on accurate information and detail. Other aspects of this writing include a preference for writing in the third person, paraphrased source information, and the use of headings and subheadings. Sources are usually cited in **APA** format.

✳ academic literacies
◼ rhetorical situations
▲ genres
⬢ fields
○ processes
◆ strategies
● research MLA / APA
◻ media / design

A Sample of Writing in Nursing: A Case Study

Patient Status. ......• Ms. D is a morbidly obese 67 year old female, 240 lbs, 5'2" with type II diabetes mellitus. She was transferred from a nursing home to the hospital for pneumonia, but also suffers from congestive heart disease, sleep apnea, psoriasis, and osteoarthritis. She has a weak but productive cough with tonsil suction, and she was on breathing treatments with albuterol. Her skin is very dry and thin with several lesions and yeast infections, and the deep folds of her lower abdomen bled during the bed bath. She did not want to wear her breathing mask at night and refused to get out of bed. She cried when encouraged to use the bathroom or to move her legs. She expressed great fear of returning to the nursing home.

Careful description of patient's condition.

Detailed observation using precise terms.

Behavior as well as medical conditions taken into account.

From the outset, we realized that Ms. D needed care beyond physical therapy and treatment for pneumonia; we realized that her obesity and refusal to participate in her health care expressed important patterns of her life. Morbid obesity does not happen overnight; it is a progressive pattern associated with activity levels, diet, and self-care practices, as well as other possible physiological and psychosocial dimensions. Johnson's (1980) Behavioral System Model, which outlines seven behavioral subsystems, was helpful in providing a perspective of the complexity of Ms. D's health needs. We also assessed that Ms. D lacked confidence in taking care of herself (reflecting the *achievement subsystem*) and lacked a sense of family support from her two sons (*affiliative subsystem*). Her fear of returning to the nursing home coupled with her need for ongoing care challenged her sense of interdependency as addressed in Johnson's *dependency subsystem*.

Patient Assessment.

Use of paraphrased scholarly source to aid assessment.

Adapted from "Esthetic Knowing with a Hospitalized Morbidly Obese Patient," by R. Brinkley, K. Ricker, and K. Tuomey, Fall 2007, Journal of Undergraduate Nursing Scholarship, 9, no. 1, http://www.juns.nursing.arizona.edu/articles/Fall%202007/Esthetic%20knowing.htm

Typical Organization of Case Studies in Health Sciences and Nursing

Case studies, typical assignments in these fields, usually include the following elements:

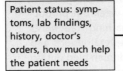

Patient status: symptoms, lab findings, history, doctor's orders, how much help the patient needs	→	Assessment: why the patient is being cared for; origins of current situation; when symptoms started, how the patient has been treated, the expected outcome	→	Care plan: what has been done, how current care is working, how care might be improved

part 5

Processes

To create anything, we generally break the work down into a series of steps. We follow a recipe (or the directions on a box) to bake a cake; we break a song down into different parts and the music into various chords to arrange a piece of music. So it is when we write. We rely on various processes to get from a blank screen or page to a finished product. The chapters that follow offer advice on some of these processes—from WRITING AS INQUIRY and GENERATING IDEAS to DRAFTING to GETTING RESPONSE to EDITING to COMPILING A PORTFOLIO, and more.

Processes

Writing as Inquiry **27**

Sometimes we write to say what we think. Other times, however, we write in order to figure out what we think. Much of the writing you do in college will be the latter. Even as you learn to write, you will be writing to learn. This chapter is about writing with a spirit of inquiry—approaching writing projects with curiosity, moving beyond the familiar, keeping your eyes open, tackling issues that don't have easy answers. It's about starting with questions and going from there—and taking risks. As Mark Twain once said, "Sail away from the safe harbor. . . . Explore. Dream. Discover." This chapter offers strategies for doing just that with your writing.

Starting with Questions

The most important thing is to start with questions—with what you don't know rather than with what you do know. Your goal is to learn about your subject and then to learn more. If you're writing about a topic you know well, you want to expand on what you already know. In academic writing, good topics arise from important questions, issues, and problems that are already being discussed. As a writer, you need to find out what's being said about your topic and then see your writing as a way of entering that larger conversation.

So start with questions, and don't expect to find easy answers. If there were easy answers, there would be no reason for discussion—or for you to write. For purposes of inquiry, the best questions can't be answered by looking in a reference book. Instead, they are ones that help you explore what you think—and why. As it happens, many of the strategies in this book can help you ask questions of this kind. Following are some questions to get you started:

academic literacies

rhetorical situations

genres

fields

processes

strategies

research MLA / APA

media / design

432–42 **How can it be DEFINED?** What is it, and what does it do? Look it up in a dictionary; check *Wikipedia*. Remember, though, that these are only starting points. How *else* can it be defined? What more is there to know about it? If your topic is being debated, chances are that its very definition is subject to debate. If, for instance, you're writing about gay marriage, how you define marriage will affect how you approach the topic.

443–51 **How can it be DESCRIBED?** What details should you include? From what vantage point should you describe your topic? If, for example, your topic is the physiological effects of running a marathon, what are those effects—on the lungs, heart muscles, nerves, brain, and so on? How will you describe the physical experience of running over twenty-six miles from the runner's point of view?

457–61 **How can it be EXPLAINED?** What does it do? How does it work? If you're investigating the use of performance-enhancing drugs by athletes, for example, what exactly are the effects of these drugs? What makes them dangerous—and are they always dangerous or only in certain conditions? Why are they illegal—and should they be illegal?

424–31 **What can it be COMPARED with?** Again using performance-enhancing drugs by athletes as an example, how does taking such supplements compare with wearing high-tech footwear or uniforms? Does such a comparison make you see taking steroids or other performance-enhancing drugs in a new light?

392–96 **What may have CAUSED it? What might be its EFFECTS?** Who or what does it affect? What causes cerebral palsy in children, for example? What are its symptoms? If children with cerebral palsy are not treated, what might be the consequences?

418–23 **How can it be CLASSIFIED?** Is it a topic or issue that can be placed into categories of similar topics or issues? What categories can it be placed into? Are there legal and illegal performance-enhancing supplements (human growth hormone and steroids, for instance), and what's the difference? Are some safe and others less safe? Classifying your topic in this way can help you consider its complexities.

How can it be ANALYZED? What parts can the topic be divided into? For example, if you are exploring the health effects of cell phone use, you might ask these questions: What evidence suggests that cell phone radiation causes cancer? What cancers are associated with cell phone use? What do medical experts and phone manufacturers say? How can cell phone users reduce their risk?

▲ 98–130

How can it be interpreted? What does it really mean? How do you interpret it, and how does your interpretation differ from others? What evidence supports your interpretation, and what argues against it? Imagine you're exploring the topic of sports injuries among young women. Do these injuries reflect a larger cultural preoccupation with competition? a desire to win college scholarships? something else?

What expectations does it raise? What will happen next? What makes you think so? If this happens, how will it affect those involved? For instance, will the governing bodies of professional sports require more testing of athletes' blood, urine, and hair than they do now? Will such tests be unfair to athletes taking drugs for legitimate medical needs?

What are the different POSITIONS on it? What controversies or disagreements exist, and what evidence is offered for the various positions? What else might be said? Are there any groups or individuals who seem especially authoritative? If so, you might want to explore what they have said.

▲ 157–84

What are your own feelings about it? What interests you about the topic? How much do you already know about it? For example, if you're an athlete, how do you feel about competing against others who may have taken supplements? If a friend has problems with drugs, do those problems affect your thinking about drugs in sports? How do you react to what others say about the topic? What else do you want to find out?

Are there other ways to think about it? Is what seems true in this case also true in others? How can you apply this subject in another situation? Will what works in another situation also work here? What do you have to do to adapt it? Imagine you are writing about traffic fatalities. If replacing stop signs with roundabouts or traffic circles reduced traffic fatalities in England, could doing so also reduce accidents in the United States?

334–35 You can also start with the journalist's **QUESTIONS**: *Who? What? When? Where? Why? How?* Asking questions from these various perspectives can help you deepen your understanding of your topic by leading you to see it from many angles.

Keeping a Journal

337–38 One way to get into the habit of using writing as a tool for inquiry is to keep a **JOURNAL**. You can use a journal to record your observations, reactions, whatever you wish. Some writers find journals especially useful places to articulate questions or speculations. You may be assigned by teachers to do certain work in a journal, but in general, you can use a journal to write for yourself. Note your ideas, speculate, digress—go wherever your thoughts lead you.

Keeping a Blog

667 You may also wish to explore issues or other ideas online in the form of a **BLOG**. Most blogs have a comments section that allows others to read and respond to what you write, leading to potentially fruitful discussions. You can also include links to other websites, helping you connect various strands of thought and research. The blogs of others, along with online discussion forums and groups, may also be useful sources of opinion on your topic, but keep in mind that they probably aren't authoritative research sources. There are a number of search engines that can help you find blog posts related to specific topics, including *Google Blog Search, Ask,* and *IceRocket.* You can create your own blog on sites such as *Blogger, Tumblr, Svbtle,* or *WordPress.*

academic literacies

rhetorical situations

genres

fields

processes

strategies

research MLA / APA

media / design

Collaborating 28

Whether you're working in a face-to-face group, posting on an online discussion board, or exchanging drafts with a classmate, you likely spend a lot of time working with others on writing tasks. Even if you do much of your writing sitting alone at a computer, you probably get help from others at various stages in the writing process—and provide help as well. Two heads can be better than one—and learning to work well with a team is as important as anything else you'll learn in college. This chapter offers some guidelines for collaborating successfully with other writers.

Some Ground Rules for Face-to-Face Group Work

- Make sure everyone is facing everyone else and is physically part of the group. Doing that makes a real difference in the quality of the interactions—think how much better conversation works when you're sitting around a table than it does when you're sitting in a row.

- Thoughtfulness, respect, and tact are key, since most writers (as you know) are sensitive and need to be able to trust those commenting on their work. Respond to the contributions of others as you would like others to respond to yours.

- Each meeting needs an agenda—and careful attention paid to time. Appoint one person as timekeeper to make sure all necessary work gets done in the available time.

- Appoint another person to be group leader or facilitator. That person needs to make sure everyone gets a chance to speak, no one dominates the discussion, and the group stays on task.

- Appoint a member of the group to record the group's discussion, jotting down the major points as they come up and then writing a **SUMMARY** of the discussion that the group members then approve.

534–35

Online Collaboration

Sometimes you'll work with one or more people online. Working together online offers many advantages, including the ability to collaborate without being in the same place at the same time. Nonetheless, it also presents some challenges that differ from those of face-to-face group work. When sharing writing or collaborating with others online in other ways, consider the following suggestions:

- As with all online communication, remember that you need to choose your words carefully to avoid inadvertently hurting someone's feelings. Without facial expressions, gestures, and other forms of body language and without tone of voice, your words carry all the weight.

57–60

- Remember that the **AUDIENCE** for what you write may well extend beyond your group—your work might be forwarded to others, so there is no telling who else might read it.
- Decide as a group how best to deal with the logistics of exchanging drafts and comments. You can cut and paste text directly into email, send it as an attachment to a message, or post it to your class course management system site or a file-sharing site like *Dropbox* or *Google Docs*. You may need to use a combination of methods, depending on each group member's access to equipment and software. In any case, name your files carefully so that everyone knows which version to use.

Writing Conferences

Conferences with instructors or writing tutors can be an especially helpful kind of collaboration. These one-on-one sessions often offer the most strongly focused assistance you can get—and truly valuable instruction. Here are some tips for making the most of conference time:

- *Come prepared.* Bring all necessary materials, including the draft you'll be discussing, your notes, any outlines—and, of course, any questions.

- *Be prompt.* Your instructor or tutor has set aside a block of time for you, and once that time is up, there's likely to be another student writer waiting.

- *Listen carefully, discuss your work seriously, and try not to be defensive.* Your instructor or tutor is only trying to help you produce the best piece possible. If you sense that your work is being misunderstood, explain what you're trying to say. Don't get angry! If a sympathetic reader who's trying to help can't understand what you mean, maybe you haven't conveyed your meaning well enough.

- *Take notes.* During the conference, jot down keywords and suggestions. Immediately afterward, flesh out your notes so you'll have a complete record of what was said.

- *Reflect on the conference.* Afterward, think about what you learned. What do you have to do now? Create a plan for revising or doing further work, and write out questions you will ask at your next conference.

Group Writing Projects

Creating a document with a team is common in business and professional work and in some academic fields as well. Here are some tips for making collaboration of this kind work well:

- *Define the task as clearly as possible.* Make sure everyone understands and agrees with the stated goals.

- *Divide the task into parts.* Decide which parts can be done by individuals, which can be done by a subgroup, and which need to be done by everyone together.

- *Assign each group member certain tasks.* Try to match tasks to each person's skills and interests and to divide the work equally.

- *Establish a deadline for each task.* Allow time for unforeseen problems before the project deadline.
- *Try to accommodate everyone's style of working.* Some people value discussion; others want to get right down to the writing. There's no best way to get work done; everyone needs to be conscious that their way is not the only way.
- *Work for consensus—not necessarily total agreement.* Everyone needs to agree that the plan to get the task done is doable and appropriate—if not exactly the way you would do it if you were working alone.
- *Make sure everyone performs.* Sometimes your instructor may help, but the group itself may have to develop a way to ensure that the work gets done well and fairly. During the course of the project, it's sometimes helpful for each group member to write an assessment both of the group's work and of individual members' contributions.

Generating Ideas and Text **29**

All good writing revolves around ideas. Whether you're writing a job-application letter, a sonnet, or an essay, you'll always spend time and effort generating ideas. Some writers can come up with a topic, put their thoughts in order, and flesh out their arguments in their heads; but most of us need to write out our ideas, play with them, tease them out, and examine them from some distance and from multiple perspectives. This chapter offers activities that can help you do just that. *Freewriting*, *looping*, *listing*, and *clustering* can help you explore what you know about a subject; *cubing* and *questioning* nudge you to consider a subject in new ways; and *outlining*, *letter writing*, *journal keeping*, and *discovery drafting* offer ways to generate a text.

Freewriting

An informal method of exploring a subject by writing about it, freewriting ("writing freely") can help you generate ideas and come up with materials for your draft. Here's how to do it:

1. Write as quickly as you can without stopping for 5 to 10 minutes (or until you fill a screen or page).

2. If you have a subject to explore, write it at the top and then start writing about it, but if you stray, don't worry—just keep writing. If you don't have a subject yet, just start writing and don't stop until the time is up. If you can't think of anything to say, write that ("I can't think of anything to say") again and again until you do—and you will!

3. Once the time is up, read over what you've written, and underline or highlight passages that interest you.

4. Write some more, starting with one of those underlined or highlighted passages as your new topic. Repeat the process until you've come up with a usable topic.

Looping

Looping is a more focused version of freewriting; it can help you explore what you know about a subject. You stop, reflect on what you've written, and then write again, developing your understanding in the process. It's good for clarifying your knowledge and understanding of a subject and finding a focus. Here's what you do:

1. Write for 5 to 10 minutes on whatever you know about your subject. This is your first loop.

2. Read over what you wrote, and then write a single sentence summarizing the most important or interesting idea. You might try completing one of these sentences: "I guess what I was trying to say was . . ." or "What surprises me most in reading what I wrote is . . ." This will be the start of another loop.

3. Write again for 5 to 10 minutes, using your summary sentence as your beginning and your focus. Again, read what you've written, and then write a sentence capturing the most important idea—in a third loop.

Keep going until you have enough understanding of your topic to be able to decide on a tentative focus—something you can write about.

Listing

Some writers find it useful to keep lists of ideas that occur to them while they are thinking about a topic. Follow these steps:

1. Write a list of potential ideas about a topic. Don't try to limit your list—include anything that interests you.

2. Look for relationships among the items on your list: what patterns do you see? If other ideas occur to you, add them to the list.

3. Arrange the items in an order that makes sense for your purpose and can serve as the beginning of an outline for your writing.

Clustering or Mapping Ideas

Clustering (also called idea mapping) is a way of generating and connecting ideas visually. It's useful for seeing how various ideas relate to one another and for developing subtopics. The technique is simple:

1. Write your topic in the middle of a sheet of paper and circle it.

2. Write ideas relating to that topic around it, circle them, and connect them to the central circle.

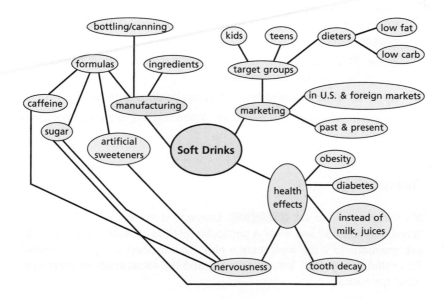

3. Write down examples, facts, or other details relating to each idea, and join them to the appropriate circles.

4. Keep going until you can't think of anything else relating to your topic.

You should end up with various ideas about your topic, and the clusters will allow you to see how they relate to one another. In the example cluster on the topic of "soft drinks" on the previous page, note how some ideas link not only to the main topic or related topics but also to other ideas.

Cubing

A cube has six sides. You can examine a topic as you might a cube, looking at it in these six ways:

443–51
- **DESCRIBE** it. What's its color? shape? age? size? What's it made of?

424–31
- **COMPARE** it to something else. What is it similar to or different from?

418–23
- Associate it with other things. What does it remind you of? What connections does it have to other things? How would you **CLASSIFY** it?

98–130
- **ANALYZE** it. How is it made? Where did it come from? Where is it going? How are its parts related?

- Apply it. What is it used for? What can be done with it?

157–84
- **ARGUE** for or against it. Choose a position relating to your subject, and defend it.

Questioning

334–35
It's always useful to ask **QUESTIONS**. One way is to start with *What? Who? When? Where? How?* and *Why?* A particular method of exploring a topic is to ask questions as if the topic were a play. This method is especially useful for exploring literature, history, the arts, and the social sciences. Start with these questions:

- **What?** What happens? How is it similar to or different from other actions?
- **Who?** Who are the actors? Who are the participants, and who are the spectators? How do the actors affect the action, and how are they affected by it?
- **When?** When does the action take place? How often does it happen? What happens before, after, or at the same time? Would it be different at another time? Does the time have historical significance?
- **Where?** What is the setting? What is the situation, and what makes it significant?
- **How?** How does the action occur? What are the steps in the process? What techniques are required? What equipment is needed?
- **Why?** Why did this happen? What are the actors' motives? What end does the action serve?

Using Genre Features

Genres typically include particular kinds of information and organize it in particular ways. One way to generate ideas and text, then, is to identify the key features of the genre in which you're writing and use them to guide you as you write. Of course, you may alter the genre's features or combine two or more genres in order to achieve your purpose, but the overall shape and content of the genre can give you a way to develop and organize your ideas and research.

Outlining

You may create an *informal outline* by simply listing your ideas and numbering them in the order in which you want to write about them. You might prefer to make a *working outline*, to show the hierarchy of relationships among your ideas. While still informal, a working outline distinguishes your main ideas and your support, often through simple indentation:

First main idea
   Supporting evidence or detail
   Supporting evidence or detail
Second main idea
   Supporting evidence or detail
   Supporting evidence or detail

A *formal outline* shows the hierarchy of your ideas through a system of indenting, numbering, and lettering. Remember that when you divide a point into more specific subpoints, you should have at least two of them—you can't divide something into only one part. Also, try to keep items at each level parallel in structure. Formal outlines work this way:

Thesis statement
   I. First reason
      A. Supporting evidence
         1. Detail of evidence
         2. Detail of evidence
      B. Supporting evidence
   II. Another reason

Here is a formal outline of the first part of the research report by Dylan Borchers on pages 588–96, "Against the Odds: Harry S. Truman and the Election of 1948," that shows how he organized it:

   I. Introduction: Outcome of 1948 election
   II. Bad predictions by pollsters
      A. Pollsters stopped polling.
      B. Dewey supporters became overconfident.
      C. Truman supporters were either energized or stayed home.
   III. Dewey's campaign overly cautious
      A. He was overconfident.
      B. His message was vague—he avoided taking stands.

IV. Dewey's public appearances poor
    A. He was seen as aloof, uncomfortable with crowds.
    B. He made blunders.
    C. His speeches were dull.

Writing out a formal outline can be helpful when you're dealing with a complex subject; as you revise your drafts, though, be flexible and ready to change your outline as your understanding of your topic develops.

Letter Writing

Sometimes the prospect of writing a report or essay can be intimidating. You may find that simply explaining your topic to someone will help you get started. In that case, write a letter or email to someone you know—your best friend, a parent or grandparent, a sibling—in which you discuss your subject. Explain it in terms that your reader can understand. Use the unsent letter to rehearse your topic; make it a kind of rough draft that you can then revise and develop to suit your actual audience.

Keeping a Journal

Some writers find that writing in a journal helps them generate ideas. Making note of your ideas, thoughts, feelings, or the events of your day can provide a wealth of topics, and a journal can also be a good place to explore what you think and why you think as you do.

Journals are private—you are the only audience—so you can feel free to write whatever comes to mind. And you can do more than write. If you choose a paper journal, doodle or draw in it, and keep clippings or scraps of paper between the pages; if you keep your journal on a computer, copy and paste interesting images or text you find online. Whatever form your journal takes, feel free to play with its contents, and don't worry about errors or grammar. The goal is to generate ideas; let yourself wander without censoring yourself or fretting that your writing is incorrect or incomplete or incoherent. That's okay.

331–32 ◉
332–33
334

One measure of the success of journaling and other personal writing is length: journal entries, **FREEWRITING**, **LISTING**, **CUBING**, and other types of informal writing are like warm-up exercises to limber you up and get you thinking. If you don't give them enough time and space, they may not do what you want them to. Often, students' best insights appear at the end of their journal entries. Had they stopped before that point, they would never have had those good ideas.

After you've written several journal entries, one way to study the ideas in them is to highlight useful patterns in different colors. For example, journal entries usually include some questioning and speculating, as well as summarizing and paraphrasing. Try color-coding each of these, sentence by sentence, phrase by phrase: yellow for summaries or paraphrases, green for questions, blue for speculations. Do any colors dominate? If, for example, your entries are mostly yellow, you may be restating the course content or quoting from the textbook too much and perhaps need to ask more questions. If you're generating ideas for an essay, you might assign colors to ideas or themes to see which ones are the most promising.

Discovery Drafting

340–42 ◉

Some writers do best by jumping in and writing. Here are the steps to take if you're ready to write a preliminary **DRAFT**:

1. Write your draft quickly, in one sitting if possible.

2. Assume that you are writing to discover what you want to say and how you need to say it—and that you will make substantial revisions in a later part of the process.

3. Don't worry about grammatical or factual correctness—if you can't think of a word, leave a blank space to fill in later. If you're unsure of a date or spelling, put a question mark in parentheses as a reminder to check it later. Just write.

IF YOU NEED MORE HELP

See each of the **GENRE** chapters for specific strategies for generating text in each genre.

▲ 73

30 Drafting

At some point, you need to write out a draft. By the time you begin drafting, you've probably written quite a bit—in the form of notes, lists, outlines, and other kinds of informal writing. This chapter offers some hints on how to write a draft—and reminds you that as you draft, you may well need to get more information, rethink some aspect of your work, or follow new ideas that occur to you as you write.

Establishing a Schedule with Deadlines

479–80

Don't wait until the last minute to write. Computers crash, printers jam. Life intervenes in unpredictable ways. You increase your chances of success immensely by setting and meeting **DEADLINES**: Research done by ____; rough draft done by ____; revisions done by ____; final draft edited, proofread, and submitted by ____. How much time you need varies with each writing task—but trying to compress everything into twenty-four or forty-eight hours before the deadline is asking for trouble.

Getting Comfortable

When are you at your best? When do you have your best ideas? For major writing projects, consider establishing a schedule that lets you write when you stand the best chance of doing good work. Schedule breaks for exercise and snacks. Find a good place to write, a place where you've got a good surface on which to spread out your materials, good lighting, a comfortable chair, and the right tools (computer, pen, paper) for the job. Often, however, we must make do: you may have to do your drafting in a busy computer lab or classroom. The trick is to make yourself as comfortable as you can manage. Sort out what you *need* from what you *prefer*.

academic literacies · rhetorical situations · genres · fields · processes · strategies · research MLA / APA · media / design

Starting to Write

All of the above advice notwithstanding, don't worry so much about the trappings of your writing situation that you don't get around to writing. Write. Start by **FREEWRITING**, start with a first sentence, start with awful writing that you know you'll discard later—but write. That's what gets you warmed up and going.

⦿ 331–32

Write quickly in spurts.   Write quickly with the goal of writing a complete draft, or a complete section of a longer draft, in one sitting. If you need to stop in the middle, make some notes about where you were headed when you stopped so that you can easily pick up your train of thought when you begin again.

Break down your writing task into small segments.   Big projects can be intimidating. But you can always write one section or, if need be, one paragraph or even a single sentence—and then another and another. It's a little like dieting. If I think I need to lose twenty pounds, I get discouraged and head for the doughnuts; but if I decide that I'll lose one pound and I lose it, well, I'll lose another—*that* I can do.

Expect surprises.   Writing is a form of thinking; the words you write lead you down certain roads and away from others. You may end up somewhere you didn't anticipate. Sometimes that can be a good thing—but sometimes you can write yourself into a dead end or out onto a tangent. Just know that this is natural, part of every writer's experience, and it's okay to double back or follow a new path that opens up before you.

Expect to write more than one draft.   A first sentence, first page, or first draft represents your attempt to organize into words your thoughts, ideas, feelings, research findings, and more. It's likely that some of that first try will not achieve your goals. That's okay—having writing on screen or on paper that you can change, add to, and cut means you're part of the way there. As you revise, you can fill in gaps and improve your writing and thinking.

Dealing with Writer's Block

You may sit down to write but find that you can't—nothing occurs to you; your mind is blank. Don't panic; here are some ways to get started writing again:

- Think of the assignment as a problem to be solved. Try to capture that problem in a single sentence: "How do I explain the context for my topic?" "What is the best way to organize my argument?" "What am I trying to do in the conclusion?"

- Start early and break the writing task into small segments drafted over several days. Waiting until the night before an assignment is due can create panic—and writer's block.

- Stop trying: take a walk, take a shower, do something else. Come back in a half hour, refreshed.

- Open a new document on your computer or get a fresh piece of paper and **FREEWRITE**, or try **LOOPING** or **LISTING**. What are you trying to say? Just let whatever comes come—you may write yourself out of your box.

- If you usually write on your computer, turn it off, get out paper and pencil, and write by hand.

- Try a graphic approach: try **CLUSTERING**, or draw a chart of what you want to say; draw a picture; doodle.

- Do some **RESEARCH** on your topic to see what others have said about it.

- Talk to someone about what you are trying to do. If there's a writing center at your school, talk to a tutor: **GET RESPONSE**. If there's no one to talk to, talk to yourself. It's the act of talking—using your mouth instead of your hands—that can free you up.

331–33
333–34
477
348–50
331–39
343–47
348–55

> **IF YOU NEED MORE HELP**
>
> See Chapter 29 on **GENERATING IDEAS AND TEXT** if you find you need more material. And once you have a draft, see Chapter 31 on **ASSESSING YOUR OWN WRITING** and Chapter 32 **GETTING RESPONSE AND REVISING** for help evaluating your draft.

academic literacies | rhetorical situations | genres | fields | processes | strategies | research MLA / APA | media / design

Assessing Your Own Writing **31**

In school and out, our work is continually assessed by others. Teach-ers determine whether our writing is strong or weak; supervisors decide whether we merit raises or promotions; even friends and relatives size up in various ways the things we do. As writers, we need to assess our own work—to step back and see it with a critical eye. By developing stan-dards of our own and being conscious of the standards others use, we can assess—and shape—our writing, making sure it does what we want it to do. This chapter will help you assess your own written work.

What we write for others must stand on its own because we usually aren't present when it is read—we rarely get to explain to readers why we did what we did and what it means. So we need to make our writ-ing as clear as we can before we submit, post, display, or publish it. It's a good idea to assess your writing in two stages, first considering how well it meets the needs of your particular rhetorical situation, then study-ing the text itself to check its focus, argument, organization, and clarity. Sometimes some simple questions can get you started:

> What works?
> What still needs work?
> Where do I need to say more (or less)?

Considering the Rhetorical Situation

PURPOSE   What is your purpose for writing? If you have multiple purposes, list them, and then note which ones are the most important. How well does your draft achieve your purpose(s)? If you're writing for an assignment, what are

55–56

the requirements of the assignment, and does your draft meet those requirements?

57–60　AUDIENCE　To whom are you writing? What do those readers need and expect, as far as you can tell? Does your draft answer their needs? Do you define any terms and explain any concepts they won't know?

61–65　GENRE　What is the genre, and what are the key features of that genre? Does your draft include each of those features? If not, is there a good reason?

66–68　STANCE　Is your attitude toward your topic and your audience clear? Does your language project the personality and tone that you want?

69–71　MEDIA / DESIGN　What medium (print? spoken? electronic?) or combination of media is your text intended for, and how well does your writing suit it? How well does the design of the text suit your purpose and audience? Does it meet any requirements of the genre or of the assignment, if you're writing for one?

Examining the Text Itself

Look carefully at your text to see how well it says what you want it to say. Start with its focus, and then examine its reasons and evidence, organization, and clarity, in that order. If your writing lacks focus, the revising you'll do to sharpen the focus is likely to change everything else; if it needs more reasons and evidence, the organization may well change.

Consider your focus.　Your writing should have a clear point, and every part of the writing should support that point. Here are some questions that can help you see if your draft is adequately focused:

387–89
- What is your **THESIS**? Even if it is not stated directly, you should be able to summarize it for yourself in a single sentence.

academic literacies　rhetorical situations　genres　fields　processes　strategies　research MLA / APA　media / design

- Is your thesis narrow or broad enough to suit the needs and expectations of your audience?

- How does the **BEGINNING** focus attention on your thesis or main point?

  373–80

- Does each paragraph support or develop that point? Do any paragraphs or sentences stray from your focus?

- Does the **ENDING** leave readers thinking about your main point? Is there another way of concluding the essay that would sharpen your focus?

  380–85

Consider the support you provide for your argument. Your writing needs to give readers enough information to understand your points, follow your argument, and see the logic of your thinking. How much information is enough will vary according to your audience. If they already know a lot about your subject or are likely to agree with your point of view, you may need to give less detail. If, however, they are unfamiliar with your topic or are skeptical about your views, you will probably need to provide much more.

- What **REASONS** and **EVIDENCE** do you give to support your thesis? Where might more information be helpful? If you're writing online, could you provide links to it?

  400–401

- What key terms and concepts do you **DEFINE**? Are there any other terms your readers might need to have explained? Could you do so by providing links?

  432–42

- Where might you include more **DESCRIPTION** or other detail?

  443–51

- Do you make any **COMPARISONS**? Especially if your readers will not be familiar with your topic, it can help to compare it with something more familiar.

  424–31

- If you include **NARRATIVE**, how is it relevant to your point?

  462–70

- See Part 6 for other useful **STRATEGIES**.

  371

Consider the organization. As a writer, you need to lead readers through your text, carefully structuring your material so that they will be able to follow your argument.

- Analyze the structure by **OUTLINING** it. An informal outline will do since you mainly need to see the parts, not the details.

  335–37

- Is your text complete? Does your genre require an **ABSTRACT**, a **WORKS-CITED LIST**, or any other elements?

  626
  MLA 558–86

- What **TRANSITIONS** help readers move from idea to idea and paragraph to paragraph? Do you need more?

  391

- If there are no **HEADINGS**, would adding them help orient readers?

  650–52

Check for clarity. Nothing else matters if readers can't understand what you write. Following are some questions that can help you see whether your meaning is clear and your text is easy to read:

- Does your **TITLE** announce the subject of your text and give some sense of what you have to say? If not, would a more direct title strengthen your argument?

  386–87

- Do you state your **THESIS** directly? If not, will readers easily understand what your main point is? Try stating your thesis outright, and see if it makes your argument easier to follow.

  387–89

- Does your **BEGINNING** tell readers what they need to understand your text, and does your **ENDING** help them make sense of what they've just read?

  373–80
  380–85

- How does each paragraph relate to the ones before and after? Are those relationships clear—or do you need to add **TRANSITIONS**?

  391

- Do you vary your sentences? If all the sentences are roughly the same length or follow the same subject-verb-object pattern, your text probably lacks any clear emphasis and might even be difficult to read.

- Are **VISUALS** clearly labeled, positioned near the text they relate to, and referred to clearly in the text?

  653–63

- If you introduce materials from other sources, have you clearly distinguished **QUOTED**, **PARAPHRASED**, or **SUMMARIZED** ideas from your own?

  526–38

- Do you **DEFINE** all the words that your readers may not know?

  432–42

academic literacies
rhetorical situations
genres
fields
processes
strategies
research MLA / APA
media / design

- Does your punctuation make your writing more clear or less? Incorrect punctuation can make writing difficult to follow or, worse, change the meaning from what you intended. As a best-selling punctuation manual reminds us, there's a considerable difference between "eats, shoots, and leaves" and "eats shoots and leaves."

Thinking about Your Process

Your growth as a writer depends on how well you understand what you do when you write so that you can build on good habits. After you finish a writing project, consider the following questions to help you see the process that led to its creation—and find ways to improve the process next time:

- How would you tell the story of your thinking? Try writing these sentences: "When I first began with my topic, I thought _____. But as I did some thinking, writing, and research about the topic, my ideas changed and I thought _____."
- At some point in your writing, did you have to choose between two or more alternatives? What were they, and how did you choose?
- What was the most difficult problem you faced while writing? How did you go about trying to solve it?
- Whose advice did you seek while researching, organizing, drafting, revising, and editing? What advice did you take, and what did you ignore? Why?

Assessing a Body of Your Work

If you are required to submit a portfolio of your writing as part of a class, you will likely need to write a letter or essay that introduces the portfolio's contents and describes the processes that you used to create them and that ASSESSES THE WRITING IN YOUR PORTFOLIO. See Chapter 34 for detailed advice and a good example of a portfolio self-assessment.

361–70

32 Getting Response and Revising

If we want to learn to play a song on the guitar, we play it over and over again until we get it right. If we play basketball or baseball, we likely spend hours shooting foul shots or practicing a swing. Writing works the same way. Making meaning clear can be tricky, and you should plan on revising and, if need be, rewriting in order to get it right. When we speak with someone face-to-face or on the phone or text a friend, we can get immediate response and restate or adjust our message if we've been misunderstood. In most other situations when we write, that immediate response is missing, so we need to seek out responses from readers to help us revise. This chapter includes a list of guidelines for those readers to consider, along with various strategies for subsequent revising and rewriting.

Giving and Getting Peer Response

When you meet with other students in pairs or small groups to respond to one another's work, in class or online, you have the opportunity to get feedback on your work from several readers who can help you plan revisions. At the same time, you learn from reading others' work how they approached the writing task—you're not writing in a vacuum. Some students wonder why class time is being taken up by peer response, assuming that their instructor's opinion is the only one that counts, but seeing the work of others and learning how others see your work can help you improve the clarity and depth of your writing. The key to responding effectively is to be as specific in your response as possible and avoid being either too harsh or too complimentary. These guidelines can help:

- Read your peer review partner's draft first from beginning to end as an interested reader, trying to understand the information and ideas.

348

Don't look for problems. In fact, a good rule of thumb is this: read your partner's drafts in the same spirit that you want yours to be read.

- Before starting a second reading, ask your partner what questions they have about the draft or if you should focus on a particular aspect or part of the draft.

- As you read the draft again, take notes on a separate sheet of paper. Your notes might include positive comments ("I like the way you. . . . "), negative comments ("This sentence seems out of place"; "Is _____ the best word to use?"), and questions ("I'm not sure what you mean by _____"; "Would this paragraph work better on p. 2?").

- When you can, do more than identify issues. Offer suggestions or possible alternatives.

- When it's your draft's turn to be discussed, listen carefully to your partner's responses, take notes, and ask for clarification if necessary. Do not take issue with your partner's responses or argue over them; even if you're sure that what you wrote is perfectly clear, it's worth taking a second look if your partner has trouble understanding it.

Getting Effective Response

Ask your readers to consider some of the specific elements in the list below, but don't restrict them to those elements. Caution: if a reader says nothing about any of these elements, don't be too quick to assume that you needn't think about them yourself.

- What did you think when you first saw the **TITLE**? Is it interesting? informative? appropriate? Will it attract other readers' attention? ◆ 386–87

- Does the **BEGINNING** grab your attention? If so, how does it do so? Does it give enough information about the topic? offer necessary background information? How else might the piece begin? ◆ 373–80

- Is there a clear **THESIS**? What is it? ◆ 387–89

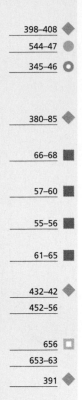
398–408
544–47
345–46
380–85
66–68
57–60
55–56
61–65
432–42
452–56
656
653–63
391

- Is there sufficient **SUPPORT** for the thesis? Is there anywhere you'd like to have more detail? Is the supporting material sufficiently **DOCUMENTED**?

- Does the text have a clear pattern of **ORGANIZATION**? Does each part relate to the thesis? Does each part follow from the one preceding it? Was the text easy to follow? How might the organization be improved?

- Is the **ENDING** satisfying? What did it leave you thinking? How else might the piece end?

- Can you tell the writer's **STANCE** or attitude toward the subject and audience? What words convey that attitude? Is it consistent throughout?

- How well does the text meet the needs and expectations of its **AUDIENCE**? Where might readers need more information, guidance, or clarification? How well does it achieve its **PURPOSE**? Does every part of the text help achieve the purpose? Could anything be cut? Should anything be added? Does the text meet the requirements of its **GENRE**? Should anything be added, deleted, or changed to meet those requirements?

- Do terms need **DEFINING**? Would examples, additional detail, explanations, **DIALOGUE**, or some other strategies help you understand the draft?

- Are **CHARTS**, **GRAPHS**, or **TABLES** clear and readable? If there are no **VISUALS**, should there be?

- Are sentences complete and grammatical? Are **TRANSITIONS** helpful or needed? Is the punctuation correct?

- Can any words or phrases be sharpened? Are verbs mostly active? Is language that refers to others appropriate? Are all words spelled correctly?

Revising

Once you have studied your draft with a critical eye and, if possible, gotten responses from other readers, it's time to revise. Major changes may be necessary, and you may need to generate new material or do some rewriting. But assume that your draft is good raw material that you can revise

✴ academic literacies
■ rhetorical situations
▲ genres
● fields
○ processes
◆ strategies
● research MLA / APA
☐ media / design

to achieve your purposes. Revision should take place on several levels, from global (whole-text issues) to particular (the details). Work on your draft in that order, starting with the elements that are global in nature and gradually moving to smaller, more particular aspects. This allows you to use your time most efficiently and take care of bigger issues first. In fact, as you deal with the larger aspects of your writing, many of the smaller ones will be taken care of along the way.

Give yourself time to revise.   When you have a due date, set deadlines for yourself that will give you time—preferably several days but as much as your schedule permits—to work on the text before it has to be delivered. Also, get some distance. Often when you're immersed in a project, you can't see the big picture because you're so busy creating it. If you can, get away from your writing for a while and think about something else. When you return to it, you're more likely to see it freshly. If there's not time to put a draft away for several days or more, even letting it sit overnight or for a few hours can help.

As you revise, assume that nothing is sacred. Bring a critical eye to all parts of a draft, not only to those parts pointed out by your reviewers. Content, organization, sentence patterns, individual words—all are subject to improvement. Be aware that a change in one part of the text may require changes in other parts.

At the same time, don't waste energy struggling with writing that simply doesn't work; you can always discard it. Look for the parts of your draft that do work—the parts that match your purpose and say what you want to say. Focus your efforts on those bright spots, expanding and developing them.

Revise to sharpen your FOCUS.   Examine your THESIS to make sure it matches your PURPOSE as you now understand it. Read each paragraph to ensure that it contributes to your main point; you may find it helpful to OUTLINE your draft to help you see all the parts. One way to do this is to highlight one sentence in each paragraph that expresses the paragraph's main idea. Then copy and paste the highlighted sentences into a new document. Does one state the thesis of the entire essay? Do the rest relate to the thesis? Are they in the best order? If not, you need to either

344–45
387–89
55–56

335–37

modify the parts of the draft that don't advance your thesis or revise your thesis to reflect your draft's focus and to rearrange your points so they advance your discussion more effectively.

373–85 Read your **BEGINNING AND ENDING** carefully; make sure that the first paragraphs introduce your topic and provide any needed contextual information and that the final paragraphs provide a satisfying conclusion.

Revise to strengthen the argument.   If readers find some of your claims unconvincing, you need to provide more information or more **SUPPORT**. 345 You may need to define terms you've assumed they will understand, offer additional examples, or provide more detail by describing, explaining 371 processes, adding dialogue, or using some other **STRATEGIES**. Make sure you show as well as tell—and don't forget that you might need to do so literally, with visuals like photos, graphs, or charts. You might try freewriting, clustering, or other ways of **GENERATING IDEAS AND TEXT**. If you need 331–39 477 to provide additional evidence, you might need to do additional **RESEARCH**.

345–46 **Revise to improve the ORGANIZATION.**   If you've outlined your draft, number each paragraph, and make sure each one follows from the one before. If anything seems out of place, move it, or if necessary, cut it completely. Check to see if you've included appropriate **TRANSITIONS** or 391 **HEADINGS** to help readers move through the text, and add them as needed. 650–52 Check to make sure your text meets readers' expectations of the **GENRE** 61–65 you're writing in.

346–47 **Revise for CLARITY.**   Be sure readers will be able to understand what you're 386–87 saying. Look closely at your **TITLE** to be sure it gives a sense of what the 387–89 text is about and at your **THESIS**: will readers recognize your main point? If you don't state a thesis directly, consider whether you should. Provide any necessary background information and **DEFINE** any key terms. Make 432–42 sure you've integrated any **QUOTATIONS**, **PARAPHRASES**, or **SUMMARIES** into 526–38 your text smoothly. Are all paragraphs focused around one main point? Do the sentences in each paragraph contribute to that point? Finally, con-

academic literacies | rhetorical situations | genres | fields | processes | strategies | research MLA / APA | media / design

sider whether there are any data that would be more clearly presented in a **CHART**, **TABLE**, or **GRAPH**.

☐ 656

One way to test whether your text is clear is to switch audiences: write what you're trying to express as if you were talking to an eight-year-old. Your final draft probably won't be written that way, but the act of explaining your ideas to a young audience or readers who know nothing about your topic can help you discover any points that may be unclear.

Revise VISUALS.   Make sure images are as close as possible to the discussion to which they relate and that the information in the visual is explained in your text. Each image should be numbered and have a title or caption that identifies it and explains its significance. Each part of a **CHART**, **GRAPH**, or **TABLE** should be clearly labeled to show what it represents. If you didn't create the image yourself, make sure to cite its source, and if you're posting your work online, obtain permission from the copyright owner.

☐ 653–63

☐ 656

Read and reread—and reread.   Take some advice from writing theorist Donald Murray:

> Nonwriters confront a writing problem and look away from the text to rules and principles and textbooks and handbooks and models. Writers look at the text, knowing that the text itself will reveal what needs to be done and what should not yet be done or may never be done. The writer reads and rereads and rereads, standing far back and reading quickly from a distance, moving in close and reading slowly line by line, reading again and again, knowing that the answers to all writing problems lie within the evolving text.
>
> —Donald Murray, *A Writer Teaches Writing*

Rewriting

Some writers find it useful to try rewriting a draft in various ways or from various perspectives just to explore possibilities. Try it! If you find that your original plan works best for your purpose, fine. But you may find that another way will work better. Especially if you're not completely satisfied with your draft, consider the following ways of rewriting. Experiment with your rhetorical situation:

- Rewrite your draft from different points of view, through the eyes of different people perhaps or through the eyes of an animal or even from the perspective of an object. See how the text changes (in the information it presents, its perspective, its voice).

57–60 ■
- Rewrite for a different **AUDIENCE**. How might an email detailing a recent car accident be written to a friend, an insurance agent, a parent?

66–68 ■
- Rewrite in a different **TONE**. If the first draft was temperate and judicious, be extreme; if it was polite, be more direct. If the first draft was in standard English, rewrite it more informally.

61–65
70 ■
- Rewrite the draft in a different **GENRE** or **MEDIUM**. Rewrite an essay as a letter, story, poem, speech, comic strip, *PowerPoint* presentation. Which genre and medium work best to reach your intended audience and achieve your purpose?

Ways of rewriting a narrative

452–56 ◆
- Rewrite one scene completely in **DIALOGUE**.
- Start at the end of the story and work back to the beginning, or start in the middle and fill in the beginning as you work toward the end.

Ways of rewriting a textual analysis

424–31 ◆
- **COMPARE** the text you're analyzing with another text (which may be in a completely different genre—film, TV, song lyrics, computer games, poetry, fiction, whatever).
- Write a parody of the text you're analyzing. Be as silly and as funny as you can while maintaining the structure of the original text. Alternatively, write a parody of your analysis, using evidence from the text to support an outrageous analysis.

Ways of rewriting a report

- Rewrite for a different **AUDIENCE**. For example, explain a concept to your grandparents; describe the subject of a profile to a visitor from another planet.

57–60

- Be silly. Rewrite the draft as if for *The Daily Show* or the *Onion*, or rewrite it as if it were written by Bart Simpson.

Ways of rewriting an argument

- Rewrite taking another **POSITION**. Argue as forcefully for that position as you did for your actual one, acknowledging and refuting your original position. Alternatively, write a rebuttal to your first draft from the perspective of someone with different beliefs.

157–84

- Rewrite your draft as a **STORY** —make it real in the lives of specific individuals. (For example, if you were writing about abortion rights, you could write a story about a young pregnant woman trying to decide what she believes and what to do.) Or rewrite the argument as a fable or parable.

462–70

- Rewrite the draft as a letter responding to a hostile reader, trying at least to make them understand what you have to say.

- Rewrite the draft as an angry letter to someone or as a table-thumping dinner-with-the-relatives discussion. Write from the most extreme position possible.

- Write an **ANALYSIS** dof the topic of your argument in which you identify, as carefully and as neutrally as you can, the various positions people hold on the issue.

118–19

Once you've rewritten a draft in any of these ways, see whether there's anything you can use. Read each draft, considering how it might help you achieve your purpose, reach your audience, and convey your stance. Revise your actual draft to incorporate anything you think will make your text more effective, whether it's other genres or a different perspective.

33 Editing and Proofreading

Your ability to produce clear, error-free writing shows something about your ability as a writer and also leads readers to make assumptions about your intellect, your work habits, even your character. Readers of job-application letters and résumés, for example, may reject applications if they contain a single error, for no other reason than it's an easy way to narrow the field of potential candidates. In addition, they may well assume that applicants who present themselves sloppily in an application will do sloppy work on the job. This is all to say that you should edit and proofread your work carefully.

Editing

Editing is the stage where you work on the details of your paragraphs, sentences, words, and punctuation to make your writing as clear, precise, correct—and effective—as possible. Your goal is not to achieve "perfection" (whatever that may be) so much as to make your writing as effective as possible for your particular purpose and audience. Consult a good writing handbook for detailed advice, but use the following guidelines to help you check your drafts systematically for some common errors with paragraphs, sentences, and words:

Editing paragraphs

389–90

- Does each paragraph focus on one point? Does it have a **TOPIC SENTENCE** that announces that point, and if so, where is it located? If it's not the first sentence, should it be? If there's no clear topic sentence, should there be one?

356

- Does every sentence relate to the main point of the paragraph? If any sentences do not, should they be deleted, moved, or revised?
- Is there enough detail to develop the paragraph's main point? How is the point developed—with narrative? definition? some other **STRATEGY**?

371

- Where have you placed the most important information—at the beginning? the end? in the middle? The most emphatic spot is at the end, so in general that's where to put information you want readers to remember. The second most emphatic spot is at the beginning.
- Are any paragraphs especially long or short? Consider breaking long paragraphs if there's a logical place to do so—maybe an extended example should be in its own paragraph, for instance. If you have paragraphs of only a sentence or two, see if you can add to them or combine them with another paragraph, unless you're using a brief paragraph to provide emphasis.
- Check the way your paragraphs fit together. Does each one follow smoothly from the one before? Do you need to add any **TRANSITIONS**?

391

- Do the **BEGINNING** paragraphs catch readers' attention? In what other ways might you begin your text?

373–80

- Do the final paragraphs provide a satisfactory **ENDING**? How else might you conclude your text?

380–85

Editing sentences

- Is each sentence complete? Does it have someone or something (the subject) performing some sort of action or expressing a state of being (the verb)? Does each sentence begin with a capital letter and end with a period, question mark, or exclamation point?
- Check your use of the passive voice. Although there are some rhetorical situations in which the passive voice ("The prince was killed by a rival") is more appropriate than the active voice ("A rival killed the prince") because you want to emphasize an action rather than who performed it, you'll do well to edit it out unless you have a good reason for using it.

- Check for parallelism. Items in a list or series should be parallel in form—all nouns (lions, tigers, bears), all verbs (hopped, skipped, jumped), all clauses (he came, he saw, he conquered), and so on.

- Do many of your sentences begin with *it* or *there?* Too often these words make your writing wordy and vague or even conceal needed information. Why write "There are reasons we voted for him" when you can say "We had reasons to vote for him"?

- Are your sentences varied? If they all start with the subject or are the same length, your writing might be dull and maybe even hard to read. Try varying your sentence openings by adding **TRANSITIONS**, introductory phrases or clauses. Vary sentence lengths by adding detail to some or combining some sentences.

- Make sure you've used commas correctly. Is there a comma after each introductory element? ("After the lead singer quit, the group nearly disbanded. However, they then produced a string of hits.") Do commas set off nonrestrictive elements—parts that aren't needed to understand the sentence? ("The books I read in middle school, like the Harry Potter series, became longer and more challenging.") Are compound sentences connected with a comma? ("I'll eat broccoli steamed, but I prefer it roasted.")

Editing words

- Are you sure of the meaning of every word? Use a dictionary; be sure to look up words whose meanings you're not sure about. And remember your audience—do you use any terms they'll need to have defined?

- Is any of your language too general or vague? Why write that you competed in a race, for example, if you could say you ran the 4 × 200 relay?

- What about the **TONE?** If your stance is serious (or humorous or critical or something else), make sure that your words all convey that attitude.

- Do any pronouns have vague or unclear antecedents? If you use "he" or "they" or "it" or "these," will readers know whom or what the words refer to?

- Have you used any clichés —expressions that are used so frequently that they are no longer fresh? "Live and let live," avoiding something

391 ◆

66–68 ■

academic literacies · rhetorical situations · genres · fields · processes · strategies · research MLA / APA · media / design

"like the plague," and similar expressions are so predictable that your writing will almost always be better off without them.

- Be careful with language that refers to others. Make sure that your words do not stereotype any individual or group. Mention age, gender, race, religion, sexual orientation, and so on only if they are relevant to your subject. When referring to an ethnic group, make every effort to use the terms members of the group prefer.

- Edit out language that might be considered sexist. Have you used words like *manpower* or *policemen* to refer to people who may be female? If so, substitute less gendered words such as *personnel* or *police officers*. Do your words reflect any gender stereotypes—for example, that all engineers are male, or all nurses female? If you mention someone's gender, is it even necessary? If not, eliminate the unneeded words.

- How many of your verbs are forms of *be* and *do*? If you rely too much on these words, try replacing them with more specific verbs. Why write "She did a proposal for" when you could say "She proposed"?

- Do you ever confuse *its* and *it's*? Use *it's* when you mean *it is* or *it has*. Use *its* when you mean *belonging to it*.

Proofreading

Proofreading is the final stage of the writing process, the point where you clean up your work to present it to your readers. Proofreading is like checking your appearance in a mirror before going into a job interview: being neat and well groomed looms large in creating a good first impression, and the same principle applies to writing. Misspelled words, missing pages, mixed-up fonts, and other lapses send a negative message about your work—and about you. Most readers excuse an occasional error, but by and large readers are an intolerant bunch: too many errors will lead them to declare your writing—and maybe your thinking—flawed. There goes your credibility. So proofread your final draft with care to ensure that your message is taken as seriously as you want it to be.

Up to this point, you've been told *not* to read individual words on the page and instead to read for meaning. Proofreading demands the opposite: you must slow down your reading so that you can see every word, every punctuation mark.

- Use your computer's grammar checker and spelling checker, but only as a first step, and know that they're not very reliable. Computer programs don't read writing; instead, they rely on formulas and banks of words, so what they flag (or don't flag) as mistakes may or may not be accurate. If you were to write, "My brother was diagnosed with a leaning disorder," *leaning* would not be flagged as misspelled because it is a word (and might even be a disorder), even though it's the wrong word in that sentence.

- To keep your eyes from jumping ahead, place a ruler or piece of paper under each line as you read. Use your finger or a pencil as a pointer.

- Some writers find it helpful to read the text one sentence at a time, beginning with the last sentence and working backward.

- Read your text out loud to yourself—or better, to others, who may *hear* problems you can't see. Alternatively, have someone else read your text aloud to you while you follow along on the screen or page.

- Ask someone else to read your text. The more important the writing is, the more important this step is.

- If you find a mistake after you've printed out your text and are unable to print out a corrected version, make the change as neatly as possible in pencil or pen.

Compiling a Portfolio **34**

Artists maintain portfolios of their work to show gallery owners, collectors, and other potential buyers. Money managers work with investment portfolios of stocks, bonds, and various mutual funds. And often as part of a writing class, student writers compile portfolios of their work. As with a portfolio of paintings or drawings, a portfolio of writing includes a writer's best work and, sometimes, preliminary and revised drafts of that work, along with a statement by the writer articulating why they consider it good. The *why* is as important as the work, for it provides you with an occasion for assessing your overall strengths and weaknesses as a writer. This chapter offers guidelines to help you compile both a *writing portfolio* and a *literacy portfolio*, a project that writing students are sometimes asked to complete as part of a literacy narrative.

Considering the Rhetorical Situation

As with the writing you put in a portfolio, the portfolio itself is generally intended for a particular audience but could serve a number of different purposes. It's a good idea, then, to consider these and the other elements of your rhetorical situation when you begin to compile a portfolio.

PURPOSE	Why are you creating this portfolio? To show your learning? To create a record of your writing? As the basis for a grade in a course? To organize your research? To explore your literacy? For something else?	55–56
AUDIENCE	Who will read your portfolio? What will your readers expect it to contain? How can you help them understand the context or occasion for each piece of writing you include?	57–60

GENRE

What genres of writing should the portfolio contain? Do you want to demonstrate your ability to write one particular type of writing or in a variety of genres? Will your introduction to or assessment of the portfolio be in the form of a letter or an essay?

STANCE

How do you want to portray yourself in this portfolio? What items should you include to create this impression? What stance do you want to take in your written assessment of its contents? Thoughtful? Enthusiastic? Something else?

MEDIA / DESIGN

Will your portfolio be in print? Or will it be electronic? Will it include multiple media? Whichever medium you use, how can you help readers navigate its contents? What design elements will be most appropriate to your purpose and medium?

A WRITING PORTFOLIO

What to Include

A portfolio developed for a writing course typically contains examples of your best work in that course, including any notes, outlines, preliminary drafts, and so on, along with your own assessment of your performance in the course. You might include any of the following items:

- freewriting, outlines, and other work you did to generate ideas
- drafts, rough and revised
- in-class writing assignments
- source material—copies of articles and online sources, observation notes, interview transcripts, and other evidence of your research
- tests and quizzes

- responses to your drafts
- conference notes, error logs, lecture notes, and other course materials
- electronic material, including visuals, blogs, and multimedia texts
- reflections on your work

What you include will vary depending on what your instructor asks for. You may be asked to include three or four of your best papers or everything you've written. You may also be asked to show work in several different genres. In any case, you will usually need to choose, and to do that you will need to have criteria for making your choices. Don't base your decision solely on grades (unless grades are one criterion); your portfolio should reflect your assessment of your work, not your instructor's. What do you think is your best work? your most interesting work? your most ambitious work? Whatever criteria you use, you are the judge.

Organizing a Portfolio

If you set up a way to organize your writing at the start of the course, you'll be able to keep track of it throughout the course, making your job at term's end much easier. Remember that your portfolio presents you as a writer, presumably at your best. It should be neat, well organized, and easy to navigate. Your instructor may provide explicit guidelines for organizing your portfolio. If not, here are some guidelines:

Paper portfolios.   Choose something in which to gather your work. You might use a two-pocket folder, a three-ring binder, or a file folder, or you may need a box, basket, or some other container to accommodate bulky or odd-shaped items.

Label everything. Label each piece at the top of the first page, specifying the assignment, the draft, and the date: "Proposal, Draft 1, 9/12/18"; "Text Analysis, Final Draft, 10/10/18"; "Portfolio Self-Assessment, Final Draft, 11/11/18"; and so on. Write this information neatly on the page, or put it on a Post-it note. For each assignment, arrange your materials chronologically, with your earliest material (freewriting, for example) on the bottom, and each successive item (source materials, say, then your outline, then your first draft, and so on) on top of the last, ending with your final draft on top. That way readers can see how your writing changed from draft to draft.

Electronic portfolios. You might also create an electronic portfolio, or e-portfolio. E-portfolios typically consist of a network of **LINKED** documents that might include not only your writing and reflections on that writing, but also sources, writing, and art you did for other courses or for your own enjoyment, audio and video clips, and other resources. Tools that can help you create an e-portfolio include:

661–62 ▢

- *Online tools.* Several websites, including *Weebly* and *Wix*, offer free tools to help you create a preformatted e-portfolio. For example, *GoogleSites* provides templates you can use to build an e-portfolio, uploading documents, images, and videos from your computer.

- *Blogging tools.* You can create an e-portfolio using a blogging platform, like *Tumblr* or *WordPress*, which allows you to upload files and create a network of linked pages. Readers can then comment on your e-portfolio, just as they might on your blog entries.

- *Wikis.* Wiki-based e-portfolios differ from blog-based ones in the level of interactivity they allow. In addition to commenting, readers may—if you allow them—make changes and add information. *PBworks* is one free provider, as is *WikiSpaces*.

- *Courseware.* Your school may use a learning platform, such as *Blackboard*, *Brightspace*, or *Moodle*, that allows you to create an e-portfolio of your work.

It's also possible to create an electronic portfolio using word processing, spreadsheet, or presentation software. The programs available for your use and the requirements for publishing your portfolio vary from school to school and instructor to instructor; ask your instructor or your school's help desk for assistance (and see Chapter 59 on **WRITING ONLINE** for general guidance).

664–72 ▢

Assessing Your Portfolio

An important part of your portfolio is your written self-assessment of your work. This is an opportunity to assess your work with a critical eye and to think about what you're most proud of, what you most enjoyed doing, what you want to improve. It's your chance to think about and say what you've learned during the class. Some instructors may ask you to write out your assessment in essay form, as an additional sample of your writing; others will want you to put it in letter form, which usually allows for a more relaxed and personal tone. Whatever form it takes, your statement should cover the following ground:

- *An evaluation of each piece of writing in the portfolio.* Consider both strengths and weaknesses, and give examples from your writing to support what you say. What would you change if you had more time? Which is your favorite piece, and why? your least favorite?

- *An assessment of your overall writing performance.* What do you do well? What still needs improvement? What do you *want* your work to say about you? What *does* your work say about you?

- *A discussion of how the writing you did in this course has affected your development as a writer.* How does the writing in your portfolio compare with writing you did in the past? What do you know now that you didn't know before? What can you do that you couldn't do before?

- *A description of your writing habits and process.* What do you usually do? How well does it work? What techniques seem to help you most, and why? Which seem less helpful? Cite passages from your drafts that support your conclusions.

- *An analysis of your performance in the course.* How did you spend your time? Did you collaborate with others? participate in peer review? have any conferences with your instructor? visit the writing center? Consider how these or any other activities contributed to your success.

A Sample Self-Assessment

Here is a self-assessment written by Nathaniel Cooney as part of his portfolio for his first-year writing class at Wright State University.

2 June 2018

Dear Reader,

It is my hope that in reading this letter you will gain an understanding of the projects contained in this portfolio. I enclose three works that I have submitted for an introductory writing class at Wright State University, English 102, Writing in Academic Discourse: an informative report, an argument paper, and a genre project based largely on the content of the argument paper. I selected the topics of these works for two reasons: First, they address issues that I believe to be relevant in terms of both the intended audience (peers and instructors of the course) and the times when they were published. Second, they speak to issues that are important to me personally. Below I present general descriptions of the works, along with my review of their strengths and weaknesses.

My purpose in writing the informative report "Higher Standards in Education Are Taking Their Toll on Students" was to present a subject in a factual manner and to support it with well-documented research. My intent was not to argue a point. However, because I chose a narrowly focused topic and chose information to support a thesis, the report tends to favor one side of the issue over the other. Because as a student I have a personal stake in the changing standards in the formal education system, I chose to research recent changes in higher education and their effects on students. Specifically, I examine students' struggles to reach a standard that seems to be moving further and further beyond their grasp.

I believe that this paper could be improved in two areas. The first is a bias that I think exists because I am a student presenting information from the point of view of a student. It is my hope, however, that my inclusion of unbiased sources lessens this problem somewhat and, furthermore, that it presents the

academic literacies　rhetorical situations　genres　fields　processes　strategies　research MLA / APA　media / design

reader with a fair and accurate collection of facts and examples that supports the thesis. My second area of concern is the overall balance in the paper between outside sources supporting my own thoughts and outside sources supporting opposing points of view. Rereading the paper, I notice many places where I may have worked too hard to include sources that support my ideas.

The second paper, "Protecting Animals That Serve," is an argument intended not only to take a clear position on an issue but also to argue for that position and convince the reader that it is a valid one. That issue is the need for legislation guaranteeing that certain rights of service animals be protected. I am blind and use a guide dog. Thus, this issue is especially important to me. During the few months that I have had him, my guide dog has already encountered a number of situations where intentional or negligent treatment by others has put him in danger. At the time I was writing the paper, a bill was being written in the Ohio House of Representatives that, if passed, would protect service animals and establish consequences for those who violated the law. The purpose of the paper, therefore, was to present the reader with information about service animals, establish the need for the legislation in Ohio and nationwide, and argue for passage of such legislation.

I think that the best parts of my argument are the introduction and the conclusion. In particular, I think that the conclusion does a good job of not only bringing together the various points but also conveying the significance of the issue for me and for others. In contrast, I think that the area most in need of further attention is the body of the paper. While I think the content is strong, I believe the overall organization could be improved. The connections between ideas are unclear in places, particularly in the section that acknowledges opposing viewpoints. This may be due in part to the fact that I had difficulty understanding the reasoning behind the opposing argument.

The argument paper served as a starting point for the genre project, for which the assignment was to revise one paper written for this class in a different genre. My genre project consists of a poster and a brochure. As it was for the argument paper, my primary goal was to convince my audience of the importance of a particular issue and viewpoint—specifically, to convince my audience to support House Bill 369, the bill being introduced in the Ohio legislature that would create laws to protect the rights of service animals in the state.

Perhaps both the greatest strength and the greatest weakness of the genre project is my use of graphics. Because of my blindness, I was limited in my use of some graphics. Nevertheless, the pictures were carefully selected to capture the attention of readers and, in part, to appeal to their emotions as they viewed and reflected on the material.

I put a great deal of time, effort, and personal reflection into each project. While I am hesitant to say that they are finished and while I am dissatisfied with some of the finer points, I am satisfied with the overall outcome of this collection of works. Viewing it as a collection, I am also reminded that writing is an evolving process and that even if these works never become exactly what I envisioned them to be, they stand as reflections of my thoughts at a particular time in my life. In that respect, they need not be anything but what they already are, because what they are is a product of who I was when I wrote them. I hope that you find the papers interesting and informative and that as you read them, you, too, may realize their significance.

Respectfully,

Nathaniel J. Cooney

Nathaniel J. Cooney

Enclosures (3)

Cooney describes each of the works he includes and considers their strengths and weaknesses, citing examples from his texts to support his assessment.

A LITERACY PORTFOLIO

As a writing student, you may be asked to think back to the time when you first learned to read and write or to remember significant books or other texts you've read, and perhaps to put together a portfolio that chronicles your development as a reader and writer. You may also be asked to put together a literacy portfolio to accompany a **LITERACY NARRATIVE**.

▲ 75–97

What you include in such a portfolio will vary depending on what you've kept over the years and what your family has kept. You may have all of your favorite books, stories you dictated to a preschool teacher, notebooks in which you practiced writing the alphabet. Or you may have almost nothing. What you have or don't have is unimportant in the end: what's important is that you gather what you can and arrange it in a way that shows how you think about your development and growth as a literate person. What have been your experiences with reading and writing? What's your earliest memory of learning to write? If you love to read, what led you to love it? Who was most responsible for shaping your writing ability? Those are some of the questions you'll ask if you write a literacy narrative. You might also compile a literacy portfolio as a good way to generate ideas and text for that assignment.

What to Include in a Literacy Portfolio

- school papers
- drawings and doodles from preschool
- favorite books
- photographs you've taken
- drawings
- poems
- letters
- journals and diaries
- lists
- reading records or logs

- electronic texts you've created
- marriage vows
- speeches you've given
- awards you've received

Organizing a Literacy Portfolio

You may wish to organize your material chronologically, but there are other methods of organization to consider as well. For example, you might group items according to where they were written (at home, at school, at work), by genre (stories, poems, essays, letters, notes), or even by purpose (pleasure, school, work, church, and so on). Arrange your portfolio in the way that best conveys who you are as a literate person. Label each item you include, perhaps with a Post-it note, to identify what it is, when it was written or read, and why you've included it in your portfolio. Or you might create an e-portfolio, scanning print items to include in it with electronic items.

Reflecting on Your Literacy Portfolio

- Why did you choose each item?
- Is anything missing? Are there any other important materials that should be here?
- Why is the portfolio organized as it is?
- What does the portfolio show about your development as a reader and writer?
- What patterns do you see? Are there any common themes you've read or written about? Any techniques you rely on? Any notable changes over time?
- What are the most significant items, and why?

part 6

Strategies

Whenever we write, we draw on many different strategies to articulate what we have to say. We may DEFINE
key terms, DESCRIBE people or places, and EXPLAIN how
something is done. We may COMPARE one thing
to another. Sometimes we may choose a pertinent story
to NARRATE, and we may even want to include some
DIALOGUE. The chapters that follow offer advice on how
to use these and OTHER BASIC STRATEGIES for developing
and organizing the texts you write.

Strategies

Beginning and Ending 35

Whenever we pick up something to read, we generally start by looking at the first few words or sentences to see if they grab our attention, and based on them we decide whether to keep reading. Beginnings, then, are important, both attracting readers and giving them some information about what's to come. When we get to the end of a text, we expect to be left with a sense of closure, of satisfaction—that the story is complete, our questions have been answered, the argument has been made. So endings are important, too. This chapter offers advice on how to write beginnings and endings.

Beginning

How you begin depends on your **RHETORICAL SITUATION**, especially your purpose and audience. Academic audiences generally expect your introduction to establish context, explaining how the text fits into some larger conversation, addresses certain questions, or explores an aspect of the subject. Most introductions also offer a brief description of the text's content, often in the form of a thesis statement. The following opening of an essay on the effect of texting on student writing does all of this:

■ 53

> It's taking over our lives. We can do it almost anywhere—walking to class, waiting in line at the grocery store, or hanging out at home. It's quick, easy, and convenient. It has become a concern of doctors, parents, and teachers alike. What is it? It's texting!
>
> Text messaging—or texting, as it's more commonly called—is the process of sending and receiving typed messages via a cellular phone. It is a common means of communication among teenagers and is even becoming popular in the business world because it allows quick messages

to be sent without people having to commit to a telephone conversation. A person is able to say what is needed, and the other person will receive the information and respond when it's convenient to do so.

In order to more quickly type what they are trying to say, many people use abbreviations instead of words. The language created by these abbreviations is called textspeak. Some people believe that using these abbreviations is hindering the writing abilities of students, and others argue that texting is actually having a positive effect on writing. In fact, it seems likely that texting has no significant effect on student writing.   —Michaela Cullington, "Does Texting Affect Writing?"

If you're writing for a nonacademic audience or genre—for a newspaper or a website, for example—your introduction may need to entice your readers to read on by connecting your text to their interests through shared experiences, anecdotes, or some other attention-getting device. Cynthia Bass, writing a newspaper article about the Gettysburg Address on its 135th anniversary, connects that date—the day her audience would read it—to Lincoln's address. She then develops the rationale for thinking about the speech and introduces her specific topic: debates about the writing and delivery of the Gettysburg Address:

November 19 is the 135th anniversary of the Gettysburg Address. On that day in 1863, with the Civil War only half over and the worst yet to come, Abraham Lincoln delivered a speech now universally regarded as both the most important oration in U.S. history and the best explanation—"government of the people, by the people, for the people"—of why this nation exists.

We would expect the history of an event so monumental as the Gettysburg Address to be well established. The truth is just the opposite. The only thing scholars agree on is that the speech is short—only ten sentences—and that it took Lincoln under five minutes to stand up, deliver it, and sit back down.

Everything else—when Lincoln wrote it, where he wrote it, how quickly he wrote it, how he was invited, how the audience reacted—has been open to debate since the moment the words left his mouth.

—Cynthia Bass, "Gettysburg Address: Two Versions"

Ways of Beginning

Explain the larger context of your topic.   Most essays are part of an ongoing conversation, so you might begin by outlining the context of the subject to which your writing responds. An essay exploring the "emotional climate" of the United States after Barack Obama became president in 2008 begins by describing the national moods during some of his predecessors' administrations:

> Every president plays a symbolic, almost mythological role that's hard to talk about, much less quantify—it's like trying to grab a ball of mercury. I'm not referring to using the bully pulpit to shape the national agenda but to the way that the president, as America's most inescapably powerful figure, colors the emotional climate of the country. John Kennedy and Ronald Reagan did this affirmatively, expressing ideals that shaped the whole culture. Setting a buoyant tone, they didn't just change movies, music, and television; they changed attitudes. Other presidents did the same, only unpleasantly. Richard Nixon created a mood of angry paranoia, Jimmy Carter one of dreary defeatism, and George W. Bush, especially in that seemingly endless second term, managed to do both at once.
>
> —John Powers, "Dreams from My President"

State your thesis.   Sometimes the best beginning is a clear **THESIS** stating your position, like the following statement in an essay arguing that fairy tales and nursery rhymes introduce us to "the rudiments and the humanness of engineering":

387–89

> We are all engineers of sorts, for we all have the principles of machines and structures in our bones. We have learned to hold our bodies against the forces of nature as surely as we have learned to walk. We calculate the paths of our arms and legs with the computer of our brain, and we catch baseballs and footballs with more dependability than the most advanced weapons systems intercept missiles. We may wonder if human evolution may not have been the greatest engineering feat of all time. And though many of us forget how much we once knew about the principles and practices of engineering, the nursery rhymes and fairy tales of our youth preserve the evidence that we did know quite a bit.
>
> —Henry Petroski, "Falling Down Is Part of Growing Up"

Forecast your organization. You might begin by briefly outlining the way in which you will organize your text. The following example from a scholarly paper on the role of immigrants in the U.S. labor market offers background on the subject and describes the points that the writer's analysis will discuss:

> Debates about illegal immigration, border security, skill levels of workers, unemployment, job growth and competition, and entrepreneurship all rely, to some extent, on perceptions of immigrants' role in the U.S. labor market. These views are often shaped as much by politics and emotion as by facts.
>
> To better frame these debates, this short analysis provides data on immigrants in the labor force at the current time of slowed immigration, high unemployment, and low job growth and highlights eight industries where immigrants are especially vital. How large a share of the labor force are they and how does that vary by particular industry? How do immigrants compare to native-born workers in their educational attainment and occupational profiles?
>
> The answers matter because our economy is dependent on immigrant labor now and for the future. The U.S. population is aging rapidly as the baby boom cohort enters old age and retirement. As a result, the labor force will increasingly depend upon immigrants and their children to replace current workers and fill new jobs. This analysis puts a spotlight on immigrant workers to examine their basic trends in the labor force and how these workers fit into specific industries and occupations of interest.
>
> —Audrey Singer, "Immigrant Workers in the U.S. Labor Force"

Offer background information. If your readers may not know as much as you do about your topic, giving them information to help them understand your position can be important, as David Guterson does in an essay on the Mall of America:

> Last April, on a visit to the new Mall of America near Minneapolis, I carried with me the public-relations press kit provided for the benefit of reporters. It included an assortment of "fun facts" about the mall: 140,000 hot dogs sold each week, 10,000 permanent jobs, 44 escalators and 17 elevators, 12,750 parking places, 13,300 short tons of steel, $1 million in cash disbursed weekly from 8 automatic-teller machines.

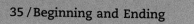

The rotunda of the Mall of America.

Opened in the summer of 1992, the mall was built on the 78-acre site of the former Metropolitan Stadium, a five-minute drive from the Minneapolis–St. Paul International Airport. With 4.2 million square feet of floor space—including twenty-two times the retail footage of the average American shopping center—the Mall of America was "the largest fully enclosed combination retail and family entertainment complex in the United States."

—David Guterson, "Enclosed. Encyclopedic. Endured. One Week at the Mall of America"

653–63 ▢

VISUALS can also help provide context. For example, this essay on the Mall of America might have included a photo like the one on the preceding page to convey the size of the structure.

Define key terms or concepts.   The success of an argument often hinges

432–42 ◆

on how key terms are **DEFINED**. You may wish to provide definitions up front, as an advocacy website, *Health Care Without Harm*, does in a report on the hazards of fragrances in health-care facilities:

To many people, the word "fragrance" means something that smells nice, such as perfume. We don't often stop to think that scents are chemicals. Fragrance chemicals are organic compounds that volatilize, or vaporize into the air—that's why we can smell them. They are added to products to give them a scent or to mask the odor of other ingredients. The volatile organic chemicals (VOCs) emitted by fragrance products can contribute to poor indoor air quality (IAQ) and are associated with a variety of adverse health effects.

—"Fragrances," *Health Care Without Harm*

Connect your subject to your readers' interests or values.   You'll always want to establish common ground with your readers, and sometimes you may wish to do so immediately, in your introduction, as in this example:

We all want to feel safe. Most Americans lock their doors at night, lock their cars in parking lots, try to park near buildings or under lights, and wear seat belts. Many invest in expensive security systems, carry pepper spray or a stun gun, keep guns in their homes, or take self-defense classes. Obviously, safety and security are important issues in American life.

—Andy McDonie, "Airport Security: What Price Safety?"

Start with something that will provoke readers' interest.   Anna Quindlen opens an essay on feminism with the following eye-opening assertion:

> Let's use the F word here. People say it's inappropriate, offensive, that it puts people off. But it seems to me it's the best way to begin, when it's simultaneously devalued and invaluable.
> Feminist. Feminist, feminist, feminist.
>
> —Anna Quindlen, "Still Needing the F Word"

Start with an anecdote.   Sometimes a brief NARRATIVE helps bring a topic to life for readers. See, for example, how an essay on the dozens, a type of verbal contest played by some African Americans, begins:

462–70

> Alfred Wright, a nineteen-year-old whose manhood was at stake on Longwood Avenue in the South Bronx, looked fairly calm as another teenager called him Chicken Head and compared his mother to Shamu the whale.
> He fingered the gold chain around his thin neck while listening to a detailed complaint about his sister's sexual abilities. Then he slowly took the toothpick out of his mouth; the jeering crowd of young men quieted as he pointed at his accuser.
> "He was so ugly when he was born," Wright said, "the doctor smacked his mom instead of him."
>
> —John Tierney, "Playing the Dozens"

Ask a question.   Instead of a thesis statement, you might open with a question about the topic your text will explore, as this study of the status of women in science does:

> Are women's minds different from men's minds? In spite of the women's movement, the age-old debate centering around this question continues. We are surrounded by evidence of de facto differences between men's and women's intellects—in the problems that interest them, in the ways they try to solve those problems, and in the professions they choose. Even though it has become fashionable to view such differences as environmental in origin, the temptation to seek an explanation in terms of innate differences remains a powerful one.
>
> —Evelyn Fox Keller, "Women in Science: A Social Analysis"

Jump right in. Occasionally you may wish to start as close to the key action as possible. See how one writer jumps right into his profile of a blues concert:

> Long Tongue, the Blues Merchant, strolls onstage. His guitar rides side-saddle against his hip. The drummer slides onto the tripod seat behind the drums, adjusts the high-hat cymbal, and runs a quick, off-beat tattoo on the tom-tom, then relaxes. The bass player plugs into the amplifier, checks the settings on the control panel, and nods his okay. Three horn players stand off to one side, clustered, lurking like brilliant sorcerer-wizards waiting to do magic with their musical instruments.
>
> —Jerome Washington, "The Blues Merchant"

Ending

Endings are important because they're the last words readers read. How you end a text will depend in part on your RHETORICAL SITUATION. You may end by wrapping up loose ends, or you may wish to give readers something to think about. Some endings do both, as Cynthia Bass does in a report on the debate over the Gettysburg Address. In her two final paragraphs, she first summarizes the debate and then shows its implications:

> What's most interesting about the Lincoln-as-loser and Lincoln-as-winner versions is how they marshal the same facts to prove different points. The invitation asks Lincoln to deliver "a few appropriate remarks." Whether this is a putdown or a reflection of the protocol of the time depends on the "spin"—an expression the highly politicized Lincoln would have readily understood—which the scholar places on it.
>
> These diverse histories should not in any way diminish the power or beauty of Lincoln's words. However, they should remind us that history, even the history of something as deeply respected as the Gettysburg Address, is seldom simple or clear. This reminder is especially useful today as we watch expert witnesses, in an effort to divine what the founders meant by "high crimes and misdemeanors," club one another with conflicting interpretations of the same events, the same words, the same precedents, and the same laws.
>
> —Cynthia Bass, "Gettysburg Address: Two Versions"

53

Bass summarizes the dispute about Lincoln's address and then moves on to discuss the role of scholars in interpreting historical events. Writing in 1999 during President Bill Clinton's impeachment hearings, she concludes by pointing out the way in which expert government witnesses often offer conflicting interpretations of events to suit their own needs. The ending combines several strategies to bring various strands of her essay together, leaving readers to interpret her final words themselves.

Ways of Ending

Restate your main point.   Sometimes you'll simply **SUMMARIZE** your central idea, as in this example from an essay arguing that we have no "inner" self and that we should be judged by our actions alone:

534–35

> The inner man is a fantasy. If it helps you to identify with one, by all means, do so; preserve it, cherish it, embrace it, but do not present it to others for evaluation or consideration, for excuse or exculpation, or, for that matter, for punishment or disapproval.
>
> Like any fantasy, it serves your purposes alone. It has no standing in the real world which we share with each other. Those character traits, those attitudes, that behavior—that strange and alien stuff sticking out all over you—*that's the real you!*
>
> —Willard Gaylin, "What You See Is the Real You"

Discuss the implications of your argument.   The following conclusion of an essay on the development of Post-it notes leads readers to consider how failure sometimes leads to innovation:

> Post-it notes provide but one example of a technological artifact that has evolved from a perceived failure of existing artifacts to function without frustrating. Again, it is not that form follows function but, rather, that the form of one thing follows from the failure of another thing to function as we would like. Whether it be bookmarks that fail to stay in place or taped-on notes that fail to leave a once-nice surface clean and intact, their failure and perceived failure is what leads to the true evolution of artifacts. That the perception of failure may take

centuries to develop, as in the case of loose bookmarks, does not reduce the importance of the principle in shaping our world.

—Henry Petroski, "Little Things Can Mean a Lot"

462–70

End with an anecdote, maybe finishing a NARRATIVE that was begun earlier in your text or adding one that illustrates the point you are making. See how Sarah Vowell uses a story to end an essay on students' need to examine news reporting critically:

> I looked at Joanne McGlynn's syllabus for her media studies course, the one she handed out at the beginning of the year, stating the goals of the class. By the end of the year, she hoped her students would be better able to challenge everything from novels to newscasts, that they would come to identify just who is telling a story and how that person's point of view affects the story being told. I'm going to go out on a limb here and say that this lesson has been learned. In fact, just recently, a student came up to McGlynn and told her something all teachers dream of hearing. The girl told the teacher that she was listening to the radio, singing along with her favorite song, and halfway through the sing-along she stopped and asked herself, "What am I singing? What do these words mean? What are they trying to tell me?" And then, this young citizen of the republic jokingly complained, "I can't even turn on the radio without thinking anymore."
>
> —Sarah Vowell, "Democracy and Things Like That"

Refer to the beginning.   One way to bring closure to a text is to bring up something discussed in the beginning; often the reference adds to or even changes the original meaning. For example, Amy Tan opens an essay on her Chinese mother's English by establishing herself as a writer and lover of language who uses many versions of English in her writing:

> I am not a scholar of English or literature. I cannot give you much more than personal opinions on the English language and its variations in this country or others.
>   I am a writer. And by that definition, I am someone who has always loved language. I am fascinated by language in daily life. I spend a

great deal of my time thinking about the power of language—the way it can evoke an emotion, a visual image, a complex idea, or a simple truth. Language is the tool of my trade. And I use them all—all the Englishes I grew up with.

At the end of her essay, Tan repeats this phrase, but now she describes language not in terms of its power to evoke emotions, images, and ideas but in its power to evoke "the essence" of her mother. When she began to write fiction, she says,

> [I] decided I should envision a reader for the stories I would write. And the reader I decided upon was my mother, because these were stories about mothers. So with this reader in mind—and in fact she did read my early drafts—I began to write stories using all the Englishes I grew up with: the English I spoke to my mother, which for lack of a better term might be described as "simple"; the English she used with me, which for lack of a better term might be described as "broken"; my translation of her Chinese, which could certainly be described as "watered down"; and what I imagined to be her translation of her Chinese if she could speak in perfect English, her internal language, and for that I sought to preserve the essence, but neither an English nor a Chinese structure. I wanted to capture what language ability tests can never reveal: her intent, her passion, her imagery, the rhythms of her speech and the nature of her thoughts.
>
> —Amy Tan, "Mother Tongue"

Note how Tan not only repeats "all the Englishes I grew up with" but also provides parallel lists of what those Englishes can do for her: "evoke an emotion, a visual image, a complex idea, or a simple truth," on the one hand, and, on the other, capture her mother's "intent, her passion, her imagery, the rhythms of her speech and the nature of her thoughts."

Propose some action, as in the following conclusion of a report on the consequences of binge drinking among college students:

> The scope of the problem makes immediate results of any interventions highly unlikely. Colleges need to be committed to large-scale and long-term behavior-change strategies, including referral of alcohol abusers

to appropriate treatment. Frequent binge drinkers on college campuses are similar to other alcohol abusers elsewhere in their tendency to deny that they have a problem. Indeed, their youth, the visibility of others who drink the same way, and the shelter of the college community may make them less likely to recognize the problem. In addition to addressing the health problems of alcohol abusers, a major effort should address the large group of students who are not binge drinkers on campus who are adversely affected by the alcohol-related behavior of binge drinkers.

—Henry Wechsler et al., "Health and Behavioral Consequences of Binge Drinking in College: A National Survey of Students at 140 Campuses"

Considering the Rhetorical Situation

As a writer or speaker, think about the message that you want to articulate, the audience you want to reach, and the larger context you are writing in.

55–56 ■ **PURPOSE**   Your purpose will affect the way you begin and end. If you're trying to persuade readers to do something, you may want to open by clearly stating your thesis and end by calling for a specific action.

57–60 ■ **AUDIENCE**   Who do you want to reach, and how does that affect the way you begin and end? You may want to open with an intriguing fact or anecdote to entice your audience to read a profile, for instance, whereas readers of a report may expect it to conclude with a summary of your findings.

61–65 ■ **GENRE**   Does your genre require a certain type of beginning or ending? Arguments, for example, often provide a statement of the thesis near the beginning; proposals typically end with a call for some solution.

66–68 ■ **STANCE**   What is your stance, and can your beginning and ending help you convey that stance? For example, beginning an argument on the distribution of AIDS medications to underdeveloped countries with an anecdote may demonstrate concern for the human costs of the disease, whereas starting with a statistical analysis may suggest the stance of a careful researcher. Ending a proposal by weighing the advantages and disadvantages of the solution you propose may make you seem reasonable.

MEDIA / DESIGN Your medium may affect the way you begin and end. A web text, for instance, may open with a homepage listing a menu of the site—and giving readers a choice of where they will begin. With a print text, you get to decide how it will begin and end.

69–71

IF YOU NEED MORE HELP

See also the guides to writing in Chapters 10–13 for ways of beginning and ending a LITERACY NARRATIVE, an essay ANALYZING TEXT, a REPORT, or an ARGUMENT.

75–97
98–130
131–56
157–84

36 Guiding Your Reader

Traffic lights, street signs, and lines on the road help drivers find their way. Readers need similar guidance—to know, for example, whether they're reading a report or an argument, an evaluation or a proposal. They also need to know what to expect: What will the report be about? What perspective will it offer? What will this paragraph cover? What about the next one? How do the two paragraphs relate to each other?

When you write, then, you need to provide cues to help your readers navigate your text and understand the points you're trying to make. This chapter offers advice on guiding your reader and, specifically, on using titles, *thesis statements*, *topic sentences*, and *transitions*.

Titles

A title serves various purposes, naming a text and providing clues to the content. It also helps readers decide whether they want to read further, so it's worth your while to come up with a title that attracts interest. Some titles include subtitles. You generally have considerable freedom in choosing a title, but always you'll want to consider the RHETORICAL SITUATION to be sure your title serves your purpose and appeals to the audience you want to reach.

Some titles simply announce the subject of the text:

"Black Men and Public Space"
The Pencil
"Why Colleges Shower Their Students with A's"
"Does Texting Affect Writing?"

53

Some titles provoke readers or otherwise entice them to read:

> "Kill 'Em! Crush 'Em! Eat 'Em Raw!"
> "Thank God for the Atom Bomb"
> "What Are Homosexuals For?"

Sometimes writers add a subtitle to explain or illuminate the title:

> *Aria: Memoir of a Bilingual Childhood*
> "It's in Our Genes: The Biological Basis of Human Mating Behavior"
> "From Realism to Virtual Reality: Images of America's Wars"

Sometimes when you're starting to write, you'll think of a title that helps you generate ideas and write. More often, though, a title is one of the last things you'll write, when you know what you've written and can craft a suitable name for your text.

Thesis Statements

A thesis identifies the topic of your text along with the claim you are making about it. A good thesis also helps readers understand an essay by forecasting its overall shape. In fact, some instructors call thesis statements *forecasting statements*. Working to create a sharp thesis can help you focus both your thinking and your writing. Here are four steps for moving from a topic to a thesis statement:

1. State your topic as a question. You may have an idea for a topic, such as "gasoline prices," "analysis of 'real women' ad campaigns," or "famine." Those may be good topics, but they're not thesis statements, primarily because none of them actually makes a statement. A good way to begin moving from topic to thesis statement is to turn your topic into a question:

> What causes fluctuations in gasoline prices?
>
> Are ads picturing "real women" who aren't models effective?
>
> What can be done to prevent famine in East Africa?

2. Turn your question into a position. A thesis statement is an assertion—it takes a stand or makes a claim. Whether you're writing a report or an argument, you are saying, "This is the way I see . . . ," "My research shows . . . ," or "This is what I believe about . . ." Your thesis statement announces your position on the question you are raising about your topic, so a relatively easy way of establishing a thesis is to answer your own question:

> Gasoline prices fluctuate for several reasons.
>
> Ads picturing "real women" instead of models are effective because women can easily identify with them.
>
> The most recent famine in Somalia could have been avoided if certain measures had been taken.

3. Narrow your thesis. A good thesis is specific, guiding you as you write and showing your audience exactly what your essay will cover, often in the same order you will cover it. The preceding thesis statements need to be qualified and focused—they need to be made more specific. For example:

> Gasoline prices fluctuate because of production procedures, consumer demand, international politics, and oil companies' policies.
>
> Dove's "Campaign for Self-Esteem" and Cover Girl's ads featuring Queen Latifah work because consumers can identify with the women's bodies and admire the women's confidence in displaying them.
>
> The 2017 famine in Somalia could have been avoided if farmers had received training in more effective methods and had planted drought-resistant crops and if other nations had provided more aid more quickly.

334–35 ◉
A good way to narrow a thesis is to ask **QUESTIONS** about it: *Why* do gasoline prices fluctuate? *How* could the Somalia famine have been avoided? The answers will help you craft a narrow, focused thesis.

4. Qualify your thesis. Sometimes you want to make a strong argument and to state your thesis bluntly. Often, however, you need to acknowledge that your assertions may be challenged or may not be unconditionally true. In those cases, consider limiting the scope of your thesis by adding to it such terms as *may, probably, apparently, very likely, sometimes,* and *often.*

Gasoline prices *very likely* fluctuate because of production procedures, consumer demand, international politics, and oil companies' policies.

Dove's and Cover Girl's ad campaigns featuring "real women" *may* work because consumers can identify with the women's bodies and admire the women's confidence in displaying them.

The 2017 famine in Somalia could *probably* have been avoided if farmers had received training in more effective methods and had planted drought-resistant crops and if other nations had provided more aid more quickly.

Thesis statements are typically positioned at or near the end of a text's introduction, to let readers know at the outset what is being claimed and what the text will be aiming to prove. While a thesis often forecasts your organization, it doesn't necessarily do so; the organization may be more complex than the thesis itself. For example, Notre Dame University student Sarah Dzubay's essay, "An Outbreak of the Irrational," contains this thesis statement:

The movement to opt out of vaccinations is irrational and dangerous because individuals advocating for their right to exercise their personal freedom are looking in the wrong places for justification and ignoring the threat they present to society as a whole.

The essay that follows includes discussions of herd immunity; a socioeconomic profile of parents who choose not to vaccinate their children; outlines of the rationales those parents use to justify their choice, which include fear of autism, fear of causing other health problems, and political and ethical values; and a conclusion that parents who refuse to vaccinate their children are unreasonable and selfish. The paper delivers what the thesis promises but includes important information not mentioned in the thesis itself.

Topic Sentences

Just as a thesis statement announces the topic and position of an essay, a topic sentence states the subject and focus of a paragraph. Good paragraphs focus on a single point, which is summarized in a topic sentence. Usually, but not always, the topic sentence begins the paragraph:

> *Graduating from high school or college is an exciting, occasionally even traumatic event.* Your identity changes as you move from being a high school teenager to a university student or a worker; your connection to home loosens as you attend school elsewhere, move to a place of your own, or simply exercise your right to stay out later. You suddenly find yourself doing different things, thinking different thoughts, fretting about different matters. As recent high school graduate T. J. Devoe puts it, "I wasn't really scared, but having this vast range of opportunity made me uneasy. I didn't know *what* was gonna happen." Jenny Petrow, in describing her first year out of college, observes, "It's a tough year. It was for all my friends."
>
> —Sydney Lewis, *Help Wanted: Tales from the First Job Front*

Sometimes the topic sentence may come at the end of the paragraph or even at the end of the preceding paragraph, depending on the way the paragraphs relate to one another. Other times a topic sentence will summarize or restate a point made in the previous paragraph, helping readers understand what they've just read as they move on to the next point. See how the linguist Deborah Tannen does this in the first paragraphs of an article on differences in men's and women's conversational styles:

> I was addressing a small gathering in a suburban Virginia living room—a women's group that had invited men to join them. Throughout the evening, one man had been particularly talkative, frequently offering ideas and anecdotes, while his wife sat silently beside him on the couch. Toward the end of the evening, I commented that women frequently complain that their husbands don't talk to them. This man quickly concurred. He gestured toward his wife and said, "She's the talker in our family." The room burst into laughter; the man looked puzzled and hurt. "It's true," he explained. "When I come home from work I have nothing to say. If she didn't keep the conversation going, we'd spend the whole evening in silence."
>
> *This episode crystallizes the irony that although American men tend to talk more than women in public situations, they often talk less at home.* And this pattern is wreaking havoc with marriage.
>
> —Deborah Tannen, "Sex, Lies, and Conversation: Why Is It So Hard for Men and Women to Talk to Each Other?"

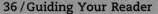

Transitions

Transitions help readers move from thought to thought—from sentence to sentence, paragraph to paragraph. You are likely to use a number of transitions as you draft; when you're **EDITING**, you should make a point of checking transitions. Here are some common ones:

356–59

- **To signal causes and effects:** accordingly, as a result, because, consequently, hence, so, then, therefore, thus
- **To signal comparisons:** also, in the same way, like, likewise, similarly
- **To signal changes in direction or expectations:** although, but, even though, however, in contrast, instead, nevertheless, nonetheless, on the contrary, on the one hand . . . on the other hand, still, yet
- **To signal examples:** for example, for instance, indeed, in fact, such as
- **To signal sequences or similarities:** again; also; and; and then; besides; finally; furthermore; last; moreover; next; too; first, second, third, etc.
- **To signal time relations:** after, as soon as, at first, at the same time, before, eventually, finally, immediately, later, meanwhile, next, simultaneously, so far, soon, then, thereafter
- **To signal a summary or conclusion:** as a result, as we have seen, finally, in a word, in any event, in brief, in conclusion, in other words, in short, in the end, in the final analysis, on the whole, therefore, thus, to summarize

---

IF YOU NEED MORE HELP

See also Chapter 58 on **USING VISUALS, INCORPORATING SOUND** for ways of creating visual signals for your readers.

653–63

37 Analyzing Causes and Effects

Analyzing causes helps us think about why something happened, whereas thinking about effects helps us consider what might happen. When we hear a noise in the night, we want to know what caused it. Children poke sticks into holes to see what will happen. Researchers try to understand the causes of diseases. Writers often have occasion to consider causes or effects as part of a larger topic or sometimes as a main focus: in a **PROPOSAL**, we might consider the effects of reducing tuition or the causes of recent tuition increases; in a **MEMOIR**, we might explore why the person we had a date with failed to show up.

Usually we can only speculate about *probable* causes or *likely* effects. In writing about causes and effects, then, we are generally **ARGUING** for those we consider plausible, not proven. This chapter will help you analyze causes and effects in writing—and to do so in a way that suits your rhetorical situation.

Determining Plausible Causes and Effects

What causes ozone depletion? Sleeplessness? Obesity? And what are their effects? Those are of course large, complex topics, but whenever you have reason to ask why something happened or what could happen, there will likely be several possible causes and just as many predictable effects. There may be obvious causes, though often they will be less important than others that are harder to recognize. (Eating too much may be an obvious cause of being overweight, but *why* people eat too much has several less obvious causes: portion size, advertising, lifestyle, and psychological disorders are only a few possibilities.) Similarly, short-term effects are often less important than long-term ones. (A stomachache may be an

246–55
224–32

397–417

academic literacies

rhetorical situations

genres

fields

processes

strategies

research MLA / APA

media / design

effect of eating too much candy, but the chemical imbalance that can result from consuming too much sugar is a much more serious effect.)

LISTING, CLUSTERING, and OUTLINING are useful processes for analyzing causes. And at times you might need to do some RESEARCH to identify possible causes or effects and to find evidence to support your analysis. When you've identified potential causes and effects, you need to analyze them. Which causes and effects are primary? Which seem to be secondary? Which are most relevant to your PURPOSE and are likely to convince your AUDIENCE? You will probably have to choose from several possible causes and effects for your analysis because you won't want or need to include all of them.

332–34
477

55–56
57–60

Arguing for Causes or Effects

Once you've identified several possible causes or predictable effects, you need to ARGUE that some are more plausible than others. You must provide convincing support for your argument because you usually cannot *prove* that x causes y or that y will be caused by z; you can only show, with good reasons and appropriate evidence, that x is likely to cause y or that y will likely follow from z. See, for example, how an essay on the psychological basis for risk taking speculates about two potential causes for the popularity of extreme sports:

397–417

> Studies now indicate that the inclination to take high risks may be hardwired into the brain, intimately linked to arousal and pleasure mechanisms, and may offer such a thrill that it functions like an addiction. The tendency probably affects one in five people, mostly young males, and declines with age. It may ensure our survival, even spur our evolution as individuals and as a species. Risk taking probably bestowed a crucial evolutionary advantage, inciting the fighting and foraging of the hunter-gatherer. . . .
>
> As psychologist Salvadore Maddi, PhD, of the University of California at Davis warns, "High-risk takers may have a hard time deriving meaning and purpose from everyday life." Indeed, this peculiar form of dissatisfaction could help explain the explosion of high-risk sports in America and other postindustrial Western nations. In unstable cultures, such as those at war or suffering poverty, people rarely seek

out additional thrills. But in a rich and safety-obsessed country like America, land of guardrails, seat belts, and personal-injury lawsuits, everyday life may have become too safe, predictable, and boring for those programmed for risk taking.　　　　　　　—Paul Roberts, "Risk"

Roberts suggests that genetics is one likely cause of extreme sports and that an American obsession with safety is perhaps a cause of their growing popularity. Notice, however, that he presents these as likely or possible, not certain, by choosing his words carefully: "studies now *indicate*"; "the inclination to take high risks *may be* hardwired"; "[r]isk taking *probably* bestowed a crucial evolutionary advantage"; "this . . . dissatisfaction *could help* explain." Like Roberts, you will almost always need to qualify what you say about causes and effects—to say that something *could explain* (rather than saying it "explains") or that it *suggests* (rather than "shows"). Causes and effects can seldom be proved definitively, so you need to acknowledge that your argument is not the last word on the subject.

Ways of Organizing an Analysis of Causes and Effects

Your analysis of causes and effects may be part of a proposal or some other genre of writing, or you may write a text whose central purpose is to analyze causes or speculate about effects. While there are many ways to organize an analysis of causes and effects, three common ways are to state a cause and then discuss its effects, to state an effect and then discuss its causes, and to identify a chain of causes and effects.

Identify a cause and then discuss its effects. If you were writing about climate change, you might first show that many scientists fear it will have several effects, including more violent storms, the extinction of various kinds of plants, and elevated sea levels.

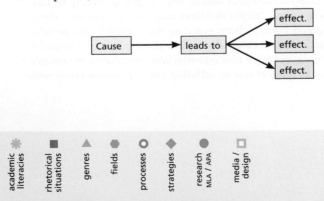

Identify an effect and then trace its causes. If you were writing about school violence, for example, you might argue that it is a result of sloppy dress, informal teacher-student relationships, low academic standards, and disregard for rules.

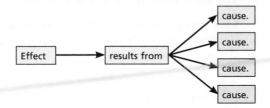

Identify a chain of causes and effects. You may sometimes discuss a chain of causes and effects. If you were writing about the right to privacy, for example, you might consider the case of Megan's law. A convicted child molester raped and murdered a girl named Megan; the crime caused New Jersey legislators to pass the so-called Megan's law (an effect), which requires that convicted sex offenders be publicly identified. As more states enacted versions of Megan's law, concern for the rights of those who are identified developed—the effect became a cause of further effects.

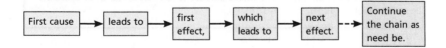

Considering the Rhetorical Situation

As a writer or speaker, you need to think about the message that you want to articulate, the audience you want to reach, and the larger context you are writing in.

PURPOSE   Your main purpose may be to analyze the causes and effects of something. But sometimes you'll have another goal that calls for such analysis — a business report, for

■ 55–56

example, might need to explain what caused a decline in sales.

57–60 ■ **AUDIENCE**   Who is your intended audience, and how will analyzing causes help you reach them? Do you need to tell them why some event happened or what effects resulted?

61–65 ■ **GENRE**   Does your genre require you to analyze causes? Proposals, for example, often need to consider the effects of a proposed solution.

66–68 ■ **STANCE**   What is your stance, and could analyzing causes or effects show that stance? Could it help demonstrate your seriousness or show that your conclusions are reasonable?

69–71 ■ **MEDIA / DESIGN**   You can rely on words to analyze causes, but sometimes a drawing will help readers *see* how causes lead to effects.

321 ○

IF YOU NEED MORE HELP

See also the **PROCESSES** chapters for help generating ideas, drafting, and so on if you need to write an entire text whose purpose is to analyze causes or speculate about effects.

Arguing 38

Basketball fans argue about who's better, LeBron James or Steph Curry. Political candidates argue that they have the most experience or best judgment. A toilet paper ad argues that "you deserve a little luxury in your life, and so does your bottom." As you likely realize, we are surrounded by arguments, and much of the work you do as a college student requires you to read and write arguments. When you write a **LITERARY ANALYSIS**, for instance, you argue for a particular interpretation. In a **PROPOSAL**, you argue for a particular solution to a problem. Even a **PROFILE** argues that a subject should be seen in a certain way. This chapter offers advice on some of the key elements of making an argument, from developing an arguable thesis and identifying good reasons and evidence that supports those reasons to building common ground and dealing with viewpoints other than your own.

211–23
246–55
233–45

Reasons for Arguing

We argue for many reasons, and they often overlap: to convince others that our position on a subject is reasonable, to influence the way they think about a subject, to persuade them to change their point of view or to take some sort of action. In fact, many composition scholars and teachers believe that all writing makes an argument.

As a student, you'll be called on to make arguments continually: when you participate in class discussions, when you take an essay exam, when you post a comment to an online discussion or a blog. In all these instances, you are adding your opinions to some larger conversation, arguing for what you believe—and why.

Arguing Logically: Claims, Reasons, and Evidence

398–408 ◆

The basic building blocks of argument are **CLAIMS**, **REASONS**, and **EVIDENCE** that supports those reasons. Using these building blocks, we can construct a strong logical argument, also known as *logos*.

Claims. Good arguments are based on arguable claims—statements that reasonable people may disagree about. Certain kinds of statements cannot be argued:

- *Verifiable statements of fact.* Most of the time, there's no point in arguing about facts like "the earth is round" or "George H. W. Bush was America's forty-first president." Such statements contain no controversy, no potential opposition—and so no interest for an audience. However, you might argue about the basis of a fact. For example, until recently it was a fact that our solar system had nine planets, but when further discoveries led to a change in the definition of *planet*, Pluto no longer qualified.

- *Issues of faith or belief.* By definition, matters of faith cannot be proven or refuted. If you believe in reincarnation or don't believe there is an afterlife, there's no way I can convince you otherwise. However, in a philosophy or religion course you may be asked to argue, for example, whether or not the universe must have a cause.

- *Matters of simple opinion or personal taste.* If you think cargo pants are ugly, no amount of arguing will convince you to think otherwise. If you've downloaded every Taylor Swift album and think she's the greatest singer ever, you won't convince your Nirvana-loving parents to like her, too. If matters of taste are based on identifiable criteria, though, they may be argued in an **EVALUATION**, where "Tom Cruise is a terrible actor" is more than just your opinion—it's an assertion you can support with evidence.

202–10 ▲

You may begin with an opinion: "I think wearing a helmet makes riding a bike more dangerous, not less." As it stands, that statement can't be considered a claim—it needs to be made more reasonable and informed. To do that, you might reframe it as a question—"Do bike riders who wear helmets get injured more often than those who don't?"—that may be answered as you do research and start to write. Your opinion or question should lead

✳ academic literacies   ▪ rhetorical situations   ▲ genres   ● fields   ○ processes   ◆ strategies   ● research MLA / APA   ▫ media / design

you to an arguable claim, however, one that could be challenged by another thoughtful person. In this case, for example, your research might lead you to a focused, qualified claim: *Contrary to common sense, wearing a helmet while riding a bicycle increases the chances of injury, at least to adult riders.*

Qualifying a claim. According to an old saying, there are two sides to every story. Much of the time, though, arguments don't sort themselves neatly into two sides, pro and con. No matter what your topic, your argument will rarely be a simple matter of being for or against; in most cases, you'll want to qualify your claim—that it is true in certain circumstances, with certain conditions, with these limitations, and so on. Qualifying your claim shows that you're reasonable and also makes your topic more manageable by limiting it. The following questions can help you qualify your claim.

- *Can it be true in some circumstances or at some times but not others?* For example, freedom of speech should generally be unrestricted, but individuals can sue for slander or libel.

- *Can it be true only with certain conditions?* For instance, cell phones and computer monitors should be recycled, but only by licensed, domestic recyclers.

- *Can it be true for some groups or individuals but not others?* For example, nearly everyone should follow a low-carb diet, but some people, such as diabetics, should avoid it.

SOME WORDS FOR QUALIFYING A CLAIM

sometimes	nearly	it seems/seemingly
rarely	usually	some
in some cases	more or less	perhaps
often	for the most part	possibly
routinely	in many cases	in most cases

Drafting a thesis statement. Once your claim is focused and appropriately qualified, it can form the core of your essay's **THESIS STATEMENT**, which announces your position and forecasts the path your argument will follow. For example, here is the opening paragraph of an essay by the

387–89

executive director of the National Congress of American Indians arguing that the remains of Native Americans should be treated with the same respect given to others. The author outlines the context of her argument and then presents her thesis (here, in italics):

> What if museums, universities and government agencies could put your dead relatives on display or keep them in boxes to be cut up and otherwise studied? What if you believed that the spirits of the dead could not rest until their human remains were placed in a sacred area? The ordinary American would say there ought to be a law—and there is, for ordinary Americans. *The problem for American Indians is that there are too many laws of the kind that make us the archeological property of the United States and too few of the kind that protect us from such insults.* —Susan Shown Harjo, "Last Rites for Indian Dead: Treating Remains Like Artifacts Is Intolerable"

Reasons. Your claim must be supported by reasons that your audience will accept. A reason can usually be linked to a claim with the word *because*:

CLAIM	+	*BECAUSE*	+	REASON
College students should strive to graduate		*because*		they will earn far more over their lifetimes than those who do not.

Keep in mind that you likely have a further reason, a rule or principle that underlies the reason you link directly to your claim. In this argument, the underlying reason is that isolation from other people is bad. If your audience doesn't accept that principle, you may have to back it up with further reasons or evidence.

To come up with good reasons, start by stating your position and then answering the question *why?*

CLAIM: College students should strive to graduate. *Why?*

REASON: (Because) They will earn far more over their lifetimes than those who do not. *Why?*

UNDERLYING REASON: The economy values college graduates and pays them more.

academic literacies

rhetorical situations

genres

fields

processes

strategies

research MLA / APA

media / design

As you can see, this exercise can continue indefinitely as the underlying reasons grow more and more general and abstract. You can do the same with other positions:

CLAIM: Smoking should be banned. *Why?*

REASON: (Because) It is harmful to smokers and also to nonsmokers.

UNDERLYING REASON: People should be protected from harmful substances.

Evidence. Evidence to support your reasons can come from various sources. In fact, you may need to use several kinds of evidence to persuade your audience that your claim is true. Some of the most common types of evidence include facts, statistics, examples, authorities, anecdotes, scenarios, case studies, textual evidence, and visuals.

Facts are ideas that are proven to be true. Facts can include observations or scholarly research (your own or someone else's), but they need to be accepted as true. If your audience accepts the facts you present, they can be powerful means of persuasion. For example, an essay on junk email offers these facts to demonstrate the seasonal nature of spam:

> The flow of spam is often seasonal. It slows in the spring, and then, in the month that technology specialists call "black September"—when hundreds of thousands of students return to college, many armed with new computers and access to fast Internet connections—the levels rise sharply.
>
> —Michael Specter, "Damn Spam"

Specter offers this fact with only a general reference to its origin ("technology specialists"), but given what most people know—or think they know—about college students, it rings true. A citation from a study published by a "technology specialist" would offer even greater credibility.

Statistics are numerical data, usually produced through research, surveys, or polls. Statistics should be relevant to your argument, as current as possible, accurate, and from a reliable source. An argument advocating that Americans should eat less meat presents these data to support the writer's contention that we eat far too much of it:

> Americans are downing close to 200 pounds of meat, poultry, and
> fish per capita per year (dairy and eggs are separate, and hardly insig-
> nificant), an increase of 50 pounds per person from 50 years ago.
> We each consume something like 110 grams of protein a day, about
> twice the federal government's recommended allowance; of that,
> about 75 grams come from animal protein. (The recommended level
> is itself considered by many dietary experts to be higher than it needs
> to be.) It's likely that most of us would do just fine on around 30 grams
> of protein a day, virtually all of it from plant sources.
>
> —Mark Bittman, "Rethinking the Meat-Guzzler"

Bittman's statistics demonstrate the extent to which Americans have
increased their meat consumption over the last half century, the proportion of our diets that comes from meat, and, by comparison, how much
protein our bodies require—and summarize the heart of his argument in
stark numeric terms.

Examples are specific instances that illustrate general statements. In a
book on life after dark in Europe, a historian offers several examples to
demonstrate his point that three hundred years ago, night—without artificial lighting—was treacherous:

> Even sure-footed natives on a dark night could misjudge the lay of
> the land, stumbling into a ditch or off a precipice. In Aberdeenshire,
> a fifteen-year-old girl died in 1739 after straying from her customary
> path through a churchyard and tumbling into a newly dug grave. The
> Yorkshireman Arthur Jessop, returning from a neighbor's home on a
> cold December evening, fell into a stone pit after losing his bearings.
>
> —A. Roger Ekirch, *At Day's Close: Night in Times Past*

Ekirch illustrates his point and makes it come alive for readers by citing
two specific individuals' fates.

Authorities are experts on your subject. To be useful, authorities must be
reputable, trustworthy, and qualified to address the subject. You should
EVALUATE any authorities you consult carefully to be sure they have the
credentials necessary for readers to take them seriously. When you cite

511–18

academic literacies
rhetorical situations
genres
fields
processes
strategies
research MLA / APA
media / design

experts, you should clearly identify them and the origins of their authority in a SIGNAL PHRASE, as does the author of an argument that deforested land can be reclaimed:

535–38

> Reed Funk, professor of plant biology at Rutgers University, believes that the vast areas of deforested land can be used to grow millions of genetically improved trees for food, mostly nuts, and for fuel. Funk sees nuts used to supplement meat as a source of high-quality protein in developing-country diets,
>
> —Lester R. Brown, *Plan B 2.0: Rescuing a Planet under Stress and a Civilization in Trouble*

Brown cites Funk, an expert on plant biology, to support his argument that humans need to rethink the global economy in order to create a sustainable world. Without the information on Funk's credentials, though, readers would have no reason to take his proposal seriously.

Anecdotes are brief NARRATIVES that your audience will find believable and that contribute directly to your argument. Anecdotes may come from your personal experience or the experiences of others. In an essay arguing that it's understandable when athletes give in to the temptation to use performance-enhancing drugs, sports blogger William Moller uses an anecdote to show that the need to perform can outweigh the potential negative consequences of using drugs:

462–70

> I spent my high school years at a boarding school hidden among the apple orchards of Massachusetts. Known for a spartan philosophy regarding the adolescent need for sleep, the school worked us to the bone, regularly slamming us with six hours of homework. I pulled a lot more all-nighters (of the scholastic sort) in my years there than I ever did in college. When we weren't in class, the library, study hall, or formal sit-down meals, we were likely found on a sports field. We also had school on Saturday, beginning at 8 a.m. just like every other non-Sunday morning.
>
> Adding kindling to the fire, the students were not your laid-back types; everyone wanted that spot at the top of the class, and social life was rife with competition. The type A's that fill the investment banking,

legal, and political worlds—those are the kids I spent my high school years with.

And so it was that midway through my sophomore year, I found myself on my third all-nighter in a row, attempting to memorize historically significant pieces of art out of E. H. Gombrich's *The Story of Art.* I had finished a calculus exam the day before, and the day before that had been devoted to world history. And on that one cold night in February, I had had enough. I had hit that point where you've had so little sleep over such a long time that you start seeing spots, as if you'd been staring at a bright light for too long. The grade I would compete for the next day suddenly slipped in importance, and I began daydreaming about how easy the real world would be compared to the hell I was going through.

But there was hope. A friend who I was taking occasional study breaks with read the story in the bags beneath my eyes, in the slump of my shoulders, the nervous drumming of my fingers on the chair as we sipped flat, warm Coke in the common room. My personal *deus ex machina,** he handed me a small white pill.

I was very innocent. I matured way after most of my peers, and was probably best known for being the kid who took all the soprano solos away from the girls in the choir as a first-year student. I don't think I had ever been buzzed, much less drunk. I'd certainly never smoked a cigarette. And knowing full well that what I was doing could be nothing better than against the rules (and less importantly, illegal) I did what I felt I needed to do, to accomplish what was demanded of me. And it worked. I woke up and regained focus like nothing I'd ever experienced. Unfortunately, it also came with serious side effects: I was a hypersensitized, stuffed-up, sweaty, wide-eyed mess, but I studied until the birds started chirping. And I aced my test.

Later I found out the pill was Ritalin, and it was classified as a class 3 drug.† I did it again, too—only a handful of times, as the side effects were so awful. But every time it was still illegal, still against

---

Deus ex machina: In ancient Greek and Roman drama, a god introduced into the plot to resolve complications.

†*Class 3 drug:* Drug that is illegal to possess without a prescription.

the rules. And as emphasized above, I was much more worried about the scholastic consequences if I were discovered abusing a prescription drug than the fact that I was breaking the law. Though I was using it in a far different manner than the baseball players who would later get caught with it in their systems, it was still very clearly a "performance-enhancing drug."

Just like every other person on this planet, I was giving in to the incentive scheme that was presented to me. The negative of doing poorly on the test was far greater than the negative of getting caught, discounted by the anesthetic of low probability.

—William Moller, "We, the Public,
Place the Best Athletes on Pedestals"

Moller uses this anecdote to demonstrate the truth of his argument, that given the choice between "breaking the rules and breaking my grades" or "getting an edge" in professional sports, just about everyone will choose to break the rules.

Scenarios are hypothetical situations. Like anecdotes, "what if" scenarios can help you describe the possible effects of particular actions or offer new ways of looking at a particular state of affairs. For example, a mathematician presents this lighthearted scenario about Santa Claus in a tongue-in-cheek argument that Christmas is (almost) pure magic:

Let's assume that Santa only visits those who are children in the eyes of the law, that is, those under the age of 18. There are roughly 2 billion such individuals in the world. However, Santa started his annual activities long before diversity and equal opportunity became issues, and as a result he doesn't handle Muslim, Hindu, Jewish and Buddhist children. That reduces his workload significantly to a mere 15% of the total, namely 378 million. However, the crucial figure is not the number of children but the number of homes Santa has to visit. According to the most recent census data, the average size of a family in the world is 3.5 children per household. Thus, Santa has to visit 108,000,000 individual homes. (Of course, as everyone knows, Santa only visits good children, but we can surely assume that, on an average, at least one child of the 3.5 in each home meets that criterion.)

—Keith Devlin, "The Mathematics of Christmas"

Devlin uses this scenario, as part of his mathematical analysis of Santa's yearly task, to help demonstrate that Christmas is indeed magical—because if you do the math, it's clear that Santa's task is physically impossible.

Case studies and observations feature detailed reporting about a subject. Case studies are in-depth, systematic examinations of an occasion, a person, or a group. For example, in arguing that class differences exist in the United States, sociologist Gregory Mantsios presents studies of three "typical" Americans to show "enormous class differences" in their lifestyles.

Observations offer detailed descriptions of a subject. Here's an observation of the emergence of a desert stream that flows only at night:

At about 5:30 water came out of the ground. It did not spew up, but slowly escaped into the surrounding sand and small rocks. The wet circle grew until water became visible. Then it bubbled out like a small fountain and the creek began.

—Craig Childs, *The Secret Knowledge of Water*

Childs presents this and other observations in a book that argues (among other things) that even in harsh, arid deserts, water exists, and knowing where to find it can mean the difference between life and death.

526–38

Textual evidence includes QUOTATIONS, PARAPHRASES, and SUMMARIES. Usually, the relevance of textual evidence must be stated directly, as excerpts from a text may carry several potential meanings. For example, here is an excerpt from a student essay analyzing the function of the raft in *Huckleberry Finn* as "a platform on which the resolution of conflicts is made possible":

[T]he scenes where Jim and Huck are in consensus on the raft contain the moments in which they are most relaxed. For instance, in chapter twelve of the novel, Huck, after escaping capture from Jackson's Island, calls the rafting life "solemn" and articulates their experience as living "pretty high" (Twain 75–76). Likewise, subsequent to escaping the unresolved feud between the Grangerfords and Shepherdsons in chapter eighteen, Huck is unquestionably at ease on the raft: "I was powerful glad to get away from the feuds. . . . We said there warn't no home like a raft, after all. Other places do seem so cramped up and smothery, but a raft don't. You feel mighty free and easy and comfortable on a raft" (Twain 134).

—Dave Nichols, "'Less All Be Friends': Rafts as Negotiating Platforms in Twain's *Huckleberry Finn*"

Huck's own words support Nichols's claim that he can relax on a raft. Nichols strengthens his claim by quoting evidence from two separate pages, suggesting that Huck's opinion of rafts pervades the novel.

Visuals can be a useful way of presenting evidence. Remember, though, that charts, graphs, photos, drawings, and other **VISUAL TEXTS** seldom speak for themselves and thus must be explained in your text. Below, for example, is a photograph of a poster carried by demonstrators at the 2008 Beijing Summer Olympics, protesting China's treatment of Tibetans.

653–63

If you were to use this photo in an essay, you would need to explain that the poster combines the image of a protester standing before a tank during the 1989 Tiananmen Square uprising with the Olympic logo, making clear to your readers that the protesters are likening China's treatment of Tibetans to its brutal actions in the past. Similarly, you could use this image of an American flag made from license plates in an argument about America's dependence on the auto industry.

Choosing appropriate evidence. The kinds of evidence you provide to support your argument depends on your RHETORICAL SITUATION. If your purpose is, for example, to convince readers to accept the need for a proposed solution, you'd be likely to include facts, statistics, and anecdotes. If you're writing for an academic audience, you'd be less likely to rely on anecdotes, preferring authorities, textual evidence, statistics, and case studies instead. And even within academic communities different disciplines and genres may focus primarily on different kinds of evidence. If you're not sure what counts as appropriate evidence, ask your instructor for guidance.

53 ■

Arguing with a Hostile Audience

Academic arguments are often presented to an audience that is presumed to be open-minded and fair, and the goal of such arguments is to demonstrate that your position is plausible and reasonable. Sometimes, though, your goal is to change people's minds, to try to get them to see some issue differently. That can be more of a challenge, because your audience likely has good reasons for thinking as they do, or their views reflect their basic values, and they may well feel defensive, angry, or threatened when you challenge them. These situations call for different argumentative strategies, such as Rogerian argument.

Rogerian argument. This method of presenting an argument is based on the work of psychologist Carl Rogers. This method assumes that common ground—areas of shared values or beliefs—exist between people who disagree. If they can find that common ground, they're more likely to come to some agreement or compromise position.

Since the goal of a Rogerian argument is to find compromise, it is organized differently than a traditional argument. First you must show that you understand the position of your opponents, and then you offer your position. Here's how a typical Rogerian argument is organized; be aware that each section may require several paragraphs:

Introduction. Here, you introduce the issue, acknowledging the various sides of the controversy, being as fair as you can.

Describe the opposing view. In this section, you try to capture the opposing view as accurately and as neutrally as you can. There may be circumstances when that view might be valid, and you should include them, too. Your goal here is to show that you understand the opposing view and why your readers hold that view convincingly enough that they will agree that it's accurate. By doing so, you establish your credibility and honest desire to understand those whose views differ from yours.

387–89 ◆

State your THESIS **and support it.** Now it's time to outline your position and defend it with reasons and evidence. As with a traditional argument, your goal here is to show that you have thought carefully about your posi-

66–68 ■

tion and researched it thoroughly. As with all arguing, your TONE should show your openness to ideas and avoid sounding as if you and you alone know the truth about the issue or that you are intellectually or morally superior to your opponent.

Conclude. In your concluding section, you bring the two perspectives you've just outlined together to show how, while your opponent's views have merit, your position deals with the issue or solves the problem better—or how a compromise position, somewhere in the middle, allows both sides to benefit.

You may find value in using Rogerian techniques in traditional arguments, including seeking common ground, describing issues and positions in neutral terms, and addressing those with opposing views respectfully and with goodwill.

Convincing Readers You're Trustworthy

For your argument to be convincing, you need to establish your own credibility with readers (also known as *ethos*)—to demonstrate your knowledge about your topic, to show that you and your readers share some common ground, and to show yourself to be evenhanded in the way you present your argument.

Building common ground. One important element of gaining readers' trust is to identify some common ground, some values you and your audience share. For example, to introduce a book arguing for the compatibility of science and religion, author Chet Raymo offers some common memories:

> Like most children, I was raised on miracles. Cows that jump over the moon; a jolly fat man that visits every house in the world in a single night; mice and ducks that talk; little engines that huff and puff and

academic literacies

rhetorical situations

genres

fields

processes

strategies

research MLA / APA

media / design

say, "I think I can"; geese that lay golden eggs. This lively exercise of credulity on the part of children is good practice for what follows—for believing in the miracle stories of traditional religion, yes, but also for the practice of poetry or science.

—Chet Raymo, *Skeptics and True Believers: The Exhilarating Connection between Science and Religion*

Raymo presents childhood stories and myths that are part of many people's shared experiences to help readers find a connection between two realms that are often seen as opposed.

Incorporating other viewpoints. To show that you have carefully considered the viewpoints of others, including those who may agree or disagree with you, you should incorporate those viewpoints into your argument by acknowledging, accommodating, or refuting them.

Acknowledging other viewpoints. One essential part of establishing your credibility is to acknowledge that there are viewpoints different from yours and to represent them fairly and accurately. Rather than weakening your argument, acknowledging possible objections to your position shows that you've thought about and researched your topic thoroughly. For example, in an essay about his experience growing up homosexual, writer Andrew Sullivan admits that not every young gay man or woman has the same experience:

I should add that many young lesbians and homosexuals seem to have had a much easier time of it. For many, the question of sexual identity was not a critical factor in their life choices or vocation, or even a factor at all. —Andrew Sullivan, "What Is a Homosexual?"

In response to a reasonable objection, Sullivan qualifies his assertions, making his own stance appear to be reasonable.

Accommodating other viewpoints. You may be tempted to ignore views you don't agree with, but in fact it's important to demonstrate that you are aware of them and have considered them carefully. You may find yourself conceding that opposing views have some merit and qualifying your claim or even making them part of your own argument. See, for example, how a philosopher arguing that torture is sometimes "not merely permissible but morally mandatory" addresses a major objection to his position:

> The most powerful argument against using torture as a punishment or to secure confessions is that such practices disregard the rights of the individual. Well, if the individual is all that important—and he is— it is correspondingly important to protect the rights of individuals threatened by terrorists. If life is so valuable that it must never be taken, the lives of the innocents must be saved even at the price of hurting the one who endangers them.
>
> —Michael Levin, "The Case for Torture"

Levin acknowledges his critics' argument that the individual is indeed important but then asserts that if the life of one person is important, the lives of many people must be even more important. In effect, he uses an opposing argument to advance his own.

Refuting other viewpoints. Often you may need to refute other arguments and make a case for why you believe they are wrong. Are the values underlying the argument questionable? Is the reasoning flawed? Is the evidence inadequate or faulty? For example, an essay arguing for the elimination of college athletics scholarships includes this refutation:

> Some argue that eliminating athletics scholarships would deny opportunity and limit access for many students, most notably black athletes. The question is, access to what? The fields of competition or an opportunity to earn a meaningful degree? With the six-year graduation rates of black basketball players hovering in the high 30-percent range, and black football players in the high 40-percent range, despite years of "academic reform," earning an athletics

scholarship under the current system is little more than a chance to play sports.
                                              —John R. Gerdy, "For True Reform,
                                                  Athletics Scholarships Must Go"

Gerdy bases his refutation on statistics showing that for more than half of African American college athletes, the opportunity to earn a degree by playing a sport is an illusion.

When you incorporate differing viewpoints, be careful to avoid the **FALLACIES** of attacking the person making the argument or refuting a competing position that no one seriously entertains. It is also important that you not distort or exaggerate opposing viewpoints. If *your* argument is to be persuasive, other arguments should be represented fairly.

◆ 414–16

Appealing to Readers' Emotions

Logic and facts, even when presented by someone who seems reasonable and trustworthy, may not be enough to persuade readers. Many successful arguments include an emotional component that appeals to readers' hearts as well as to their minds. Advertising often works by appealing to its audience's emotions, as in this paragraph from a Volvo ad:

> Choosing a car is about the comfort and safety of your passengers, most especially your children. That's why we ensure Volvo's safety research examines how we can make our cars safer for everyone who travels in them—from adults to teenagers, children to babies. Even those who aren't even born yet.　　　　　　　　　　　　—*Volvo.com*

This ad plays on the fear that children—or a pregnant mother—may be injured or killed in an automobile accident.

Keep in mind that emotional appeals, also known as *pathos*, can make readers feel as though they are being manipulated and, consequently, less likely to accept an argument. For most kinds of academic writing, use emotional appeals sparingly.

Checking for Fallacies

Fallacies are arguments that involve faulty reasoning. It's important to avoid fallacies in your writing because they often seem plausible but are usually unfair or inaccurate and make reasonable discussion difficult. Here are some of the most common fallacies:

- *Ad hominem* arguments attack someone's character rather than address the issues. (*Ad hominem* is Latin for "to the man.") It is an especially common fallacy in political discourse and elsewhere: "Jack Turner has no business talking about the way we run things in this city. He's just another flaky liberal." Whether or not Turner is a "flaky liberal" has no bearing on the worth of his argument about "the way we run things in this city"; insulting one's opponents isn't an argument against their positions.

- *Bandwagon appeals* argue that because others think or do something, we should, too. For example, an advertisement for a breakfast cereal claims that it is "America's favorite cereal." It assumes that readers want to be part of the group and implies that an opinion that is popular must be correct.

- *Begging the question* is a circular argument. It assumes as a given what is trying to be proved, essentially asserting that A is true because A is true. Consider this statement: "Affirmative action can never be fair or just because you cannot remedy one injustice by committing another." This statement begs the question because to prove that affirmative action is unjust, it assumes that it is an injustice.

- *Either-or* arguments, also called *false dilemmas*, are oversimplifications that assert there can be only two possible positions on a complex issue. For example, "Those who oppose our actions in this war are enemies of freedom" inaccurately assumes that if someone opposes the war in question, they oppose freedom. In fact, people might have many other reasons for opposing the war.

- *False analogies* compare things that resemble each other in some ways but not in the most important respects—for example, "Trees pollute the air just as much as cars and trucks do." Although it's true that plants emit hydrocarbons, and hydrocarbons are a component of smog, they also produce oxygen, whereas motor vehicles emit gases that combine with hydrocarbons to form smog. Vehicles pollute the air; trees provide the air that vehicles' emissions pollute.

- *Faulty causality,* also known as *post hoc, ergo propter hoc* (Latin for "after this, therefore because of this"), assumes that because one event followed another, the first event caused the second—for example, "Legalizing same-sex marriage in Sweden led to a decline in the marriage rate of opposite-sex couples." The statement contains no evidence to show that the first event caused the second.

- *Straw man* arguments misrepresent an opposing position to make it ridiculous or extreme and thus easy to refute, rather than dealing with the actual position. For example, if someone argues that funding for supplemental nutrition assistance should be cut, a straw man response would be, "You want the poor to starve," transforming a proposal to cut a specific program into an exaggerated argument that the proposer hasn't made.

- *Hasty generalizations* are conclusions based on insufficient or inappropriately qualified evidence. This summary of a research study is a good example: "Twenty randomly chosen residents of Brooklyn, New York, were asked whether they found graffiti tags offensive; fourteen said yes, five said no, and one had no opinion. Therefore, 70 percent of Brooklyn residents find tagging offensive." In Brooklyn, a part of New York City with a population of over two million, twenty residents is far too small a group from which to draw meaningful conclusions. To be able to generalize, the researcher would have had to survey a much greater percentage of Brooklyn's population.

- *Slippery slope* arguments assert that one event will inevitably lead to another, often cataclysmic event without presenting evidence that such a chain of causes and effects will in fact take place. Here's an example: "If the state legislature passes this 2 percent tax increase, it won't be long before all the corporations in the state move to other states and leave thousands unemployed." According to this argument, if taxes are raised, the state's economy will be ruined—not a likely scenario, given the size of the proposed increase.

Considering the Rhetorical Situation

To argue effectively, you need to think about the message that you want to articulate, the audience you want to persuade, the effect of your stance, and the larger context you are writing in.

55–56 ■	**PURPOSE**	What do you want your audience to do? To think a certain way? To take a certain action? To change their minds? To consider alternative views to their current ones? To accept your position as plausible? To see that you have thought carefully about an issue and researched it appropriately?
57–60 ■	**AUDIENCE**	Who is your intended audience? What do they likely know and believe about your topic? How personal is it for them? To what extent are they likely to agree or disagree with you? Why? What common ground can you find with them? How should you incorporate other viewpoints they have? What kind of evidence are they likely to accept?
61–65 ■	**GENRE**	What genre will help you achieve your purpose? A position paper? An evaluation? A review? A proposal? An analysis?
66–68 ■	**STANCE**	What's your attitude toward your topic, and why? What strategies will help you to convey that stance? How do you want your audience to perceive you? As an authority on your topic? As someone much like them? As calm? reasonable? impassioned or angry? something else?

MEDIA/DESIGN What media will you use, and how do your media affect your argument? If you're writing on paper, does your argument call for photos or charts? If you're giving an oral presentation, should you put your reasons and support on slides? If you're writing online, should you add links to sites representing other positions or containing evidence that supports your position?

69–71

39 Classifying and Dividing

Classification and division are ways of organizing information: various items may be classified according to their similarities, or a single topic may be divided into parts. We might classify different kinds of flowers as annuals or perennials, for example, and classify the perennials further as dahlias, daisies, roses, and peonies. We might also divide a flower garden into distinct areas: for herbs, flowers, and vegetables.

Writers often use classification and division as ways of developing and organizing material. This book, for instance, classifies comparison, definition, description, and several other common ways of thinking and writing as strategies. It divides the information it provides about writing into seven parts: "Rhetorical Situations," "Genres," and so on. Each part further divides its material into various chapters. Even if you never write a book, you will have occasion to classify and divide material in **ANNOTATED BIBLIOGRAPHIES**, essays **ANALYZING TEXTS**, and other kinds of writing. This chapter offers advice for classifying and dividing information for various purposes—and in a way that suits your own rhetorical situation.

190–98
98–130

Classifying

When we classify something, we group it with similar things. A linguist would classify French, Spanish, and Italian as Romance languages, for example—and Russian, Polish, and Bulgarian as Slavic languages. In a phony news story from the *Onion* about a church bake sale, the writer classifies the activities observed there as examples of the seven deadly sins:

academic literacies · rhetorical situations · genres · fields · processes · strategies · research MLA / APA · media / design

GADSDEN, AL—The seven deadly sins—avarice, sloth, envy, lust, gluttony, pride, and wrath—were all committed Sunday during the twice-annual bake sale at St. Mary's of the Immaculate Conception Church.

—"All Seven Deadly Sins Committed at Church Bake Sale," *Onion*

The article goes on to categorize the participants' behavior in terms of the sins, describing one parishioner who commits the sin of pride by bragging about her cookies and others who commit the sin of envy by envying the popularity of the prideful parishioner's baked goods (the consumption of which leads to the sin of gluttony). In all, the article notes, "347 individual acts of sin were committed at the bake sale," and every one of them can be classified as one of the seven deadly sins.

Dividing

As a writing strategy, division is a way of breaking something into parts—and a way of making the information easy for readers to follow and understand. See how this example about children's ways of nagging divides their tactics into seven categories:

James U. McNeal, a professor of marketing at Texas A&M University, is considered America's leading authority on marketing to children. In his book *Kids as Customers* (1992), McNeal provides marketers with a thorough analysis of "children's requesting styles and appeals." He [divides] juvenile nagging tactics into seven major categories. A *pleading* nag is one accompanied by repetitions of words like "please" or "mom, mom, mom." A *persistent* nag involves constant requests for the coveted product and may include the phrase "I'm gonna ask just one more time." *Forceful* nags are extremely pushy and may include subtle threats, like "Well, then, I'll go and ask Dad." *Demonstrative* nags are the most high risk, often characterized by full-blown tantrums in public places, breath holding, tears, a refusal to leave the store. *Sugar-coated* nags promise affection in return for a purchase and may rely on seemingly heartfelt declarations, like "You're the best dad in the world." *Threatening* nags are youthful forms of blackmail, vows of eternal hatred and of running away if something isn't bought. *Pity* nags claim the child will be heartbroken, teased, or socially stunted if the parent refuses to buy a certain item. "All of these appeals and styles may be used in combination," McNeal's research has discovered, "but kids tend to stick to one or two of each that prove most effective . . . for their own parents."

—Eric Schlosser, *Fast Food Nation:*
The Dark Side of the All-American Meal

Here the writer announces the division scheme of "seven major categories." Then he names each tactic and describes how it works. Notice the italics: each tactic is italicized, making it easy to recognize and follow. Take away the italics, and the divisions would be less visible.

Creating Clear and Distinct Categories

When you classify or divide, you need to create clear and distinct categories. If you're writing about music, you might divide it on the basis of the genre (rap, rock, classical, gospel), artist (male or female, group or solo), or instruments (violins, trumpets, bongos, guitars). These categories must be distinct so that no information overlaps or fits into more than one category, and they must include every member of the group you're discussing. The simpler the criteria for selecting the categories, the better. The nagging categories in the example from *Fast Food Nation* are based on only one criterion: a child's verbal behavior.

Sometimes you may want to highlight your categories visually to make them easier to follow. Eric Schlosser does that by italicizing each category: the *pleading* nag, the *persistent* nag, the *forceful* nag, and so on. Other **DESIGN** elements—bulleted lists, pie charts, tables, images—might also prove useful.

644–52

academic literacies · rhetorical situations · genres · fields · processes · strategies · research MLA / APA · media / design

Sometimes you might show categories visually, as in the following chart. The differences among the six varieties pictured are visible at a glance, and the chart next to the photos shows the best uses for each variety—and its level of tartness.

The photographs allow us to see the differences among the varieties at a glance. Although the varieties shown here are arranged according to the tartness of their flavor, they could have been arranged in other ways too—alphabetically or by shape or size.

	EATING	BAKING	COOKING	
Red Delicious	✔	✔		LESS TART
Honeycrisp	✔	✔	✔	
Red Rome		✔	✔	
Braeburn	✔		✔	
McIntosh	✔	✔	✔	MORE TART

All photos © New York Apple Association

For another example, see how *The World of Caffeine* authors Bennett Alan Weinberg and Bonnie K. Bealer use a two-column list to show what they say are the differing cultural connotations of coffee and tea:

Coffee Aspect	Tea Aspect
Male	Female
Boisterous	Decorous
Indulgence	Temperance
Hardheaded	Romantic
Topology	Geometry
Heidegger	Carnap
Beethoven	Mozart
Libertarian	Statist
Promiscuous	Pure

—Bennett Alan Weinberg and Bonnie K. Bealer,
The World of Caffeine

Considering the Rhetorical Situation

As a writer or speaker, you need to think about the message that you want to articulate, the audience you want to reach, and the larger context you are writing in.

55–56 ■ **PURPOSE** Your purpose for writing will affect how you classify or divide information. Weinberg and Bealer classify coffee as "boisterous" and tea as "decorous" to help readers understand the cultural styles the two beverages represent, whereas J. Crew might divide sweaters into cashmere, wool, and cotton to help shoppers find and buy clothing from their website.

57–60 ■ **AUDIENCE** Who do you want to reach, and will classifying or dividing your material help them follow your discussion?

✳ academic literacies   ■ rhetorical situations   ▲ genres   ◆ fields   ○ processes   ◆ strategies   ● research MLA / APA   □ media / design

GENRE   Does your genre call for you to categorize or divide information? A long report might need to be divided into sections, for instance.

61–65

STANCE   Your stance may affect the way you classify information. Weinberg and Bealer's classification of coffee as "Beethoven" and tea as "Mozart" reflects a stance that focuses on cultural analysis (and assumes an audience familiar with the difference between the two composers). If the authors were botanists, they might categorize the two beverages in terms of their biological origins ("seed based" and "leaf based").

66–68

MEDIA / DESIGN   You can classify or divide in paragraph form, but sometimes a pie chart or list will show the categories better.

69–71

IF YOU NEED MORE HELP

See also **CLUSTERING**, **CUBING**, and **LOOPING**, three methods of generating ideas discussed in Chapter 29 that can be especially helpful for classifying material. And see all the **PROCESSES** chapters for guidelines on drafting, revising, and so on if you need to write a classification essay.

332–34
321

40 Comparing and Contrasting

Comparing things looks at their similarities; contrasting them focuses on their differences. It's a kind of thinking that comes naturally and that we do constantly—for example, comparing Houston with Dallas, iPhones with Androids, or three paintings by Renoir. And once we start comparing, we generally find ourselves contrasting—Houston and Dallas have differences as well as similarities.

246–55
202–10

As a student, you'll often be asked to compare and contrast paintings or poems or other things. As a writer, you'll have cause to compare and contrast in most kinds of writing. In a **PROPOSAL**, for instance, you will need to compare your solution with other possible solutions; or in an **EVALUATION**, such as a movie review, you might contrast the film you're reviewing with some other film. This chapter offers advice on ways of comparing and contrasting things for various writing purposes and for your own rhetorical situations.

Most of the time, we compare obviously similar things: laptops we might purchase, three competing political candidates, two versions of a film. Occasionally, however, we might compare things that are less obviously similar. See how John McMurtry, an ex–football player, compares football with war in an essay arguing that the attraction football holds for spectators is based in part on its potential for violence and injury:

> The family resemblance between football and war is, indeed, striking. Their languages are similar: "field general," "long bomb," "blitz," "take a shot," "front line," "pursuit," "good hit," "the draft," and so on. Their principles and practices are alike: mass hysteria, the art of intimidation, absolute command and total obedience, territorial aggression, censorship, inflated insignia and propaganda, blackboard maneuvers and strategies, drills, uniforms, marching bands, and training

academic literacies

rhetorical situations

genres

fields

processes

strategies

research MLA / APA

media / design

camps. And the virtues they celebrate are almost identical: hyper-aggressiveness, coolness under fire, and suicidal bravery.

—John McMurtry, "Kill 'Em! Crush 'Em! Eat 'Em Raw!"

McMurtry's comparison helps focus readers' attention on what he's arguing about football in part because it's somewhat unexpected. But the more unlikely the comparison, the more you might be accused of comparing apples and oranges. It's important, therefore, that the things we compare be legitimately compared—as is the case in the following comparison of the health of the world's richest and poorest people:

> World Health Organization (WHO) data indicate that roughly 1.2 billion people are undernourished, underweight, and often hungry. At the same time, roughly 1.2 billion people are overnourished and overweight, most of them suffering from excessive caloric intake and exercise deprivation. So while 1 billion people worry whether they will eat, another billion should worry about eating too much.
>
> Disease patterns also reflect the widening gap. The billion poorest suffer mostly from infectious diseases—malaria, tuberculosis, dysentery, and AIDS. Malnutrition leaves infants and small children even more vulnerable to such infectious diseases. Unsafe drinking water takes a heavier toll on those with hunger-weakened immune systems, resulting in millions of fatalities each year. In contrast, among the billion at the top of the global economic scale, it is diseases related to aging and lifestyle excesses, including obesity, smoking, diets rich in fat and sugar, and exercise deprivation, that cause most deaths.
>
> —Lester R. Brown, *Plan B 2.0: Rescuing a Planet*
> *under Stress and a Civilization in Trouble*

While the two groups of roughly a billion people each undoubtedly have similarities, this selection from a book arguing for global action on the environment focuses on the stark contrasts.

Two Ways of Comparing and Contrasting

Comparisons and contrasts may be organized in two basic ways: block and point by point.

The block method.   One way is to discuss separately each item you're comparing, giving all the information about one item and then all the information about the next item. A report on Seattle and Vancouver, for example, compares the firearm regulations in each city using a paragraph about Seattle and then a paragraph about Vancouver:

> Although similar in many ways, Seattle and Vancouver differ markedly in their approaches to the regulation of firearms. In Seattle, handguns may be purchased legally for self-defense in the street or at home. After a thirty-day waiting period, a permit can be obtained to carry a handgun as a concealed weapon. The recreational use of handguns is minimally restricted.
>
>   In Vancouver, self-defense is not considered a valid or legal reason to purchase a handgun. Concealed weapons are not permitted. Recreational uses of handguns (such as target shooting and collecting) are regulated by the province, and the purchase of a handgun requires a restricted-weapons permit. A permit to carry a weapon must also be obtained in order to transport a handgun, and these weapons can be discharged only at a licensed shooting club. Handguns can be transported by car, but only if they are stored in the trunk in a locked box.
>
> —John Henry Sloan et al., "Handgun Regulations, Crime, Assaults, and Homicide: A Tale of Two Cities"

The point-by-point method.   The other way to compare things is to focus on specific points of comparison. In this paragraph, humorist David Sedaris compares his childhood with his partner's, discussing corresponding aspects of the childhoods one at a time:

> Certain events are parallel, but compared with Hugh's, my childhood was unspeakably dull. When I was seven years old, my family moved to North Carolina. When he was seven years old, Hugh's family moved to the Congo. We had a collie and a house cat. They had a monkey and two horses named Charlie Brown and Satan. I threw stones at stop signs. Hugh threw stones at crocodiles. The verbs are the same, but he definitely wins the prize when it comes to nouns and objects. An eventful day for my mother might have involved a trip to the dry

cleaner or a conversation with the potato-chip deliveryman. Asked one ordinary Congo afternoon what she'd done with her day, Hugh's mother answered that she and a fellow member of the Ladies' Club had visited a leper colony on the outskirts of Kinshasa.

—David Sedaris, "Remembering My Childhood on the Continent of Africa"

Using Graphs and Images to Present Comparisons

Some comparisons can be easier to understand if they're presented visually, as a **CHART**, **GRAPH**, or **ILLUSTRATION**. For example, this excerpt from a chart from the Gallup polling company's website shows the percentage of Americans who identified themselves as Republicans, Independents, or Democrats in 2012, broken down by race and ethnicity:

653–63

Racial and Ethnic Composition of U.S., by Party ID

	Republican	Independent	Democrat
Non-Hispanic white	89%	70%	60%
Non-Hispanic black	2%	8%	22%
Hispanic	6%	16%	13%
Asian	1%	3%	2%
Other	1%	1%	1%
Undesignated	1%	2%	2%

Gallup Daily tracking, January–December 2012

—*GALLUP*

The following bar graph, from an economics textbook, compares the incomes of various professions in the United States, both with one another and with the average U.S. income (defined as 100 percent). Again, it would be possible to write out this information in a paragraph—but it is much easier to understand it this way:

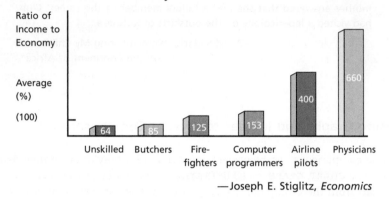

—Joseph E. Stiglitz, *Economics*

Sometimes photographs can make a comparison. The two photos below show a street in Houston before and after Hurricane Harvey in 2017.

Roadway in Houston before the 2017 hurricane (left) and after (right).

academic literacies

rhetorical situations

genres

fields

processes

strategies

research MLA / APA

media / design

Using Figurative Language to Make Comparisons

Another way we make comparisons is with figurative language: words and phrases used in a nonliteral way to help readers see a point. Three kinds of figurative language that make comparisons are similes, metaphors, and analogies. When Robert Burns wrote that his love was "like a red, red rose," he was comparing his love with a rose and evoking an image—in this case, a simile—that helps us understand his feelings for her. A simile makes a comparison using *like* or *as*. In the following example, from an article in the food section of the *New York Times*, a restaurant critic uses several similes (underlined) to help us visualize an unusual food dish:

> Once upon a time, possibly at a lodge in Wyoming, possibly at a butcher shop in Maurice, Louisiana, or maybe even at a plantation in South Carolina, an enterprising cook decided to take a boned chicken, a boned duck, and a boned turkey, stuff them one inside the other <u>like Russian dolls</u>, and roast them. He called his masterpiece turducken. . . .
>
> A well-prepared turducken is a marvelous treat, a free-form poultry terrine layered with flavorful stuffing and moistened with duck fat. When it's assembled, it looks <u>like a turkey</u> and it roasts <u>like a turkey</u>, but when you go to carve it, you can slice through it <u>like a loaf of bread</u>. In each slice you get a little bit of everything: white meat from the breast; dark meat from the legs, duck, carrots, bits of sausage, bread, herbs, juices, and chicken, too.
>
> —Amanda Hesser, "Turkey Finds Its Inner Duck (and Chicken)"

Metaphors make comparisons without such connecting words as *like* or *as*. See how desert ecologist Craig Childs uses a metaphor to help us understand the nature of water during a flood in the Grand Canyon:

> Water splashed off the desert and ran all over the surface, looking for the quickest way down. It was too swift for the ground to absorb. When water flows like this, it will not be clean tap water. It will be <u>a gravy of debris</u>, snatching everything it finds.
>
> —Craig Childs, *The Secret Knowledge of Water*

Calling the water "a gravy of debris" allows us to see the murky liquid as it streams through the canyon.

Analogies are extended similes or metaphors that compare something unfamiliar with something more familiar. Arguing that corporations should not patent parts of DNA whose function isn't yet clear, a genetics professor uses the familiar image of a library to explain an unfamiliar concept:

> It's like having a library of books and randomly tearing pages out. You may know which books the pages came from but that doesn't tell you much about them.　—Peter Goodfellow, quoted in John Vidal and John Carvel, "Lambs to the Gene Market"

Sometimes analogies are used for humorous effect as well as to make a point, as in this passage from a critique of history textbooks:

> Another history text—this one for fifth grade—begins with the story of how Henry B. Gonzalez, who is a member of Congress from Texas, learned about his own nationality. When he was ten years old, his teacher told him he was an American because he was born in the United States. His grandmother, however, said, "The cat was born in the oven. Does that make him bread?"
>
> —Frances FitzGerald, *America Revised: History Schoolbooks in the Twentieth Century*

The grandmother's question shows how an intentionally ridiculous analogy can be a source of humor—and can make a point memorably.

Considering the Rhetorical Situation

As a writer or speaker, you need to think about the message that you want to articulate, the audience you want to reach, and the larger context you are writing in.

55–56 ■

PURPOSE　　Sometimes your main purpose for writing will be to compare two or more things. Other times, you may want to compare several things for some other purpose—to compare your views with those of others in an argument essay or to compare one text with another as you analyze them.

academic literacies
rhetorical situations
genres
fields
processes
strategies
research MLA / APA
media / design

AUDIENCE   Who is your audience, and will comparing your topic with   57–60
a more familiar one help them to follow your discussion?

GENRE   Does your genre require you to compare something?   61–65
Evaluations often include comparisons—one book to
another in a review, or ten different cell phones in *Consumer Reports*.

STANCE   Your stance may affect any comparisons you make.   66–68
How you compare two things—evenhandedly, or clearly
favoring one over the other, for example—will reflect
your stance.

MEDIA / DESIGN   Some things you will want to compare with words alone   69–71
(lines from two poems, for instance), but sometimes you
may wish to make comparisons visually (two images juxtaposed on a page, or several numbers plotted on a line
graph).

IF YOU NEED MORE HELP

See **LOOPING** and **CUBING**, two methods of generating ideas discussed in Chapter 29   332
that can be especially helpful for comparing and contrasting. If you're writing an   334
essay whose purpose is to compare two or more things, see also the **PROCESSES**   321
chapters for help drafting, revising, and so on.

41 Defining

Defining something says what it is—and what it is not. A terrier, for example, is a kind of dog. A fox terrier is a small dog now generally kept as a pet but once used by hunters to dig for foxes. Happiness is a jelly doughnut, at least according to Homer Simpson. All of those are definitions. As writers, we need to define any terms our readers may not know. And sometimes you'll want to stipulate your own definition of a word in order to set the terms of an **ARGUMENT**—as Homer Simpson does with a definition that's not found in any dictionary. This chapter details strategies for using definitions in your writing to suit your own rhetorical situations.

397–417

Formal Definitions

Sometimes to make sure readers understand you, you will need to provide a formal definition. If you are using a technical term that readers are unlikely to know or if you are using a term in a specific way, you need to say then and there what the word means. The word *mutual*, for example, has several dictionary meanings:

> **Definition of MUTUAL**
>
> **1a:** directed by each toward the other or the others • *mutual* affection
> **b:** having the same feelings one for the other • they had long been *mutual* enemies
> **c:** shared in common • enjoying their *mutual* hobby
> **d:** joint • to their *mutual* advantage
> **2:** characterized by intimacy • *mutual* contacts
> **3:** of or relating to a plan whereby the members of an organization share in the profits and expenses; specifically: of, relating to, or taking

academic literacies | rhetorical situations | genres | fields | processes | strategies | research MLA / APA | media / design

the form of an insurance method in which the policyholders constitute the members of the insuring company

—*Merriam-Webster.com*

The first two meanings are commonly understood and probably require no definition. But if you were to use *mutual* in the third sense, it might—depending on your audience. A general audience would probably need the definition; an audience from the insurance industry would not. A website that gives basic financial advice to an audience of non-specialists, for instance, offers a specific definition of the term *mutual fund*:

> *Mutual funds* are financial intermediaries. They are companies set up to receive your money and then, having received it, to make investments with the money.
>
> —Bill Barker, "A Grand, Comprehensive
Overview to Mutual Funds Investing"

But even writers in specialized fields routinely provide formal definitions to make sure their readers understand the way they are using certain words. See how two writers define the word *stock* as it pertains to their respective (and very different) fields:

> Stocks are the basis for sauces and soups and important flavoring agents for braises. Admittedly, stock making is time consuming, but the extra effort yields great dividends.
>
> —Tom Colicchio, *Think Like a Chef*

> Want to own part of a business without having to show up at its office every day? Or ever? Stock is the vehicle of choice for those who do. Dating back to the Dutch mutual stock corporations of the sixteenth century, the modern stock market exists as a way for entrepreneurs to finance businesses using money collected from investors. In return for ponying up the dough to finance the company, the investor becomes a part owner of the company. That ownership is represented by stock—specialized financial "securities," or financial instruments, that are "secured" by a claim on the assets and profits of a company.
>
> —"Investing Basics: Stocks," *Motley Fool*

To write a formal definition

- Use words that readers are likely to be familiar with.
- Don't use the word being defined in the definition.
- Begin with the word being defined; include the general category to which the term belongs and the attributes that make it different from the others in that category.

For example:

Term	General Category	Distinguishing Attributes
Stock is	a specialized financial "security"	that is "secured" by a claim.
Photosynthesis is	a process	by which plants use sunlight to create energy.
Astronomers are	scientists	who study celestial objects and phenomena.
Zach Galifianakis,	an actor,	has been featured in several films, including *The Hangover* and *Birdman.*

Note that the category and distinguishing attributes cannot be stated too broadly; if they were, the definition would be too vague to be useful. It wouldn't be helpful in most circumstances, for example, to say, "Zach Galifianakis is a man who has acted" or "Photosynthesis is something having to do with plants."

Extended Definitions

Sometimes you need to provide a more detailed definition. Extended definitions may be several sentences long or several paragraphs long and may include pictures or diagrams. Sometimes an entire essay is devoted to defining a difficult or important concept. Here is one writer's extended definition of *meme*:

> Richard Dawkins first came up with the idea of a meme in his 1976 book *The Selfish Gene*. Essentially, memes are ideas that evolve according to the same principles that govern biological evolution. Think about all the ideas that you have in your head right now. They are all memes, and they all came from somewhere. Some of them will have come from friends and some will have come from the internet or television. Examples of memes are musical tunes, jokes, trends, fashions, catch phrases, and car designs. Now, the memes that inhabit your mind are in competition with all the other memes in the *memepool* (the collection of all existing memes). This means that they are all competing to get themselves copied into other people's minds. Some of these memes do quite well. Every time you whistle your favorite tune or utter a useful catch phrase, you are facilitating the spread of those memes. Every time you wear something that is "in fashion" you are helping the idea of that fashion enter other people's minds. Consider the first four notes of Beethoven's 5th symphony, or the "Happy Birthday" song. These are ideas that inhabit our minds and have been very successful at replicating. Not only have these memes found their way into literally millions of minds, they have also managed to leave copies of themselves on paper, in books, on audiotape, on compact disks, and in computer hard-drives.
>
> There is a limited amount of memetic storage space on this planet, so only the best memes manage to implant themselves. Memes that are good at replicating tend to leave more copies of themselves in minds and in other mediums such as books. Memes that are not so good at replicating tend to die out. We can imagine what sorts of memes have become extinct. Ancient songs that were once sung and never written down are one example. Another example is the many stories that were once told but have since slipped into oblivion.
>
> —Brent Silby, "What Is a Meme?"

That definition includes a description of the basic features and behavior of memes, examples of them, and the origin of the term. We can assume that it's written for a general audience, one that doesn't know anything about memes.

Abstract concepts often require extended definitions because by nature they are more complicated to define. There are many ways of writing an extended definition, depending in part on the term being defined and on your audience and purpose. The following examples show some of the methods that can be used for composing extended definitions of *democracy*.

Explore the word's origins. Where did the word come from? When did it first come into use? In the following example, from an essay considering what democracy means in the twenty-first century, the writer started by looking at the word's first known use in English. Though it's from an essay written for a first-year writing course and thus for a fairly general audience, it's a definition that might pique any audience's interest:

> According to the *Oxford English Dictionary*, the term *democracy* first appeared in English in a thirteenth-century translation of Aristotle's works—specifically, in his *Politics*, where he stated that the "underlying principle of democracy is freedom" and that "it is customary to say that only in democracies do men have a share in freedom, for that is what every democracy makes its aim." By the sixteenth century, the word was used much as it is now. One writer in 1586, for instance, defined it in this way: "where free and poore men being the greater number, are lords of the estate."
>
> —Susanna Mejía, "What Does Democracy Mean Now?"

Here's another example, this one written for a scholarly audience, from an essay about women, participation, democracy, and the information age:

> The very word *citizenship* carries with it a connotation of place, a "citizen" being, literally, the inhabitant of a city. Over the years the word has, of course, accumulated a number of associated meanings . . . and the word has come to stand in for such concepts as participation, equality, and democracy. The fact that the concept of locality is deeply embedded in the word *citizen* suggests that it is also fundamental to our current understanding of these other, more apparently abstract words.
>
> In Western thought, the concepts of citizenship, equality, and democracy are closely interlinked and can be traced back to a common source, in Athens in the fifth century B.C. Perhaps it is no accident that it was the same culture which also gave us, in its theater, the

Norman Rockwell's 1943 painting Freedom of Speech *presents a visual defini-* *tion of democracy: a citizen stands to speak at a public meeting while his fellow* *citizens listen attentively.*

concept of the unity of time and space. The Greek city-state has been represented for centuries as the ideal model of democracy, with free and equal access for all citizens to decision making. Leaving aside, for the moment, the question of who was included, and who excluded from this notion of citizenship, we can see that the sense of place is fundamental to this model. Entitlement to participate in the democratic process is circumscribed by geography; it is the inhabitants of the geographical entity of the city-state, precisely defined and bounded, who have the rights to citizenship. Those who are not defined as inhabitants of that specific city-state are explicitly excluded, although, of course, they may have the right to citizenship elsewhere.

—Ursula Huws, "Women, Participation, and Democracy in the Information Society"

Provide details. What are its characteristics? What is it made of? See how a historian explores the basic characteristics of democracy in a book written for an audience of historians:

As a historian I am naturally disposed to be satisfied with the meaning which, in the history of politics, men have commonly attributed to the word—a meaning, needless to say, which derives partly from the experience and partly from the aspirations of mankind. So regarded, the term *democracy* refers primarily to a form of government, and it has always meant government by the many as opposed to government by the one—government by the people as opposed to government by a tyrant, a dictator, or an absolute monarch. . . . Since the Greeks first used the term, the essential test of democratic government has always been this: the source of political authority must be and remain in the people and not in the ruler. A democratic government has always meant one in which the citizens, or a sufficient number of them to represent more or less effectively the common will, freely act from time to time, and according to established forms, to appoint or recall the magistrates and to enact or revoke the laws by which the community is governed.   —Carl Becker, *Modern Democracy*

Compare it with other words. How is this concept like other similar
424–31 ◆
things? How does it differ? What is it *not* like? **COMPARE AND CONTRAST**

academic literacies
rhetorical situations
genres
fields
processes
strategies
research MLA / APA
media / design

it. See how a political science textbook defines a *majoritarian democracy* by comparing its characteristics with those of a *consensual democracy*:

> A majoritarian democracy is one
>
> 1. having only two major political parties, not many
> 2. having an electoral system that requires a bare majority to elect one clear winner in an election, as opposed to a proportional electoral system that distributes seats to political parties according to the rough share of votes received in the election
> 3. a strong executive (president or prime minister) and cabinet that together are largely independent of the legislature when it comes to exercising the executive's constitutional duties, in contrast to an executive and cabinet that are politically controlled by the parties in the legislature and therefore unable to exercise much influence when proposing policy initiatives.
>
> —Benjamin Ginsberg, Theodore J. Lowi, and Margaret Weir,
> *We the People: An Introduction to American Politics*

And here's an example in which democracy is contrasted with various other forms of governments of the past:

> Caesar's power derived from a popular mandate, conveyed through established republican forms, but that did not make his government any the less a dictatorship. Napoleon called his government a democratic republic, but no one, least of all Napoleon himself, doubted that he had destroyed the last vestiges of the democratic republic.
>
> —Carl Becker, *Modern Democracy*

Give examples. See how the essayist E. B. White defines democracy by giving some everyday examples of considerate behavior, humility, and civic participation—all things he suggests constitute democracy:

> It is the line that forms on the right. It is the don't in "don't shove." It is the hole in the stuffed shirt through which the sawdust slowly trickles; it is the dent in the high hat. Democracy is the recurrent suspicion that more than half of the people are right more than half of the time. . . . Democracy is a letter to the editor.   —E. B. White, "Democracy"

White's definition is elegant because he uses examples that his readers will know. His characteristics—metaphors, really—define democracy not as a conceptual way of governing but as an everyday part of American life.

418–23 ◆ **Classify it.** Often it is useful to divide or CLASSIFY a term. The ways in which democracy unfolds are complex enough to warrant entire textbooks, of course, but the following definition, from a political science textbook, divides democracy into two kinds, representative and direct:

> A system of government that gives citizens a regular opportunity to elect the top government officials is usually called a representative democracy or republic. A system that permits citizens to vote directly on laws and policies is often called a direct democracy. At the national level, America is a representative democracy in which citizens select government officials but do not vote on legislation. Some states, however, have provisions for direct legislation through popular referendum. For example, California voters in 1995 decided to bar undocumented immigrants from receiving some state services.
>
> —Benjamin Ginsberg, Theodore J. Lowi, and Margaret Weir,
> *We the People: An Introduction to American Politics*

Stipulative Definitions

Sometimes a writer will stipulate a certain definition, essentially saying, "This is how I'm defining x." Such definitions are not usually found in a dictionary—and at the same time are central to the argument the writer is making. Here is one example, from an essay by Toni Morrison. Describing a scene from a film in which a newly arrived Greek immigrant, working as a shoe shiner in Grand Central Terminal, chases away an African American competitor, Morrison calls the scene an example of "race talk," a concept she then goes on to define:

This is race talk, the explicit insertion into everyday life of racial signs and symbols that have no meaning other than pressing African Americans to the lowest level of the racial hierarchy. Popular culture, shaped by film, theater, advertising, the press, television, and literature, is heavily engaged in race talk. It participates freely in this most enduring and efficient rite of passage into American culture: negative appraisals of the native-born black population. Only when the lesson of racial estrangement is learned is assimilation complete. Whatever the lived experience of immigrants with African Americans—pleasant, beneficial, or bruising—the rhetorical experience renders blacks as noncitizens, already discredited outlaws.

All immigrants fight for jobs and space, and who is there to fight but those who have both? As in the fishing ground struggle between Texas and Vietnamese shrimpers, they displace what and whom they can. Although U.S. history is awash in labor battles, political fights and property wars among all religious and ethnic groups, their struggles are persistently framed as struggles between recent arrivals and blacks. In race talk the move into mainstream America always means buying into the notion of American blacks as the real aliens. Whatever the ethnicity or nationality of the immigrant, his nemesis is understood to be African American.   —Toni Morrison, "On the Backs of Blacks"

The following example is from a book review of Nancy L. Rosenblum's *Membership and Morals: The Personal Uses of Pluralism in America*, published in the *American Prospect*, a magazine for readers interested in political analysis. In it a Stanford law professor outlines a definition of "the democracy of everyday life":

Democracy, in this understanding of it, means simply treating people as equals, disregarding social standing, avoiding attitudes of either deference or superiority, making allowances for others' weaknesses, and resisting the temptation to respond to perceived slights. It also means protesting everyday instances of arbitrariness and unfairness—from the rudeness of the bakery clerk to the sexism of the car dealer or the racism of those who vandalize the home of the first black neighbors on the block.   —Kathleen M. Sullivan, "Defining Democracy Down"

Considering the Rhetorical Situation

As a writer or speaker, you need to think about the message that you want to articulate, the audience you want to reach, and the larger context you are writing in.

55–56 **PURPOSE**   Your purpose for writing will affect any definitions you include. Would writing an extended definition help you explain something? Would stipulating definitions of key terms help you shape an argument? Could an offbeat definition help you entertain your readers?

57–60 **AUDIENCE**   What audience do you want to reach, and are there any terms your readers are unlikely to know (and therefore need to be defined)? Are there terms they might understand differently from the way you're defining them?

61–65 **GENRE**   Does your genre require you to define terms? Chances are that if you're reporting information you'll need to define some terms, and some arguments rest on the way you define key terms.

66–68 **STANCE**   What is your stance, and do you need to define key terms to show that stance clearly? How you define *fetus*, for example, is likely to reveal your stance on abortion.

69–71 **MEDIA / DESIGN**   Your medium will affect the form your definitions take. In a print text, you will need to define terms in your text; if you're giving a speech or presentation, you might also provide images of important terms and their definitions. In an electronic text, you may be able to define terms by linking to an online dictionary definition.

IF YOU NEED MORE HELP

321 See also the **PROCESSES** chapters for help generating ideas, drafting, revising, and so on if you are writing a whole essay dedicated to defining a term or concept.

---

academic literacies   rhetorical situations   genres   fields   processes   strategies   research MLA / APA   media / design

Describing **42**

When we describe something, we indicate what it looks like—and sometimes how it sounds, feels, smells, and tastes. Descriptive details are a way
of showing rather than telling, of helping readers see (or hear, smell, and
so on) what we're writing about—that the sky is blue, that Miss Havisham
is wearing an old yellowed wedding gown, that the chemicals in the beaker
have reacted and smell like rotten eggs. You'll have occasion to describe
things in most of the writing you do—from describing a favorite hat in
a **MEMOIR** to detailing a chemical reaction in a lab report. This chapter
will help you work with description—and, in particular, help you think
about the use of *detail*, about *objectivity and subjectivity*, about *vantage point*,
about creating a clear *dominant impression*, and about using description to
fit your rhetorical situation.

224–32

Detail

The goal of using details is to be as specific as possible, providing information that will help your audience imagine the subject or make sense of
it. See, for example, how Nancy Mairs, an author with multiple sclerosis,
describes the disease in clear, specific terms:

> During its course, which is unpredictable and uncontrollable, one may
> lose vision, hearing, speech, the ability to walk, control of bladder and/
> or bowels, strength in any or all extremities, sensitivity to touch, vibra-
> tion, and/or pain, potency, coordination of movements—the list of pos-
> sibilities is lengthy and, yes, horrifying. One may also lose one's sense
> of humor. That's the easiest to lose and the hardest to survive without.
>   In the past ten years, I have sustained some of these losses. Char-
> acteristic of MS are sudden attacks, called exacerbations, followed by

remissions, and these I have not had. Instead, my disease has been slowly progressive. My left leg is now so weak that I walk with the aid of a brace and a cane, and for distances I use an Amigo, a variation on the electric wheelchair that looks rather like an electrified kiddie car. I no longer have much use of my left hand. Now my right side is weakening as well. I still have the blurred spot in my right eye. Overall, though, I've been lucky so far. —Nancy Mairs, "On Being a Cripple"

Mairs's gruesome list demonstrates, through *specific details*, how the disease affects sufferers generally and her in particular. We know far more after reading this text than we do from the following more general description, from a National Multiple Sclerosis Society brochure:

> Multiple sclerosis is a chronic, unpredictable disease of the central nervous system (the brain, optic nerves, and spinal cord). It is thought to be an autoimmune disorder. This means the immune system incorrectly attacks the person's healthy tissue.
>
> MS can cause blurred vision, loss of balance, poor coordination, slurred speech, tremors, numbness, extreme fatigue, problems with memory and concentration, paralysis, and blindness. These problems may be permanent, or they may come and go.
>
> —National Multiple Sclerosis Society, *Just the Facts*

Specific details are also more effective than labels, which give little meaningful information. Instead of saying that someone is a "moron" or "really smart," it's better to give details so that readers can understand the reasons behind the label: what does this person *do* or *say* that makes them deserve this label? See, for example, how the writer of a news story about shopping on the day after Thanksgiving opens with a description of a happy shopper:

> Last Friday afternoon, the day ritualized consumerism is traditionally at its most frenetic, Alexx Balcuns twirled in front of a full-length mirror at the Ritz Thrift Shop on West Fifty-seventh Street as if inhabited by the soul of Eva Gabor in *Green Acres*. Ms. Balcuns was languishing in a $795 dyed-mink parka her grandmother had just bought her. Ms. Balcuns is six.
>
> —Ginia Bellafante, "Staying Warm and Fuzzy during Uncertain Times"

The writer might simply have said, "A spoiled child admired herself in the mirror." Instead, she shows her subject twirling and "languishing" in a "$795 dyed-mink parka" and seemingly possessed by the soul of a glamorous actress—all details that create a far more vivid description.

Sensory details help readers imagine sounds, odors, tastes, and physical sensations in addition to sights. In the following example, writer Scott Russell Sanders recalls sawing wood as a child. Note how visual details, odors, and even the physical sense of being picked up by his father mingle to form a vivid scene:

> As the saw teeth bit down, the wood released its smell, each kind with its own fragrance, oak or walnut or cherry or pine—usually pine because it was the softest, easiest for a child to work. No matter how weathered and gray the board, no matter how warped and cracked, inside there was this smell waiting, as of something freshly baked. I gathered every smidgen of sawdust and stored it away in coffee cans, which I kept in a drawer of the workbench. When I did not feel like hammering nails I would dump my sawdust on the concrete floor of the garage and landscape it into highways and farms and towns, running miniature cars and trucks along miniature roads. Looming as huge as a colossus, my father worked over and around me, now and again bending down to inspect my work, careful not to trample my creations. It was a landscape that smelled dizzyingly of wood. Even after a bath my skin would carry the smell, and so would my father's hair, when he lifted me for a bedtime hug.
>
> —Scott Russell Sanders, *The Paradise of Bombs*

Whenever you describe something, you'll select from many possible details you might use. Simply put, to exhaust all the details available to describe something is impossible—and would exhaust your readers as well. To focus your description, you'll need to determine the kinds of details appropriate for your subject. They will vary, depending on your **PURPOSE**. See, for example, how the details might differ in three different genres:

55–56

- For a **MEMOIR** about an event, you might choose details that are significant for you, that evoke the sights, sounds, and other sensations that give meaning to your event.

224–32

233–45 ▲

- For a **PROFILE**, you're likely to select details that will reinforce the dominant impression you want to give, that portray the event from the perspective you want readers to see.

- For a *lab report*, you need to give certain specifics—what equipment was used, what procedures were followed, what exactly were the results.

Deciding on a focus for your description can help you see it better, as you'll look for details that contribute to that focus.

Objectivity and Subjectivity

Descriptions can be written with objectivity, with subjectivity, or with a mixture of both. Objective descriptions attempt to be uncolored by personal opinion or emotion. Police reports and much news writing aim to describe events objectively; scientific writing strives for objectivity in describing laboratory procedures and results. See, for example, the following objective account of what happened at the World Trade Center on September 11, 2001:

> ### World Trade Center Disaster—Tuesday, September 11, 2001
>
> On Tuesday, September 11, 2001, at 8:45 a.m. New York local time, One World Trade Center, the north tower, was hit by a hijacked 767 commercial jet airplane loaded with fuel for a transcontinental flight. Two World Trade Center, the south tower, was hit by a similar hijacked jet eighteen minutes later, at 9:03 a.m. (In separate but related attacks, the Pentagon building near Washington, D.C., was hit by a hijacked 757 at 9:43 a.m., and at 10:10 a.m. a fourth hijacked jetliner crashed in Pennsylvania.) The south tower, WTC 2, which had been hit second, was the first to suffer a complete structural collapse, at 10:05 a.m., 62 minutes after being hit itself, 80 minutes after the first impact. The north tower, WTC 1, then also collapsed, at 10:29 a.m., 104 minutes after being hit. WTC 7, a substantial forty-seven-story office building in its own right, built in 1987, was damaged by the collapsing towers, caught fire, and later in the afternoon also totally collapsed.
>
> —"World Trade Center," *GreatBuildings.com*

✳ academic literacies
■ rhetorical situations
▲ genres
● fields
○ processes
◆ strategies
● research MLA / APA
□ media / design

Subjective descriptions, on the other hand, allow the writer's opinions and emotions to come through. A house can be described as comfortable, with a lived-in look, or as rundown and in need of a paint job and a new roof. Here's a subjective description of the planes striking the World Trade Center, as told by a woman watching from a nearby building:

> Incredulously, while looking out [the] window at the damage and carnage the first plane had inflicted, I saw the second plane abruptly come into my right field of vision and deliberately, with shimmering intention, thunder full-force into the south tower. It was so close, so low, so huge and fast, so intent on its target that I swear to you, I swear to you, I felt the vengeance and rage emanating from the plane.
>
> —Debra Fontaine, "Witnessing"

Vantage Point

Sometimes you'll want or need to describe something from a certain vantage point. Where you locate yourself in relation to what you're describing will determine what you can perceive (and so describe) and what you can't. You may describe your subject from a *stationary vantage point*, from which you (and your readers) see your subject from one angle only, as if you were a camera. This description of one of three photographs that captured a woman's death records only what the camera saw from one angle at one particular moment:

> The first showed some people on a fire escape—a fireman, a woman and a child. The fireman had a nice strong jaw and looked very brave. The woman was holding the child. Smoke was pouring from the building behind them. A rescue ladder was approaching, just a few feet away, and the fireman had one arm around the woman and one arm reaching out toward the ladder.
>
> —Nora Ephron, "The Boston Photographs"

By contrast, this description of a drive to an Italian villa uses a *moving vantage point*; the writer recounts what he saw as he passed through a gate in a city wall, moving from city to country:

La Pietra—"the stone"—is situated one mile from the Porta San Gallo, an entry to the Old City of Florence. You drive there along the Via Bolognese, twisting past modern apartment blocks, until you come to a gate, which swings open—and there you are, at the upper end of a long lane of cypresses facing a great ocher palazzo; with olive groves spreading out on both sides over an expanse of fifty-seven acres. There's something almost comically wonderful about the effect: here, the city, with its winding avenue; there, on the other side of a wall, the country, fertile and gray green.   —James Traub, "Italian Hours"

The description of quarries in the following section uses *multiple vantage points* to capture the quarries from many perspectives.

Dominant Impression

With any description, your aim is to create some dominant impression—the overall feeling that the individual details add up to. The dominant impression may be implied, growing out of the details themselves. For example, Scott Russell Sanders's memory of the smell of sawdust creates a dominant impression of warmth and comfort: the "fragrance . . . as of something freshly baked," sawdust "stored . . . away in coffee cans," a young boy "lifted . . . for a bedtime hug." Sometimes, though, a writer will state the dominant impression directly, in addition to creating it with details. In an essay about Indiana limestone quarries, Sanders makes the dominant impression clear from the start: "They are battlefields."

The quarries will not be domesticated. They are not backyard pools; they are battlefields. Each quarry is an arena where violent struggles have taken place between machines and planet, between human ingenuity and brute resisting stone, between mind and matter. Waste rock litters the floor and brim like rubble in a bombed city. The ragged pits might have been the basements of vanished skyscrapers. Stones weighing tens of tons lean against one another at precarious angles, as if they have been thrown there by some gigantic strength and have not yet finished falling. Wrecked machinery hulks in the weeds, grimly rusting, the cogs and wheels, twisted rails, battered engine housings, trackless bulldozers and burst boilers like junk from an armored regiment. Everywhere the ledges are scarred from drills, as if from an artillery barrage or machine-gun strafing. Stumbling onto one of these abandoned quarries and gazing at the ruins, you might be left wondering who had won the battle, men or stone.

—Scott Russell Sanders, *The Paradise of Bombs*

The rest of his description, full of more figurative language ("like rubble in a bombed city," "like junk from an armored regiment," "as if from an artillery barrage or machine-gun strafing") reinforces the direct "they are battlefields" statement.

The orange sunset and expanse of sky and water in this Michigan tourism ad create a dominant impression of spaciousness and warmth, while the text invites readers to visit a Michigan beach and enjoy watching the sun set, rather than watching television.

Organizing Descriptions

You can organize descriptions in many ways. When your description is primarily visual, you will probably organize it spatially: from left to right, top to bottom, outside to inside. One variation on this approach is to begin with the most significant or noteworthy feature and move outward from that center, as Ephron does in describing a photo. Or you may create a chronological description of objects as you move past or through them in space, as Traub does in his description of his drive. You might even pile up details to create a dominant impression, as Sanders and Mairs do, especially if your description draws on senses besides vision.

Considering the Rhetorical Situation

As a writer or speaker, you need to think about the message that you want to articulate, the audience you want to reach, and the larger context you are writing in.

55–56 ■ **PURPOSE**
Your purpose may affect the way you use description. If you're arguing that a government should intervene in another country's civil war, for example, describing the anguish of refugees from that war could make your argument more persuasive. If you're analyzing a painting, you will likely need to describe it.

57–60 ■ **AUDIENCE**
Who is your audience, and will they need detailed description to understand the points you wish to make?

61–65 ■ **GENRE**
Does your genre require description? A lab report generally calls for you to describe materials and results; a memoir about Grandma should probably describe her— her smile, her dress, her apple pie.

66–68 ■ **STANCE**
The way you describe things can help you convey your stance. For example, the details you choose can show you to be objective (or not), careful or casual.

MEDIA / DESIGN Your medium will affect the form your description can take. In a print or spoken text, you will likely rely on words, though you may also include visuals. In an electronic text, you can easily provide links to visuals as well as audio clips and so may need fewer words of your own.

69–71

IF YOU NEED MORE HELP

See also **FREEWRITING**, **CUBING**, and **LISTING**, three methods of generating ideas that can be especially helpful for developing detailed descriptions. Sometimes you may be assigned to write a whole essay describing something: see the **PROCESSES** chapters for help drafting, revising, and so on.

331–34
321

---

43 Dialogue

224–32 ▲
233–45
211–23
157–84

Dialogue is a way of including people's own words in a text, letting readers hear those people's voices—not just what you say about them. **MEMOIRS** and **PROFILES** often include dialogue, and many other genres do as well: **LITERARY ANALYSES** often quote dialogue from the texts they analyze, and essays **ARGUING A POSITION** might quote an authoritative source as support for a claim. This chapter provides brief guidelines for the conventions of paragraphing and punctuating dialogue and offers some good examples of how you can use dialogue most effectively to suit your own rhetorical situations.

Why Add Dialogue?

Dialogue is a way of bringing in voices other than your own, of showing people and scenes rather than just telling about them. It can add color and texture to your writing, making it memorable. Most important, however, dialogue should be more than just colorful or interesting. It needs to contribute to your rhetorical purpose, to support the point you're making. See how dialogue is used in the following excerpt from a magazine profile of the Mall of America, how it gives us a sense of the place that the journalist's own words could not provide:

> Two pubescent girls in retainers and braces sat beside me sipping coffees topped with whipped cream and chocolate sprinkles, their shopping bags gathered tightly around their legs, their eyes fixed on the passing crowds. They came, they said, from Shakopee—"It's nowhere," one of them explained. The megamall, she added, was "a buzz at first, but now it seems pretty normal. 'Cept my parents are like Twenty Questions every time I want to come here. 'Specially since the shooting."

academic literacies · rhetorical situations · genres · fields · processes · strategies · research MLA / APA · media / design

On a Sunday night, she elaborated, three people had been wounded when shots were fired in a dispute over a San Jose Sharks jacket. "In the *mall*," her friend reminded me. "Right here at megamall. A shooting."
"It's like nowhere's safe," the first added.

—David Guterson, "Enclosed. Encyclopedic. Endured.
One Week at the Mall of America"

Of course it was the writer who decided whom and what to quote, and Guterson deliberately chose words that capture the young shoppers' speech patterns, quoting fragments ("In the *mall*. . . . Right here at megamall. A shooting"), slang ("a buzz at first," "my parents are like Twenty Questions"), even contractions ("'Cept," "'Specially").

Integrating Dialogue into Your Writing

There are certain conventions for punctuating and paragraphing dialogue:

- *Punctuating.* Enclose each speaker's words in quotation marks, and put any end punctuation—periods, question marks, and exclamation marks—inside the closing quotation mark. Whether you're transcribing words you heard or making them up, you will sometimes need to add punctuation to reflect the rhythm and sound of the speech. In the last sentence of the example below, see how Chang-Rae Lee adds a comma after "Well" and italicizes "*practice*" to show intonation—and attitude.

- *Paragraphing.* When you're writing dialogue that includes more than one speaker, start a new paragraph each time the speaker changes.

- *Signal phrases.* Sometimes you'll need to introduce dialogue with SIGNAL PHRASES—"I said," "she asked," and so on—to make clear who is speaking. At times, however, the speaker will be clear enough, and you won't need any signal phrases.

535–38

Here is a conversation between a mother and her son that illustrates each of the conventions for punctuating and paragraphing dialogue:

"Whom do I talk to?" she said. She would mostly speak to me in Korean, and I would answer back in English.

"The bank manager, who else?"

"What do I say?"

"Whatever you want to say."

"Don't speak to me like that!" she cried.

"It's just that you should be able to do it yourself," I said.

"You know how I feel about this!"

"Well, maybe then you should consider it *practice*," I answered lightly, using the Korean word to make sure she understood.

—Chang-Rae Lee, "Coming Home Again"

Interviews

Interviews are a kind of dialogue, with different conventions for punctuation. When you're transcribing an interview, give each speaker's name each time they speak, starting a new line but not indenting, and do not use quotation marks. Here is an excerpt from a National Public Radio interview that radio journalist Audie Cornish conducted with writer Susan Cain:

> **Audie Cornish:** In the 1940s and '50s, the message to most Americans was, don't be shy. And in the era of reality television, Twitter and relentless self-promotion, it seems that cultural mandate is in overdrive.
>
> A new book tells the story of how things came to be this way, and it's called *Quiet: The Power of Introverts in a World that Can't Stop Talking*. The author is Susan Cain, and she joins us from the NPR studios in New York to talk more about it. Welcome, Susan.
>
> **Susan Cain:** Thank you. It's such a pleasure to be here, Audie.
>
> **Cornish:** Well, we're happy to have you. And to start out—I think we should get this on the record—do you consider yourself an introvert or an extrovert?
>
> **Cain:** Oh, I definitely consider myself an introvert, and that was part of the fuel for me to write the book.
>
> **Cornish:** And what's the difference between being an introvert versus being shy? I mean, what's your definition?
>
> **Cain:** So introversion is really about having a preference for lower-stimulation environments—so just a preference for quiet, for less noise, for less action—whereas extroverts really crave more stimulation in order to feel at their best. And what's important to understand

about this is that many people believe that introversion is about being antisocial. And that's really a misperception because actually, it's just that introverts are differently social. So they would prefer to have, you know, a glass of wine with a close friend as opposed to going to a loud party full of strangers.

Now shyness, on the other hand, is about a fear of negative social judgment. So you can be introverted without having that particular fear at all, and you can be shy but also be an extrovert.

Cornish: And in the book, you say that there's a spectrum. So if some people are listening and they think, well, I, too, like a glass of wine and a party. It's like we all have these tendencies.

Cain: Yeah, yeah. That's an important thing. And, in fact, Carl Jung, the psychologist who first popularized these terms all the way back in the 1920s—even he said there's no such thing as a pure introvert or a pure extrovert, and he said such a man would be in a lunatic asylum.

Cornish: That makes me worry because I took your test in the book and I'm like, 90 percent extroverted, basically.

[soundbite of laughter].

—"Quiet, Please: Unleashing 'The Power of Introverts'"

In preparing the interview transcript for publication, NPR had to add punctuation, which of course was not part of the oral conversation, and probably deleted pauses and verbal expressions such as *um* and *uh*. At the same time, the editor kept informal constructions, such as incomplete sentences, which are typical answers to questions ("Yeah") to maintain the oral flavor of the interview and to reflect Cain's voice.

Considering the Rhetorical Situation

As a writer or speaker, you need to think about the message that you want to articulate, the audience you want to reach, and the larger context of your writing.

PURPOSE Your purpose will affect any use of dialogue. Dialogue can help bring a profile to life and make it memorable. Interviews with experts or firsthand witnesses can add credibility to a report or argument.

55–56

57–60 ■	**AUDIENCE**	Whom do you want to reach, and will dialogue help? Sometimes actual dialogue can help readers hear human voices behind facts or reason.
61–65 ■	**GENRE**	Does your genre require dialogue? If you're evaluating or analyzing a literary work, for instance, you may wish to include dialogue from that work. If you're writing a profile of a person or event, dialogue can help you bring your subject to life. Similarly, an interview with an expert can add credibility to a report or argument.
66–68 ■	**STANCE**	What is your stance, and can dialogue help you communicate that stance? For example, excerpts of an interview may allow you to challenge someone's views and make your own views clear.
69–71 ■	**MEDIA / DESIGN**	Your medium will affect the way you present dialogue. In a print text, you will present dialogue through written words. In an oral or electronic text, you might include actual recorded dialogue.

IF YOU NEED MORE HELP

506–7 ●
526–38
See also the guidelines on **INTERVIEWING EXPERTS** for advice on setting up and recording interviews and those on **QUOTING, PARAPHRASING,** and **SUMMARIZING** for help deciding how to integrate dialogue into your text.

✳ academic literacies
■ rhetorical situations
▲ genres
◆ fields
○ processes
◆ strategies
● research MLA / APA
□ media / design

Explaining Processes 44

When you explain a process, you tell how something is (or was) done—how a bill becomes a law, how an embryo develops—or you tell someone how to do something—how to throw a curve ball, how to write a memoir. This chapter focuses on those two kinds of explanations, offering examples and guidelines for explaining a process in a way that works for your rhetorical situation.

Explaining a Process Clearly

Whether the process is simple or complex, you'll need to identify its key stages or steps and explain them one by one, in order. The sequence matters because it allows readers to follow your explanation; it is especially important when you're explaining a process that others are going to follow. Most often you'll explain a process chronologically, from start to finish. **TRANSITIONS**—words like *first*, *next*, *then*, and so on—are often necessary, therefore, to show readers how the stages of a process relate to one another and to indicate time sequences. Finally, you'll find that verbs matter; they indicate the actions that take place at each stage of the process.

◆ 391

Explaining How Something Is Done

All processes consist of steps, and when you explain how something is done, you describe each step, generally in order, from first to last. Here, for example, is an explanation of how french fries are made, from an essay published in the *New Yorker*:

> Fast-food French fries are made from a baking potato like an Idaho russet, or any other variety that is mealy, or starchy, rather than waxy. The potatoes are harvested, cured, washed, peeled, sliced, and then blanched—cooked enough so that the insides have a fluffy texture but not so much that the fry gets soft and breaks. Blanching is followed by drying, and drying by a thirty-second deep fry, to give the potatoes a crisp shell. Then the fries are frozen until the moment of service, when they are deep-fried again, this time for somewhere around three minutes. Depending on the fast-food chain involved, there are other steps interspersed in this process. McDonald's fries, for example, are briefly dipped in a sugar solution, which gives them their golden-brown color; Burger King fries are dipped in a starch batter, which is what gives those fries their distinctive hard shell and audible crunch. But the result is similar. The potato that is first harvested in the field is roughly 80 percent water. The process of creating a French fry consists, essentially, of removing as much of that water as possible—through blanching, drying, and deep-frying— and replacing it with fat.
>
> —Malcolm Gladwell, "The Trouble with Fries"

Gladwell clearly explains the process of making French fries, showing us the specific steps—how the potatoes "are harvested, cured, washed, peeled, sliced," and so on—and using clear transitions—"followed by," "then," "until," "when"—and action verbs to show the sequence. His last sentence makes his stance clear, pointing out that the process of creating a French fry consists of removing as much of a potato's water as possible "and replacing it with fat."

Explaining How to Do Something

In explaining how to do something, you are giving instruction so that others can follow the process themselves. See how Martha Stewart explains the process of making french fries. She starts by listing the ingredients and then describes the steps:

4 medium baking potatoes
2 tablespoons olive oil
$1^1/_2$ teaspoons salt
$^1/_4$ teaspoon freshly ground pepper
malt vinegar (optional)

1. Heat oven to 400 degrees. Place a heavy baking sheet in the oven. Scrub and rinse the potatoes well, and then cut them lengthwise into $^1/_2$-inch-wide batons. Place the potato batons in a medium bowl, and toss them with the olive oil, salt, and pepper.

2. When baking sheet is hot, about 15 minutes, remove from the oven. Place prepared potatoes on the baking sheet in a single layer. Return to oven, and bake until potatoes are golden on the bottom, about 30 minutes. Turn potatoes over, and continue cooking until golden all over, about 15 minutes more. Serve immediately.

—Martha Stewart, *Favorite Comfort Food*

Stewart's explanation leaves out no details, giving a clear sequence of steps and descriptive verbs that tell us exactly what to do: "Heat," "Place," "Scrub and rinse," and so on. After she gives the recipe, she even goes on to explain the process of *serving* the fries—"Serve these French fries with a bowl of malt vinegar"—and reminds us that "they are also delicious dipped in spicy mustard, mayonnaise, and, of course, ketchup."

Explaining a Process Visually

Some processes are best explained **VISUALLY**, with diagrams or photographs. See, for example, how a blogger explains one process of shaping dough into a bagel—giving the details in words and then showing us in photos how to do it:

🔲 653–63

Gently press dough to deflate it a bit and divide into 6 equal portions.

Roll each portion into a rope about 1/2-inch in diameter.

Wrap the dough around your hand like this.

Seal the ends together by rolling back and forth on the counter a few times.

Place bagels on a lined sheet pan. Allow to rise, uncovered.

—Patricia Reitz, *ButterYum*

Photos by Patricia Reitz (butteryum.org).

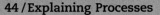

Considering the Rhetorical Situation

As always, you need to think about the message that you want to articulate, the audience you want to reach, and the larger context you are writing in.

PURPOSE   Your purpose for writing will affect the way you explain a process. If you're arguing that we should avoid eating fast food, you might explain the process by which chicken nuggets are made. But to give information about how to fry chicken, you would explain the process quite differently.   ■ 55–56

AUDIENCE   Whom are you trying to reach, and will you need to provide any special background information or to interest them in the process before you explain it?   ■ 57–60

GENRE   Does your genre require you to explain a process? In a lab report, for example, you'll need to explain processes used in the experiment. You might want to explain a process in a profile of an activity or a proposal for a solution.   ■ 61–65

STANCE   If you're giving practical directions for doing something, you'll want to take a straightforward "do this, and then do that" perspective. If you're writing to entertain, you'll need to take a clever or amusing stance.   ■ 66–68

MEDIA / DESIGN   Your medium will affect the way you explain a process. In a print text, you can use both words and images. On the web, you may have the option of showing an animation of the process as well.   ■ 69–71

IF YOU NEED MORE HELP

See also **PROFILES** if you are writing about an activity that needs to be explained. See **NARRATING** for more advice on organizing an explanation chronologically. Sometimes you may be assigned to write a whole essay or report that explains a process; see **PROCESSES** for help drafting, revising, and so on.

▲ 233–45
◆ 462–70
○ 321

45 Narrating

157–84 ▲

233–45 ▲

Narratives are stories. As a writing strategy, a good narrative can lend support to most kinds of writing—in a **POSITION PAPER** arguing for Title IX compliance, for example, you might include a brief narrative about an Olympic sprinter who might never have had an opportunity to compete on a track-and-field team without Title IX. Or you can bring a **PROFILE** of a favorite coach to life with an anecdote about a pep talk they once gave before a championship track meet. Whatever your larger writing purpose, you need to make sure that any narratives you add support that purpose— they should not be inserted simply to tell an interesting story. You'll also need to compose them carefully—to put them in a clear *sequence*, include *pertinent detail*, and make sure they are appropriate to your particular rhetorical situation.

Sequencing

When we write a narrative, we arrange events in a particular sequence. Writers typically sequence narratives in chronological order, reverse chronological order, or as a flashback.

Use chronological order.   Often you may tell the story chronologically, starting at the beginning of an event and working through to the end, as Maya Angelou does in this brief narrative from an essay about her high school graduation:

> The school band struck up a march and all classes filed in as had been rehearsed. We stood in front of our seats, as assigned, and on a signal from the choir director, we sat. No sooner had this been accomplished

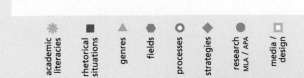

academic literacies · rhetorical situations · genres · fields · processes · strategies · research MLA / APA · media / design

than the band started to play the national anthem. We rose again and sang the song, after which we recited the pledge of allegiance. We remained standing for a brief minute before the choir director and the principal signaled to us, rather desperately I thought, to take our seats. —Maya Angelou, "Graduation"

Use reverse chronological order. You may also begin with the final action and work back to the first, as Aldo Leopold does in this narrative about cutting down a tree:

Now our saw bites into the 1890s, called gay by those whose eyes turn cityward rather than landward. We cut 1899, when the last passenger pigeon collided with a charge of shot near Babcock, two counties to the north; we cut 1898, when a dry fall, followed by a snowless winter, froze the soil seven feet deep and killed the apple trees; 1897, another drouth year, when another forestry commission came into being; 1896, when 25,000 prairie chickens were shipped to market from the village of Spooner alone; 1895, another year of fires; 1894, another drouth year; and 1893, the year of "the Bluebird Storm," when a March blizzard reduced the migrating bluebirds to near zero.

—Aldo Leopold, *A Sand County Almanac*

RÉSUMÉS are one genre where we generally use reverse chronological order, listing the most recent jobs or degrees first and then working backward. Notice, too, that we usually write these as narratives—telling what we have done rather than just naming positions we have held:

▲ 264–79

Sept. 2018–present	*Student worker*, Department of Information Management, Central State University, Wilberforce, OH. Compile data and format reports using Excel, Word, and university database.
June–Sept. 2018	*Intern*, QuestPro Corporation, West Louisville, KY. Assisted in development of software.
Sept. 2017–June 2018	*Bagger*, Ace Groceries, Elba, KY. Bagged customers' purchases.

Use a flashback. You can sometimes put a flashback in the middle of a narrative, to tell about an incident that illuminates the larger narrative. Terry Tempest Williams does this in an essay about the startling incidence of breast cancer in her family: she recalls a dinnertime conversation with her father right after her mother's death from cancer, when she learned for the first time what caused all of the cancer in her family:

> Over dessert, I shared a recurring dream of mine. I told my father that for years, as long as I could remember, I saw this flash of light in the night in the desert. That this image had so permeated my being, I could not venture south without seeing it again, on the horizon, illuminating buttes and mesas.
>
> "You did see it," he said.
>
> "Saw what?" I asked, a bit tentative.
>
> "The bomb. The cloud. We were driving home from Riverside, California. You were sitting on your mother's lap. She was pregnant. In fact, I remember the date, September 7, 1957. We had just gotten out of the Service. We were driving north, past Las Vegas. It was an hour or so before dawn, when this explosion went off. We not only heard it, but felt it. I thought the oil tanker in front of us had blown up. We pulled over and suddenly, rising from the desert floor, we saw it, clearly, this golden-stemmed cloud, the mushroom. The sky seemed to vibrate with an eerie pink glow. Within a few minutes, a light ash was raining on the car."
>
> I stared at my father. This was new information to me.
>
> —Terry Tempest Williams, "The Clan of the One-Breasted Women"

Williams could have simply announced this information as a fact—but see how much more powerful it is when told in narrative form.

Use time markers. Time markers help readers follow a sequence of events. The most obvious time markers are those that simply label the time, as the narrative entries in a diary, journal, or log might. For example, here is the final part of the narrative kept in a diary by a doomed Antarctic explorer:

WEDNESDAY, MARCH 21: Got within eleven miles of depot. Monday night; had to lay up all yesterday in severe blizzard. Today forlorn hope, Wilson and Bowers going to depot for fuel.

MARCH 22 and 23: Blizzard bad as ever—Wilson and Bowers unable to start—tomorrow last chance—no fuel and only one or two [days] of food left—must be near the end. Have decided it shall be natural—we shall march for the depot with or without our effects and die in our tracks.

THURSDAY, MARCH 29: Since the 21st we have had a continuous gale from W.S.W. and S.W. We had fuel to make two cups of tea apiece and bare food for two days on the 20th. Every day we have been ready to start for our depot eleven miles away, but outside the door of the tent it remains a scene of whirling drift. I do not think we can hope for any better things now. We shall stick it out to the end, but we are getting weaker, of course, and the end cannot be far. It seems a pity, but I do not think I can write more. . . .

Last Entry: For God's sake look after our people.

—Robert F. Scott, *Scott's Last Expedition: The Journals*

More often you will integrate time markers into the prose itself, as is done in this narrative about a woman preparing and delivering meals to workers at a cotton gin:

She made her plans meticulously and in secret. <u>One early evening</u> to see if she was ready, she placed stones in two five-gallon pails and carried them three miles to the cotton gin. She rested a little, and then, discarding some rocks, she walked in the darkness to the sawmill five miles farther along the dirt road. <u>On her way back</u> to her little house and her babies, she dumped the remaining rocks along the path.

<u>That same night</u> she worked into the early hours boiling chicken and frying ham. She made dough and filled the rolled-out pastry with meat. <u>At last</u> she went to sleep.

<u>The next morning</u> she left her house carrying the meat pies, lard, an iron brazier, and coals for a fire. <u>Just before lunch</u> she appeared in an empty lot behind the cotton gin. <u>As the dinner noon bell rang</u>, she

dropped the savors into boiling fat, and the aroma rose and floated
over to the workers who spilled out of the gin, covered with white
lint, looking like specters.

—Maya Angelou, *Wouldn't Take Nothing for My Journey Now*

Use transitions. Another way to help readers follow a narrative is with
TRANSITIONS, words like *first, then, meanwhile, at last,* and so on. See how
the following paragraphs from Langston Hughes's classic essay about
meeting Jesus use transitions (and time markers) to advance the action:

391 ◆

> <u>Suddenly</u> the whole room broke into a sea of shouting, <u>as</u> they saw
> me rise. Waves of rejoicing swept the place. Women leaped in the air.
> My aunt threw her arms around me. The minister took me by the hand
> and led me to the platform.
>
> <u>When</u> things quieted down, in a hushed silence, punctuated by
> a few ecstatic "Amens," all the new young lambs were blessed in the
> name of God. <u>Then</u> joyous singing filled the room. <u>That night</u>, for the
> last time in my life but one—for I was a big boy twelve years old—I
> cried.   —Langston Hughes, "Salvation"

Including Pertinent Detail

When you include a narrative in your writing, you must decide which
details you need—and which ones you don't need. For example, you don't
want to include so much detail that the narrative distracts the reader from
the larger text. You must also decide whether you need to include any
background, to set the stage for the narrative. The amount of detail you
include depends on your audience and purpose: How much detail does
your audience need? How much detail do you need to make your meaning clear? In an essay on the suspicion African American men often face
when walking at night, a journalist deliberately presents a story without
setting the stage at all:

> My first victim was a woman—white, well dressed, probably in her
> late twenties. I came upon her late one evening on a deserted street

in Hyde Park, a relatively affluent neighborhood in an otherwise mean, impoverished section of Chicago. As I swung onto the avenue behind her, there seemed to be a discreet, uninflammatory distance between us. Not so. She cast back a worried glance. To her, the youngish black man—a broad six feet two inches with a beard and billowing hair, both hands shoved into the pockets of a bulky military jacket—seemed menacingly close. After a few more quick glimpses, she picked up her pace and was soon running in earnest. Within seconds she disappeared into a cross street.   —Brent Staples, "Black Men and Public Space"

Words like "victim" and phrases like "came upon her" lead us to assume the narrator is scary and perhaps dangerous. We don't know why he is walking on the deserted street because he hasn't told us: he simply begins with the moment he and the woman encounter each other. For his purposes, that's all the audience needs to know at first, and details of his physical appearance that explain the woman's response come later, after he tells us about the encounter. Had he given us those details at the outset, the narrative would not have been nearly so effective. In a way, Staples lets the story sneak up on us, as the woman apparently felt he had on her.

Other times you'll need to provide more background information, as an MIT professor does when she uses an anecdote to introduce an essay about young children's experiences with electronic toys. First the writer tells us a little about Merlin, the computer tic-tac-toe game that the children in her anecdote play with. As you'll see, the anecdote would be hard to follow without the introduction:

Among the first generation of computational objects was Merlin, which challenged children to games of tic-tac-toe. For children who had only played games with human opponents, reaction to this object was intense. For example, while Merlin followed an optimal strategy for winning tic-tac-toe most of the time, it was programmed to make a slip every once in a while. So when children discovered strategies that allowed them to win and then tried these strategies a second time, they usually would not work. The machine gave the impression of not being "dumb enough" to let down its defenses twice. Robert, seven, playing with his friends on the beach, watched his friend Craig perform the "winning trick," but when he tried it, Merlin did not slip up and the game ended in a draw. Robert, confused and frustrated, threw Merlin into the sand and said, "Cheater. I hope your brains break." He was overheard by Craig and Greg, aged six and eight, who salvaged the by-now very sandy toy and took it upon themselves to set Robert straight. "Merlin doesn't know if it cheats," says Craig. "It doesn't know if you break it, Robert. It's not alive." Greg adds, "It's smart enough to make the right kinds of noises. But it doesn't really know if it loses. And when it cheats, it don't even know it's cheating." Jenny, six, interrupts with disdain: "Greg, to cheat you have to know you are cheating. Knowing is part of cheating."

—Sherry Turkle, "Cuddling Up to Cyborg Babies"

Opening and Closing with Narratives

373–80 ◆

Narratives are often useful as **BEGINNINGS** to essays and other kinds of writing. Everyone likes a good story, so an interesting or pithy narrative can be a good way to get your audience's attention. In the following introductory paragraph, a historian tells a gruesome but gripping story to attract our attention to a subject that might not otherwise merit our interest, bubonic plague:

In October 1347, two months after the fall of Calais, Genoese trading ships put into the harbor of Messina in Sicily with dead and dying men at the oars. The ships had come from the Black Sea port of Caffa (now Feodosiya) in the Crimea, where the Genoese maintained a trading post. The diseased sailors showed strange black swellings about the size of an egg or an apple in the armpits and groin. The swellings oozed blood and pus and were followed by spreading boils and black blotches on the skin from internal bleeding. The sick suffered severe pain and died quickly, within five days of the first symptoms. As the disease spread, other symptoms of continuous fever and spitting of blood appeared instead of the swellings or buboes. These victims coughed and sweated heavily and died even more quickly, within three days or less, sometimes in twenty-four hours. In both types everything

✳ academic literacies

■ rhetorical situations

▲ genres

● fields

○ processes

◆ strategies

● research MLA / APA

□ media / design

that issued from the body—breath, sweat, blood from the buboes and lungs, bloody urine, and blood-blackened excrement—smelled foul. Depression and despair accompanied the physical symptoms, and before the end "death is seen seated on the face."

—Barbara Tuchman, "This Is the End of the World: The Black Death"

Imagine how different the preceding paragraph would be if it weren't in the form of a narrative. Imagine, for example, that Tuchman began by defining bubonic plague. Would that have gotten your interest? The piece was written for a general audience; how might it have been different if it had been written for scientists? Would they need (or appreciate) the story told here?

Narrative can be a good way of **ENDING** a text, too, by winding up a discussion with an illustration of the main point. Here, for instance, is a concluding paragraph from an essay on American values and Las Vegas weddings.

◆ 380–85

I sat next to one . . . wedding party in a Strip restaurant the last time I was in Las Vegas. The marriage had just taken place; the bride still wore her dress, the mother her corsage. A bored waiter poured out a few swallows of pink champagne ("on the house") for everyone but the bride, who was too young to be served. "You'll need something with more kick than that," the bride's father said with heavy jocularity to his new son-in-law; the ritual jokes about the wedding night had a certain Panglossian character, since the bride was clearly several months pregnant. Another round of pink champagne, this time not on the house, and the bride began to cry. "It was just as nice," she sobbed, "as I hoped and dreamed it would be."

—Joan Didion, "Marrying Absurd"

No doubt Didion makes her points about American values clearly and cogently in the essay. But concluding with this story lets us *see* (and hear) what she is saying about Las Vegas wedding chapels, which sell "'nice-ness,' the facsimile of proper ritual, to children who do not know how else to find it, how to make the arrangements, how to do it 'right.'"

Considering the Rhetorical Situation

As a writer or speaker, you need to think about the message that you want to articulate, the audience you want to reach, and the larger context you are writing in.

55–56 ■ **PURPOSE** — Your purpose will affect the way you use narrative. For example, in an essay about seat belt laws, you might tell about the painful rehabilitation of a teenager who was not wearing a seat belt and was injured in an accident in order to persuade readers that seat belt use should be mandatory.

57–60 ■ **AUDIENCE** — Whom do you want to reach, and do you have an anecdote or other narrative that will help them understand your topic or persuade them that your argument has merit?

61–65 ■ **GENRE** — Does your genre require you to include narrative? A memoir about an important event might be primarily narrative, whereas a reflection about an event might focus more on the significance of the event than on what happened.

66–68 ■ **STANCE** — What is your stance, and do you have any stories that would help you convey that stance? A funny story, for example, can help create a humorous stance.

69–71 ■ **MEDIA/DESIGN** — In a print or spoken text, you will likely be limited to brief narratives, perhaps illustrated with photos or other images. In an electronic text, you might have the option of linking to full-length narratives or visuals available on the web.

IF YOU NEED MORE HELP

See also the **PROCESSES** chapters if you are assigned to write a narrative essay and need help drafting, revising, and so on. Two special kinds of narratives are **LAB REPORTS** (which use narrative to describe the steps in an experiment from beginning to end) and **RÉSUMÉS** (which essentially tell the story of the work we've done, at school and on the job).

321 ○

Glossary
264–79 ▲

✳ academic literacies

■ rhetorical situations

▲ genres

● fields

○ processes

◆ strategies

● research MLA / APA

□ media / design

Taking Essay Exams **46**

Essay exams present writers with special challenges. You must write quickly, on a topic presented to you on the spot, to show your instructor what you know about a specific body of information. This chapter offers advice on how to take essay exams.

Considering the Rhetorical Situation

PURPOSE   In an essay exam, your purpose is to show that you have mastered certain material and that you can analyze and apply it in an essay. You may need to make an argument or simply to convey information on a topic.   ■ 55–56

AUDIENCE   Will your course instructor be reading your exam, or a teaching assistant? Sometimes standardized tests are read by groups of trained readers. What specific criteria will your audience use to evaluate your writing?   ■ 57–60

GENRE   Does the essay question specify or suggest a certain genre? In a literature course, you may need to write a compelling literary analysis of a passage. In a history course, you may need to write an argument for the significance of a key historical event. In an economics course, you may need to contrast the economies of the North and South before the Civil War. If the essay question doesn't specify a genre, look for keywords such as *argue*, *evaluate*, or *explain*, which point to a certain genre.   ■ 61–65

STANCE   In an essay exam, your stance is usually unemotional, thoughtful, and critical.   ■ 66–68

69–71 **MEDIA/DESIGN** Since essay exams are usually handwritten on lined paper or in an exam booklet, legible handwriting is a must. If you are taking an online test, write your essays in a word-processing program, edit there, and then paste them into the exam.

Analyzing Essay Questions

Essay questions usually include key verbs that specify the kind of writing you'll need to do—argue a position, compare two texts, and so on. Here are some of the most common kinds of writing you'll be asked to do on an essay exam:

- *Analyze.* Break an idea, theory, text, or event into its parts and examine them. For example, a world history exam might ask you to **ANALYZE** European imperialism's effect on Africa in the late nineteenth century and discuss how Africans responded.

98–130

- *Apply.* Consider how an idea or concept might work out in practice. For instance, a film studies exam might ask you to apply the concept of auteurism—a theory of film that sees the director as the primary creator, whose body of work reflects a distinct personal style—to two films by Clint Eastwood. An economics exam might ask you to apply the concept of opportunity costs to a certain supplied scenario.

- *Argue/prove/justify.* Offer reasons and evidence to support a position. A philosophy exam, for example, might ask you to **ARGUE** whether or not all stereotypes contain a "kernel of truth" and whether believing a stereotype is ever justified.

397–417

- *Classify.* Group something into categories. For example, a marketing exam might ask you to **CLASSIFY** shoppers in categories based on their purchasing behavior, motives, attitudes, or lifestyle patterns.

418–23

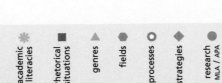

academic literacies   rhetorical situations   genres   fields   processes   strategies   research MLA / APA   media / design

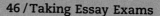

- *Compare/contrast.* Explore the similarities and/or differences between two or more things. An economics exam, for example, might ask you to **COMPARE** the effectiveness of patents and tax incentives in encouraging technological advances.

  424–31

- *Critique.* **ANALYZE** and **EVALUATE** a text or argument, considering its strengths and weaknesses. For instance, an evolutionary biology exam might ask you to critique John Maynard Smith's assertion that "scientific theories say nothing about what is right but only about what is possible" in the context of the theory of evolution.

  98–130
  202–10

- *Define.* Explain what a word or phrase means. An art history exam, for example, might ask you to **DEFINE** negative space and discuss the way various artists use it in their work.

  432–42

- *Describe.* Tell about the important characteristics or features of something. For example, a sociology exam might ask you to **DESCRIBE** Erving Goffman's theory of the presentation of self in ordinary life, focusing on roles, props, and setting.

  443–51

- *Evaluate.* Determine something's significance or value. A drama exam, for example, might ask you to **EVALUATE** the setting, lighting, and costumes in a filmed production of *Macbeth*.

  202–10

- *Explain.* Provide reasons and examples to clarify an idea, argument, or event. For instance, a rhetoric exam might ask you to explain the structure of the African American sermon and discuss its use in writings of Frederick Douglass and Martin Luther King Jr.

- *Summarize/review.* Give the major points of a text or idea. A political science exam, for example, might ask you to **SUMMARIZE** John Stuart Mill's concept of utilitarianism and its relation to freedom of speech.

  534–35

- *Trace.* Explain a sequence of ideas or order of events. For instance, a geography exam might ask you to trace the patterns of international migration since 1970 and discuss how these patterns differ from those of the period between 1870 and World War I.

Some Guidelines for Taking Essay Exams

Before the exam

16–17 ✳

- **Read** over your class notes and course texts strategically, **ANNOTATING** them to keep track of details you'll want to remember.

327–28 ○

- **Collaborate** by forming a **STUDY GROUP** to help one another master the course content.

519–23 ●

- **Review** key ideas, events, terms, and themes. Look for common themes and **CONNECTIONS** in lecture notes, class discussions, and any read-ings—they'll lead you to important ideas.

- **Ask** your instructor about the form the exam will take: how long it will be, what kind of questions will be on it, how it will be evaluated, and so on. Working with a study group, write questions you think your instructor might ask, and then answer the questions together.

331–32 ○

- **Warm up** just before the exam by **FREEWRITING** for 10 minutes or so to gather your thoughts.

During the exam

- **Scan the questions** to determine how much each part of the test counts and how much time you should spend on it. For example, if one essay is worth 50 points and two others are worth 25 points each, you'll want to spend half your time on the 50-point question.

- **Read over** the entire test before answering any questions. Start with the question you feel most confident answering, which may or may not be the first question on the test.

- **Don't panic.** Sometimes when students first read an essay question, their minds go blank, but after a few moments they start to recall the information they need.

- **Plan.** Although you won't have much time for revising or editing, you still need to plan and allow yourself time to make some last-minute

changes before you turn in the exam. So apportion your time. For a three-question essay test in a two-hour test period, you might divide your time like this:

Total Exam Time—120 minutes
Generating ideas—20 minutes (6–7 minutes per question)
Drafting—85 minutes (45 for the 50-point question,
                            20 for each 25-point question)
Revising, editing, proofreading—15 minutes

Knowing that you have built in time at the end of the exam period can help you remain calm as you write, as you can use that time to fill in gaps or reconsider answers you feel unsure about.

- *Jot down the main ideas* you need to cover in answering the question on scratch paper or on the cover of your exam book, number those ideas in the order you think makes sense—and you have an outline for your essay. If you're worried about time, plan to write the most important parts of your answers early on. If you don't complete your answer, refer your instructor to your outline to show where you were headed.

- *Turn the essay question into your introduction,* like this:

    Question: How did the outcomes of World War II differ from those of World War I?

    Introduction: The outcomes of World War II differed from those of World War I in three major ways: World War II affected more of the world and its people than World War I did, distinctions between citizens and soldiers were eroded, and the war's brutality made it impossible for Europe to continue to claim cultural superiority over other cultures.

- *State your thesis explicitly,* provide **REASONS** and **EVIDENCE** to support your thesis, and use transitions to move logically from one idea to the next. Restate your main point in your conclusion. You don't want to give what one professor calls a "garbage truck answer," dumping everything you know into a blue book and expecting the instructor to sort it all out.

◆ 400–408

- **Write on every other line** and only on one side of each page so that you'll have room to make additions or corrections. If you're typing on a computer, double space.
- **If you have time left, go over your exam,** looking for ideas that need elaboration as well as for grammatical and punctuation errors.

After the exam.　If your instructor doesn't return your exam, consider asking for a conference to go over your work so you can learn what you did well and where you need to improve—important knowledge to take with you into your next exam.

academic
literacies

rhetorical
situations

genres

fields

processes

strategies

research
MLA / APA

media /
design

part 7

Doing Research

We do research all the time, for many different reasons. We search the web for information about a new computer, ask friends about the best place to get coffee, try on several pairs of jeans before deciding which ones to buy. You have no doubt done your share of library research before now, and you probably have visited a number of schools' websites before deciding which college you wanted to attend. Research, in other words, is something you do every day. The following chapters offer advice on the kind of research you'll need to do for your academic work and, in particular, for research projects.

Doing Research

Getting a Start on Research **47**

When you need to do research, it's sometimes tempting to jump in and start looking for information right away. However, doing research is complex and time-consuming. Research-based writing projects usually require you to follow several steps. You need to come up with a topic (or to analyze the requirements of an assigned topic) and come up with a research question to guide your research efforts. Once you do some serious, focused research to find the information you need, you'll be ready to turn your research question into a tentative thesis and sketch out a rough outline. After doing whatever additional research you need to fill in your outline, you'll write a draft—and get some response to that draft. You may then need to do additional research before revising. Once you revise, you'll need to edit and proofread. In other words, there's a lot to do. You need a schedule.

Establishing a Schedule and Getting Started

A good place to start a research project is by creating a time line for getting all this work done, perhaps using the form on the next page. Once you have a schedule, you can get started. The sections that follow offer advice on considering your rhetorical situation, coming up with a topic, and doing preliminary research; developing a research question, a tentative thesis, and a rough outline; and creating a working bibliography and keeping track of your sources. The chapters that follow offer guidelines for **FINDING SOURCES**, **EVALUATING SOURCES**, and **SYNTHESIZING IDEAS**.

459–510
511–18
519–25

academic literacies ❋ | rhetorical situations ■ | genres ▲ | fields ◆ | processes ○ | strategies ◆ | research MLA / APA ● | media / design ☐

Scheduling a Research Project

Complete by:

Analyze your rhetorical situation.	_____
Choose a possible topic or analyze the assignment.	_____
Plan a research strategy and do preliminary research.	_____
Come up with a research question.	_____
Schedule interviews and other field research.	_____
Find sources.	_____
Read sources and take notes.	_____
Do any field research.	_____
Come up with a tentative thesis and outline.	_____
Write a draft.	_____
Get response.	_____
Do any additional research.	_____
Revise.	_____
Prepare a list of works cited.	_____
Edit.	_____
Proofread the final draft.	_____
Submit the final draft.	_____

Considering the Rhetorical Situation

As with any writing task, you need to start by considering your purpose, your audience, and the rest of your rhetorical situation:

55–56 ■ **PURPOSE**   Is this project part of an assignment—and if so, does it specify any one purpose? If not, what is your broad purpose? To inform? argue? analyze? A combination?

57–60 ■ **AUDIENCE**   To whom are you writing? What does your audience likely know about your topic, and is there any background information you'll need to provide? What opinions or attitudes do your readers likely hold? What kinds of evidence will they find persuasive? How do you want them to respond to your writing?

GENRE Are you writing to report on something? to compose a profile? to make a proposal? an argument? What are the requirements of your genre in terms of the number and kind of sources you must use?
61–65

STANCE What is your attitude toward your topic? What accounts for your attitude? How do you want to come across? Curious? Critical? Positive? Something else?
66–68

MEDIA / DESIGN What medium or media will you use? Print? Spoken? Electronic? Will you need to create any charts, photographs, video, presentation software slides, or other visuals?
69–71

Coming Up with a Topic

If you need to choose a topic, consider your interests as they relate to the course for which you're writing. What do you want to learn about? What do you have questions about? What topics from the course have you found intriguing? What community, national, or global issues do you care about? Once you've thought of a potential topic, use the questions in Chapter 27, **WRITING AS INQUIRY**, to explore it and find an angle on it that you can write about—and want to.
323–26

If your topic is assigned, you need to make sure you understand exactly what it asks you to do. Read the assignment carefully, looking for keywords: does it ask you to **ANALYZE**, **COMPARE**, **EVALUATE**, **SUMMARIZE**, or **ARGUE**? If the assignment offers broad guidelines but allows you to choose within them, identify the requirements and the range of possible topics and define your topic within those constraints.
98–130
424–31
202–10
534–35
397–417

For example, in an American history course, your instructor might ask you to "discuss social effects of the Civil War." Potential but broad topics might include poverty among Confederate soldiers or former slaveholders, the migration of members of those groups to Mexico or Northern cities, the establishment of independent African American churches, or the spread of the Ku Klux Klan—to name only a few of the possibilities.

Think about what you know about your topic. Chances are you already know something about your topic, and articulating that knowledge can help you see possible ways to focus your topic or come up with potential sources of information. **FREEWRITING**, **LISTING**, **CLUSTERING**, and **LOOPING** are all good ways of tapping your knowledge of your topic. Consider where you might find information about it: Have you read about it in a textbook? heard stories about it on the news? visited websites focused on it? Do you know anyone who knows about this topic?

331–34 ○

Narrow the topic. As you consider possible topics, look for ways to narrow your topic's focus to make it specific enough to discuss in depth. For example:

> **Too general:** fracking
>
> **Still too general:** fracking and the environment
>
> **Better:** the potential environmental effects of extracting natural gas through the process of hydraulic fracturing, or fracking

If you limit your topic, you can address it with specific information that you'll be more easily able to find and manage. In addition, a limited topic will be more likely to interest your audience than a broad topic that forces you to use abstract, general statements. For example, it's much harder to write well about "the environment" than it is to address a topic that explores a single environmental issue.

Consulting with Librarians and Doing Preliminary Research

Consulting with a reference librarian at your school and doing some preliminary research in the library can save you time in the long run. Reference librarians can direct you to the best scholarly sources for your topic and help you focus your topic by determining appropriate search terms and

495–98 ●
KEYWORDS—significant words that appear in the title, abstract, or text of

potential sources and that you can use to search for information on your topic in library catalogs, in databases, and on the web. These librarians can also help you choose the most appropriate reference works, sources that provide general overviews of the scholarship in a field. General internet searches can be time-consuming, as they often result in thousands of possible sites—too many to weed out efficiently, either by revising your search terms or by going through the sites themselves, many of which are unreliable. Library databases, on the other hand, include only sources that already have been selected by experts, and searches in them usually present manageable numbers of results.

Wikipedia can often serve as a jumping-off point for preliminary research, but since its entries are written and edited by people who may not have expertise in the subject, it is not considered a reliable academic source. Specialized encyclopedias, however, usually present subjects in much greater depth and provide more scholarly references that might suggest starting points for your research. Even if you know a lot about a subject, doing preliminary research can open you to new ways of seeing and approaching it, increasing your options for developing and narrowing your topic.

Coming Up with a Research Question

Once you've surveyed the territory of your topic, you'll likely find that your understanding of the topic has become broader and deeper. You may find that your interests have changed and your research has led to surprises and additional research. That's okay: as a result of exploring avenues you hadn't anticipated, you may well come up with a better topic than the one you'd started with. At some point, though, you need to develop a research question—a specific question that you will then work to answer through your research.

To write a research question, review your analysis of the **RHETORICAL SITUATION**, to remind yourself of any time constraints or length consider-ations. Generate a list of questions beginning with *What? When? Where? Who? How? Why? Would? Could?* and *Should?* Here, for example, are some questions

53

about the tentative topic "the potential environmental effects of extracting natural gas through the process of hydraulic fracturing, or fracking":

> *What* are the environmental effects of fracking?
>
> *When* was fracking introduced as a way to produce natural gas?
>
> *Where* is fracking done, and how does this affect the surrounding people and environment?
>
> *Who* will benefit from increased fracking?
>
> *How* much energy does fracking use?
>
> *Why* do some environmental groups oppose fracking?
>
> *Would* other methods of extracting natural gas be safer?
>
> *Could* fracking cause earthquakes?
>
> *Should* fracking be expanded, regulated, or banned?

Select one question from your list that you find interesting and that suits your rhetorical situation. Use the question to guide your research.

Drafting a Tentative Thesis

387–89 ◆

Once your research has led you to a possible answer to your research question, try formulating that answer as a tentative **THESIS**. You need not be committed to the thesis; in fact, you should not be. The object of your research should be to learn about your topic, not to find information that simply supports what you already think you believe. Your tentative thesis may (and probably will) change as you learn more about your subject, consider the many points of view on it, and reconsider your topic and, perhaps, your goal: what you originally planned to be an argument for considering other points of view may become a call to action. However tentative, a thesis allows you to move forward by clarifying your purpose for doing research. Here are some tentative thesis statements on the topic of fracking:

> Fracking is a likely cause of earthquakes in otherwise seismically stable regions of the country.
>
> The federal government should strictly regulate the production of natural gas by fracking.

Fracking can greatly increase our supplies of natural gas, but other methods of producing energy should still be pursued.

As with a research question, a tentative thesis should guide your research efforts—but be ready to revise it as you learn still more about your topic. Research should be a process of **INQUIRY** in which you approach your topic with an open mind, ready to learn and possibly change. If you hold too tightly to a tentative thesis, you risk focusing only on evidence that supports your view, making your writing biased and unconvincing.

323–26

Creating a Rough Outline

After you've created a tentative thesis, write out a rough **OUTLINE** for your research project. Your outline can be a simple list of topics you want to explore, something that will help you structure your research efforts and organize your notes and other materials. As you read your sources, you can use your outline to keep track of what you need to find and where the information you do find fits into your argument. Then you'll be able to see if you've covered all the ideas you intended to explore—or whether you need to rethink the categories on your outline.

335–37

Keeping a Working Bibliography

A working bibliography is a record of all the sources you consult. You should keep such a record so that you can find sources easily when you need them and then cite any that you use. Your library likely offers tools to store source information you find in its databases and catalog, and software such as *Zotero* or *EasyBib* can also help you save, manage, and cite your sources. You may find it helpful to print out bibliographical data you find useful or to keep your working bibliography on index cards or in a notebook. However you decide to compile your working bibliography, include all the information you'll need later to document any sources you use; follow the **DOCUMENTATION** style you'll use when you write so that

544–47

Information for a Working Bibliography

FOR A BOOK

Library call number

Author(s) or editor(s)

Title and subtitle

Publication information: city, publisher, year of publication

Other information: edition, volume number, translator, and so on

If your source is an essay in a collection, include its author, title, and page numbers.

FOR A SOURCE FROM A DATABASE

Publication information for the source, as listed above

Name of database

DOI (digital object identifier) or URL of original source, such as the periodical in which an article was published.

Stable URL or permalink for database

Date you accessed source

FOR AN ARTICLE IN A PRINT PERIODICAL

Author(s)

Title and subtitle

Name of periodical

Volume number, issue number, date

Page numbers

FOR A WEB SOURCE

URL

Author(s) or editor(s) if available

Name of site

Sponsor of site

Date site was first posted or last updated

Date you accessed site

If the source is an article or book reprinted on the web, include its title, the title and publication information of the periodical or book, where it was first published, and any page numbers.

you won't need to go back to your sources to find the information. Some databases make this step easy by preparing rough-draft citations in several styles that you can copy, paste, and edit.

On the previous page is most of the basic information you'll want to include for each source in your working bibliography. Go to wwnorton.com/write/fieldguide for templates you can use to keep track of this information.

Keeping Track of Your Sources

- *Staple together photocopies and printouts.* It's easy for individual pages to get shuffled or lost on a desk or in a backpack. Keep a stapler handy, and fasten pages together as soon as you copy them or print them out.

- *Bookmark web sources* or save them using a free bookmark management tool available through several library databases. For database sources, use the *DOI* or *stable URL*, *permalink*, or *document URL* (the terms used by databases vary)—not the URL in the "Address" or "Location" box in your browser, which will expire after you end your online session.

- *Label everything.* Label your copies with the source's author and title.

- *Highlight sections you plan to use.* When you sit down to draft, your goal will be to find what you need quickly, so as soon as you decide you might use a source, highlight the paragraphs or sentences that you think you'll use. If your instructor wants copies of your sources to see how you used them, you've got them ready. If you're using PDF copies, you can highlight or add notes using *Adobe Reader*.

- *Use your rough outline to keep track of what you've got.* In the margin of each highlighted section, write the number or letter of the outline division to which the section corresponds. (It's a good idea to write it in the same place consistently so you can flip through a stack of copies and easily see what you've got.) Alternatively, attach sticky notes to each copy, using a different color for each main heading in your outline.

- *Keep everything in an online folder, file folder, or box.* Keep everything related to your research in one place. If you create online subfolders or create folders that correspond to your rough outline, you'll be able to organize your material, at least tentatively. And if you highlight, label, and use sticky notes, your material will be even better organized, making writing a draft easier. The folder or box will also serve you well if you are required to create a portfolio that includes your research notes, copies of sources, and drafts.

- *Use a reference manager.* Web-based reference or citation management software allows you to create and organize a personal database of resources. You can import references from databases to a personal account, organize them, and draft citations in various formats. *RefWorks, EndNote, Mendeley,* and *Zotero* are four such systems; check with your librarian to see what system your library supports, or search online, as several of them are available for free. Be aware, though, that the citations generated are often inaccurate and need to be checked carefully for content and format. So treat them as rough drafts and plan to edit them.

489–510 ⬤

511–18

> **IF YOU NEED MORE HELP**
>
> See the guidelines on **FINDING SOURCES** once you're ready to move on to in-depth research and those on **EVALUATING SOURCES** for help thinking critically about the sources you find.

academic literacies

rhetorical situations

genres

fields

processes

strategies

research MLA / APA

media / design

Finding Sources 48

To analyze media coverage of the 2016 Democratic National Convention, you examine news stories and blogs published at the time. To write an essay interpreting a poem by Maya Angelou, you study the poem and read several critical interpretations in literary journals. To write a report on career opportunities in psychology, you interview a graduate of your university who is working in a psychology clinic. In each of these cases, you go beyond your own knowledge to consult additional sources of information.

This chapter offers guidelines for locating a range of sources—print and online, general and specialized, published and firsthand. Keep in mind that as you do research, finding and **EVALUATING SOURCES** are two activities that usually take place simultaneously. So this chapter and the next one go hand in hand.

511–18

Kinds of Sources

Primary and secondary sources. Your research will likely lead you to both primary and secondary sources. *Primary sources* include historical documents, literary works, eyewitness accounts, field reports, diaries, letters, and lab studies, as well as any original research you do through interviews, observation, experiments, or surveys. *Secondary sources* include scholarly books and articles, reviews, biographies, textbooks, and other works that interpret or discuss primary sources. Novels and films are primary sources; articles interpreting them are secondary sources. The Declaration of Independence is a primary historical document; a historian's description of the events surrounding the Declaration's writing is secondary. A published report of scientific findings is primary; a critique of that report is secondary.

Whether a work is considered primary or secondary sometimes depends on your topic and purpose. If you're analyzing a poem, a critic's article interpreting the poem is a secondary source—but if you're investigating that critic's work, the article would be a primary source for your own study and interpretation.

Secondary sources are often useful because they can help you understand and evaluate primary source material. Whenever possible, however, you should find and use primary sources, because secondary sources can distort or misrepresent the information in primary sources. For example, a seemingly reputable secondary source describing the 1948 presidential election asserted that the *New York Times* ran a headline reading, "Thomas E. Dewey's Election as President Is a Foregone Conclusion." But the actual article was titled "Talk Is Now Turning to the Dewey Cabinet," and it began by noting "[the] *popular view that* Gov. Thomas E. Dewey's election as President is a foregone conclusion." Here the secondary source got not only the headline wrong but also distorted the source's intended meaning by leaving out an important phrase. Your research should be as accurate and reliable as it can be; using primary sources whenever you can helps ensure that it is.

Scholarly and popular sources. Scholarly sources are written by academic experts or scholars in a particular discipline and are *peer-reviewed*— evaluated by other experts in the same discipline for their factual accuracy and lack of bias. They are also written largely *for* experts in a discipline, as a means of sharing research, insights, and in-depth analysis with one another; that's why they must meet high standards of accuracy and objectivity and adhere to the discipline's accepted research methods, including its style for documenting sources. Scholarly articles are usually published in academic journals; scholarly books may be published by university presses or by other academically focused publishers.

Popular sources include just about all other online and print publications, from websites to magazines to books written for nonspecialists. These sources generally explain or provide opinion on current events or topics of general interest; when they discuss scholarly research, they tend to simplify the concepts and facts, providing definitions, narratives, and examples to make them understandable to nonspecialist audiences. They are often written by journalists or other professional writers who may specialize in a particular area but who report or comment on the scholarship of others rather than doing any themselves. Their most important difference from scholarly sources is that popular sources are not reviewed by other experts in the field being discussed, although editors or fact-checkers review the writing before it's published.

In most of your college courses, you'll be expected to rely primarily on scholarly sources rather than popular ones. However, if you're writing about a very current topic or need to provide background information on a topic, a mix of scholarly and popular sources may be appropriate. To see how scholarly and popular sources differ in appearance, look at the Documentation Map for scholarly journals (p. 564) and at the illustrations on pages 492–93. Here's a guide to determining whether or not a potential source is scholarly:

IDENTIFYING SCHOLARLY SOURCES: WHAT TO LOOK FOR

- *Author.* Look for the author's scholarly credentials, including affiliations with academic or other research-oriented institutions.

- *Peer review.* Look for a list of reviewers at the front of the journal or on the journal's or publisher's website. If you don't find one, the source is probably not peer-reviewed.

- *Source citations.* Look for a detailed list of works cited or references at the end of the source and citations either parenthetically within the text or in footnotes or endnotes. (Popular sources may include a reference list but seldom cite sources within the text, except in signal phrases.)

- *Publisher.* Look for publishers that are professional scholarly organizations, such as the Modern Language Association or the Organization of American Historians, that are affiliated with universities or colleges, or that have a stated academic mission.

- *Language and content.* Look for abstracts (one-paragraph summaries of the contents) at the beginning of articles and for technical or specialized language and concepts that readers are assumed to be familiar with.

- *Other clues.* Look for little or no advertising on websites or within the journal; for a plain design with few or no illustrations, especially in print sources; and for listing in academic databases when you limit your search to *academic*, *peer-reviewed*, or *scholarly sources.*

Scholarly Source

Published in an academic journal.

Includes an abstract.

Cites academic research with consistent documentation style.

Describes research methods, includes numerical data.

Multiple authors who are academics.

Includes complete references list.

Journal List > NIHPA Author Manuscripts > PMC2918908

NIH Public Access
Author Manuscript
Accepted for publication in a peer reviewed journal

About Author manuscripts　　　Submit a manuscript

J Res Pers. Author manuscript; available in PMC 2011 August 1.
Published in final edited form as:
J Res Pers. 2010 August 1; 44(4): 478–484.
doi: 10.1016/j.jrp.2010.06.001

PMCID: PMC2918908
NIHMSID: NIHMS218233

Sounds like a Narcissist: Behavioral Manifestations of Narcissism in Everyday Life

Nicholas S. Holtzman, Simine Vazire, and Matthias R. Mehl

Author information ►　Copyright and License information ►

See other articles in PMC that cite the published article.

Abstract

Little is known about narcissists' everyday behavior. The goal of this study was to describe how narcissism is manifested in everyday life. Using the Electronically Activated Recorder (EAR), we obtained naturalistic behavior from participants' everyday lives. The results suggest that the defining characteristics of narcissism that have been established from questionnaire and laboratory-based studies are borne out in narcissists' day-to-day behaviors. Narcissists do indeed behave in more extraverted and less agreeable ways than non-narcissists, skip class more (among narcissists high in exploitativeness/entitlement only), and use more sexual language. Furthermore, we found that the link between narcissism and disagreeable behavior is strengthened when controlling for self-esteem, thus extending prior questionnaire-based findings (Paulhus, Robins, Trzesniewski, & Tracy, 2004) to observed, real-world behavior.

Keywords: narcissism, behavior, personality traits, sexual behavior, language use

Narcissists love attention. Lucky for them, they have recently received a considerable amount of it from academic psychologists, especially in laboratory settings (e.g., Back, Schmukle, & Egloff, 2010; Bushman & Baumeister, 1998; Campbell, Foster, & Finkel, 2002; Miller et al., 2009). This laboratory research has led to several wide-reaching theories about why narcissists do what they do (Holtzman & Strube, 2010a; Morf & Rhodewalt, 2001; Twenge & Campbell, 2009; Vazire & Funder, 2006). Despite all this attention from researchers, however, we still know little about what narcissists actually do in their everyday lives. The aim of this paper is to help create an empirical basis for a more complete understanding of narcissism by exploring behavioral manifestations of narcissism in everyday life. Thus, we intend to answer a simple, yet largely unanswered question: What do narcissists do on a day-to-day basis?

Method

Participants

Participants were 80 undergraduate students at the University of Texas at Austin (79 provided valid EAR data), recruited mainly from introductory psychology courses and by flyers in the psychology department. The sample was 54% female, and the ethnic composition of the sample was 65% White, 21% Asian, 11% Latino, and 3% of another ethnicity. Participants ranged from 18 to 24 years old ($M = 18.7$, $SD = 1.4$). Participants were compensated $50. Data from this sample were also reported in Vazire and Mehl (2008), where further information can be found about the study.[1]

Narcissistic Personality Inventory (NPI)

The NPI is a 40-item test of narcissism that is reliable and well-validated (Raskin & Terry, 1988). The items on this forced-choice test contain pairs of statements such as "Sometimes I tell good stories" (non-narcissistic) versus "Everybody likes to hear my stories" (narcissistic). In our study, the NPI exhibited good reliability ($\alpha = .83$). As seen in Table 1, we also calculated means and reliabilities for four facets (Emmons, 1987).

Table 1
Means, Standard Deviations, Gender-Differences, and Reliabilities for the NPI and NPI Facets

Contributor Information

Nicholas S. Holtzman, Washington University in St. Louis.

Simine Vazire, Washington University in St. Louis.

Matthias R. Mehl, University of Arizona.

References

1. Back MD, Schmukle SC, Egloff B. Why are narcissists so charming at first sight? Decoding the narcissism-popularity link at zero acquaintance. Journal of Personality and Social Psychology. 2010;98:132–145. [PubMed]
2. Baumeister RF, Vohs KD, Funder DC. Psychology as the science of self-reports and finger movements: Whatever happened to actual behavior? Perspectives on Psychological Science. 2007;2:396–403.

PubReader format:
click here to try

Formats:
Article | PubReader | ePub (beta) | PDF (330K)

Related citations in PubMed
Impulsivity and the self-defeating behavior of narcissists.
[Pers Soc Psychol Rev. 2006]
Why are narcissists so charming at first sight? Decoding the narcissism-popularity link at zero acquai [J Pers Soc Psychol. 2010]
The performance of narcissists rises and falls with perceived opportunity for glory. [J Pers Soc Psychol. 2002]
An empirical typology of narcissism and mental health in late adolescence. [J Adolesc. 2006]
Animal models of obsessive-compulsive disorder: rationale to understanding psychobiology and [Psychiatr Clin North Am. 2006]
See reviews ...
See all ...

Cited by other articles in PMC
Evidence for the criterion validity and clinical utility of the Pathological Narcissism Inventory [Assessment. 2012]
See all...

Links
MedGen
PubMed

Recent activity
Turn Off　Clear
Sounds like a Narcissist: Behavioral Manifestations of Narcissism in Everyday Li ...
PMC
See more ...

Does self-love lead to love for others? A story of narcissistic game playing. [J Pers Soc Psychol. 2002]
Interpersonal and intrapsychic adaptiveness of trait self-enhancement: a mixed blessing? [J Pers Soc Psychol. 1998]

Knowing me, knowing you: the accuracy and unique predictive validity of self-ratings and other-ratin[J Pers Soc Psychol. 2008]

A principal-components analysis of the Narcissistic Personality Inventory and further evidence of its [J Pers Soc Psychol. 1988]
Narcissism: theory and measurement. [J Pers Soc Psychol. 1987]

academic literacies　　rhetorical situations　　genres　　fields　　processes　　strategies　　research MLA / APA　　media / design

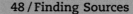

Popular Source

Published in general-interest periodical or website.

Catchy, provocative title; no abstract.

Author not an academic or other subject matter expert.

Academic experts cited but not documented.

Print and online sources.   Some sources are available only in print; some are available only online. But many print sources are also available on the web. You'll find print sources in your school's library, but chances are that many reference books and academic journal articles in your library will also be available online. In general, for academic writing it's best to try to find most of your online sources through the library's website rather than commercial search sites, which may lead you to unreliable sources and cause you to spend much more time sorting and narrowing search results.

Searching in Academic Libraries

College and university libraries typically offer several ways to search their holdings. Take a look at this search box, from the homepage of the Houston Community College libraries:

This box allows you to search through all the library's holdings at once an option that may be a good way to get started. You may already know, though, that you need to focus your search on one type of source, such as scholarly articles, leading you to choose the Articles search tab.

This box lets you shape and limit your search in several ways: by selecting a specific database, by choosing to search only for full-text articles and only peer-reviewed articles, and by searching within a specific journal. "Ask a Librarian" options can be very useful; many libraries offer email, texting, chat, and phone conversations with reference librarians when you need help but aren't working in the library.

Searching Effectively Using Keywords

Whether you're searching for books, articles in periodicals, or other material available on the web, chances are you'll conduct most of your search online. Most materials produced since the 1980s and most library catalogs are online, and most periodical articles can be found by searching electronic indexes and databases. In each case, you can search for authors, titles, or subjects.

To search online, you'll need to come up with keywords. Keywords are significant words that stand for an idea or concept. The key to searching efficiently is to use keywords and combinations of them that will focus your searches on the information you need—but not too much of it. Often you'll start out with one general keyword that will yield far too many results; then you'll need to switch to more specific terms or combinations (*homeopathy* instead of *medicine* or *secondary education Japan* instead of *education Japan*).

Other times your keyword search won't yield enough sources; then you'll need to use broader terms or combinations (*education Japan* instead of *secondary education Japan*) or substitute synonyms (*home remedy* instead of *folk medicine*). Sometimes you'll need to learn terms used in academic disciplines or earlier in history for things you know by other names, such as *myocardial infarction* rather than *heart attack* or *the Great War* instead of *World War I*. Or look through the sources that turn up in response to other terms to see what keywords you might use in subsequent searches. Searching requires flexibility, in the words you use and the methods you try.

Finding keywords using word clouds.   One way to find keywords to help you narrow and focus your topic is to create a word cloud, a visual representation of words used in a text; the more often a word is used,

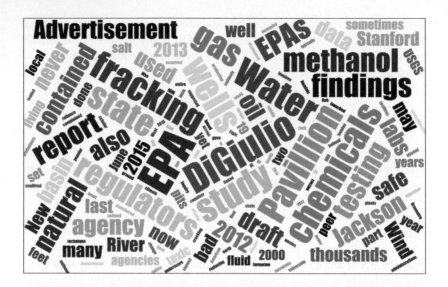

the larger it looks in the word cloud. Several websites, including *Tagxedo*, *Wordle*, and *TagCrowd*, let you create word clouds. Examining a word cloud created from an article in a reference work may help you see what terms are used to discuss your topic—and may help you see new possible ways to narrow it. Above, for example, is a word cloud derived from an article in *Scientific American* discussing fracking. Many of the terms—*fracking*, *water*, *gas*, *wells*, *drilling*—are just what you'd expect. However, some terms—*USGS*, *DiGiulio*, *coalfired*—may be unfamiliar and lead to additional possibilities for research. For instance, *DiGiulio* is the last name of an expert on fracking whose publications might be worth examining, while *USGS* is an acronym for the United States Geological Survey, a scientific government agency.

Finding keywords using databases.　Once you've begun searching for and finding possible sources, you can expand your list of possible keywords by skimming the "detailed record" or "metadata" page for any scholarly

✳ academic literacies
■ rhetorical situations
▲ genres
⬤ fields
◯ processes
◆ strategies
⬤ research MLA / APA
▢ media / design

articles you find, where full bibliographic information on the source may be found. A search for *fracking* resulted in this source:

Note the list of author-supplied keywords, which offers options for narrowing and focusing your topic. Each keyword is a link, so simply clicking on it will produce a new list of sources.

Advanced keyword searching. Most search sites have "advanced search" options that will help you focus your research. Some allow you to ask questions in conversational language: *What did Thomas Jefferson write about slavery?* Others allow you to focus your search by using specific words or symbols. Here are some of the most common ones:

- Type quotation marks around words to search for an exact phrase— "Thomas Jefferson."

- Type AND to specify that more than one keyword must appear in sources: Jefferson AND Adams. Some search engines require a plus sign instead: +Jefferson +Adams.

- Type OR if you're looking for sources that include any of several terms: Jefferson OR Adams OR Madison.

- Type NOT to find sources *without* a certain word: Jefferson NOT Adams. Some search engines call for a minus sign (actually, a hyphen) instead: +Jefferson –Adams.

- Type an asterisk to search for words in different form. For example, teach* will yield sources containing *teacher* and *teaching*.

Reference Works

The reference section of your school's library is the place to find encyclopedias, dictionaries, atlases, almanacs, bibliographies, and other reference works in print. Many of these sources are also online and can be accessed from any computer that is connected to the internet. Others are available only in the library. Remember, though, that whether in print or online, reference works are only a starting point, a place where you can get an overview of your topic.

General reference works.   Consult encyclopedias for general background information on a subject, dictionaries for definitions of words, atlases for maps and geographic data, and almanacs for statistics and other data on current events. These are some works you might consult:

The New Encyclopaedia Britannica

The Columbia Encyclopedia

Webster's Third New International Dictionary

Oxford English Dictionary

National Geographic Atlas of the World

Statistical Abstract of the United States

The World Almanac and Book of Facts

Caution: *Wikipedia* is a popular online research tool, but since anyone can edit its entries, you can't be certain of its accuracy. Use it for general overviews, but look elsewhere—including *Wikipedia*'s own references and citations—for authoritative sources.

Specialized reference works.   You can also go to specialized reference works, which provide in-depth information on a single field or topic. These may also include authoritative bibliographies, leading you to more specific works. A reference librarian can refer you to specialized encyclopedias in particular fields, but good places to start are online collections of many topic-specific reference works that offer overviews of a topic, place it in a larger context, and sometimes provide links to potential academic sources. Collections that are available through libraries include the following:

CQ Researcher offers in-depth reports on topics in education, health, the environment, criminal justice, international affairs, technology, the economy, and social trends. Each report gives an overview of a particular topic, outlines of the differing positions on it, and a bibliography of resources on it.

Gale Virtual Reference Library (GVRL) offers thousands of full-text specialized encyclopedias, almanacs, articles, and ebooks.

Oxford Reference contains hundreds of dictionaries, encyclopedias, and other reference works on a wide variety of subjects, as well as timelines with links to each item mentioned on each timeline.

SAGE Knowledge includes many encyclopedias and handbooks on topics in the social sciences.

Bibliographies. Bibliographies provide an overview of what has been published on a topic, listing published works along with the information you'll need to find each work. Some are annotated with brief summaries of each work's contents. You'll find bibliographies at the end of scholarly articles and books, and you can also find book-length bibliographies, both in the reference section of your library and online. Check with a reference librarian for bibliographies on your research topic.

Books / Searching the Library Catalog

The library catalog is your primary source for finding books. Almost all library catalogs are computerized and can be accessed through the library's website. You can search by author, title, subject, or keyword. The image below shows the result of a keyword search for material on looted art in Nazi Germany. This search of the library's catalog revealed six items—print books and ebooks—on the topic; to access information on each one, the researcher must simply click on the title or thumbnail image. The image on the next page shows detailed information for one source: bibliographic data about author, title, and publication;

related subject headings (which may lead to other useful materials in the library)—and more. Library catalogs also supply a call number, which identifies the book's location on the library's shelves.

Ebooks / Finding Books Online

Many books in the library catalog are available online. Some may be downloaded to a tablet or mobile device. In addition, thousands of classic works that are in the public domain—no longer protected by copyright—may be read online. *Bartleby*, *Google Books*, *Open Library*, and *Project Gutenberg* are four collections of public-domain works. Here are some other sources of ebooks:

Hathi Trust Digital Library offers access to millions of ebooks, about a third of them in the public domain, contributed by university libraries.

Internet Archive includes millions of ebooks as well as audio, video, music, software, images, and the Way Back Machine, which archives historical webpages.

The *Gale Virtual Reference Library (GVRL)*, *Oxford Reference*, and *SAGE Knowledge* all contain large ebook collections.

Periodicals / Searching Indexes and Databases

To find journal, magazine, and newspaper articles, you will need to search periodical indexes and databases. Indexes provide listings of articles organized by topics; many databases provide the full texts. Some indexes are in print and can be found in the reference section of the library; most are online. Some databases are available for free; most of the more authoritative ones, however, are available only by subscription and so must be accessed through a library.

Many databases now include not only scholarly articles but also dissertations, theses, book chapters, book reviews, and conference proceedings. Dissertations and theses are formal works of scholarship done as requirements for graduate degrees; book reviews offer critical evaluations of scholarly and popular books; and conference proceedings are papers presented, usually orally, at scholarly meetings.

When you access a source through a database, the URL or link address is different each time you log in, so if you want to return to a source, look for a *stable URL*, *permalink*, or *document URL* option and choose it to copy and paste into your list of sources.

General indexes and databases. A reference librarian can help you determine which databases will be most helpful to you, but here are some useful ones:

> *Academic Search Complete* and *Academic Search Premier* are multidisciplinary indexes and databases containing the full text of articles in thousands of journals and indexing of even more, with abstracts of their articles.

> *FirstSearch* offers access to millions of full-text, full-image articles in dozens of databases covering many disciplines.

> *InfoTrac* offers millions of full-text articles in a broad spectrum of disciplines and on a wide variety of topics from thousands of scholarly and popular periodicals, including the *New York Times*.

> *JSTOR* archives scanned copies of entire publication runs of scholarly journals in many disciplines, but it may not include current issues of the journals.

LexisNexis contains full-text publications and articles from a large number of newspapers and business and legal resources.

ProQuest Central provides access to full-text articles from thousands of books, scholarly journals, conference papers, magazines, newspapers, blogs, podcasts, and websites and a large collection of dissertations and theses.

Single-subject indexes and databases. The following are just a sample of what's available; check with a reference librarian for indexes and databases in the subject you're researching.

America: History and Life indexes scholarly literature on the history and culture of the United States and Canada.

BIOSIS Previews provides abstracts and indexes for thousands of sources on a wide variety of biological and medical topics.

ERIC is the U.S. Department of Education's Educational Resource Information Center database. It includes hundreds of journal titles as well as conference papers, technical reports, and other resources on education.

Historical Abstracts includes abstracts of articles on the history of the world, excluding the United States and Canada, since 1450.

Humanities International Index contains bibliographic references to more than 2,200 journals dealing with the humanities.

MLA International Bibliography indexes scholarly articles on modern languages, literature, folklore, and linguistics.

PsycINFO indexes scholarly literature in a number of disciplines relating to the behavioral and social sciences.

PubMed includes millions of citations for biomedical literature, many with links to full-text content.

Print indexes. You may need to consult print indexes to find articles published before the 1980s. Here are six useful ones:

The Readers' Guide to Periodical Literature (print, 1900–; online, 1983–)

InfoTrac Magazine Index (print, 1988–; online, 1973–)

The New York Times Index (print and online, 1851–)

Humanities Index (print, 1974–; online, 1984–)

Social Sciences Index (print, 1974–; online, 1983–)

General Science Index (print, 1978–; online, 1984–)

Images, Sound, and More

Your library likely subscribes to various databases that allow you to find and download video, audio, and image files. Here is a sampling:

AP Images provides access to photographs taken for the Associated Press, the cooperative agency of thousands of newspapers and radio and television stations worldwide.

ArtStor provides images in the arts, architecture, humanities, and sciences.

Dance in Video offers hundreds of videos of dance productions and documentaries on dance.

Education in Video includes thousands of videos of teaching demonstrations, lectures, documentaries, and footage of students and teachers in their classrooms.

Naxos Music Library contains more than 130,000 classical, jazz, and world music recordings, as well as libretti and synopses of hundreds of operas and other background information.

Theatre in Video provides videos of hundreds of performances of plays and film documentaries.

The following indexes and databases are freely available on the internet:

The WWW Virtual Library is a catalog of websites on a wide range of subjects, compiled by volunteers with expertise in particular subject areas.

CSA Discovery Guides provide comprehensive information on current issues in the arts and humanities, natural sciences, social sciences, and technology, with an overview of each subject, key citations with abstracts, and links to websites.

Voice of the Shuttle, or *VoS,* offers information on subjects in the humanities, arranged to mirror "the way the humanities are organized for research and teaching as well as the way they are adapting to social, cultural, and technological changes."

The Library of Congress offers online access to information on a wide range of subjects, including academic subjects, as well as prints, photographs, and government documents.

JURIST is a university-based online gateway to authoritative legal instruction, information, scholarship, and news.

Searching the Web

The web provides access to countless sites containing information posted by governments, educational institutions, organizations, businesses, and individuals. Such websites are different from other sources—including the kinds of online sources you access through indexes and databases—in two key ways: (1) their content varies greatly in its reliability and (2) they are not stable, which means that what you see on a site today may be different (or gone) tomorrow. Anyone who wants to can post material on the web, so you need to evaluate carefully what you find there to eliminate sources that are not current, lack credibility, or are primarily advertisements or promotional in nature.

Because it is so vast and dynamic, finding what you need on the web for academic writing can be a challenge. The primary way of finding information on the web is with a search site. You may find the most suitable results for academic writing by using *Google Scholar*, a search site that finds scholarly literature, including peer-reviewed papers, technical reports, and abstracts. Here are other ways of searching the web:

- *Keyword searches*. *Google*, *Yahoo!*, *Microsoft Edge*, and most other search sites all scan the web looking for keywords that you specify.
- *Subject directories*. *Google*, *Yahoo!*, and some other search sites offer directories that arrange information by topics, much like a library cataloging system. Such directories allow you to broaden or narrow your search if you need to—for example, a search for "birds" can be broadened to "animals" or narrowed to "blue-footed booby."
- *Metasearches*. *Yippy*, *Dogpile*, and *ZapMeta* are metasearch sites that allow you to use several search engines simultaneously. They are best for searching broadly; use a single search site for the most precise results.
- **Twitter** *searches*. In addition to *Twitter* Search, you can find *Twitter* content through search sites such as *Social Mention* and *Keyhole*.

Each search site and metasearch site has its own protocols for searching; most have an "advanced search" option that will help you search more productively. Remember, though, that you need to be careful about EVALUATING SOURCES that you find on the web because the web is unregulated and no one independently verifies the information posted on its sites.

511–18

Doing Field Research

Sometimes you'll need to do your own research, to go beyond the information you find in published sources and gather data by doing field research. Three kinds of field research you might want to consider are interviews, observations, and questionnaires.

Interviewing experts.   Some kinds of writing—a profile of a living person, for instance—almost require that you conduct an interview. And sometimes you may just need to find information that you haven't been able to find in published sources. To get firsthand information on the experience of serving as a soldier in Afghanistan, you might interview your cousin who served a tour of duty there; to find current research on pesticide residues in food, you might need to interview a toxicologist. Whatever your goal, you can conduct interviews in person, using video-calling software such as *Skype* or *FaceTime*, by telephone, through email, or by mail. In general, you will want to use interviews to find information you can't find elsewhere. Below is some advice on planning and conducting an interview.

Before the interview

55–56

1. Once you identify someone you want to interview, email or phone to ask the person, stating your **PURPOSE** for the interview and what you hope to learn.
2. Once you've set up an appointment, send a note or email confirming the time and place. If you wish to record the interview, be sure to ask for permission to do so. If you plan to conduct the interview by mail or email, state when you will send your questions.
3. Write out questions. Plan questions that invite extended response and supporting details: "What accounts for the recent spike in gasoline prices?" forces an explanation, whereas "Is the recent spike in gas prices a direct result of global politics?" is likely to elicit only a yes or a no.

At the interview

4. Record the full name of the person you interview, along with the date, time, and place of the interview; you'll need this information to cite and document the interview accurately.

academic
literacies

rhetorical
situations

genres

fields

processes

strategies

research
MLA / APA

media /
design

5. Take notes, even if you are recording the interview.
6. Keep track of time: don't take more than you agreed to beforehand unless both of you agree to keep talking. End by thanking your subject and offering to provide a copy of your final product.

After the interview

7. Flesh out your notes with details as soon as possible after the interview, while you still remember them. What did you learn? What surprised you? Summarize both the interviewee's words and your impressions.
8. Make sure you've reproduced quotations from the interview accurately and fairly. Avoid editing quotations in ways that distort the speaker's intended meaning.
9. Be sure to send a thank-you note or email.

Observation. Some writing projects are based on information you get by observing something. For a sociology report, you may observe how students behave in large lectures. For an education course, you may observe one child's progress as a writer over a period of time. The following advice can help you conduct observations.

Before observing

1. Think about your research **PURPOSE**: What are you looking for? What do you expect to find? How will your presence as an observer affect what you observe? What do you plan to do with what you find?
2. If necessary, set up an appointment. You may need to ask permission of the people you wish to observe and of your school as well. (Check with your instructor about your school's policy in this area.) Be honest and open about your goals and intentions; college students doing research assignments are often welcomed where others may not be.

While observing

3. If you're taking notes on paper, you may want to divide each page down the middle vertically and write only on the left side of the page, reserving the right side for information you will fill in later. If you're using a laptop, you can set up two columns or a split screen.

55–56

4. Note descriptive details about the setting. What do you see? What do you hear? Do you smell anything? Get down details about color, shape, size, sound, and so on. Consider photographing or making a sketch of what you see.

443–51 ◆

5. Who is there, and what are they doing? **DESCRIBE** what they look like, and make notes about what they say. Note any significant demographic details—about gender, race, occupation, age, dress, and so on.

6. What is happening? Who's doing what? What's being said? Make note of these kinds of **NARRATIVE** details.

462–70 ◆

After observing

7. As soon as possible after you complete your observations, use the right side of your notes to fill in gaps and include additional details.

98–130 ▲

8. **ANALYZE** your notes, looking for patterns. Did some things appear or happen more than once? Did anything stand out? surprise or puzzle you? What did you learn?

Questionnaires and surveys. Various kinds of questionnaires and surveys can provide information or opinions from a large number of people. For a political science course, you might conduct a survey to ask students who they plan to vote for. Or, for a marketing course, you might distribute a questionnaire asking what they think about an advertising campaign. The advice in this section will help you create useful questionnaires and surveys.

Define your goal. The goal of a questionnaire or survey should be limited and focused, so that every question will contribute to your research question. Also, people are more likely to respond to a brief, focused survey.

Define your sample. A survey gets responses from a representative sample of the whole group. The answers to these questions will help you define that sample:

1. Who should answer the questions? The people you contact should represent the whole population. For example, if you want to survey undergraduate students at your school, your sample should reflect your school's enrollment in terms of gender, year, major, age, ethnicity, and so forth as closely as possible.

2. How many people make up a representative sample? In general, the larger your sample, the more the answers will reflect those of the whole group. But if your population is small—200 students in a history course, for example—your sample must include a large percentage of that group.

Decide on a medium. Will you ask the questions face-to-face? over the phone? on a website such as *SurveyMonkey*? by mail? by email? Face-to-face questions work best for simple surveys or for gathering impersonal information. You're more likely to get responses to more personal questions with printed or online questionnaires, which should be neat and easy to read. Phone interviews may require well-thought-out scripts that anticipate possible answers and make it easy to record these answers.

Design good questions. The way you ask questions will determine the usefulness of the answers you get, so take care to write questions that are clear and unambiguous. Here are some typical question types:

- *Multiple-choice*
  What is your current age?
  ____ 15–20 ____ 21–25 ____ 26–30 ____ 31–35 ____ Other

- *Rating scale*
  How would you rate the service at the campus bookstore?
  ____ Excellent ____ Good ____ Fair ____ Poor

- *Agreement scale*
  How much do you agree with the following statements?

	Strongly Agree	Agree	Disagree	Strongly Disagree
The bookstore has sufficient numbers of textbooks available.	❑	❑	❑	❑

	Strongly Agree	Agree	Disagree	Strongly Disagree
Staff at the bookstore are knowledgeable.	❑	❑	❑	❑
Staff at the bookstore are courteous.	❑	❑	❑	❑

- *Open-ended*

   How often do you visit the campus bookstore?

   How can the campus bookstore improve its service?

Include all potential alternatives when phrasing questions to avoid biasing the answers. And make sure each question addresses only one issue—for example, "Bookstore staff are knowledgeable and courteous" could lead to the response "knowledgeable, agree; courteous, disagree."

When arranging questions, place easier ones at the beginning and harder ones near the end (but if the questions seem to fall into a different natural order, follow it). Make sure each question asks for information you will need—if a question isn't absolutely necessary, omit it.

Include an introduction.   Start by stating your survey's purpose and how the results will be used. It's also a good idea to offer an estimate of the time needed to complete the questions. Remind participants of your deadline.

Test the survey or questionnaire.   Make sure your questions elicit the kinds of answers you need by asking three or four people who are part of your target population to answer them. They can help you find unclear instructions, questions that aren't clear or that lack sufficient alternatives, or other problems that you should correct to make sure your results are useful. But if you change the questionnaire as a result of their responses, don't include their answers in your total.

IF YOU NEED MORE HELP

511–18 See **EVALUATING SOURCES** for help determining their usefulness. See also Chap-
526–28 ter 49 for help **TAKING NOTES** on your sources.

---

academic
literacies

rhetorical
situations

genres

fields

processes

strategies

research
MLA / APA

media /
design

Searching the *Health Source* database for information on the incidence of meningitis among college students, you find seventeen articles. A *Google* search on the same topic produces over 600,000 hits. How do you decide which sources to read? This chapter presents advice on evaluating sources—first to determine whether a source might be useful for your purposes and is worth looking at more closely and then to read with a critical eye the ones you choose.

Considering Whether a Source Might Be Useful

Think about your **PURPOSE**. Are you trying to persuade readers to believe or do something? to inform them about something? If the former, it will be especially important to find sources representing various positions; if the latter, you may need sources that are more factual or informative. Reconsider your **AUDIENCE**. What kinds of sources will they find persuasive? If you're writing for readers in a particular field, what counts as evidence in that field? Following are some questions that can help you judge whether a possible source you've found deserves your time and attention:

55–56

57–60

- **Is it reliable?** Is it **SCHOLARLY**? peer-reviewed? published in a reputable journal or magazine, or by a reputable publisher? Did you find it in a library database? on the web? Evaluating web-based texts may require more work than using results from library databases. But whatever kind of search you do, skim the results quickly to evaluate their reliability.

490–93

- **Is it relevant?** How does the source relate to your purpose? What will it add to your work? Look at the title and at any introductory material— a preface, abstract, or introduction—to see what the source covers.

- *What are the author's credentials?* How is the author qualified to write on the subject? Are they associated with a particular position on the issue? See whether the source mentions other works this author has written. In any case, you might do a web search to see what else you can learn about the author.

66–68 ■

- *What is the* STANCE*?* Consider whether a source covers various perspectives or advocates one particular point of view. Does its title suggest a certain slant? If it's online, you might check to see whether it includes links to other sites and, if so, what their perspectives are. You'll want to consult sources with a variety of viewpoints.

- *Who is the publisher or sponsor?* If it's a book, what kind of company published it; if an article, what kind of periodical did it appear in? Books published by university presses and articles in scholarly journals are reviewed by experts before they are published. Books and articles written for the general public typically do not undergo rigorous review—and they may lack the kind of in-depth discussion that is useful for research.

  If the source is online, is the site maintained by an organization? an interest group? a government agency? an individual? Look for clues in the URL: *.edu* is used mostly by colleges and universities, *.gov* by government agencies, *.org* by nonprofit organizations, *.mil* by the military, and *.com* by commercial organizations. Evaluate the publisher's or sponsor's motives: to present information even-handedly? to promote a certain point of view, belief, or position? to sell something?

- *What is the level?* Can you understand the material? Texts written for a general audience might be easier to understand but not authoritative enough for academic work. Texts written for scholars will be more authoritative but may be hard to comprehend.

- *When was it published?* See when books and articles were published. Check to see when online sources were created and last updated. (If the site lists no date, see if links to other sites still work.) Recent does not necessarily mean better—some topics may require very current information whereas others may call for older sources.

- *Does it include other useful information?* Is there a bibliography that might lead you to other sources? How current are the sources it cites?
- *Is it available?* Is it a source you can get hold of? If it's a book and your school's library doesn't have it, can you get it through interlibrary loan?

Once you've decided that a source should be examined more closely, use the following questions to give it critical scrutiny.

Reading Sources with a Critical Eye

- *What ARGUMENTS does the author make?* Does the author present a number of different positions, or do they argue for a particular position? Do you need to ANALYZE THE ARGUMENT?

  ▲ 157–84

  ✳ 26–27

- *How persuasive do you find the argument?* What reasons and evidence does the author provide in support of any position(s)? Are there citations or links—and if so, are they credible? Is any evidence presented without citations? Do you find any of the author's assumptions questionable? How thoroughly does the author consider opposing arguments?

- *What is the author's STANCE?* Does the author strive for objectivity, or does the content or language reveal a particular bias? Does the author consider opposing views and treat them fairly?

  ■ 66–68

- *Do you recognize ideas you've run across in other sources?* Does the source leave out any information or perspective that other sources include—or include any that other sources leave out?

- *Does this source support or challenge your own position—or does it do both?* Does it support your thesis? offer a different argument altogether? Does it represent a position you may need to ACKNOWLEDGE or REFUTE? Don't reject a source just because it challenges your views; your sources should reflect a variety of views on your topic, showing that you've considered the subject thoroughly.

  ▲ 178

  178

- *What can you tell about the intended AUDIENCE and PURPOSE?* Is the author writing to a general audience, to a subset of that audience, to specialists in a particular field? Are you a member of that audience? If

  ■ 57–60

  55–56

not, does that affect the way you interpret what you read? Is the main purpose to inform readers about a topic or to argue a certain point?

Comparing Sources

You may find that two or more of your sources present similar information or arguments. How do you decide which one to use? Compare them, using these questions as a guide:

- *Which source is most current?* Generally, a more recent source is better than an older one, because the newer source includes information or data that is more up to date—and may include (or refute) the information in the earlier source. Be aware, though, that in some fields, such as literary criticism, decades-old sources may still be important.

398–408 ◆

- *Which argument is more persuasive?* Examine the **CLAIMS**, **REASONS**, and **EVIDENCE** presented in each source. Which source's argument is most logical? Which one has the best supporting reasons and evidence? Which one best **ACKNOWLEDGES**, **ACCOMMODATES**, or **REFUTES** opposing arguments?

411–13 ◆

- *Which author or authors are most authoritative?* An expert in the subject is more authoritative than, say, a journalist writing on the subject. An article published in a scholarly journal is more authoritative than one published in a general-circulation magazine or website. The journalist's article may be easier to read and more interesting, but you're best off looking for the best information—not the best read.

66–68 ■

- *Which source has the most appropriate* **STANCE**? In general, look for sources that strive for objectivity, rather than a particular bias. Also, be aware that we all tend to favor information that agrees with our views—and that may lead us to choose sources we agree with rather than sources that present all sides of an issue.

- *Which source best fits your needs?* All other things being equal, the best source to choose is the one that will give you the information you need, support the argument you're making, and perhaps provide useful quotations to add to your writing. The best source will show that you've done appropriate research and will enhance your own credibility as a thinker, reader, researcher, and writer.

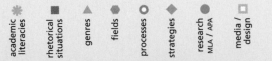

A Note of Caution: False News

As you read to find sources or simply to find out what's happening in the world, you need to be on guard against false or "fake" news. False news—propaganda, hoaxes, misinformation, and lies—includes satires and counterfeit news stories. Satires, which range from Jonathan Swift's "A Modest Proposal" to *Onion* stories like "NFL to Curb Excessive Celebrations by Removing Areas of Players' Brains Responsible for Emotions" and episodes of *The Daily Show*, offer humorous exaggerations to expose and criticize people and governments. Counterfeit news stories, though, are malicious fabrications created usually for political ends. World War II Nazi propaganda and recent fraudulent stories such as "Pope Francis Endorses Donald Trump," a story that went viral on Facebook, are intended to mislead readers. Further complicating things, some politicians and other public figures have taken to calling news reports with which they disagree and even entire newspapers and networks "fake news"—even though the stories reported are verifiably true and the news outlets are considered trustworthy.

Although false news has been around at least since the invention of the printing press, the internet and social media have led to a huge increase in false news stories, especially during the 2016 presidential election, seriously challenging and muddying "real" news. Each false story can rapidly multiply over sites such as *Facebook* and *Twitter* and through email. As a reader and researcher, you need to be able to see whether or not a story is false. As a writer, you risk harming your credibility if you cite a false news story as evidence.

All news outlets have a bias, but some are more trustworthy than others. Here is some advice on how to determine whether a potential news source is unfairly biased or can be safely used as a source in your own research.

Investigate the source. Some news media outlets' political bias is well known, but to determine the bias of other sources, you may have to do some research: Read the "About" pages of online sources to see how the source characterizes itself, who owns or runs it, and how the site may be contacted. A site without such information (or with only a link to a personal email account) is probably not a good source. If a site includes a disclaimer to the effect of, "We are not responsible for the reliability or accuracy of this information," assume that it's a site to avoid.

- See what websites that evaluate news sources say about the bias of the source. These sites rate the bias of sources using a combination of research into the content of a news source and votes on the site's judgment by the website's readers. While these sites acknowledge that such judgments are by nature subjective, they present a rough consensus on the direction and extent of bias.

- See whether the site appears in lists of websites that post fake or satirical stories. FactCheck.org and Wikipedia are two sites that publish such lists.

- Check the URL of online sources. Counterfeit websites mimic real news sources but either alter the URL (Breaking-CNN.com imitates CNN.com) or add a .co or .ma to a legitimate URL (usatoday.com.co or Bloomberg.com.ma). While reputable sites usually end in .org, .net, or .com, these endings don't necessarily mean the site is trustworthy — so exercise caution, especially with .com addresses.

- Check to see if other news media are reporting the same story. If the story appears in only one source, it's likely false.

- Check the date of the story and dates within the story. Sometimes old stories resurface as "news." They aren't any truer now than they were then.

- Do a search for the story's author. Does the author appear to be an expert on your topic? Does the author write for or belong to other organizations or sites that are biased or suspect? What other articles has the author written? If there's no author listed, the site is probably not trustworthy.

Use Your Own Judgment.   Sometimes you need to judge the trustworthiness of your sources yourself. Begin by assessing the story's plausibility: how likely is it to be true, given what you already know about the world? For example, the likelihood of a U.S. senator's father being involved in the assassination of President John F. Kennedy or that vast, secret conspiracies are running the world is pretty slim—though such stories are common on the internet and believed by some people.

A story that seems designed to generate a strong emotional response in readers, especially anger or fear, rather than appealing to logic or sound evidence, may be false. For example, stories circulating on the internet asserting that childhood immunizations cause autism—and even that the president enacted a temporary ban on vaccinations—prey on parents' fears for their children's safety. But they are completely false.

You should also consider the source in light of the rhetorical situation:

PURPOSE
Consider the headline: Is it inflammatory or outrageous? Read beyond the headline. Does the story match the headline? Is the piece meant to inform? persuade? entertain? confirm readers' current beliefs? Is the story written to manipulate your emotions by making you angry? sad? Something else?

55–56

AUDIENCE
For whom is the piece written? Would this piece be considered reliable by the extreme political partisans on one side or another? To what extent does the piece confirm or challenge the expectations of its readers? Does the story appear only on social media, or is it also on other publication sites?

57–60

GENRE
Is the genre of the piece appropriate for its purpose and audience? If it's an argument, does it offer multiple perspectives on the topic? What evidence is offered—and can it be confirmed through links, references, or other sources? Do links or references actually exist and support the claims in the story? Does the information in the piece appear in other, reputable publications?

61–65

STANCE
What is the author's attitude toward the subject: objective? serious? angry? outraged? astonished? amused? snide? disrespectful? Is the author's tone appropriate for the content of the story?

66–68

69–71

MEDIA/DESIGN Does the website appear to be well designed or the work of an amateur? Does the headline or the story use ALL CAPS? Are photographs, charts, or tables included in the story? Do they seem real—again, do they appear in other, reputable sources—or doctored? Could a photograph, for example, have been Photoshopped?

Consider, too, the effect of your own biases. Does the story confirm what you already believe? Confirmation bias (our tendency to believe things that match what we already believe) makes us more likely to accept stories that confirm our beliefs and to discount information that doesn't. Be wary of assuming a story or article is trustworthy just because you agree with the author—you need to step back and make sure your own beliefs aren't clouding your judgment.

As a final check, you can go to sites whose purpose is investigating news for its veracity. Some to visit:

- FactCheck.org
- Snopes.com
- PolitiFact.com
- *The Washington Post* Fact Checker
- AllSides.com
- mediabiasfactcheck.com

IF YOU NEED MORE HELP

526–38
539–43

See **QUOTING, PARAPHRASING, AND SUMMARIZING** for help in taking notes on your sources and deciding how to use them in your writing. See also **ACKNOWLEDGING SOURCES, AVOIDING PLAGIARISM** for advice on giving credit to the sources you use.

Synthesizing Ideas **50**

To **ANALYZE** the works of a poet, you show how she uses similar images 98–130 in three different poems to explore a recurring concept. To solve a crime, a detective studies several eyewitness accounts to figure out who did it. To trace the history of photojournalism, a professor **COMPARES** the uses of 424–31 photography during the Civil War and during the Vietnam War. These are all cases where someone *synthesizes*—brings together material from two or more sources in order to generate new information or to support a new perspective. When you do research, you need to go beyond what your sources say; you need to use what they say to inspire and support *what you want to say.* This chapter focuses on how to synthesize ideas you find in other sources as the basis for your own ideas.

Reading for Patterns and Connections

Your task as a writer is to find as much information as you can on your topic—and then to sift through all that you have found to determine and support what you yourself will write. In other words, you'll need to synthesize ideas and information from the sources you've consulted to figure out first what arguments *you* want to make and then to provide support for those arguments.

 When you synthesize, you group similar bits of information together, looking for patterns or themes or trends and trying to identify the key points. In the brief report on the following page, writer Jude Stewart synthesizes several pieces of research on boredom. Stewart's report originally appeared in *The Atlantic*, which uses an abbreviated documentation style.

Boredom has, paradoxically, become quite interesting to academics lately. The International Interdisciplinary Boredom Conference gathered humanities scholars in Warsaw for the fifth time in April. In early May, its less scholarly forerunner, London's Boring Conference, celebrated seven years of delighting in tedium. At this event, people flock to talks about toast, double yellow lines, sneezing, and vending-machine sounds, among other snooze-inducing topics.

What, exactly, is everybody studying? One widely accepted psychological definition of boredom is "the aversive experience of wanting, but being unable, to engage in satisfying activity." [1] But how can you quantify a person's boredom level and compare it with someone else's? In 1986, psychologists introduced the Boredom Proneness Scale, [2] designed to measure an individual's overall propensity to feel bored (what's known as "trait boredom"). By contrast, the Multidimensional State Boredom Scale, [3] developed in 2008, measures a person's feelings of boredom in a given situation ("state boredom"). A German-led team has since identified five types of state boredom: indifferent, calibrating, searching, reactant, and apathetic (indifferent boredom—characterized by low arousal—was the mellowest, least unpleasant kind; reactant—high arousal—was the most aggressive and unpleasant). [4] Boredom may be miserable, but let no one call it simple.

Boredom has been linked to behavior issues, including bad driving, [5] mindless snacking, [6] binge-drinking, [7] risky sex, [8] and problem gambling. [9] In fact, many of us would take pain over boredom. One team of psychologists discovered that two-thirds of men and a quarter of women would rather self-administer electric shocks than sit alone with their thoughts for 15 minutes. [10] Probing this phenomenon, another team asked volunteers to watch boring, sad, or neutral films, during which they could self-administer electric shocks. The bored volunteers shocked themselves more and harder than the sad or neutral ones did. [11]

But boredom isn't all bad. By encouraging contemplation and daydreaming, it can spur creativity. An early, much-cited study gave participants abundant time to complete problem-solving and word-association exercises. Once all the obvious answers were exhausted, participants gave more and more inventive answers to fend off boredom. [12] A British study took these findings one step further, asking subjects to complete a creative challenge (coming up with a list of alternative

This question allows Stewart to bring together four ways boredom can be measured.

Stewart synthesizes seven different studies under one category, "behavior issues."

One study builds on a previous study.

Again, Stewart creates a category that includes two different studies.

Stewart shows how one study relates to an earlier one's findings.

uses for a household item). One group of subjects did a boring activity first, while the others went straight to the creative task. Those whose boredom pumps had been primed were more prolific. [13]

In our always-connected world, boredom may be an elusive state, but it is a fertile one. Watch paint dry or water boil, or at least put away your smartphone for a while. You might unlock your next big idea.

Conclusion brings together all the research, creating a synthesis of the findings of all 13 sources.

The Studies

[1] Eastwood et al., "The Unengaged Mind" (*Perspectives on Psychological Science*, Sept. 2012)

[2] Farmer and Sundberg, "Boredom Proneness" (*Journal of Personality Assessment*, Spring 1986)

[3] Fahlman et al., "Development and Validation of the Multidimensional State Boredom Scale" (*Assessment*, Feb. 2013)

[4] Goetz et al., "Types of Boredom" (*Motivation and Emotion*, June 2014)

[5] Steinberger et al., "The Antecedents, Experience, and Coping Strategies of Driver Boredom in Young Adult Males" (*Journal of Safety Research*, Dec. 2016)

[6] Havermans et al., "Eating and Inflicting Pain Out of Boredom" (*Appetite*, Feb. 2015)

[7] Biolcati et al., "'I Cannot Stand the Boredom'" (*Addictive Behaviors Reports*, June 2016)

[8] Miller et al., "Was Bob Seger Right?" (*Leisure Sciences*, Jan. 2014)

[9] Mercer and Eastwood, "Is Boredom Associated with Problem Gambling Behaviour?" (*International Gambling Studies*, April 2010)

[10] Wilson et al., "Just Think: The Challenges of the Disengaged Mind" (*Science*, July 2014)

[11] Nederkoorn et al., "Self-Inflicted Pain Out of Boredom" (*Psychiatry Research*, March 2016)

[12] Schubert, "Boredom as an Antagonist of Creativity" (*Journal of Creative Behavior*, Dec. 1977)

[13] Mann and Cadman, "Does Being Bored Make Us More Creative?" (*Creativity Research Journal*, May 2014)

—Jude Stewart, "Boredom Is Good for You: The Surprising Benefits of Stultification"

Here are some tips for reading to identify patterns and connections:

- Read all your sources with an open mind. Withhold judgment, even of sources that seem wrong-headed or implausible. Don't jump to conclusions.

534–35
- Take notes and write a brief **SUMMARY** of each source to help you see relationships, patterns, and connections among your sources. Take notes on your own thoughts, too.

- Pay attention to your first reactions. You'll likely have many ideas to work with, but your first thoughts can often lead somewhere that you 331–34 will find interesting. Try **FREEWRITING**, **CLUSTERING**, or **LISTING** to see where they lead. How do these thoughts and ideas relate to your topic? 335–37 Where might they fit into your rough **OUTLINE**?

- Try to think creatively, and pay attention to thoughts that flicker at the edge of your consciousness, as they may well be productive.

- Be playful. Good ideas sometimes come when we let our guard down or take ideas to extremes just to see where they lead.

Ask yourself these questions about your sources:

- What sources make the strongest arguments? What makes them so strong?

- Do some arguments recur in several sources?

- Which arguments do you agree with? disagree with? Of those you disagree with, which ones seem strong enough that you need to 411 **ACKNOWLEDGE** them in your text?

- Are there any disagreements among your sources?

- Are there any themes you see in more than one source?

- Are any data—facts, statistics, examples—or experts cited in more than one source?

- Do several of your sources use the same terms? Do they use the terms similarly, or do they use them in different ways?

academic literacies rhetorical situations genres fields processes strategies research MLA / APA media / design

- What have you learned about your topic? How have your sources affected your thinking on your topic? Do you need to adjust your **THESIS**? If so, how?

387–89

- Have you discovered new questions you need to investigate?

- Keep in mind your **RHETORICAL SITUATION**—have you found the information you need that will achieve your purpose, appeal to your audience, and suit your genre and medium?

53

What is likely to emerge from this questioning is a combination of big ideas, including new ways of understanding your topic and insights into recent scholarship about it, and smaller ones, such as how two sources agree with each other but not completely and how the information in one source supports or undercuts the argument of another. These ideas and insights will become the basis for your own ideas and for what *you* have to say about the topic.

Synthesizing Ideas Using Notes

You may find that identifying connections among your sources is easier if you examine them together rather than reading them one by one. For example, taking notes on note cards and then laying the cards out on a desk or table (or on the floor) lets you see passages that seem related. Doing the same with photocopies or printouts of your sources can help you identify similarities as well.

In doing research for an essay arguing that the sale of assault weapons should be banned, you might find several sources that address the scope of U.S. citizens' right to bear arms. On the next page are notes taken on three such sources: Joe Klein, a journalist writing in *Time.com*; Antonin Scalia, a former U.S. Supreme Court justice, quoted in an online news article; and Drew Westen, a professor of psychology writing in a blog sponsored by the *New York Times*. Though the writers hold very different views, juxtaposing these notes and highlighting certain passages show a common thread running through the sources. In this example, all three sources might be used to support the thesis that restrictions on the owning of weapons—but not an outright ban—are both constitutional and necessary.

Source 1

Limits of gun ownership

Although the U.S. Constitution includes the right to bear arms, that right is not absolute. "No American has the right to own a stealth bomber or a nuclear weapon. Armor-piercing bullets are forbidden. The question is where you draw a reasonable bright line."
— Klein, "How the Gun Won" — quote

Source 4

Limits of gun ownership

Supreme Court Justice Antonin M. Scalia has noted that when the Constitution was written and ratified, some weapons were barred. So limitations could be put on owning some weapons, as long as the limits are consistent with those in force in 1789.
— Scalia, quoted in Woods — paraphrase

Source 3

Limits of gun ownership

Westen's "message consulting" research has shown that Americans are ambivalent about guns but react very positively to a statement of principle that includes both the right to own guns and restrictions on their ownership, such as prohibiting large ammunition clips and requiring all gun purchasers to undergo background checks for criminal behavior or mental illness.
— Westen — paraphrase

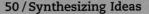

Synthesizing Information to Support Your Own Ideas

If you're doing research to write a **REPORT**, your own ideas will be communicated primarily through which information you decide to include from the sources you cite and how you organize that information. If you're writing a **TEXTUAL ANALYSIS**, your synthesis may focus on the themes, techniques, or other patterns you find. If you're writing a research-based **ARGUMENT**, on the other hand, your synthesis of sources must support the position you take in that argument. No matter what your genre, the challenge is to synthesize information from your research to develop ideas about your topic and then to support those ideas.

131–56
98–130
157–84

Entering the Conversation

As you read and think about your topic, you will come to an understanding of the concepts, interpretations, and controversies relating to your topic—and you'll become aware that there's a larger conversation going on. When you begin to find connections among your sources, you will begin to see your own place in that conversation, to discover your own ideas and your own stance on your topic. This is the exciting part of a research project, for when you write out your own ideas on the topic, you will find yourself entering that conversation. Remember that your **STANCE** as an author needs to be clear: simply stringing together the words and ideas of others isn't enough. You need to show readers *how* your source materials relate to one another and to your thesis.

66–68

> **IF YOU NEED MORE HELP**
> See Chapter 51, **QUOTING, PARAPHRASING, AND SUMMARIZING**, for help in integrating source materials into your own text. See also Chapter 52 on **ACKNOWL-EDGING SOURCES, AVOIDING PLAGIARISM** for advice on giving credit to the sources you cite.

526–38
539–43

51 Quoting, Paraphrasing, and Summarizing

In an oral presentation about the rhetoric of Abraham Lincoln, you quote a memorable line from the Gettysburg Address. For an essay on the Tet Offensive in the Vietnam War, you paraphrase arguments made by several commentators and summarize some key debates about that war. When you work with the ideas and words of others, you need to clearly distinguish those ideas and words from your own and give credit to their authors. This chapter will help you with the specifics of quoting, paraphrasing, and summarizing source materials that you use in your writing.

Taking Notes

When you find material you think will be useful, take careful notes. How do you determine how much to record? You need to write down enough information so that when you refer to it later, you will be reminded of its main points and have a precise record of where it comes from.

- *Use a computer file, note cards, or a notebook,* labeling each entry with the information that will allow you to keep track of where it comes from—author, title, and the pages or the URL (or DOI [digital object identifier]). You needn't write down full bibliographic information (you can abbreviate the author's name and title) since you'll include that information in your WORKING BIBLIOGRAPHY.

- *Take notes in your own words, and use your own sentence patterns.* If you make a note that is a detailed PARAPHRASE, label it as such so that you'll know to provide appropriate DOCUMENTATION if you use it.

485–87

531–34
544–47

academic literacies | rhetorical situations | genres | fields | processes | strategies | research MLA / APA | media / design

- *If you find wording that you'd like to quote,* be sure to enclose it in quotation marks to distinguish your source's words from your own. Double-check your notes to be sure any quoted material is accurately quoted—and that you haven't accidentally **PLAGIARIZED** your sources.

539–43

- *Label each note with a number to identify the source and a subject heading* to relate the note to a subject, supporting point, or other element in your essay. Doing this will help you to sort your notes easily and match them up with your rough outline. Restrict each note to a single subject.

Here are a few examples of one writer's notes on a source discussing synthetic dyes, bladder cancer, and the use of animals to determine what causes cancers. Each note includes a subject heading and brief source information and identifies whether the source is quoted or paraphrased.

Source 3

Synthetic dyes

The first synthetic dye was mauve, invented in 1854 and derived from coal. Like other coal-derived dyes, it contained aromatic amines.
Steingraber, "Pesticides," 976 — paraphrase

Source 3

Synthetic dyes & cancer

Bladder cancer was common among textile workers who used dyes. Steingraber: "By the beginning of the twentieth century, bladder cancer rates among this group of workers had skyrocketed."
Steingraber, "Pesticides," 976 — paraphrase and quote

> **Source 3**
>
> Synthetic dyes & cancer
>
> In 1938, Wilhelm Hueper exposed dogs to aromatic amines and showed that the chemical caused bladder cancer. Steingraber, "Pesticides," 976 — paraphrase

Deciding Whether to Quote, Paraphrase, or Summarize

340–42

528–31

531–34

534–35

When it comes time to **DRAFT**, you'll need to decide *how* to use any source you want to include—in other words, whether to quote, paraphrase, or summarize it. You might follow this rule of thumb: **QUOTE** texts when the wording is worth repeating or makes a point so well that no rewording will do it justice, when you want to cite the exact words of a known authority on your topic, when an authority's opinions challenge or disagree with those of others, or when the source is one you want to emphasize. **PARAPHRASE** sources that are not worth quoting but contain details you need to include. **SUMMARIZE** longer passages whose main points are important but whose details are not.

Quoting

Quoting a source is a way of weaving someone else's exact words into your text. You need to reproduce the source exactly, though you can modify it to omit unnecessary details (with ellipses) or to make it fit smoothly into your text (with brackets). You also need to distinguish quoted material from your own by enclosing short quotations in quotation marks, setting off longer quotes as a block, and using appropriate **SIGNAL PHRASES**.

535–38

Incorporate short quotations into your text, enclosed in quotation marks. If you are following **MLA STYLE**, short quotations are defined as four typed

MLA 548–96

lines or fewer; if using **APA STYLE**, as below, short means fewer than forty words.

APA 597–636

> Gerald Graff (2003) has argued that colleges make the intellectual life seem more opaque than it needs to be, leaving many students with "the misconception that the life of the mind is a secret society for which only an elite few qualify" (p. 1).

If you are quoting three lines or fewer of poetry, run them in with your text, enclosed in quotation marks. Separate lines with slashes, leaving one space on each side of the slashes.

> Emma Lazarus almost speaks for the Statue of Liberty with the words inscribed on its pedestal: "Give me your tired, your poor, / Your huddled masses yearning to breathe free, / The wretched refuse of your teeming shore" (58).

Set off long quotations block style.   If you are using MLA style, set off quotations of five or more typed lines by indenting the quote one-half inch from the left margin. If you are using APA style, indent quotations of forty or more words one-half inch (or five to seven spaces) from the left margin. In either case, do not use quotation marks, and put any parenthetical documentation *after* any end punctuation.

> Nonprofit organizations such as Oxfam and Habitat for Humanity rely on visual representations of the poor. What better way to get our attention, asks rhetorician Diana George:
>
> > In a culture saturated by the image, how else do we convince Americans that—despite the prosperity they see all around them—there is real need out there? The solution for most nonprofits has been to show the despair. To do that they must represent poverty as something that can be seen and easily recognized: fallen down shacks and trashed out public housing, broken windows, dilapidated porches, barefoot kids with stringy hair, emaciated old women and men staring out at the camera with empty eyes. (210)

If you are quoting four or more lines of poetry, they need to be set off block style in the same way.

Indicate any omissions with ellipses. You may sometimes delete words from a quotation that are unnecessary for your point. Insert three ellipsis marks (leaving a space before the first and after the last one) to indicate the deletion. If you omit a sentence or more in the middle of a quotation, put a period before the three ellipsis dots. Be careful not to distort the source's meaning, however.

> Faigley points out that Gore's "Information Superhighway" metaphor "associated the economic prosperity of the 1950s and . . . 1960s facilitated by new highways with the potential for vast . . . commerce to be conducted over the Internet" (253).

> According to Welch, "Television is more acoustic than visual. . . . One can turn one's gaze away from the television, but one cannot turn one's ears from it without leaving the area where the monitor leaks its aural signals into every corner" (102).

Indicate additions or changes with brackets. Sometimes you'll need to change or add words in a quotation—to make the quotation fit grammatically within your sentence, for example, or to add a comment. In the following example, the writer changes the passage "one of our goals" to clarify the meaning of "our."

> Writing about the dwindling attention among some composition scholars to the actual teaching of writing, Susan Miller notes that "few discussions of writing pedagogy take it for granted that one of [writing teachers'] goals is to teach how to write" (480).

Here's an example of brackets used to add explanatory words to a quotation:

> Barbosa observes that Buarque's lyrics have long included "many a metaphor of *saudades* [yearning] so characteristic of *fado* music" (207).

Use punctuation correctly with quotations. When you incorporate a quotation into your text, you have to think about the end punctuation in the quoted material and also about any punctuation you need to add when you insert the quote into your own sentence.

Periods and commas. Put periods or commas *inside* closing quotation marks, except when you have parenthetical documentation at the end, in which case you put the period or comma after the parentheses.

> "Country music," Tichi says, "is a crucial and vital part of the American identity" (23).

After long quotations set off block style with no quotation marks, however, the period goes *before* the documentation, as in the example on page 529.

Question marks and exclamation points. These go *inside* closing quotation marks if they are part of the quoted material but *outside* when they are not. If there's parenthetical documentation at the end of the quotation, any punctuation that's part of your sentence comes after it.

> Speaking at a Fourth of July celebration in 1852, Frederick Douglass asked, "What have I, or those I represent, to do with your national independence?" (35).

> Who can argue with W. Charisse Goodman's observation that media images persuade women that "thinness equals happiness and fulfill-ment" (53)?

Colons and semicolons. These always go *outside* closing quotation marks.

> It's hard to argue with W. Charisse Goodman's observation that media images persuade women that "thinness equals happiness and fulfillment"; nevertheless, American women today are more overweight than ever (53).

Paraphrasing

When you paraphrase, you restate information from a source in your own words, using your own sentence structures. Paraphrase when the source material is important but the original wording is not. Because it includes all the main points of the source, a paraphrase is usually about the same length as the original.

Here is a paragraph about synthetic dyes and cancer, followed by two paraphrases of it that demonstrate some of the challenges of paraphrasing:

ORIGINAL SOURCE

In 1938, in a series of now-classic experiments, exposure to synthetic dyes derived from coal and belonging to a class of chemicals called aromatic amines was shown to cause bladder cancer in dogs. These results helped explain why bladder cancers had become so prevalent among dyestuffs workers. With the invention of mauve in 1854, synthetic dyes began replacing natural plant-based dyes in the coloring of cloth and leather. By the beginning of the twentieth century, bladder cancer rates among this group of workers had skyrocketed, and the dog experiments helped unravel this mystery. The International Labor Organization did not wait for the results of these animal tests, however, and in 1921 declared certain aromatic amines to be human carcinogens. Decades later, these dogs provided a lead in understanding why tire-industry workers, as well as machinists and metalworkers, also began falling victim to bladder cancer: aromatic amines had been added to rubbers and cutting oils to serve as accelerants and antirust agents.

—Sandra Steingraber, "Pesticides, Animals, and Humans"

The following paraphrase borrows too much of the language of the original or changes it only slightly, as the highlighted words and phrases show:

UNACCEPTABLE PARAPHRASE: WORDING TOO CLOSE

Now-classic experiments in 1938 showed that when dogs were exposed to aromatic amines, chemicals used in synthetic dyes derived from coal, they developed bladder cancer. Similar cancers were prevalent among dyestuffs workers, and these experiments helped to explain why. Mauve, a synthetic dye, was invented in 1854, after which cloth and leather manufacturers replaced most of the natural plant-based dyes with synthetic dyes. By the early twentieth century, this group of workers had skyrocketing rates of bladder cancer, a mystery the dog experiments helped to unravel. As early as 1921, though, before the test results proved the connection, the International Labor Organization had labeled certain aromatic amines carcinogenic. Even so, decades later many metalworkers, machinists, and tire-industry workers began developing bladder cancer. The animal tests helped researchers understand that rubbers and cutting oils contained aromatic amines as accelerants and antirust agents (Steingraber 976).

The next paraphrase uses original language but follows the sentence structure of Steingraber's text too closely:

UNACCEPTABLE PARAPHRASE: SENTENCE STRUCTURE TOO CLOSE

In 1938, several pathbreaking experiments showed that being exposed to synthetic dyes that are made from coal and belong to a type of chemicals called aromatic amines caused dogs to get bladder cancer. These results helped researchers identify why cancers of the bladder had become so common among textile workers who worked with dyes. With the development of mauve in 1854, synthetic dyes began to be used instead of dyes based on plants in the dyeing of leather and cloth. By the end of the nineteenth century, rates of bladder cancer among these workers had increased dramatically, and the experiments using dogs helped clear up this oddity. The International Labor Organization anticipated the results of these tests on animals, though, and in 1921 labeled some aromatic amines carcinogenic. Years later these experiments with dogs helped researchers explain why workers in the tire industry, as well as metalworkers and machinists, also started dying of bladder cancer: aromatic amines had been put into rubbers and cutting oils as rust inhibitors and accelerants (Steingraber 976).

Patchwriting, a third form of unacceptable paraphrase, combines the other two. Composition researcher Rebecca Moore Howard defines it as "copying from a source text and then deleting some words, altering grammatical structures, or plugging in one-for-one synonym-substitutes." Here is a patchwrite of the first two sentences of the original source: (The source's exact words are shaded in yellow; paraphrases are in blue.)

PATCHWRITE

Scientists have known for a long time that chemicals in the environment can cause cancer. For example, in 1938, in a series of important experiments, being exposed to synthetic dyes made out of coal and belonging to a kind of chemicals called aromatic amines was shown to cause dogs to develop bladder cancer. These experiments explain why this type of cancer had become so common among workers who handled dyes.

Here is an acceptable paraphrase of the entire passage:

ACCEPTABLE PARAPHRASE

Biologist Sandra Steingraber explains that pathbreaking experiments in 1938 demonstrated that dogs exposed to aromatic amines (chemicals used in coal-based synthetic dyes) developed cancers of the bladder that were similar to cancers common among dyers in the textile industry. After mauve, the first synthetic dye, was invented in 1854, leather and cloth manufacturers replaced most natural dyes made from plants with synthetic dyes, and by the early 1900s textile workers had very high rates of bladder cancer. The experiments with dogs proved the connection, but years before, in 1921, the International Labor Organization had labeled some aromatic amines carcinogenic. Even so, years later many metal-workers, machinists, and workers in the tire industry started to develop unusually high rates of bladder cancer. The experiments with dogs helped researchers understand that the cancers were caused by aromatic amines used in cutting oils to inhibit rust and in rubbers as accelerants (976).

Some guidelines for paraphrasing

- *Use your own words and sentence structure.* It is acceptable to use some words from the original, but as much as possible, the phrasing and sentence structures should be your own.

- *Introduce paraphrased text with* SIGNAL PHRASES.

- *Put in quotation marks any of the source's original phrasing that you use.*

- *Indicate the source.* Although the wording may be yours, the ideas and information come from another source; be sure to name the author and include DOCUMENTATION to avoid the possibility of PLAGIARISM.

535–38

MLA 551–57
APA 600–604
539–43

Summarizing

A summary states the main ideas in a source concisely and in your own words. Unlike a paraphrase, a summary does not present all the details, and it is generally as brief as possible. Summaries may boil down an entire book or essay into a single sentence, or they may take a paragraph or more to present the main ideas. Here, for example, is a one-sentence summary of the Steingraber paragraph:

> Steingraber explains that experiments with dogs demonstrated that aromatic amines, chemicals used in synthetic dyes, cutting oils, and rubber, cause bladder cancer (976).

In the context of an essay, the summary might take this form:

> Medical researchers have long relied on experiments using animals to expand understanding of the causes of disease. For example, biologist and ecologist Sandra Steingraber notes that in the second half of the nineteenth century, the rate of bladder cancer soared among textile workers. According to Steingraber, experiments with dogs demonstrated that synthetic chemicals in dyes used to color the textiles caused the cancer (976).

Some guidelines for summarizing

- *Include only the main ideas; leave out the details.* A summary should include just enough information to give the reader the gist of the original. It is always much shorter than the original, sometimes even as brief as one sentence.

- *Use your own words.* If you quote phrasing from the original, enclose the phrase in quotation marks.

- *Indicate the source.* Although the wording may be yours, the ideas and information come from another source. Name the author, either in a signal phrase or parentheses, and include an appropriate **IN-TEXT CITATION** to avoid the possibility of **PLAGIARISM**.

MLA 551–57
APA 600–604

542–43

Introducing Source Materials Using Signal Phrases

You need to introduce quotations, paraphrases, and summaries clearly, usually letting readers know who the author is—and, if need be, something about their credentials. Consider this sentence:

> Professor and textbook author Elaine Tyler May argues that many high school history books are too bland to interest young readers (531).

The beginning ("Professor and textbook author Elaine Tyler May argues") functions as a *signal phrase*, telling readers who is making the assertion and why she has the authority to speak on the topic—and making clear that everything between the signal phrase and the parenthetical citation comes from that source. Since the signal phrase names the author, the parenthetical citation includes only the page number; had the author not been identified in the signal phrase, she would have been named in the parentheses:

> Even some textbook authors believe that many high school history books are too bland to interest young readers (May 531).

MLA and APA have different conventions for constructing signal phrases. In MLA, the language you use in a signal phrase can be neutral—like *X says* or *Y thinks* or *according to Z*. Or it can suggest something about the **STANCE**—the source's or your own. The example above referring to the textbook author uses the verb *argues*, suggesting that what she says is open to dispute (or that the writer believes it is). How would it change your understanding if the signal verb were *observes* or *suggests*?

66–68 ◼

In addition to the names of sources' authors, signal phrases often give readers information about institutional affiliations and positions authors have, their academic or professional specialties, and any other information that lets readers judge the credibility of the sources. You should craft each signal phrase you use so as to highlight the credentials of the author. Here are some examples:

> A study done by Anthony M. Armocida, professor of psychology at Duke University, showed that . . .

The signal phrase identifies the source's author, his professional position, and his university affiliation, emphasizing his title.

> Science writer Isaac McDougal argues that . . .

This phrase acknowledges that the source's author may not have scholarly credentials but is a published writer; it's a useful construction if the source doesn't provide much information about the writer.

Writing in *Psychology Today,* Amanda Chao-Fitz notes that . . .

This is the sort of signal phrase you use if you have no information on the author; you establish credibility on the basis of the publication in which the source appears.

If you're writing using APA style, signal phrases are typically briefer, giving only the author's last name and the date of publication:

According to Benzinger (2010), . . .

Quartucci (2011) observed that . . .

SOME COMMON SIGNAL VERBS

acknowledges	claims	disagrees	observes
admits	comments	disputes	points out
advises	concludes	emphasizes	reasons
agrees	concurs	grants	rejects
argues	confirms	illustrates	reports
asserts	contends	implies	responds
believes	declares	insists	suggests
charges	denies	notes	thinks

Verb tenses. MLA and APA also have different conventions regarding the tenses of verbs in signal phrases. MLA requires present-tense verbs (*writes, asserts, notes*) in signal phrases to introduce a work you are quoting, paraphrasing, or summarizing.

In *Poor Richard's Almanack,* Benjamin Franklin <u>notes</u>, "He that cannot obey, cannot command" (739).

If, however, you are referring to the act of writing or saying something rather than simply quoting someone's words, you might not use the present tense. The writer of the following sentence focuses on the year in which the source was written—therefore, the verb is necessarily in the past tense:

Back in 1941, Kenneth Burke <u>wrote</u> that "the ethical values of work are in its application of the competitive equipment to cooperative ends" (316).

If you are following APA style, use the past tense or present-perfect tense to introduce sources composed in the past.

Dowdall, Crawford, and Wechsler (1998) <u>observed</u> that women attending women's colleges are less likely to engage in binge drinking than are women who attend coeducational colleges (p. 713).

APA requires the present tense, however, to discuss the results of an experiment or to explain conclusions that are generally agreed on.

The findings of this study <u>suggest</u> that excessive drinking has serious consequences for college students and their institutions.

The authors of numerous studies <u>agree</u> that smoking and drinking among adolescents are associated with lower academic achievement.

IF YOU NEED MORE HELP

See Chapter 52 for help **ACKNOWLEDGING SOURCES** and giving credit to the sources you use. See also the **SAMPLE RESEARCH PAPERS** to see how sources are cited in MLA and APA styles. And see Chapter 3 if you're writing a **SUMMARY/ RESPONSE** essay.

539–43 ●
MLA 587–96 ●
APA 626–36
33–44 ✳

Acknowledging Sources, **52**
Avoiding Plagiarism

Whenever you do research-based writing, you find yourself entering a conversation—reading what many others have had to say about your topic, figuring out what you yourself think, and then putting what you think in writing—"putting in your oar," as the rhetorician Kenneth Burke once wrote. As a writer, you need to *acknowledge* any words and ideas that come from others—to give credit where credit is due, to recognize the various authorities and many perspectives you have considered, to show readers where they can find your sources, and to situate your own arguments in the ongoing conversation. Using other people's words and ideas without acknowledgment is *plagiarism,* a serious academic and ethical offense. This chapter will show you how to acknowledge the materials you use and avoid plagiarism.

Acknowledging Sources

When you insert in your text information that you've obtained from others, your reader needs to know where your source's words or ideas begin and end. Therefore, you should usually introduce a source by naming the author in a **SIGNAL PHRASE** and then provide brief **DOCUMENTATION** of the specific material from the source in a parenthetical reference following the material. (Sometimes you can put the author's name in the parenthetical reference as well.) You need only brief documentation of the source here, since your readers will find full bibliographic information about it in your list of **WORKS CITED** or **REFERENCES**.

535–38

MLA 551–57

APA 600–604

MLA 558–86

APA 605–23

539

Sources that need acknowledgment. You almost always need to acknowledge any information that you get from a specific source. Material you should acknowledge includes the following:

- *Direct quotations.* Unless they are well known (see p. 542 for some examples), any quotations from another source must be enclosed in quotation marks, cited with brief bibliographic information in parentheses, and usually introduced with a signal phrase that tells who wrote or said it and provides necessary contextual information, as in the following sentence:

    > In a dissenting opinion on the issue of racial preferences in college admissions, Supreme Court justice Ruth Bader Ginsburg argues, "The stain of generations of racial oppression is still visible in our society, and the determination to hasten its removal remains vital" (*Gratz v. Bollinger*).

- *Arguable statements and information that may not be common knowledge.* If you state something about which there is disagreement or for which arguments can be made, cite the source of your statement. If in doubt about whether you need to give the source of an assertion, provide it. As part of an essay on "fake news" programs, for example, you might make the following assertion:

    > The satire of *The Daily Show* complements the conservative bias of FOX News, since both have abandoned the stance of objectivity maintained by mainstream news sources, contends Michael Hoyt, executive editor of the *Columbia Journalism Review* (43).

Others might argue with the contention that the FOX News Channel offers biased reports of the news, so the source of this assertion needs to be acknowledged. In the same essay, you might present information that should be cited because it's not widely known, as in this example:

> According to a report by the Pew Research Center, 12 percent of Americans under thirty got information about the 2012 presidential campaign primarily from "fake news" and comedy shows like *The Daily Show* and *Saturday Night Live* (2).

academic literacies

rhetorical situations

genres

fields

processes

strategies

research MLA / APA

media / design

- *The opinions and assertions of others.* When you present the ideas, opinions, and assertions of others, cite the source. You may have rewritten the concept in your own words, but the ideas were generated by someone else and must be acknowledged, as they are here:

  > David Boonin, writing in the *Journal of Social Philosophy*, asserts that, logically, laws banning marriage between people of different races are not discriminatory since everyone of each race is affected equally by them. Laws banning same-sex unions are discriminatory, however, since they apply only to people with a certain sexual orientation (256).

- *Any information that you didn't generate yourself.* If you did not do the research or compile the data yourself, cite your source. This goes for interviews, statistics, graphs, charts, visuals, photographs—anything you use that you did not create. If you create a chart using data from another source, you need to cite that source.

- *Collaboration with and help from others.* In many of your courses and in work situations, you'll be called on to work with others. You may get help with your writing at your school's writing center or from fellow students in your writing courses. Acknowledging such collaboration or assistance, in a brief informational note, is a way of giving credit—and saying thank you. See guidelines for writing notes in the **MLA** and **APA** sections of this book.

MLA 557–58
APA 605

Sources that don't need acknowledgment. Widely available information and common knowledge do not require acknowledgment. What constitutes common knowledge may not be clear, however. When in doubt, provide a citation, or ask your instructor whether the information needs to be cited. You generally do not need to cite the following:

- *Information that most readers are likely to know.* You don't need to acknowledge information that is widely known or commonly accepted as fact. For example, in a literary analysis, you wouldn't cite a source saying that Harriet Beecher Stowe wrote *Uncle Tom's Cabin*; you can assume your readers already know that. On the other hand, you should cite the source from which you got the information that the book was first published in installments in a magazine and then, with revisions, in book form, because that information isn't common knowledge. As you do research in areas you're not familiar with, be aware that what constitutes common knowledge isn't always clear; the history of the novel's publication would be known to Stowe scholars and would likely need no acknowledgment in an essay written for them. In this case, too, if you aren't sure whether to acknowledge information, do so.

- *Information and documents that are widely available.* If a piece of information appears in several sources or reference works or if a document has been published widely, you needn't cite a source for it. For example, the date when astronauts Neil Armstrong and Buzz Aldrin landed a spacecraft on the moon can be found in any number of reference works. Similarly, the Declaration of Independence and the Gettysburg Address are reprinted in thousands of sources, so the ones where you found them need no citation.

- *Well-known quotations.* These include such famous quotations as Lady Macbeth's "Out, damned spot!" and John F. Kennedy's "Ask not what your country can do for you; ask what you can do for your country." Be sure, however, that the quotation is correct. Winston Churchill is said to have told a class of schoolchildren, "Never, ever, ever, ever, ever, ever, ever give up. Never give up. Never give up. Never give up." His actual words, however, are much different and begin "Never give in."

- *Material that you created or gathered yourself.* You need not cite photographs that you took, graphs that you composed based on your own findings, or data from an experiment or survey that you conducted— though you should make sure readers know that the work is yours.

A good rule of thumb: *when in doubt, cite your source.* You're unlikely to be criticized for citing too much—but you may invite charges of plagiarism by citing too little.

Avoiding Plagiarism

When you use the words or ideas of others, you need to acknowledge who and where the material came from; if you don't credit those sources, you are guilty of plagiarism. Plagiarism is often committed unintentionally—as when a writer paraphrases someone else's ideas in language that is too close to the original. It is essential, therefore, to know what constitutes plagiarism: (1) using another writer's words or ideas without acknowledging the source, (2) using another writer's exact words without quotation marks, and (3) paraphrasing or summarizing someone else's ideas using language or sentence structures that are too close to theirs.

To avoid plagiarizing, take careful **NOTES** as you do your research, clearly labeling as quotations any words you quote directly and being careful to use your own phrasing and sentence structures in paraphrases and summaries. Be sure you know what source material you must **DOCUMENT**, and give credit to your sources, both in the text and in a list of **REFERENCES** or **WORKS CITED**.

526–28

544–47
APA 605–23
MLA 558–86

Be aware that it's easy to plagiarize inadvertently when you're working with online sources, such as full-text articles, that you've downloaded or cut and pasted into your notes. Keep careful track of these materials, since saving copies of your sources is so easy. Later, be sure to check your draft against the original sources to make sure your quotations are accurately worded—and take care, too, to include quotation marks and document the source correctly. Copying online material right into a document you are writing and forgetting to put quotation marks around it or to document it (or both) is all too easy to do. You must acknowledge information you find on the web just as you must acknowledge all other source materials.

And you must recognize that plagiarism has consequences. Scholars' work will be discredited if it too closely resembles another's. Journalists found to have plagiarized lose their jobs, and students routinely fail courses or are dismissed from their school when they are caught cheating—all too often by submitting as their own essays that they have purchased from online "research" sites. If you're having trouble completing an assignment, seek assistance. Talk with your instructor, or if your school has a writing center, go there for advice on all aspects of your writing, including acknowledging sources and avoiding plagiarism.

53 Documentation

In everyday life, we are generally aware of our sources: "I read it on Megan McArdle's blog." "Amber told me it's your birthday." "If you don't believe me, ask Mom." Saying how we know what we know and where we got our information is part of establishing our credibility and persuading others to take what we say seriously.

The goal of a research project is to study a topic, combining what we learn from sources with our own thinking and then composing a written text. When we write up the results of a research project, we cite the sources we use, usually by quoting, paraphrasing, or summarizing, and we acknowledge those sources, telling readers where the ideas came from. The information we give about sources is called documentation, and we provide it not only to establish our credibility as researchers and writers but also so that our readers, if they wish to, can find the sources themselves.

Understanding Documentation Styles

The Norton Field Guide covers the documentation styles of the Modern Language Association (MLA) and the American Psychological Association (APA). MLA style is used chiefly in the humanities; APA is used in the social sciences, sciences, education, and nursing. Both are two-part systems, consisting of (1) brief in-text parenthetical documentation for quotations, paraphrases, or summaries and (2) more-detailed documentation in a list of sources at the end of the text. MLA and APA require that the end-of-text documentation provide the following basic information about each source you cite:

- author, editor, or creator of the source
- title of source (and of publication or site where it appears)
- place of publication (for print sources; APA only)
- name of publisher
- date of publication
- retrieval information (for online sources)

MLA and APA are by no means the only documentation styles. Many other publishers and organizations have their own style, among them the University of Chicago Press and the Council of Science Editors. We focus on MLA and APA here because those are styles that college students are often required to use. On the following page are examples of how the two parts—the brief parenthetical documentation in your text and the more detailed information at the end—correspond in each of these systems.

The examples here and throughout this book are color-coded to help you see the crucial parts of each citation: tan for author and editor, yellow for title, and gray for publication information: place of publication, name of publisher, date of publication, page number(s), and so on.

As the examples of in-text documentation show, in either MLA or APA style you should name the author either in a signal phrase or in parentheses following the source information. But there are several differences between the two styles in the details of the documentation. In MLA, the author's full name is used in a signal phrase; in APA, only the last name is used. In APA, the abbreviation *p.* is used with the page number, which is provided only for a direct quotation; in MLA, a page number (if there is one) is always given, but with no abbreviation before it. Finally, in APA the date of publication always appears just after the author's name.

Comparing the MLA and APA styles of listing works cited or references also reveals some differences: MLA includes an author's first name while APA gives only initials; MLA puts the date near the end while APA places it right after the author's name; APA requires the place of publication while MLA usually does not; MLA capitalizes most of the words in a book's title and subtitle while APA capitalizes only the first words and proper nouns and proper adjectives in each.

MLA Style

IN-TEXT DOCUMENTATION

As Lester Faigley puts it, "The world has become a bazaar from which to shop for an individual 'lifestyle'" (12).

As one observer suggests, "The world has become a bazaar from which to shop for an individual 'lifestyle'" (Faigley 12).

WORKS-CITED DOCUMENTATION

Faigley, Lester. *Fragments of Rationality: Postmodernity and the Subject of Composition.* U of Pittsburgh P, 1992.

APA Style

IN-TEXT DOCUMENTATION

As Faigley (1992) suggested, "The world has become a bazaar from which to shop for an individual 'lifestyle'" (p. 12).

As one observer has noted, "The world has become a bazaar from which to shop for an individual 'lifestyle'" (Faigley, 1992, p. 12).

REFERENCE-LIST DOCUMENTATION

Faigley, L. (1992). *Fragments of rationality: Postmodernity and the subject of composition.* Pittsburgh, PA: University of Pittsburgh Press.

author   title   publication

Some of these differences are related to the nature of the academic fields in which the two styles are used. In humanities disciplines, the authorship of a text is emphasized, so both first and last names are included in MLA documentation. Scholarship in those fields may be several years old but still current, so the publication date doesn't appear in the in-text citation. In APA style, as in many documentation styles used in the sciences, education, and engineering, emphasis is placed on the date of publication because in these fields, more recent research is usually preferred over older studies. However, although the elements are arranged differently, both MLA and APA—and other documentation styles as well—require similar information about author, title, and publication.

54 MLA Style

MLA style calls for (1) brief in-text documentation and (2) complete bibliographic information in a list of works cited at the end of your text. The models and examples in this chapter draw on the eighth edition of the *MLA Handbook*, published by the Modern Language Association in 2016. For additional information, visit style.mla.org.

A DIRECTORY TO MLA STYLE

In-Text Documentation   551

Throughout this chapter, you'll find models and examples that are color-coded to help you see how writers include source information in their texts and in their lists of works cited: tan for author, editor, translator, and other contributors; yellow for titles; gray for publication information—date of publication, page number(s) or other location information, and so on.

IN-TEXT DOCUMENTATION

Brief documentation in your text makes clear to your reader what you took from a source and where in the source you found the information.

In your text, you have three options for citing a source: QUOTING, PARAPHRASING, and SUMMARIZING. As you cite each source, you will need to decide whether or not to name the author in a signal phrase—"as Toni Morrison writes"—or in parentheses—"(Morrison 24)."

526–38

The first examples below show basic in-text documentation of a work by one author. Variations on those examples follow. The examples illustrate the MLA style of using quotation marks around titles of short works and italicizing titles of long works.

1. AUTHOR NAMED IN A SIGNAL PHRASE

If you mention the author in a SIGNAL PHRASE, put only the page number(s) in parentheses. Do not write *page* or *p*.

535–38

> McCullough describes John Adams's hands as those of someone used to manual labor (18).

2. AUTHOR NAMED IN PARENTHESES

If you do not mention the author in a signal phrase, put their last name in parentheses along with the page number(s). Do not use punctuation between the name and the page number(s).

> Adams is said to have had "the hands of a man accustomed to pruning his own trees, cutting his own hay, and splitting his own firewood" (McCullough 18).

Whether you use a signal phrase and parentheses or parentheses only, try to put the parenthetical documentation at the end of the sentence or as close as possible to the material you've cited—without awkwardly interrupting the sentence. Notice that in the example above, the parenthetical reference comes after the closing quotation marks but before the period at the end of the sentence.

3. TWO OR MORE WORKS BY THE SAME AUTHOR

If you cite multiple works by one author, include the title of the work you are citing either in the signal phrase or in parentheses. Give the full title if it's brief; otherwise, give a short version.

> Kaplan insists that understanding power in the Near East requires "Western leaders who know when to intervene, and do so without illusions" (*Eastward* 330).

Put a comma between author and title if both are in the parentheses.

> Understanding power in the Near East requires "Western leaders who know when to intervene, and do so without illusions" (Kaplan, *Eastward* 330).

4. AUTHORS WITH THE SAME LAST NAME

Give the author's first and last names in any signal phrase, or add the author's first initial in the parenthetical reference.

author   title   publication

Imaginative applies not only to modern literature but also to writing of all periods, whereas *magical* is often used in writing about Arthurian romances (A. Wilson 25).

5. TWO OR MORE AUTHORS

For a work with two authors, name both, either in a signal phrase or in parentheses.

> Carlson and Ventura's stated goal is to introduce Julio Cortázar, Marjorie Agosín, and other Latin American writers to an audience of English-speaking adolescents (v).

For a work by three or more authors, name the first author followed by *et al.*

> One popular survey of American literature breaks the contents into sixteen thematic groupings (Anderson et al. A19-24).

6. ORGANIZATION OR GOVERNMENT AS AUTHOR

Acknowledge the organization either in a signal phrase or in parentheses. It's acceptable to shorten long names.

> The US government can be direct when it wants to be. For example, it sternly warns, "If you are overpaid, we will recover any payments not due you" (Social Security Administration 12).

7. AUTHOR UNKNOWN

If you don't know the author, use the work's title or a shortened version of the title in the parenthetical reference.

> A powerful editorial in last week's paper asserts that healthy liver donor Mike Hurewitz died because of "frightening" faulty postoperative care ("Every Patient's Nightmare").

8. LITERARY WORKS

When referring to literary works that are available in many different editions, give the page numbers from the edition you are using, followed by
information that will let readers of any edition locate the text you are citing.

NOVELS. Give the page and chapter number, separated by a semicolon.

> In *Pride and Prejudice,* Mrs. Bennet shows no warmth toward Jane and
> Elizabeth when they return from Netherfield (105; ch. 12).

VERSE PLAYS. Give act, scene, and line numbers, separated with periods.

> Macbeth continues the vision theme when he says, "Thou hast no
> speculation in those eyes / Which thou dost glare with" (3.3.96-97).

POEMS. Give the part and the line numbers (separated by periods). If a poem
has only line numbers, use the word *line(s)* only in the first reference.

> Whitman sets up not only opposing adjectives but also opposing nouns
> in "Song of Myself" when he says, "I am of old and young, of the foolish
> as much as the wise, / . . . a child as well as a man" (16.330-32).

> One description of the mere in *Beowulf* is "not a pleasant place" (line
> 1372). Later, it is labeled "the awful place" (1378).

9. WORK IN AN ANTHOLOGY

Name the author(s) of the work, not the editor of the anthology—either
in a signal phrase or in parentheses.

> "It is the teapots that truly shock," according to Cynthia Ozick in her
> essay on teapots as metaphor (70).

> In *In Short: A Collection of Creative Nonfiction,* readers will find both an
> essay on Scottish tea (Hiestand) and a piece on teapots as metaphors (Ozick).

author   title   publication

10. ENCYCLOPEDIA OR DICTIONARY

Acknowledge an entry in an encyclopedia or dictionary by giving the author's name, if available. For an entry without an author, give the entry's title in parentheses. If entries are arranged alphabetically, no page number is needed.

> According to *Funk & Wagnall's New World Encyclopedia*, early in his
> career Kubrick's main source of income came from "hustling chess
> games in Washington Square Park" ("Kubrick, Stanley").

11. LEGAL AND HISTORICAL DOCUMENTS

For legal cases and acts of law, name the case or act in a signal phrase or in parentheses. Italicize the name of a legal case.

> In 2005, the Supreme Court confirmed in *MGM Studios, Inc. v. Grokster,*
> *Ltd.* that peer-to-peer file sharing is copyright infringement.

Do not italicize the titles of laws, acts, or well-known historical documents such as the Declaration of Independence. Give the title and any relevant articles and sections in parentheses. It's fine to use common abbreviations such as *art.* or *sec.* and to abbreviate well-known titles.

> The president is also granted the right to make recess appointments
> (US Const., art. 2, sec. 2).

12. SACRED TEXT

When citing a sacred text such as the Bible or the Qur'an for the first time, give the title of the edition, and in parentheses give the book, chapter, and verse (or their equivalent), separated by periods. MLA recommends abbreviating the names of the books of the Bible in parenthetical references. Later citations from the same edition do not have to repeat its title.

> The wording from *The New English Bible* follows: "In the beginning of
> creation, when God made heaven and earth, the earth was without form
> and void, with darkness over the face of the abyss, and a mighty wind
> that swept over the surface of the waters" (Gen. 1.1-2).

13. MULTIVOLUME WORK

If you cite more than one volume of a multivolume work, each time you cite one of the volumes, give the volume *and* the page number(s) in parentheses, separated by a colon and a space.

> Sandburg concludes with the following sentence about those paying last respects to Lincoln: "All day long and through the night the unbroken line moved, the home town having its farewell" (4: 413).

If your works-cited list includes only a single volume of a multivolume work, give just the page number in parentheses.

14. TWO OR MORE WORKS CITED TOGETHER

If you're citing two or more works closely together, you will sometimes need to provide a parenthetical reference for each one.

> Tanner (7) and Smith (viii) have looked at works from a cultural perspective.

If you include both in the same parentheses, separate the references with a semicolon.

> Critics have looked at both *Pride and Prejudice* and *Frankenstein* from a cultural perspective (Tanner 7; Smith viii).

15. SOURCE QUOTED IN ANOTHER SOURCE

When you are quoting text that you found quoted in another source, use the abbreviation *qtd. in* in the parenthetical reference.

> Charlotte Brontë wrote to G. H. Lewes: "Why do you like Miss Austen so very much? I am puzzled on that point" (qtd. in Tanner 7).

16. WORK WITHOUT PAGE NUMBERS

For works without page numbers, including many online sources, identify the source using the author or other information either in a signal phrase or in parentheses.

author   title   publication

> Studies show that music training helps children to be better at multitask-
> ing later in life ("Hearing the Music").

If the source has chapter, paragraph, or section numbers, use them with the abbreviations *ch., par.,* or *sec.*: ("Hearing the Music," par. 2). Alternatively, you can refer to a heading on a screen to help readers locate text.

> Under the heading "The Impact of the Railroad," Rawls notes that the
> transcontinental railroad was called an iron horse and a greedy octopus.

For an audio or a video recording, give the hours, minutes, and seconds (separated by colons) as shown on the player: (00:05-08:30).

17. AN ENTIRE WORK OR A ONE-PAGE ARTICLE

If you cite an entire work rather than a part of it, or if you cite a single-page article, there's no need to include page numbers.

> Throughout life, John Adams strove to succeed (McCullough).

NOTES

Sometimes you may need to give information that doesn't fit into the text itself—to thank people who helped you, to provide additional details, to refer readers to other sources, or to add comments about sources. Such information can be given in a *footnote* (at the bottom of the page) or an *endnote* (on a separate page with the heading *Notes* just before your works-cited list). Put a superscript number at the appropriate point in your text, signaling to readers to look for the note with the corresponding number. If you have multiple notes, number them consecutively throughout your paper.

TEXT

> This essay will argue that small liberal arts colleges should not recruit
> athletes and, more specifically, that giving student athletes preferential
> treatment undermines the larger educational goals.[1]

NOTE

1. I want to thank all those who have contributed to my thinking on this topic, especially my classmates and my teacher Marian Johnson.

LIST OF WORKS CITED

A works-cited list provides full bibliographic information for every source cited in your text. See page 587 for guidelines on formatting this list and pages 595–96 for a sample works-cited list.

Core Elements

The new MLA style provides a list of "core elements" for documenting sources, advising writers to list as many of them as possible in the order that MLA specifies. We've used these general principles to provide templates and examples for documenting fifty-three kinds of sources college writers most often need to cite and the following general guidelines for how to treat each of the core elements.

AUTHORS AND OTHER CONTRIBUTORS

- If there is one author, list the name last name first: Morrison, Toni.

- If there are two authors, list the first author last name first and the second one first name first: Lunsford, Andrea, and Lisa Ede. Put their names in the order given in the work.

- If there are three or more authors, give the first author's name followed by *et al.*: Rose, Mike, et al.

- Include any middle names or initials: Heath, Shirley Brice; Toklas, Alice B.

- If you're citing an editor, translator, or others who are not authors, specify their role. For works with multiple contributors, put the one whose work you wish to highlight before the title, and list any others you want to mention after the title. For contributors named before the title, put the label after the name: Fincher, David, director. For

author   title   publication

those named after the title, specify their role first: directed by David Fincher.

TITLES

- Include any subtitles and capitalize all the words in titles and subtitles except for articles (*a, an, the*), prepositions (*to, at, from,* and so on), and coordinating conjunctions (*and, but, for, or, nor, yet*)—unless they are the first or last word of a title or subtitle.

- Italicize the titles of books, periodicals, and other long whole works (*Pride and Prejudice, Wired*), even if they are part of a larger work.

- Enclose in quotation marks the titles of short works and sources that are part of larger works: "Letter from Birmingham Jail."

- To document a source that has no title, describe it without italics or quotation marks: Letter to the author, Review of doo wop concert.

PUBLICATION INFORMATION

- Write publishers' names in full, but omit words like *Company* or *Inc.*

- For university presses, use *U* for "University" and *P* for "Press": Princeton UP, U of California P.

DATES

- Whether to give just the year or to include the month and day depends on the source. Give the full date that you find there.

- For books, give the year of publication: 1948. If a book lists more than one date, use the most recent one.

- Periodicals may be published annually, monthly, seasonally, weekly, or daily. Give the full date that you find in the periodical: 2016, Apr. 2016, Spring 2016, 16 Apr. 2016.

- Abbreviate the months except for May, June, and July: Jan., Feb., Mar., Apr., Aug., Sept., Oct., Nov., Dec.

- Because online sources often change or even disappear, provide the date on which you accessed them: Accessed 6 June 2017.

- If an online source includes the time when it was posted or modified, include the time along with the date: 18 Oct. 2014, 9:20 a.m.

LOCATION

- For most print articles and other short works, help readers locate the source by giving a page number or range of pages: p. 24, pp. 24-35. For those that are not on consecutive pages, give the first page number with a plus sign: pp. 24+.

- For online sources, give the URL, omitting *http://* or *https://*. If a source has a permalink, give that.

- For sources found in a database, give the DOI for any that have one. Otherwise, give the URL.

- For physical objects that you find in a museum, archive, or some other place, give the name of the place and its city: Menil Collection, Houston. Omit the city if it's part of the place's name: Boston Public Library.

- For performances or other live presentations, name the venue and its city: Mark Taper Forum, Los Angeles. Omit the city if it's part of the place's name: Berkeley Repertory Theatre.

PUNCTUATION

- Use a period after the author name(s) that start an entry (Morrison, Toni.) and the title of the source you're documenting (*Beloved*.).

- Use a comma between the author's last and first names: Morrison, Toni.

- Sometimes you'll need to provide information about more than one work for a single source—for instance, when you cite an article from a periodical that you access through a database. MLA refers to the periodical and database (or any other entity that holds a source) as "containers." Use commas between elements within each container and put a period at the end of each container. For example:

  Semuels, Alana. "The Future Will Be Quiet." *The Atlantic,* Apr. 2016,
     pp. 19-20. *ProQuest,* search.proquest.com/docview/
     1777443553?accountid+42654. Accessed 5 Apr. 2018.

author   title   publication

The guidelines below should help you document kinds of sources you're likely to use. The first section shows how to acknowledge authors and other contributors and applies to all kinds of sources—print, online, or others. Later sections show how to treat titles, publication information, location, and access information for many specific kinds of sources. In general, provide as much information as possible for each source—enough to tell readers how to find a source if they wish to access it themselves.

Authors and Other Contributors

When you name authors and other contributors in your citations, you are crediting them for their work and letting readers know who's in on the conversation. The following guidelines for citing authors and other contributors apply to all sources you cite: in print, online, or in some other media.

1. ONE AUTHOR

Author's Last Name, First Name. *Title*. Publisher, Date.

Anderson, Curtis. *The Long Tail: Why the Future of Business Is Selling Less of More*. Hyperion, 2006.

2. TWO AUTHORS

1st Author's Last Name, First Name, and 2nd Author's First and Last Names. *Title*. Publisher, Date.

Lunsford, Andrea, and Lisa Ede. *Singular Texts/Plural Authors: Perspectives on Collaborative Writing*. Southern Illinois UP, 1990.

3. THREE OR MORE AUTHORS

1st Author's Last Name, First Name, et al. *Title*. Publisher, Date.

Sebranek, Patrick, et al. *Writers INC: A Guide to Writing, Thinking, and Learning*. Write Source, 1990.

4. TWO OR MORE WORKS BY THE SAME AUTHOR

Give the author's name in the first entry, and then use three hyphens in the author slot for each of the subsequent works, listing them alphabetically by the first important word of each title.

> Author's Last Name, First Name. *Title That Comes First Alphabetically.* Publisher, Date.
>
> - - -. *Title That Comes Next Alphabetically.* Publisher, Date.
>
> Kaplan, Robert D. *The Coming Anarchy: Shattering the Dreams of the Post Cold War.* Random House, 2000.
>
> - - -. *Eastward to Tartary: Travels in the Balkans, the Middle East, and the Caucasus.* Random House, 2000.

5. AUTHOR AND EDITOR OR TRANSLATOR

> Author's Last Name, First Name. *Title.* Role by First and Last Names, Publisher, Date.
>
> Austen, Jane. *Emma.* Edited by Stephen M. Parrish, W. W. Norton, 2000.
>
> Dostoevsky, Fyodor. *Crime and Punishment.* Translated by Richard Pevear and Larissa Volokhonsky, Vintage Books, 1993.

Start with the editor or translator if you are focusing on their contribution rather than the author's.

> Pevear, Richard, and Larissa Volokhonsky, translators. *Crime and Punishment.* By Fyodor Dostoevsky, Vintage Books, 1993.

6. NO AUTHOR OR EDITOR

When there's no known author or editor, start with the title.

> *The Turner Collection in the Clore Gallery.* Tate Publications, 1987.
>
> "Being Invisible Closer to Reality." *The Atlanta Journal-Constitution,* 11 Aug. 2008, p. A3.

author   title   publication

7. ORGANIZATION OR GOVERNMENT AS AUTHOR

> Organization Name. *Title.* Publisher, Date.

> Diagram Group. *The Macmillan Visual Desk Reference.* Macmillan, 1993.

For a government publication, give the name of the government first, followed by the names of any department and agency.

> United States, Department of Health and Human Services, National
> Institute of Mental Health. *Autism Spectrum Disorders.*
> Government Printing Office, 2004.

When the organization is both author and publisher, start with the title and list the organization only as the publisher.

> *Stylebook on Religion 2000: A Reference Guide and Usage Manual.*
> Catholic News Service, 2002.

Articles and Other Short Works

Articles, essays, reviews, and other short works are found in journals, magazines, newspapers, other periodicals, and books—all of which you may find in print, online, or in a database. For most short works, you'll need to provide information about the author, the titles of both the short work and the longer work, any page numbers, and various kinds of publication information, all explained below.

8. ARTICLE IN A JOURNAL

PRINT

> Author's Last Name, First Name. "Title of Article." *Name of Journal,*
> Volume, Issue, Date, Pages.

Documentation Map (MLA)
Article in a Print Journal

Marge Simpson, Blue-Haired Housewife: ◄── Title of article
Defining Domesticity on *The Simpsons*

JESSAMYN NEUHAUS ◄── Author

MORE THAN TWENTY SEASONS AFTER ITS DEBUT AS A SHORT ON *THE Tracy Ullman Show* in 1989, pundits, politicians, scholars, journalists, and critics continue to discuss and debate the meaning and relevance of *The Simpsons* to American society. For academics and educators, the show offers an especially dense pop culture text, inspiring articles and anthologies examining *The Simpsons* in light of American religious life, the representation of homosexuality in cartoons, and the use of pop culture in the classroom, among many other topics (Dennis; Frank; Henry "The Whole World's Gone Gay"; Hobbs; Kristiansen). Philosophers and literary theorists in particular are intrigued by the quintessentially postmodern self-aware form and content of *The Simpsons* and the questions about identity, spectatorship, and consumer culture it raises (Alberti; Bybee and Overbeck; Glynn; Henry "The Triumph of Popular Culture"; Herron; Hull; Irwin et al.; Ott; Parisi).

Simpsons observers frequently note that this TV show begs one of the fundamental questions in cultural studies: can pop culture ever provide a site of individual or collective resistance or must it always ultimately function in the interests of the capitalist dominant ideology? Is *The Simpsons* a brilliant satire of virtually every cherished American myth about public and private life, offering dissatisfied Americans the opportunity to critically reflect on contemporary issues (Turner 435)? Or is it simply another TV show making money for the Fox Network? Is *The Simpsons* an empty, cynical, even nihilistic view of the world, lulling its viewers into laughing hopelessly at the pointless futility of

Volume ──┐ ├── Issue

Name of journal ──► *The Journal of Popular Culture*, Vol. 43, No. 4, 2010 ◄── Year
© 2010, Wiley Periodicals, Inc.

563–71
for more
on citing
articles
MLA style

Neuhaus, Jessamyn. "Marge Simpson, Blue-Haired Housewife: Defining Domesticity on *The Simpsons*." *The Journal of Popular Culture*, vol. 43, no. 4, 2010, pp. 761-81.

Cooney, Brian C. "Considering *Robinson Crusoe*'s 'Liberty of Conscience' in an Age of Terror." *College English,* vol. 69, no. 3, Jan. 2007, pp. 197-215.

ONLINE

Author's Last Name, First Name. "Title of Article." *Name of Journal,* Volume, Issue, Date, Pages (if any), URL. Accessed Day Month Year.

Gleckman, Jason. "Shakespeare as Poet or Playwright? The Player's Speech in *Hamlet.*" *Early Modern Literary Studies,* vol. 11, no. 3, Jan. 2006, purl.oclc.org/emls/11-3/glechaml.htm. Accessed 31 Mar. 2018.

9. ARTICLE IN A MAGAZINE

PRINT

Author's Last Name, First Name. "Title of Article." *Name of Magazine,* Date, Pages.

Neyfakh, Leon. "The Future of Getting Arrested." *The Atlantic,* Jan.-Feb. 2015, pp. 26+.

ONLINE

Author's Last Name, First Name. "Title of Article." *Name of Magazine,* Date on web, Pages (if any), URL. Accessed Day Month Year.

Khazan, Olga. "Forgetting and Remembering Your First Language." *The Atlantic,* 24 July 2014, www.theatlantic.com/international/archive/2014/07/learning-forgetting-and-remembering-your-first-language/374906/. Accessed 2 Apr. 2018.

10. ARTICLE IN A NEWSPAPER

PRINT

Author's Last Name, First Name. "Title of Article." *Name of Newspaper,* Date, Pages.

Saulny, Susan, and Jacques Steinberg. "On College Forms, a Question of Race Can Perplex." *The New York Times,* 14 June 2011, p. A1.

To document a particular edition of a newspaper, list the edition (*late ed., natl. ed.,* and so on) after the date. If a section of the newspaper is numbered, put that detail after the edition information.

Burns, John F., and Miguel Helft. "Under Pressure, YouTube Withdraws Muslim Cleric's Videos." *The New York Times,* 4 Nov. 2010, late ed., sec. 1, p. 13.

ONLINE

Author's Last Name, First Name. "Title of Article." *Name of Newspaper,* Date on web, URL. Accessed Day Month Year.

Banerjee, Neela. "Proposed Religion-Based Program for Federal Inmates Is Canceled." *The New York Times,* 28 Oct. 2006, www.nytimes .com/2006/10/28/us/28prison.html?_r=0. Accessed 4 Apr. 2018.

11. ARTICLE ACCESSED THROUGH A DATABASE

Author's Last Name, First Name. "Title of Article." *Name of Periodical,* Volume, Issue, Date, Pages. *Name of Database,* DOI or URL. Accessed Day Month Year.

Stalter, Sunny. "Subway Ride and Subway System in Hart Crane's 'The Tunnel.'" *Journal of Modern Literature,* vol. 33, no. 2, Jan. 2010, pp. 70-91. *JSTOR,* doi: 10.2979/jml.2010.33.2.70. Accessed 30 Mar. 2018.

author   title   publication

Documentation Map (MLA)
Article in an Online Magazine

URL

Name of magazine

Title of article

Author

Date

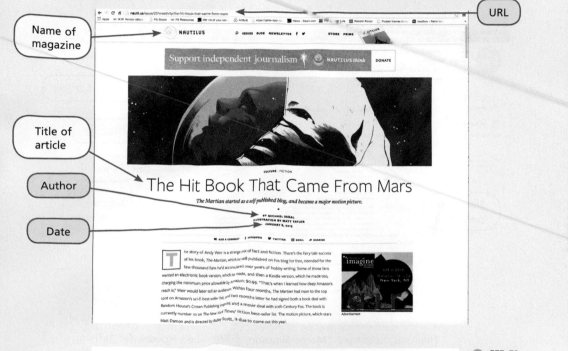

Segal, Michael. "The Hit Book That Came from Mars." *Nautilus*,
8 Jan. 2015, nautil.us/issue/20/creativity/the-hit-book-that
-came-from-mars. Accessed 10 Oct. 2018.

577–79
for more
on citing
websites
MLA style

Documentation Map (MLA)

Journal Article Accessed through a Database

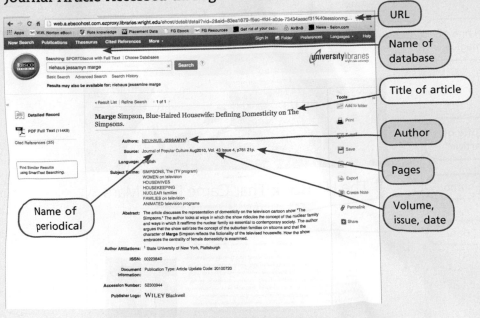

URL

Name of database

Title of article

Author

Pages

Volume, issue, date

Name of periodical

Neuhaus, Jessamyn. "Marge Simpson, Blue-Haired Housewife: Defining Domesticity on *The Simpsons*." *Journal of Popular Culture*, vol. 43, no. 4, Aug. 2010, pp. 761-81. *SPORT Discus with Full Text*, ezproxy .libraries.wright.edu/login?url=http://search.ebscohost.com/login.aspx? direct=true&db=a9h&AN=52300944&site=ehost-live. Accessed 24 Mar. 2018.

12. ENTRY IN A REFERENCE WORK

PRINT

Author's Last Name, First Name (if any). "Title of Entry." *Title of Reference Book,* edited by Editor's First and Last Names (if any), Edition number, Publisher, Date, Pages.

"California." *The New Columbia Encyclopedia*, edited by William H. Harris and Judith S. Levey, 4th ed., Columbia UP, 1975, pp. 423-24.

"Feminism." *Longman Dictionary of American English*, Longman, 1983, p. 252.

If there's no author given, start with the title of the entry.

ONLINE

Document online reference works the same as print ones, adding the URL and access date after the date of publication.

"Baseball." *The Columbia Electronic Encyclopedia,* edited by Paul Lagassé, 6th ed., Columbia UP, 2012. www.infoplease.com/encyclopedia. Accessed 25 May 2018.

13. EDITORIAL

PRINT

"Title of Editorial." Editorial. *Name of Periodical,* Date, Page.

"Gas, Cigarettes Are Safe to Tax." Editorial. *The Lakeville Journal,* 17 Feb. 2005, p. A10.

ONLINE

"Title of Editorial." Editorial. *Name of Periodical,* Date on web, URL. Accessed Day Month Year.

"Keep the Drinking Age at 21." Editorial. *Chicago Tribune*, 28 Aug. 2008, articles.chicagotribune.com/2008-08-26/news/0808250487 _1_binge-drinking-drinking-age-alcohol-related-crashes. Accessed 26 Apr. 2015.

14. LETTER TO THE EDITOR

Author's Last Name, First Name. "Title of Letter (if any)." Letter. *Name of Periodical,* Date on web, URL. Accessed Day Month Year.

Pinker, Steven. "Language Arts." Letter. *The New Yorker,* 4 June 2012, www.newyorker.com/magazine/2012/06/04/language-arts-2. Accessed 6 Apr. 2018.

15. REVIEW

PRINT

Reviewer's Last Name, First Name. "Title of Review." Review of *Title,* by Author's First and Last Names. *Name of Periodical,* Date, Pages.

Frank, Jeffrey. "Body Count." Review of *The Exception,* by Christian Jungersen. *The New Yorker,* 30 July 2007, pp. 86-87.

If a review has no author or title, start with what's being reviewed:

Review of *Ways to Disappear,* by Idra Novey. *The New Yorker,* 28 Mar. 2016, p. 79.

author   title   publication

ONLINE

Reviewer's Last Name, First Name. "Title of Review." Review of *Title*,
   by Author's First and Last Name. *Name of Periodical*, Date, URL.
   Accessed Day Month Year.

Donadio, Rachel. "Italy's Great, Mysterious Storyteller." Review
   of *My Brilliant Friend*, by Elena Ferrante. *The New York Review
   of Books*, 18 Dec. 2014, www.nybooks.com/articles/2014
   /12/18/italys-great-mysterious-storyteller. Accessed 28 Sept. 2017.

16. COMMENT ON AN ONLINE ARTICLE

Commenter. Comment on "Title of Article." *Name of Periodical*,
   Date posted, Time posted, URL. Accessed Day Month Year.

Nick. Comment on "The Case for Reparations." *The Atlantic*, 22 May
   2014, 3:04 p.m., www.theatlantic.com/business/archive/2014/05
   /how-to-comment-on-reparations/371422/#article-comments.
   Accessed 8 May 2018.

Books and Parts of Books

For most books, you'll need to provide information about the author, the
title, the publisher, and the year of publication. If you found the book
inside a larger volume, a database, or some other work, be sure to specify
that as well.

Documentation Map (MLA)
Print Book

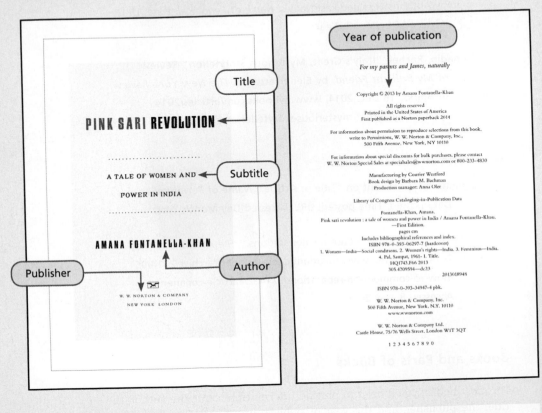

571–77
for more
on citing
books
MLA style

Fontanella-Khan, Amana. *Pink Sari Revolution: A Tale of Women and Power in India.* W. W. Norton, 2013.

17. BASIC ENTRIES FOR A BOOK

PRINT

Author's Last Name, First Name. *Title.* Publisher, Year of publication.

Watson, Brad. *Miss Jane.* W. W. Norton, 2016.

EBOOK

Document an ebook as you would a print book, but add information about the ebook—or the type of ebook if you know it.

Watson, Brad. *Miss Jane.* Ebook, W. W. Norton, 2016.

Watson, Brad. *Miss Jane.* Kindle ed., W. W. Norton, 2016.

IN A DATABASE

Author's Last Name, First Name. *Title.* Publisher, Year of publication. *Name of Database,* DOI or URL. Accessed Day Month Year.

Anderson, Sherwood. *Winesburg, Ohio.* B. W. Huebsch, 1919. *Bartleby.com,* www.bartleby.com/156/. Accessed 8 Apr. 2018.

18. ANTHOLOGY

Last Name, First Name, editor. *Title.* Publisher, Year of publication.

Hall, Donald, editor. *The Oxford Book of Children's Verse in America.* Oxford UP, 1985.

19. WORK(S) IN AN ANTHOLOGY

Author's Last Name, First Name. "Title of Work." *Title of Anthology,* edited by First and Last Names, Publisher, Year of publication, Pages.

Achebe, Chinua. "Uncle Ben's Choice." *The Seagull Reader: Literature,* edited by Joseph Kelly, W. W. Norton, 2005, pp. 23-27.

TWO OR MORE WORKS FROM ONE ANTHOLOGY

Prepare an entry for each selection by author and title, followed by the anthology editors' last names and the pages of the selection. Then include an entry for the anthology itself (see no. 18).

> Author's Last Name, First Name. "Title of Work." Anthology Editors' Last Names, Pages.

> Hiestand, Emily. "Afternoon Tea." Kitchen and Jones, pp. 65-67.

> Ozick, Cynthia. "The Shock of Teapots." Kitchen and Jones, pp. 68-71.

20. MULTIVOLUME WORK

ALL VOLUMES

> Author's Last Name, First Name. *Title of Work.* Publisher, Year(s) of publication. Number of vols.

> Churchill, Winston. *The Second World War.* Houghton Mifflin, 1948-53. 6 vols.

SINGLE VOLUME

> Author's Last Name, First Name. *Title of Work.* Vol. number, Publisher, Year of publication. Number of vols.

> Sandburg, Carl. *Abraham Lincoln: The War Years.* Vol. 2, Harcourt, Brace and World, 1939. 4 vols.

21. BOOK IN A SERIES

> Author's Last Name, First Name. *Title of Book.* Edited by First and Last Names, Publisher, Year of publication. Series Title.

> Walker, Alice. *Everyday Use.* Edited by Barbara T. Christian, Rutgers UP, 1994. Women Writers: Texts and Contexts.

author   title   publication

22. GRAPHIC NARRATIVE

> Author's Last Name, First Name. *Title*. Publisher, Year of publication.

> Bechdel, Alison. *Fun Home: A Family Tragicomedy*. Houghton Mifflin, 2006.

If the work has both an author and an illustrator, start with the one whose work is more relevant to your research, and label the role of anyone who's not an author.

> Pekar, Harvey. *Bob & Harv's Comics*. Illustrated by R. Crumb, Running Press, 1996.

> Crumb, R., illustrator. *Bob & Harv's Comics*. By Harvey Pekar, Running Press, 1996.

23. SACRED TEXT

If you cite a specific edition of a religious text, you need to include it in your works-cited list.

> *The New English Bible with the Apocrypha*. Oxford UP, 1971.

> *The Torah: A Modern Commentary*. Edited by W. Gunther Plaut, Union of American Hebrew Congregations, 1981.

24. EDITION OTHER THAN THE FIRST

> Author's Last Name, First Name. *Title*. Name or number of edition, Publisher, Year of publication.

> Fowler, H. W. *A Dictionary of Modern English*. 2nd ed., Oxford UP, 1965.

25. REPUBLISHED WORK

> Author's Last Name, First Name. *Title*. Year of original publication. Current publisher, Year of republication.

> Bierce, Ambrose. *Civil War Stories*. 1909. Dover, 1994.

26. FOREWORD, INTRODUCTION, PREFACE, OR AFTERWORD

Part Author's Last Name, First Name. Name of Part. *Title of Book,*
by Author's First and Last Names, Publisher, Year of publication,
Pages.

Tanner, Tony. Introduction. *Pride and Prejudice,* by Jane Austen, Penguin,
1972, pp. 7-46.

27. PUBLISHED LETTER

Letter Writer's Last Name, First Name. Letter to First and Last
Names. Day Month Year. *Title of Book,* edited by First and Last
Names, Publisher, Year of publication, Pages.

White, E. B. Letter to Carol Angell. 28 May 1970. *Letters of E. B. White,*
edited by Dorothy Lobarno Guth, Harper and Row, 1976, p. 600.

28. PAPER AT A CONFERENCE

PAPER PUBLISHED IN CONFERENCE PROCEEDINGS

Author's Last Name, First Name. "Title of Paper." *Title of Published
Conference Proceedings,* edited by First and Last Names, Publisher,
Year of publication, Pages.

Flower, Linda. "Literate Action." *Composition in the Twenty-first Century:
Crisis and Change,* edited by Lynn Z. Bloom et al., Southern Illinois
UP, 1996, pp. 249-60.

PAPER HEARD AT A CONFERENCE

Author's Last Name, First Name. "Title of Paper." *Title of Conference,*
Day Month Year, Location, City.

Hern, Katie. "Inside an Accelerated Reading and Writing Classroom."
Conference on Acceleration in Developmental Education, 15 June
2016, Sheraton Inner Harbor Hotel, Baltimore.

author   title   publication

29. DISSERTATION

> Author's Last Name, First Name. *Title*. Diss. Institution, Year, Publisher,
>   Year of publication.

> Goggin, Peter N. *A New Literacy Map of Research and Scholarship in
>   Computers and Writing*. Diss. Indiana U of Pennsylvania, 2000,
>   University Microfilms International, 2001.

For an unpublished dissertation, put the title in quotation marks, and end with the institution and the year.

> Kim, Loel. "Students Respond to Teacher Comments: A Comparison of
>   Online Written and Voice Modalities." Diss. Carnegie Mellon U, 1998.

Websites

Many sources are available in multiple media—for example, a print periodical that is also on the web and contained in digital databases—but some are published only on websites. This section covers the latter.

30. ENTIRE WEBSITE

> Last Name, First Name, role. *Title of Site*. Publisher, Date, URL.
>   Accessed Day Month Year.

> Zalta, Edward N., principal editor. *Stanford Encyclopedia of Philosophy*.
>   Metaphysics Research Lab, Center for the Study of Language, Stanford
>   U, 1995-2015, plato.stanford.edu/index.html. Accessed 21 Apr. 2018.

PERSONAL WEBSITE

> Author's Last Name, First Name. *Title of Site*. Date, URL. Accessed Day
>   Month Year.

> Heath, Shirley Brice. *Shirley Brice Heath*. 2015, shirleybriceheath.net.
>   Accessed 6 June 2018.

Documentation Map (MLA)

Work on a Website

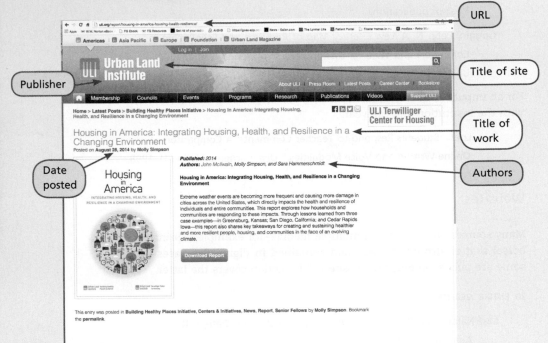

URL

Title of site

Publisher

Title of work

Date posted

Authors

McIlwain, John, et al. "Housing in America: Integrating Housing, Health, and Resilience in a Changing Environment." *Urban Land Institute,* Urban Land Institute, 28 Aug. 2014, uli.org/report/housing-in -america-housing-health-resilience. Accessed 16 Nov. 2017.

31. WORK ON A WEBSITE

Author's Last Name, First Name (if any). "Title of Work." *Title of Site,*
Publisher, Date, URL. Accessed Day Month Year.

"Global Minnesota: Immigrants Past and Present." *Immigration History*
Research Center, U of Minnesota, 2015, cla.umn.edu.ihrc. Accessed
25 May 2018.

32. BLOG ENTRY

Author's Last Name, First Name. "Title of Blog Entry." *Title of*
Blog, Date, URL. Accessed Day Month Year.

Hollmichel, Stefanie. "Bringing Up the Bodies." *So Many Books,* 10 Feb.
2014, somanybooksblog.com/2014/02/10/bring-up-the-bodies/.
Accessed 12 Feb. 2018.

Document a whole blog as you would an entire website (no. 30) and a
comment on a blog as you would a comment on an online article (no. 16).

33. WIKI

"Title of Entry." *Title of Wiki,* Publisher, Date, URL. Accessed Day Month
Year.

"Pi." *Wikipedia,* Wikimedia Foundation, 28 Aug. 2013, en.wikipedia.org/
wiki/Pi. Accessed 25 Oct. 2018.

Personal Communication and Social Media

34. PERSONAL LETTER

Sender's Last Name, First Name. Letter to the author. Day Month Year.

Quindlen, Anna. Letter to the author. 11 Apr. 2017.

35. EMAIL

Sender's Last Name, First Name. "Subject Line." Received by First and
Last Names, Day Month Year.

Smith, William. "Teaching Grammar—Some Thoughts." Received by
Richard Bullock, 19 Nov. 2018.

36. TEXT MESSAGE

Sender's Last Name, First Name. Text message. Received by First and Last
Names, Day Month Year.

Douglass, Joanne. Text message. Received by Kim Yi, 4 June 2017.

37. POST TO AN ONLINE FORUM

Author. "Subject line" or "Full text of short untitled post." *Name of
Forum,* Day Month Year, URL.

@somekiryu. "What's the hardest part about writing for you?" *Reddit,*
22 Apr. 2016, redd.it/4fyni0.

38. POST TO *TWITTER, FACEBOOK,* OR OTHER SOCIAL MEDIA

Author. "Full text of short untitled post" or "Title" or Descriptive label.
Name of Site, Day Month Year, Time, URL.

@POTUS (Barack Obama). "I'm proud of the @NBA for taking a stand
against gun violence. Sympathy for victims isn't enough—change
requires all of us speaking up." *Twitter,* 23 Dec. 2015, 1:21 p.m.,
twitter.com/POTUS/status/679773729749078016.

Black Lives Matter. "Rise and Grind! Did you sign this petition yet?
We now have a sign on for ORGANIZATIONS to lend their
support." *Facebook,* 23 Oct. 2015, 11:30 a.m., www.facebook.com
/BlackLivesMatter/photos/a.294807204023865.1073741829.
180212755483311/504711973033386/?type=3&theater.

@quarterlifepoetry. Illustrated poem about girl at Target. *Instagram,*
22 Jan. 2015, www.instagram.com/p/yLO6fSurRH/.

author   title   publication

Audio, Visual, and Other Sources

39. ADVERTISEMENT

PRINT

Name of Product or Company. Advertisement or Description of ad.
   Title of Periodical Date, Page.

Cal Alumni Association. Sports Merchandise ad. *California*, Spring 2018, p. 3.

AUDIO OR VIDEO

Name of Product or Company. Advertisement or Description of ad.
   Date. *Name of Host Site*, URL. Accessed Day Month Year.

Chrysler. Super Bowl commercial. 6 Feb. 2011. *YouTube*,
   www.youtube.com/watch?v=SKLZ254Y_jtc. Accessed 1 May 2018.

40. ART

ORIGINAL

Artist's Last Name, First Name. *Title of Art*. Year created, Site, City.

Van Gogh, Vincent. *The Potato Eaters*. 1885, Van Gogh Museum, Amsterdam.

REPRODUCTION

Artist's Last Name, First Name. *Title of Art*. Year created. *Title of Book*,
   by First and Last Names, Publisher, Year of publication, Page.

Van Gogh, Vincent. *The Potato Eaters*. 1885. *History of Art: A Survey of
   the Major Visual Arts from the Dawn of History to the Present Day*,
   by H. W. Janson, Prentice-Hall/Harry N. Abrams, 1969, p. 508.

ONLINE

Artist's Last Name, First Name. *Title of Art*. Year created. *Name of Site*,
   URL. Accessed Day Month Year.

Warhol, Andy. *Self-portrait*. 1979. *J. Paul Getty Museum*, www.getty
   .edu/art/collection/objects/106971/andy-warhol-self-portrait-
   american-1979/. Accessed 20 Jan. 2018.

41. CARTOON

PRINT

Author's Last Name, First Name. "Title of Cartoon." *Title of Periodical,*
Date, Page.

Chast, Roz. "The Three Wise Men of Thanksgiving." *The New Yorker,*
1 Dec. 2003, p. 174.

ONLINE

Author's Last Name, First Name. "Title of Cartoon." *Title of Site,*
Date, URL. Accessed Day Month Year.

Munroe, Randall. "Up Goer Five." *xkcd,* 12 Nov. 2012, xkcd.com/1133/.
Accessed 22 Apr. 2018.

42. SUPREME COURT CASE

First Plaintiff v. First Defendant. *United States Reports* citation. Name of
Court, Year of decision, URL. Accessed Day Month Year.

District of Columbia v. Heller. 554 US 570. Supreme Court of the US, 2008,
www.lawcornell.edu/supct/html/07-290.ZS.html. Accessed 3 June 2018.

43. FILM

Name individuals based on the focus of your project—the director, the
screenwriter, the cinematographer, or someone else.

Title of Film. Role by First and Last Names, Production Studio, Date.

Breakfast at Tiffany's. Directed by Blake Edwards, Paramount, 1961.

STREAMING

Title of Film. Role by First and Last Names, Production Studio,
Date. *Streaming Service,* URL. Accessed Day Month Year.

Interstellar. Directed by Christopher Nolan, Paramount, 2014. *Amazon
Prime Video,* www.amazon.com/Interstellar-Matthew-McConaughey/
dp/B00TU9UFTS. Accessed 2 May 2018.

44. INTERVIEW

If the interview has a title, put it in quotation marks following the subject's name.

BROADCAST

Subject's Last Name, First Name. Interview or "Title of Interview."
  Title of Program, Network, Day Month Year.

Gates, Henry Louis, Jr. Interview. *Fresh Air,* NPR, 9 Apr. 2002.

PUBLISHED

Subject's Last Name, First Name. Interview or "Title of Interview." *Title
  of Publication,* Date, Pages.

Stone, Oliver. Interview. *Esquire,* Nov. 2004, pp. 170-71.

PERSONAL

Subject's Last Name, First Name. Personal interview. Day Month Year.

Roddick, Andy. Personal interview. 17 Aug. 2013.

45. MAP

"Title of Map." Publisher, URL. Accessed Day Month Year.

"National Highway System." US Department of Transportation Federal
  Highway Administration, www.fhwa.dot.gov/planning/images/nhs.pdf.
  Accessed 10 May 2018.

46. MUSICAL SCORE

Composer's Last Name, First Name. *Title of Composition.* Year of
  composition. Publisher, Year of publication.

Stravinsky, Igor. *Petrushka.* 1911. W. W. Norton, 1967.

47. ONLINE VIDEO

Author's Last Name, First Name. *Title. Name of Host Site,* Date, URL.
  Accessed Day Month Year.

Westbrook, Adam. *Cause/Effect: The Unexpected Origins of Terrible Things.* *Vimeo*, 9 Sept. 2014, vimeo.com/105681474. Accessed 20 Dec. 2017.

48. ORAL PRESENTATION

Presenter's Last Name, First Name. "Title of Presentation." Sponsoring Institution, Date, Location.

Cassin, Michael. "Nature in the Raw—The Art of Landscape Painting." Berkshire Institute for Lifelong Learning, 24 Mar. 2005, Clark Art Institute, Williamstown.

49. PODCAST

If you accessed a podcast online, give the URL and date of access; if you accessed it through a service such as *iTunes* or *Spotify*, indicate that instead.

Last Name, First Name, role. "Title of Episode." *Title of Program,* season, episode, Sponsor, Date, URL. Accessed Day Month Year.

Koenig, Sarah, host. "DUSTWUN." *Serial,* season 2, episode 1, WBEZ, 10 Dec. 2015, serialpodcast.org/season-two/1/dustwun. Accessed 23 Apr. 2018.

Foss, Gilad, writer and performer. "Aquaman's Brother-in-Law." *Superhero Temp Agency,* season 1, episode 1, 16 Apr. 2015. *iTunes.*

50. RADIO PROGRAM

Last Name, First Name, role. "Title of Episode." *Title of Program,* Station, Day Month Year of broadcast, URL. Accessed Day Month Year.

Glass, Ira, host. "In Defense of Ignorance." *This American Life*, WBEZ, 22 Apr. 2016, thisamericanlife.org/radio-archives/episode/585 /in-defense-of-ignorance. Accessed 2 May 2018.

51. SOUND RECORDING

ONLINE

Last Name, First Name. "Title of Work." *Title of Album,* Distributor, Date. *Name of Audio Service.*

Simone, Nina. "To Be Young, Gifted and Black." *Black Gold*, RCA Records,
    1969. *Spotify*.

CD

Last Name, First Name. "Title of Work." *Title of Album,* Distributor, Date.

Brown, Greg. "Canned Goods." *The Live One,* Red House, 1995.

52. TV SHOW

ORIGINAL BROADCAST

"Title of Episode." *Title of Show,* role by First and Last Names,
    season, episode, Network, Day Month Year.

"Stormborn." *Game of Thrones,* written by Bryan Cogman, season 7,
    episode 2, HBO, 23 July 2017.

DVD

"Title of Episode." Broadcast Year. *Title of DVD,* role by First and Last
    Names, season, episode, Production Studio, Release Year, disc number.

"The Pants Tent." 2003. *Curb Your Enthusiasm: Season One*, performance
    by Larry David, season 1, episode 1, HBO Video, 2006, disc 1.

ONLINE

"Title of Episode." *Title of Show,* season, episode, role by First and Last
    Names (if any), Production Studio, Day Month Year. *Name of Host
    Site,* URL. Accessed Day Month Year.

"Shadows in the Glass." *Marvel's Daredevil*, season 1, episode 8, Netflix,
    10 Apr. 2015. *Netflix*, www.netflix.com/watch/80018198?trackId
    =13752289&tctx=0%2C7%2Cbcfd6259-6e64-4d51-95ab
    -2a9f747eabf0-158552415. Accessed 3 Nov. 2018.

53. VIDEO GAME

Last Name, First Name, role. *Title of Game.* Distributor, Date of release.
    Gaming System or Platform.

Metzen, Chris, and James Waugh, writers. *StarCraft II: Legacy of the Void.* Blizzard Entertainment, 2015. OS X.

FORMATTING A RESEARCH PAPER

Name, course, title.   MLA does not require a separate title page. In the upper left-hand corner of your first page, include your name, your professor's name, the name of the course, and the date. Center the title of your paper on the line after the date; capitalize it as you would a book title.

Page numbers.   In the upper right-hand corner of each page, one-half inch below the top of the page, include your last name and the page number. Number pages consecutively throughout your paper.

Font, spacing, margins, and indents.   Choose a font that is easy to read (such as Times New Roman) and that provides a clear contrast between regular and italic text. Double-space the entire paper, including your works-cited list. Set one-inch margins at the top, bottom, and sides of your text; do not justify your text. The first line of each paragraph should be indented one-half inch from the left margin.

Long quotations.   When quoting more than three lines of poetry, more than four lines of prose, or dialogue between characters in a drama, set off the quotation from the rest of your text, indenting it one-half inch (or five spaces) from the left margin. Do not use quotation marks, and put any parenthetical documentation *after* the final punctuation.

> In *Eastward to Tartary*, Kaplan captures ancient and contemporary Antioch for us:
>
>> At the height of its glory in the Roman-Byzantine age, when it had an amphitheater, public baths, aqueducts, and sewage pipes, half a million people lived in Antioch. Today the population is only 125,000. With sour relations between Turkey and Syria, and unstable politics throughout the Middle East, Antioch is now a backwater—seedy and tumbledown, with relatively few tourists. I found it altogether charming. (123)

author   title   publication

In the first stanza of Arnold's "Dover Beach," the exclamations make clear
that the speaker is addressing someone who is also present in the scene:

> Come to the window, sweet is the night air!
> Only, from the long line of spray
> Where the sea meets the moon-blanched land,
> Listen! You hear the grating roar
> Of pebbles which the waves draw back, and fling. (6-10)

Be careful to maintain the poet's line breaks. If a line does not fit on one
line of your paper, put the extra words on the next line. Indent that line
an additional quarter inch (or two spaces).

Illustrations.   Insert illustrations close to the text that discusses them.
For tables, provide a number (*Table* 1) and a title on separate lines above
the table. Below the table, provide a caption and information about the
source. For graphs, photos, and other figures, provide a figure number
(*Fig.* 1), caption, and source information below the figure. If you give only
brief source information (such as a parenthetical note), or if the source is
cited elsewhere in your text, include it in your list of works cited. Be sure
to make clear how any illustrations relate to your point.

List of Works Cited.   Start your list on a new page, following any notes.
Center the title and double-space the entire list. Begin each entry at the
left margin, and indent subsequent lines one-half inch (or five spaces).
Alphabetize the list by authors' last names (or by editors' or translators'
names, if appropriate). Alphabetize works with no author or editor by
title, disregarding *A*, *An*, and *The*. To cite more than one work by a single
author, list them as in no. 4 on page 562.

SAMPLE RESEARCH PAPER

The following report was written by Dylan Borchers for a first-year writing
course. It's formatted according to the guidelines of the MLA (style.mla.org).

Last name and page number.

Borchers   1

Dylan Borchers

Professor Bullock

English 102, Section 4

4 May 2018

Against the Odds:

Harry S. Truman and the Election of 1948

Just over a week before Election Day in 1948, a *New York Times* article noted "[t]he popular view that Gov. Thomas E. Dewey's election as President is a foregone conclusion" (Egan). This assessment of the race between incumbent Democrat Harry S. Truman and Dewey, his Republican challenger, was echoed a week later when *Life* magazine published a photograph whose caption labeled Dewey "The Next President" (Photo of Truman 37). In a *Newsweek* survey of fifty prominent political writers, each predicted Truman's defeat, and *Time* correspondents declared that Dewey would carry 39 of the 48 states (Donaldson 210). Nearly every major media outlet across the United States endorsed Dewey and lambasted Truman. As historian Robert H. Ferrell observes, even Truman's wife, Bess, thought he would be beaten (270).

The results of an election are not so easily predicted, as the famous photograph in fig. 1 shows. Not only did Truman win the election, but he won by a significant margin, with 303 electoral votes and 24,179,259 popular votes, compared to Dewey's 189 electoral votes and 21,991,291 popular votes (Donaldson 204-07). In fact, many historians and political analysts argue that Truman

Marginal annotations:

Title centered.

Double-spaced throughout.

No page number needed for one-page source.

Author named in signal phrase, page number in parentheses.

1" 1/2" 1" 1" 1"

Borchers   2

Fig. 1. President Harry S. Truman holds up an edition of the *Chicago Daily Tribune* that mistakenly announced "Dewey Defeats Truman" (Rollins).

Illustration is positioned close to the text to which it relates, with figure number, caption, and parenthetical documentation.

would have won by an even greater margin had third-party Progressive candidate Henry A. Wallace not split the Democratic vote in New York State and Dixiecrat Strom Thurmond not won four states in the South (McCullough 711). Although Truman's defeat was heavily predicted, those predictions themselves, Dewey's passiveness as a campaigner, and Truman's zeal turned the tide for a Truman victory.

In the months preceding the election, public opinion polls predicted that Dewey would win by a large margin. Pollster Elmo Roper stopped polling in September, believing there was no reason to continue, given a seemingly inevitable Dewey landslide. Although the margin narrowed as the election drew near, the other pollsters

1″

No signal phrase; author and page number in parentheses.

predicted a Dewey win by at least 5 percent (Donaldson 209). Many historians believe that these predictions aided the president in the long run. First, surveys showing Dewey in the lead may have prompted some of Dewey's supporters to feel overconfident about their candidate's chances and therefore to stay home from the polls on Election Day. Second, these same surveys may have energized Democrats to mount late get-out-the-vote efforts ("1948 Truman-Dewey Election"). Other analysts believe that the overwhelming predictions of a Truman loss also kept at home some Democrats who approved of Truman's policies but saw a Truman loss as inevitable. According to political analyst Samuel Lubell, those Democrats may have saved Dewey from an even greater defeat (Hamby, *Man* 465). Whatever the impact on the voters, the polling numbers had a decided effect on Dewey.

Paragraphs indented $\frac{1}{2}$ inch or 5 spaces.

Historians and political analysts alike cite Dewey's overly cautious campaign as one of the main reasons Truman was able to achieve victory. Dewey firmly believed in public opinion polls. With all indications pointing to an easy victory, Dewey and his staff believed that all he had to do was bide his time and make no foolish mistakes. Dewey himself said, "When you're leading, don't talk" (Smith 30). Each of Dewey's speeches was well crafted and well rehearsed. As the leader in the race, he kept his remarks faultlessly positive, with the result that he failed to deliver a solid message or even mention Truman or any of Truman's policies. Eventually, Dewey began to be perceived as aloof and stuffy. One

Borchers 4

observer compared him to the plastic groom on top of a wedding cake (Hamby, "Harry S. Truman"), and others noted his stiff, cold demeanor (McCullough 671-74).

Two works cited within the same sentence.

As his campaign continued, observers noted that Dewey seemed uncomfortable in crowds, unable to connect with ordinary people. And he made a number of blunders. One took place at a train stop when the candidate, commenting on the number of children in the crowd, said he was glad they had been let out of school for his arrival. Unfortunately for Dewey, it was a Saturday ("1948: The Great Truman Surprise"). Such gaffes gave voters the feeling that Dewey was out of touch with the public.

Title used when there's no known author.

Again and again through the autumn of 1948, Dewey's campaign speeches failed to address the issues, with the candidate declaring that he did not want to "get down in the gutter" (Smith 515). When told by fellow Republicans that he was losing ground, Dewey insisted that his campaign not alter its course. Even *Time* magazine, though it endorsed and praised him, conceded that his speeches were dull (McCullough 696). According to historian Zachary Karabell, they were "notable only for taking place, not for any specific message" (244). Dewey's numbers in the polls slipped in the weeks before the election, but he still held a comfortable lead over Truman. It would take Truman's famous whistle-stop campaign to make the difference.

Few candidates in US history have campaigned for the presidency with more passion and faith than Harry Truman. In the autumn of 1948, he wrote to his sister, "It will be the greatest campaign any President ever made. Win, lose, or draw, people will know where I stand" (91). For thirty-three days, Truman traveled the nation, giving hundreds of speeches from the back of the *Ferdinand Magellan* railroad car. In the same letter, he described the pace: "We made about 140 stops and I spoke over 147 times, shook hands with at least 30,000 and am in good condition to start out again tomorrow for Wilmington, Philadelphia, Jersey City, Newark, Albany and Buffalo" (91). McCullough writes of Truman's campaign:

> No President in history had ever gone so far in quest of support from the people, or with less cause for the effort, to judge by informed opinion. . . . As a test of his skills and judgment as a professional politician, not to say his stamina and disposition at age sixty-four, it would be like no other experience in his long, often difficult career, as he himself understood perfectly. More than any other event in his public life, or in his presidency thus far, it would reveal the kind of man he was. (655)

He spoke in large cities and small towns, defending his policies and attacking Republicans. As a former farmer and relatively late bloomer, Truman was able to connect with the public. He developed an energetic style, usually speaking from notes rather than from a prepared speech, and often mingled with the crowds that met his train. These crowds grew larger as the campaign

Quotations of more than 4 lines indented $\frac{1}{2}$ inch and double-spaced.

Parenthetical reference after final punctuation.

progressed. In Chicago, over half a million people lined the streets
as he passed, and in St. Paul the crowd numbered over 25,000.
When Dewey entered St. Paul two days later, he was greeted by
only 7,000 supporters ("1948 Truman-Dewey Election"). Reporters
brushed off the large crowds as mere curiosity seekers wanting to
see a president (McCullough 682). Yet Truman persisted, even if
he often seemed to be the only one who thought he could win. By
going directly to the American people and connecting with them,
Truman built the momentum needed to surpass Dewey and win the
election.

The legacy and lessons of Truman's whistle-stop campaign
continue to be studied by political analysts, and politicians today
often mimic his campaign methods by scheduling multiple visits
to key states, as Truman did. He visited California, Illinois, and
Ohio 48 times, compared with 6 visits to those states by Dewey.
Political scientist Thomas M. Holbrook concludes that his strategic
campaigning in those states and others gave Truman the electoral
votes he needed to win (61, 65).

The 1948 election also had an effect on pollsters, who, as
Elmo Roper admitted, "couldn't have been more wrong." *Life*
magazine's editors concluded that pollsters as well as reporters and
commentators were too convinced of a Dewey victory to analyze
the polls seriously, especially the opinions of undecided voters
(Karabell 256). Pollsters assumed that undecided voters would vote
in the same proportion as decided voters—and that turned out

to be a false assumption (Karabell 257). In fact, the lopsidedness of the polls might have led voters who supported Truman to call themselves undecided out of an unwillingness to associate themselves with the losing side, further skewing the polls' results (McDonald et al. 152). Such errors led pollsters to change their methods significantly after the 1948 election.

Work by 3 or more authors is shortened using et al.

After the election, many political analysts, journalists, and historians concluded that the Truman upset was in fact a victory for the American people, who, the *New Republic* noted, "couldn't be ticketed by the polls, knew its own mind and had picked the rather unlikely but courageous figure of Truman to carry its banner" (T.R.B. 3). How "unlikely" is unclear, however; Truman biographer Alonzo Hamby notes that "polls of scholars consistently rank Truman among the top eight presidents in American history" (*Man* 641). But despite Truman's high standing, and despite the fact that the whistle-stop campaign is now part of our political landscape, politicians have increasingly imitated the style of the Dewey campaign, with its "packaged candidate who ran so as not to lose, who steered clear of controversy, and who made a good show of appearing presidential" (Karabell 266). The election of 1948 shows that voters are not necessarily swayed by polls, but it may have presaged the packaging of candidates by public relations experts, to the detriment of public debate on the issues in future presidential elections.

1″   Borchers   8

Works Cited

Donaldson, Gary A. *Truman Defeats Dewey.* UP of Kentucky, 1999.

Egan, Leo. "Talk Is Now Turning to the Dewey Cabinet." *The New York Times,* 20 Oct. 1948, p. 8E, www.nytimes.com/timesmachine/1948/10/26/issue.html. Accessed 18 Apr. 2017.

Ferrell, Robert H. *Harry S. Truman: A Life.* U of Missouri P, 1994.

Hamby, Alonzo L., editor. "Harry S. Truman: Campaigns and Elections." *American President,* Miller Center, U of Virginia, 11 Jan. 2012, millercenter.org/president/biography/truman-campaigns-and-elections. Accessed 17 Mar. 2017.

- - -. *Man of the People: A Life of Harry S. Truman.* Oxford UP, 1995.

Holbrook, Thomas M. "Did the Whistle-Stop Campaign Matter?" *PS: Political Science and Politics,* vol. 35, no. 1, Mar. 2002, pp. 59-66.

Karabell, Zachary. *The Last Campaign: How Harry Truman Won the 1948 Election.* Alfred A. Knopf, 2000.

McCullough, David. *Truman.* Simon and Schuster, 1992.

McDonald, Daniel G., et al. "The Spiral of Silence in the 1948 Presidential Election." *Communication Research,* vol. 28, no. 2, Apr. 2001, pp. 139-55.

"1948: The Great Truman Surprise." *The Press and the Presidency,* Dept. of Political Science and International Affairs, Kennesaw State U, 29 Oct. 2003, kennesaw.edu/pols.3380/pres/1984.html. Accessed 10 Apr. 2017.

Heading centered.

Double-spaced.

Alphabetized by authors' last names.

Each entry begins at the left margin; subsequent lines are indented one-half inch.

Multiple works by a single author listed alphabetically by title. For second and subsequent works, replace author's name with three hyphens.

Sources beginning with numerals are alphabetized as if the number were spelled out.

"1948 Truman-Dewey Election." *American Political History*, Eagleton
Institute of Politics, Rutgers, State U of New Jersey,
1995-2012, www.eagleton.rutgers.edu/research/
americanhistory/ap_trumandewey.php. Accessed 18 Apr. 2017.

Photo of Truman in San Francisco. *Life*, 1 Nov. 1948, p. 37. *Google
Books*, books.google.com/books?id=ekoEAAAAMBAJ&printsec
=frontcover#v=onepage&q&f=false. Accessed 20 Apr. 2017.

Rollins, Byron. "President Truman with *Chicago Daily Tribune
Headline of 'Dewey Defeats Truman.'*" Associated Press,
4 Nov. 1948. *Harry S. Truman Library & Museum*, www
.trumanlibrary.org/photographs/view.php?id=25248. Accessed
20 Apr. 2017.

Roper, Elmo. "Roper Eats Crow; Seeks Reason for Vote Upset."
Evening Independent, 6 Nov. 1948, p. 10. *Google News*,
news.google.com/newspapers?nid=PZE8UkGerEcC&dat
=19481106&printsec=frontpage&hl=en. Accessed 13 Apr. 2017.

Smith, Richard Norton. *Thomas E. Dewey and His Times*. Simon and
Schuster, 1982.

T.R.B. "Washington Wire." *The New Republic*, 15 Nov. 1948, pp. 3-4.
EBSCOhost, search.ebscohost.com/login.aspx?direct=true&db
=tsh&AN=14779640&site=ehost-live. Accessed 20 Apr. 2017.

Truman, Harry S. "Campaigning, Letter, October 5, 1948." *Harry S.
Truman*, edited by Robert H. Ferrell, CQ P, 2003, p. 91.

A range of dates is given for web projects developed over a period of time.

Every source used is in the list of works cited.

APA Style 55

American Psychological Association (APA) style calls for (1) brief documentation in parentheses near each in-text citation and (2) complete documentation in a list of references at the end of your text. Throughout this chapter, you'll find models and examples that are color-coded to help you see how writers include source information in their texts and reference lists: tan for author or editor, yellow for title, gray for publication information: place of publication, publisher, date of publication, page number(s), and so on. These models and examples draw on the *Publication Manual of the American Psychological Association*, 6th edition (2009). Additional information is available at www.apastyle.org.

A DIRECTORY TO APA STYLE

In-Text Documentation   600

author   title   publication

IN-TEXT DOCUMENTATION

Brief documentation in your text makes clear to your reader precisely what you took from a source and, in the case of a quotation, precisely where (usually, on which page) in the source you found the text you are quoting.

526–38

PARAPHRASES and SUMMARIES are more common than QUOTATIONS in APA-style projects. As you cite each source, you will need to decide whether to name the author in a signal phrase—"as McCullough (2001) wrote"—or in parentheses—"(McCullough, 2001)." Note that APA requires you to use the past tense or present perfect tense for verbs in SIGNAL PHRASES: "Moss (2003) argued," "Moss (2003) has argued."

535–38

1. AUTHOR NAMED IN A SIGNAL PHRASE

If you are quoting, you must give the page number(s). You are not required to give the page number(s) with a paraphrase or a summary, but APA encourages you to do so, especially if you are citing a long or complex work; most of the models in this chapter do include page numbers.

AUTHOR QUOTED

Put the date in parentheses right after the author's name; put the page in parentheses as close to the quotation as possible.

> McCullough (2001) described John Adams as having "the hands of a man accustomed to pruning his own trees, cutting his own hay, and splitting his own firewood" (p. 18).

Notice that in this example, the parenthetical reference with the page number comes *after* the closing quotation marks but *before* the period at the end of the sentence.

AUTHOR PARAPHRASED OR SUMMARIZED

Put the date in parentheses right after the author's name; follow the date with the page.

> John Adams's hands were those of a laborer, according to McCullough (2001, p. 18).

2. AUTHOR NAMED IN PARENTHESES

If you do not mention an author in a signal phrase, put their name, a comma, and the year of publication in parentheses as close as possible to the quotation, paraphrase, or summary.

AUTHOR QUOTED

Give the author, date, and page in one parenthesis, or split the information between two parentheses.

> One biographer (McCullough, 2001) has said John Adams had "the hands of a man accustomed to pruning his own trees, cutting his own hay, and splitting his own firewood" (p. 18).

AUTHOR PARAPHRASED OR SUMMARIZED

Give the author, date, and page in one parenthesis toward the beginning or the end of the paraphrase or summary.

> John Adams's hands were those of a laborer (McCullough, 2001, p. 18).

3. AUTHORS WITH THE SAME LAST NAME

If your reference list includes more than one person with the same last name, include initials in all documentation to distinguish the authors from one another.

> Eclecticism is common in contemporary criticism (J. M. Smith, 1992, p. vii).

4. TWO AUTHORS

Always mention both authors. Use *and* in a signal phrase, but use an ampersand (&) in parentheses.

> Carlson and Ventura (1990) wanted to introduce Julio Cortázar, Marjorie Agosín, and other Latin American writers to an audience of English-speaking adolescents (p. v).

> According to the Peter Principle, "In a hierarchy, every employee tends to rise to his level of incompetence" (Peter & Hull, 1969, p. 26).

5. THREE OR MORE AUTHORS

In the first reference to a work by three to five persons, name all contributors. Use *and* in a signal phrase, but use an ampersand (&) in parentheses. In subsequent references, name the first author followed by *et al.*, Latin for "and others." Whenever you refer to a work by six or more contributors, name only the first author, followed by *et al.*

> Faigley, George, Palchik, and Selfe (2004) have argued that where there used to be a concept called *literacy*, today's multitude of new kinds of texts has given us *literacies* (p. xii).

> Peilen et al. (1990) supported their claims about corporate corruption with startling anecdotal evidence (p. 75).

6. ORGANIZATION OR GOVERNMENT AS AUTHOR

If an organization has a long name that is recognizable by its abbreviation, give the full name and the abbreviation the first time you cite the source. In subsequent references, use only the abbreviation. If the organization does not have a familiar abbreviation, always use its full name.

FIRST REFERENCE

(American Psychological Association [APA], 2008)

SUBSEQUENT REFERENCES

(APA, 2008)

7. AUTHOR UNKNOWN

Use the complete title if it is short; if it is long, use the first few words of the title under which the work appears in the reference list.

> *Webster's New Biographical Dictionary* (1988) identifies William James as "American psychologist and philosopher" (p. 520).

> A powerful editorial asserted that healthy liver donor Mike Hurewitz died because of "frightening" faulty postoperative care ("Every Patient's Nightmare," 2007).

8. TWO OR MORE WORKS CITED TOGETHER

If you cite multiple works in the same parenthesis, place them in the order that they appear in your reference list, separated by semicolons.

> Many researchers have argued that what counts as "literacy" is not necessarily learned at school (Heath, 1983; Moss, 2003).

9. TWO OR MORE WORKS BY AN AUTHOR IN THE SAME YEAR

If your list of references includes more than one work by the same author published in the same year, order them alphabetically by title, adding lowercase letters ("a," "b," and so on) to the year.

> Kaplan (2000a) described orderly shantytowns in Turkey that did not resemble the other slums he visited.

10. SOURCE QUOTED IN ANOTHER SOURCE

When you cite a source that was quoted in another source, let the reader know that you used a secondary source by adding the words *as cited in*.

> During the meeting with the psychologist, the patient stated repeatedly that he "didn't want to be too paranoid" (as cited in Oberfield & Yasik, 2004, p. 294).

11. WORK WITHOUT PAGE NUMBERS

Instead of page numbers, some electronic works have paragraph numbers, which you should include (preceded by the abbreviation *para.*) if you are referring to a specific part of such a source. In sources with neither page nor paragraph numbers, refer readers to a particular part of the source if possible, perhaps indicating a heading and the paragraph under the heading.

> Russell's dismissals from Trinity College at Cambridge and from City College in New York City have been seen as examples of the controversy that marked his life (Irvine, 2006, para. 2).

12. AN ENTIRE WORK

You do not need to give a page number if you are directing readers' attention to an entire work.

> Kaplan (2000) considered Turkey and Central Asia explosive.

When you are citing an entire website, give the URL in the text. You do not need to include the website in your reference list. To cite part of a website, see no. 20 on page 614.

> Beyond providing diagnostic information, the website for the Alzheimer's Association includes a variety of resources for family and community support of patients suffering from Alzheimer's disease (http://www.alz.org).

13. PERSONAL COMMUNICATION

Document email, telephone conversations, interviews, personal letters, messages from nonarchived discussion sources, and other personal texts as *personal communication*, along with the person's initial(s), last name, and the date. You do not need to include such personal communications in your reference list.

> L. Strauss (personal communication, December 6, 2013) told about visiting Yogi Berra when they both lived in Montclair, New Jersey.

author   title   publication

NOTES

You may need to use content notes to give an explanation or information that doesn't fit into your text. To signal a content note, place a superscript numeral at the appropriate point in your text. If you have multiple notes, number them consecutively throughout your text. Put the notes themselves on a separate page with the heading *Notes*, after your reference list. Here is an example from *In Search of Solutions: A New Direction in Psychotherapy* (2003).

TEXT WITH SUPERSCRIPT

An important part of working with teams and one-way mirrors is taking the consultation break, as at Milan, BFTC, and MRI.[1]

CONTENT NOTE

[1]It is crucial to note here that while working within a team is fun, stimulating, and revitalizing, it is not necessary for successful outcomes. Solution-oriented therapy works equally well when working solo.

REFERENCE LIST

A reference list provides full bibliographic information for every source cited in your text with the exception of entire websites and personal communications. See page 626 for guidelines on preparing such a list; for a sample reference list see pages 635–36.

Print Books

For most books, you'll need to provide the author, the publication date, the title and any subtitle, and the place of publication and publisher.

IMPORTANT DETAILS FOR DOCUMENTING PRINT BOOKS

- **AUTHORS**: Use the author's last name, but replace the first and middle names with initials (D. Kinder for Donald Kinder).

- **DATES**: If more than one year is given, use the most recent one.

- **TITLES**: Capitalize only the first word and proper nouns and proper adjectives in titles and subtitles.

- **PUBLICATION PLACE**: Give city followed by state (abbreviated) or country, if outside the United States (for example, Boston, MA; London, England; Toronto, Ontario, Canada). If more than one city is given, use the first. Do not include the state or country if the publisher is a university whose name includes that information.

- **PUBLISHER**: Use a shortened form of the publisher's name (Little, Brown for Little, Brown and Company), but retain *Association*, *Books*, and *Press* (American Psychological Association, Princeton University Press).

1. ONE AUTHOR

Author's Last Name, Initials. (Year of publication). *Title*. Publication City, State or Country: Publisher.

Louis, M. (2003). *Moneyball: The art of winning an unfair game*. New York, NY: Norton.

2. TWO OR MORE WORKS BY THE SAME AUTHOR

If the works were published in different years, list them chronologically.

Lewis, B. (1995). *The Middle East: A brief history of the last 2,000 years*. New York, NY: Scribner.

Lewis, B. (2003). *The crisis of Islam: Holy war and unholy terror*. New York, NY: Modern Library.

If the works were published in the same year, list them alphabetically by title, adding "a," "b," and so on to the year (see p. 608).

Documentation Map (APA)
Print Book

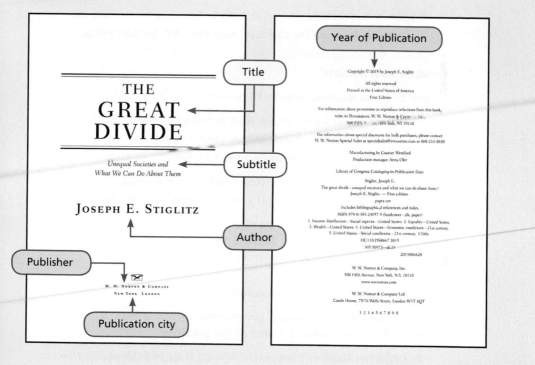

Stiglitz, J. E. (2015). *The great divide: Unequal societies and what we can do about them.* New York, NY: Norton.

605–11

for more on citing books APA style

Kaplan, R. D. (2000a). *The coming anarchy: Shattering the dreams of the post cold war.* New York, NY: Random House.

Kaplan, R. D. (2000b). *Eastward to Tartary: Travels in the Balkans, the Middle East, and the Caucasus.* New York, NY: Random House.

3. TWO OR MORE AUTHORS

For two to seven authors, include all names.

First Author's Last Name, Initials, Next Author's Last Name, Initials, & Final Author's Last Name, Initials. (Year of publication). *Title.* Publication City, State or Country: Publisher.

Leavitt, S. D., & Dubner, S. J. (2005). *Freakonomics: A rogue economist explores the hidden side of everything.* New York, NY: Morrow.

For a work by eight or more authors, name just the first six authors, followed by three ellipsis points, and end with the final author (see no. 21 for an example from a magazine article).

4. ORGANIZATION OR GOVERNMENT AS AUTHOR

Sometimes an organization or a government agency is both author and publisher. If so, use the word *Author* as the publisher.

Organization Name or Government Agency. (Year of publication). *Title.* Publication City, State or Country: Publisher.

Catholic News Service. (2002). *Stylebook on religion 2000: A reference guide and usage manual.* Washington, DC: Author.

5. AUTHOR AND EDITOR

Author's Last Name, Initials. (Year of edited edition). *Title.* (Editor's Initials Last Name, Ed.). Publication City, State or Country: Publisher. (Original work[s] published Year[s])

author   title   publication

Dick, P. F. (2008). *Five novels of the 1960s and 70s.* (J. Lethem, Ed.). New York, NY: Library of America. (Original works published 1964–1977)

6. EDITED COLLECTION

First Editor's Last Name, Initials, Next Editor's Last Name, Initials, & Final Editor's Last Name, Initials. (Eds.). (Year of edited edition). *Title.* Publication City, State or Country: Publisher.

Raviv, A., Oppenheimer, L., & Bar-Tal, D. (Eds.). (1999). *How children understand war and peace: A call for international peace education.* San Francisco, CA: Jossey-Bass.

7. WORK IN AN EDITED COLLECTION

Author's Last Name, Initials. (Year of publication). Title of article or chapter. In Initials Last Name (Ed.), *Title* (pp. pages). Publication City, State or Country: Publisher.

Harris, I. M. (1999). Types of peace education. In A. Raviv, L. Oppenheimer, & D. Bar-Tal (Eds.), *How children understand war and peace: A call for international peace education* (pp. 46–70). San Francisco, CA: Jossey-Bass.

8. UNKNOWN AUTHOR

Title. (Year of publication). Publication City, State or Country: Publisher.

Webster's new biographical dictionary. (1988). Springfield, MA: Merriam-Webster.

If the title page of a work lists the author as *Anonymous*, treat the reference-list entry as if the author's name were Anonymous, and alphabetize it accordingly.

9. EDITION OTHER THAN THE FIRST

Author's Last Name, Initials. (Year). *Title* (name or number ed.). Publication City, State or Country: Publisher.

Burch, D. (2008). *Emergency navigation: Find your position and shape your course at sea even if your instruments fail* (2nd ed.). Camden, ME: International Marine/McGraw-Hill.

10. TRANSLATION

Author's Last Name, Initials. (Year of publication). *Title* (Translator's Initials Last Name, Trans.). Publication City, State or Country: Publisher. (Original work published Year)

Hugo, V. (2008). *Les misérables* (J. Rose, Trans.). New York, NY: Modern Library. (Original work published 1862)

11. MULTIVOLUME WORK

Author's Last Name, Initials. (Year). *Title* (Vols. numbers). Publication City, State or Country: Publisher.

Nastali, D. P., & Boardman, P. C. (2004). *The Arthurian annals: The tradition in English from 1250 to 2000* (Vols. 1–2). New York, NY: Oxford University Press USA.

ONE VOLUME OF A MULTIVOLUME WORK

Author's Last Name, Initials. (Year). *Title of whole work (Vol. number).* Publication City, State or Country: Publisher.

Spiegelman, A. (1986). *Maus* (Vol. 1). New York, NY: Random House.

12. ARTICLE IN A REFERENCE BOOK

UNSIGNED

Title of entry. (Year). In *Title of reference book* (Name or number ed., Vol. number, pp. pages). Publication City, State or Country: Publisher.

Macrophage. (2003). In *Merriam-Webster's collegiate dictionary* (11th ed., p. 745). Springfield, MA: Merriam-Webster.

author   title   publication

SIGNED

Author's Last Name, Initials. (Year). Title of entry. In *Title of reference
    book* (Vol. number, pp. pages). Publication City, State or Country:
    Publisher.

Wasserman, D. E. (2006). Human exposure to vibration. In *International
    encyclopedia of ergonomics and human factors* (Vol. 2, pp. 1800–
    1801). Boca Raton, FL: CRC.

Print Periodicals

For most articles, you'll need to provide information about the author; the
date; the article title and any subtitle; the periodical title; and any volume
or issue number and inclusive page numbers.

IMPORTANT DETAILS FOR DOCUMENTING PRINT PERIODICALS

- **AUTHORS:** List authors as you would for a book (see pp. 606–9).
- **DATES:** For journals, give year only. For magazines and newspapers,
  give year followed by a comma and then month or month and day.
- **TITLES:** Capitalize article titles as you would for a book. Capitalize the
  first and last words and all principal words of periodical titles. Do not
  capitalize *a, an, the,* or any prepositions or coordinating conjunctions
  unless they begin the title of the periodical.
- **VOLUME AND ISSUE:** For journals and magazines, give volume or volume and issue, depending on the journal's pagination method. For
  newspapers, do not give volume or issue.
- **PAGES:** Use *p.* or *pp.* for a newspaper article but not for a journal or
  magazine article. If an article does not fall on consecutive pages, give
  all the page numbers (for example, 45, 75–77 for a journal or magazine;
  pp. C1, C3, C5–C7 for a newspaper).

13. **ARTICLE IN A JOURNAL PAGINATED BY VOLUME**

> Author's Last Name, Initials. (Year). Title of article. *Title of Journal,*
> *volume,* pages.

> Gremer, J. R., Sala, A., & Crone, E. E. (2010). Disappearing plants: Why
> they hide and how they return. *Ecology, 91,* 3407–3413.

14. **ARTICLE IN A JOURNAL PAGINATED BY ISSUE**

> Author's Last Name, Initials. (Year). Title of article. *Title of Journal,*
> *volume*(issue), pages.

> Weaver, C., McNally, C., & Moerman, S. (2001). To grammar or not to
> grammar: That is *not* the question! *Voices from the Middle, 8*(3),
> 17–33.

15. **ARTICLE IN A MAGAZINE**

If a magazine is published weekly, include the day and the month. If there
are a volume number and an issue number, include them after the magazine title.

> Author's Last Name, Initials. (Year, Month Day). Title of article. *Title of*
> *Magazine, volume*(issue), page(s).

> Gregory, S. (2008, June 30). Crash course: Why golf carts are more
> hazardous than they look. *Time, 171*(26), 53.

If a magazine is published monthly, include the month(s) only.

16. **ARTICLE IN A NEWSPAPER**

If page numbers are consecutive, separate them with a hyphen. If not,
separate them with a comma.

> Author's Last Name, Initials. (Year, Month Day). Title of article. *Title of*
> *Newspaper,* p(p). page(s).

> Schneider, G. (2005, March 13). Fashion sense on wheels. *The Washington*
> *Post,* pp. F1, F6.

author   title   publication

17. ARTICLE BY AN UNKNOWN AUTHOR

Title of article. (Year, Month Day). *Title of Periodical, volume*(issue),
page(s) or p(p). page(s).

Hot property: From carriage house to family compound. (2004,
December). *Berkshire Living, 1*(1), 99.

Clues in salmonella outbreak. (2008, June 21). *The New York Times,* p. A13.

18. BOOK REVIEW

Reviewer's Last Name, Initials. (Date of publication). Title of review
[Review of by the book *Title of Work*, by Author's Initials Last Name].
Title of Periodical, volume(issue), page(s).

Brandt, A. (2003, October). Animal planet [Review of the book
Intelligence of apes and other rational beings, by D. R. Rumb
& D. A. Washburn]. *National Geographic Adventure, 5*(10), 47.

If the review does not have a title, include the bracketed information about
the work being reviewed, immediately after the date of publication.

19. LETTER TO THE EDITOR

Author's Last Name, Initials. (Date of publication). Title of letter [Letter to
the editor]. *Title of Periodical, volume*(issue), page(s) or p(p). page(s).

Hitchcock, G. (2008, August 3). Save our species [Letter to the editor].
San Francisco Chronicle, p. P-3.

Online Sources

Not every online source gives you all the data that APA would like to see
in a reference entry. Ideally, you will be able to list author's or editor's
name; date of first electronic publication or most recent revision; title of
document; information about print publication if any; and retrieval information: DOI (digital object identifier, a string of letters and numbers that

identifies an online document) or URL. In some cases, additional information about electronic publication may be required (title of site, retrieval date, name of sponsoring institution).

IMPORTANT DETAILS FOR DOCUMENTING ONLINE SOURCES

- **AUTHORS:** List authors as you would for a print book or periodical.
- **TITLES:** For websites and electronic documents, articles, or books, capitalize titles and subtitles as you would for a book; capitalize periodical titles as you would for a print periodical.
- **DATES:** After the author, give the year of the document's original publication on the web or of its most recent revision. If neither of those years is clear, use *n.d.* to mean "no date." For undated content or content that may change (for example, a wiki entry), include the month, day, and year that you retrieved the document. You don't need to include the retrieval date for content that's unlikely to change.
- **DOI OR URL:** Include the DOI instead of the URL in the reference whenever one is available. If no DOI is available, provide the URL of the homepage or menu page. If you do not identify the sponsoring institution, you do not need a colon before the URL or DOI. Don't include any punctuation at the end of the URL or DOI. When a URL won't fit on the line, break the URL before most punctuation, but do not break *http://.*

20. WORK FROM A NONPERIODICAL WEBSITE

Author's Last Name, Initials. (Date of publication). Title of work. *Title of site.* DOI or Retrieved Month Day, Year [if necessary], from URL

Cruikshank, D. (2009, June 15). Unlocking the secrets and powers of the brain. *National Science Foundation.* Retrieved from http://www.nsf.gov /discoveries/disc_summ.jsp?cntn_id=114979&org=NSF

When citing an entire website, include the URL in parentheses within the text. Do not include the website in your list of references.

author   title   publication

Documentation Map (APA)
Work from a Website

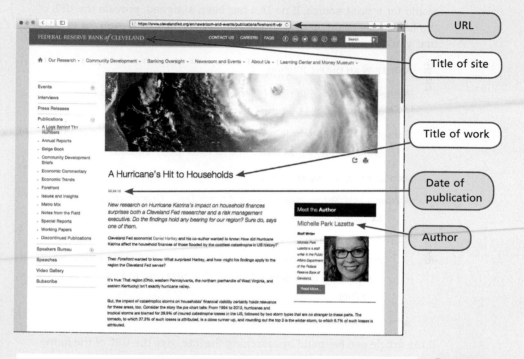

URL

Title of site

Title of work

Date of publication

Author

Lazette, M. P. (2015, February 25). A hurricane's hit to households. *Federal Reserve Bank of Cleveland*. Retrieved from https://www.clevelandfed.org/en/Newsroom%20and%20Events/Publications/Forefront/Katrina.aspx

613–21
for more
on citing
websites
APA style

21. ARTICLE IN AN ONLINE PERIODICAL

When available, include the volume number and issue number as you would for a print source. If no DOI has been assigned, provide the URL of the homepage or menu page of the journal or magazine, even for articles that you access through a database.

ARTICLE IN AN ONLINE JOURNAL

Author's Last Name, Initials. (Year). Title of article. *Title of Journal, volume*(issue), pages. DOI or Retrieved from URL

Corbett, C. (2007). Vehicle-related crime and the gender gap. *Psychology, Crime & Law, 13*, 245–263. doi:10.1080/10683160600822022

ARTICLE IN AN ONLINE MAGAZINE

Author's Last Name, Initials. (Year, Month Day). Title of article. *Title of Magazine, volume*(issue). DOI or Retrieved from URL

Barreda, V. D., Palazzesi, L., Tellería, M. C., Katinas, L., Crisci, J. N., Bromer, K., . . . Bechis, F. (2010, September 24). Eocene Patagonia fossils of the daisy family. *Science, 329*, 1621. doi:10.1126/science .1193108

ARTICLE IN AN ONLINE NEWSPAPER

If the article can be found by searching the site, give the URL of the homepage or menu page.

Author's Last Name, Initials. (Year, Month Day). Title of article. *Title of Newspaper.* Retrieved from URL

Collins, G. (2012, September 12). Game time. *The New York Times.* Retrieved from http://www.nytimes.com

22. ARTICLE AVAILABLE ONLY THROUGH A DATABASE

Some sources, such as an out-of-print journal or rare book, can be accessed only through a database. When no DOI is provided, give either the name of the database or its URL. (See p. 619 for a template and example.)

author   title   publication

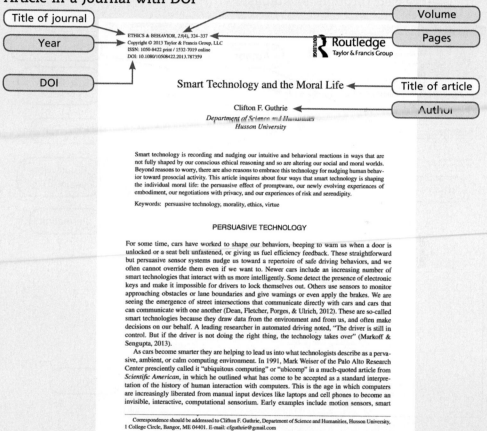

Documentation Map (APA)
Article in a Journal with DOI

Title of journal

Year

DOI

Volume

Pages

Title of article

Author

ETHICS & BEHAVIOR, 23(4), 324–337
Copyright © 2013 Taylor & Francis Group, LLC
ISSN: 1050-8422 print / 1532-7019 online
DOI: 10.1080/10508422.2013.787359

Routledge
Taylor & Francis Group

Smart Technology and the Moral Life

Clifton F. Guthrie
Department of Science and Humanities
Husson University

Smart technology is recording and nudging our intuitive and behavioral reactions in ways that are not fully shaped by our conscious ethical reasoning and so are altering our social and moral worlds. Beyond reasons to worry, there are also reasons to embrace this technology for nudging human behavior toward prosocial activity. This article inquires about four ways that smart technology is shaping the individual moral life: the persuasive effect of promptware, our newly evolving experiences of embodiment, our negotiations with privacy, and our experiences of risk and serendipity.

Keywords: persuasive technology, morality, ethics, virtue

PERSUASIVE TECHNOLOGY

For some time, cars have worked to shape our behaviors, beeping to warn us when a door is unlocked or a seat belt unfastened, or giving us fuel efficiency feedback. These straightforward but persuasive sensor systems nudge us toward a repertoire of safe driving behaviors, and we often cannot override them even if we want to. Newer cars include an increasing number of smart technologies that interact with us more intelligently. Some detect the presence of electronic keys and make it impossible for drivers to lock themselves out. Others use sensors to monitor approaching obstacles or lane boundaries and give warnings or even apply the brakes. We are seeing the emergence of street intersections that communicate directly with cars and cars that can communicate with one another (Dean, Fletcher, Porges, & Ulrich, 2012). These are so-called smart technologies because they draw data from the environment and from us, and often make decisions on our behalf. A leading researcher in automated driving noted, "The driver is still in control. But if the driver is not doing the right thing, the technology takes over" (Markoff & Sengupta, 2013).

As cars become smarter they are helping to lead us into what technologists describe as a pervasive, ambient, or calm computing environment. In 1991, Mark Weiser of the Palo Alto Research Center presciently called it "ubiquitous computing" or "ubicomp" in a much-quoted article from *Scientific American*, in which he outlined what has come to be accepted as a standard interpretation of the history of human interaction with computers. This is the age in which computers are increasingly liberated from manual input devices like laptops and cell phones to become an invisible, interactive, computational sensorium. Early examples include motion sensors, smart

Correspondence should be addressed to Clifton F. Guthrie, Department of Science and Humanities, Husson University, 1 College Circle, Bangor, ME 04401. E-mail: cfguthrie@gmail.com

Guthrie, C. F. (2013). Smart Technology and the Moral Life. *Ethics & Behavior*, *23*(4), 324–337. doi:10.1080/10508422.2013.787359

611–13, 616
for more
on citing
journals
APA style

614
for more
on DOIs

Documentation Map (APA)
Article Accessed through a Database with DOI

616, 619
for more
on citing an
article in a
database
APA style

Guthrie, C. F. (2013). Smart technology and the moral life. *Ethics &
Behavior, 23*(4), 324–337. doi:10.1080/10508422.2013.787359

author   title   publication

> Author's Last Name, Initials. (Year). Title of article. *Title of Journal,*
> *volume*(issue), pages. DOI or Retrieved from Name of database
> or URL

> Simpson, M. (1972). Authoritarianism and education: A comparative
> approach. *Sociometry, 35*(2), 223–234. Retrieved from http://www.jstor
> .org/stable/2786619

23. ARTICLE OR CHAPTER IN A WEB DOCUMENT OR ONLINE REFERENCE WORK

For a chapter in a web document or an article in an online reference
work, give the URL of the chapter or entry if no DOI is provided.

> Author's Last Name, Initials. (Year). Title of entry. In Initials Last Name
> (Ed.), *Title of reference work*. DOI or Retrieved from URL

> Korfmacher, C. (2006). Personal identity. In J. Fieser & B. Dowden (Eds.),
> *Internet encyclopedia of philosophy*. Retrieved from http://www.iep
> .utm.edu/person-i/

24. ELECTRONIC BOOK

> Author's Last Name, Initials. (Year). *Title of book*. DOI or Retrieved from URL

> TenDam, H. (n.d.). *Politics, civilization & humanity*. Retrieved from http://
> onlineoriginals.com/showitem.asp?itemID=46&page=2

For an ebook based on a print version, include a description of the digital
format in brackets after the book title.

> Blain, M. (2009). *The sociology of terror: Studies in power, subjection,*
> *and victimage ritual* [Adobe Digital Editions version]. Retrieved
> from http://www.powells.com/sub/AdobeDigitalEditionsPolitics
> .html?sec_big_link=1

25. WIKI ENTRY

Give the entry title and the date of posting, or *n.d.* if there is no date. Then
include the retrieval date, the name of the wiki, and the URL for the entry.

Title of entry. (Year, Month Day). Retrieved Month Day, Year, from Title
of wiki: URL

Discourse. (n.d.). Retrieved November 8, 2013, from Psychology Wiki:
http://psychology.wikia.com/wiki/Discourse

26. ONLINE DISCUSSION SOURCE

If the name of the list to which the message was posted is not part of the
URL, include it after *Retrieved from*. The URL you provide should be for the
archived version of the message or post.

Author's Last Name, Initials. (Year, Month Day). Subject line of message
[Descriptive label]. Retrieved from URL

Baker, J. (2005, February 15). Re: Huffing and puffing [Electronic
mailing list message]. Retrieved from American Dialect Society
electronic mailing list: http://listserv.linguistlist.org/cgi-bin
/wa?A2=ind0502C&L=ADS-L&P=R44

Do not include email or other nonarchived discussions in your list of
references. Simply give the sender's name in your text. See no. 13 on
page 604 for guidelines on identifying such sources in your text.

27. BLOG ENTRY

Author's Last Name, Initials. (Year, Month Day). Title of post [Blog post].
Retrieved from URL

Collins, C. (2009, August 19). Butterfly benefits from warmer springs?
[Blog post]. Retrieved from http://www.intute.ac.uk/blog
/2009/08/19/butterfly-benefits-from-warmer-springs/

28. ONLINE VIDEO

Last Name, Initials (Writer), & Last Name, Initials (Producer). (Year, Month
Day posted). *Title* [Descriptive label]. Retrieved from URL

Coulter, J. (Songwriter & Performer), & Booth, M. S. (Producer). (2006,
    September 23). *Code Monkey* [Video file]. Retrieved from http://
    www.youtube.com/watch?v=v4Wy7gRGgeA

29. PODCAST

Writer's Last Name, Initials. (Writer), & Producer's Last Name, Initials.
    (Producer). (Year, Month Day). Title of podcast. *Title of site or
    program* [Audio podcast]. Retrieved from URL

Britt, M. A. (Writer & Producer). (2009, June 7). Episode 97: Stanley
    Milgram study finally replicated. *The Psych Files Podcast* [Audio
    podcast]. Retrieved from http://www.thepsychfiles.com/

Other Kinds of Sources

30. FILM, VIDEO, OR DVD

Last Name, Initials (Producer), & Last Name, Initials (Director). (Year). *Title*
    [Motion picture]. Country: Studio.

Wallis, H. B. (Producer), & Curtiz, M. (Director). (1942). *Casablanca*
    [Motion picture]. United States: Warner.

31. MUSIC RECORDING

Composer's Last Name, Initials. (Year of copyright). Title of song. On *Title
    of album* [Medium]. City, State or Country: Label.

Veloso, C. (1997). Na baixado sapateiro. On *Livros* [CD]. Los Angeles, CA:
    Nonesuch.

32. PROCEEDINGS OF A CONFERENCE

Author's Last Name, Initials. (Year of publication). Title of paper. In
    Proceedings Title (pp. pages). Publication City, State or Country:
    Publisher.

Heath, S. B. (1997). Talking work: Language among teens. In *Symposium about Language and Society—Austin* (pp. 27–45). Austin: Department of Linguistics at the University of Texas.

33. TELEVISION PROGRAM

Last Name, Initials (Writer), & Last Name, Initials (Director). (Year). Title of episode [Descriptive label]. In Initials Last Name (Producer), *Series title*. City, State or Country: Network.

Dunkle, R. (Writer), & Lange, M. (Director). (2012). Hit [Television series episode]. In E. A. Bernero (Executive Producer), *Criminal minds.* New York, NY: NBC.

34. SOFTWARE OR COMPUTER PROGRAM

Title and version number [Computer software]. (Year). Publication City, State or Country: Publisher.

Elder Scrolls V: Skyrim [Computer software]. (2011). Rockwood, MD: Bethesda.

35. GOVERNMENT DOCUMENT

Government Agency. (Year of publication). *Title*. Publication City, State or Country: Publisher.

U.S. Department of Health and Human Services, Centers for Disease Control and Prevention. (2009). *Fourth national report on human exposure to environmental chemicals.* Washington, DC: Government Printing Office.

ONLINE GOVERNMENT DOCUMENT

Government Agency. (Year of publication). *Title* (Publication No. [if any]). Retrieved from URL

author   title   publication

U.S. Department of Health and Human Services, National Institutes of
Health, National Institute of Mental Health. (2006). *Bipolar disorder*
(NIH Publication No. 06-3679). Retrieved from http://www.nimh.nih
.gov/health/publications/bipolar-disorder/nimh-bipolar-adults.pdf

36. DISSERTATION

Include the database name and accession number for dissertations that
you retrieve from a database.

> Author's Last Name, Initials. (Year). *Title of dissertation* (Doctoral
> dissertation). Retrieved from Name of database. (accession number)

> Knapik, M. (2008). *Adolescent online trouble-talk: Help-seeking in
> cyberspace* (Doctoral dissertation). Retrieved from ProQuest
> Dissertation and Theses database. (AAT NR38024)

For a dissertation that you access on the web, include the name of institution
after *Doctoral dissertation*. For example: (Doctoral dissertation, University of
North Carolina). End your documentation with *Retrieved from* and the URL.

37. TECHNICAL OR RESEARCH REPORT

> Author's Last Name, Initials. (Year). *Title of report* (Report number).
> Publication City, State or Country: Publisher.

> Elsayed, T., Namata, G., Getoor, L., & Oard, D. W. (2008). *Personal name
> resolution in email: A heuristic approach* (Report No. LAMP-TR-150).
> College Park: University of Maryland.

Sources Not Covered by APA

To document a source for which APA does not provide guidelines, look at
models similar to the source you have cited. Give any information readers
will need in order to find it themselves—author; date of publication; title;
publisher; information about electronic retrieval (DOI or URL); and any
other pertinent information. You might want to try your reference note
yourself, to be sure it will lead others to your source.

FORMATTING A PAPER

Title page. APA generally requires a title page. At the upper left-hand corner of the page, include "Running head:" and a shortened version of your title in capital letters. The page number (1) should go in the upper right-hand corner. Center the full title of the paper, your name, and the name of your school on separate lines about halfway down the page. You may add an "Author Note" at the bottom of the page to provide course information, acknowledgments, or contact information.

Page numbers. Use a shortened title in capital letters in the upper left-hand corner of each page; place the page number in the upper right-hand corner. Number pages consecutively throughout your paper.

Fonts, spacing, margins, and indents. Use a serif font (such as Times New Roman or Bookman) for the text, and a sans serif font (such as Calibri or Verdana) for figure labels. Double-space the entire paper, including any notes and your list of references. Leave one-inch margins at the top, bottom, and sides of your text; do not justify the text. Paragraphs should be indented one-half inch (or five to seven spaces) from the left margin. APA recommends using two spaces after end-of-sentence punctuation.

Headings. Though they are not required in APA style, headings can help readers follow your organization. The first level of heading should be bold, centered, and capitalized as you would any other title; the second level of heading should be bold and flush with the left margin; the third level should be bold and indented, with only the first letter and proper nouns capitalized and with a period at the end of the heading, with the text following on the same line.

First-Level Heading

Second-Level Heading

    Third-level heading.

Long quotations.   Indent quotations of more than forty words to one-half inch (or five to seven spaces) from the left margin. Do not use quotation marks, and place page number(s) in parentheses after the end punctuation.

> Kaplan (2000) captured ancient and contemporary Antioch for us:
>> At the height of its glory in the Roman-Byzantine age, when it had an amphitheater, public baths, aqueducts, and sewage pipes, half a million people lived in Antioch. Today the population is only 125,000. With sour relations between Turkey and Syria, and unstable politics throughout the Middle East, Antioch is now a backwater—seedy and tumbledown, with relatively few tourists. (p. 123)
>
> Antioch's decline serves as a reminder that the fortunes of cities can change drastically over time.

Illustrations.   For each table, provide a number (*Table 1*) and a descriptive title on separate lines above the table; below the table, include a note with information about the source. For figures—charts, diagrams, graphs, photos, and so on—include a figure number (*Figure 1*) and information about the source in a note below the figure. Number tables and figures

Table 1
Hours of Instruction Delivered per Week

	American classrooms	Japanese classrooms	Chinese classrooms
First grade			
Language arts	10.5	8.7	10.4
Mathematics	2.7	5.8	4.0
Fifth grade			
Language arts	7.9	8.0	11.1
Mathematics	3.4	7.8	11.7

Note. Adapted from "Peeking Out from Under the Blinders: Some Factors We Shouldn't Forget in Studying Writing," by J. R. Hayes, 1991, National Center for the Study of Writing and Literacy (Occasional Paper No. 25). Retrieved from National Writing Project website: http://www.nwp.org/

separately, and be sure to refer to any illustrations in your text and clarify how they relate to the rest of your text.

Abstract.   An abstract is a concise summary of your paper that briefly introduces readers to your topic and main points. Most scholarly journals require an abstract; check with your instructor about their preference. Put your abstract on the second page, with the word *Abstract* centered at the top. Unless your instructor specifies a length, limit your abstract to 250 words or fewer.

Keywords.   Keywords are the words or phrases that describe the most important elements of your paper and that researchers would likely use to find papers like yours in databases. They may include individual words, combinations of words, and acronyms—whatever will provide a brief summary of the topics covered in your paper. The keywords list should follow the abstract; italicize the word *Keywords* and indent it five spaces as you would a new paragraph.

List of references.   Start your list on a new page after the text but before any endnotes. Center the title and double-space the entire list. Each entry should begin at the left margin, and subsequent lines should be indented one-half inch (or five to seven spaces). Alphabetize the list by authors' last names (or by editors' names, if appropriate). Alphabetize works that have no author or editor by title, disregarding *A*, *An*, and *The*. Be sure every source listed is cited in the text; don't include sources that you consulted but didn't cite.

SAMPLE RESEARCH PAPER

Analisa Johnson wrote the following paper for a first-year writing course. It is formatted according to the guidelines of the *Publication Manual of the American Psychological Association,* 6th edition (2009). While APA guidelines are used widely in linguistics and the social sciences, exact requirements may vary from discipline to discipline and course to course. If you're unsure about what your instructor wants, ask for clarification.

Running head: PRISON NURSERY PROGRAMS   1

Page number.

"Running head:" and shortened title.

The Benefits of Prison Nursery Programs

Analisa Johnson

Boston University

Title, name, and school name.

**Heading
centered.**

Abstract

The rising population of women in prisons has resulted in the births of some 2,000 babies per year to women behind bars. Female prisoners suffer from a number of inadequacies in their health care, but changes in birthing practices and the provision of nursery programs in prisons could yield important benefits. Currently, nine states offer such programs, and research conducted in these states has shown a number of positive effects. Fully 86.3% of women who have come through these programs remain in their communities after 3 years. Likewise, preschool performance of their children shows better emotional / behavioral adjustment than that of children who have been sent to foster care. Finally, estimates show that the annual costs of such programs are approximately 40% less than that of foster care.

Keywords: birthing practices, correctional, foster care, health care, incarceration, mother–child bond, mother–child attachment, nursery program, prenatal care, preschool, prison, recidivism, sentencing project, shackles

**Limited to 250
words or fewer.**

**"Keywords:" in
italics, indented.**

PRISON NURSERY PROGRAMS   3

The Benefits of Prison Nursery Programs

Over the past 40 years or so, the United States has seen a steady increase in incarcerated individuals, with 2.2 million people currently in prisons and jails nationwide, according to statistics on prisons and the criminal justice system provided by the Sentencing Project (2017, p. 2). In particular, the number of incarcerated females has risen dramatically, at a rate 50% higher than that of men since the early 1980s. As recently as 2015, there were nearly 112,000 incarcerated women across the nation (Sentencing Project, 2017, p. 4). While there is a plethora of health care issues that women face when locked up, one of the most concerning is that of reproductive health, specifically pregnancy and birth in prison. Roughly 1 in 25 women entering prison or jail is pregnant (Yager, 2015). As a result, the number of babies born behind bars has also grown at an alarming rate. It is estimated that up to 2,000 infants are born to incarcerated mothers each year, only to be taken from them a scant 24 hours after birth and placed either with a family member or, more often, in the foster care system (Sufrin, 2012). Current scholarly sources have proven prison nursery programs—which allow mothers to keep their infants with them while they serve out their sentences—to be a very effective method in dealing with the issue of incarcerated mothers. Despite this fact, there are only nine nursery programs currently operational in America. In order to make prison nursery programs more prevalent, better education is needed for correctional administrators about the effectiveness of nursery programs.

Title centered.

Double-spaced throughout.

First-level head-ings boldface, centered.

Inadequacies of Prison Health Care for Pregnant Women

Paragraphs indented $\frac{1}{2}$ inch or 5 to 7 spaces.

When it comes to women's health care in the prison system, there are many inadequate areas, but two that are of great importance are prenatal care and birthing practices.

Prenatal Care

Authors referred to by last name.

Hotelling (2008) discussed the lack of quality health care provided to expectant mothers behind bars. Despite adequate health care being mandated to all inmates through the Eighth Amendment to the Constitution, women still make up a lesser percentage of total incarcerated individuals than men, a fact that is used by correctional staff to justify providing scarcer health care and rehabilitative programs for incarcerated women (para. 3). In addition, prisons aren't subject to any sort of external review of their standards of inmate care, so they are not encouraged to improve health care services, especially if they are seen as costly

In-text citation of web article with-out pagination.

(para. 10). As a result, many incarcerated women face unnecessarily high-risk pregnancies (para. 6).

Second-level headings bold-face, flush with left margin.

Birthing Practices

Another practice that increases the risk of complications in pregnancy in prison is the custom of shackling female inmates during labor, delivery, and postpartum. This practice is both degrading and inhumane and can pose a problem for health care providers in case of an emergency. In an official position statement made by the Association of Women's Health, Obstetric and Neonatal Nurses condemning the use of shackles on pregnant

PRISON NURSERY PROGRAMS   5

women, the board of directors noted that the unnecessary practice can interfere with the ability of nurses and health care providers to deliver the proper care and treatment (2011, p. 817). Only 18 states in the United States currently ban the shackling of expectant mothers in prison while they give birth (American Civil Liberties Union, 2012). The remaining 32 states are left to their own devices, in some cases shackling mothers with no regard to the recommendations of nurses and other health care providers. This poor treatment of female inmates and lack of proper health and prenatal care is cause for concern. When looking at the nine states that currently operate prison nursery programs—California, Illinois, Indiana, Nebraska, New York, Ohio, South Dakota, Washington, and West Virginia—one-third do not have laws in place that prevent the shackling of inmates while giving birth (Sufrin, 2012).

Prison Nursery Programs

In order to effectively spread awareness of prison nursery programs, it must be clear exactly what they are and how they serve incarcerated mothers. Prison nursery programs offer women who become incarcerated while pregnant the option to keep and parent their child while they serve their sentences. Getting into these programs can be a rigorous process; with limited spots available, prospective mothers must have a nonviolent conviction, no record of child abuse, and be roughly within 18 months of completing their sentence—which is the maximum amount of time a child can stay with their mother behind bars (Stein, 2010, p. 11).

Author name in parentheses when no signal phrase is used.

PRISON NURSERY PROGRAMS 6

Benefits

When mothers do get into these programs, there are many benefits to be had for both themselves and their children. For starters, mothers are provided with parenting classes, support groups, substance abuse counseling, and complementary day-care services to attend these classes. Many prisons also provide high school and college courses for those mothers who have not yet completed their education (Wertheimer, 2005). Lastly, vocational programs are also offered, which aid in the job search once the women are released from prison. These enrichment and rehabilitative classes are an important part of reintegrating these women back into society upon their release from prison.

Recidivism

As a result of the programs, many of the mothers have been shown to have a reduced recidivism rate. An astounding 86.3% of women exiting a prison nursery program remained in the community three years following their release (Goshin, Byrne, & Henninger, 2014, "Results," para. 3). This is a proven positive for both the mothers and their children.

The Mother-Child Bond

In addition, prison nursery programs have been proven to foster the imperative mother–child attachment bond. Jbara (2012) noted that the attachment bond is crucial to a child's psychological development (p. 1827). The American Psychological Society found that "infants who bond securely with their mothers become

Author named in a signal phrase, publication date in parentheses after the name.

PRISON NURSERY PROGRAMS   7

more self-reliant and have higher self-esteem as toddlers" (as

cited in Jbara, 2012, p. 1827).

Preschool Outcomes

Goshin, Byrne, and Blanchard-Lewis (2014) described a study

examining the long-term effects of early childhood life in prison

on infants ages 1 to 18 months. These data were compared to

those of children who were separated from their mother due to

incarceration. Goshin, Byrne, and Blanchard-Lewis found that

"children who spent time with their mothers in a prison nursery

had significantly lower mean anxious / depressed and withdrawn

behavior scores than children who were separated from their

mothers in infancy or toddlerhood because of incarceration" (2014,

p. 149). This is promising evidence for the effectiveness of prison

nursery programs and shows that there are not only benefits to

be had in the short term but also in the long-term development of

children.

Longer Lasting Results

Still, the mother–child attachment bond is not merely

something beneficial if fostered. Lack of attachment can actually

produce detrimental effects on the child: "Studies have shown

that children who fail to sufficiently bond with their mothers are

more likely to suffer from developmental delay, an inability to

connect with others, and a greater likelihood of being convicted

of a crime later in life" (Jbara, 2012, p. 1826). Clearly, mother–child

separation is not good for the child, the mother, or the state, which

*Source quoted in
another source
identified with
"as cited in."*

would not only be putting more children into foster care but also more individuals into incarceration, two avenues paid for by the government.

Cost of Prison Nursery Programs

Many may question the costliness of these programs on prison facilities. While it may seem as if implementing prison nursery programs across the country would be an expensive endeavor, it is important to consider by comparison the costs of putting children in foster care. On average, according to the report "Children in Foster Care," the total financial cost for one child to remain in foster care per year in Oregon is about $26,600 (Fixsen, 2011, p. 3). Conversely, Yager (2015) summarized the findings of Joseph Carlson, a professor at the University of Nebraska at Kearney who evaluated Nebraska's prison nursery program: "He calculated that nursery supplies, staff salaries, and medical expenses would total about 40% less each year than foster care for the babies who would otherwise end up there, and predicted more-significant savings from a decline in recidivism" (as cited in Yager, para. 34). Rapidly increasing the number of prison nursery programs across the country may result in some extra money spent in the short run, but it will provide benefits in the long run, both financially and socially.

Implementing Programs

While it seems obvious that more of these programs should be implemented nationwide, in order for this to happen, understanding of the benefits of these programs must be more

PRISON NURSERY PROGRAMS   9

widespread. Implementing such programs may also lead scholars
to consider the ultimate question: Should the prison system be
punitive or rehabilitative in nature? One significant example of
the benefits of a rehabilitative prison system is the prison nursery
program.

References

American Civil Liberties Union Foundation. (2012). *The shackling
    of pregnant women & girls in U.S. prisons, jails & youth detention
    centers* [Briefing paper]. Retrieved from https://www.aclu.org
    /files/assets/anti-shackling_briefing_paper_stand_alone.pdf

Association of Women's Health, Obstetric and Neonatal Nurses.
    (2011). *Shackling incarcerated pregnant women* [Position
    statement]. Retrieved from http://www.jognn.org/article
    /S0884-2175(15)30763-2/pdf

Fixsen, A. (2011). *Children in foster care*. Retrieved from A Family for
    Every Child website: http://www.afamilyforeverychild.org/
    wp=content/uploads/2018/04/children_in_foster_care.pdf

Goshin, L. S., Byrne, M. W., & Blanchard-Lewis, B. (2014). Preschool
    outcomes of children who lived as infants in a prison nursery.
    The Prison Journal, 94(2), 139–158. doi:10.1177/0032885514524692

Goshin, L. S., Byrne, M. W., & Henninger, A. M. (2014). Recidivism
    after release from a prison nursery program. *Public Health
    Nursing, 33*(2), 109–117. doi:10.1111/phn.12072

Heading
centered.

Alphabetized
by authors'
last names or
first word of
organization.

All lines after the
first line of each
entry indented.

PRISON NURSERY PROGRAMS   10

Hotelling, B. A. (2008). Perinatal needs of pregnant incarcerated
    women. *The Journal of Perinatal Education, 17*(2), 37–44.
      doi:10.1624/105812408X298372

Jbara, A. E. (2012). The price they pay: Protecting the mother–
    child relationship through the use of prison nurseries and
    residential parenting programs. *Indiana Law Journal, 87*(4),
    1825–1845.

Sentencing Project. (2017). *Trends in U.S. corrections* [Fact sheet].
    Retrieved from http://sentencingproject.org/wp
    -content/uploads/2016/01/Trends-in-US-Corrections.pdf

Stein, D. J. (2010, July/August). Babies behind bars: Nurseries for
    incarcerated mothers and their children. *Children's Voice, 19*(4),
    10–13. Retrieved from https://search-proquest-com.ezproxy
    .bu.edu/docview/866359865?accountid=9676

Sufrin, C. (2012, July 1). *Incarcerated women and reproductive health
    care* [Video file]. Retrieved from https://www.youtube.com
    /watch?v=WNx1ntLyI2Q

Wertheimer, L. (2005, November 5). *Prenatal care behind bars* [Audio
    file]. Retrieved from http://www.npr.org/templates/story/story
    .php?storyId=4990886

Yager, S. (2015, July/August). Prison born. *The Atlantic.* Retrieved
    from https://www.theatlantic.com/magazine/archive/2015/07
    /prison-born/395297/

All sources cited in the text are listed.

part 8

Media / Design

Consciously or not, we design all the texts we write,
choosing typefaces, setting up text as lists or charts,
deciding whether to add headings—and then whether
to center them or align them on the left. Sometimes
our genre calls for certain design elements—essays
begin with titles, letters begin with salutations ("Dear
Auntie Em"). Other times we design texts to meet the
demands of particular audiences, formatting documentation in MLA or APA or some other style, setting type
larger for young children, and so on. And our designs
always depend upon our medium. A memoir might take
the form of an essay in a book, be turned into a bulleted
list for a slide presentation, or include links to images or
other pages if presented on a website. The chapters
in this part offer advice for CHOOSING MEDIA;
working with DESIGN, IMAGES, and SOUND;
WRITING ONLINE; and GIVING PRESENTATIONS.

Media/Design

Choosing Media 56

USA Today reports on contract negotiations between automakers and auto-workers with an article that includes a large photo and a colorful graph; the article on the same story on the *New York Times* website includes a video of striking workers. In your economics class, you give a presentation about the issue that includes *Prezi* slides.

These examples show how information about the same events can be delivered using three different media: print (*USA Today*), digital (*nytimes.com*), and spoken (the main medium for your class presentation). They also show how different media offer writers different modes of expressing meaning, ranging from words to images to sounds and hyperlinks. A print text can include written words and still visuals; online, the same text can also incorporate links to moving images and sound as well as to other written materials. A presentation with slides can include both spoken and written words, can incorporate video and audio elements—and can also include print handouts.

In college writing, the choice of medium often isn't up to you: your instructor may require a printed essay or a classroom talk, a website, or some combination of media. Sometimes, though, you'll be the one deciding. Because your medium will play a big part in the way your audience receives and reacts to your message, you'll need to think hard about what media best suit your audience, purpose, and message. This chapter will help you choose media when the choice is yours.

academic literacies

rhetorical situations

genres

fields

processes

strategies

research MLA / APA

media / design

Print

When you have a choice of medium, print has certain advantages over spoken and digital text in that it's more permanent and doesn't depend on audience access to technology. Depending on your own access to technology, you can usually insert photos or other visuals and can present data and other information as graphs or charts. Obviously, though, print documents are more work than digital ones to update or change, and they don't allow for sound, moving images, or links to other materials.

Digital

Online writing is everywhere: on course learning management systems and class websites; in virtual discussion groups and wikis; in emails, text messages, tweets, and other social media. And when you're taking an online course, you are, by definition, always using a digital medium. Remember that this medium has advantages as well as limitations and potential pitfalls. You can add audio, video, and links—but your audience may not have the same access to technology that you do. These are just some of the things you'll need to keep in mind when deciding, say, whether to include or link to videos or a site that has restricted access. Also, digital texts that circulate online, through blogs, websites, email, or social media, can take on a life of their own; others may forward, like, retweet, or repost your text to much larger audiences than you originally considered.

Spoken

If you deliver your text orally, as a speech or presentation, you have the opportunity to use your tone of voice, gestures, and physical bearing to establish credibility. But you must write your text so that it's easy to understand when it is heard rather than read. Speaking from memory or from notecards, rather than reading a script or essay, often makes it easier for the audience to follow your talk. The spoken medium can be used alone with a live, face-to-face audience, but it's often combined with print, in the form of handouts, or with digital media, in the form of presentation software like *PowerPoint* or *Prezi*, or designed for remote audiences in formats like webcasts, webinars, podcasts, or video-calling services such as *Skype*.

Multimedia

It's increasingly likely that you'll be assigned to create a multimedia text, one that includes some combination of print, oral, and digital elements. It's also possible that you'll have occasion to write a multimodal text, one that uses more than one mode of expression: words, images, audio, video, links, and so on. The words *multimedia* and *multimodal* are often used interchangeably, but *multimodal* is the term that's used most often in composition classes, whereas *multimedia* is the one used in other disciplines and in industry. In composition classes, the word generally refers to writing that includes more than just words.

For example, let's say that in a U.S. history class you're assigned to do a project about the effects of the Vietnam War on American society. You might write an essay using words alone to discuss such effects as increased hostility toward the military and government, generational conflict within families and society at large, and increased use of recreational drugs. But you could also weave such a text together with many other materials to create a multimodal composition.

If you're using print, for example, you could include photographs from the Vietnam era, such as of antiwar protests or military funerals. Another possibility might be a timeline that puts developments in the war in the context of events going on simultaneously elsewhere in American life, such as in fashion and entertainment or in the feminist and civil rights movements. If you're posting your project online, you might also incorporate video clips of TV news coverage of the war and clips from films focusing on it or its social effects, such as *Apocalypse Now* or *Easy Rider*. Audio elements could include recorded interviews with veterans who fought in the war, people who protested against it, or government officials who were involved in planning or overseeing it. Many of these elements could be inserted into your document as links.

If your assignment specifies that you give an oral presentation, you could play some of the music of the Vietnam era, show videos of government officials defending the war and demonstrators protesting it, maybe hang some psychedelic posters from the era.

You might do something similar with your own work by creating an electronic, or e-portfolio. Tips for compiling an **E-PORTFOLIO** may be found in Chapter 34.

361–70 ○

Considering the Rhetorical Situation

55–56 ■

PURPOSE　What's your purpose, and what media will best suit that purpose? A text or email may be appropriate for inviting a friend to lunch, but neither would be ideal for demonstrating to a professor that you understand a complex historical event; for that, you'd likely write a report, either in print or online—and you might include photos or maps or other such texts to provide visual context.

57–60 ■

AUDIENCE　What media are your audience likely to expect—and be able to access? A blog may be a good way to reach people who share your interest in basketball or cupcakes, but to reach your grandparents, you may want to put a handwritten note in the mail. Some employers and graduate school admissions officers require applicants to submit résumés and applications online, while others prefer to receive them in print form.

61–65 ■

GENRE　Does your genre require a particular medium? If you're giving an oral presentation, you'll often be expected to include slides. Academic essays are usually formatted to be printed out, even if they are submitted electronically. An online essay based on field research might include audio files of those you've interviewed, but if your essay

were in print, you'd need to quote (or paraphrase or summarize) what they said.

STANCE   If you have a choice of media, think about whether a   66–68
particular medium will help you convey your stance. A
print document in MLA format, for instance, will make
you seem scholarly and serious. Tweeting or blogging,
however, might work better for a more informal stance.
Presenting data in charts will sometimes help you establish your credibility as a knowledgeable researcher

Once you decide on the media and modes of expression you're using, you'll
need to design your text to take advantage of their possibilities and to deal
with their limitations. The next chapters will help you do that.

57 Designing Text

You're trying to figure out why a magazine ad you're looking at is so funny, and you realize that the text's font is deliberately intended to make you laugh. An assignment for a research paper in psychology specifies that you are to follow APA format. Your classmates complain that the *PowerPoint* slides you use for a presentation are hard to read because there's not enough contrast between the words and the background. Another says you include too many words on each slide. Whether you're putting together your résumé, creating a website for your intramural soccer league, or writing an essay for a class, you need to think about how you design what you write.

Sometimes you can rely on established conventions: in MLA and APA styles, for example, there are specific guidelines for margins, headings, and the use of single-, double-, or triple-spaced lines of text. But often you'll have to make design decisions on your own—and not just about words and spacing. If what you're writing includes photos, charts, tables, graphs, or other visuals, you'll need to integrate these with your written text in the most attractive and effective way; online, you may also need to decide where and how to include video clips and links. You might even use scissors, glue, and staples to attach objects to a poster or create pop-ups in a brochure.

No matter what your text includes, its design will influence how your audience responds to it and therefore how well it achieves your purpose. This chapter offers general advice on designing print and online texts.

Considering the Rhetorical Situation

As with all writing tasks, your rhetorical situation should affect the way you design a text. Here are some points to consider:

PURPOSE   How can you design your text to help achieve your purpose? If you're reporting information, for instance, you may want to present statistical data in a chart or table rather than in the main text to help readers grasp it more quickly. If you're trying to get readers to care about an issue, a photo or pull quote—a brief selection of text "pulled out" and reprinted in a larger font—might help you do so.   55–56

AUDIENCE   How can you make your design appeal to your intended audience? By using a certain font style or size to make your text look stylish, serious, or easy to read? What kind of headings—big and bold, simple and restrained?—would your readers expect or find helpful? What colors would appeal to them?   57–60

GENRE   Are you writing in a genre that has design conventions, such as an annotated bibliography, a lab report, or a résumé? Do you need to follow a format such as those prescribed in MLA or APA style?   61–65

STANCE   How can your design reflect your attitude toward your audience and subject? Do you need a businesslike font or a playful one? Would tables and graphs help you establish your credibility? How can illustrations help you convey a certain tone?   66–68

Some Basic Principles of Design

Be consistent. To keep readers oriented while reading documents or browsing multiple webpages, any design elements should be used consistently. In a print academic essay, that task may be as simple as using the same font throughout for your main text and using boldface or italics for headings. If you're writing for the web, navigation buttons and other major elements should be in the same place on every page. In a presentation, each slide should use the same background and the same font unless there's a good reason to introduce differences.

Keep it simple. One of your main design goals should be to help readers see quickly—even intuitively—what's in your text and how to find specific information. Adding headings to help readers see the parts, using consistent colors and fonts to help them recognize key elements, setting off steps in lists, using white space to set off blocks of text or to call attention to certain elements, and (especially) resisting the temptation to fill pages with fancy graphics or unnecessary animations—these are all ways of making your text simple to read.

Look, for example, at a furniture store's simple, easy-to-understand webpage design on the next page. This webpage contains considerable information: a row of links across the top, directing readers to various products; a search option; a column down the right side that provides details about the chair shown in the wide left-hand column; thumbnail photos below the chair and ordering information; and more details across the bottom. Despite the wealth of content, the site's design is both easy to figure out and, with the generous amount of white space, easy on the eyes.

Aim for balance. On the webpage on the following page, the photo takes up about a quarter of the screen and is balanced by a narrower column of text, and the product information tabs and text across the page bottom balance the company logo and search box across the top. For a page without images, balance can be created through the use of margins, headings, and spacing. In the journal page shown on page 564, notice how using white space around the article title and the author's name, as well as setting both in larger type and the author's name in all capital letters, helps to balance them vertically against the large block of text below. The large initial letter of the text also helps to balance the mass of smaller type that follows. MLA and APA styles have specific design guidelines for academic research papers that cover these elements. A magazine page might create a sense of balance by using pull quotes and illustrations to break up dense vertical columns of text.

Use color and contrast carefully. Academic readers usually expect black text on a white background, with perhaps one other color for headings. Presentation slides and webpages are most readable with a plain, light-colored background and dark text that provides contrast. Remember that

not everyone can see all colors and that an online text that includes several colors might be printed out and read in black and white; make sure your audience will be able to distinguish any color variations well enough to grasp your meaning. Colored lines on a graph, for example, should be distinguishable even if readers cannot see the colors. Red-green contrasts are especially hard to see and should be avoided.

Use available templates.   Good design takes time, and most of us do not have training as designers. If you're pressed for time or don't feel up to the challenge of designing your own text, take advantage of the many templates available. In *Microsoft Word*, for example, you can customize "styles" to specify the font, including its size and color; single- or double-spacing; paragraph indentations; and several other features that will then automatically apply to your document. Websites that host personal webpages and blogs offer dozens of templates that you can use or modify to suit your needs. And presentation software offers many templates that can simplify creating slides.

Some Elements of Design

Fonts.   You can usually choose from among many fonts, and the one you choose will affect how well the audience can read your text and how they will perceive your TONE. Times Roman will make a text look businesslike or academic; *Comic Sans* will make it look playful. For most academic writing, you'll want to use a font size between 10 and 12 points and a serif font (such as Times Roman or Bookman) rather than a sans serif font (such as Arial, Verdana, or Calibri) because serif fonts are generally easier to read. Reserve sans serif for headings and parts of the text that you want to highlight. Decorative fonts (such as *Magneto*, *Amaze*, Chiller, and Jokerman) should be used sparingly and only when they're appropriate for your audience, purpose, and the rest of your RHETORICAL SITUATION. If you use more than one font, use each one consistently: one for HEADINGS, one for captions, one for the main body of your text. Don't go overboard—you won't often have reason to use more than two or, at most, three fonts in any one text.

Every font has regular, **bold**, and *italic* forms. In general, choose regular for the main text and lower-level headings, bold for major head-

66–68 ◼

53 ◼
650–52 ◻

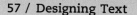

ings, and italic within the main text to indicate titles of books and other long works and, occasionally, to emphasize words or brief phrases. Avoid italicizing or boldfacing entire sentences or paragraphs, especially in academic writing. If you are following **MLA**, **APA**, or some other style format, be sure your use of fonts conforms to its requirements.

MLA 548–96

APA 597–636

Finally, consider the line spacing of your text. Generally, academic writing is double-spaced, whereas **JOB LETTERS** and **RÉSUMÉS** are usually single-spaced. Some kinds of **REPORTS** may call for single-spacing; check with your instructor if you're not sure. You'll often need to add extra space to set off parts of a text—items in a list, for instance, or headings.

264–79

131–56

Layout.   Layout is the way text is arranged on a page. An academic essay, for example, will usually have a title centered at the top, one-inch margins all around, and double-spacing. A text can be presented in paragraphs— or in the form of **LISTS**, **TABLES**, **CHARTS**, **GRAPHS**, and so on. Sometimes you'll need to include other elements as well: headings, images and other graphics, captions, lists of works cited.

649–50

656

Paragraphs.   Dividing text into paragraphs focuses information for readers and helps them process it by dividing it into manageable chunks. If you're writing a story for a print newspaper with narrow columns, for example, you'll divide your text into shorter paragraphs than you would if you were writing an academic essay. In general, indent paragraphs five to seven spaces (one-half inch) when your text is double-spaced; either indent or skip a line between single-spaced paragraphs.

Lists.   Put into list form information that you want to set off and make easily accessible. Number the items in a list when the sequence matters (in instructions, for example); use bullets when the order is not important. Set off lists with an extra line of space above and below, and add extra space between the items if necessary for legibility. Here's an example:

> Darwin's theory of how species change through time derives from three postulates, each of which builds on the previous one:
>
> 1. The ability of a population to expand is infinite, but the ability of any environment to support populations is always finite.

2. Organisms within populations vary, and this variation affects the ability of individuals to survive and reproduce.
3. The variations are transmitted from parents to offspring.

—Robert Boyd and Joan B. Silk, *How Humans Evolved*

Do not set off text as a list unless there's a good reason to do so, however. Some lists are more appropriately presented in paragraph form, especially when they give information that is not meant to be referred to more than once. In the following example, there is no reason to highlight the information by setting it off in a list—and bad news is softened by putting it in paragraph form:

> I regret to inform you that the Scholarship Review Committee did not approve your application for a Board of Rectors scholarship for the following reasons: your grade-point average did not meet the minimum requirements; your major is not among those eligible for consideration; and the required letter of recommendation was not received before the deadline.

Presented as a list, that information would be needlessly emphatic.

Headings.   Headings make the structure of a text easier to follow and help readers find specific information. Some genres require standard headings—announcing an **ABSTRACT**, for example, or a list of **WORKS CITED**. Other times you will want to use headings to provide an overview of a section of text. You may not need any headings in brief texts, but when you do, you'll probably want to use one level at most, just to announce major topics. Longer texts, information-rich genres such as brochures or detailed **REPORTS**, and websites may require several levels of headings. If you decide to include headings, you will need to decide how to phrase them, what fonts to use, and where to position them.

185–89 ▲
587 ●

131–56 ▲

Phrase headings concisely.   Make your headings succinct and parallel in structure. You might make all the headings nouns (**Mushrooms**), noun phrases (**Kinds of Mushrooms**), gerund phrases (**Recognizing Kinds of**

Mushrooms), or questions (**How Do I Identify Mushrooms?**). Whatever form you decide on, use it consistently for each heading. Sometimes your phrasing will depend on your purpose. If you're simply helping readers find information, use brief phrases:

HEAD	**Forms of Social Groups among Primates**
SUBHEAD	*Solitary Social Groups*
SUBHEAD	*Monogamous Social Groups*

If you want to address your readers directly with the information in your text, consider writing your headings as questions:

How can you identify edible mushrooms?
Where can you find edible mushrooms?
How can you cook edible mushrooms?

Make headings visible. Headings need to be visible, so if you aren't following an academic style like MLA or APA, consider making them larger than the regular text, putting them in **bold** or *italics*, or using <u>underlining</u>— or a different font. For example, you could use a serif font like Times Roman for your main text and a sans serif font like Arial for your headings. On the web, consider making headings a different color from the body text. When you have several levels of headings, use capitalization, bold, and italics to distinguish among the various levels:

First-Level Head
Second-Level Head
Third-level head

APA format requires that each level of heading appear in a specific style: centered bold uppercase and lowercase for the first level, flush-left bold uppercase and lowercase for the second level, and so on.

● APA 624

Position headings appropriately. If you're following APA format, center first-level headings. If you are not following a prescribed format, you get to decide where to position your headings: centered, flush with the left margin, or even alongside the text in a wide left-hand margin. Position each level of head consistently throughout your text. Generally, online headings are positioned flush left.

White space.   Use white space to separate the various parts of a text. In general, use one-inch margins for the text of an essay or report. Unless you're following MLA or APA format, include space above headings, above and below lists, and around photos, graphs, and other visuals. See the two **SAMPLE RESEARCH PAPERS** in this book for examples of the formats required by MLA and APA.

MLA 587–96 ●
APA 626–36

Evaluating a Design

55–56 ■

Does the design suit your PURPOSE?   Does the overall look of the design help convey the text's message, support its argument, or present information?

57–60 ■

How well does the design meet the needs of your AUDIENCE?   Will the overall appearance of the text appeal to the intended readers? Is the font large enough for them to read? Are there headings to help them find their way through the text? Does the design help readers find the information they need?

61–65 ■

How well does the text meet any GENRE requirements?   Can you tell by looking at the text that it is an academic essay, a lab report, a résumé, a blog? Do its fonts, margins, headings, and page layout meet the require-ments of **MLA**, **APA**, or whatever style is being followed?

MLA 586–87 ●
APA 624–26

66–68 ■

How well does the design reflect your STANCE?   Do the page layout and fonts convey the appropriate tone—serious, playful, adventuresome, con-servative, or whatever other tone you intended?

Using Visuals, Incorporating Sound 58

For an art history class, you write an essay comparing two paintings by Willem de Kooning. For a business class, you create a proposal to improve department communication in a small local firm and incorporate diagrams to illustrate the new procedure. For a visual rhetoric class, you take an autobiographical photograph and include a two-page analysis of how the picture distills something essential about you. For an engineering class project, you design a model of a bridge and give an in-class presentation explaining the structures and forces involved, which you illustrate with slides. For a psychology assignment, you interview several people who've suffered foreclosures on their homes in recent years about how the experience affected them—and then create an online text weaving together a slideshow of photos of the people outside their former homes, a graph of foreclosure rates, video and audio clips from the interviews, and your own insights.

All of these writing tasks require you to incorporate and sometimes to create visuals and sound. Many kinds of visuals can be included in print documents: photos, drawings, diagrams, graphs, charts, and more. And with writing that's delivered online or as a spoken presentation, your choices expand to include audio and video, voice-over narration, and links to other materials.

Visuals and sound aren't always appropriate, however, or even possible—so think carefully before you set out to include them. But they can help you make a point in ways that words alone cannot. Election polling results are easier to see in a bar graph than in a paragraph; photos of an event may convey its impact more powerfully than words alone; an audio clip can make a written analysis of an opera easier to understand. This chapter provides some tips for using visuals and incorporating sound in your writing.

Considering the Rhetorical Situation

53 ■

Use visuals and sounds that are appropriate for your audience, purpose, and the rest of your RHETORICAL SITUATION. If you're trying to persuade voters in your town to back a proposal on an issue they don't know much about, for example, you might use dramatic pictures just to get their attention. But when it's important to come across as thoughtful and objective, maybe you need a more subdued look—or to make your points with written words alone. A newspaper article on housing prices might include a bar or line graph and also some photos. A report on that topic for an economics class would probably have graphs with no photos; a spoken presentation for a business class might use a dynamic graph that shows prices changing over time and an audio voice over for pictures of a neighborhood; a community website might have graphs, links to related sites, and a video interview with a home owner.

In your academic writing, especially, be careful that any visuals you use support your main point—and don't just serve to decorate the text. (Therefore, avoid clip art, which is primarily intended as decoration and comes off as unsophisticated and childish.) Images should validate or exemplify what you say elsewhere with written words and add information that words alone can't provide as clearly or easily.

Using Visuals

Photos, drawings, diagrams, videos, tables, pie charts, bar graphs—these are many kinds of visuals you could use. Visuals can offer support, illustration, evidence, and comparison and contrast in your document.

397–417 ◆
462–70
457–61

Photographs.   Photos can support an ARGUMENT, illustrate NARRATIVES and PROCESSES, present other points of view, and help readers "place" your information in time and space. You may use photos you take yourself, or you can download photos and other images from the internet—within limits. Most downloadable photos are copyrighted, meaning that you can use them without obtaining permission from the copyright owner only if

An essay discussing the theme of mother and child might compare this paint-ing from the Italian Renaissance (left) with a modern photograph such as Dorothea Lange's Migrant Mother *(right).*

you are doing so for academic purposes, to fulfill an assignment. If you are going to publish your text, either in print or on the web, you must have permission. You can usually gain permission by emailing the copyright holder, but that often entails a fee, so think carefully about whether you need the image. Consider, too, the file size of digital images; large files can clog readers' email in-boxes, take a long time to display on their screens, or be hard for you to upload in the first place, so you may have to com-press an image in a zip file or reduce its resolution (which can diminish its sharpness).

Videos.　If you're writing online, you can include video clips for readers to play. If you're using a video already available online, such as on *YouTube*, you can show the opening image with an arrow for readers to click on to start the video, or you can simply copy the video's URL and paste it into your text as a **LINK**. In either case, you need to introduce the video in your text with a **SIGNAL PHRASE**. As with any other source, you need to provide an in-text citation and full documentation.

▢　661–62
●　535–38

If you want to include a video you made yourself, you can edit it using such programs as *iMovie* or *Shotcut*. Once you're ready to insert it into your online document, the easiest way is to first upload it to *YouTube*, choosing the Private setting so only those you authorize may view it, and then create a link in your document.

Graphs, charts, and tables.   Statistical and other numerical information is often best presented in graphs, charts, and tables. If you can't find the right one for your purpose, you can create your own, as long as it's based on sound data from reliable sources. To do so, you can use various spreadsheet programs such as *Excel* or online chart and graph generators such as *Plot.ly* or *Venngage*.

645 □
646

In any case, remember to follow basic design principles: be **CONSISTENT**, label all parts clearly, and **KEEP THE DESIGN SIMPLE**, so readers can focus on the information and not be a distracted by a needlessly complex

646–48 □

design. In particular, use color and contrast wisely to emphasize what's most significant. Choose **COLORS** that are easy to distinguish from one another—and that remain so if the graph or chart is printed out in black and white. (Using distinct gradations of color from light to dark will show well in black and white.) Some common kinds of graphs, charts, and tables are shown on the facing page.

Diagrams, maps, flowcharts, and timelines.   Information about place and time is often presented in diagrams, maps, flowcharts, and timelines. If you're using one of these infographics from the web or elsewhere,

544–47 ●

be sure to **DOCUMENT** it. Otherwise you can create one of these yourself. Make diagrams and maps as simple as possible for the point you're making. Unnecessarily complex maps can be more of a distraction than a help. To draw a flowchart, you can use the Shape tab on the Insert section of *Microsoft Word*. For timelines, make sure the scale accurately depicts the passage of time about which you are writing and avoids gaps and bunches.

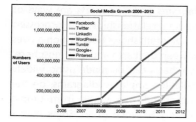

Line graphs are a good way of showing changes in data over time. Each line here represents a different social media platform. Plotting the lines together allows readers to compare the data at different points in time. Be sure to label the *x* and *y* axes and limit the number of lines to avoid confusion.

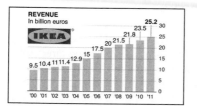

Bar graphs are useful for comparing quantitative data, measurements of how much or how many. The bars can be horizontal or vertical. This graph shows IKEA's earnings between 2000 and 2011. Some software offers 3-D and other special effects, but simple graphs are often easier to read.

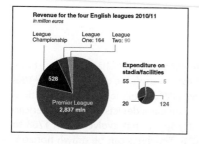

Pie charts can be used to show how a whole is divided into parts or how parts of a whole relate to one another. These two pie charts show and compare the revenue of four 2010–11 English soccer leagues and their expenditures. The segments in a pie should always add up to 100 percent, and each segment should be clearly labeled.

ECONOMY WATCH
A snapshot of key figures for the world's largest economies.

COUNTRY	GDP in billions in 2010	GDP GROWTH Y/year (%)	CURRENT ACC'T/GDP in 2010 (%)	INFLATION Year over year (%)	JOBLESS (%)
U.S.	$14,658	2.0‡	-3.2	3.5	8.6
Euro zone	12,474*	1.4	-0.2*	3.0	10.3
China	5,878	9.1	5.2	5.5	4.1§
Japan	5,459	5.6‡	3.6	-0.1	4.5
Germany	3,316	2.5	5.3	2.8†	6.9
France	2,583	1.7	-2.1	2.5†	9.7
Britain	2,247	0.5	-2.5	5.0	8.3
Italy	2,055	0.8	-2.1*	3.7†	8.5
Brazil	1,601*	2.1	-1.5*	6.6	5.8
Canada	1,574	3.5‡	-3.1	2.9	7.4
India	1,538	6.9	-3.2	9.7	n.a.
Russia	1,222*	4.8	4.1*	6.8	6.4
Mexico	1,039	4.5	-0.7*	3.5	5.0
South Korea	833*	3.5	3.9*	4.2	3.1

* Actual figures of 2009   ** Harmonized figures   † Quarter on quarter annualized   ‡ Urban end September

Tables are useful for displaying numerical information concisely, especially when several items are being compared. The table here presents economic information for fourteen countries: 2010 GDP, GDP growth, current account GDP, inflation, and joblessness. Presenting information in columns and rows permits readers to find data and identify relationships among them.

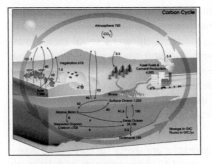

Diagrams and flowcharts are ways of showing relationships and processes. This diagram shows how carbon moves between the Earth and its atmosphere. Flowcharts can be made using widely available templates; diagrams, on the other hand, can range from simple drawings to works of art. Some simple flowcharts may be found in the genres chapters.

Maps show physical locations. This map shows the annual average direct solar resources for each of the U.S. states. Maps can be drawn to scale or purposefully out of scale to emphasize a point.

350–4

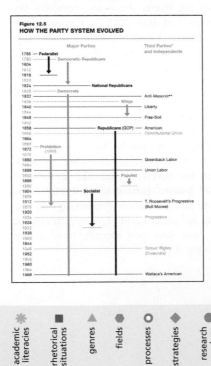

Timelines show change over time. These are useful to demonstrate **CAUSE** and **EFFECT** relationships or evolution. This timeline depicts how the American party system has evolved from 1788 to 2016. Timelines can be drawn horizontally or vertically.

academic literacies
rhetorical situations
genres
fields
processes
strategies
research MLA / APA
media / design

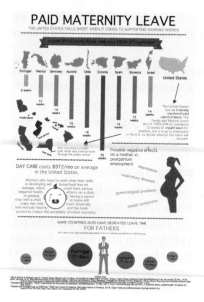

Infographics are eye-catching visual representations of information that help simplify a complicated subject. Infographics typically include an engaging title; a design that reflects the content being displayed; and a balance of charts, graphs, and other elements; readable fonts, and the sources of your information. Several websites offer templates to help you design and execute infographics, including *Piktochart*, *Infogram*, and several others.

SOME TIPS FOR USING VISUALS

- Position images as close as possible to the discussion to which they relate. In *Microsoft Word*, simply position your cursor where you want to insert an image; click the appropriate type of visual from the menu on the Insert tab; choose the appropriate image from your files; and click Insert. You may then need to adjust the way the text flows or wraps around the image: in the Page Layout tab, choose the appropriate option in Wrap Text.

- In academic writing, number all images, using separate sequences of numbers for figures (photos, graphs, diagrams, video clips, and drawings) and tables: Fig. 1, Fig. 2; Table 1, Table 2. Follow style guidelines (e.g., **MLA** or **APA**) for where to place the figure or table number and caption.

  ● MLA 587
  APA 625–26

- Explain in your written text whatever information you present in an image—don't expect it to speak for itself. Refer to the image before it appears, identifying it and summarizing its point. For example: "As Table 1 shows, Italy's economic growth rate has been declining for thirty years."

- Provide a title or caption for each image to identify it and explain its significance for your text. For example: "Table 1: Italy's Economic Growth Rate, 1985–2015."

- Label the parts of visuals clearly to ensure that your audience will understand what they show. For example, label each section of a pie chart to show what it represents.

- Cite the source of any images you don't create yourself. You need not document visuals you create, based on data from your own experimental or field research, but if you use data from a source to create a graph or chart, **CITE THE SOURCE** of the data.

539–42

- In general, you may use visuals created by someone else in your academic writing as long as you include full **DOCUMENTATION**. If you post your writing online, however, you must first obtain permission from the copyright owner and include permission information. For example: *Photo courtesy of Victoria and Albert Museum, London.* Copyright holders will often tell you how they want the permission sentence to read.

544–47

Incorporating Sound

Audio clips, podcasts, and other sound files can serve various useful purposes in online writing and spoken presentation. Music, for example, can create a mood for your text, giving your audience hints about how to interpret the meaning of your words and images or what emotional response you're evoking. Other types of sound effects—such as background conversations, passing traffic, birdsongs, crowd noise at sports events—can provide a sense of immediacy, of being part of the scene or event you're describing. Spoken words can serve as the primary way you present an online text or as an enhancement of or even a counterpoint to a written text. (And if your audience includes visually impaired people, an audio track can allow or help them to follow the text.)

You can download or link to various spoken texts online, or you can record voice and music as podcasts using programs such as *GarageBand* and *Audacity*. Remember to provide an **IN-TEXT CITATION** and full **DOCUMENTATION** of any sound material you obtain from another source.

MLA 551–57
APA 600–604
544–47

Adding Links

If you're writing an online text in which you want to include images, video, or sound material available on the web, it's often easier and more effective to create links to them within the text than to embed them by copying and pasting. Rather than provide the URL for the link, use relevant words to make it easier for a reader to decide to click on the link. (See the example below where the links are marked by blue color and words such as "Francis Davis Millet and Millet family papers.") Such links allow readers to see the materials' original context and to explore it if they wish. Be selective in the number of links you include: too many links can dilute a text.

The example below shows a blog post from the Archives of American Art with links to additional detail and documentation.

John Singer Sargent

This lively caricature from the Francis Davis Millet and Millet family papers features an artist fervently painting his subject, just in the background. Most likely it is John Singer Sargent at work on his painting *Carnation, Lily, Lily, Rose*. His posture and the expression on his face suggest an exuberance that matches the action of the paint dripping and splashing as it prepares to meet the canvas with energetic strokes.

Caricature of an artist painting vigorously, ca. 1885-1886. Francis Davis Millet and Millet family papers. Archives of American Art, Smithsonian Institution.

535–38

SOME TIPS FOR CREATING LINKS

- Indicate links with underlining and color (most often blue), and introduce them with a **SIGNAL PHRASE**.
- Don't include your own punctuation in a link. In the example on page 661, the period is not part of the link.
- Try to avoid having a link open in a new browser window. Readers expect links to open in the same window.

Editing Carefully—and Ethically

You may want to edit a photograph, cropping to show only part of it or using *Photoshop* or similar programs to enhance the colors or otherwise alter it. Similarly, you may want to edit a video, podcast, or other audio file to shorten it or remove irrelevant parts. If you are considering making a change of this kind, however, be sure not to do so in a way that misrepresents the content. If you alter a photo, be sure the image still represents the subject accurately; if you alter a recording of a speech or interview, be sure the edited version maintains the speaker's intent. Whenever you alter an image, a video, or a sound recording, tell your readers how you have changed it.

The same goes of editing charts and graphs. Changing the scale on a bar graph, for example, can change the effect of the comparison, making the quantities being compared seem very similar or very different, as shown in the two bar graphs of identical data in Figures 1 and 2.

Both charts show the increase in average housing costs in the United States between 2000 and 2015. However, by making the baseline in Figure 1 $200,000 instead of zero, the increase appears to be far greater than it was in reality. Just as you shouldn't edit a quotation or a photograph in a way that might misrepresent its meaning, you should not present statistical data in a way that could mislead readers.

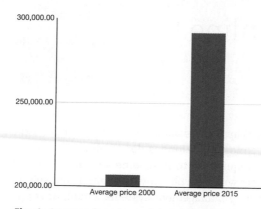

Fig. 1. Average housing prices in the United States, 2000–2015 (exaggerated).

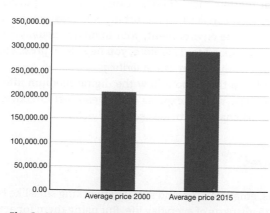

Fig. 2. Average housing prices in the United States, 2000–2015 (presented accurately).

59 Writing Online

Email. *Facebook. Snapchat, Instagram, Pinterest, Youtube.* Texts. Tweets. It may seem as if almost all writing is done online now. In college courses, you may still be required to turn in some writing assignments on paper, but more and more writing is not only done online but submitted that way too through learning management systems, email, or some other online system. You may rarely use email, but your professor may require you to do so. And many classes are being taught online, with little or no face-to-face communication between instructors and students.

Online, your instructor and classmates usually cannot see or hear you—and that matters more than you might think. A puzzled look or a smile of recognition can start an important conversation in a face-to-face class, but in an online environment, your audience usually has only your written words to respond to. Therefore, you need to express your thoughts and feelings as clearly as you can *in writing*.

So it's useful to think about how the digital medium affects the way we write—and how we can express ourselves most effectively when we write online. This chapter provides some advice.

Online Genres

For most of us, email, texting, and social networking sites like *Facebook* and *Twitter* are already parts of everyday life. But using them for academic purposes may require some careful attention. Following are some guidelines.

Email.   When emailing faculty members and school administrators, you are writing in an academic context, so your messages should reflect it: use an appropriate salutation ("Dear Professor Hagzanian"); write clearly

academic literacies ■ rhetorical situations ▲ genres ● fields ○ processes ◆ strategies ● research MLA / APA □ media / design

and concisely in complete sentences; use standard capitalization and punctuation; proofread; and sign your full name. If you are requesting something from your professor—to read a draft or to write a letter of recommendation—be sure to give enough notice well in advance of the deadline. If you're writing about a specific course or group work, identify the course or group explicitly. Also, craft a specific subject line; instead of writing "Question about paper," be specific: "Profile organization question." If you change topics, change your subject line as well rather than simply replying to an old email. And be careful before you hit Send—you want to be good and sure that your email neither says something you'll regret later (don't send an email when you're angry!) nor includes anything you don't want the whole world reading (don't put confidential or sensitive information in email).

Texts.   Texting is inherently informal and often serves as an alternative to a phone call. Since texting often takes place as a conversation in real time (and phone keyboards can be hard to use), those who write texts often use acronyms, shorthand, and emoticons—ROTFL (rolling on the floor laughing), OST (on second thought), 2nite (tonight), 10Q (thank you), :) (happy)—to get their meaning across quickly and efficiently. If you use these abbreviations, though, be sure your readers will understand them!

Social media.   You may take a course that involves using *Facebook* or another social media site as a way for class members to communicate or as part of a **LEARNING MANAGEMENT SYSTEM**. If so, you need to consider your rhetorical situation to make sure your course postings represent you as a respectful (and respectable) member of the class. Also, remember that many employers and graduate school administrators routinely check job applicants' social media pages, so don't post writing or photos that you wouldn't want a potential employer to see.

☐ 670–72

Websites.   Websites are groups of webpages organized around a homepage and connected to one another (and to other websites) through links, which take users automatically from one page to another. While it's possible to create your own websites from scratch, free website builders such as

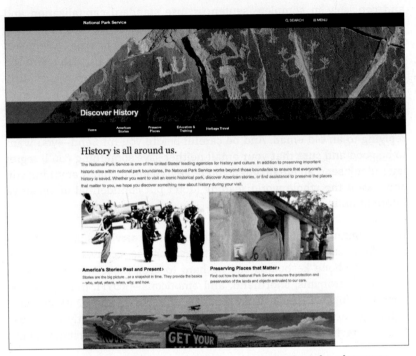

The homepage of Discover History, the National Park Service cultural resource program, provides a navigation menu that leads to various sections of the site. Links connect to pages describing Park Service programs.

Weebly, Google Sites, or *Wix* make it easy to create a site by providing templates for homepages, page designs, and navigation systems.

    One key element in a website is the use of links to bring material from other sources into your text. You can link to the definition of a key term, for instance, rather than defining it yourself, or you can summarize a source and link to the full text rather than quoting or paraphrasing it. Providing links lets readers decide whether they need or want to see more detailed information—or not.

This blog, hosted by the Smithsonian Institution, focuses on marine biology and includes video, audio, slideshows, and written narratives.

Blogs.   Blogs are websites that generally focus on a single topic—politics, celebrities, gaming, baseball, you name it. They're maintained and updated regularly by individuals or groups who post opinions, reflections, information, and more—with writing, photos, video and audio files, and links to other sites. Blogs are an easy way to share your writing with others—and to invite response. Free blog hosting sites such as *WordPress*, *Tumblr*, or *Blogger* offer templates that let you create a blog and post to it easily, and some learning management systems include blogging capability as well.

If your blog is public, anyone can read it, including potential employers, so just as with *Facebook* and other social media, you'll want to be careful about how you present yourself and avoid posting anything that others could see as offensive. (Think twice before posting when you're angry or upset.) You may want to activate privacy settings that let you restrict access to some of the content or that make your blog unsearchable by *Google* and other search tools. Also, assume that what you post in a blog is permanent: your friends, family, employer—anyone—may read a posting years in the future, even if the blog is no longer active.

Wikis. Wikis are websites that allow a group to work collaboratively, with all users free to add, edit, and delete content. *Wikipedia*, the online encyclopedia, is one of the most famous wikis: its content is posted and edited by people all over the world. You may be asked to contribute to a class wiki, such as the one below from a writing course at Bloomsburg University of Pennsylvania. Students post their work to the wiki, and everyone in the class has access to everyone else's writing and can comment on or revise it. When contributing to a wiki, you should be careful to write precisely, edit carefully, and make sure your research is accurate and appropriately cited—others may be quick to question and rewrite your work if it's sloppy or inaccurate. Free wiki apps include *MediaWiki*, *PmWiki*, and *DokuWiki*.

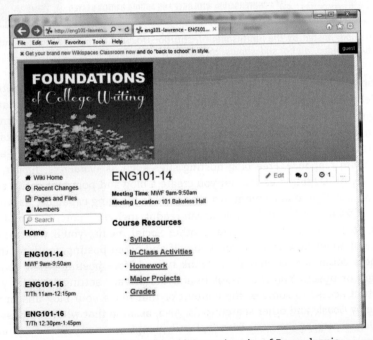

A writing-course wiki from Bloomsburg University of Pennsylvania.

Managing Online Course Work

Because so much of your college work will be done online—at the very least, you'll do most of your writing on a computer and submit some assignments via email—it's important to set up some procedures for yourself. In a single writing course, for example, you may write three or four drafts of four essays—that's twelve to sixteen documents. To keep track of your files, you'll need to create folders, establish consistent file names, and back up your work.

Creating folders. Create a folder for each course, and name it with the course title or number and the academic term: ENG 101 Fall 2018. Within each course folder, create a folder for each major assignment. Save your work in the appropriate folder, so you can always find it.

Saving files. Your word processor likely saves documents to a specific format identified by a three- or four-letter ending automatically added to the file name: .doc, .docx, .txt, and so on. However, this default format may not be compatible with other programs. If you're not sure what format you'll need, use the Save As command to save each document in Rich Text Format, or .rtf, which most word processors can read.

Naming files. If you are expected to submit files electronically, your instructor may ask you to name them in a certain way. If not, devise a system that will let you easily find the files, including multiple drafts of your writing. For example, you might name your files using *Your last name + Assignment + Draft number + Date:* Jones Evaluation Draft 2 10-5-2018.docx. You'll then be able to find a particular file by looking for the assignment, the draft number, or the date. Saving all your drafts as separate files will make it easy to include them in a portfolio; also, if you lose a draft, you'll be able to use the previous one to reconstruct it.

Backing up your work. Hard drives fail, laptops and tablets get dropped, flash drives are left in public computers. Because files stored in computers can be damaged or lost, you should save your work in several places: on your computer, on a flash drive or portable hard drive, in space supplied by your school, or online. You can also ensure that an extra copy of your work exists by emailing a copy to yourself.

Finding Basic Course Information

You'll need to learn some essential information about any online courses you take:

- *The phone number for the campus help desk* or technology center. Check the hours of operation, and keep the number handy.
- *The syllabus,* list of assignments, and calendar with deadlines.
- *Where to find tutorials* for your school's learning management system and other programs you may need help with.
- *How and when you can contact your instructor*—in person during office hours? by phone or email?—and how soon you can expect a response.
- *What file format you should use* to submit assignments—.doc, .docx, .rtf, .pdf, something else?—and how to submit them.
- *How to use the spellcheck function* on your word processor or learning management system.
- *How to participate in online discussions*—will you use a discussion board? a chat function in a learning management system? a blog? a social network? something else?

Using Learning Management Systems

Whether you're in a face-to-face, hybrid, or online class, you may be asked to do some or all of your classwork online using a learning management system such as *Blackboard, Moodle,* or *Canvas.* An LMS is a web-based educational tool that brings together all the course information your instructor wants you to have, along with features that allow you to participate in

A course homepage from Wright State University's Pilot LMS.

the class in various ways. Your school's LMS likely includes the following features that you'll be expected to use:

A course homepage contains posts from your instructor; a calendar with due dates for assignments; and links to the course syllabus, other course content, and additional features available on the site.

A discussion board allows you to communicate with classmates even if everyone isn't logged in to the board at the same time. These conversations may be organized in "threads" so that posts on a particular topic appear together and may be read in order. When you contribute to a threaded discussion, treat it as an ongoing conversation: you need not introduce the topic but can simply add your comments.

A chat tool allows you to engage in written conversations in real time, with all participants logged in simultaneously. In a classroom, doing this may be like texting with many others at once, so the rules for class discussion apply: be patient while waiting for a response; focus on the topic being discussed; avoid sarcasm or personal attacks.

A dropbox is a place where you submit assignments online. If your course dropbox has folders for each assignment, be sure to upload your assignment into the correct folder. Keep in mind that systems go down, so don't wait until the last minute to submit a file. It's a good idea to double-check that the file you've submitted has been uploaded; often you can simply exit the dropbox and then return to it to see that your file is where it should be.

Online portfolios. Many LMSs allow you to create an online portfolio where you may post your coursework as well as photos, personal information, and links to other websites.

Additional features. An LMS may also include email; a space to keep a journal; a whiteboard for posting images, graphics, and presentations; a gradebook; a social network (sometimes called a Ning) for class members only; and other features that can help you keep track of your work in a class.

Giving Presentations 60

In a marketing class, you give a formal presentation that includes slides and handouts as part of a research project on developing brand loyalty to clothing labels among college students. As a candidate for student government, you deliver several speeches to various campus groups that are simultaneously broadcast over the web. At a good friend's wedding, after you make a toast to the married couple, another friend who couldn't attend in person toasts them remotely using *Skype*; a third guest records both toasts on his cell phone and uploads them to *Facebook*. Whether or not you include digital and print media, whenever you are called on to give a spoken presentation, you need to make your points clear and memorable. This chapter offers guidelines to help you prepare and deliver effective presentations. We'll start with two good examples.

ABRAHAM LINCOLN
Gettysburg Address

Given by the sixteenth president of the United States, at the dedication of the Gettysburg battlefield as a memorial to those who died in the Civil War, this is one of the most famous speeches ever delivered in the United States.

Four score and seven years ago our fathers brought forth on this continent, a new nation, conceived in Liberty, and dedicated to the proposition that all men are created equal.

Now we are engaged in a great civil war, testing whether that nation, or any nation so conceived and so dedicated, can long endure.

We are met on a great battle-field of that war. We have come to dedicate a portion of that field, as a final resting place for those who here gave their lives that that nation might live. It is altogether fitting and proper that we should do this.

But, in a larger sense, we can not dedicate—we can not consecrate—we can not hallow—this ground. The brave men, living and dead, who struggled here, have consecrated it, far above our poor power to add or detract. The world will little note, nor long remember what we say here, but it can never forget what they did here. It is for us the living, rather, to be dedicated here to the unfinished work which they who fought here have thus far so nobly advanced. It is rather for us to be here dedicated to the great task remaining before us—that from these honored dead we take increased devotion to that cause for which they gave the last full measure of devotion—that we here highly resolve that these dead shall not have died in vain—that this nation, under God, shall have a new birth of freedom—and that government of the people, by the people, for the people, shall not perish from the earth.

You won't likely be called on to deliver such an address, but the techniques Lincoln used—brevity, rhythm, recurring themes—are ones you can use in your own spoken texts. The next example represents the type of spoken text we are sometimes called on to deliver at important occasions in the lives of our families.

JUDY DAVIS

Ours Was a Dad . . .

This short eulogy was given at the funeral of the writer's father, Walter Boock. Judy Davis lives in Davis, California, where she was for many years the principal of North Davis Elementary School.

Elsa, Peggy, David, and I were lucky to have such a dad. Ours was a dad who created the childhood for us that he did not have for himself.

academic literacies ● rhetorical situations ● genres ● fields ● processes ● strategies ● research MLA / APA ● media / design

The dad who sent us airborne on the soles of his feet, squealing with delight. The dad who built a platform in the peach tree so we could eat ourselves comfortably into peachy oblivion. The dad who assigned us chores and then did them with us. The dad who felt our pain when we skinned our knees.

Ours was the dad who took us camping, all over the U.S. and Canada, but most of all in our beloved Yosemite. The one who awed us with his ability to swing around a full pail of water without spilling a drop and let us hold sticks in the fire and draw designs in the night air with hot orange coals.

Our dad wanted us to feel safe and secure. On Elsa's eighth birthday, we acquired a small camping trailer. One very blustery night in Minnesota, Mom and Dad asleep in the main bed, David suspended in the hammock over them, Peggy and Elsa snuggled in the little dinette bed, and me on an air mattress on the floor, I remember the most incredible sense of well-being: our family all together, so snug, in that little trailer as the storm rocked us back and forth. It was only in the morning that I learned about the tornado warnings. Mom and Dad weren't sleeping: they were praying that when morning came we wouldn't find ourselves in the next state.

Ours was the dad who helped us with homework at the round oak table. He listened to our oral reports, taught us to add by looking for combinations of 10, quizzed us on spelling words, and when our written reports sounded a little too much like the *World Book* encyclopedia, he told us so.

Ours was a dad who believed our round oak table that seated   5 twelve when fully extended should be full at Thanksgiving. Dad called the chaplain at the airbase, asked about homesick boys, and invited them to join our family. Or he'd call International House in Berkeley to see if someone from another country would like to experience an American Thanksgiving. We're still friends with the Swedish couple who came for turkey forty-five years ago. Many people became a part of our extended family around that table. And if twelve around the table was good, then certainly fourteen would be better. Just last fall, Dad commissioned our neighbor Randy to make yet another leaf for the table. There were fourteen around the table for Dad's last Thanksgiving.

Ours was a dad who had a lifelong desire to serve. He delivered Meals on Wheels until he was eighty-three. He delighted in picking up the day-old doughnuts from Mr. Rollen's shop to give those on his route an extra treat. We teased him that he should be receiving those meals himself! Even after walking became difficult for him, he continued to drive and took along an able friend to carry the meals to the door.

Our family, like most, had its ups and downs. But ours was a dad who forgave us our human failings as we forgave him his. He died in peace, surrounded by love. Elsa, Peggy, David, and I were so lucky to have such a dad.

This eulogy, in honor of the writer's father, provides concrete and memorable details that give the audience a clear image of the kind of man he was. The repetition of the phrase "ours was a dad" provides a rhythm and unity that moves the text forward, and the use of short, conventional sentences makes the text easy to understand—and deliver.

Key Features / Spoken Presentations

A clear structure. Spoken texts need to be clearly organized so that your audience can follow what you're saying. The **BEGINNING** needs to engage their interest, make clear what you will be talking about, and perhaps forecast the central parts of your talk. The main part of the text should focus on a few main points—only as many as your listeners can be expected to absorb and retain. (Remember, they can't go back to reread!) The **ENDING** is especially important: it should leave your audience with something, to remember, think about, or do. Davis ends as she begins, saying that she and her sisters and brother "were so lucky to have such a dad." Lincoln ends with a dramatic resolution: "that government of the people, by the people, for the people, shall not perish from the earth."

Signpost language to keep your audience on track. You may need to provide cues to help your listeners follow your text, especially **TRANSITIONS** that lead them from one point to the next. Sometimes you'll also want to stop and **SUMMARIZE** a complex point to help your audience keep track of your ideas and follow your development of them.

373–80

380–85

391

534–35

A tone to suit the occasion. Lincoln spoke at a serious, formal event, the dedication of a national cemetery, and his address is formal and even solemn. Davis's eulogy is more informal in **TONE**, as befits a speech given for friends and loved ones. In a presentation to a panel of professors, you probably would want to take an academic tone, avoiding too much slang and speaking in complete sentences. If you had occasion to speak on the very same topic to a neighborhood group, however, you would likely want to speak more casually.

66–68

Repetition and parallel structure. Even if you're never called on to deliver a Gettysburg Address, you will find that repetition and parallel structure can lend power to a presentation, making it easier to follow—and more likely to be remembered. "We can not dedicate—we can not consecrate—we can not hallow": the repetition of "we can not" and the parallel forms of the three verbs are one reason these words stay with us more than 150 years after they were written and delivered. These are structures any writer can use. See how the repetition of "ours was a dad" in Davis's eulogy creates a rhythm that engages listeners and at the same time unifies the text.

Slides and other media. Depending on the way you deliver your presentation, you will often want or need to use other media—*PowerPoint*, *Prezi*, or other presentation slides, video and audio clips, handouts, flip charts, whiteboards, and so on—to present certain information and to highlight key points.

Considering the Rhetorical Situation

As with any writing, you need to consider your rhetorical situation when preparing a presentation:

PURPOSE Consider what your primary purpose is. To inform? persuade? entertain? evoke another kind of emotional response?

55–56

AUDIENCE   57–60

Think about whom you'll be addressing and how well you know them. Will they be interested, or will you need to get them interested? Are they likely to be friendly? How can you get and maintain their attention, and how can you establish common ground with them? How much will they know about your subject—will you need to provide background or define any terms?

GENRE   61–65

The genre of your text will affect the way you structure and present it. If you're making an argument, for instance, you'll need to consider counterarguments—and, depending on the way you're giving the presentation, perhaps to allow for questions and comments from members of the audience who hold other opinions. If you're giving a report, you may have reasons to prepare handouts with detailed information you don't have time to cover in your spoken text, or links to online documents or websites.

STANCE   66–68

Consider the attitude you want to express. Is it serious? thoughtful? passionate? well informed? humorous? something else? Choose your words and any other elements of your presentation accordingly. Whatever your attitude, your presentation will be received better by your listeners if they perceive you as comfortable and sincere.

A Brief Guide to Writing Presentations

Whether you're giving a poster presentation at a conference or an oral report in class, what you say will differ in important ways from what you might write for others to read. Here are some tips for composing an effective presentation.

academic literacies   rhetorical situations   genres   fields   processes   strategies   research MLA / APA   media / design

Budget your time.   A five-minute presentation calls for about two and a half double-spaced pages of writing, and ten minutes means only four or five pages. Your introduction and conclusion should each take about one-tenth of the total time available; time for questions (if the format allows for them) should take about one-fifth; and the body of the talk, the rest. In a ten-minute presentation, then, allot one minute for your introduction, one minute for your conclusion, and two minutes for questions, leaving six minutes for the body of your talk.

Organize and draft your presentation.   Readers can go back and reread if they don't understand or remember something the first time through a text. Listeners can't. Therefore, it's important that you structure your presentation so that your audience can follow your text—and remember what you say.

- *Craft an introduction* that engages your audience's interest and tells them what to expect. Depending on your rhetorical situation, you may want to **BEGIN** with humor, with an anecdote, or with something that reminds them of the occasion for your talk or helps them see the reason for it. In any case, you always need to summarize your main points, provide any needed background information, and outline how you'll proceed.

  ◆ 373–80

- *In the body of your presentation,* present your main points in more detail and support them with **REASONS** and **EVIDENCE**. As you draft, you may well find that you have more material than you can present in the time available, so you'll need to choose the most important points to focus on and leave out the rest.

  ◆ 400–401
  401–8

- *Let your readers know you're concluding* (but try to avoid saying "in conclusion"), and then use your remaining time to restate your main points and to explain why they're important. End by saying "thank you" and offering to answer questions or take comments if the format allows for them.

Consider whether to use visuals.   You may want or need to include some visuals to help listeners follow what you're saying. Especially when you're presenting complex information, it helps to let them see it as well as hear it. Remember, though, that visuals should be a means of conveying information, not mere decoration.

DECIDING ON THE APPROPRIATE VISUALS

- *Slides* are useful for listing main points and for projecting illustrations, tables, and graphs.

- *Videos, animations, and sounds* can add additional information to your presentations.

- *Flip charts, whiteboards, or chalkboards* allow you to create visuals as you speak or to keep track of comments from your audience.

- *Posters* sometimes serve as the main part of a presentation, providing a summary of your points. You then offer only a brief introduction and answer any questions. You should be prepared to answer questions from any portion of your poster.

- *Handouts* can provide additional information, lists of works cited, or copies of any slides you show.

What visual tools (if any) you decide to use is partly determined by how your presentation will be delivered. Will you be speaking to a crowd or a class, delivering your presentation through a podcast, or creating an interactive presentation for a web conference? Make sure that any necessary equipment and programs are available—and that they work. If at all possible, check out any equipment in the place where you'll deliver your presentation before you go live. If you bring your own equipment for a live presentation, make sure you can connect to the internet if you need to and that electrical outlets are in reach of your power cords. Also, make sure that your visuals can be seen. You may have to rearrange the furniture or the screen to make sure everyone can see.

    And finally, have a backup plan. Computers fail; projector bulbs burn out; marking pens run dry. Whatever your plan is, have an alternative in case any problems occur.

Presentation software. *PowerPoint, Keynote,* and other presentation software can include images, video, and sound in addition to displaying written text. They are most useful for linear presentations that move audiences along one slide at a time. Cloud-based programs like *Prezi* also allow you to arrange words or slides in various designs, group related content together, and zoom in and out. Here are some tips for writing and designing slides:

- *Use LISTS or images, not paragraphs.* Use slides to emphasize your main points, not to reproduce your talk onscreen: keep your audience's attention focused on what you're saying. A list of brief points, presented one by one, reinforces your words. An image can provide additional information that your audience can take in quickly. ☐ 649–50

- *Make your text easy for your audience to read.* FONTS should be at least 18 points, and larger than that for headings. Projected slides are easier to read in sans serif fonts like Arial, Helvetica, and Tahoma than in serif fonts like Times New Roman. And avoid using all capital letters, which can be hard to read. ☐ 648–49

- *Choose colors carefully.* Your text and any illustrations must contrast with the background. Dark content on a light background is easier to read than the reverse. And remember that not everyone sees all colors; be sure your audience doesn't need to be able to see particular colors or contrasts in order to get your meaning. Red-green and blue-yellow contrasts are especially hard for some people to see and should be avoided.

- *Use bells and whistles sparingly, if at all.* Presentation software offers lots of decorative backgrounds, letters that fade in and out or dance across the screen, and sound effects. These features can be more distracting than helpful; use them only if they help to make your point.

- *Mark your text.* In your notes or prepared text, mark each place where you need to click a mouse to call up the next slide.

This Prezi presentation rotates, includes audio and video, and zooms in and out to let viewers take a closer look.

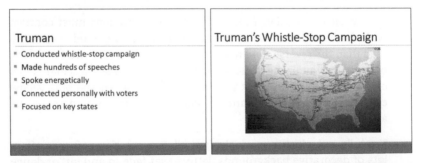

Two PowerPoint slides on the U.S. presidential election of 1948. The slide on the left outlines the main points; the one on the right shows a map of Truman's whistle-stop campaign, providing a graphic illustration of the miles he traveled as he campaigned to be president.

Handouts. When you want to give your audience information they can refer to later—reproductions of your visuals, bibliographic information about your sources, printouts of your slides—do so in the form of handouts. Refer to the handouts in your presentation, but unless they include material your audience needs to consult before or as you talk, wait until you are finished to distribute them so as not to distract listeners. Clearly label everything you give out, including your name and the date and title of the presentation.

Delivering a Presentation

The success of a presentation often hinges on how you deliver it. As you work on your spoken texts, bear in mind the following points:

Practice. Practice, practice, and then practice some more. The better you know your talk, the more confident you will be, and your audience will respond positively to that confidence. If you're reading a prepared text, try to write it as if you were talking. Then practice by recording it as you read it; listen for spots that sound as if you're reading, and work on your delivery to sound more relaxed. As you practice, pay attention to keeping within your time limit. If possible, rehearse your talk with a small group of friends to test their response and to get used to speaking in front of an audience.

Speak clearly. When you're giving a spoken presentation, your first goal is to be understood by your audience. If listeners miss important words or phrases because you don't pronounce them distinctly, your talk will not succeed. Make sure, too, that your pace matches your audience's needs. Often you'll need to make yourself speak more slowly than usual to explain complex material (or to compensate for nerves); sometimes you may need to speed up to keep your audience's attention. In general, though, strive for a consistent pace throughout, one that ensures you don't have to rush at the end.

Pause for emphasis.   In writing, you have white space and punctuation to show readers where an idea or discussion ends. When speaking, you need to pause to signal the end of a thought, to give listeners a moment to consider something you've said, or to get them ready for a surprising or amusing statement.

Stand up (or sit up) straight and look at your audience.   If you're in the same physical space as your audience, try to maintain some eye contact with them. If that's uncomfortable, fake it: pick a spot on the wall just above the head of a person in the back of the room, and focus on it. You'll appear as if you're looking at your audience even if you're not looking them in the eye. And if you stand or sit up straight, you'll project the sense that you have confidence in what you're saying. If you appear to believe in your words, others will, too. If you're speaking via an online forum like *Skype*, look at the computer's camera — not at the screen. Also, make sure the camera is positioned at your eye level, so you aren't looking down at it (and showing your viewers the ceiling behind you!).

Use gestures for emphasis.   If you're not used to speaking in front of a group, you may let your nervousness show by holding yourself stiffly, elbows tucked in. To overcome some of that nervousness, take some deep breaths, try to relax, and move your arms and the rest of your body as you would if you were talking to a friend. Use your hands for emphasis: most public speakers use one hand to emphasize specific points and both hands to make larger gestures. Watch politicians on C-SPAN to see how people who speak on a regular basis use gestures as part of their overall delivery.

Acknowledgments

IMAGE ACKNOWLEDGMENTS

Page 40: Jacob MacLeod; p. 75: Courtesy of Emily Vallowe; p. 81: Meghan Hickey; p. 84: Ana-Jamileh Kassfy; p. 102: Courtesy of Danielle Allen. © Laura Rose Photography; p. 107: Photo by Kenneth Irby. Courtesy of The Poynter Institute; p. 120: urbanbuzz/Shutterstock.com; p. 121: TOLES © 2007 The Washington Post. Reprinted with permission of ANDREW MCMEEL SYNDICATION. All rights reserved; p. 123: AP Photo/Jeffrey Phelps; p. 124 (both): Courtesy of Ann C. Johns, Ph.D./University of Texas at Austin; p. 131: Michaela Cullington; p. 139: Frankie Schembri; p. 140: Coki10/Shutterstock; p. 143: Courtesy of Jon Marcus, photo by Andrew Kubica; p. 144: Wesley Hitt/Getty Images; p. 157: Joanna MacKay; p. 162: Evan Agostini/Invision/EP Photo; p. 164: Bettmann/Corbis via Getty Images; p. 165: Jafar Fallahi; p. 192: Photo courtesy of www.donlaurencephotography.com; p. 204: Francois Duhamel/© STX Entertainment/Courtesy Everett Collection; p. 211: Keystone Pictures USA/Alamy Stock Photo; p. 212: Matthew M. Miller; p. 224: John Amis/AP; p. 233: Courtesy of Ernie Smith; p. 234: Patryk Michalski/Shutterstock; p. 235: Library of Congress; p. 246: Michael H. Granof; p. 250: Courtesy Dena Betz; p. 256: Courtesy Adam Karsten; p. 257: Courtesy Adalena Kavanagh; p. 258: Courtesy Julia Black; p. 259: Courtesy Darcy Vebber; p. 280: AP Photo/Evan Agostini; p. 377: Jim Mone/AP; p. 407: © Reagan Louie; p. 408: AaronFoster.com; p. 421: All photos © New York Apple Association; p. 428 (left): F. Carter Smith/Bloomberg via Getty Images; p. 428 (right): Richard Carson/REUTERS/Newscom; p. 437: Photo by Swim Ink 2, LLC/CORBIS/Corbis via Getty Images; p. 449: Michigan Economic Development Corporation; p. 460 (all): Patricia Reitz (butteryum.org); p. 492 (all): Nicholas S. Holtzman, Simine Vazire, Matthias R. Mehl. "Sounds Like a Narcissist: Behavioral Manifestations of Narcissism in Everyday Life." *Journal of Research in Personality*; p. 494 (both): Houston Community College; p. 497: Permission to publish courtesy of EBSCO; pp. 500–501: Wright State University Libraries; p. 567: Michael Segal, "The Hit Book That Came from Mars." *Nautilus*. Nautilus Think, 8 January 2015. Web. 10 October 2016; p. 568: Jessamyn Neuhaus, "Marge Simpson, Blue-Haired Housewife Defining Domesticity on *The Simpsons*." *Journal of Popular Culture* 43.4 (2010); p. 572: Amana Fontanella-Khan, *Pink Sari Revolution: A Tale of Women and Power in India*. New York: Norton, 2013; p. 578: John McIlwain, Molly Simpson, and Sara Hammerschmidt. "Housing in America: Integrating Housing, Health, and Resilience in a Changing Environment." *Urban Land Institute*. Urban Land Institute, 2014. Web. 17 Sept. 2016; p. 589: Bettmann/Getty Images; p. 607: Joseph E. Stiglitz, *The Great Divide: Unequal Societies and What We Can Do about Them*. New York: Norton, 2015; p. 615: M. P. Lazette,

(2015, February 25). "A Hurricane's Hit to Households." Federal Reserve Bank of Cleveland. Retrieved from www.clevelandfed.org/en/Newsroom%20and%20 Events/Publications/Forefront/Katrina.aspx; pp. 617–18: C. F. Guthrie, (2013). "Smart Technology and the Moral Life." *Ethics & Behavior*, 23, 324–37. https://www .tandfonline.com/doi/full/10.1080/10508422.2013.78735 9; p. 647: Used with the permission of Inter IKEA Systems B.V; p. 655 (left): National Gallery of Art; p. 655 (right): Library of Congress; p. 657 (all): RNGS/ RTR/Newscom; p. 658 (top): NASA Image Collection/ Alamy Stock Photo; p. 658 (center): This map was created by the National Renewable Energy; Laboratory for the U.S. Department of Energy; p. 661: Caricature of an artist painting vigorously, ca. 1885–1886. Francis Davis Millet and Millet family papers, 1858–1984, bulk 1858–1955. Archives of American Art, Smithsonian Institution; p. 666: Courtesy of National Park Service. No protection is claimed in original US government works; p. 667: Smithsonian National Museum of History; p. 668: Courtesy of Ann M. Lawrence, PhD, University of South Florida; p. 671: Courtesy Richard Bullock; p. 673: Library of Congress; p. 674: Courtesy of Judy Davis.

TEXT ACKNOWLEDGMENTS

Danielle Allen: From *Our Declaration: A Reading of the Declaration of Independence in Defense of Equality* by Danielle Allen. Copyright © 2014 by Danielle Allen. Used by permission of Liveright Publishing Corporation.

Cynthia Bass: Excerpt from "Gettysburg Address: Two Versions," *The San Francisco Examiner*, November 19, 1997. Reprinted by permission of the author.

Michael Benton, Mark Dolan & Rebecca Zisch: "Teen Film$: An Annotated Bibliography" from *Journal of Popular Film and Television*, Vol. 25, No. 2, Summer 1997, pp. 83–88. Reprinted by permission of the publisher Taylor & Francis Ltd, http://www .tandfonline.com

Hannah Berry: "The Fashion Industry: Free to Be an Individual." Copyright © 2012 by Hannah Berry.

Dylan Borchers: "Against the Odds: Harry S. Truman and the Election of 1948." Copyright © 2009 by Dylan Borchers.

Rick Bragg: "All Over But the Shoutin'" from *All Over But the Shoutin'* by Rick Bragg, copyright © 1997 by Rick Bragg. Used by permission of Pantheon Books, an imprint of the Knopf Doubleday Publishing Group, a division of Penguin Random House LLC. All rights reserved.

Rachel Brinkley, Kenneth Ricker, and Kelly Tuomey: From "Esthetic Knowing with a Hospitalized Morbidly Obese Patient," *Journal of Undergraduate Nursing Scholarship*, Vol. 9, No. 1, Fall 2007. Reprinted by permission of The University of Arizona College of Nursing.

Cameron Carroll: "Zombie Film Scholarship: A Review of the Literature" from UMW Blogs (http://www .umwblogs.org/). Reprinted by permission of the author.

Roy Peter Clark: "Why It Worked: A Rhetorical Analysis of Obama's Speech on Race" from Poynter.org, October 20, 2017. Reprinted by permission of the author.

Nathaniel Cooney: "Self-Assessment." Copyright © 2013 by Nathaniel Cooney.

Michaela Cullington: "Texting and Writing," *Young Scholars in Writing*, Vol. 8, 2011. Reprinted by permission of University of Missouri Press.

Daniel Felsenfeld: "Rebel Music" from *The New York Times*, March 26, 2010 © 2010 The New York Times. All rights reserved. Used by permission and protected by the Copyright Laws of the United States. The printing, copying,

Glossary / Index

A

Note: This glossary / index defines key terms and concepts and directs you to pages in the book where you can find specific information on these and other topics. Please note the words set in SMALL CAPITAL LETTERS are themselves defined in the glossary / index.

B

background information. *See* context

balance of sources, 195

bandwagon appeal, 414   A logical FAL-LACY that argues for thinking or acting a certain way just because others do.

Barker, Bill, 433

Bartleby, 501

Bass, Cynthia, 374, 380–81

be, forms of, overreliance on, 359

Bealer, Bonnie K., 422

because, with reasons for claims, 400

Becker, Carl, 438, 439

begging the question, 414   A logical FALLACY that involves arguing in a circle, assuming as a given what the writer is trying to prove.

beginnings

genres

literacy narratives, 93

narration, 468–69

position papers, 180–81

reports, 152–53

textual analyses, 127

rhetorical situation and, 373–74, 384–85

strategies

anecdotes, 379

asking questions, 379

background information, 376–78

connecting to readers' interests, 378

defining key concepts, 378

explaining context, 375

forecasting organization, 376

jumping right in, 380

provoking interest, 379

stating thesis, 375

believing and doubting game, 20–21

Bellafante, Ginia, 444–45

Benton, Michael, 190–92

Berry, Hannah, 99–102

bibliography. *See also* annotated bibliography

as research source, 500

working, 485–86

biology, proposal in, 310

BIOSIS Previews, 503

Bittman, Mark, 401–2

"Black Men and Public Space" (Staples), 466–67

block method of comparing and contrasting, 426

block quotation, 529   In a written work, a long quotation that is set off, or indented, from the main text and presented without quotation marks. In MLA style: set off text more than four typed lines, indented five spaces (or one-half inch) from the left margin; in APA style, set off quotes of forty or more words, indented five spaces (or one-half inch) from the left margin. *See also* quotation

blogs

as genre, 667

for writing ideas, 326

"The Blues Merchant" (Washington), 380

book reviews, 502

books

documenting, APA style

online, 619

print, 605–11

F

implications, discussing, 381–82

IMRaD, 303, 311, 318　An acronym representing sections of scientific reports: Introduction (asks a question), methods (tells about experiments), results (states findings), and discussion (tries to make sense of findings in light of what was already known). In some fields, an abstract, literature review, and list of references may also be required.

indefinite pronoun　A PRONOUN—such as *all, anyone, anything, everyone, everything, few, many, nobody, nothing, one, some,* and *something*—that does not refer to a specific person or thing.

independent clause　A CLAUSE, containing a SUBJECT and a VERB, that can stand alone as a sentence: *She sang. The world-famous soprano sang several popular arias.*

indexes, library, 502–3

infinitive　To plus the base form of the verb: *to come, to go.* An infinitive can function as a NOUN (*He likes to run first thing in the morning*); an ADJECTIVE (*She needs a campaign to run*); or an ADVERB (*He registered to run in the marathon*).

infographics, 659–60
informal outlines, 335

informal writing　Writing not intended to be evaluated, sometimes not even to be read by others. Informal writing is produced primarily to explore ideas or to communicate casually with friends and acquaintances. *See also* formal writing

informative abstracts, 185–86, 188, 189

InfoTrac, 502
InfoTrac Magazine Index, 503

inquiry, writing as, 323–26　A PROCESS for investigating a topic by posing questions, searching for multiple answers, and keeping an open mind.
　　journals, 326
　　starting with questions, 323–26

integrating dialogue, 453–54
integrating sources
　　deciding whether to quote, paraphrase, or summarize, 528
　　paraphrasing, 531–34
　　quoting
　　　　incorporating short quotations, 528–29
　　　　indicating omissions, 530
　　　　punctuation, 530–31
　　　　setting off long quotations, 529
　　signal phrases, 535–38
　　summarizing, 534–35
　　taking notes, 526–28

interjection　A word expressing surprise, resignation, agreement, and other emotions. It can be attached to a sentence or stand on its own: <u>Well,</u> if you insist. <u>Ouch!</u>

Internet Archive, 501
internet research
　　e-books, 501
　　general guidelines, 505
　　vs. library databases, 482–83

interpretation, 114, 216–17, 221, 325　The act of making sense of something or explaining what one thinks it means. Interpretation is the goal of writing a LITERARY ANALYSIS or TEXTUAL ANALYSIS.

layout, 649 The way text is arranged on a page or screen—for example, in paragraphs, in lists, on charts, with headings.

letter writing, 337 A PROCESS of GENERATING IDEAS AND TEXT by going through the motions of writing to someone to explain a topic.

linking verb A VERB that expresses a state of being (*appear, be, feel, seem*).

listing, 332–33 A PROCESS for GENERATING IDEAS AND TEXT by making lists while thinking about a topic, finding relationships among the notes, and arranging the notes as an OUTLINE.

literacy narrative, 75–97 A writing GENRE that explores the writer's experiences with reading and writing. Key Features: well-told story • vivid detail • indication of the narrative's significance

literary analysis, 211–23 A writing GENRE that examines a literary text (most often fiction, poetry, or drama) and argues for a particular INTERPRETATION of the text. Key Features: arguable THESIS • careful attention to the language of the text • attention to patterns or themes • clear interpretation • MLA style. *See also* analysis; textual analysis

multimedia, 504–5 Using more than one medium of delivery, such as print, speech, or electronic. Often used interchangeably with MULTIMODAL.

multimodal, 504–5 Using more than one mode of expression, such as words, images, sound, links, and so on. Often used interchangeably with MULTIMEDIA.

multiple perspectives, incorporating, 6
  genres and
    arguments, 411–13
    evaluations, 208
    position papers, 178
  Rogerian argument, 409
multiple vantage points, 448–49
Murray, Donald, 353
"mutual" *(Merriam-Webster.com)*, 432–33

N

narration, 75–97 A STRATEGY for presenting information as a story, for telling "what happened." It is a pattern most often associated with fiction, but it shows up in all kinds of writing. When used in an essay, a REPORT, or another academic GENRE, narration is used to support a point—not merely tell an interesting story for its own sake. It must also present events in some kind of sequence and include only pertinent detail. Narration can serve as the ORGANIZING principle for a whole text. *See also* literacy narrative
  in beginnings and endings, 468–69
  detail and, 466–68
  genres and
    literary analyses, 218
    profiles, 244
  rhetorical situation and, 470

sequencing
  chronological order, 462–63
  flashbacks, 464
  reverse chronological order, 463
  time markers, 464–66
  transitions, 466
narratives
  anecdotes as, 403–5
  rewriting, 354
narrowing a topic, 150
National Geographic Atlas of the World, 499
National Multiple Sclerosis Society, 444
Naxos Music Library, 504
New Encyclopedia Britannica, 499
New York Times Index, 503
Nichols, Dave, 406–7
Nizamoff, Jenna, 312

noncount noun A word that names something that cannot be counted or made plural: *information, rice.*

nonessential element, 358 A word, PHRASE, or CLAUSE that gives additional information but that is not necessary for understanding the basic meaning of a sentence: *I learned French, which is a Romance language online.* Nonessential elements should be set off by commas.

nonrestrictive element. *See* nonessential
    element
notes
  in documentation
    APA style, 605
    MLA style, 557–58
  taking
    guidelines, 526–28
    plagiarism and, 543
    synthesizing ideas using, 522–24

noun A word that names a person, place, thing, or idea (*teacher, Zadie Smith, forest, Amazon River, notebook, democracy*).

nursing, academic writing for, 318–20

O

object A word or phrase that follows a PREPOSITION or that receives the action of a VERB. In the sentence *I handed him the mail on the table,* him is an indirect object and *mail* is a direct object of the verb *handed; table* is an object of the preposition *on.*

organizing Arranging parts of a text so that the text as a whole has COHERENCE. The text may use one STRATEGY throughout or may combine several strategies to create a suitable organization.

phrase A group of words that lacks a
SUBJECT, a VERB, or both.

The use of another
person's words, ideas, or sentence structures without appropriate credit and
DOCUMENTATION. Plagiarism is a serious
breach of ethics.

point of view The choice a writer makes
of whether to use the first person *(I, we)*,
the second person *(you)*, or the third person *(he, she, it, they, a student, the students)*.

portfolio, 361–70 A collection of writing
selected by a writer to show their work,
including a statement assessing the work
and explaining what it demonstrates.

position, 398–400 A statement that
asserts a belief or CLAIM. In an ARGUMENT,
a position needs to be stated in a THESIS
or clearly implied, and it requires support
with REASONS and EVIDENCE. *See also* arguing a position

post hoc, ergo propter hoc. See faulty
    causality

predicate In a sentence or CLAUSE, the
VERB and the words that tell more about
the verb — MODIFIERS, COMPLEMENTS, and
OBJECTS. In the sentence *Mario forcefully
stated his opinion,* the predicate is *forcefully
stated his opinion.*

preposition A word or group of words
that tells about the relationship of a NOUN
or PRONOUN to another word in the sentence. Some common prepositions are
*after, at, before, behind, between, by, for, from,
in, of, on, to, under, until, with,* and *without.*

arguing (cont.)
   key features, 676–77
   rhetorical situation, 677–78
presentation slides, 677

present participle   A VERB form used with a HELPING VERB to create progressive TENSES (*is writing*) or used alone as an ADJECTIVE (*a living organism*). The present participle of a verb always ends in -*ing*.

present perfect   A TENSE used to indicate actions that took place at no specific time in the past or that began in the past and continue into the present: *I have often wondered how I can make my love of language into a career. He has cried every day since his companion of fifty years died.*

present tense, 221, 538
previewing texts, 12–13, 116

primary source, 300–301, 489–90   A source such as a literary work, historical document, work of art, or performance that a researcher examines firsthand. Primary sources also include experiments and FIELD RESEARCH. A researcher would likely consider the Declaration of Independence a primary source and a textbook's description of how the document was written a SECONDARY SOURCE.

print indexes, 503
print vs. online research sources, 493
proceedings, conference, 502

process, 321–70   In writing, a series of actions that may include GENERATING IDEAS AND TEXT, DRAFTING, REVISING, EDITING, and PROOFREADING. *See also* explaining a process *and specific processes*

profile, 233–45   A GENRE that presents an engaging portrait of a person, place, or event based on firsthand FIELD RESEARCH. Key Features: interesting subject • necessary background • interesting angle • firsthand account • engaging details
   key features, 239–41
   with other genres, 284
   reading: "A Brief History of the
      Modern-Day Straw, the World's
      Most Wasteful Commodity,"
      233–39
   strategies for
      argument, 397
      description, 446
      dialogue, 452
      narration, 462
   writing guide, 241–45

Project Gutenberg, 501

pronoun   A word that takes the place of a NOUN, such as *she, anyone, whoever.*

proofreading, 359–60   The final PROCESS of writing, when a writer checks for correct spelling and punctuation as well as for page order, missing text, and consistent use of FONTS. *See also* editing; revising; rewriting

proposal, 246–55   A GENRE that argues for a solution to a problem or suggests some action. Key Features: well-defined problem • recommended solution • answers to anticipated questions • call to action • appropriate TONE. *See also* topic proposal
   abstract for, 186, 188, 189
   for annotated bibliography, 196
   key features, 249–50
   with other genres, 284

Q

R

reason Support for a CLAIM or POSITION.
A reason, in turn, requires its own support
in the form of EVIDENCE.

references The list of sources at the end
of a text prepared in APA STYLE.

reflection, 256–63 A GENRE of writing
that presents a writer's thoughtful, personal exploration of a subject. Key Features: topic intriguing to the writer • some
kind of structure • specific details • speculative TONE

relative pronoun A PRONOUN such as
that, which, who, whoever, whom, or *whomever*
that introduces a SUBORDINATE CLAUSE: *The
professor <u>who</u> gave the lecture is my adviser.*

reporting, 131–56 A writing GENRE that
presents information to readers on a subject. Key Features: tightly focused TOPIC •
accurate, well-researched information •

response, 348–50 A PROCESS of writing
in which a reader gives the writer their
thoughts about the writer's title, beginning,
THESIS, support and DOCUMENTATION,
ORGANIZING, STANCE, treatment of AUDI-
ENCE, achievement of PURPOSE, handling of
the GENRE, ending, and other matters.

résumé, 264–73 A GENRE that summarizes someone's academic and employment history, generally written to submit
to potential employers. Key Features:
organization that suits goals and experience • succinctness • design that highlights key information.

secondary source, 300–301, 489–90 An
ANALYSIS or INTERPRETATION of a PRIMARY
SOURCE. In writing about the Revolution-
ary War, a researcher would likely consider the Declaration of Independence a
primary source and a textbook's description of how the document was written a
secondary source.

sentence fragment A group of words
that is capitalized and punctuated as a
sentence but is not one, either because it
lacks a SUBJECT, a VERB, or both, or because
it begins with a word that makes it a SUB-
ORDINATE CLAUSE.

sexist language, 359 Language that stereotypes or ignores women or men or
needlessly calls attention to gender.

signal phrase A phrase used to attribute
quoted, paraphrased, or summarized
material to a source, as in "she said" or
"according to Kristof."

    with dialogue, 453

    identifying authorities with, 403

    integrating sources and, 535–38

    MLA style and, 551

simile, 429 A figure of speech that uses
like or *as* to compare two items: *See also*
figurative language; metaphor

singular *they* The use of *they, them,* and
their to refer to a person whose gender is
unknown or not relevant to the context.
Traditionally, *they* has referred only to
plural items, but the use of the singular
they is now becoming more accepted.

subject A word or word group, usually including at least one NOUN or PRONOUN plus its MODIFIERS, that tells who or what a sentence or CLAUSE is about. In the sentence *A frustrated group of commuters waited for the late bus,* the subject is *A frustrated group of commuters.*

subject directories, web, 505
subjective descriptions, 446–47

subordinate clause A clause that begins with a SUBORDINATING WORD and therefore cannot stand alone as a sentence: *She feels good when she exercises. My roommate, who was a physics major, tutors students in science.*

subordinating word A word, such as a RELATIVE PRONOUN or a subordinating conjunction, that introduces a SUBORDINATE CLAUSE: *The ice sculpture melted because the ballroom was too hot.* Common subordinating words include *although, as, because, if, since, that, which,* and *why.*

Sullivan, Andrew, 411
Sullivan, Kathleen M., 441

summary, 33–35, 534–35 The use of one's own words and sentence structure to condense someone else's text into a briefer version that gives the main ideas of the original. As with PARAPHRASING and QUOTATION, summarizing requires DOCUMENTATION.
    essay questions, 473
    genres
        abstracts, 187, 188
        textual analyses, 116
    integrating sources, 528, 534–35

as reading strategy, 20
signal phrases, 535–37
textual evidence, 406–7
transitions, 391

summary and response essay, 33–44 A GENRE of writing that demonstrates one's ability to convey a text's main ideas in condensed form and to engage with those ideas by ARGUING a position, ANALYZING the text, or writing a REFLECTION on its content. Key Features: clearly identified author and title • concise summary of the text • an explicit response • support for that response
    key features, 42–43
    sample essay: "Guns and Cars Are Different" (McLeod), 40–42
    writing guide, 43–44

support. *See* evidence
survey research, 508–10
The Swerve (Greenblatt), 296

synthesizing ideas, 519–25 Bringing together ideas and information from multiple sources in order to discover patterns and gain new insights and perspectives.
    reading across fields of study, 297
    in reading process, 519–23
    in reports, 147
    to support own ideas, 525
    using notes, 523–24

T

tables, 656, 657
taking notes
    integrating sources, 526–28
    plagiarism and, 543
    synthesizing ideas using, 522–24

tone, 66–68   The way a writer's or speaker's STANCE toward the readers and subject is reflected in the text.

topic, 387   The specific subject written about in a text. A topic should be narrow enough to cover, not too broad or general, and needs to be developed appropriately for its AUDIENCE and PURPOSE.

topic proposal, 253–55   A statement of intent to examine a topic; also called a proposal ABSTRACT. Some instructors require a topic proposal in order to assess the feasibility of the writing project that a student has in mind. Key Features: concise discussion of the subject • clear statement of the intended focus • rationale for choosing the subject • mention of resources

topic sentence, 389–90   A sentence, often at the beginning of a paragraph, that states the paragraph's main point. The details in the rest of the paragraph should support the topic sentence.

transition, 391   A word or PHRASE that helps to connect sentences and paragraphs and to guide readers through a text. Transitions can help to show comparisons (*also, similarly*); contrasts (*but, instead*); examples (*for instance, in fact*); sequence (*finally, next*); time (*at first, meanwhile*); and more.

Submitting Papers for Publication by W. W. Norton & Company

We are interested in receiving writing from college students to consider including in our textbooks as examples of student writing. Please send this form with the work that you would like us to consider to Marilyn Moller, Student Writing, W. W. Norton & Company, 500 Fifth Avenue, New York NY 10110. For questions, or to submit electronically, email us at composition@wwnorton.com

Text Submission Form

Student's name _____

School _____

Address _____

Department _____

Course _____

Writing assignment the text responds to _____

_____

_____

_____

_____

Instructor's name _____

(continued next page)

Please write a few sentences about what your primary purposes were for writing this text. Also, if you wish, tell us what you think you learned about writing from the experience writing it.

_____

_____

_____

_____

_____

_____

_____

_____

Contact Information

Please provide the information below so that we can contact you if your work is selected for publication.

Name _____

Permanent address _____

Email _____

Phone _____

A Directory to MLA Style